LIFE
DEATH
LOVE
HATE
PLEASURE
PAIN

LIFE DEATH LOVE H

ATE PLEASURE PAIN

Selected Works from the Museum of Contemporary Art, Chicago, Collection

Foreword
Robert Fitzpatrick *Pritzker Director*

Principal authors
Elizabeth A. T. Smith *James W. Alsdorf Chief Curator*
Alison Pearlman *Former Assistant Curator*
Julie Rodrigues Widholm *Curatorial Assistant*

Contributors
Francesco Bonami *Manilow Senior Curator*
Staci Boris *Associate Curator*
Sylvia Chivaratanond *Curatorial Assistant*
Monika Gehlawat *Former Marjorie Susman Curatorial Fellow*
Lela Hersh *Director of Collections and Exhibitions*
Dominic Molon *Associate Curator*
Heather Ring *Former Curatorial Intern*
Michael Rooks *Assistant Curator*
Jenni Sorkin *Former Curatorial Intern*
Tricia Van Eck *Curatorial Coordinator*
Lynne Warren *Curator*

This catalogue was published in conjunction with the exhibition *Life, Death, Love, Hate, Pleasure, Pain: Selected Works from the MCA Collection* held at the Museum of Contemporary Art, Chicago, from November 16, 2002 to April 20, 2003.

Support for the publication of this catalogue has been generously provided by Donna and Howard Stone, the Elizabeth F. Cheney Foundation, Ruth Horwich, Lannan Foundation, and Furthermore, a program of the J. M. Kaplan Fund.

The Museum of Contemporary Art (MCA) is a nonprofit, tax-exempt organization. The MCA's exhibitions, programming, and operations are member supported and privately funded through contributions from individuals, corporations, and foundations. Additional support is provided through the Illinois Arts Council, a state agency; and CityArts Program 4 Grant from the City of Chicago Department of Cultural Affairs. Additional significant support is provided by the State of Illinois. Air transportation services are provided by American Airlines, the official airline of the Museum of Contemporary Art.

Produced by the Publications Department of the Museum of Contemporary Art, Chicago. Designed by Hal Kugeler, Director. Edited by Kari Dahlgren, Associate Director, with Trisha Beck, Editorial Assistant.

Printed by Snoeck-Ducaju & Zoon, Ghent, Belgium

Color separations by Professional Graphics, Rockford, Illinois

Library of Congress Catalog Card Number: 2002111378

ISBN 0-933856-73-3 (hard cover)
ISBN 0-933856-74-1 (soft cover)

This catalogue is distributed by D.A.P./Distributed Art Publishers. 155 Sixth Avenue, 2nd floor New York, New York 10013-1507 Phone: 212.627.1999 Fax: 212.627.9484

The type for this catalogue was set in Scala Sans, designed by Martin Majoor for the Vredenberg Concert Hall in Utrecht. This neohumanist typeface was issued publicly by Font Shop International, Berlin, in 1994.

Contents

This book is dedicated to the founding
trustees and benefactors of the Museum
of Contemporary Art, Chicago.

Foreword

The Spirit of our Time

The fabric of history is an endless patchwork of stories unfolding into the present. Art collections tell such stories, about the people who have assembled them, the institutions that care for them, and the artists they represent, commingling individual narratives to create a rich, multidimensional conversation that spans generations. When the trustees of the Museum of Contemporary Art decided to build a collection in 1974, they understood the importance of preserving objects and ideas in order to understand not just the past, but also the present. Their decision to form a collection for the museum was intuitive: passionate collectors themselves, they were moved to share their own experiences of discovery and passion for art with a larger audience.

They began by organizing informal gatherings at each others' homes to talk about art, inviting artists and critics as well. By the late 1950s a lively, peripatetic forum fostered the exchange of information and ideas across Chicago, generating a proliferation of new and discerning collectors who inspired and competed with one another. Over the next several decades, collectors led by Joseph and Jory Shapiro, Edwin and Lindy Bergman, Ruth and Leonard Horwich, Mary and Earle Ludgin, Lewis Manilow, and Beatrice and Robert Mayer not only assembled phenomenal art collections but became the MCA's

founders and first patrons. They joined with many others to nurture the museum's early development, and contributed substantially to form a core collection with strengths in surrealism, Chicago art, minimalism, and conceptual art.

The MCA acquired surrealist masterpieces from the Shapiro, Bergman, and Ludgin collections, and the majority of our extraordinary group of sculptures and mobiles by Alexander Calder are gifts and long-term loans from the Horwich family. The MCA's holdings of art from the 1960s were significantly bolstered by gifts from Beatrice Mayer, while Susan and Lewis Manilow contributed works by earlier artists with roots in Chicago such as H. C. Westermann and Leon Golub. Since then, the Manilows have added many notable works in a variety of media by a new generation of internationally renowned artists.

For nearly three decades, many others have been instrumental in strengthening core areas of the Collection and establishing new branches that reflect the multiplicity of practices that characterize the art of today. Since the beginning of the Collection, its development has proceeded in quantum leaps rather than step by step. With the initial influx of important paintings and sculptures by the founding patrons of the museum, and the further development of the core interests they encompass, the Collection experienced an enormous impetus for growth with the Gerald S. Elliott bequest of ninety-six outstanding works in 1995, an unparalleled gift representing seminal artists working over the last forty years. On the heels of the Elliott bequest, the Lannan Foundation gift of eighty-six works contributed to the MCA's already substantial holdings of mostly American art from a younger generation.

Many artists are represented in the Collection by works of singular quality such as Jasper Johns's *In Memory of My Feelings Frank O'Hara* and Robert Rauschenberg's iconic painting *Retroactive II*, both gifted to the MCA by Stefan Edlis and Gael Neeson. These gifts, along with Jeff Koons's *Rabbit*, reveal Edlis and Neeson's discerning focus on American artists whose explorations were formative in the shift from abstract expressionism to pop art and its continuing permutations today. Other donors of outstanding pieces

Original Language, 2001, with works by Richard Serra, Alighiero e Boetti, Jeff Koons, Giuseppe Gabellone, Bruce Nauman, and Andreas Gursky

Life, Death, Love, Hate, Pleasure, Pain

from the 1960s onward include gifts by Anne and Will Hokin, Helyn and Ralph Goldenberg, and Paul and Dorie Sternberg. Important paintings of the 1980s were provided by Camille Oliver-Hoffmann in memory of her late husband Paul Oliver-Hoffmann, and several prime examples of recent conceptual photography have entered the Collection thanks to Pamela and Michael Alper. In addition, a remarkable gift of seventy-five photographs from Donna and Howard Stone has substantially enhanced the emphasis on photography that has become a hallmark of the Collection, including important works by American and European artists from the late 1960s to the present with an emphasis on the 1990s.

We are particularly proud of the number and quality of works in the Collection that were made by Chicago artists. Through the generosity of many donors, including the founding patrons, Walter and Dawn Clark Netsch, Muriel Kallis Newman, the Ruttenberg family, and Ruth S. Nath, the MCA has extensive holdings of works by Chicago imagists as well as significant examples of younger Chicagoans, an emphasis that continues to grow in the Collection.

The acquisition of work by young and emerging artists is a vital part of our mission. Helping to advance this goal have been the efforts of Sandy and Jack Guthman, Andrea and James Gordon, Daryl Gerber Stokols and Jeff Stokols, George and Lori Bucciero, Barbara and Tom Ruben, and others. The support of Carol and Douglas Cohen, Nancy and Sandy Koltun, Ken Griffin, and Sara Albrecht have made it possible for the museum to commission and purchase a variety of new art and show it frequently in the galleries and public spaces of the MCA. Building on past support from the Men's Council and ongoing support from MCA's Women's Board, the Collectors Forum has also been aggressive in their drive to acquire very recent art for the MCA by young artists, some of whom have not been previously collected by American institutions.

The MCA's ability to develop the Collection is also enhanced thanks to contributions of multiple donors.

Recent purchases have been made possible by the collective efforts of donors including Judith Neisser, Nancy Lauter and Fred McDougal, Penny Pritzker and Bryan Traubert, Ed and Jackie Rabin, Paul Beitler, and Marjorie and Louis Susman, as well as the National Endowment for the Arts and the Illinois Arts Council. Meanwhile, the Bernice and Kenneth Newberger Fund has enabled works by young artists to be purchased directly by the museum. In addition, corporate support from the Maremont Corporation, LaSalle Bank, AT&T, the Sara Lee Foundation, and Refco has enabled the museum to purchase significant photographic works, and Marshall Field's has contributed a stunning Calder mobile to the MCA's sizeable group of his works.

Until recently, the museum had no permanent endowment for acquisitions, which is essential for the intelligent, long-term building of the Collection. Now, thanks to a significant gift from Stefan Edlis and Gael Neeson, we have begun building such endowments. The Edlis/Neeson Art Acquisition Fund's inaugural commission and purchase of Maurizio Cattelan's *Felix* is a prodigious indication of what is to follow.

I owe an enormous debt to James W. Alsdorf Chief Curator Elizabeth Smith, who has not only guided this catalogue project but has organized a stunning exhibition to accompany it. Her efforts, and those of Manilow Senior Curator Francesco Bonami, have brought a new and clearer focus to the Collection and to our acquisition policy. Together they have provided judicious leadership in defining future directions for the MCA Collection. Collection Committee Chair Donna Stone and her predecessor Jack Guthman have been instrumental in supporting and guiding the process. MCA Board Chair Sally Meyers Kovler and her predecessors Penny Pritzker and Allen Turner have also provided valuable leadership in building the Collection.

While all members of the MCA curatorial team have contributed their consummate skills and knowledge to the contents of this catalogue, along with the invaluable assistance of members of the registrarial staff, special acknowledgment is reserved for Curatorial Assistant Julie Rodrigues Widholm

and former Assistant Curator Alison Pearlman for their diligence and perseverance in bringing this project to fruition.

This project could not have proceeded without the generosity of the Elizabeth F. Cheney Foundation, which recognized the significance of this publication from the beginning and has underwritten its research, writing, and editing phases. In addition to donations of works of art for the Collection, the Lannan Foundation has also made a generous contribution to support this publication. The MCA also owes enormous gratitude to Furthermore Foundation for its equally valuable support of the production process, enabling us to print a book of enduring quality. Most importantly, we owe thanks to Donna and Howard Stone and Ruth Horwich for generously providing support for the catalogue and accompanying exhibition.

Finally, I reserve for last my heartfelt thanks to the MCA trustees and donors, who have demonstrated an extraordinary commitment in their support of the MCA since its inception in 1967. While many are mentioned above and in the pages to follow, there are many others who have helped to create the shape of our collection and continue to make valuable contributions to it. The MCA Collection and this volume are testaments to their dedication, tireless enthusiasm, and remarkable vision.

Robert Fitzpatrick
Pritzker Director
Museum of Contemporary Art,
Chicago

LIFE DEATH LOVE H

ATE PLEASURE PAIN

A Spectrum of Contemporary Art at the MCA, Chicago

Elizabeth A.T. Smith

What attracts me is a certain awesomeness
and presence which relates to the spirit of our time —
to the human condition: the ups, the downs,
the disruption, the chaos, the ambivalence.

— Gerald S. Elliott, interviewed by Judith Neisser, 1987

The MCA Collection tells an ever-developing story of the ways art responds to and reflects the cerebral, emotive, and social aspects of human experience. Beyond its art historical significance, the Collection marks a commitment to preserve for posterity the most eloquent artistic expressions of what it means to live in our time. References to "life, death, love, hate, pleasure, pain" — a phrase borrowed from a work in the Collection by Bruce Nauman (p. 83) — emanate from and reverberate within the most compelling works of art from any era. Yet the art produced in recent decades resonates with much more ambivalence and ambiguity about these fundamental human states. Mirroring the uncertainties of our age and triggering our reflective responses, these works indeed embody the awesomeness and presence of human experience, as well as its disruption and chaos, as described by noted collector Gerald S. Elliott, whose 1995 bequest to the MCA forms a cornerstone of the Collection.

Regionally inflected yet national and international in its scope, the MCA Collection manifests notable strengths in historical examples of late surrealism, pop art, minimalism, and conceptual art from the 1940s through the 1970s; important holdings of work from the 1980s that can be loosely grouped under the rubric of postmodernism; and growing coherence within the plurality of directions in painting, sculpture, photography, video, installation, and related media today's artists explore. While initially the Collection was lovingly if haphazardly assembled through the largesse of the museum's early founders, increasingly it has come to reflect not only the passions of devoted patrons but also those of curators and directors who have strategically guided its focus in more recent years. Founded in 1967, the MCA built its Collection slowly and, during its early years, sporadically. While concentrating on generating an identity for the fledgling museum and on creating the stability to present a dynamic avant-garde program in contemporary art, the Board of Trustees did not officially vote to establish a permanent collection until 1974.[1]

Elizabeth A. T. Smith

Ten years later the MCA published *Selections from the Permanent Collection, Vol. 1*, the first cata-logue of its major holdings, many of which were related to pioneering early exhibitions. *Collective Vision: Creating a Contemporary Art Museum,* published in 1996 to coincide with the opening of the MCA's current building on Chicago Avenue, offered an updated treatment of key works in the mu-seum's growing collection. Yet a large number of gaps in the MCA's holdings necessitated an al-phabetical rather than a chronological or thematic organization of that catalogue.

Vast differences characterize the current volume, which reveals the Collection as an increas-ingly substantive and focused trajectory of the art of an approximately sixty-five-year period. Organized chronologically, it begins with works that prefigure developments in the post–World War II period, continues through the latter decades of the twentieth century, and concludes with recently acquired examples by some of the most outstanding of today's artists. Early in its history, the MCA defined it-self as a forerunner in the development of an avant-garde sensibility among American contemporary art museums; a continuing emphasis on the new and experimental stems from this spirit. Strengths established by earlier generations of patrons, foremost among them Joseph and Jory Shapiro and Gerald S. Elliott, continue to be consciously and thoughtfully expanded, refined, and realigned to reflect this vision. Moreover, the MCA's innovative exhibition program, with its emphasis on the work of younger and mid-career artists, continues to provide a fertile point of departure for its curators as they build the Collection. This volume highlights approximately 190 works by 130 artists, selected from the museum's complete hold-ings of more than five thousand works in all media, including artists' books, that from today's perspective are most significant to the art of the past half-century and representative of the way in which the Collection has evolved from the vantage point of the pursuit of the new in Chicago.

Installation view, 2002, with works by Vito Acconci, Dieter Roth, Mariko Mori, and Beat Streuli

Foundations of the MCA Collection:
Late Surrealism and Its Patrons

At the outset, the MCA Collection grew entirely from gifts that reflected the tastes of the vanguard of Chicago's early contemporary art collectors, reflecting their predilection for surrealism.[2] The phenomenon of Chicago collectors' receptivity to surrealism beginning around 1950 has been cogently analyzed by a number of scholars including Katharine Kuh, a noted Art Institute of Chicago curator who wrote in 1985, "I have long wondered why Chicago collectors turn to Surrealism with such intense loyalty and why Chicago artists in recent years have specialized in highly subjective imagery. . . . Why, in this center of tangible industrialization, have Surrealism, Dadaism, and various peripheral forms flourished? Could it be that the city's very materialism and overpowering vitality are responsible for driving some Chicagoans to psychic escape routes?"[3] In an unpublished master's thesis of 1992, Michele McCrillis offered a detailed and penetrating assessment of why Chicagoans gravitated toward surrealism, attributing it to the direct influence of artists Jean Dubuffet (p. 46) and Roberto Matta (p. 42), who lectured and exhibited in Chicago in the early and mid-1950s, and to the desire on the part of independent-minded Chicagoans to distinguish their interests from those of East Coast collectors whose focus was the New York school.[4] This legacy of independence persists in the attitudes of a current generation of Chicago collectors, but it has evolved substantially as the city has established itself as a leader in the contemporary art arena, due in no small part to the MCA's generative role.

Joseph and Jory Shapiro were foremost among these intensely committed early patrons and founders of the MCA. They formed an extensive collection of surrealist and related works, many with a figurative emphasis, by predominately European artists. With an unparalleled passion and enthusiasm for the art of his time, Joseph Shapiro played a key role in educating other Chicagoans — often opening his Oak Park home to individuals or groups — and inciting the interest of those who would go on to become major

Alexander Calder in Focus, 2000

Elizabeth A. T. Smith

collectors and patrons in their own right. Describing his commitment to the work of such artists as Max Ernst (p. 34), Victor Brauner (p. 38), Matta, Yves Tanguy, René Magritte (p. 50), Joseph Cornell, Balthus, Francis Bacon (p. 44), Dubuffet, and others, Shapiro stated of his and his wife's interest, first established in the 1950s: "We like poetic, metaphysical works expressing the unseen inner self instead of visible reality. We like art of inherent ambiguity and complexity. The lure of the fantastic, the enigmatic, and mystery of the poetic vision brought us into the orbit of Surrealism."[5] Among the late surrealist works collected by the Shapiros that later became gifts or bequests to the MCA are Ernst's *Loplop Introducing a Bird* (1929/1957), Hans Bellmer's *La toupie (The Top)* (1938/1968), and Brauner's *L'objet qui rêve II (The Object that Dreams II)* (1938). These, together with various benefactors' gifts of postwar examples of late surrealism — Wifredo Lam's *Anamu* (1942), Matta's *A Grave Situation* (1946) and *Let's Phosphoresce by Intellection #1* (1950), Dubuffet's *La verrue sous le nez (The Wart under the Nose)* (1951) and Magritte's *Les merveilles de la nature (The Wonders of Nature)* (1953) — provide an underpinning for later developments represented in the Collection, especially with regard to the evolution of contemporary art in Chicago. Not only did surrealism directly influence many Chicago-based artists from the 1950s onward, particularly the imagists, with their emphasis on fantasy, figuration, humor, and scatology, but a surrealist sensibility also resounded in works created in the 1960s by such artists as Marisol (p. 68) and Claes Oldenburg (p. 74), affiliated with the "neo-dada" strain of assemblage and pop art, respectively. More recently, affinities to surrealism can be discerned throughout a wider spectrum of work in photography, film, and sculpture by artists ranging from Cindy Sherman (p. 138) to Matthew Barney (p. 294) to Maurizio Cattelan (p. 310).

A notable collection of works by Alexander Calder (p. 48) further distinguishes the MCA's collection of art created at or around mid-century. *Brass in the Sky* (1947), *Snow Flurry II* (1951), *Polychrome and Horizontal Bluebird* (1954), and *Cascading Snow* (1961), along with fifteen long-term loans of key works by Calder from the Leonard and Ruth Horwich Family, have been displayed at the MCA for a significant portion of each year since 1996 and are visitor favorites. This rich amalgam of mobiles, stabiles, figurative works, and drawings straddle surrealism, abstraction, and related tendencies that emerged in this transitional era between the late modernism of mid-century and the early contemporary period. These works underscore Calder's importance as a major innovator in bridging figurative and nonfigurative references to create a highly distinctive language of abstract form.

13

While the MCA Collection holds a plethora of key works from the late 1930s to the early 1950s, it contains fewer examples of the New York–based movements abstract expressionism and abstract imagism. Among its exceptional works from this period are Franz Kline's *Vawdavitch* (1955, p. 52), a signature painting that exemplifies this artist's vocabulary of rigorous, dynamic abstraction. Ad Reinhardt's *Abstract Painting* (1962, p. 64), the language of which is considerably more reductive, prefigures the minimalist sensibilities of many artists who came of age in the 1960s and beyond; a 1998 exhibition project at the MCA by artist Byron Kim, for instance, used Reinhardt's painting as a specific point of departure. These works by Kline and Reinhardt represent two poles of abstraction — action painting and the abstract "sublime" — American artists of the New York school explored during the immediate postwar period; both are highly important examples of these artists' approaches, which were fundamental to the development of later directions in painting. Yet their singularity in the MCA Collection reveals how the collecting interests of Chicagoans in this period ran counter to the prevailing tendencies of their counterparts in New York or Los Angeles. From the 1950s through the 1970s, many Chicagoans sought opportunities to collect in ways that were distinctive and even maverick. Even today, only a handful of private collections in the city emphasize works associated with the New York school.

Instead, the figurative emphasis of artists like Dubuffet, Matta, and Francis Bacon, whose *Study for a Portrait* (1949, p. 45) is an outstanding work by this important British painter, attracted

H. C. Westermann, 2001

the patrons whose tastes formed the cornerstone of the MCA Collection and appealed to the nascent sensibilities of artists beginning to make their mark in Chicago in the 1950s. Among the earliest works in the Collection created by a Chicago resident are paintings by June Leaf (p. 104), whose work, presented in a 1978 retrospective at the MCA, would continue to evolve in the 1960s and 1970s with a distinctive focus

Elizabeth A. T. Smith

on eccentric, carnivalesque images of women. A pronounced figurative emphasis also distinguishes the sculptures and drawings of H. C. Westermann (p. 54), of whose work the MCA holds sixteen pieces, the largest collection of Westermann objects in a public collection, spanning the 1940s to 1979. Westermann's work has been the subject of two MCA-originated exhibitions, one in 1969 and the second, a 2001 retrospective that toured extensively within the United States, which was accompanied by a catalogue raisonné constituting the definitive scholarship on the artist. Westermann's alternatively deadpan and heartfelt treatment of a wide range of subjects, from Hollywood films to the symbolism of home to the horrors of war, manifested in his idiosyncratic, exquisitely crafted sculptures and incisive drawings, is exemplified by such key pieces as *Mad House* and *Memorial to the Idea of Man If He Was an Idea* (both 1958). Highly influential for a generation of younger artists, his work appealed strongly to the sensibility of Chicago collectors. While works by Leaf, Westermann, and others active in the 1950s reveal affinities with the ideas of artists such as Dubuffet, Matta, and Bacon, they were grounded much more strongly in an American sensibility rooted in time, place, historical circumstance, and the personal experiences of each artist. Their reception to and reworking of images from popular culture and the vernacular also foreshadowed developments that would emerge in a more pronounced way in the 1960s.

Art of the 1960s: From Mass Culture to Minimalism

A number of seminal works in the MCA Collection indicate the pervasiveness and growing influence of mass culture that began to emerge strongly in the art of the early 1960s. These include Jasper Johns's *In Memory of My Feelings — Frank O'Hara* (1961, p. 62) and Robert Rauschenberg's *Retroactive II* (1963, p. 70), both of which exemplify the transitional idiom of "hand-painted pop," in which expressive painterly techniques are conjoined with a more controlled approach as well as with imagery of everyday life and the mass media, and in the case of Johns, as an homage to his friend the poet Frank O'Hara. These paintings and Andy Warhol's *Troy Diptych* (1962, p. 66) and *Jacqueline Kennedy* (1964) — the latter a promised gift to the MCA — mirror the nature of American culture during a period of economic and political hegemony marked by the complexities and uncertainties of societal change. Reflecting artists' fascination with and responses to the explosive societal events and technological innovations of the era as well as the increasingly prominent culture of celebrity, these works are iconic examples of art in which images from popular culture and the mass media were increasingly central

Developments in sculpture of the 1960s probed the transformative potential of the common object, the everyday, and the ostensibly banal. A group of notable works with roots in the tradition of assemblage includes pieces by the artist Marisol (p. 68), who in 1968 donated the first work to the MCA — *Six Women* (1965–66) — even before the official establishment of the Collection. This work and her *Jazz Wall* (c. 1962) exemplify Marisol's unique approach to figurative sculpture that centered in a humorous, expressive way on portraiture. Claes Oldenburg's *Green Beans* (1964, p. 74) and *Sculpture in the Form of a Fried Egg* (1966/1971, p. 75) are equally witty manipulations of banal objects that exploit scale and materiality to disjunctive, surreal effects. *Man in Bar* (1969, p. 114) is a prime example of George Segal's casts of human forms in ghostly white plaster, positioned in eloquent tableaux to evoke the loneliness characteristic of contemporary urban life. Christo (p. 76) developed a startlingly original approach to the assemblage and installation tradition by using fabric to transform and transfigure the common object as in *Orange Store Front* (1964–65) and *Museum of Contemporary Art Packed (Chicago) — Project for January–March 1969* (1968). He developed the latter as a study for an exhibition in which the entire MCA building was wrapped in canvas — an event that stands out as a highlight in the MCA's early history of experimentation with innovative, avant-garde practices.

An exhibition of works by Dan Flavin (p. 72) at the MCA in 1967–68 was another of the most controversial exhibitions in the museum's early history. While audiences at the time struggled to comprehend Flavin's use of simple neon light tubes as material for art, his experimental use of light as a medium, interest in industrially fabricated materials, and rigorously reductive aesthetics were formative contributions to what became known as minimalism. Developed as a counterpoint to expressionist and pop tendencies and reflecting an urge toward pure abstraction and object-hood, prime examples of minimalist painting and sculpture in the Collection include Robert Ryman's *Untitled No. 25* (1960, p. 61), Flavin's *the alternative diagonals of March 2, 1964 (to Donald Judd)* (1964, p. 73), Robert Irwin's *Untitled* (1965–67, p. 87), Carl Andre's *Zinc-Lead Plain* (1969, p. 110), and Donald Judd's *Untitled* (1970, p. 125) as well as several other examples of his work spanning 1965 to 1984. The emphatic geometric simplicity, insistent seriality, and mass-produced appearance of Judd's objects, together with his extensive body of writings on such issues as materiality, wholeness, and illusion versus illusionism fundamentally redefined the theory and practice of art in this decade.

Additional works of the 1960s in the MCA Collection reflect the more expansive, expressive vocabulary of what would become identified as postminimalism. Robert Morris's *Portal* (1965, p. 79) is grounded in minimalism but employs a form with multiple associations, from the

16

vernacular to the more broadly cultural and historical. Lee Bontecou's untitled 1966 sculpture (p. 88) is a major abstract work by an artist who came to prominence in the early 1960s and whose sculptures and drawings from that decade onward increasingly reflected her complex responses to the interaction between nature and culture. Throughout the 1960s Richard Serra (p. 108) and Robert Smithson (p. 90) pioneered radical ways of working with industrial materials and with ideas about the meaning of time, site, and the very action of art-making. Serra's *Prop* is joined in the Collection by Smithson's *A Nonsite (Franklin, New Jersey)*, both from 1968, as well as additional major pieces by Smithson including *Mirror Stratum* (1966) and a film documenting the artist's monumental landscape sculpture *The Spiral Jetty* (1970). These works, as well as Vito Acconci's *Stretch* (1969, p. 112) and his later *House of Used Parts* (1985, p. 113), are exceptional examples of these artists' innovations in the genres of large-scale installations and interventions directly within the physical landscape that established them as leading figures of their generation. A number of these artists have been the subject of exhibitions at the MCA; *Vito Acconci: A Retrospective* in 1980 and *Robert Smithson: Sculpture* in 1981 included several of the works now in the Collection, while Bontecou's work was presented in an early survey of 1972 and will be the subject of an MCA-organized retrospective in 2004. Richard Tuttle's *Purple Octagon* (1967, p. 99) probes the nature of nongeometric form and the painterliness of a nonpainting material, conditions the artist continues to explore. A younger generation including Tom Friedman (p. 300), Arturo Herrera (p. 302), and Richard Rezac, who work in both two and three dimensions, display similarly improvisational attitudes in their sculptures, installations, and drawings, building upon precedents established by Tuttle.

A selection of twenty works spanning 1965 to 1989 by Bruce Nauman (p. 80) distinguishes the MCA as the largest institutional home of works by this pioneering figure in postminimal and conceptual art. Nauman's restless experimentalism, which has spanned many media and areas of inquiry, continues to be central in the thinking of today's artists. The Collection encompasses a suite of eleven photographs of 1966–67 documenting a series of quasi-sculptural, quasi-performative actions testing ideas about the function

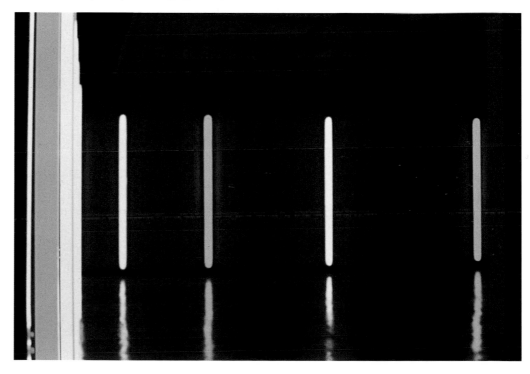

Dan Flavin: Pink and "Gold," 1967–68

and purpose of making art; sculptures, including the iconic *Henry Moore Bound to Fail* (1967/1970), *Three Dead-End Adjacent Tunnels, Not Connected* (1979), and *Hanging Carousel (George Skins a Fox)* (1988); and video installations such as *Rats and Bats (Learned Helplessness in Rats II)* (1988). The neon work *Life, Death, Love, Hate, Pleasure, Pain* (1983) is among Nauman's most defining explorations of the relationship between language and image. Its powerful simplicity of form and medium, conjoined with its circularity of linguistic reference to fundamental states of human existence and emotion, renders this work an incisive, emblematic, and complex contemporary artistic statement.

Like Nauman, Sol LeWitt (p. 92) advanced the understanding of what can constitute a work of art beginning in the 1960s. A founder of conceptual art, he articulated ideas about seriality and concepts as generators of form, privileging the rational over the emotive and the systematic over the arbitrary in theoretical writings and works ranging from the three-dimensional *Serial Project, Set D* (1966) to *Wall Drawing No. 358* (1981). Conceptual art is unquestionably the most significant contemporary development to have emerged in recent decades; many of today's most compelling works of art depend on a fusion of conceptual practices first established in the 1960s with far more intuitive attitudes and responses to various cultural, social, and emotional stimuli, resulting in works that are simultaneously rigorous and evocative. The MCA's presentation of major exhibitions of LeWitt's work in 1978 and 2000 reflects his continuing significance as a conceptual artist as well as the impact his wall drawing technique has had on the work of a younger generation in-

terested in the idea of site and reproducibility as a generator of form. Joseph Kosuth (p. 228), also a pioneer of conceptual art with a focus on language, is represented in the Collection with *No Number #6 (On Color, Blue)* (1991) exemplifying the commitment to the conflation of language and image he first explored in the 1960s.

Modeling The Future: The New Museum and Key Works from the Permanent Collection, 1992, with works by Andy Warhol, Robert Smithson, and Joseph Beuys

Elizabeth A. T. Smith

Unmasking, Deconstructing, Provoking: Art of the 1970s

The 1970s marked the beginning of a period of pluralism in contemporary art, characterized by the coexistence of numerous tendencies rather than the dominance of a single movement. Works in the MCA Collection by artists ranging from Europeans Marcel Broodthaers (p. 116), Joseph Beuys (p. 122), and Dieter Roth (p. 102) to Americans Richard Artschwager (p. 126), Claire Zeisler (p. 106), John Cage (p. 148), Jackie Ferrara (p. 128), Ed Paschke (p. 118), Jim Nutt (p. 120), and Christina Ramberg (p. 132) intriguingly reveal the multiplicity of interests and vocabularies that developed during this transitional period. Broodthaers pioneered a hermetic visual language that commingled literary and mass-cultural references in works such as *1833......Le manuscrit (1833......The Manuscript)* (1969–1970), while Beuys's *Filzanzug (Felt Suit)* (1970) exemplifies this artist's visionary engagement with materiality and symbolism in a quest for social, cultural, and philosophical regeneration. A large group of 1970s artist's books by Roth formed the subject of an exhibition at the MCA in 1984 and were donated by the artist to the Collection. Artschwager's *Polish Rider I* (1970–71), a prime example from within this artist's eclectic oeuvre in which he ambiguously recasts historical subject matter in contemporary terms, joins Ferrara's *Stacked Pyramid* (1972), which refers to elemental geometric forms with a range of cultural associations.

An energetic group of artists working in Chicago, including Roger Brown (p. 134), Paschke, Nutt, and Ramberg, began to capture the attention of the collecting community in the late 1960s and 1970s. The MCA produced important early shows of these artists' works, notably *Don Baum Says "Chicago Needs Famous Artists,"* curated by artist Don Baum in 1969, and *Chicago Imagist Art* in 1972. Significant early paintings by Paschke, including *Japanese Cowboy* (1969) and *Adria* (1976), are standouts from among the sixteen examples at the MCA that chronicle his contributions to imagism in Chicago. The subject of Paschke's painting *Adria* is Chicago historian and collector Dennis Adrian, who has long championed work by Paschke, Nutt, Westermann, and others working in a figurative vein. Likewise, fellow Chicagoan Nutt enjoys significant representation in the MCA Collection. His work has been the subject of two exhibitions at the MCA: *Jim Nutt Retrospective* in 1974 and a later show of his portraits in 1999. *Summer Salt* (1970), a gift of Adrian, exemplifies the artist's insistence on fantasy, scatological humor, and references to popular culture in his characteristic figurative style. While also grouped with the Chicago imagists, Ramberg diverged from their interests with her images of women drawn from popular cultural sources; her *Sleeve Mountain #1 and #2* (1973) is an important example of the highly charged approach that set her apart from her male peers and allied her concerns more closely with artists exploring feminist themes in the early 1970s.

A group of photographs from the *Silueta* series (1973–77/1991, p. 130) by Ana Mendieta reflects her engagement with performative activities centering on feminist concerns but also encompassing landscape, ritual, and issues of ephemerality. Equally innovative and site-specific work of a very different type was produced by artist Gordon Matta-Clark (p. 150) in Chicago in 1978 — the subject of an exhibition for which the artist made radical physical interventions within the space of the MCA itself, profoundly altering the building by making deep cuts within its walls. Matta-Clark's actions were documented in films and in photographs that he often collaged, as in *Circus or the Caribbean Orange* (1978). His approach to what he termed "anarchitecture" — a combination of anarchy and architecture — rethought conventional ideas about site-specific interventions combining architecture, sculpture, and performance to create political and social commentary.

Circus, or *The Caribbean Orange: Gordon Matta-Clark,* 1978

More conventional in their three-dimensionality are sculptures from the late 1970s and early 1980s by artists Martin Puryear (p. 144), Richard Hunt (p. 154), Magdalena Abakanowicz (p. 158), and Jackie Winsor (p. 156). Puryear's *Untitled* (1975–78) and Hunt's *Farmer's Dream* (1980) typify these artists' rigorous experiments with predominantly abstract forms in wood and Corten steel, respectively. In contrast, Winsor's *Cheesecloth Piece* (1981) is among her preeminent explorations with the admixture of geometric form and an experimental array of often delicate, organic materials. *Cage* (1981) is a highly characteristic work by Abakanowicz, who has consistently abstracted the figures within her work to reflect political and psychological meaning. Her disquieting sculptures were the subject of a solo exhibition at the MCA in 1982, as was Puryear's work in 1980.

Leon Golub (p. 58) has been similarly emphatic in his commitment to communicating political and social ideas in painting, insistently foregrounding the

Elizabeth A. T. Smith

human figure. His 1979 *Mercenaries I* presents menacing, larger-than-life renditions of gun-toting mercenary soldiers who boldly confront viewers. With a long history in and significance to Chicago, Golub is additionally represented in the Collection with the classically inspired *Reclining Youth* (1959) and other early examples from his extensive series of paintings of heads. His work was the subject of a retrospective presented at the MCA in 1974. Figures from marginalized or subcultural groups populate Larry Clark's photographic series including *Tulsa* (1961–1971/1980, p. 136) and *Kids* (1995), and John Ahearn's portrait sculptures, such as *Clyde* (1981, p. 165). While Clark documents the activities of teenage drug addicts in his native Tulsa, Oklahoma — a group of which Clark himself was a part — Ahearn's work seeks to honor and dignify members of a lower socioeconomic community within which he himself has lived and worked but from which he remained apart.

Art of the 1980s: From Banality to Hyperbole

Artists working during the 1980s pursued an astonishing variety of directions in their work. The dualities of banality — the mass media, consumerism, and everyday life — and hyperbole — associated with both the bombastic aspects of neo-expressionism and the intense theoretical ruminations of postmodernism — bookend a large spectrum of related ideas and endeavors. Beginning in the 1970s but not becoming fully defined until the 1980s, postmodernism took many forms and manifested widely diverse sensibilities relative to the self-conscious use of appropriation and imagery from the media, the impact of which was becoming increasingly pervasive in the culture at large.

In 1975 Cindy Sherman (p. 138), then a young artist, made five photographs modeled on the familiar genre of black-and-white head shots in which she posed with various facial expressions and props to present an array of characters. *Untitled, A, B, C, D,* and *E* are the earliest in an extensive group of works by Sherman in the MCA Collection that initiated her explorations into the fluidity of identity. Her *Untitled Film Stills* are among the defining works of postmodernism in which the artist, chameleon-like, adopted a variety of female roles drawn from B movies, using the standard genre of the eight-by-ten inch film still. Sherman's works of the 1980s undermine conventional assumptions about beauty and children's literature, using fashion photography and fairy tales as points of departure. Brilliantly parodying social and cultural mores with her simultaneously grotesque and seductive images, Sherman is one of contemporary art's formative figures, whose work continues to be crucial to a generation of younger artists. Her work was the subject of a major retrospective co-organized by the MCA and The Museum of Contemporary Art, Los Angeles, in 1998.

Richard Prince's *Untitled (Sunset)* (1981, p. 166) is a definitive example of the adoption of readymade advertising imagery taken out of context to call attention to the way it carries meaning. This emphasis on the multivalence and ambiguity of meaning and an awareness of its constructed nature are foremost aspects of the postmodern thinking that shaped art in the 1980s. Jeff Koons (p. 168) is another of the leading artists of this generation to appropriate and recast imagery from mass culture. The MCA holds several major sculptures by Koons from the mid-1980s — widely considered the period when he made his most crucial innovations — some of which were included in an influential early exhibition of his work presented by the MCA in 1988. *New Hoover Deluxe Shampoo Polishers . . .* (1981/87), *Lifeboat* (1985), and *Pink Panther* (1988) have been recently joined by another notable sculpture from this decade, *Rabbit* (1986). These works embody and extend the spirit of engagement with mass culture first pioneered in the contemporary period by the pop artists and consummately expressed by Andy Warhol, but that also stems from the work of early twentieth-century figures such as Marcel Duchamp, who used objects from non-art contexts to investigate the nature of what constitutes art itself. In a related vein, Sherrie Levine's intimately scaled *Untitled (Gold Knots: 1)* (1985, p. 186) poses Duchampian questions about the nature and meaning of art, originality, and interpretation, while provocative sculptural approaches to similar issues are found in other representative three-dimensional works spanning the 1980s: Tony Cragg's *Red Bottle* (1982, p. 172) and *St. George and the Dragon* (1985), Haim Steinbach's *Untitled (cabbage, pumpkin, pitchers) #1* (1986, p. 188), and Tony Tasset's *Button Progression* (1986, p. 192) and *Abstraction with Wedges* (1990).

The MCA Collection encompasses several key monumental paintings of the 1980s by American and European artists who used heroic scale and subject matter ranging from history and culture to the body, sexuality, and identity as a counterpoint to the reductive urges of the preceding generation of minimalists. Reintroducing iconography into painting by an emphasis on the figure or on psychologically charged references to the human subject, this tendency, labeled neo-expressionism but also stemming in large part from the subjectivity and hybridity of postmodernism, was a pronounced feature of painting during the 1980s. Major examples at the MCA include Julian Schnabel's *Aorta* (1981, p. 160), David Salle's *Din* (1984, p. 182), and Anselm Kiefer's *Banner* (1990, p. 214). Sigmar Polke's large-scale *Ashes to Ashes* (1992, p. 236), while not linked specifically to neo-expressionism, similarly probes hybrid approaches to distinct visual motives within the same painting. Chuck Close's monumental painting *Cindy* (1988, p. 200) presents this artist's characteristically larger-than-life focus on the physiognomies of his art-world friends — in this case, a portrait of artist Cindy Sherman, who herself has become an emblem of the shifting, mutable nature of identity through her own work.

Elizabeth A. T. Smith

Conceptual Photography:
An Emphasis Spanning Decades

In 1995, with his bequest of 105 major works including the entire group of Bruce Nauman hold-ings, collector Gerald S. Elliott catapulted the MCA Collection to a new level of substantive en-gagement with major movements and directions in contemporary art from the 1960s to the 1980s. In addition to the works by Nauman, his gift included many other outstanding examples of min-imalism, conceptual art and photography, and neo-expressionism by both American and European artists, redefining the MCA Collection. Stimulated initially by the presence of key works from the Elliott bequest, MCA curators have increasingly focused on conceptual photography in exhibitions and in subsequent collection building to reflect the genre's expanded status in the art world since the 1960s from its flowering in the later 1980s to its continued importance today. Notable early conceptual photographs bequeathed by Elliott include Ed Ruscha's documentation of the Sunset Strip in photographs (1966, p. 94; the MCA also owns this work in book form) and Dan Graham's *Bedroom Dining Room Model House* (1967, p. 96). These works take vernacular culture and archi-tecture as their subjects, foreshadowing the approaches of artists such as Catherine Opie, who came to prominence in the 1990s and whose work often focuses on architecture as the basis for social and cultural commentary. Many of the aforementioned works by Cindy Sherman from the 1970s and 1980s also entered the Collection as part of the bequest, as did a series by the parent figures of conceptual photography in Europe, Bernd and Hilla Becher (p. 174). *Cooling Towers* (1983) embodies their system-atic approach beginning in the 1950s to documenting archi-tectural typologies, particularly those that have both historical and formal significance.

The genre of conceptual photography has continued to develop in new and more com-plex directions. Particularly in the 1980s and 1990s, many artists used conceptual art and photography as a means of ex-amining assumptions about

Conceptual Photography from the Gerald S. Elliott Collection, 1993, with works by Cindy Sherman and Bernd and Hilla Becher

racial or sexual identity, building on premises explored and articulated in postmodern theory. A number of important works revolving around the subject of identity from the 1980s include Gilbert and George's *Winter Pissing* (1983, p. 180), an example of the duo's celebratory emphasis of gay identity from the outset of their work in the early 1960s. Jenny Holzer's *Truisms* (1983, p. 176), a work in the form of an LED sign, and Barbara Kruger's *Untitled (We construct the chorus of missing persons)* (1983, p. 178), raise questions about meaning through manipulations of text and imagery from the mass media. Adrian Piper's *Cornered* (1988, p. 204) confronts assumptions about racial identity by directly addressing the viewer, whereas *Flipside* (1991), *She* (1992), and *Bio* (1992) by Lorna Simpson (p. 240) provocatively juxtapose photographs and text to challenge viewers' readings of imagery associated with race. John Baldessari's use of found imagery from movie stills, as in *Fish and Ram* (1988, p. 198), functions in similar ways, as do Louise Lawler's *Between Reagan and Bush* (1989, p. 208) and David Robbins's *Talent* (1986, p. 190). In this latter work, a variety of headshots of artists from the 1980s are configured and titled to evoke comparisons to the status of celebrities, playfully suggesting their commodification as media stars during that era.

The Bechers have been highly influential teachers to a generation of German artists including Thomas Struth (p. 210), Andreas Gursky (p. 290), and Thomas Ruff (p. 196), whose larger-than-life-sized frontal portraits begun in the late 1980s demonstrate a related strategy of objectivity and formalism. Ruff's portraits in the MCA Collection formed part of his first experiments with startlingly large scale, an element with great influence on the work of his colleagues and contemporaries who gravitated to a similar use of this device for its vivid, dramatic impact. Ruff's hallmark portraits of the late 1980s, striking in their sharpness and clarity emphasized by their overblown scale, are joined in the Collection by a more recent example of his work — *d.p.b.02* (1999), from a series of images of important works of modern architecture by Ludwig Mies van der Rohe, in this case a softly focused, almost atmospheric view of the re-created 1928–29 German Pavilion at the Barcelona Exposition. These works reveal aspects of the profound shifts that have occurred in Ruff's oeuvre, both in subject matter and style, as he continues a ceaselessly investigatory pursuit of the possibilities of the photographic medium.

Several important photographic works spanning more than a decade by Struth are also featured in the MCA Collection. Struth's intensive, probing focus on the meaning of social spaces such as cathedrals, museums, temples, and other sites of historical and cultural importance is exemplified in his *Kunsthistorisches Museum I, Vienna* (1989–1990) and in the later *Todai-Ji, Hall of the Great Buddha, Nara* (1996) and *Milan Cathedral (Interior), Milan* (1998). Likewise, Struth's early views of streetscapes and the family portraits he has made throughout his work, a number of which are also in the Collection, further manifest his preoccupation with the intertwining of conceptual and formal approaches with social issues as he seeks to define the character and psychological implications of specific places or groupings.

Art of the 1990s: Reflections in the Mirror of American Culture

Partially in response to the stimulus of readying for its new building, the MCA Collection enjoyed unprecedented growth during the first part of the 1990s, most spectacularly through the afore-mentioned Elliott bequest. Escalating this momentum in the second half of the decade, the Lannan Foundation's 1997 gift to the MCA of eighty-five works of contemporary art included eleven ex-amples by Cindy Sherman, twenty-three by Jim Shaw, and seven by Chris Burden (p. 224), among other important pieces, profoundly enriching the Collection's scope in the realm of very recent work. A standout from among the Foundation's gifts is *The Other Vietnam Memorial* (1991), a major sculpture by Burden, who had undertaken a controversial and memorable perform-ance at the MCA in 1975. This powerful, large-scale sculpture refers to the Vietnam Veterans' Memorial in Washington, D.C., but it does so from the perspective of the "other" — an implicit critique of U.S. policies and attitudes that link this work to others by Burden from the 1990s that address the theme of war as an institution. Further investigations of recent history and cultural episodes — especially a fascination with the antihero — emerge in works that treat these subjects in ways ranging from the specific to the broadly allusive and ambiguous. Cady Noland's *Chainsaw Cut Cowboy Head* (1990, p. 218) treats the fabled figure of the American cowboy as an amalgam of disparate and discarded parts, while Jack Pierson's *Scarface* (1991, p. 230) similarly uses in-dustrial castoffs to create a text-based portrait of a legendary American antihero. Matthew Barney's *The Cabinet of Frank Gilmore* (1999, p. 294) is derived from the story of Gary Gilmore, the subject of the 1979 book *The Executioner's Song* by Norman Mailer. This sculpture functions as a portrait of Gilmore's father Frank, a character in Barney's film *Cremaster 2* (1999), by employing references to ma-terials and symbols that recur throughout the film. Many of these works, and others focusing on the complex nature of social and cultural memory, were presented in the 1999–2000 Collection-based MCA exhibition *Age of Influence: Reflections in the Mirror of*

California Scheming, 1998, with works by Mike Kelley and Chris Burden

American Culture, which centered on artists' various responses to a wide spectrum of issues stemming from the spread of American influence in recent years.

Additional works addressing instances of social conflict include Jeff Wall's *Pleading* (1988, p. 206), which presents an ambiguous, yet highly charged scene from the urban landscape — an altercation between individuals on a city street — in the artist's characteristic use of backlit photographic transparency. Alfredo Jaar (p. 226) has also repeatedly used lightboxes in his work to underscore and dramatize his images of human subjects in third world contexts. In his haunting installation *Geography=War* (1991), photographs of a geopolitical disaster in Nigeria suspended above metal barrels filled with water glow with the appeal of advertisements, their reflections appearing to float. Other works in which visual beauty and wrenching political and social commentary coexist in exquisite tension are two major animated films by William Kentridge (p. 252) — *Felix in Exile* (1994) and *History of the Main Complaint* (1996) — together with fourteen drawings related to the latter film, that address the tenuous nature of personal and historical memory in the artist's native South Africa. Many of these works formed part of a landmark retrospective of Kentridge's work coorganized by and presented at the MCA in 2001.

Several major pieces in the MCA Collection by artists Glenn Ligon (p. 242), Kara Walker (p. 272), and Kerry James Marshall (p. 270) provocatively refer to episodes in African-American history and cultural memory. Ligon's series *Narratives* and *Runaways* (both 1993) and his painting *White #11* (1994) probe historical treatises from the era of slavery as well as more recent literary works by authors addressing the subject of the invisibility of the African-American male. Like Ligon, Walker employs

and slyly undermines a familiar historical genre — the cut-paper silhouette — to make pointed references to slavery and the condition of victim and victimizer as a troublesome, ambiguous psychological phenomenon that persists in our culture. Her epic work *Presenting Negro Scenes Drawn Upon My Passage Through the South . . .* (1997) presents a dazzling, seductive

Age of Influence: Reflections in the Mirror of American Culture, 2000, with works by David Hammons and Kara Walker

Elizabeth A. T. Smith

panorama in which acts of violence and degradation reveal themselves in a sinister, quasi-narrative format. Less strident than Walker but equally ambivalent, Marshall's *Souvenir I* (1997) draws on the tradition of history painting to simultaneously honor and critique the legacy of the Civil Rights movement in America, addressing its meaning and relevance from today's perspective.

Social and cultural issues pertaining to identity and phenomena including the pervasiveness of AIDS-related deaths stimulated the production of key works in the 1990s by such artists as Felix Gonzalez-Torres (p. 216). His *Untitled (The End)* of 1990 is an ephemeral piece in which visitors can take away components of a renewable stack of paper, memorializing the loss of life to AIDS by symbolizing the ebbing away of life and the generosity of enrichment to those touched by that life. This theme of loss and anguish resounds in Jim Hodges's *The end from where you are* (1998, p. 278), created for and presented in a 1999 exhibition of the artist's work at the MCA. Arturo Herrera's *Behind the House III* (1999, p. 302), Hiroshi Sugimoto's photographic series *Time Exposed* (1991, p. 238), and Tatsuo Miyajima's sculptural installation *Counter Circle No. 19* (1993, p. 248), convey related ideas encompassing the passage of time and the circularity and ephemerality of existence. Jin Soo Kim's sculpture *Wall (from imprints)* (1994–98, p. 260) updates the concerns of an earlier strain of postminimalism in her emphasis on process to create evocative objects of delicate wire forms, while Ann Hamilton's *(the capacity of absorption • video)*, *(dissections . . . they said it was an experiment • video)*, *(linings • video)*, *(aleph • video)*, a group of works from 1993 (p. 202), revels in ambiguous ritualistic bodily actions.

Another notable sensibility of art of the 1990s is the use of a deliberately raw, crude, or childlike technique to suggest abjecthood and anomie. While in certain respects this approach also characterizes that of the earlier Chicago imagists, it has manifested itself in distinct ways throughout the work of a number of predominantly American artists who first began to make art in the late 1970s and 1980s. Mike Kelley's sculptural installation *Craft Morphology Flow Chart* (1991, p. 222), Ken Warneke's painting *The Tyranny of Everyday Life* (1990, p. 220), Tony Oursler's sculpture/video installation *Guilty* (1995, p. 266), and Raymond Pettibon's idiosyncratic drawings juxtaposing fragmentary images and text, spanning 1978 to 1995 (p. 152), offer humorous but quirky, antiformal, and even crude representations of the pathos and drama of everyday existence. A related sensibility marks the photographic and video work of Jeanne Dunning, which is extensively represented in the Collection. Dunning's *The Pink* (1996, p. 258) presents a seductive yet highly repellent field of what appears to be organic matter, while *The Toe-Sucking Video* (1994) is a patently absurdist endurance test of quasi-infantile, quasi-erotic activity

27

Various works in the MCA Collection from the late 1990s to the present evince the vibrancy and pluralism of directions within the most recent manifestations of contemporary art. Photography and mediated imagery remain central to the practice of many artists working today. Andreas Gursky (p. 290) is a foremost practitioner, known for his use of digital manipulation to enhance the qualities of large-scale photographs that in many respects approximate the properties of painting. Gursky's spectacular image of *Chicago Board of Trade II* (1999), which treats the landscape of global capitalism with startling visual impact and conceptual resonance, has become an emblematic work for the MCA; he is represented in the MCA Collection with several additional works including the coolly minimal *Prada III* (1998) and *Avenue of the Americas* (2001) as well as an example from the late 1980s. Other recent photographs by artists such as Sharon Lockhart (p. 288), whose work was the subject of an MCA-organized exhibition in 2001, rely on the traditions of conceptual art and cinema but are also characterized by a keen attention to formalism.

The MCA's holdings continue to expand in the area of sculpture and three-dimensional work. Recent examples that have entered the Collection display an astonishing stylistic variety, yet have in common their embodiment of a multiplicity of cultural and contextual references and, in some instances, an almost surrealist sense of the absurd. Dan Peterman (p. 282), who explores the possibilities of recycled materials and functionality in his sculpture and installations, produced *Accessories to an Event (plaza)* in 1998 as a commission from the MCA to stimulate activity on the museum's front plaza. Also incorporating recycled or found objects as a major component of his work, David Hammons recombined Thai Buddhist figures with the humble materials of a safety pin and string in *Praying to Safety* (1997, p. 274) to suggest an interplay of related ideas and cultural connotations. In *Alien Obsessives, Mum, Dad and the Kids* (1998, p. 286), Yinka Shonibare probes cross-cultural readings not only of the concept of "alien," but also the origin of the cloth that covers the figures — which conventionally signifies Africanism — to humorous effect. The absurd also functions as a profound component of the work of such sculptors as Tom Friedman (p. 300) and Maurizio Cattelan (p. 310). Constructed of cardboard and Styrofoam balls, Friedman's *Untitled* (1999) suggests a giant childlike robot, while Maurizio Cattelan's *Felix* (2001) draws on the tradition of pop art in its exaggerated scale and overt humor, as well as its site-specific implications — a hallmark of much of Cattelan's work that recalls the earlier pop artist Claes Oldenburg.

Several important recent video installations by artists including Shirin Neshat (p. 280) and Doug Aitken populate the MCA Collection, indicating the growing prominence of this medium as a compelling way to convey meaning and imagery at a cinematic scale. Stan Douglas's video installation *Evening* (1994, p. 250) extends the investigations of earlier artists' fascination with the media, exploring its contradictions and its shaping of our perceptions about the society in which we live. Pipilotti Rist's video projection *Sip My Ocean* (1996, p. 268) oscillates between haunting beauty, tedium, and a jarring sense of angst-ridden depravity. Experimental approaches to harnessing the properties of video, photo-based, and digital media occur in the work of Mariko Mori (p. 264), whose *Birth of a Star* (1995) combines sound and photographic imagery of a half-alien, half-human female for which the artist herself modeled — an approach that owes much to the example of Cindy Sherman — to comment on cultural and psychological phenomena of hybridity. Likewise, Iñigo Manglano-Ovalle's video and sculptural installation *Le Baiser (The Kiss)* (1999, p. 256) incorporates the artist's own image, transformed in relationship to an iconic architectural work by Ludwig Mies van der Rohe. Juxtaposing video projection and music within a large-scale sculptural framework, *Le Baiser* blurs the boundaries of media and exploits their hybrid possibilities to create an evocative three-dimensional environment in which multiple references to aspects of the human condition emerge. An additional example of combinations of media is Donald Moffett's *What Barbara Jordan Wore* (p. 312), developed for a 2002 exhibition at the MCA in which abstract painting merged with video projection and sound for an unprecedented treatment of the subject of a leading late twentieth-century political figure and the ethical dimensions of her thinking.

As this book goes to press, the Collection continues to grow with recent acquisitions of work by younger and mid-career artists who are extending and provocatively redefining the language of art. During the past two years the MCA's acquisitions have encompassed examples of photography by Beat Streuli (p. 298), Thomas Demand (p. 306), Catherine Opie, Giuseppe Gabellone (p. 304), Dawoud Bey, and others, including a notable collection of seventy-five photographic works from the 1960s to the present from Howard and Donna Stone that deepen and extend the already-established emphasis on conceptual photography in the Collection; paintings by Gary Hume (p. 232), Judy Ledgerwood (p. 262), and Laura Owens; video installations and projections by Paul Pfeiffer (p. 296) and Jason Salavon (p. 308), and sculptures by Gary Simmons, Helen Mirra, James Angus, and Damian Ortega. Many of these works have been featured in recent MCA exhibitions.

Building on the precedents established by an earlier generation of patrons and curators, the artistic program of the MCA continues to emphasize research into the most compelling and

29

substantive new developments in today's art and how it conveys meaning about the times in which we live. Through an emphatic strategy of acquiring works from exhibitions, the curatorial vision for the ongoing growth of the Collection is continuously to enhance and underscore the vital relationship between these intertwined branches of its artistic program. Over time, this strategy will continue to result in a unique identity for the MCA Collection, highlighting the museum's ongoing dedication to originating innovative, thought-provoking, and substantive exhibitions that reflect the spirit of our time — "the ups, the downs, the disruption, the chaos, the ambivalence" of the human condition. Interrelating recent history with the emerging tendencies that are themselves continuously becoming historical, the MCA Collection embodies a living, vital resource in which the present continuously inflects and informs our understanding of the past, in a dynamic and mutable framework that mirrors the shifting nature of contemporary art itself.

People See Paintings, 2002, with works by Cady Noland, Jo Baer, Thomas Ruff, Sharon Lockhart, Kenneth Noland, Georg Baselitz, and Leon Golub

Elizabeth A.T. Smith

1 This decision is documented in the minutes of an MCA Permanent Collection Committee meeting, June 26, 1974.

2 For more on this, see Joseph Randall Shapiro's introduction to *The Mr. and Mrs. Joseph Randall Shapiro Collection*, exh. cat. (Chicago: The Art Institute), p. 9.

3 Katharine Kuh, "An Appreciation," in *The Mr. and Mrs. Joseph Randall Shapiro Collection* (note 2), p. 14.

4 Michelle M. McCrillis, *Matta in Chicago: A Reexamination of the Career of Roberto Matta Echaurren in the 1950s* (Master's thesis, The School of The Art Institute of Chicago, 1992).

5 Shapiro (note 2), p. 9.

The author wishes to thank the MCA curators and other colleagues who have contributed valuable and inspired insights to this essay. Special thanks are also owed to the former curators of the MCA who nurtured the Collection's growth. This publication and the entire collection-building emphasis of the MCA have resulted from their creativity and passion, as well as their dedication of time, energy, and expertise.

SELECTED WORKS FROM

THE MCA COLLECTION

Max Ernst

French, b. Germany 1891–1976

Loplop Introducing a Bird
1929/1957
Plaster, oil, and wood
40¼ × 48½ in. (102.2 × 123.2 cm)
Ed: 2/6
Gift of Joseph and Jory Shapiro
1991.25

Inspired by the expatriate artists who founded Dada in the Zurich bar Cabaret Voltaire in 1916, a group of artists in Cologne assembled under the Dada banner in 1919 to express their outrage at the war in Europe, attacking conventional standards of aesthetics and behavior. Their leader was Max Ernst. He soon became acquainted with the French writer André Breton (1896–1966) and Paul Eluard (French, 1895–1952), chief proponents of the Paris Dada circle and central figures in the nascent surrealist movement.

Ernst moved to Paris in 1922 to join them. He became a major influence in the articulation of Breton's *Manifeste du surréalisme,* written in October 1924: "Surrealism [is] pure psychic automatism, by which an attempt is made to express, either verbally, in writing, or in any other manner, the true functioning of thought. The dictation of thought, in the absence of all control by the reason, excludes any aesthetic or moral preoccupation."[1]

In 1929, Ernst used the Dada-inspired technique of collage to produce his first "collage novel," *La femme 100 têtes* — a surrealist narrative assembled mainly from images cut out of cheap romance novels of the period. He first introduced the character "Loplop" in this work as an alter ego for himself. Like *Dada,* the word *Loplop* is itself a nonsensical invention.

Ernst produced a separate series of unique collages in which Loplop serves as a cabaret *aboyeur* or sideshow barker, presenting another element (usually a picture) within the picture. This idea may be traced back to the sixteenth- and seventeenth-century Northern European tradition of trompe l'oeil, in which a painting of a drawn curtain reveals a painting in the painting. Ernst often returned to this device in his work to communicate the surrealists' notion of an interior reality — the dream or subconscious — in a continuum parallel with the physical world.

Many historians have conjectured about the origin of Loplop in Ernst's oeuvre, particularly the Ernst scholar Werner Spies, who dedicated an entire volume to the subject. Ernst himself gave conflicting explanations. He told

Joseph Shapiro, the donor of *Loplop Introducing a Bird*, of his memory of a childhood pet cockatoo. He claimed that the bird's spirit entered his consciousness at the moment of his sister's birth, when the bird is said to have died. Ernst also recounted in a letter to his son that Loplop was the name of the boy's rocking horse — taking the name from the words "gallop, gallop." This explanation draws a parallel with both the name "Dada," a child's expression for a hobby horse, and with the name of a recurring motif in the oeuvre of fellow surrealist René Magritte (p. 50), the *bilboquet*, which is also the name of a children's toy. Regardless of Loplop's origins, the character is a doppelgänger for the artist and represents a conduit to the subconscious realm.

Loplop Introducing a Bird is a plaster cast taken from a work first made in 1929 and severely damaged during World War II. During the restoration of the original, Ernst made six separate casts of the piece. He would typically work on several variations on a motif when experimenting with a new technique or guiding principal. He painted each cast with a different subject that Loplop introduces, and so each of these later works is distinct. Two of them were acquired by Chicago collectors, a testament to the enthusiastic interest in and support of surrealists in the city. One was in the collection of Edwin and Lindy Bergman, and *Loplop Introducing a Bird* was purchased by Joseph and Jory Shapiro.

The bird-man in this work introduces a multicolored parrot in a cage. The muscular figure of Loplop stands in sharp contrast to the fragmented suggestion of Loplop in the collages of the 1930s. The caged bird represents the latent potential of the subconscious to transcend the physical world undeniably present in the rugged texture of the bas-relief surrounding the cage — the world in which Loplop himself exists. MR

1 André Breton, *Manifeste du surréalisme*, 1924, in Maurice Nadeau and Richard Howard, trans. *The History of Surrealism*, New York: Macmillan, 1965, p. 89.

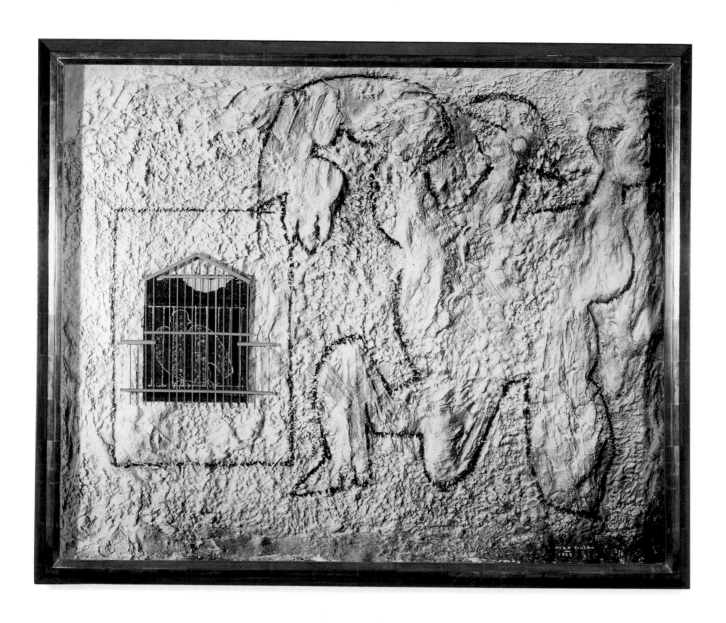

Hans Bellmer

German, 1902–1975

La toupie (The Top)
1938/1968
Oil on bronze
13¼ × 6¹³⁄₁₆ × 6 in. (33.7 × 17.3 × 15.2 cm)
Edition of 8 aside from 2 artist's proofs
Gift of Joseph and Jory Shapiro
1998.34

Hans Bellmer spent his youth and early adulthood in Berlin, where he associated with the Dadaists and identified with their irreverent spirit and leftist politics. In the 1930s he made occasional trips to Paris, where he formed lasting ties with the surrealists. In 1938, when the fascist regime in Germany made life there intolerable, Bellmer moved permanently to France.

Bellmer, like other surrealists, chose eroticism as a central theme in his work. He perceived the erotic not simply as sexual passion but as the link between pleasure and the forbidden, a connection that had political connotations during the rise of fascism. Drawing on the psychoanalytic theories of Sigmund Freud, the surrealists saw art as a means of liberating repressed erotic impulses. For Bellmer, liberation from repression implied both familial and political modes of antiauthoritarianism. Bellmer was strongly affected by his turbulent relationship with his stern and puritanical father, against whom he ultimately rebelled by dropping out of engineering school, thus forfeiting family financial support. In the 1930s, when Bellmer was developing the work that would distinguish his oeuvre, he witnessed the rise of fascism and was branded a "degenerate artist" by the Nazis while living in Germany. In response, Bellmer declared by the end of the 1930s that he would never work in the service of the state.

Although Bellmer's primary media were photography and drawing, the artist produced five sculptures in the late 1930s, all based on the doll figure. *First Doll* (1934) was Bellmer's first mature surrealist work. Bellmer photographed each stage in his construction of the doll. That series of photographs was published in the surrealist journal *Minotaure* in December 1934, winning him recognition and acceptance among the surrealists. The final sculpture was titled *La toupie (The Top)*. Bellmer made a small model for a sculpture from his drawings, which was destroyed, and in 1968 re-created the sculpture in bronze and painted-bronze editions.

What distinguished Bellmer's approach from other surrealists' use of surrogate humans — such as mannequins, robots, and puppets — was the degree to which he reconfigured and multiplied body parts in unnatural ways. According to Bellmer, the subconscious mind understands body imagery as words in a sentence, scrambling them to represent psychic truths. In a 1957 statement of his ideas and methods, Bellmer described the body in the unconscious as an anagram, its psychic significance revealed only in isolation and displacement from its ordinary position. *La toupie (The Top)* demonstrates Bellmer's further conviction that, in the unconscious, desire becomes fixated on a psychically significant fragment (the breast, for example) causing that object to multiply in the imagery of the subconscious.

Bellmer found support for his belief in the body as anagram in ancient statuary. He compared the statue of Diana on the temple at Ephesus in the sixth century BC to a spinning top, and made drawings in 1938 in which he modeled *La toupie (The Top)* with titles referring to Diana of Ephesus. Bellmer translated the ancient statue with breasts into a representation of a modern machine, in which Diana of Ephesus becomes a top that spins on a ball joint. In doing so, Bellmer not only represents the multiplication of the fetish objects but also wittily associates the metaphors of biological and mechanical reproduction. A P

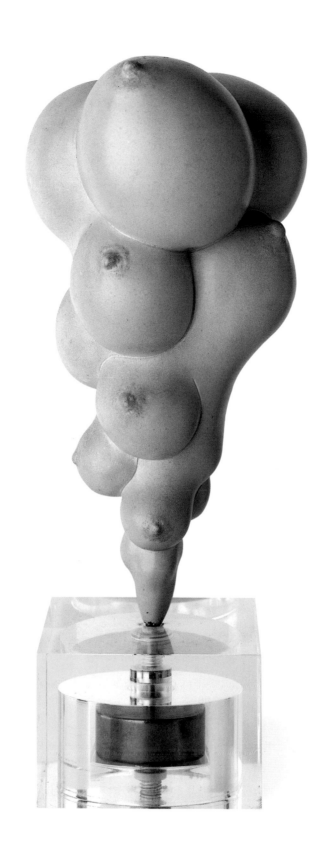

Victor Brauner

Romanian, 1903–1966

L'objet qui rêve II
(The Object that Dreams II)
1938
Oil on canvas
31¾ × 25⅝ in. (80.6 × 65.1 cm)
Gift of Joseph and Jory Shapiro
1992.53

Victor Brauner joined the circle of surrealists led by André Breton (French, 1896–1966) in 1933, shortly after leaving his native Romania for Paris in 1930. He consistently participated in surrealist activities and exhibitions until 1948. The surrealists sought liberation from conventional artistic expression, especially naturalistic subject matter, and Brauner gravitated toward their experiments with images drawn from the recesses of the psyche. In retrospective commentary, Brauner hinted at the reason for his break with the group; as he developed increasingly idiosyncratic imagery, his need for identification with the group became less important. Brauner also acknowledged that the contradiction between idealized individualism and group solidarity was a continual source of tension among the surrealists.

This tension is also evident in surrealist imagery. Like other members of the group, Brauner believed that the individual's dream and fantasy life was the wellspring of the collective unconscious, which, in turn, was the source of revolutionary truths that had been repressed in the process of socialization. He mixed dream imagery with ancient mythological symbol systems, and created hybrids of abstracted human-animal forms reminiscent of the ritual art forms of non-Western cultures, such as Oceanic and African masks. For the surrealists, eyes symbolized transcendental as well as physical understanding, and like Wifredo Lam (p. 40), Brauner positioned eyes prominently within his compositions. The eye motif took on a personal significance for Brauner; he lost one of his own in an accident in 1938.

In *L'objet qui rêve II*, eyes are a central feature. The female figure's eyes are closed, as though she is unconscious. The figure of the frog, however, is alert, with open eyes that are depicted directly under the closed eyes of the larger figure. The open-eyed frog suggests that the female figure's psyche has been awakened in the process of dreaming. For the catalogue *Victor Brauner:*

Paintings from 1932 to 1958 (1959), Brauner wrote this to accompany the work:

> A daydream in honor of Woman shown as a moving flame-Life. The frog is a mutation of the great humid depths which gives to mortal existence the immortality of thought; thus, in her turn, Woman becomes the great initiator."[1]

The statement parallels the enigmatic sensuality with which Brauner imbued the image.

A drawing study Brauner made for this work the same year, titled *L'objet qui rêve (The Object that Dreams)*, reveals a great deal about Brauner's way of arriving at his cryptically suggestive imagery. In this study, Brauner depicts the furry-limbed figure with breasts, genitals, and a spiny tail; the painting replaces those explicit depictions of sexual characteristics with the symbolic frog figure. This substitution follows the concept of "displacement," which Freud used to describe a common process in the formulation of dreams, whereby the real erotic basis of a thought is allowed expression via symbolism. Brauner intended his works to serve as catalysts for viewers to explore their notions of sexuality and eroticism. AP

1 Richard L. Feigen, *Victor Brauner: Paintings from 1932–1958*, exh. cat. (Chicago: Richard L. Feigen & Co., 1959), unpag.

Wifredo Lam

Cuban, 1902–1982

Anamu
1942
Oil on canvas
60 × 50 in. (152.4 × 127 cm)
Gift of Joseph and Jory Shapiro
1991.26

Wifredo Lam was a pioneer of the African movement of self-reclamation, or negritude, in art. He is acknowledged by many art historians as the first artist to express African aspects of the culture of the Americas from an indigenous perspective. Among his greatest achievements is his synthesis of Afro-Cuban aesthetics and religious symbolism with mainstream artistic modernism, including cubism and surrealism. Cultural hybridity was integral to nearly every aspect of Lam's life — from his genealogy as the son of a Chinese father and an Afro-Cuban mother to his artistic influences and identifications.

Lam spent much of his youth in Segua La Grande, Cuba, living with his mother and godmother. They exposed him to the beliefs and customs of Santería, an Afro-Cuban religion derived from African slaves in Cuba who fused Yoruba deities with Roman Catholic saints. When Lam studied art at the Academy in Madrid, Spain, from 1923 to 1937, he was disturbed by the separation and hierarchical distinction made in the Western tradition between so-called "primitive" arts and the art of ostensibly "mature" cultures.

Lam found a way out of such strictures in modernism. Moved by an exhibition of work by Pablo Picasso (Spanish, 1881–1973) in Madrid in 1936, Lam sought out and began a life-long friendship with the artist when he moved to Paris in 1938 in exile from the Spanish Civil War. The Parisian avant-garde revered African art; it was through Picasso's collection of African sculpture that Lam first learned about the African art that would thereafter inspire his imagery. Through Picasso, Lam also met the surrealist André Breton (French, 1896–1966) and his circle, whose intellectual and aesthetic sensibilities both affirmed Lam's sense of wonder about his Afro-Cuban heritage and offered him a model for representing the intangible forces of spirit and nature.

When Lam left France in 1941 following the Nazi occupation, he returned to Cuba. There he found validation of his interests in expressing the beauty and power of Afro-Cuban culture in the company of a group of ethnographers, folklorists, and other intellectuals who were part of the Afro-Cuban movement. It was then that Lam developed the motifs that we now recognize as his distinctive imagery.

Anamu represents this pivotal turn in Lam's art, around 1942. That year, he began to create images of hybrid beings — seated or standing figures combined with animal, human, and plant elements. In *Anamu,* the standing figure resembles a plant stalk with offshoots of palm fronds and animal or human appendages. The word *anamú* refers to a wild plant used in Santerían medicines and rituals to ward off evil. Central to the Afro-Cuban worldview is the belief in the unity and spiritual power of nature. Lam's hybrid forms integrate references to aspects of nature while including culturally specific references to African art. In *Anamu,* the pointed oval face of the figure, which Lam used repeatedly, was inspired by an African sculpture type found in the region from the Congo Basin to Nigeria. Unlike Picasso, the surrealists, or the abstract expressionists of the 1940s and 1950s who used totemic imagery mainly to arrive at a new formal language in abstraction, Lam sought to maintain the reference to the cultural source of his imagery. AP

Matta

Roberto Matta
Chilean, b. 1911

A Grave Situation
1946
Oil on canvas
55 × 77⅛ in. (139.7 × 195.9 cm)
Gift of the Mary and Earle Ludgin Collection
1998.30

Let's Phosphoresce by Intellection #1
1950
Oil on canvas
58 × 69⅝ in. (147.3 × 176.8 cm)
Gift of Mr. and Mrs. E. A. Bergman
1976.45

One of the youngest members of the surrealist circle, Chilean-born Roberto Matta was part of a community of artists in exile in New York from 1939 to 1948. Fusing surrealist-inspired painting techniques with references to the physical landscape, architecture, and the human figure, Matta sought to depict "reality in a state of perpetual transformation."[1] He succeeded in conjoining his portrayal of man's inner life with references to events in the world around him, from the horrors of war to advances in science and technology and their influence on human life. It is the realm of psychic space that has most deeply preoccupied the artist throughout his career and that characterizes his major works in the MCA Collection.

A Grave Situation demonstrates the artist's use of personal iconography to comment on man and society in the aftermath of World War II. It encapsulates an anguished social commentary within the framework of a psychological landscape fraught with tension and transformation. Beginning in 1945, Matta used overt references to figures in his paintings to address world events within his predominantly abstract visual language. An abstracted, totemic figure dominates the center of the composition, arms outstretched and straining against the confines of an architectural enclosure. This skeletal, primitivistic figure, in a gesture of agonized supplication, represents a universal idea of man. Derived from sources including Northwest Native American totems and the ritualistic figures of New Caledonia, as well as a sculpture by Alberto Giacometti (Swiss, 1901–1966), a cast of which Matta owned, this universal figure appears often in Matta's works of this period.

A Grave Situation also reveals the artist's unorthodox use of color; a lurid orange pervades the painting, evoking

the otherworldly and conveying the idea of psychic space. Art historian William Rubin has linked Matta's use of color to the influence of the mystic Eliphas Levi, whose writings referred to the concept of a universal "astral light" that seems to resonate from within Matta's canvases; the surrealist André Breton (French, 1896–1966) noted Matta's contributions as revolutionizing pictorial space and saw in his use of color new ways of portraying the world.

During his New York years, Matta interacted not only with the older generation of exiled European surrealists including Yves Tanguy (American, b. France 1900–1955) and Marcel Duchamp (French, 1887–1968), both of whom were highly influential on his own work, but also with a younger generation of American artists that included Robert Motherwell (1915–1991), Jackson Pollock (1912–1956), William Baziotes

(1912–1956), and Arshile Gorky (1905–1948). Matta played a pivotal role within this circle by virtue of his youth, his ability to speak English, and his exuberant personality, but most importantly through the revelatory impact of his paintings and drawings on the young Americans. His influence in introducing many young New York artists to surrealist practices during the early 1940s, stimulating the development of what later became known as abstract expressionism, has been termed catalytic.

A Grave Situation typifies Matta's commitment during the later 1940s to the making of art that directly addressed aspects of contemporary reality and the turbulent social and psychological tenor of the world around him, marking the beginning of his work's divergence from the concerns of the New York school artists. By 1950, when he painted *Let's Phosphoresce by Intellection #1*, Matta had returned to live in Europe and was continuing to explore his unique per-

sonal language of painting, which, in its enigmatic references to science, metaphysics, politics, and the persistent use of the human figure, differed markedly from the "tragic and timeless" emphasis found in the work of his American contemporaries. ES

1 Gordon Onslow-Ford, "Notes on Matta and Painting (1937–1941)," in Germana Ferrari, *Entretiens Morphologiques, Notebook No. 1, 1936–1944* (London: Lugano-Svizzera and Sistan, 1987), pp. 23–25.

43

Francis Bacon

British, b. Ireland 1909–1992

Study for a Portrait
1949
Oil on canvas
58¹³⁄₁₆ × 51⁷⁄₁₆ in. (149.4 × 130.6 cm)
Gift of Joseph and Jory Shapiro
1976.44

Francis Bacon's figurative paintings have long been regarded as preeminent examples of the portrayal of life's anguish and futility, especially as felt during World War II. His use of garish color, aggressive painting style, and agitated, often screaming subjects conveys a disturbing view of the human condition.

Portraiture is the predominant genre in Bacon's oeuvre. Although he is best known for his series of portraits of popes based on historical paintings such as *Pope Innocent X* (1650) by Diego Velázquez (Spanish, 1599–1660), Bacon also drew inspiration from an astonishingly wide variety of sources, including paintings of modern businessmen, painted studies of animals, works by Vincent Van Gogh (Dutch, 1853–1890), studies by Eadweard Muybridge (English, 1830–1904) of figures in motion, and the crucifixion of Christ for his subjects. He created portraits of people he knew, including Mick Jagger and Lucien Freud (German, b. 1922), as well as anonymous portraits.

Study for a Portrait was featured in Bacon's first solo exhibition at the Hanover Gallery in London along with his related *Head* series (I–VI). Critics viewed the 1949 exhibition as a culmination of the influences of surrealism, existentialism, and the tragic postwar mood. *Study for a Portrait* (formerly known as *Man in a Blue Box*, donor Joseph Shapiro's title for the work) displays many of the conventions characteristic of Bacon's portrait paintings.

Like papal portraits of the sixteenth century, which place a figure in front of a solid, ambiguous background, the businessman in *Study for a Portrait*, identifiable by his suit and tie, hovers within a dark green field. The only illusion of spatial depth is created by the transparent box in which he sits. Bacon did not work from models, rather he referred to reproductions of images and his memory. The silent scream suggested by the man's wide open mouth is often traced back to a still that hung in Bacon's studio from Sergei Eisenstein's 1925 film *The Battleship Potemkin* of a nurse screaming as her eye is shot. He often claimed that his paintings reflected his nervous state at the time of painting. He eschewed predominant artistic trends of the 1950s and 1960s, although working from memory relates his work to the abstract expressionists.

Bacon's stylistic and thematic motifs endured, although his late paintings became more abstracted and grotesque, as well as more vivid in color. His work was consistent throughout his career in its emotive painterly expression and underlying tone of anxiety and suffering.
JRW

Jean Dubuffet

French, 1901–1985

La verrue sous le nez
(The Wart under the Nose)
1951
Oil on board
28¾ × 23⅝ in. (73 × 60 cm)
Gift of Mr. and Mrs. E. A. Bergman
1978.43

Jean Dubuffet's outspoken nature, bold writings, and paintings and sculptures, as well as his seminal collection of Art Brut (raw art) — works of art by the mentally ill and others who produced inventive and spontaneous art — make him one of the most compelling figures of twentieth-century Europe. Dubuffet felt strongly that *true* or *pure* art focuses on the commonplace and rejects traditional and learned Western notions of beauty, logic, and analysis. His great passion for the objects and people that he observed overwhelmed him to the point that, after his early academic training, he stopped making art and became involved in his family's wine business, among other pursuits. In 1942, however, Dubuffet resumed painting, determined to emulate the spirit of Art Brut. Like the work he had started collecting, the art that Dubuffet sought to produce was denatured (free from cultural influences), depicting such subjects as the human figure, animals, cityscapes, and domestic objects.

Dubuffet painted *La verrue sous le nez* in 1951; it is one of several renderings of the human head from the 1940s and early 1950s. The MCA work presents the face of an anonymous person, though Dubuffet also produced a number of portraits during this time. Using his typical technique, Dubuffet coarsely incised the outlines of the facial features in thick layers of a variety of brown, red, and blue pigments, without regard to perspective, proportion, or veracity. His energetic buildup of layers of paint produced the effect of a raw or unfinished surface. The form is rather simple and childlike, with squiggles for the misplaced ears, a stylized hat that flows directly into the head, the trunk of the figure no more than an unarticulated mass, and the wart itself difficult to find within the irregularities of the painted surface. Along with a related work of the same year, *Tête aux soufflures (Head with Blisters)*, and others of this time, *La verrue sous le nez* can be understood as

a strident rejection of the classical definition of beauty, as well as an example of the artist's insistence on prosaic subject matter. Dubuffet wrote,

> I am not interested in what is exceptional and this extends to all domains. I feed on the banal. The more banal a thing may be, the better it suits me. Luckily, I do not consider myself exceptional in any way. In my paintings, I wish to recover the vision of an average and ordinary man, and, it is without using techniques beyond the grasp of an ordinary man . . . that I have tried to constitute great celebrations. [1]

These paintings can also be considered in terms of Dubuffet's fascination with the nature of his materials — it is probable that the titles came after the completion of the paintings and that the material peculiarities of each surface brought to mind the physiognomic traits singled out. Dubuffet perceived paint as a living substance itself and endeavored to work in tandem with his materials and their inherent properties.

The year 1951 was important for Dubuffet: he presented his philosophy in the form of a lecture, "Anticultural Positions," at The Arts Club of Chicago in conjunction with one of his first exhibitions in the United States. His engagement with tenets of non-Western thought as well as art outside of the mainstream were eagerly embraced by many artists and collectors in Chicago interested in a roughly rendered, nonacademic figurative art. SB

1 Margit Rowell, in *Jean Dubuffet: A Retrospective* (New York: Solomon R. Guggenheim Museum), p. 15.

Alexander Calder

American, 1898–1976

Snow Flurry II
1951
Painted sheet metal and steel wire
96 × 96 in. diameter (243.8 × 243.8 cm)
Gift of Ruth and Leonard J. Horwich
1983.80

Polychrome and Horizontal Bluebird
1954
Painted sheet metal and steel wire
39 × 63 in. diameter (99.1 × 160 cm)
Gift of Ruth Horwich
1991.92

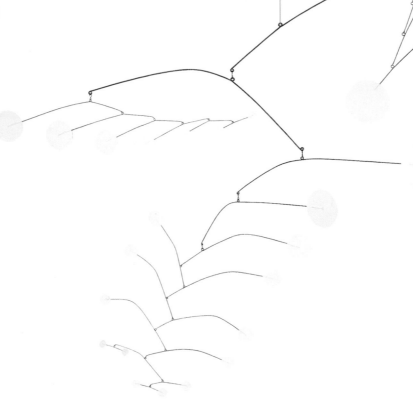

48

The Leonard and Ruth Horwich Family Loan of works by Alexander Calder, which includes mobiles, sculptures in metal, bronze, and wood, and works on paper, together with the major mobiles in the MCA Collection, *Untitled* (1944), *Brass in the Sky* (1947), *Snow Flurry II*, and *Polychrome and Horizontal Bluebird*, survey almost the entirety of Calder's career and reveal his tremendous range. One of the twentieth century's most prominent artists, Calder is best known for his innovation of the mobile: a hanging assembly of wire and sheet metal that responds to currents of air. While Calder came from a family of successful artists, he earned a degree in engineering before devoting himself to art. Early in his career he made numerous mechanical toys, which in part inspired the kinetic and dynamic qualities of his mobiles, including the famous *Circus* developed during the early 1930s, now on

permanent display at the Whitney Museum of American Art, New York.

A sense of delight and wonder is reflected both in Calder's characteristic use of bright, primary colors and organic and geometric forms, a vocabulary that has roots in his association with the surrealists and other modernists in Paris in the 1920s and 1930s. Among Calder's acquaintances were Jean Arp (French, 1887–1966), Joan Miró (Spanish, 1893–1983), Fernand Léger (French, 1881–1955), Man Ray (American, 1890–1976), and Piet Mondrian (Dutch, 1872–1944). Calder shared these artists' penchant for abstracting natural forms, rendering them as simplified geometric and organic shapes, and juxtaposing these forms in whimsical, fantastic combinations. His work also has connections to such surrealist masters as René Magritte (p. 50), Wifredo Lam (p. 40), Jean Dubuffet (p. 46), and Roberto Matta (p. 42).

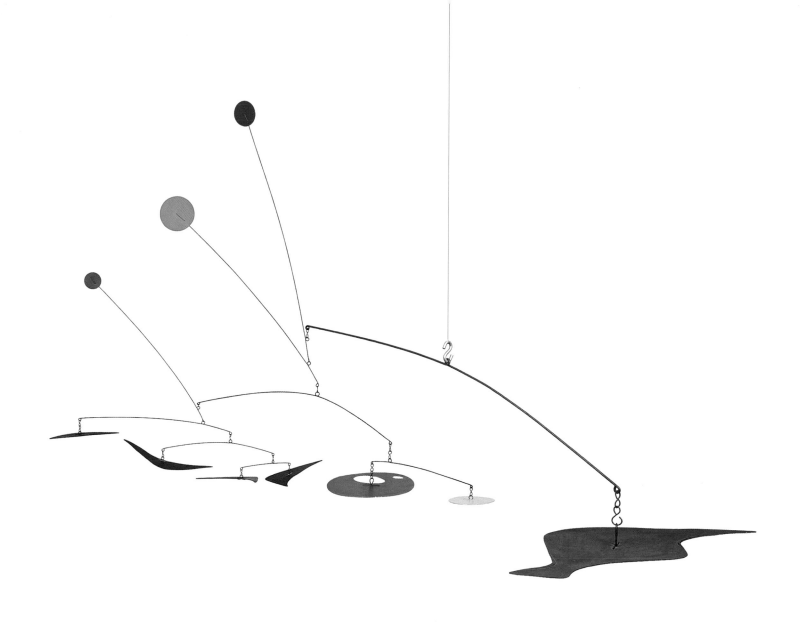

Calder used modest materials, most characteristically sheet metal and wire in his stabiles — stationary works that suggest movement — as well as in freestanding mobiles with moving elements on a static base such as *Performing Seal* (1950). He also made extensive use of found objects, such as the broken bits of bottles and glass that make up the charming *Little Face* (c. 1945). Later in his career he created monumental pieces such as *Brass in the Sky*. This work is the artist's only large-scale unpainted brass mobile.

While Calder attended the Art Students League in New York in the late 1920s, he painted and made wood carvings. When he began making mobiles and stabiles out of sheet metal, he also used found objects in his work, particularly driftwood and broken glass. Yet Calder's use of materials hardly formed a neat, linear progression throughout

his career. For example, although he was well into his production of often dazzlingly elaborate mobiles by the 1940s, he also made bronze sculptures from plaster casts during this period, such as *A Detached Person* (1944/1968). In addition, he used the found objects more characteristic of his earlier mobiles and stabiles in later works, such as *Bird* (c. 1952, from the Leonard and Ruth Horwich Family Loan), made from old coffee cans. Furthermore, Calder's use of materials and formats was radically limited by the onset of World War II, when the sheet metal he typically used for his mobiles became scarce.

Calder's range and resourcefulness over his long career was nevertheless grounded in consistent artistic concerns. His central preoccupation was with the disparity between form, masses, and movement and how he could shape this dynamism through relatively simple means. Like the organic forms and objects that inspired him,

especially those that are naturally buoyant in water or air, such as leaves, fish, birds, and snowflakes, Calder's art contains a multiplicity of experience. Indeed, the artist saw his mobiles as microcosms of the universe.

Chicago has long had a special affection for the art of Alexander Calder. Two of his significant early solo exhibitions were held at The Arts Club and The Renaissance Society in 1935. The Chicago collectors the Horwichs amassed one of the largest private Calder collections in the world, and the MCA mounted a major Calder retrospective in 1974, the year that two public works by Calder were dedicated in Chicago — *Flamingo,* the sculpture in the Federal Plaza, and *Universe,* the kinetic mural in the foyer of the Sears Tower (rededicated in 1999). LW

René Magritte

Belgian, 1898–1967

Les merveilles de la nature
(The Wonders of Nature)
1953
Oil on canvas
30½ × 38⅝ in. (77.5 × 98.1 cm)
Gift of Joseph and Jory Shapiro
1982.48

Although he was not a member of the original surrealist group of artists based in Paris and formed with the leadership of André Breton (French, 1896–1966) in 1924, René Magritte was indisputably the chief proponent of surrealism among the group of Belgian artists who closely aligned themselves with Breton's group. In 1927, Magritte moved from Brussels to a Paris suburb, Perreux-sur-Marne, after his first solo exhibition, held at the Galerie Le Centaure in Brussels, was panned by critics. There he met the French surrealists and began a close association with members of the group, particularly Breton. Although this association was short-lived, it established him as a kindred spirit and a worthy, if non-ordained, member of the group. With the penning of the second surrealist manifesto in 1929, Magritte was formally accepted into the group along with Salvador Dalí (Spanish, 1904–1989). He quickly tired of the polemics that characterized both Breton and the surrealists, however, and he returned to Brussels in 1930.

Debate concerning Magritte's designation as a surrealist continued sporadically as late as the 1960s. Critics argued that his work was literal, literary-minded, and had more to do with semiology than with the "omnipotence of the dream, and in the disinterested play of thought."[1] His first word pictures of 1929, which included *La Trahison des images (The Treachery of Images,* or *"This is not a pipe")* were revolutionary and tremendously influential to philosophers such as Georges Bataille and Henri Michaux, and later to Michel Foucault. Magritte himself wrote "I consider valid the linguistic attempt to say that my pictures were conceived as material signs of freedom of thought."[2]

Adding to the paradoxical nature of Magritte's word-pictures, the application of linguistic and semiological theory to his work was facilitated in part by his collagelike juxtapositions of disparate or impossible objects in irreconcilable settings. Max Ernst (p. 34) once described Magritte's paintings as "collages painted entirely by hand."[3] Magritte's titles also explored the nuances and subtleties of language, describing impenetrable mysteries. This extended beyond his imagery in titles such as *Les merveilles de la nature (The Wonders of Nature),* a painting of two inverted and petrified half human–half fish figures sitting with their backs to the sea as a phantom ship courses the waves on the horizon. Paradoxically, the figures in Magritte's painting are supernatural rather than natural wonders.

Magritte painted this work in 1953 specifically for an exhibition on the theme of the mermaid, *Exposition sur le thème La Sirène,* at La Sirène gallery in Brussels. His invention of the inverted mermaid originated several years earlier, however, in an illustration for the 1945 La Boétie edition of *Les Chants de Maldoror* by the Comte de Lautréamont (Isidore Ducasse) in which a mermaid sits alone by the sea as a derelict ship flails against tempestuous waves. A merman first appeared in his work in 1947 with a painting titled *Le Vieux canonnier (The Old Gunner),* which depicts the figure, peg-legged, sitting beside the sea and embracing a naked youth. Like the earlier illustration, the subject of *Les merveilles de la nature* seems to be suggested by Lautréamont's lines:

> They howl . . . at the navigation lights to be seen on the masts of invisible vessels . . . at the great fish, which while swimming show their black backs then sink into the depths; and at man, who makes them slaves . . . No one has seen the green fissures on my forehead; nor the bones protruding from my spare features, akin to the spiky fins of some huge fish . . . why are you not with me, your quicksilver belly against my breast of aluminum, both of us seated on some rock by the shore, to meditate on this spectacle I adore !"[4]

In the same year, Magritte included the mermaid and phantom ship in his huge mural for the Casino Communal at Knokke in Belgium. He published sources from his own oeuvre for the mural, citing *Le Séducteur* (1951) as the forerunner of the phantom ship, and two works, *Le Vieux canonnier* and *L'Invention collective* (1934), as the precursors of the mermaid.

Since its acquisition by Joseph and Jory Shapiro in 1957 until more recently, the painting was known as *Le Chant d'amour* or *The Song of Love,* the spurious title given by the donors. Sarah Whitfield and Michael Raeburn restored its correct title and provenance in their 1993 publication *René Magritte Catalogue Raisonné.* MR

1 André Breton, "Manifeste du Surréalisme," 1924, in Maurice Nadeau and Richard Howard, trans. *The History of Surrealism* (New York: Macmillan, 1965), p. 89.

2 Harry Torczyner, "René Magritte," in *Magritte: Ideas and Images* (New York: Harry N. Abrams, 1979).

3 David Sylvester, *Magritte* (New York: Harry N. Abrams, 1992).

4 Isidore Ducasse (Comte de Lautréamont, pseud.) *Les Chants de Maldoror with Illustrations by René Magritte* (Brussels: La Boetie, 1948).

Franz Kline

American, 1910–1962

Franz Kline's large-scale, black-and-white paintings embody the ambience of frenzied, postwar New York City. *Vawdavitch*, with its forceful, spontaneous strokes, epitomizes Kline's expressive and dramatic oeuvre. His intuitive and introspective approach to art — and his self-destructive lifestyle that eventually led to his untimely death in 1962 — became part of the myth that defined abstract expressionism.

Born in 1910 in an industrial Pennsylvania town, Franz Kline grew up in an area surrounded by coal mines, timber companies, and railroads. He moved to New York in the late 1930s and became a regular at the Cedar Street Tavern, then a favorite haunt of artists and writers such as Jackson Pollock (American, 1912–1956), Willem de Kooning (American, b. Netherlands 1904–1997), Mark

Rothko (American, b. Russia 1903–1970) Harold Rosenberg, Jack Kerouac, and Allen Ginsberg. Kline was close friends with several important New York photographers of the time, especially Aaron Siskind (1903–1991) who paid homage to Kline in a series of important images and whose photographs of the urban landscape shared visual elements with the abstract forms that Kline painted.

Kline began his career as an academic artist, creating portraits, still lifes, landscapes, and cityscapes. His later paintings were influenced by a discovery he made after projecting one of his small graphic sketches upside down. He was said to have been astounded by the impact of the elements, the strength of the strokes in such a large format, and the absence of the representative image

Vawdavitch
1955
Oil on canvas
62¼ × 80¹¹/₁₆ (158.1 × 204.9 cm)
Gift of Claire B. Zeisler
1976.39

from the drawing. Legend has it that this was the moment when Kline became a peer member of the abstract expressionists. Some argue, however, that his major breakthrough came after seeing de Kooning's black-and-white abstract paintings of the late 1940s.

In 1955, Kline painted *Vawdavitch* as part of a series of black-and-white canvases that he produced from 1950 until his death twelve years later. Kline worked on several canvases at once, painting over and readjusting the work, the imagery evolving through the process of painting. His motions personified action painting, with large bold swipes punctuated by drips and stains. In *Vawdavitch*, Kline skillfully balanced powerful strokes of black-and-white paint with directional gestures and voids that recall the railroads and architecture of his youth. The direct and raw surface of *Vawdavitch* creates a powerful psychological portrait of the artist. While he probably conceived it in the form of small, architectonic forms on paper, Kline resolved this finished work with arm-length vigorous strokes that recalled the actions that created them. Each streak, dab, and lash of paint forms a record of Kline's unique physical engagement with this work.

Kline typically named his paintings after people and places that had an effect on his life; his dealer, Sidney Janis, recalled that *Vawdavitch* was named after one of Kline's football heroes.[1] Unlike many of his abstract expressionist peers, Kline shied away from partaking in intellectual discussions about the meaning of his art. Yet his signature paintings were considered audacious and stand out as some of the most important paintings of his time. His work was extremely influential to a younger generation of artists, including Mark di Suvero (American, b. 1933), Brice Marden (p. 145), and Robert Rauschenberg (p. 70). LH

1 Sidney Janis Gallery, letter to Museum of Contemporary Art, January 4, 1984.

H.C. Westermann

American, 1922–1981

**Memorial to the Idea of Man
If He Was an Idea**
1958
Pine, bottle caps, cast-tin toys, glass,
metal, brass, ebony, and enamel
56½ × 38 × 14¼ in. (143.5 × 96.5 × 36.2 cm)
Gift of Susan and Lewis Manilow
1993.34

**W.W.I General, W.W.II
General, W.W.III General**
1962
Pine, plywood, and fluorescent alkyd enamel
19 ¾ × 34 ½ × 13 in. (50.2 × 87.6 × 33 cm)
Gift of Mrs. Robert B. Mayer
1984.4

54

H. (Horace) C. (Clifford) Westermann is one of the most influential, yet under-recognized, figures in postwar American art. His work and his tough, no-nonsense persona earned him the respect and admiration of peers as varied as William Copley (1919–1996), Ed Kienholz (1927–1994), Donald Judd (p. 124)), Roy Lichtenstein (1923–1997), and Claes Oldenburg (p. 74). Across the Atlantic, a cult following among British artists resulted in the inclusion of Westermann's picture on the cover of the Beatles album *Sergeant Pepper's Lonely Hearts Club Band* (1967), designed by British artist Peter Blake (b. 1932). Westermann's influence continues to resound in the work of another generation of American artists, including Terry Allen (b. 1943), Bruce Nauman (p. 80), Charles Ray (b. 1953), Ed Ruscha (p. 94), Vija Celmins (American, b. Latvia 1939), and Liz Larner (b. 1960). The MCA has the largest museum collection of Westermann's objects in the world.

Westermann invented an entirely new genre of sculpture, combining the surrealist technique of assemblage, traditional sculpting practices, and design with carpentry and woodworking materials and techniques. He used common commercial and domestic products such as plate glass, plywood, galvanized sheet metal, and pile carpet as sculptural materials along with more traditional media like bronze and exotic hardwoods. At odds with the prevailing modes of abstraction in the 1950s, and later with the aesthetic purity of minimalism in the 1960s, Westermann often strove to make his sculpture pictorial or narrative by creating tableaux within vitrines or on plinth-like bases. Underscoring his working process was an indefatigable work ethic strengthened by necessity while coming of age during the Great Depression.

Memorial to the Idea of Man if He Was an Idea was Westermann's first life-sized figurative work, encapsulating many ideas and images the artist had been investigating during the 1950s. As a representation of the world or of mankind, the anthropomorphic, cabinet-like sculpture suggests society's inability to look inward with its single, one-dimensional vision. The little figure painted on the reverse of the glass inside the mouth seems to be attempting an escape, suggesting a maddening confinement within one's own skin and within

one's psyche. Such themes were taken up in Hermann Hesse's novels *Steppenwolf* (first English edition, 1929) and *Death and the Lover* (1932) (the first English translation of *Narcissus und Goldmund*), which influenced several works from this period.

Although Westermann denied that this work is a self-portrait, he spelled out his initials, "HCW," on the inside of the door with bottle caps, and placed suggestions of tattoos on the figure that are self-referential. The punning inscription "A mad cabinetmaker might" may be read as a motto referring to the structural integrity of the work, or to the creativity sometimes attributed to madness. The

work also incorporates metaphors for helplessness, such as a trapeze acrobat who, lacking arms, cannot perform on the trapeze, and a baseball player who, without a head, cannot see the ball to hit it. A ship sinks in the bottom compartment of the work as a devil laughs at its demise.

W.W.I General, W.W.II General, W.W.III General is one of a group of eight polychromed sculptures that Westermann made between 1961 and 1962. This decorative method of painting sculpture was Westermann's first

serious engagement with surface patterning, which is less pronounced but more important in his later attention to the natural patterning of wood grain. In this work, two mysterious shapes are disposed on an elliptical base in a way that suggests they are somehow derelict or debilitated. They represent two of the title's Generals, while a third is carved on the base between them. Together they comprise a militaristic triumvirate of doom. Like the Fates in Greek mythology, Clotho, Lachesis, and Atropos, Westermann's generals have ultimate control over others' lives.

This work was made in the year of the Cuban Missile Crisis, which for two

Rosebud
1963
Douglas fir, plate-glass
mirror, brass, ink,
and rubber bumpers
24¼ × 19¾ × 9¼ in.
(61.6 × 50.2 × 23.5 cm)
Partial gift of Ruth Horwich
2001.6

Billy Penn
1976
Galvanized sheet metal,
steel, pine, bronze,
and aluminum alkyd paint
79¼ × 42½ × 29⅝ in.
(201.3 × 108 × 75.2 cm)
Gift of Alan and Dorothy Press
1979.1

56

weeks in October 1961 brought the United States and the U.S.S.R. to the brink of World War III. The threat of thermonuclear war and the absurdity of hawkish members of the military who perpetuated a policy of "brinkmanship" (a term coined by President Eisenhower's Secretary of State John Foster Dulles) struck Westermann as darkly comic.

Westermann's stovepipe sculpture, *Billy Penn*, was made in 1976, the year of the United States bicentennial. Following Westermann's inclination to play on words, the title of this work is typically rich with associations: in 1681, William Penn bought rights to land on the west bank of the Delaware river, where he planned to build an ideal Christian community. He named it Pennsylvania, after his father. Penn is also famous for planning Philadelphia, the first model city in America. The geometric structure of this sculpture recalls the quadrants of the city, as its appearance evokes Philadelphia's industrial urban environment.

Westermann was also interested in themes that involve freedom and confinement: the struts or braces of *Billy Penn* evoke Penn's imprisonment in the Tower of London for his Quaker beliefs and radical preaching before he came to America. The sculpture, however, is not only about constriction, but construction, and foundations of all kinds. The struts confine the legs of the figure, but they also make a solid foundation for the square section above, a frame opening into endless possibilities, like the United States itself, built in part on Penn's foundation.

When Westermann made *Billy Penn*, he was absorbed with building his house in Brookfield Center, Connecticut. He used galvanized pipe, brand-named "Billy Penn," in the construction. The name is stamped on the sculpture near the bottom of the legs, and is echoed in a carved inscription on top. MR

Leon Golub

American, b. 1922

Reclining Youth
1959
Lacquer on canvas
78¾ × 163½ in. (200 × 415.3 cm)
Gift of Susan and Lewis Manilow
1979.52

Mercenaries I
1979
Acrylic on unstretched linen
120 × 166 in. (304.8 × 421.6 cm)
Gift of Lannan Foundation
1997.39

Since the late 1940s, painter Leon Golub has addressed power and the dynamics of male aggression. His interest in these themes comes from his conviction that great art expresses universal aspects of human experience and that great artists respond to the larger dramas unfolding in the world. Golub's preoccupation with the violent, dark side of the male psyche was shared by the abstract expressionist painters of the 1940s and 1950s, as well as other intellectuals who attempted to explain the horrors of World War II as a lashing out of the "primitive" self. Golub, however, decried the methods of the abstract expressionists, retaining his belief in the primacy of the human figure to engage the viewer's sympathy.

After earning his MFA at The School of The Art Institute of Chicago in 1950, Golub remained in the city until the mid-1950s. There, he met artists who were influenced by non-Western cultures and had already established a tradition of painting the distorted figure. Golub and his colleagues in Chicago, soon to be labeled the "Monster Roster," incorporated postwar angst into iconic figure paintings and sculptures.

In Golub's work before 1968, he strove to make his imagery universal, modeling his figures on Greek and Roman art that depicted warriors, leaders, wounded soldiers, and the victims of war. The MCA Collection includes key examples of Golub's work of this type from the late 1950s: some of the _Heads_ he painted after seeing the colossal sculptural head of the Roman emperor Constantinople in Italy, and _Reclining_

58

Youth, modeled on the famous sculpture of the Dying Gaul of Pergamon. The anonymous innocent subject of Golub's figure in *Reclining Youth* — an icon for battered idealism — is scarred by the harsh treatment of the painting's surface.

In the late 1960s, Golub became increasingly involved in the anti–Vietnam War movement. By 1972, he began to portray characters from the contemporary theater of battle in monumental compositions. He used news photos of American GIs and Vietnamese civilians as models, depicting these figures in modern dress with contemporary automatic weapons. In most cases, Golub made each figure a composite of several photographs.

With his *Mercenaries* series, beginning in 1979 with the MCA's *Mercenaries I,* and extending into the mid-1980s, Golub focused on the soldier of fortune, who found lucrative and steady employment during the 1970s and 1980s. *Mercenaries I* exposes the vanity of the "mercs" and their machismo by establishing a particular relation of the figures to the viewer. The stances, gestures, expressions, and gazes of the men are intended to suggest that we are taking their picture. Golub deliberately set up this relationship to implicate the viewer as an actor in the scene as if he were asking us, "What is your position on war?" Like the ancient dramatists, Golub aims to create pathos in the viewer, thus prompting him or her to take action.

Golub endows individuals with a sense of vitality not only through his compositional choices and choreography of gestures and expressions but also by his manner of building the surface and "skin" of the characters. Since 1953, Golub has painted the surface of his figures and then used solvents to "burn off" parts of that surface. Golub then repaints parts of the figure, often adjusting gestures and expressions. This deconstructing and reconstructing process gives the figures a raw, masklike appearance that evokes both the dynamism of our psychological makeup and the skin-flaying brutality of war. AP

59

Robert Ryman

American, b. 1930

Untitled No. 25
1960
Oil on canvas
52¾ × 52¾ in. (133.9 × 133.9 cm)
Gerald S. Elliott Collection
1995.92

Some artists use media and methods omnivorously, expanding artistic possibilities by adding to the means, while others impose rigorous limitations on their methods as a way of paradoxically expanding creative potential. Robert Ryman's work represents the latter tendency. Since approximately 1957, Ryman has limited his paintings to a white-only palette and an almost exclusively square format. What might at first seem to be restrictive rules become the basis for endless variations and experiments in types of paints and primers, brushes and brush strokes, shades of white, support materials, types of hardware for mounting the supports, compositions, sizes, and relationships of the supports to the wall. Each of these variations affects the scale and pattern of the work, defining it as a physical experience.

Untitled No. 25 is one of the earliest examples of Ryman's experiments with these limitations. Despite its intimate size, this work contains striking textural contrasts of a type that is often difficult to see in reproductions of Ryman's paintings. Thick, rough, multidirectional strokes cover most of the canvas, juxtaposed with a thin, smooth strip on the left side into which an even smoother square is painted on the lower corner. The dirty-white paint is faintly and erratically flecked with various distinct colors, a holdover from Ryman's first uses of color between 1953 and 1957, when he experimented with monochromatic painting in colors such as orange and black. According to Ryman, he finally decided on an exclusive use of white, the carrier of all colors, because of its clarity and ability to increase the visibility of the formal effects created with it. He also found that white integrated best with the white walls of the modern gallery space. Ryman's consideration of his paintings' architectural surroundings became increasingly important after this early period.

His development of an environmental approach to painting is consistent with his unconventional definition of realism. In describing his aims as "realist," Ryman means that he approaches painting as the creation of an object that refers to nothing but its physical self and its relationship to the surrounding space. This idea of realism is opposed to the long-entrenched concept of realism as representation. Ryman's literalism is closest to that of certain minimalists, especially Donald Judd p. 124); but Ryman rejects the identification of his work with minimalism. He has also been associated with mystical abstraction, exemplified by Mark Rothko (American, b. Russia 1903–1970). Although Ryman admires Rothko's work formally, he rejects any spiritual or symbolic associations with his own work.

Ryman's antisymbolic aims extend to his purely formal and architectural rationale for using white. Despite his insistence on the formal, critics and historians have repeatedly acknowledged that white carries considerable art-historical and spiritual connotations. A younger generation of artists, including Glenn Ligon (p. 242), have used color precisely for its potential for social reference. AP

Jasper Johns

American, b. 1930

Jasper Johns was one of the first major figures in American art to emerge in the wake of abstract expressionism during the late 1950s. He continues to be seen as a seminal influence on contemporary artists' tendency to complicate the ideal of direct and original self-expression in art. Along with his equally influential contemporary Robert Rauschenberg (p. 70), Johns has become known for juxtaposing different systems of representation — the verbal and the visual, the public and private, the literal and illusionistic, and the handmade and mass-produced — within works of art.

Johns's most influential body of work dates from the mid-1950s to the early 1960s. *In Memory of My Feelings — Frank O'Hara* is exemplary of Johns's attention to problems of self-expression in art. The subject of the painting is a 1956 poem, titled "In Memory of My Feelings," by the writer and critic Frank O'Hara. The poem, which O'Hara dedicated to the American painter Grace Hartigan upon the end of his relationship with her, deals with the fragility of friendship, loss, and feelings of attachment and detachment. Formally, the poem has a disjointed and, at points, numbingly dissociative quality. Its opening lines read: "My quietness has a man in it, he is transparent / he carries me quietly, like a gondola, through the streets / He has several likenesses, like stars and years, like numerals / My quietness has a number of naked selves. . . ." Johns's painting is not an illustration of the poem, but instead

**In Memory of My Feelings —
Frank O'Hara**
1961
Oil on canvas with objects
40¼ × 60 × 2⅞ in. (102.2 × 152.4 × 7.3 cm)
Partial gift of Apollo Plastics Corporation, courtesy of Stefan T. Edlis and H. Gael Neeson
1995.114.a – d

uses the poem as a layer of meaning within the work. The theme of emotional fragmentation is suggested in the painting's title, in which the phrase "my feelings" refers to the expression of someone other than Johns, someone whose feelings are dedicated to a third person. Thus O'Hara is a filter for Johns's self-expression, and poetry is a filter for painting.

References to self-revelation and concealment abound in the work. The hinges between its two halves suggest metaphoric opening and closing of the self. Some of the imagery in the painting is partially concealed, such as the barely discernable image of a skull and the stenciled words "DEAD MAN,"

perhaps a reference to the allusions to death in O'Hara's poem. Also in keeping with the poem, the painting is filled with references to connection and disconnection — not only in the hinges but in the spoon and fork bound together and suspended from a wire at its upper left edge. Johns has said that he associates cutlery with creation and destruction, as embodied in the rituals of measuring, mixing, blending, and consuming. The joined spoon and fork further act as a metaphor for the intimacy of coupling. Johns layers meaning so that each element reads differently depending on the viewer's knowledge of Johns, O'Hara, or painting itself. This layering and veiling of meaning relates to the theme of memory and the loss of access to the self and the other.

Throughout Johns's oeuvre, the play between elements that reveal and conceal aspects of the self challenges previously accepted identifications of art with personal revelations and asserts the status of art as a densely layered field of symbols and conundrums. His work has had an enormous impact on subsequent generations of artists, including Bruce Nauman (p. 80), Ed Ruscha (p. 94), and David Salle (p. 182). AP

63

Ad Reinhardt

American, 1913–1967

Abstract Painting

1962
Oil on canvas
60 × 60 in. (152.4 × 152.4 cm)
Gift of William J. Hokin
1981.44

Considered a purist and a leader in the modernist tradition, Ad Reinhardt cannot easily be delimited by the boundaries of a particular movement. Often associated with abstract expressionism, Reinhardt's paintings contradicted many of the dominant tenets of the New York movement as typified by artists such as Jackson Pollock (American, 1912–1956), Willem de Kooning (American, b. Netherlands 1904–1997), Hans Hofmann (American, b. Germany 1880–1966), and Franz Kline (p. 52). Unlike many of his contemporaries, he was an abstract artist from the beginning to the end of his career.

Reinhardt painted *Abstract Painting* as a part of his final and most widely known series of paintings. Five feet square, matte black with subtle red and blue bands forming a cross in the center, the painting presents the viewer with a visual paradox. It has an immediate power and presence with its stark blackness, yet it requires patience and acute perception to reveal its subtle imagery. Because of the visual challenge it presents — ultra-low contrast coupled with an overpowering vista of black — viewers are drawn to study the painting's visual nuances. *Abstract Painting*'s blue vertical and red horizontal bisecting bands have a value range nearly equal to the black field and require diligent viewing to perceive. In making it difficult to discern the painting's imagery, Reinhardt engages his viewers in an act of optical adjustment and discovery.

In contrast to his abstract expressionist contemporaries, Reinhardt relied less on dramatic and emotive brushwork and was more concerned with a cool, rational, and contemplative vision. In *Abstract Painting*, he reduced painting to its most essential qualities and challenged his viewers with this nearly void canvas. The reduction of form in this work highlights the physicality of the materials from which the work is made — acknowledging that paintings are first of all paint. Using a simple color field of black for this and similar paintings, Reinhardt often included unadorned

shapes such as squares, crosses, and rectangles. He liberated the paintings from all overt mimetic and symbolic references, intending the viewer to be "aware of nothing but art."[1]

Reinhardt's series of relatively bright paintings with a compressed range of lights and darks began in the late 1930s and continued until 1953. Eventually giving up color as a major component of his work, he began this investigation of nearly black paintings — including *Abstract Painting* — which he continued until his death in 1967. Cognizant of the biblical and cultural symbolism that the color (or absence of color) black carries, Reinhardt sought both to acknowledge and eliminate such references from the interpretation of his work. The painting seems impersonal, although its meditative and transcendent qualities engage viewers in highly personal experiences.

Reinhardt was the epitome of an intellectual artist — educated, well read, and well traveled, and he wrote copiously about his work. In particular, he was known for his penchant for writing heated letters to institutions, editors, and artists with whom he disagreed. The power of his work and the strength of his convictions led him to be a widely recognized and well-respected figure in the art world. LH

1 "Ad Reinhardt: Three Statements," *Artforum* 4, no. 7 (March 1966), pp. 34–35.

Andy Warhol

American, 1928 – 1987

By far the most controversial figure of 1960s pop art, and arguably the most influential, Andy Warhol recognized the importance of mass media and consumer culture in contemporary life and anticipated its explosive impact on the visual environment and cultural values. He felt it was the task of the artist to explore these subjects and, to do so, Warhol crossed multiple genres and media, as would many artists who followed him. After a successful career as an advertising designer in the 1950s, he painted, made art objects, installations, and cult films, produced a Velvet Underground record, founded *Interview* magazine, painted commissioned portraits, and relentlessly manufactured his celebrity image. He stood out among the other pop artists because he used the mass media as a medium, not just as a subject.

Troy Diptych is a pivotal early example of Warhol's art, when he made the transition from hand-painting to the silk-screening method he would use with his assistants at his New York studio, the Factory. Silk screening allowed Warhol to borrow images from the media and reproduce them repeatedly with ease, achieving a mechanical appearance. He had been experimenting with mechanical means of reproducing images on canvas beginning in 1960, using rubber stamps and subsequently stencils before settling on silk screening.

Troy Diptych
1962
Silk-screen ink on synthetic
polymer paint on canvas
81 × 110¾ in. (205.7 × 281.3 cm)
Gift of Mrs. Robert B. Mayer
1984.1.a – b

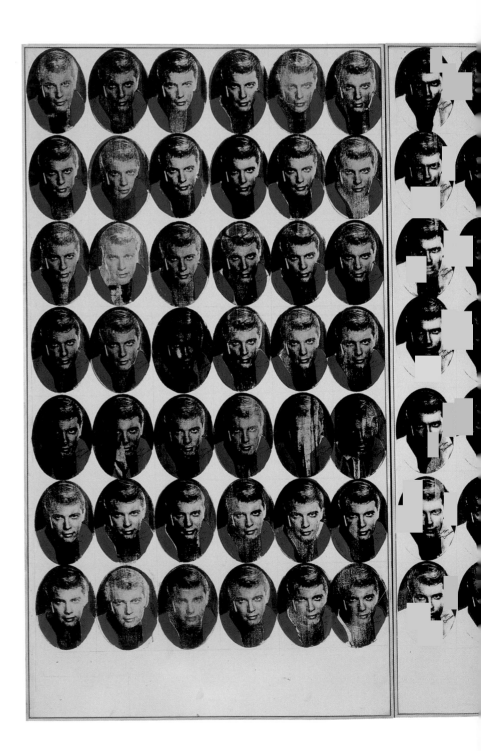

Along with other silk-screen works depicting celebrities, he made two paintings of the B-movie actor, this one and the single-panel, all-color *Troy Donahue*.

In *Troy Diptych*, Warhol explored one of his central themes, the opposition of sameness and difference. The work consists of two abutting canvases. The left panel reproduces a signed publicity photograph of Donahue in black and white in multiple across a grid structure. The right panel repeats this in bright colors. The repetition of a borrowed fan club photograph suggests the mass-produced nature of the image and the values that may be associated with it: the democracy of access to the image, on the one hand; and, on the other, the alienation from the individual, whose image the artist borrows from a mediated source. Warhol had no closer a relationship with his celebrity sitter than the viewer does. The work also seems to suggest that the mass-production of the image has a leveling effect, in terms of both the accessibility of the subject and of his individuality. Not only does the repetition of one image of a celebrity make him seem generic, but the repetition of all images of celebrities makes them all similar to one another.

The repetition of the image also demonstrates its schematic nature in spite of variations in its appearance. Changes in amounts of ink used, pressure applied to the screens, and deliberate mistakes in the registration of screens make each reproduction within one painting remarkably different. Some reproductions of Donahue are so dark that his face is obscured. Warhol also left empty spaces in some squares of the composition's grid structure. Each one of these images would have a unique expressive effect if used alone, but the combined effect of the variations is homogenizing. Warhol's play of variation and repetition critically reflects on the impact of mass culture's influence on distinctions of cultural value. AP

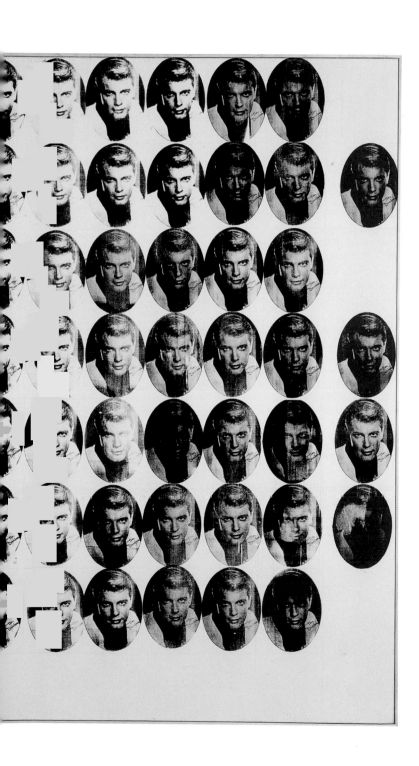

Marisol

Marisol Escobar
Venezuelan, b. France 1930

Jazz Wall
c. 1962
Paper, paint, and found objects on wood
95 × 107 × 14 in. (241.3 × 271.8 × 35.6 cm)
Partial gift of Ruth Horwich
1998.48

Marisol (Escobar), a Parisian-born artist of Venezuelan descent, picked up found objects such as discarded wooden boards or old shoes while walking the streets of New York. She combined these elements with plaster casts of her face, magazine photographs, wood carvings and loosely painted details to construct everyday scenes in life-sized tableaux. She shared this method with artists George Segal (p. 114) and Edward Kienholz (American, 1927 – 1994), with whom she was associated in the early 1960s. Unlike Segal's isolated and lonely plaster figures, however, Marisol's figure groups often generate warmth and humor, frequently conjoining famiing multiple dimensions from a frontal plane. Hans Hofmann (American, b. Germany 1880–1966), Marisol's teacher in the mid-1950s, influenced the sketched quality of her paint applications and her use of suggestive masks and facades rather than whole three-dimensional figures.[1]

Jazz Wall, an arrangement of five musicians, is an extension of relief sculpture. A seated mandolin player wearing sunglasses, two coronetists, a saxophonist, and a piano player face the viewer from a narrow stage. Marisol often chose her subjects from images in *Life* magazine, and might have spotted this unidentified jazz quintet among its pages. Complicating the distinction between painting and sculpture, these boxlike figures at once evoke the appearance of a performance while flattening toward the "wall" like a posed photograph. Suggestive representations and subtleties contribute to *Jazz Wall*'s dialogue between the real and the constructed. Actual gloves and ties recall the strange reality of snowmen or scarecrows dressed up to suggest animation. A photograph stands in for the saxophonist, while the others wear plaster casts of the artist's own face.

The symbol of the mask refers in part to the artist herself hiding behind the part she played as the artist-celebrity. She embodied a stylishness often compared to Greta Garbo or Jeanne Moreau and made appearances in the social circles of icons like Andy Warhol (p. 66). Because she satirized popular culture, nuclear families, and celebrities, critics initially placed Marisol's work under the loosely defined category of pop art. While artists like Warhol attempted to remove the "artist's hand" by imitating processes of mass production, Marisol applied wood-carving techniques influenced by Mexican, pre-Columbian, and American folk art.

Often compared to the work of surrealist artist Joseph Cornell (American, 1903–1972), Marisol's earlier works were small figurines fashioned out of terra-cotta or wood and assembled in sectioned-off boxes enclosed by glass. Her tableaux from the 1960s also recall Cornell's memory boxes: shallow frames with configurations of nostalgic found objects. The materials in Marisol's work, whether secondhand ties, masks of her face, or the photographs from which she drew her scenes, carry ambiguous histories. Marisol's sense of the absurd comes through in the central figure that appears to have two saxophones in his mouth: one held in his hands and an additional mouthpiece suggested by the photograph. Details like a plastic cup in preparation for "taking five" add endearing wit to the scene.

In *Jazz Wall,* the dichotomy between the three-dimensional boxlike quality of the figures (echoing the piano's structure) and the reaffirmation of the figures' two-dimensionality through their attachment to the support wall, or canvas, creates a similar sensation to opening a page of a child's pop-up book. The wall also echoes the fluidity and intuitiveness of jazz. H R

1 Leon Shulman, *Marisol,* exh. cat. (Worchester, Mass.: Davis Press, 1971).

Robert Rauschenberg

American, b. 1925

Retroactive II
1963
Oil, silk screen, and ink on canvas
80 × 60 in. (203.2 × 152.4 cm)
Partial gift of Stefan T. Edlis
and H. Gael Neeson
1998.49

In the early 1950s, Robert Rauschenberg began a revolution in artistic practice. With his "combines," Rauschenberg reintroduced the found object of Dada and surrealism and combined it with painted surfaces to produce hybrids of painting and sculpture. Over the decades, Rauschenberg continued to surprise with his use of new media and his inclusive approach to formats and materials, forging the heterogeneous methods that are now ubiquitous in contemporary art.

Rauschenberg also helped lay a new foundation for artists' approaches to expression in art. Reacting against the abstract expressionists' idea of art as a window to simultaneously private and universal psychic symbolism, Rauschenberg preferred to define himself as a conduit for contemporary, public symbolism. Inspired in part by John Cage (p. 148), who taught at Black Mountain College in North Carolina during the late 1940s and early 1950s, Rauschenberg adopted a receptive rather than introspective method, introducing chance into the otherwise rational and intuitive creative process. Rauschenberg's rejection of art's introspective role and his use of appropriation and chance-receptive method made him an important precursor to the postmodern methods of sampling or quoting from past art, pop culture, and mass media.

Rauschenberg adopted the technique of silk screening in the fall of 1962 in order to appropriate a great range of found imagery and to engage topical themes efficiently. The silk screen could transfer photographic imagery to other flat surfaces such as canvas, in altered sizes. Through 1964, Rauschenberg used this method, incorporating images from magazines and newspapers such as the *New York Times*, *Herald Tribune*, *Life*, *Time*, and *National Geographic*, alongside photographs he took of his immediate environment, manipulating the composition and painting over the images. Rauschenberg's earliest silk-screen paintings were black and white, reflecting the artist's tendency to restrict his palette when experimenting with a new medium. Yet by the summer of 1963, Rauschenberg was painting with a wide range of colors.

Retroactive I and *II*, both of which centrally feature the image of President John F. Kennedy from a news photograph of him holding a press conference are key examples of Rauschenberg's silk-screen paintings. By the time of Kennedy's assassination on November 22, 1963, Rauschenberg had already begun several canvases with the silk-screened image of Kennedy. Although concerned that finishing the works would appear to celebrate a murder, he ultimately decided that leaving them unfinished would be worse, a failure to honor a man he admired as an agent of positive change. In the end, Rauschenberg produced eight silk-screen paintings with the same enlarged photograph of Kennedy. In *Quote* (1964), *Retroactive I* (1964), and *Retroactive II* (1963), Rauschenberg used a press photograph of an astronaut as the other dominant image, a potent symbol of the era's optimistic fascination with cultural, societal, and scientific progress. In *Retroactive II*, as in his other silk-screen paintings, Rauschenberg juxtaposed appropriated images and with painterly gestures, creating a complex, multifaceted visual field of interlocking formal and symbolic concerns. A P

Dan Flavin
American, 1933–1996

*the alternative diagonals
of March 2, 1964 (to Donald Judd)*
1964
Fluorescent lights
145 × 12 × 4 in. (368.3 × 30.5 × 10.2 cm)
Ed: 1/3
Gerald S. Elliott Collection
1995.40

In the early 1960s, Dan Flavin began using standard lengths of fluorescent lights as his exclusive art medium. Until his death in 1996, he used this material to make works he called "situations" to emphasize their environmental character. He explored myriad possible arrangements for the fixtures: standard two-, four-, six-, and eight-foot tubes in various horizontal, vertical, and diagonal alignments; freestanding tubes arranged on floors, attached to walls, or hanging from ceilings; tubes aligned with corners of rooms or barring entrance to them; and tubes facing the viewer or the wall.

Like Donald Judd (p. 124), Flavin's friend and peer in 1960s minimalism, Flavin produced three-dimensional objects derived from painting. Both artists rejected the term "sculpture" for their work. Many of Flavin's earliest experiments using electric lights — the "icons" he made between 1961 and 1963 — are painted canvases or colored, wall-mounted rectangular surfaces with light bulbs attached around their edges or faces. Flavin's preoccupation with transforming an environment with colored fluorescent fixtures, which began in 1963, departed from the rendering of light through line, proportion, and color in the illusionistic traditions of painting. Instead, the fluorescent fixtures cast colored washes of light over floors and walls in a way reminiscent of the staining and bleeding techniques of American painters such as Mark Rothko (b. Russia 1903–1970), Morris Louis (1912–1962), Jules Olitski (b. Russia 1922), and Kenneth Noland (b. 1924).

Flavin determined the arrangement of colored lights in his artworks not only to achieve formal objectives, but, in some cases, to refer to people he admired or ideas that interested him. He made these references explicit by incorporating them in the titles of his works, as in *the alternate diagonals of March 2, 1964 (to Donald Judd)*, which

includes red and yellow, the colors Judd was using at the time. Though formally Flavin considered the diagonal to be a position of equilibrium between verticals and horizontals, he also underscored its libidinal connotations. He subtitled his first diagonal work *the diagonal of personal ecstasy* (1963). The diagonal in the Collection was created shortly after that work.

Flavin's use of light also has a religious dimension, harkening back to the age-old use of light as a metaphor for spiritual ecstasy or transcendence. Although Flavin dropped out of a Catholic seminary, rejecting the restrictions of organized religion, he did not simply reject religious ideas. Instead he transmuted religious metaphors — especially ecstasy, light, and "icons" — into the everyday, secularized terms of functional fluorescent fixtures.

Flavin adamantly rejected the artistic practice he associated with abstract expressionist painting, in which formal decisions were made intuitively. Like other minimalists such as Carl Andre (p. 110), Judd, and Sol LeWitt (p. 92), Flavin sought to eliminate arbitrariness from his art. He did so by generating a seemingly infinite variety of formal possibilities from the most reductive means, relying on mathematical or architectural systems. Flavin's use of ready-made materials led many contemporaries to think he was extending the ideas of Marcel Duchamp (French, 1887–1968) about challenging art's definition. Yet Flavin insisted that his purpose was different. He used the store-bought tubes as formal elements with which to transform the commonplace. AP

Claes Oldenburg

American, b. Sweden 1929

Green Beans
1964
Vinyl, and acrylic on plaster
Eighteen parts, each: 2 × 11¾ × 5 in.
(5.1 × 29.8 × 12.7 cm)
Gift of Anne and William J. Hokin
1996.5.a–r

Sculpture in the Form of a Fried Egg
1966/1971
Canvas, dyed cotton, and expanded
polystyrene
122 in. diameter (309.9 cm)
Gift of Anne and William J. Hokin
1986.65

Claes Oldenburg amplified the scale of everyday objects in *Green Beans* and *Sculpture in the Form of a Fried Egg* as well as public works such as *Proposed Colossal Monument for Central Park North, N.Y.C.—Teddy Bear* (1965) to create tension between the subject and its oversized presence. For *Proposed Colossal Monument* he sketched a giant teddy bear placed on the north side of Central Park, looking from Harlem to Manhattan. This, as well as many other of Oldenburg's ideas for large sculptures, such as a Good Humor ice cream bar blocking traffic on Park Avenue, exist only as drawings. Oldenburg has worked with his wife Coosje van Bruggen (American, b. Netherlands 1942) to execute more than thirty-five large public

sculptures, such as *Batcolumn* (1977) in Chicago and *Spoonbridge and Cherry* (1988) at the Walker Art Center in Minneapolis.

Oldenburg attempted to broaden conceptions of art in the 1960s by distancing himself from what he considered traditional museum art. He re-created familiar objects related to the home, store, or office, and made sculptures so large that they would not fit in galleries or private residences. His use of humor and literal references to mundane objects signaled a departure from the approaches of abstract expressionist and minimalist artists. Oldenburg derived many objects for his projects from an installation, *The Store* (1961–62), prompted by his involvement with Allan Kaprow (American, b. 1927) and with "happenings," or performances, by Jim

Dine (American, b. 1935). Despite his association with pop artists such as Andy Warhol (p. 66) and Roy Lichtenstein (American, 1923–1997), who referred to cartoons and advertising in their work, Oldenburg's larger concerns lie with the form of his sculptures as they relate to gravity and the passage of time. This aspect of Oldenburg's work also recalls elements of surrealism, such as the sagging watches in *Persistence of Memory* (1931) by Salvador Dalí (Spanish, 1904–1989).

By altering the context, scale, and material of familiar objects, such as light switches, plugs, hand-mixers, and food, Oldenburg created sensual, expressive, and humorous sculptures. *Green Beans* was part of his 1964 solo exhibition at the Sidney Janis Gallery in New York.

Oldenburg first created naturalistic food sculptures in 1961 out of plaster and enamel. In his installation *The Store,* he displayed these cakes, pies, and ice-cream sculptures within a glass case, in a gesture of forbidden temptation. In 1963, he began making vinyl food objects, such as *Giant BLT (Bacon, Lettuce, and Tomato Sandwich)*. The slippery vinyl *Green Beans* are piled into a heap, which inevitably shifts. Displayed directly on the floor, the giant green beans invite touching, a visceral reaction Oldenburg desired. *Sculpture in the Form of a Fried Egg,* a large egg made of cotton and canvas, is another example of how Oldenburg has used scale and context to disrupt the hierarchy of art materials and subjects. *Sculpture in the Form of a Fried Egg* originally appeared

in *Massage,* a 1966 "happening" at the Moderna Museet in Stockholm, Sweden as a coverlet for performer lying on a bed of balloons. The original egg no longer exists but was remade in 1971.

During the 1960s, Oldenburg's works presented an alternative to the highly finished, industrial sculptures of minimalist artists while challenging the seriousness of art and traditional art materials. With their balance of humor and psychological weight, Oldenburg's soft sculptures redefined the conventions of art in a museum context. JRW

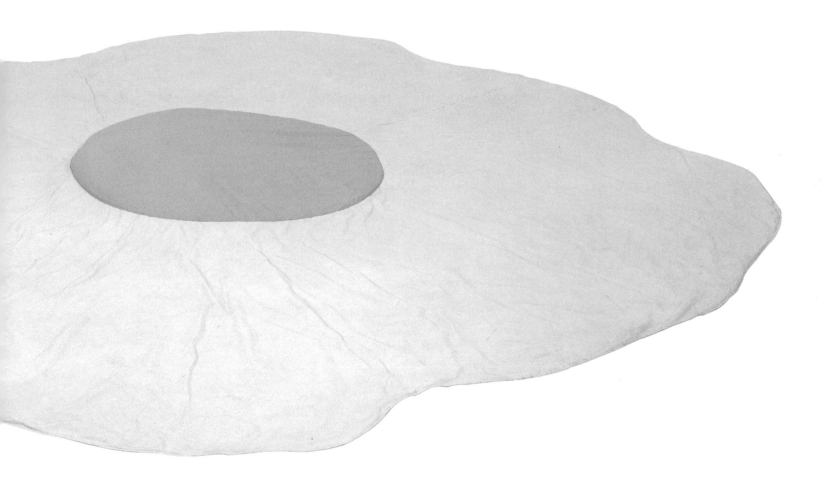

Christo

Christo Javacheff
American, b. Bulgaria 1935

Orange Store Front
1964–65
Painted wood, Masonite, Plexiglas,
galvanized metal, pegboard, fabric,
and electric lights
112½ × 101⅛ × 23⅞ in.
(285.8 × 256.8 × 60.6 cm)
Gift of Natalie and Irving Forman
1975.50

**Museum of Contemporary Art
Packed (Chicago) — Project for
January–March 1969**
Collage, 1968
Graphite, fabric, oil, polyethylene,
staples, and twine on mat board
21⅞ × 28 in. (55.6 × 71.1 cm)
Gift of William J. Hokin
1984.48

Over a forty-year career, Christo and his partner Jeanne-Claude (b. 1935) have confounded the experience of architecture through concealment, using fabric. Christo initially wrapped smaller-scale objects such as chairs and bottles. Beginning in the late 1950s, together with Jeanne-Claude, he wrapped monuments ranging from the Museum of Contemporary Art, Chicago, to the Pont-Neuf in Paris and the Berlin Reichstag. Working together on large-scale outdoor projects, they recast public buildings as aesthetic objects, forcing viewers to think about their relationship to public architecture before and after its transformation. Public involvement and reaction to Christo and Jeanne-Claude's community projects often reveal sentiments ranging from pride to hostility to intrigue and curiosity.

Christo's early works defied convention by adopting non-art, often industrial found objects, and by suggesting connections with real-life situations. For example, he made vitrines using materials such as Plexiglas, brown paper, and concealed interior lighting, foreshadowing his series of *Store Fronts,* which he first made in 1964. In these

objects he used doors salvaged from lower Manhattan buildings to create storefronts, juxtaposing architectural exteriors with gallery interiors. Like his other *Store Fronts* executed in yellow and green, *Orange Store Front* is in full architectural scale, convincingly simulating an urban commercial store window. However, the viewer's expectations and curiosity about looking into a window display are frustrated by the white cloth drape and closed door, thwarting any impulse to buy what would be on display.

The technique of wrapping and concealing evolved into a much larger scale in works such as Christo and Jeanne-Claude's wrapping of the Museum of Contemporary Art in 1969. The first such project in the United States, *Wrap In, Wrap Out* took place in the MCA's former building at 237 East Ontario. It consisted of ten thousand square feet of canvas tarpaulin and manila rope to cover the building, its floors, walls, and several pieces of furniture. The preparatory collages for this project, *Museum of Contemporary Art Packed (Chicago) — Project for January–March 1969,* and others often incorporated the actual materials of their wrapping, such as rope and fabrics, as well as site photographs and architectural measurements.

Preparatory studies, made by Christo, are vital to the artists' working process, allowing Christo and Jeanne-Claude to explore the feasibility of ideas. On occasion they also serve as records of projects that were never realized; as, for example, their proposals to wrap The Museum of Modern Art and the Whitney Museum of American Art in New York. The sale of prints and objects also raises funds for their future projects, since they do not accept public or private funding.

The works in the MCA Collection are early examples of ideas that have germinated and been explored over a lengthy career, becoming significant precedents to many younger artists creating works in public spaces. Christo and Jeanne-Claude's public projects transcend artistic, cultural, and political boundaries — their significance lies in the ideas and collaborative process of creating topographical and social interventions. *Wrap In, Wrap Out* and later works including *Running Fence* (1972–76), *Surrounded Islands* (1980–83), and *The Umbrellas, Japan-USA* (1984–1991) created new ways of experiencing the surrounding environment and offer a model for public art that is community-based and ephemeral, in stark contrast to historical monuments that have been made to withstand time. JRW

77

Robert Morris

American, b. 1931

Portal
1965
Latex on aluminum
95¾ × 48¹⁄₁₆ × 12 in.
(243.2 × 122.1 × 30.5 cm)
Gift of Mrs. Robert B. Mayer
1984.3

Robert Morris is known for his use of a tremendous range of media and methods. Like contemporaries such as Bruce Nauman (p. 80), he developed several interests simultaneously instead of progressively advancing one style or medium, becoming an important precursor to this approach. From 1961 to 1969, he produced sculptures in plywood, aluminum, felt, and steel and created performances, earthworks, lead wall works, and sculptures with sound. Morris, along with other artists who emerged in the 1960s, sought to broaden art's function, making it in response to epistemological and not just aesthetic problems. His philosophical explorations through art centered on the relationship of the body to the mind and of verbal to visual language.

Morris was regarded as a pioneer of minimalism for his work of the early and mid-1960s, along with Donald Judd (p. 124), Carl Andre (p. 110), Sol LeWitt (p. 92), Dan Flavin (p. 72), and others. In 1961, Morris created his first "unitary form," a term thereafter associated with the aesthetic language of minimalism, which Morris used to describe solid polyhedrons. These shapes remained a constant feature of Morris's minimal work. Because they are well-known geometric forms, their total shape can be instantly grasped even from a one-sided view of the structure. The lack of internal interest makes Morris's work unlike the art that preceded it, which was based on the cubist model of space as a consideration of the relationship of parts within an illusionistic space. To many commentators of the time, Morris's minimal works seemed to lack aesthetic interest altogether. Yet such shapes are ideal for emphasizing the discrepancy between the mind and body that Morris has pursued throughout his career. With his unitary forms, Morris found a way to resolve what he called the "mind-body problem" — the dichotomy between knowledge and experience. Our familiarity with geometric shapes is unchanging and independent of our surroundings, yet the sensory perception of a shape is contingent on behavior and environment.

Morris's minimal works most often consist of large plywood polyhedrons. He painted them a middle-value gray so as to achieve the most visually neutral surface possible. Typically, the shape and position of the works relates to architectural surroundings — floors, walls, and ceilings — and they are placed or suspended either parallel to or adjacent to these structures. By drawing attention to the space around the sculpture, Morris was able to demonstrate that objects, including art objects, acquire meaning only through the interaction between human beings and their surroundings.

Morris's visually spare minimal works depend on an active viewer. This is most explicit in Morris's *Portal*, a post-and-lintel passageway — one can literally walk through it. Like the other cube, slab, column, and L-beam shapes of his minimal works, the portal is recognizable as an architectural motif. As such, *Portal* adumbrates a consistent metaphor in Morris's earthworks throughout the 1970s, which often featured rearrangements of the natural landscape into passageways of various sorts, such as groups of rocks assembled into tunnel and bridgelike structures. With these works, as with *Portal*, Morris turned the artwork into an open-ended proposition that guides the movement of the spectator but leaves him or her to make critical decisions about the function and limits of the work. AP

Bruce Nauman

American, b. 1941

Untitled
1965
Fiberglass and polyester resin
Installed: 80 × 9 × 80 in.
(203.2 × 22.9 × 203.2 cm)
Gerald S. Elliott Collection
1995.69

Self-Portrait as a Fountain
from the portfolio *Eleven*
Color Photographs
1966–67
Chromogenic development print
19⅞ × 23¾ in. (50.9 × 60.3 cm)
Ed: 8/8
Gerald S. Elliott Collection
1994.11.k

Bound to Fail
from the portfolio *Eleven*
Color Photographs
1966–67
Chromogenic development print
19⅞ × 23¾ in. (50.9 × 60.3 cm)
Ed: 8/8
Gerald S. Elliott Collection
1994.11.h

Henry Moore Bound to Fail
1967/1970
Cast iron
25½ × 23 × 3½ in.
(64.8 × 58.4 × 8.9 cm)
Unnumbered edition of 9,
aside from 1 artist's proof
Gerald S. Elliott Collection
1995.71

For nearly forty years, Bruce Nauman has challenged our understanding of art, ourselves, and the world. Alongside other pioneers who emerged in the 1960s such as Robert Morris (p. 78), Vito Acconci (p. 112), Joseph Kosuth (p. 228), and Robert Irwin (p. 86), Nauman has extended the precedent of Marcel Duchamp (French, 1887–1968), who used art to expose and disrupt social conventions. He thus shifted art away from the pursuit of more traditional goals: visual beauty, technical facility within a particular medium, and the expression of the artist's "inner self." Nauman uses a wide range of media — cast sculptures, photographs, performances, films, videos, neon signs, and installations — to expose the limits of knowledge and behavior.

The MCA has one of the largest museum collections of Nauman works in the world, including twenty prime examples that were bequeathed in 1994 as part of an unparalleled gift to the museum by the late Gerald S. Elliott, noted collector and MCA trustee. These works, which span from the mid-1960s to the late 1980s, provide a significant sampling from Nauman's far-reaching and influential career.

In *Untitled*, Nauman assaulted the art-making tradition of eliminating evidence of the fabrication process by including surface imperfections in the casting process. The form is a hollow, convex surface that itself resembles a cast. By representing both the process and the product, Nauman implied that the manufacturing of an object is equally, if not more interesting than the final product. Because this idea was so central to his work, Nauman, along with other artists such as Morris and Richard Serra (p. 108), became known in the 1960s as "process artists."

The portfolio *Eleven Color Photographs* reflects on the artist's role in society. Nauman began this series near the end of 1966, just after he had graduated from the University of California at Davis and moved into a studio in San Francisco to begin his life as an artist and part-time art teacher at the San Francisco Art Institute. His transition from student to professional prompted considerable introspection about his function as an artist and what art itself should be. He wondered whether the problems of what to do as an artist were really different from the problems of what to do as a human being. The titles and images of the *Eleven Color Photographs* work together to refer to various roles that have

traditionally been attributed to artists. The title *Waxing Hot*, for instance, refers obliquely to the expectation that artists are temperamental. Nauman, however, showed the artist carefully polishing the sculpted letters H–O–T with wax. The image thus presents the subject according to an opposing model, that of the artist as a patient craftsman. *Coffee Spilled Because the Cup Was Too Hot* refers to art as a product of impulse and immediacy. Yet the precise framing of the coffee stain and staging of the cup's placement in the photograph demonstrate the contradictory idea of art as a product of precise planning. The photograph *Self-Portrait as a Fountain* likewise puts word and image in tension, with each perspective revealing a traditional artist role not accounted for by the other. The title refers to the romantic notion of the artist as a "font of creativity," while the image of Nauman aping a fountain statue recalls an alternate tradition of art as the imitation of the physical world. This image is also an homage to Marcel Duchamp, whose notorious *Fountain* (1917), a urinal turned upside-down, likewise responded to the sentimental view of the artist. *Eleven Color*

Photographs demonstrates a vital principle that Nauman exercises throughout his oeuvre — one that he learned early on while considering a career in mathematics. Inspired by mathematician Kurt Gödel's 1931 theorem, which states that any system that is consistent is incomplete, here Nauman demonstrates the incompleteness of the various expectations of an artist. The works themselves show the failure of purely visual or purely verbal expressions.

Nauman took on artistic tradition again in *Henry Moore Bound to Fail,* but this time his theme was generational revolt. Nauman, who admired the work of British sculptor Henry Moore (1898–1986) but was ambivalent about its influence on his own work, treated the inevitability of rebellion against one's predecessors sympathetically. After all, according to the logic of generational revolt, Nauman too is eventually "bound to fail." He depicted this process in one of the *Eleven Color Photographs,* titled *Bound to Fail.* To make *Henry Moore Bound to Fail*, he used the earlier photograph of himself from the back wearing a sweater and bound by rope. From the image, Nauman modeled the sculpture in wax. He made a cast iron edition of nine, one of which is in the MCA Collection. As

part of the young Nauman's struggle with his indebtedness to and desire to surpass his predecessors, in the late 1960s he named other sculptures after artists important to him, including H. C. Westermann (p. 54), his teacher William T. Wiley (American, b. 1937), and Ray Johnson (American, b. 1927).

In the beginning of the 1970s, Nauman shifted his attention to choreographing the spectator's activity. Throughout the 1970s, Nauman played the role of interior architect, creating or modeling structures that physically constrained the spectator. This reflected Nauman's increasing interest in social control and behavioral conditioning, topics he avidly read about in popular literature of behaviorist psychology and the existentialist literature of Samuel Beckett. In the early 1970s, he exhibited a series of works he referred to as "corridors," in which viewers would navigate their way through narrow passages, some with audio or video components that accentuated the viewer's sense of entrapment. Unlike Robert Morris's open-ended architectural works of this period (*Portal* [p. 79], for example),

Nauman's works exerted deliberate control over the viewer's physical experience.

Following the theme of entrapment, Nauman produced *Three Dead-End Adjacent Tunnels, Not Connected*, which was first presented at the Leo Castelli Gallery in New York in 1980 among several related works as a model for an underground tunnel. This and the other works are hollow, reinforced plaster structures. Although these particular structures have not been realized, viewers are left to imagine the terror of occupying these spaces. Nauman has related his tunnel works to Samuel Beckett's book *The Lost Ones* (1970), which describes a large number of people trapped in a space from which they cannot exit. The effect of entrapment is exacerbated by the triangular configuration of this work. Nauman considers triangles to be especially disconcerting spaces, in which one feels cornered, isolated, and claustrophobic. Also, the dead-end passages convey a sense of frustration that fascinates the artist as a response to psychological experiments.

Nauman's work since the 1970s functions in part as a series of psychological experiments on the viewer. Yet instead of leaving the viewer helpless, these works attempt to raise the viewer's consciousness of social conditioning. He often employs words in his works to show how much our thinking is conditioned by the rules of language. This idea, inspired by the philosopher Ludwig Wittgenstein, is central to his neon sign *Life, Death, Love, Hate, Pleasure, Pain,* which represents the circularity of the opposing constructs that govern our lives. The imposed nature of this cycle is reinforced by the neon medium, typically associated with advertising signage, and the inter- mittent flashing on and off of words in a circular pattern that directs the viewer's eye to different parts of the work.

Chambres d'Amis (Krefeld Piece) elaborates on Nauman's theme of social conditioning through language games. The work has three components, each installed in separate rooms. The first portion of the installation contains *One Hundred Live and Die,* an empty room in which one hears the audio tape of a sing-song recitation of one hundred combinations of a set of verbs conjoined by "and." The script is derived from a 1984 neon work of the same title, which consists of rows and columns of these combinations. The alternatively absurd and macabre statements — such as "Live and Die," "Live and Live," "Hate and Die," "Hate and Live," "Laugh and Die," "Laugh and Live" — seem like commands, yet their sequence reveals that they are in fact blindly following the rules of a language game. The second

Three Dead-End Adjacent Tunnels, Not Connected
1979
Plaster and wood
21 × 115 × 104 in. (53.3 × 292.1 × 264.2 cm)
Gerald S. Elliott Collection
1995.73

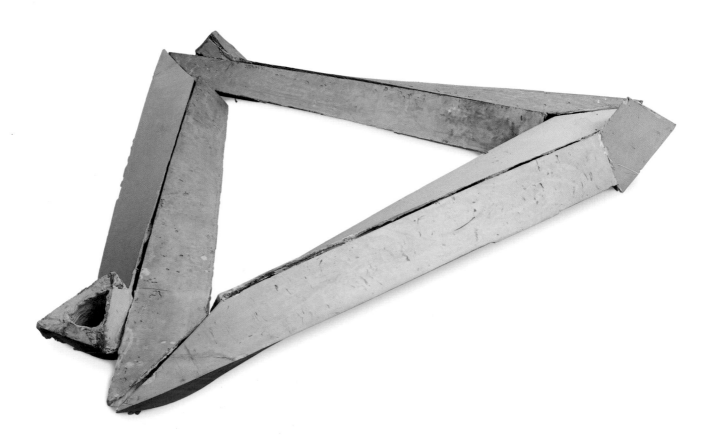

Life, Death, Love, Hate,
Pleasure, Pain
1983
Neon
70⁷⁄₈ in. diameter (180 cm)
Gerald S. Elliott Collection
1995.74

Hanging Carousel
(George Skins a Fox)
1988
Color video installation with steel
and polyurethane foam
204 in. diameter (518.2 cm)
suspended 74½ in. (189.2 cm) above the floor
Gerald S. Elliott Collection
1995.76

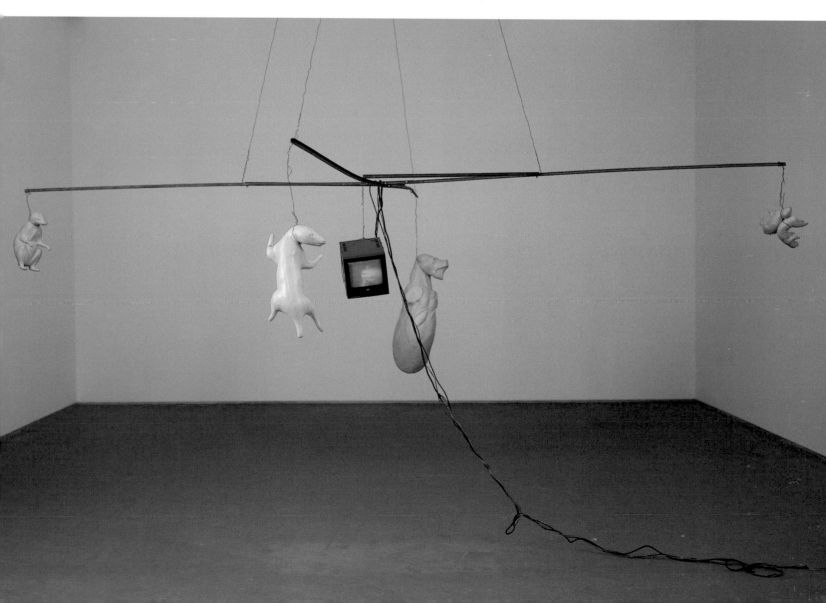

room, containing *Good Boy Bad Boy*, presents another language game. A black man and a white woman each appear on a twenty-six-inch color monitor. They both repeat conjugations of a set of statements in the same order. The statements cover a broad range of activities and emotions in four-line groupings such as "I was a good boy. You were a good boy. We were good boys. That was good." The speakers' differences of sex and race ensure that some of the statements will be absurd — for instance, they cannot both be boys — despite the speakers' faithful adherence to the language game. The final room refers to a children's language game. *Hanged Man* recalls Hangman, in which failure to correctly guess and spell a word leads to the drawn stick figure. This ordinary game, morbid in itself, is twisted further in Nauman's neon-sign version of the figure of the hanged man. The stick figure's execution is

shown in three distinct lighting phases in which the figure progressively gets an erection as he is dying. All three components of *Chambres d'Amis (Krefeld Piece)*, named after its initial exhibition title and venue, exemplify Nauman's tendency to expose the limits of social systems by disrupting their rules or by showing how following the rules to their logical conclusion can result in absurdity.

In *Hanging Carousel (George Skins a Fox)*, Nauman again used a children's game — in this case, the merry-go-round — as a point of departure. This work is one of numerous installations in which the artist has used casts of animals such as coyotes, wolves, bears, and deer like those used by taxidermists to create stuffed animals. The forms lack recognizable anatomical characteristics so they appear abstracted, perhaps reflecting the desensitization to

killing inherent to taxidermy and in society at large. Like others in this series, this work features animal forms cut into sections and suspended from the ceiling by revolving crossbars. At the central axis of the crossbar hangs a small monitor showing a man, George, methodically demonstrating how to skin a fox. Meanwhile, the work rotates like a carousel, occasionally changing direction. This perpetually puts the viewer, who wants to approach the monitor to get a better view, in danger of being hit by dangling animal parts or being tripped by the wire extending from the suspended monitor to a plug beyond the radius of the work to the gallery wall. In contrast to George's assurance of his place in the scheme of things, the viewer constantly feels like the hunted animal in relation to the threatening work of art. This work typifies Nauman's interest in activating the space of the work's display and physically directing the viewer as a component of the work of art.

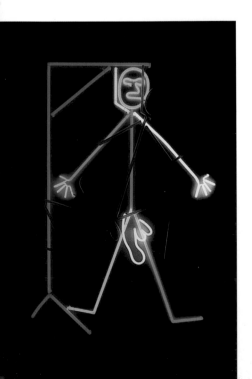

Rats and Bats (Learned Helplessness in Rats II) likewise involves the viewer in the theme of subjugation. In this and a related work of the same year, *Learned Helplessness in Rats*, Nauman attached closed-circuit video monitors to a Plexiglas chamber resembling a rat maze and projected a video onto a nearby gallery wall. A closed-circuit video camera mounted high in the gallery scans the exhibition space. The projections on the wall and the images on the monitors facing the interior of the maze alternate between prerecorded and live images of viewers looking at the work in the gallery. In the MCA's work, the video projection on the gallery wall shows a man furiously and continuously hitting a large sack with a baseball bat. The loud pounding of the bat serves as the viewer's first sensation of the work upon approaching it. Thus the viewer is immediately put in a position of subjugation. This work combines many of Nauman's characteristic methods and concerns: his ongoing interest in the relationship between the processes of physical constraint and social conditioning and the emotions of anger and frustration, as well as his attempt to control the viewer's physical relationship to the work. AP

**Chambres d'Amis
(Krefeld Piece)**
1985
Color video installation
(*Good Boy Bad Boy*),
audio tape (*One Hundred Live and Die*),
and neon (*Hanged Man*)
Dimensions variable
Gerald S. Elliott Collection
1995.75.a–c

**Rats and Bats
(Learned Helplessness
in Rats II)**
1988
Color video installation with Plexiglas
Dimensions variable
Gerald S. Elliott Collection
1995.77

Robert Irwin

American, b. 1928

Untitled
1965–67
Acrylic lacquer on shaped aluminum
60 in. diameter × 3½ in. (152.4 × 8.9 cm)
Gift of Lannan Foundation
1997.40

Like many artists of his generation, Robert Irwin defined himself artistically in reaction to formalist aesthetics. In the 1960s, artists such as Irwin began to feel constrained by formalism's basic tenet that artworks must be primarily concerned with advancing the unique characteristics of their particular medium. Irwin's generation rejected the idea that art could be defined by a set of unique and unchanging properties and, under the influence of theorists such as Ludwig Wittgenstein and Maurice Merleau-Ponty, defined art as contingent on its function within different physical environments and social contexts.

Irwin's break with formalism predated his interest in aesthetic theory, evolving out of his growing unease with the abstract expressionist painting style that had shaped his early work. By 1960, Irwin became dissatisfied with what he saw as the arbitrary products of loose brushwork and spontaneous gestures. His desire to eliminate the arbitrary soon came to encompass the structure of all painting, which he defined primarily as a figure-against-ground relationship created by a mark on a canvas or other support. Irwin disliked the illusionism resulting from this relationship and the way it created a hierarchy, privileging the figure over the ground. Irwin believed this relationship was more a product of painting conventions than a necessary condition of art. Minimalists based in New York, such as Donald Judd (p. 124) and Carl Andre (p. 110), thought similarly about illusionism in art as the Los Angeles–based Irwin did at the time.

Irwin began experimenting with ways to eliminate illusionism from his paintings. From 1962 to 1966, Irwin produced "line paintings" and "dot paintings," attempts to systematize the surface of the canvas with standardized marks, the spacing and coloring of which were chosen so that no single area was emphasized. Yet these efforts still left Irwin with one problem: no matter how he constructed the surface of his canvases, the viewer's perception of the edge of the canvas nullified his effort to eliminate illusionism. The canvas was itself a figure against a ground.

Irwin's aluminum discs of 1965 to 1967, including the MCA's *Untitled*, were pivotal works. They were the first in which he succeeded in transcending the edge of the work of art, visually and metaphorically. He chose aluminum for its evenness, spraying the concave disks with acrylic lacquer that was slightly darker just inside the edge to mitigate the appearance of the edge and counteract the concavity. In *Untitled*, he employed four floodlights positioned equidistantly and designed to shine onto the disc, producing symmetrical shadows that make the work appear to blend with its environment.

Not only was this Irwin's first use of light, it was his first attempt to manipulate the environment outside of the picture plane. Both elements subsequently became central to his art. Throughout the 1970s, Irwin produced works that had very few material components, often consisting of existing spaces altered through the use of scrims. More recently, Irwin designed the garden at the Getty Center in Los Angeles and a permanent installation of lights running the entire height of the corner of a staircase at the DIA Center for the Arts in New York. Irwin's use of light to change the perception of the environment has associated him with other artists employing the medium for similar ends, such as Dan Flavin (p. 72) and James Turrell (American, b. 1943). The slick, seductive surfaces of Irwin's discs from the 1960s have also associated his work with what has come to be called the "fetish finish" school of Los Angeles–based minimalism, which is said to emphasize the unique quality of light in that region as well as the polished surface of a Los Angeles icon, the automobile. AP

Lee Bontecou

American, b. 1931

One of the few women artists to achieve broad recognition in the 1960s, Lee Bontecou created a strikingly original body of work in sculpture that extended the tradition of assemblage and paralleled aspects of minimalism and postminimalism during the 1960s and 1970s. Throughout these decades Bontecou's predominantly abstract work incorporated an array of figurative, organic, and mechanistic references. Her sculptures, often wall-mounted yet decidedly three-dimensional, demonstrate a seemingly random dispersal of visual detail and an almost cubistic fragmentation of form. At times heroically scaled and other times intimate, these works suggest various states of transformation between the natural and the man-made, an ongoing preoccupation of Bontecou from the outset of her career.

Bontecou became widely known during the early 1960s for her welded steel sculptures in which she incorporated various fabrics, metals, and found objects to produce works that were often aggressive and sinister in appearance. The impetus behind much of her early work was a need to respond to the persistent presence of world violence and the threat of global destruction in the Cold War era. During this period Bontecou commented that her goal was to "build things that express our relation to this country — to other countries — to this world — to other worlds — in terms of myself."[1] By the mid-1960s she began to experiment with plastics, epoxy, and other synthetic materials to create molded rather than assembled forms. As her work evolved, it increasingly made overt references to natural phenomena by the use of organic forms as well as variations in materials and a

Untitled
1966
Steel, wire, oil, and epoxy on fiberglass, canvas, leather, and light
78½ × 119 × 31 in. (199.4 × 302.3 × 78.7 cm)
Gift of Robert B. Mayer Family Collection
1991.85

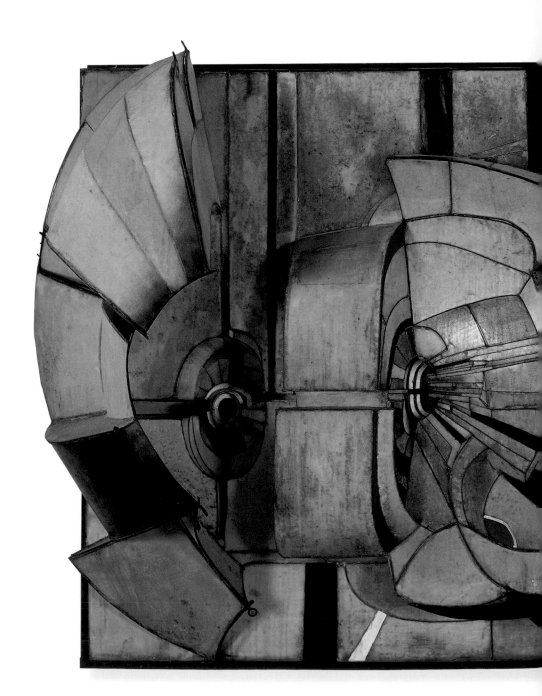

color palette incorporating black, red, gold, and ivory. Her three-dimensional works of this period, including the untitled work in the MCA Collection, evoke biological life — the shells of snails, sea creatures, and plant life — as well as the billowing, curving forms of sails.

Bontecou created *Untitled* during the period of transition between her welded sculptures of the early 1960s and a later series of vacuum-formed plastic sculptures that demonstrate her engagement with environmental issues and with destruction and regeneration in nature. In this work she introduced a complex array of materials and combined techniques of welding, assemblage, and molding. Additionally, *Untitled* is the only work Bontecou has made that incorporates artificial lighting, glowing eerily as if irradiated. Its dynamic curvature and irregular geometric shapes are consis-

tent with her sculptural concerns and interest in the relationship between the natural and the man-made, order and chaos, and delicacy and ferocity.

Bontecou, who spent summers in Nova Scotia as a child and who currently lives in rural western Pennsylvania, is fascinated by animal and plant life — a strain within her work that can be observed as early as her bronze sculptures of birds and other animal forms of the late 1950s and that persists in her most recent works. By the beginning of the 1970s, she was fully engaged in creating a body of work in which plant and animal forms, recognizable yet menacingly transformed, became dominant. Her interest in organic and biological life is also evident in the drawings she has made throughout her career in which half-plant, half-machine forms seem to endlessly transmute. Describing the intentions behind her work, Bontecou has stated,

My most persistently recurring thought is to work in a scope as far-reaching as possible; to express a feeling of freedom in all its necessary ramifications — its awe, beauty, magnitude, horror, and baseness. This feeling embraces ancient, present, and future worlds; from caves to jet engines, landscapes to outer space, from visible nature to the inner eye, all encompassed in cohesive works of my inner world. This total freedom is essential.[2] ES

1 Lee Bontecou, artist's statement in Dorothy C. Miller, ed., *Americans 1963* (New York: The Museum of Modern Art, 1963), p. 12.

2 Statement by Lee Bontecou in correspondence with the author, quoted in Elizabeth A. T. Smith, "Abstract Sinister," *Art in America* 81, no. 9 (September 1993), p. 87.

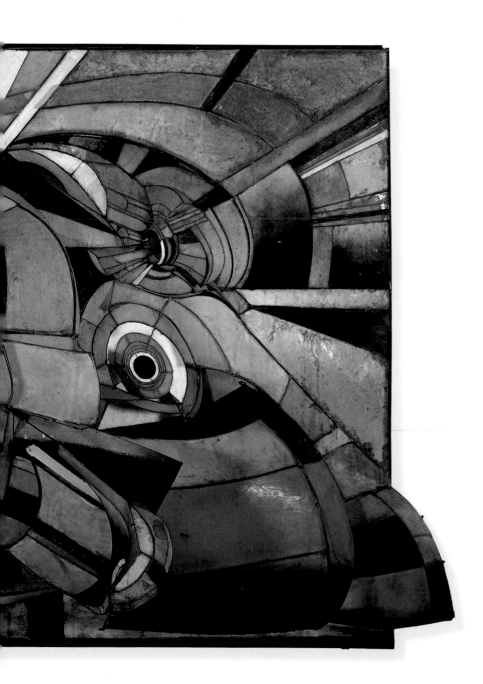

Robert Smithson

American, 1938–1973

Mirror Stratum
1966
Mirrors
10⅛ × 35 × 35 in. (25.7 × 88.9 × 88.9 cm)
Gift of Ralph I. and Helyn D. Goldenberg
1982.26

A Nonsite (Franklin, New Jersey)
1968
Painted wooden bins, limestone,
gelatin silver prints and typescript
on paper with graphite and transfer
letters, mounted on mat board
Bins installed: 16½ × 82¼ × 103 in.
(41.9 × 208.9 × 261.6 cm);
board: 40 1/16 × 30 1/16 in. (101.8 × 76.4 cm)
Gift of Susan and Lewis Manilow
1979.2.a–g

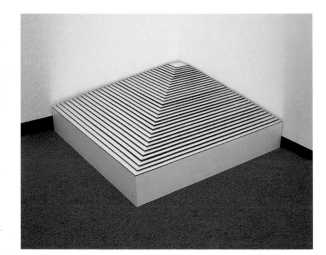

Robert Smithson, like other artists who emerged during the late 1960s, including his widow Nancy Holt (American, b. 1938) and Richard Long (p. 90), examined relationships with the environment by making work that addressed shifts in scale, displacement of indoor and outdoor elements, and organizational structures of the landscape. Some of these artists sought to impose new systems while others focused on the existing natural order. Smithson's interest in primary structures and archetypes of nature derived from an early interest in natural history museums and later in his career he found an affinity in the work of Donald Judd (p. 124) and Sol LeWitt (p. 92). The earthwork artists, however, were dissatisfied with the industrially inspired works of the minimalists. Smithson in particular voiced concerns in his highly influential writings about the increasing commodification of art and the ideologies of museum spaces and sought to make work that could circumvent both these establishments.

Smithson's early work incorporated the landscape by bringing elements of the outside in, while his later work, such as *Spiral Jetty* (1970), was executed outdoors in specific geographic locations. The year 1964 marked the beginning of a mature body of work that used what he called crystalline structures. Smithson began to use only the basic elements and forms, such as geometric shapes and spirals, of which matter is made. In outdoor works, called mirror displacements, he would place mirrors on the ground or in trees to convey ideas of infinite reflection. As he said, "if one wishes to be ingenious enough to erase time, one requires mirrors."[1] This quality is apparent in *Mirror Stratum*, a sculpture that resembles a ziggurat with each plane gradually decreasing in size. It also refers to the multilayered strata of the earth's surface, which Smithson addressed in an illustrated essay, "Strata, A Geophotographic Fiction."[2]

A Nonsite (Franklin, New Jersey) reflects Smithson's personal connection with New Jersey, where he grew up, and his view of the suburban landscape as made up of various natural minerals that have been refined into building materials. He developed an interest in the origin of raw materials, such as the zinc ore deposits found at the Franklin Furnace mines, and in removing these materials and putting them in another context, the nonsite. The nonsite is constituted by the absence of the actual site. Although this work has a minimalist aesthetic, Smithson's concern was not with its objecthood, but rather the ideas and associations of the limestone rocks and photographic representations.

A Nonsite (Franklin, New Jersey) comprises five trapezoidal bins of decreasing size filled with limestone. Hanging on the wall is a framed aerial photomap of the distribution of ore deposits divided into five sections corresponding to the bins. Smithson devised a system for the trapezoid size and shapes by drawing lines that converge off the map at a dead-end street in Franklin. Parallel lines intersect the perspective lines, resulting in the five trapezoids. Smithson believed that human actions, such as development and construction, are an inherent part of entropy and the passage of time and that the sites would at some point no longer exist except in photographs. He created the following chart[3] of the relationship between site and nonsite to indicate the conceptual associations suggested by each category:

	Site	Nonsite
1.	Open Limits	Closed Limits
2.	A Series of Points	An Array of Matter
3.	Outer Coordinates	Inner Coordinates
4.	Subtraction	Addition
5.	Indeterminate Certainty	Determinate Uncertainty
6.	Scattered Information	Contained Information
7.	Reflection	Mirror
8.	Edge	Center
9.	Some Place (physical)	No Place (abstract)
10.	Many	One

Smithson examined the natural forces of entropy in works such as *Spiral Jetty*; in the *Site/Nonsites,* he looked at the cultural forces of entropy on the landscape as he attempted to make sense of the persistent tension between nature and culture, representation and reality. J R W

1 Nancy Holt, ed., *The Writings of Robert Smithson: Essays with Illustrations* (New York: New York University Press, 1979), p. 103.

2 Ibid., 129.

3 Ibid., 115.

Sol LeWitt

American, b. 1928

Serial Project, Set D
1966
Painted steel
15½ × 55½ × 55½ in. (39.4 × 141 × 141 cm)
Gerald S. Elliott Collection
1995.59

Wall Drawing No. 358: A 12" (30 cm)
Grid Covering the Wall. Within Each 12"
(30 cm) Square, One Arc from the Corner.
(The direction of the arcs and their place-
ment are determined by the draftsman.)
1981
Crayon and graphite grid on painted wall
Dimensions variable
Gerald S. Elliott Collection
1995.62

Sol LeWitt is a pioneer of American conceptual art. He was among the first
artists and critics to name and define
the phenomenon in "Paragraphs on
Conceptual Art," a 1967 article in which
he described the new artistic practice in
the following way: "When an artist uses
a conceptual form of art, it means that
all of the planning and decisions are
made beforehand and the execution is
a perfunctory affair."[1] By this, he meant
that the physical manifestation of a work
of art is only a part of its meaning,
which one fully grasps only in combination with knowledge of the "planning
and decisions." With this idea of conceptual art — one among many definitions
that flourished in the late 1960s and
1970s — LeWitt hoped to solve what he
thought was a problem in much of
minimalist art: it presented objects without making apparent the principles
that generate them. LeWitt wanted an
art form that could overcome the
schisms between the invisible realm of
knowledge — generalizations applied
to particulars — and the visible world of
perception, the assimilation of particulars. For many artists of his generation,

including Robert Morris (p. 78) and
Bruce Nauman (p. 80), these issues became central, as art moved away from
formalist concerns with composition
and toward a quasi-scientific interest in
raising epistemological questions. In
order to engage knowledge and perception in a consistent way, LeWitt settled
on a serial method, producing a progression of forms governed by simple
formulae. By 1970, LeWitt had extended
his serial method to the full range of
formats he would continue to produce
throughout his career: three-dimensional structures, wall drawings, prints,
and artist's books.

Among the earliest works to explore
the relationship between knowledge
and perception are LeWitt's "structures,"
three-dimensional works he started
making in 1962. He began with squares,
then cubes became the primary modules. In 1966 and 1967, LeWitt began his
"serial projects" in which he stacked
cubic modules on portions of a gridded
platform and painted them white — a
color he determined, after experimenting with black, was best because it was
the least "expressive." The relationship
between the open grid and the combination of closed and open structures es-

92

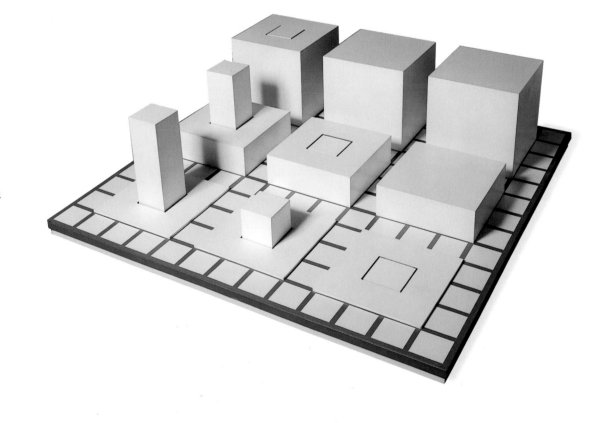

tablished a tension between inside and outside, and therefore visible and invisible dimensions. Some of LeWitt's titles for structures before the serial projects, such as *Hidden* and *Buried*, indicate his evolving concern with the relationship between visual and invisible elements. The first of LeWitt's serial projects was *Serial Project No. 1 (ABCD)*. This mega-work consists of a series of four nine-part works, each on a gridded base. In some of the works, the closed elements are contained by the open elements so both are visible. In others, open structures are set within closed ones or closed structures next to other closed ones, leaving viewers to infer what they cannot see. In 1972, this work was shown as a single unit at the Kunsthalle in Bern. The four parts have since become separate works and the final work, *Set D*, is in the MCA Collection.

LeWitt's wall drawings have allowed him to explore the synthesis of other oppositions such as the generic and the specific, theoretical and practical, rational and intuitive, controlled and spontaneous, represented and real,

and permanent and ephemeral. LeWitt created his first wall drawing in October 1968, at the Paula Cooper Gallery in New York. He has since created more than 800 wall drawings, each of them numbered according to the sequence of their creation. The wall drawings are site-contingent works. That is, their manifestation is affected by where they are executed, though they are not site-specific and can be reproduced in variable locations. LeWitt chose to draw on walls because he sees it as the most direct means of putting a drawing on view in a room. LeWitt also likes the way that making the drawing physically continuous with the exhibition space blurs the boundary between art and its surroundings.

Not only do the wall drawings challenge the traditional format of drawings, they also transcend the physical limitations of artworks as unique objects. Each of LeWitt's wall drawings is made according to a set of guidelines and a set of variables for a draftsman, not LeWitt himself, to follow. The titles of LeWitt's wall drawings all consist of a description of the work's variables, so that the viewer not only perceives the

work but understands its underlying principles. Some of the wall drawings are finite and exhaustive; they explore all of the permutations of a set of variables, such as "all two-part combinations of blue arcs from corners and sides, and blue straight, not straight, and broken lines," as in the 146th wall drawing. Others, like *No. 358* in the MCA Collection, allow the draftsman a measure of choice in the execution. For example, this work requires a black wall and white chalk arcs from the corner in each twelve-inch, or thirty-centimeter, square of a grid. The direction of the arcs is determined by the draftsman. This type of wall drawing is allographic. As in a musical performance, each execution of the same composition is unique. AP

1 Sol LeWitt, "Paragraphs on Conceptual Art," *Artforum* 5, no. 10 (June 1967), p. 79.

Ed Ruscha

American, b. 1937

Whiskey A-Go-Go from
The Sunset Strip series
1966/1995
Gelatin silver print
20 × 29 9/16 in. (50.8 × 75.1 cm)
Ed: 16/25 aside from 8 artist's proofs
Bernice and Kenneth Newberger Fund
1996.41.1

Gazzarri's Supper Club from
The Sunset Strip series
1966/1995
Gelatin silver print
19 3/4 × 29 5/16 in. (50.2 × 74.4 cm)
Ed: 16/25 aside from 8 artist's proofs
Bernice and Kenneth Newberger Fund
1996.41.2

Schwab's Pharmacy from
The Sunset Strip series
1976/1995
Gelatin silver prints
20 1/8 × 29 9/16 in. (51.1 × 75.1 cm)
Ed: 16/25 aside from 8 artist's proofs
Bernice and Kenneth Newberger Fund
1996.41.3

Greenblatt's Deli from
The Sunset Strip series
1976/1995
Gelatin silver print
20 3/16 × 29 7/8 in. (51.3 × 75.9 cm)
Ed: 16/25 aside from 8 artist's proofs
Bernice and Kenneth Newberger Fund
1996.41.4

Filthy McNasty's from
The Sunset Strip series
1976/1995
Gelatin silver print
20 1/8 × 29 7/8 in. (51.1 × 75.9 cm)
Ed: 16/25 aside from 8 artist's proofs
Bernice and Kenneth Newberger Fund
1996.41.5

Liquor Locker from
The Sunset Strip series
1976/1995
Gelatin silver print
20 1/8 × 29 7/8 in. (51.1 × 75.9 cm)
Ed: 16/25 aside from 8 artist's proofs
Bernice and Kenneth Newberger Fund
1996.41.6

Every Building on The Sunset Strip
1966
Artist's book
First edition
MCA Purchase
AB1981.584

Although Ed Ruscha has used a range of media, including painting, photography, and artist's books, the content of his work has been consistently influenced by language and the social landscape. Trained as a commercial artist, Ruscha is known today primarily for his graphic paintings in which the text either betrays or enhances the work's imagery, which is often derived from the Los Angeles landscape. His artist's books of the 1960s, such as *Every Building on The Sunset Strip*, defined the medium, showing the influence of neo-Dada, conceptualism, and minimalism, while promoting new ideas about mass-produced art. Many artists experimented with artists' books during the emergence of conceptual forms of art such as performance, video, happenings, and minimalist sculpture.

Artists' books usually adhere to the idea or format of a book and depend in some manner on reading, but do not necessarily rely on conventional linear narrative, focusing instead on ideas. In the 1960s, as an influential culture of mass media developed, artists embraced more widely distributed modes of art and related forms of communication, such as video and magazines, in part to reach a larger audience. Ruscha's freely distributed books challenged art's market value system related to the notion of unique objects. *TwentySix Gasoline Stations* (1962), Ruscha's first artist's book, was succeeded by *Various Small Fires* (1964) and *Some Los Angeles Apartments* (1965), all of which are in the MCA Collection. *Every Building on The Sunset Strip* was first published in 1966 as an edition of one thousand. Another edition of five hundred was created in 1969, and in 1971 Ruscha issued an edition of five thousand. Ruscha continued making books until 1978.

Ruscha has cited the black-and-white photographs of Walker Evans (American, 1903–1975), particularly those of buildings and signs, as an influential source. His documentary style also recalls the work of Dan Graham (p. 96), who photographed postwar suburban housing developments. Ruscha photographed each building on the Sunset Strip section of Sunset Boulevard in Los Angeles as a record of American commercial architecture in this quasi-urban context. In this work, the visual panorama of hotels, restaurants, and gas stations captures a moment in time, evoking nostalgia for what has become an idyllic myth surrounding the 1960s. The book, with its accordion-fold format, presents the photographs sequentially. A wide, horizontal band of white space divides the book in half, with each side of the street on the top and bottom. Numbers and intersecting streets identify the location of each building. The formal structure of the book suggests "cruising" down Sunset Strip; in fact, Ruscha took these photographs with an automatic camera from a pickup truck as he drove up and down Sunset Boulevard capturing every building, a practice he has repeated for several years, intermittently since 1966.

Ruscha and gallery-owner Patrick Painter issued a portfolio of the Sunset Strip photographs in 1995. Two of the images, *Whisky A-GO-GO* and *Gazzarri's Supper Club*, were in the artist's book, while the remaining four were taken from Ruscha's 1976 documentation of Sunset Boulevard. He manipulated the photographs by scratching the negatives and enhancing them with paint before sending them to the darkroom for printing. The result is a cinematic appearance of a frozen film frame. Ruscha's original photographs function as historical documents, yet, because of his surface treatment of the 1995 prints that creates a cinematic effect, the notion of time gives the images a nostalgic element of a bygone era, in which all that is left is a memory in black and white. JRW

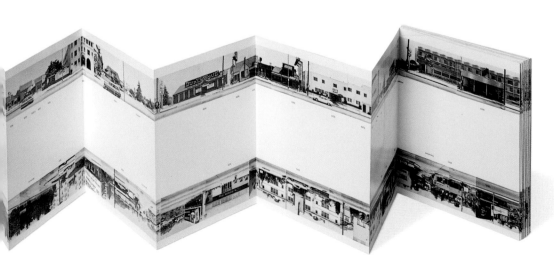

Dan Graham

American, b. 1940

Bedroom Dining Room Model House
1967
Chromogenic development prints
Two parts, each: 37¾ × 27⅝ in.
(95.9 × 70.2 cm)
Gerald S. Elliott Collection
1995.42

Influences from contemporary architecture, the suburban environment, and everyday life have consistently shaped Dan Graham's visual art and writing. Like many of his contemporaries working in the 1960s, Graham played the roles of artist and critic to engage others in theoretical, philosophical, and social dialogue. Graham's desire to link the art world more fully with society prompted him to analyze cultural phenomena such as pop music and public architecture, which he considers manifestations of a pervasive, capitalist culture, through photographs, videos, and installation works. As a writer, Graham questioned the nature of art and arts institutions, as well as the role of the viewer. He published some of his works in magazines as a means to infiltrate the mass media. For *Figurative* (1965–68), Graham bought a full-page ad in the women's magazine *Harper's Bazaar*, in which he reproduced a grocery bill. He promoted the ideas of conceptual art in other venues as well. In 1964, while manager of the John Daniels Gallery in New York, he exhibited leaders of minimal and conceptual art such as Dan Flavin (p. 72), Donald Judd (p. 124), Sol LeWitt (p. 92), and Carl Andre (p. 110).

Similar to other conceptual artists of his generation, Graham employed a documentary style in his photographs to analyze the social environment. Bernd and Hilla Becher (p. 174), for example, used black-and-white photography to categorize vernacular buildings such as cooling towers. Ed Ruscha (p. 94) documented his everyday surroundings in Los Angeles in *Every Building on The Sunset Strip* (1966).

Unlike the Bechers and Ruscha, who examined industrial or commercial architecture, Graham analyzed mass-produced suburban homes. He began his investigation of suburban architecture in the late 1960s, when he wrote an article entitled "Homes for America (Early 20th Century Possessable House to the Quasi-Discrete Cell of '66)," which appeared in *Arts Magazine*. In this article, which Graham considered a conceptual work, he analyzed the homogeneous structure of modern homes and the various "choices" available for a home buyer to make his or her home unique. Slight changes to the basic structure gave an illusion of difference, but in fact the potential for personalizing the mass-produced houses was quite limited.

Early in his career, Graham was known primarily as a photojournalist who documented suburban housing developments and other quotidian types of architecture. *Bedroom Dining Room Model House*, part of this early series, depicts a carefully decorated bedroom and dining room of a model home in Staten Island, New Jersey. The décor, with its gold scroll wallpaper, heavy wood furniture, and olive green chairs was, at the time, an idealized version of a middle-class interior. His photographs were first shown in 1966 at the Contemporary Study Wing of the Finch Museum of Art, New York, in the form of projected slides. In 1999, Graham's suburban photographs were projected in the exhibition *Blue Suburban Skies* at the Photographer's Gallery, London, reemphasizing the enduring relevance of this subject to contemporary artistic practice.

Graham continued his investigation of architecture in many later works, such as *Alterations to a Suburban Home* (1978). In this work, a model sculpture of tract housing, Graham replaced the houses' aluminum siding with glass, marking a new phase of his work in which mirrors and glass play an important role in defining social interactions within architectural space. This use of materials also recognizes and critiques the work of architects Philip Johnson (American, b. 1906), Ludwig Mies van der Rohe (American, b. Germany 1886–1969), and others using the vocabulary of modernism. Graham's later subjects include shopping malls, railway stations, urban parks, and corporate buildings — spaces in which public and private actions are conflated depending on whether one is the spectator or participant. Many of Graham's performances from the 1970s, as well as his more recent video and film works, also employ architecture to address the role of the individual within culture and collective history. JRW

Top: Bedroom of "Model Home", Staten Island, New York City 1978. Bottom: Dining Room of "Model Home", Staten Island 1978 Jane Andrews

Richard Tuttle

American, b. 1941

Purple Octagon
1967
Dyed canvas
54¹³⁄₁₆ × 55½ in. (139.2 × 141 cm)
Gift of William J. Hokin
1982.69

Richard Tuttle is part of a generation of American artists considered postminimalists who, in the late 1960s, began to make work that simultaneously extended and challenged the premises of minimalism. Like the minimalists, Tuttle made works in series and used abstract, geometric forms; what distinguishes his work is an emphasis on the process of making and displaying objects that redefines the idea of painting and sculpture, prioritizing the concept of a work and the relationship between the object, the space around it, and the viewer. Tuttle and his fellow postminimalists such as Bruce Nauman (p.80), Robert Smithson (p.90) and Jackie Winsor (p. 156) also sought to break away from the hard, industrial materials used in minimal works.

Throughout his career, Tuttle has used paper, wood, canvas, string, wire, and other materials to create objects that are neither painting nor sculpture, simply reduced to color, shape, material, and structure. In the early 1960s, he made a series of folded three-inch paper cubes

that were small enough to fit in one's hand. By the mid-1960s, he started creating wood reliefs, painting them in monochromatic colors with symbolic associations: *Water* (blue), *Fire* (red), and *Bridge* (orange), among others, which were displayed on the floor, a practice that would inform later works and mark Tuttle's interest in the spatial context of displaying artworks.

Making the transition from wood to fabric in 1967, Tuttle created ten irregularly shaped canvases, including *Purple Octagon*, followed by a series of twelve paper octagons from 1970 to 1973. Tuttle called his octagons "drawings for three-dimensional structures in space."[1] Hand-cut out of canvas from a paper pattern, each octagon has a unique character and wrinkled quality from the dying process and from being stored crumpled in a bag. By storing the work this way, Tuttle subverts the preciousness of traditional painting, while incorporating a Dadaist element of change in its appearance and installation. He in-

tended for *Purple Octagon's* placement — directly on the floor or wall — to be variable. There is no top or bottom of the work, nor a correct way to install it. Without a frame or pedestal, the work interacts with its surroundings and can be understood only in reference to the wall, the floor, the ceiling, and the viewer. As such, it represents a significant shift toward site-specific installation art that responds to the location or architectural space where it is either created or exhibited. For more than thirty years, Tuttle has attempted to expand various definitions of sculpture in space. He continues to challenge the nature of image-making by examining this fundamental question: can an abstract idea be represented by an object? SC/JRW

1 Dorothy Alexander, "Conversations with the Work and the Artist," in *Mel Bochner, Barry Le Va, Dorothea Rockburne, Richard Tuttle* (Cincinatti: Contemporary Arts Center, 1975), p. 42.

Robert Heinecken

American, b. 1931

V.N. Pin Up (#1 of 2)
1968
Black-and-white film transparency
on magazine page
12½ × 10 in. (31.8 × 25.4 cm)
Ed: 1/5
Gift of Daryl Gerber Stokols
1998.43

Emerging from the Southern California art scene of the early 1960s as one of the first conceptual photographers, Robert Heinecken has continuously blurred and challenged the boundaries of contemporary art and photography. Conceptual photography, a movement in which artists have explored the nature and meaning of the photographic in works that are not necessarily (but often are) photographs, requires consideration of theoretical, formal, and cultural elements when analyzing and interpreting an object's meaning.

V.N. Pin Up is from Heinecken's important early series, *Pin Ups* (1968–69), which consists of three works with unique variations in each edition. These works take the form of small montages of commercial photographic images overlaid with black-and-white film transparencies of a nude woman and stem from the artist's political engagement during the turbulent late 1960s. Heinecken had been a jet pilot with the Marine Corps before becoming an artist and had strong views on the United States' involvement in the Vietnam War (1961–1975), to which this work's title specifically refers. Heinecken made an overt antiwar statement by juxtaposing a black-and-white news photograph of a dead serviceman and a snippet of a newspaper article with the headline "10 Southland Men Killed in Action" that lists Los Angeles–area dead with images representing female sexuality, including a push-up bra, sleek blonde hair, and seductively smiling lips. These montaged elements are framed by a female figure in a classic pinup pose, referring to the depictions of Hollywood starlets that soldiers commonly posted in their barracks. The shadows of the nude fall in a disturbing pattern upon the face and arms of the montaged figure, appearing as bruises or an X ray that reveals the skull. The model's face is somber, though smiling lips peep out from her armpit and hip. Clearly this would be a ghastly, disturbing pinup to display, one that speaks bluntly against the war.

Heinecken founded the University of California, Los Angeles graduate photography program in 1962. The late 1960s gave rise to often violent student protests at California universities, a subject referred to in another of the *Pin Up* series, *U.C.B. Pin Up* (1969) (U.C.B. refers to the University of California, Berkeley). *V.N. Pin Up* more directly confronts the role of art-historical conventions contested at the time, particularly the female nude and the oppressio)n of women. It suggests that as young American men in the 1960s became exploited by the United States' misguided intervention in Vietnam, young women were being exploited domestically, through pornography.

Heinecken typically works in series, exploring cultural, political, and artistic subject matter. Recent works include elaborate montages of magazine advertisements that create three-dimensional reliefs. These reliefs feature updated versions of classical Indian motifs depicting Shiva and other gods. A series that spanned the 1990s used commercial, life-sized standing cutouts in which popular cultural figures including race car drivers, sports figures, and TV stars are altered to make humorous and often scathing commentaries on American consumerist culture. LW

Dieter Roth

German, 1930–1998

***Stemplekasten
(Rubber Stamp Box)***
1968
Rubber stamps, inkpads, and
instruction sheet in box
Box closed: 2½ × 11⅛ × 11⅛ in.
(6.4 × 28.2 × 28.2 cm)
Gift of the artist
1984.24

Although Dieter Roth created paintings, sculptures, videos, and sound and installation works, he is best known for his artist's books. His early transformations of the book into an artwork earned him the reputation as a pioneer among European artists. For Roth, the multiple steps involved in creating a work were inextricably linked to the finished result, an approach perfectly suited to printing.

Born in Hannover, Roth was sent to Zurich by his family during World War II and eventually settled in Basel and Reykjavik. In 1953, he published a collaborative art review, *Spirale*, which included his poems and those of concrete poet Eugen Gomringer. While Roth's poems were not well received, his visual works were. Trained as a printer and graphic designer, with a background in poetry, he began to work with the letterpress. Through his experiments with printing techniques from new commercial technologies, printing became his method and medium.

Working with ideas germinating in the 1950s and 1960s — the desire for artistic freedom, experimentation with representation, the dissolution of the boundaries separating art and life — Roth, using disparate materials, created deeply personal works that challenged the sanctity of the art object. Stripping conventional narrative and plot from books, Roth conveyed meaning through images rather than language. He also experimented with the formal conventions of a book by treating it as a sculptural

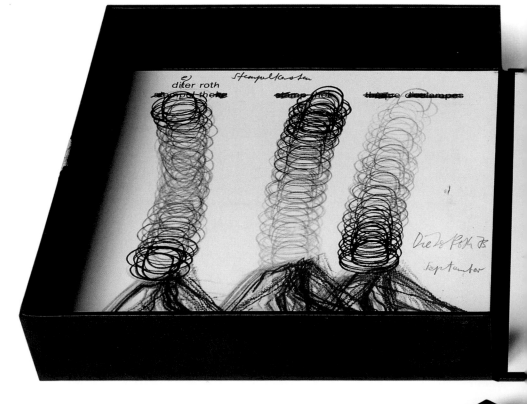

object. In a surrealistic manner, Roth created books with text printed on plastic or aluminum foil, and most famously, created *Literaturwurst,* a sausage skin filled with newspaper, lard, and spices.[1]

Stemplekasten (Rubber Stamp Box) is a product of Roth's experimentation with visual imagery, printing techniques, and process art. The linen box contains twelve stamps, two glass bottles of ink, matching black and red stamp pads, and three pages of instructions with impressions of the stamps turned ninety degrees. The stamps are labeled: I, egg, woman, chair, Arsch (ass), Trauer (sorrow), stone, god, business, memory, lust, and Herz (heart). In a fractured and absurd fashion, Roth mixes English, German, and French in the three stories, one of which is titled "Trauerarsch" ("Sad Ass"), which utilizes all of the

stamps. Roth explained this story and the others included as "symbols to interpret how you want, from stories, fairy tales, and business and love letters, to make your own stamps."[2] The use of the stamps in what he called stamp pictures, appears in his book *MUNDUCU-LUM* (1967). Through its ideogrammatic chart of symbols and the poem/etching *My Eye Is a Mouth*, Roth attempted to fuse the visual (eye) and the word (mouth) to develop a systematic structure of meaning, which can then be used by others to create future work. This synthesis of image and language also offers a code by which Roth's work can be read. TVE

1 Clive Philpot, "Contemporary Artists and Their Books," in *Artists' Books* (Stuttgart, Germany: Institute for Foreign Cultural Relations and Authors, 1995), p. 102.

2 Ina Conzen, *Dieter Roth: Die Haut der Welt,* exh. cat. (Stuttgart, Germany: Staatsgalerie, 2000), p. 114. Passage translated from the German by Andre Fiebig.

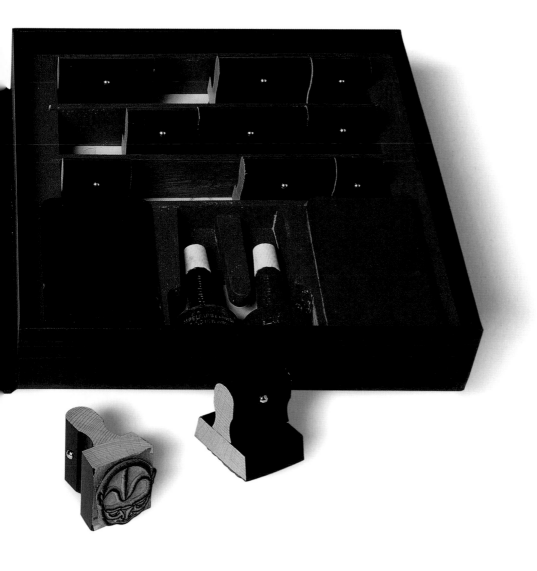

June Leaf

American, b. 1929

Ascension of Pig Lady, which was first exhibited at the Allan Frumkin Gallery in New York in 1968 as part of Leaf's first solo exhibition, is exemplary of many of her central themes. Much of Leaf's work features images of women, and in the late 1940s she experimented with painting abstracted renditions of female forms resembling tribal goddesses. She painted numerous female figures as portraits and self-portraits during the 1950s as well.

Since the mid-1960s, Leaf's work has mainly taken the form of three-dimensional constructions: freestanding figures, figures attached to one another or to painted backdrops, or actual mechanical toys, which she began creating in 1978. Leaf's constructions of the mid- and late 1960s resemble shallow stage sets, inspired in part by her exposure while in Chicago to boxes by the surrealist Joseph Cornell (American, 1903–1972), in the collection of Edwin and Lindy Bergman (currently in the The Art Institute of Chicago Collection). Leaf's own universe of fantasy retained an irreverent mixture of spirituality and vulgarity. She consistently elaborated her narratives using the lowbrow styles of carnival painting, which she saw as a child when she visited Riverview Park, a Chicago amusement park that thrived from 1907 to 1967. Leaf's statements indicate that these early experiences inspired her celebration of the link in her work between working-class life and elaborate forms of escapism.

Arguably June Leaf's best-known work, *Ascension of Pig Lady* is a hybrid of painted plywood cutouts, painted and stuffed canvas, and two-dimensional, illusionistic painting. Leaf replaced the

Ascension of Pig Lady
1968
Acrylic on canvas with hand-sewn and stuffed figures, wood, and tin
123⅜ × 174¾ × 8³⁄₁₆ in.
(313.4 × 443.9 × 20.8 cm)
Gift of Herbert and Virginia Lust
1983.12

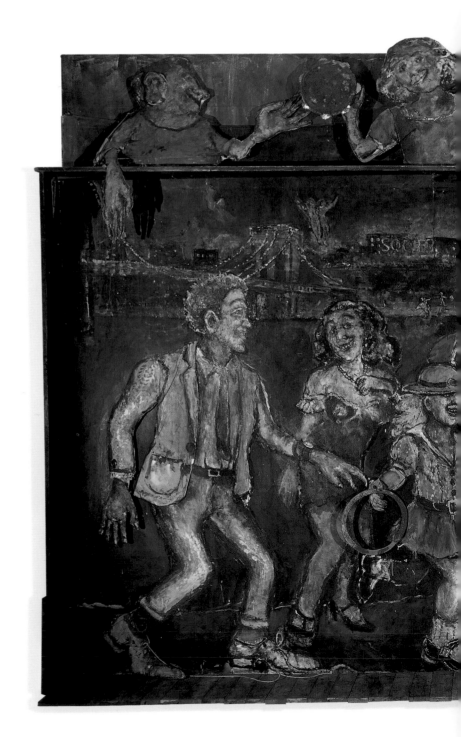

iconography of the Ascension of Christ with characters inspired by her own life and those of people she encountered while living in Chicago and New York. Leaf intended the little girl, with stick and hoop in tow, to convey her own innocence and eagerness upon going out into the larger world. Leaf's sister inspired the woman behind the young girl. The "pig lady" represents a combination of figures: a "fat lady" Leaf once saw as a child in her parent's tavern in Chicago who was sitting on a stool drinking and urinating, and a waitress she glimpsed from a bus in a New York City restaurant. The coarse, piglike features of the lady make the character's ultimate exaltation dramatic and unexpected.

Leaf altered the traditional narrative of Ascension by turning it into an allegory for the exaltation of women, especially working-class women. The work also evokes the Shakespearean adage that "life is but a stage." Two stagehands and a pair of puppet strings above and dangling over the painting's proper frame are shown in a comic effort of straining to lift the pig lady. These behind-the-scenes operators reinforce the idea that the woman's exaltation is a fiction, unlikely to happen to her in real life; they also suggest that Leaf thought of this narrative as a play. She first conceived of this work as a scenario for a play titled *The Annunciation*. In her written synopsis of the plot, the Second Coming of the Messiah manifests itself in the body of a waitress. As she is possessed with the spirit, she becomes piglike. As Leaf humorously put it, God will appear in this age as an anonymous being, such as a pig.

Leaf's interest in art forms such as carnival theater tied her work to that of the Chicago imagists. *Ascension of Pig Lady* is featured on the cover of Franz Schulze's influential 1972 book on Chicago art since 1945, *Fantastic Images*, and her work is prominently featured in it as part of what Schulze defined as the imagist tradition. Leaf came to be seen as part of the initial group of Chicago imagists, including Jim Nutt (p. 120), Barbara Rossi (American, b. 1940), Gladys Nilsson (American, b. 1940), and Ed Paschke (p. 118) — artists similarly inspired by the lurid colors and bawdy expressions of urban entertainment. Leaf also shared these artists' tendency to master traditional craft skills, ranging from old-master painting processes of underpainting and glazing to exquisite carpentry. AP

Claire Zeisler

American, 1903–1991

Rosemary
1968
Jute and wool on steel armature
60 × 48 in. diameter (152.4 × 121.9 cm)
Gift of Mrs. Robert B. Mayer
1983.35

Claire Zeisler is one of the foremost artists to bring fiber arts into the mainstream of contemporary art. Her work was included in *Woven Forms*, an exhibition at the Museum of Contemporary Crafts in New York in 1963 that drew international attention to Zeisler and her peers, including Alice Adams, Lenore Tawney, Sheila Hicks, and Dorian Zachai. Zeisler's organic sculptural forms, made with pliable natural materials, offered an alternative to the severe geometry of the minimalist objects that dominated the field of American sculpture at the time. From the 1970s to her death, Zeisler maintained a dual practice — creating large, totemlike structures with bold shapes and colors, made with the help of assistants and frequently for public environments; and small, intimate, talismanlike objects, such as found stones wrapped in soft leather and cotton threads.

Zeisler began her artistic career late in life, having her first solo exhibition at age fifty-nine. She began her formal training in Chicago at the Illinois Institute of Design in the mid-1940s with such modernist luminaries as Alexander Archipenko (American, b. Ukraine 1887–1964) and Lázsló Moholy-Nagy (Hungarian, 1895–1946) and with the weavers Bea Swartchild and Lilie Blumenau. As early as the 1930s, she started amassing what came to be noted as one of Chicago's most prominent collections of modernist art, including works by Pablo Picasso (Spanish, 1881–1973), Joan Miró (Spanish, 1893–1983), Albert Gleizes (French, 1881–1953), Paul Klee (Swiss, 1879–1940), Franz Kline (Zeisler donated Kline's painting *Vawdavitch* [p. 53] to the MCA in 1976), Robert Rauschenberg (p. 70), and Louise Nevelson (American, b. Russia 1900–1988). She also collected tribal art and antiquities, such as Hopi baskets, tribal sculpture, heraldic staffs, beaded bags, and other objects. In 1966, she began extensive travels to Central America, West Africa, India, the South Pacific, Afghanistan, Japan, and Southeast Asia, where she continued to collect art. Zeisler's broad range of cross-cultural experiences helped her to see connections between ancient and modern forms and to find ways to bridge the long-standing divide between fine art and craft in her own work.

Zeisler's distinct contribution to fiber art is her introduction of alternative methods of hand-knotting, braiding, and wrapping coarse, natural fibers such as jute, raffia, sisal, and hemp in free-standing forms. Although she began as a weaver, she was dissatisfied with flat, wall-hanging formats and found it increasingly difficult to travel with a loom. In *Rosemary*, an early example of Zeisler's signature freestanding works, square knots form a structure from which a mass of black strands falls, parting at the center to reveal a coiled and wrapped, latticelike structure that gives the work a simultaneously foreboding and intriguing opening. Zeisler developed this wrapping technique with her assistant Massae Sakai, with whom she worked closely between 1967 and 1979. Zeisler combined carefully constructed symmetry with random tangling in *Rosemary*, perhaps suggesting two opposing representations of female sexuality — graceful comportment and unbridled force.

The title refers to Roman Polanski's popular horror film of 1968, *Rosemary's Baby*, in which a tormented woman believes she has been impregnated so that her child can be used in the rituals of an evil cult. Even though Zeisler has rejected the notion that her works directly suggest female sexuality, the subject of this particular work makes the suggestion an unusually straightforward exception. *Rosemary*'s simultaneous reference to contemporary popular culture and the forms of ancient totems engage our modern and ancient selves alike, as Zeisler attempted to do throughout her career. AP

Richard Serra

American, b. 1939

Prop
1968
Lead antimony
86¼ × 60 × 57 in. (219.1 × 152.4 × 148.8 cm)
Gift of Mrs. Robert B. Mayer
1978.44 a–b

Since 1965 Richard Serra has worked against conventional approaches to experiencing art by making the viewer's physical interaction with sculpture one of its fundamental preconditions. From his early "splash" works in which molten lead flung into the corner of a room obliterated the junction of wall and floor, to his most recent monumental sculptures with vertiginous canyon walls of Corten steel, Serra has sought to abnegate prescribed functions and classifications of space, particularly as they pertain to the presentation of art in galleries, museums, and domestic settings. Involving precise engineering to construct works held together by gravity, the installation of Serra's sculptures is as important as the finished works, often requiring the professional labor of industrial workmen and taking place in situ. Serra confers the function of "art producer" to professional tradesmen, demystifying the traditional role of the artist as craftsman. This and his reductive use of materials such as lead, rubber, and steel align him with minimalist sculptors such as Carl Andre (p. 110), Donald Judd (p. 124), and Robert Morris (p. 78). Although there are direct relationships between his work and process art, minimalism, and neoconceptualism, respectively, it does not reside neatly in any one category.

Serra's early work *Prop* was given to the museum by Mrs. Robert B. Mayer. Mayer's gift presents a confluence of relationships between Serra's work and the MCA, both of which were introduced to the public as radical alternatives to the status quo in the late 1960s. Looming large over the American conscience, the year 1968 marks the first anniversary of the MCA's founding and Serra's first major exhibition with the legendary New York dealer Leo Castelli.[1] At this time, Serra first incorporated into his practice what has become a signature vocabulary of elemental components and industrial materials such as lead and steel, and he began reckoning with the physical force of gravity to create form. *Prop* is

one of Serra's seminal *Prop Pieces* of 1968–69, which were first shown together at the Solomon R. Guggenheim Museum in New York in May 1969.

"To prop" is an artistic idea that Serra has maintained ever since.[2] Emphasizing the materiality and weight of the metal objects through their precarious arrangements, he forces an immediate and bodily response to sculpture. Spatial boundaries around Serra's sculptures are demarcated emotionally by one's sense of curiosity or fear, and navigating this space is likewise contingent on the viewer's conflicting feelings of wonder and anxiety. For this reason, Serra's work has inspired comparisons with notions of the sublime in eighteenth- and nineteenth-century Romantic painting.

Serra has continued to elaborate on the essential physical properties that he explored with his *Props*, achieving stability through "the conflict and balance of forces."[3] This is evident in later works owned by the MCA including *Another Look at a Corner* (1985) and *Five Plate Pentagon* (1988), and is taken to extraordinarily dramatic lengths in the magnificent flourishes of his recent *Torqued Spirals* (2001). M R

1 Serra participated in a solo exhibition that year in Leo Castelli's warehouse on New York's Upper West Side, and in a group exhibition there organized by the minimalist sculptor Robert Morris. See Douglas Crimp, "Serra's Public Sculpture: Redefining Site Specificity," in Laura Rosenstock, ed., *Richard Serra Sculpture* (New York: The Museum of Modern Art, 1986), p. 41

2 Rosalind E. Krauss, "Richard Serra Sculpture," in *Richard Serra Sculpture* (note 1), p. 20.

3 Ibid., p. 20.

Carl Andre

American, b. 1935

In *Zinc-Lead Plain*, Carl Andre employed many significant characteristics of 1960s minimalism, including geometric shapes, industrial materials, the arrangement of modular units in simple arithmetic progressions, and the attempt to transform the viewer's physical environment.

A seminal early work of Andre's, *Zinc-Lead Plain* was first exhibited in 1970 as part of a larger work, entitled *37 Pieces of Work*, at an exhibition at the Solomon R. Guggenheim Museum in New York. The work consisted of thirty-six six-by-six-foot squares, each of which, like *Zinc-Lead Plain*, consisted of thirty-six tiles. Each component consisted of equal quantities of tiles of different materials: overall there were 219 each of

aluminum, copper, steel, magnesium, lead, and zinc. Two versions of each combination exist — six monometal and thirty bimetal "plains" — each of which were exhibited in a progression corresponding to the alphabetical order of the chemical symbol of the metal. This arrangement typifies Andre's use of existing rational systems; the order of the components of his work are never arbitrary or subjective.

Like other artists associated with minimalism, such as Donald Judd (p. 124) and Sol LeWitt (p. 92), Andre emphasized the objective and literal over the subjective and illusionistic aims of art. In minimalist works, materials are used in their original form. Minimalist artists often equated literalism with honesty and illusionism with deceit, al-

Zinc-Lead Plain
1969
Zinc and lead
Thirty-six parts, installed: 3/8 × 72 × 72 in.
(1 × 182.9 × 182.9 cm)
Gerald S. Elliott Collection
1995.26.a–jj

110

though each of the artists associated with this movement pursued a distinct ethical and aesthetic agenda.

Andre in particular developed a penchant for anaxial symmetry — namely, the construction of a work in which all modules are interchangeable. Using anaxial symmetry, Andre aimed to create nonhierarchical artworks — ones that could offer the same view from any direction, that did not value one viewpoint over another. With this, Andre was reacting against traditional monumental sculpture, which he saw as hierarchical in its authoritative verticality, heroic posturing, and its dependence on dramatic points of interest. Extending the "allover" aesthetics of American painters such as Jackson Pollock (1912–1956) and Frank Stella (b. 1936), Andre sought to make works that were equally interesting from any perspective.

Andre, who once said that the ideal sculpture is a road or causeway, saw sculpture's ability to create a literal place as its essential element. The road, for Andre, allows ultimate control of space, since one has to walk around it or on it to get somewhere; it is also without hierarchy, since it has no fixed or ideal view. Not surprisingly, most of Andre's works, including *Zinc-Lead Plain*, lie on the floor. Like roads, the works are designed to be walked on and over.

For Andre, the experience of walking across this work is as important as its visual appearance. His attention to the viewer's total sensory perception of surroundings is demonstrated by his choice of metal tiles. Zinc and lead, for instance, each have different weights. Walking across this work is therefore an experience of variable masses and sounds. Andre's work is significantly shaped by his experience in the early 1960s as a freight brakeman on the Pennsylvania Railroad and as a conductor in New Jersey. The forms of the railroad tracks seem to have inspired or reinforced his theoretical interests in modularity, anaxial symmetry, and the road. AP

Vito Acconci

American, b. 1940

Over the last three decades, Vito Acconci's conceptual work has evolved from poetry readings to body art and performance, installation, and most recently public sculpture and architecture. In the early 1970s, Acconci first used his body and later the environment as a site for performance, concentrating on the conditions involved in performative work to create installations using video and sound, such as *The Gangster Sister from Chicago* (1977). As his installations became more site specific, involving architectural elements, Acconci began to focus on architecture's effect upon the viewer. In testing the boundaries of a situation, whether physical, psychological, or political, Acconci saw the encounter between the artist and audience as a provocation of dominant systems of power and thought.

Describing his early poetry, Acconci has written that his aim was spatial: to "use language to cover a space rather than uncover a meaning."[1] Similarly, his first work of visual art — a group of photographic works made from 1969 to 1970 — recorded the physical movements of his body within various environments. In *Stretch*, Acconci oriented himself in three-dimensional space. By stretching his arms in the four cardinal directions, with a Kodak 124 Instamatic in hand, he photographed the resultant views of Central Park in New York. The text — written in chalk on foamcore and recording time, place, and actions with arrows pointing to the corresponding photos — systematically orients the viewer's eye through the work as if a

Stretch
1969
Gelatin silver prints, chalkboard spray paint, chalk, and marker on foamcore
54 × 54 in. (137.2 × 137.2 cm)
Gerald S. Elliott Collection
1995.24

House of Used Parts
1985
Aluminum ladders, doors, windows, wood, canvas, and vinyl seat cushions
108 × 72 × 72 in. (274.3 × 182.9 × 182.9 cm)
Gerald S. Elliott Collection
1995.23

visual aid to be used in a performance or as evidence explaining a sequence of actions. In his *Notebook Excerpts*, explaining the series and the multiple and systematic ways to be in space, Acconci wrote, "The real activity of these pieces — connecting my body with its surroundings — occurs somewhere between my action and the photographs." Not content with the connection, he wrote, "I would have wanted to bring about a more physical change either in myself or in the environment."[2]

In an effort to further dissolve the distinctions between individual and environment, Acconci began creating architectural furniture and public architectural projects. *House of Used Parts*, constructed with common building materials for the exhibition *Making Shelter* at Harvard University, appears to be a prefabricated playhouse with seats for four people. The ladders at each corner, serving as support columns and as

seats, lead to an upper level and suggest a jungle gym. The four doors, which open and close at the top, create a tentlike shelter. Focusing on the domestic environment, Acconci explores the roles and restraints architecture imposes upon the culture of a society. In "Home-Bodies (An Introduction to My Work, 1984–85)," he wrote "the building-blocks of a piece, are the building-blocks of a culture: these conventions are power-signs, that confirm and maintain a dominant class/race/gender. A piece, then, should take these conventions and subvert them . . . if the house makes you itch, if you do a double-take, then you snap out of the present, you can have time to think of the future and change . . . . This should be the kind of home that makes you a stranger inside it . . . "[3]

What are people expected to do when entering something that is neither house, nor shelter, nor playground, yet a combination of all three? Acconci has stipulated that not only are people allowed to sit in the piece — the piece makes no sense unless people sit in it. Despite the ambiguity of *House of Used Parts*, its openness invites people to sit within and transform the public space of a museum into a private gathering, and to question the definitions of public and private spaces. TVE

1 Vito Acconci, "Early Work: Moving My Body into Place," in Kate Linker, *Vito Acconci* (New York: Rizzoli, 1994), p. 13.

2 *Notebook Excerpts* (1969), in *Vito Acconci: Photographic Works 1969–1970*, exh. cat. (Chicago: Rhona Hoffman Gallery, 1969), unpag.

3 Vito Acconci, "Home-Bodies (An Introduction to My Work, 1984–85)," in Kate Linker, *Vito Acconci* (New York: Rizzoli, 1994), p. 140.

George Segal

American, 1924–2000

Man in Bar
1969
Plaster, tempera on metal, wood, and cloth
60½ × 24½ × 12⅜ in.
(153.7 × 62.2 × 31.4 cm)
Gift of Mr. and Mrs. E. A. Bergman
1974.12

In the 1950s, at the beginning of his artistic career, George Segal distanced himself from the abstract expressionists by making art that reflects the urban landscape. Known for his lifelike sculptures of figures and use of everyday materials, Segal was greatly influenced by Tony Smith (American, 1912–1981), his collage instructor at New York University. Segal was also interested in cubist works by Pablo Picasso (Spanish, 1881–1973) and Georges Braque (French, 1882–1963), and has even called his three-dimensional sculptural installations "literal cubism," as they allow the viewer to obtain multiple views by walking through and around them. He was also a friend of Allan Kaprow, whose "happenings" and installations of the 1960s undoubtedly encouraged Segal's interest in incorporating real-life situations into his art, positioning his work alongside that of the pop artists.

Man in Bar portrays a man sitting alone by a window in a bar, leaning his chin on his hand. His hunched posture, determined by the cast model's choice of position, suggests a melancholy mood. Segal began making these "boxes" — *Man in Bar* and *Coffee Shop* — in 1969. As relief assemblages, they differ from his earlier life-sized, three-dimensional, cast-figure installations, yet the figures, which appear alone or in groups, are immediately identifiable by their ghostly white plaster surface. Segal cast his first plaster figure, using himself as a model, in 1961. He then created an environment for the figure with a chair, table, and window. All of his sculptures are cast from live models, often friends or family, and have a personal significance to the artist. Once displayed, however, the figures in his work become anonymous.

Windows and doorways, which are common motifs in this period of Segal's work, function as symbolic boundaries between intimate, private spaces and larger, public spaces. Many of his boxes are framed in such a way that they recall brief glimpses one might see while passing by in a moving vehicle, and often Segal works from memories of such glimpses. His challenge is to re-create these scenes by incorporating found materials such as commercial signs and lettering, or the curtain rod and rings as in *Man in Bar*, in order to represent his vision of that memory. His use of old, derelict materials evokes a sense of nostalgia, while the loneliness of the ghostly figure suggests one's solitude in life. In addition to making effigies, Segal celebrates ephemeral moments and memories in his tableaux by using symbols of urban life without pop art's ironic hyper-commercialization. JRW

Marcel Broodthaers

Belgian, 1924–1976

**1833......Le manuscrit
(1833......The Manuscript)**
1969–1970
Vacuum-formed plastic
33⅝ × 47¼ in × ³⁄₁₆ in.
(85.4 × 120 × .8 cm)
Edition of 7
Restricted gift of Paul and Camille
Oliver-Hoffmann, Kunstadter Bequest Fund
in honor of Sigmund Kunstadter,
and anonymous donor
1983.68

**1833......Le manuscrit
(1833......The Manuscript)**
1969–1970
Vacuum-formed plastic
33⅝ × 47¼ × ³⁄₁₆ in.
(85.4 × 120 × .8 cm)
Edition of 7
Restricted gift of Paul and Camille
Oliver-Hoffmann, Kunstadter Bequest Fund
in honor of Sigmund Kunstadter,
and anonymous donor
1983.69

Belgian poet-turned-artist Marcel Broodthaers left an important legacy of conceptual art. Known for his wit and varied forms of work including photographs, photo-canvases, films, letters, poems, sculptures, and installations that prevent a logical or linear reading, Broodthaers examined how artworks derive their meaning through familiar images and language. He investigated social and artistic contexts such as museums and galleries while questioning systems of logic and language, creating enigmatic combinations of text and objects. His work challenged many of the traditions in art as well as the increasing commercialization of pop art based on advertisements and media.

Broodthaers proclaimed his philosophy of art making: "I too wondered whether I could not sell something and succeed in life . . . the idea of inventing something insincere finally crossed my mind and I set to work straightaway."[1]

During the 1940s, Broodthaers was a poet and part of the political resistance movement against the Nazis in Belgium. He later became part of the communist party, and his belief in Marxist ideology was central to his critique of the commercialization of art. As a testament to the absurdity of art's value system, Italian artist Piero Manzoni (1933–1963) wrote his signature on Broodthaers himself in 1962, with an accompanying certificate declaring Broodthaers a living sculpture.

Broodthaers began working on his "insincere objects" as parodies of commercial art's assimilation of the avant-garde. From 1968 to 1971, while undertaking *Musée d'Art Moderne, Departement des Aigles (Museum of Modern Art, Department of Eagles)*, the monumental

multi-installation critique of museum practice and classification systems, he created a series of industrially fabricated plastic signs and reliefs he chose for their lack of association with art. In his plastic plaques, or industrial poems, as he called them, Broodthaers questioned literary conventions and the relationship between language and images. These works were influenced in part by the uncanny use of words and pictures by René Magritte (p. 50) and the compositions of text into visual patterns by the symbolist poet Stephane Mallarmé (French, 1842–1898). The plaques are related to Broodthaers's earlier open letters, with geometric forms that recall textbook diagrams and commercial signs with letters, numbers, abstract shapes, and recognizable symbols. Broodthaers likened these works to rebuses, yet his aim was to prohibit reading through the textlike quality of the images and imagelike quality of the text. Rather, he saw them as unsolvable puzzles with no clear message.

1833......Le manuscrit is one of his industrial poems. The MCA has a red-and-black version and a gray-and-red version depicting an image of a bottle with the year 1924 on the label and a curvilinear swirl inside the bottle. Abstract square forms resembling jigsaw puzzle pieces interrupt a white background. The text *1833......Le manuscrit* appears in script on the lower edge of the plaque. Although it does not seem to suggest a clear narrative, *1833......Le manuscrit* refers to the Edgar Allan Poe story "MS. Found in a Bottle" published in 1833. In the story, a man sets sail on a ship from Batavia, Java, to the Archipelago Islands. During a sudden storm, the ship crashes and he survives by jumping aboard another passing ship as a stowaway. He keeps a diary to be placed in a bottle and thrown overboard. He writes as the ship is caught in a whirlpool and sinks near the South Pole. Although this tangential reference does not provide a definitive reading of Broodthaers's work, it provides a sense of mystery and loss that is evocative of the work itself. In light of his battle with liver disease, *1833......Le manuscrit* could also suggest a metaphor for the journey of life spinning out of control. Yet this piece, like all of Broodthaers's works, eludes conclusive interpretations. JRW

1 *Marcel Broodthaers*, exh. cat. (London: The Tate Gallery, 1980), p. 13.

Ed Paschke

American, b. 1939

Japanese Cowboy
1969
Oil on canvas
14 × 10 in. (35.6 × 25.4 cm)
Gift of Susan and Lewis Manilow
1993.8

Adria
1976
Oil on canvas
96⅛ × 74 in. (244.2 × 188 cm)
Gift of Susan and Lewis Manilow
in honor of Dennis Adrian
1988.6

Painter Ed Paschke has consistently drawn inspiration from and commented on popular media imagery. From the late 1960s to the late 1970s, Paschke's subjects were largely derived from underclass, marginal, or illicit sources — vaudevillian theater, freak shows, cult movies, and pornography — and their ephemeral forms of promotion, including cinema handbills, posters, flyers, special-interest magazines, and mail-order catalogues. Paschke's output of this period initially identified him with the Chicago group known as the imagists, including such peers as Jim Nutt (p. 120), Karl Wirsum (b. 1939), Gladys Nilsson (b. 1940), Roger Brown (p. 134), and Christina Ramberg (p. 132). Paschke shared with these artists a predilection for sensationalist media, the imagery of lowbrow entertainment, cartoons and caricature, bohemian subjects, and the projection of an irreverent, often darkly humorous view of humanity. Paschke's early work noticeably emphasizes the presentation of subjects who manipulate appearances, especially costume, to promote themselves in advertisements or on the street. His work of the late 1960s consists of montages of images drawn from ads for featured characters such as stage performers or athletes. Paschke's paintings from the early 1970s tend to feature single figures, usually underworld characters with over-the-top costumes and stances.

In the mid-1970s, however, Paschke's work began to show a greater concern with the reverse process of mediation. He examined how media — especially television — manipulate people and their perceptions of reality. Paschke's work since the mid-1970s is characterized by anonymous-looking figures in generic costumes, masks, and increasingly abstracted objects floating in abstractly patterned spaces featuring neon lines and other "electric" atmospheric effects.

The works featured here represent the beginnings of each of the two major phases of Paschke's oeuvre thus far. *Japanese Cowboy* is one of a group of paintings from 1968–69 in which he juxtaposed images of boxers and circus performers, showgirls, and porn models. To create such images, he used a

118

slide projector to enlarge or reduce his photographic sources and to create relationships among them. Paschke's sources for this work are characteristically drawn from obscure sources. In a letter to an MCA curator, Paschke explained that the cowboy comes from a handbill of a silent Western film. The cartoon thought-bubble is written in Japanese, recalling the heroic figures in Akira Kurosawa's 1954 film *Seven Samurai*. The strong, central placement of the figure emulates the star-centered presentations that are typical of movie posters. As with Paschke's other early works, the details of the figure's face and costume — the cultural specificity of the imagery's source — are important.

Adria demonstrates the beginning of Paschke's turn away from cultural specificity. As he explained in an interview, in works such as *Adria* he tried to capture the unnatural glow of color-television light. Paschke created these ghostlike figures by increasing his already laborious process of layering paint. For *Japanese Cowboy*, he began by creating a black-and-white underpainting, or cartoon, over which he painted layers of color. This traditional painting technique was made more elaborate in paintings such as *Adria*, in which Paschke added glazes of translucent color to achieve the glowing, disembodied quality. *Adria* is one of several monumental portraits that Paschke created in the mid-1970s in which the figure has an exaggerated physiognomy, is bizarrely clothed, and is set against a patterned

background to make the space appear compressed and explosive. Throughout his oeuvre, Paschke has been more concerned with artifice and drama than the accurate portrayal of individuals. For example, although this painting incorporates the face of Dennis Adrian — noted Chicago critic, teacher, curator, and friend of Paschke's — the rest of the picture is not specific to Adrian. Instead, it is nearly identical to an earlier pencil drawing, entitled *Tudor,* that had no relation to the later subject but instead refers to the Tudor style of the outlandish costume used in both pictures. Even the transformation of Adrian's name into *Adria* shows Paschke's desire to transport his subject onto a fantastic plane. A P

119

Jim Nutt

American, b. 1938

Known for his unique figurative style of grossly distorted human bodies and often scatological subject matter, Jim Nutt has been influenced by a range of sources, including comic books, tabloid advertising, and films as well as art-historical sources including Northern European painting and sculpture, ethnographic art, and contemporary masters such as Balthus (Swiss, b. France 1908–2001). *Summer Salt* is one of three works by Nutt designed to mimic a window and valance with a roll-up shade, a device from the simpler, if more trying times of the Depression and World War II eras. A panel that features small, carefully painted objects — body parts, pieces of furniture, items of clothing — forms the physical support and backdrop for a horrific, precisely rendered image of a roughly life-sized male figure painted on a piece of transparent vinyl rigged by the artist to act as a roll-up shade. Bound and gagged, his head seemingly decapitated with blood spurting out in all directions, the figure, his phallus huge and erect, sits in what seems to be an ocean of excrement. Rarely has a more explicit depiction of sadomasochism been created by a contemporary artist.

The impact of this horrific depiction is initially ameliorated by the cartoonish style of the imagery. Nutt's use of black outlines, unmodeled expanses of vibrant color, and sequences of imagery characteristic of a comic strip suggest an affinity to the work of Roy Lichtenstein (American, 1923–1997) or James Rosenquist (American, b. 1933). Yet Nutt's

Summer Salt

1970
Vinyl paint over plastic and enamel on
 wood and Masonite
61¼ × 36 × 3½ in. (155.6 × 91.4 × 8.9 cm)
Gift of Dennis Adrian
in honor of Claire B. Zeisler
1980.30.1

LEFT with shade down
RIGHT with shade up

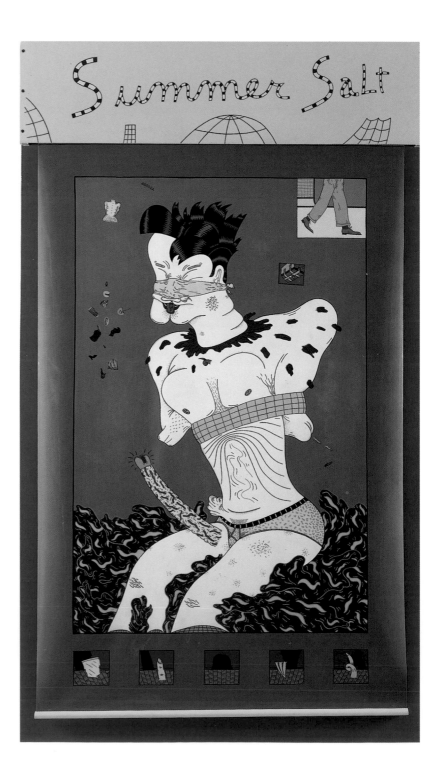

intention is less about exploring the formal aspects of this American vernacular than exploiting its playful quality to depict material of an extreme, psychosexual nature. As Lawrence Alloway has pointed out, works of this era also bear a resemblance to the display panels on pinball machines in their glossy surfaces and "slippery" color. *Summer Salt* seems to suggest a game in which the dominant player bends the game to his will.

This technique of "hinterglasmalerei" or "reverse-glass painting" was typical of Nutt's early period (roughly 1964 through 1971). Using this technique, he painted the image in reverse layers on the back side of a transparent material. To achieve the dominant figure in *Summer Salt*, Nutt created a drawing using colored pencils (*Quaffed* (1970), MCA Collection) and transferred it to the clear vinyl; the figure in *Summer Salt* is the result, the reverse of that in *Quaffed*. *Summer Salt* can be displayed both with the "shade" pulled down or rolled up to reveal the backdrop.

Born in Massachusetts, Nutt began his residence in the Chicago area when he attended The School of The Art Institute of Chicago (SAIC) in the early 1960s. He emerged with a group of other SAIC students in a seminal series of exhibitions titled *Hairy Who*. These now legendary exhibitions introduced an irreverent, high-spirited figurative style to Chicago and the world. In 1973 Nutt started his "theater" paintings (including some three-dimensional constructions such as *He's Not Allowed to Look, How-ever* (1973)), which are distinguished by painted stage curtains that frame the central composition of small figures enacting inexplicable narratives. A 1974 retrospective, which toured museums in the United States and Europe, introduced Nutt's work to the national and international audience. Since 1987, Nutt has concentrated on bust-length portraits of imaginary women with jarringly odd hairstyles and prominent noses, meticulously painted with multiple layers of acrylic glazes. Both his early works of the 1960s and 1970s and his more recent work of the 1990s feature elaborate, decorative frames designed and crafted by the artist. LW

Joseph Beuys

German, 1921–1986

Filzanzug (Felt Suit)
1970
Felt
67½ × 30¼ × 8½ in. (117.4 × 76.8 × 21.6 cm)
Ed: 87/100
Partial gift of Dr. Paul and Dorie Sternberg
1987.18.a–b

Through his work, Joseph Beuys aimed symbolically to heal the wounds inflicted by World War II and the following era of reconstruction and modernization in Germany, events he saw as creating a drastic disconnection with nature. Beuys adopted the personae of healer, shaman, and teacher through his use of related materials, such as a red cross symbol, animals, and classroom blackboards, creating modern myths through oblique meanings and symbols in his performances, objects, drawings, and multiples.

Beuys was briefly associated with Fluxus, an international group of artists that sought to create socially conscious, anti-art objects in order to conflate artistic and social concerns. Democratic ideals were of paramount importance to Beuys. He was founder and leader of social and political groups, such as the German Student Party and Organization for Direct Democracy. As a professor at the Kunstakademie Düsseldorf, Beuys welcomed students who had previously been rejected from art school. In addition to political activism, one of the hallmarks of Beuys's work was his use of specific materials to convey the concrete expression of an idea or spirituality. He sought answers to metaphysical questions about the human condition through the transformative properties of natural, common materials, such as felt, fat, fur, and honey, in his conceptual works and performances.

Filzanzug (Felt Suit), with its heavy, gray felt material, lack of buttons, and elongated arms and legs, was not designed to be a functional piece of clothing. Like most of Beuys's works, the object is secondary to its symbolism. The use of felt, a natural material made of layers of densely compressed animal hair, holds personal significance for Beuys. He was a Luftwaffe pilot in World War II, and he later told a story that, after his plane crashed, he was rescued by locals and wrapped in felt. In this context, felt conveys not only physical warmth, but spiritual warmth and salvation. Beuys wore an edition of *Felt Suit* in the performance *Isolation Unit*, an anti-Vietnam *action* (as his events were called) that took place with Terry Fox in the cellar of the Kunstakademie Düsseldorf, on October 4, 1971. Fox burned the wooden frame of a window while Beuys cradled a dead mouse in his hand. The silent performance was interrupted by Fox banging on an iron pipe, while Beuys spat fruit seeds into a silver bowl, making a delicate ringing sound. The combination of aggressive and evocative sounds metaphorically recalled the dual sides of war as both an extremely savage and ethereal experience. The ideas of physical and spiritual warmth also translated to this performance, with Beuys holding a dead mouse as a memorial to the soldiers who have died in war.

From his personal experience in World War II, as well as the radically changing social climate in Europe during the 1960s and 1970s, Beuys witnessed a world that needed to be reconnected with universal, spiritual, and natural elements of life. He did this by using archetypal symbols and ideas in a body of work that often reflected the nonsensical world around him, but also conveyed the importance of having a personal spiritual consciousness in order to make sense of such a world. JRW

123

Donald Judd

American, 1928–1994

Untitled
1970
Stainless steel and Plexiglas
Ten parts, each: 6 × 27 × 24 in.
(15.2 × 68.6 × 61 cm)
Gerald S. Elliott Collection
1995.50.a–j

Donald Judd, a key figure in the minimalist movement, began his art career as a painter and art critic before turning to sculpture in the early 1960s. He preferred not to be identified as a sculptor because of its traditional connotations; if pressed to categorize himself, he favored the term empiricist. He believed that the direct sensual experience of viewing art was the most genuine, thus aligning him more with the modern rationalists than the poetic or metaphoric work of his artist predecessors. Although he was respected as a precise craftsman, Judd's interests in sculpture were oriented primarily toward the immediate physical presence of reductive forms and materials.

Judd first showed his three-dimensional painted boxes in 1963, labeling them "functionless objects." *Untitled* (Judd rarely titled his works) is part of his best-known series of wall-hanging stacks made between 1967 and 1973. More than thirty versions of works from this series exist, ranging in primary and secondary colors of Plexiglas and a variety of metals such as stainless steel, galvanized iron, brass, and anodized aluminum. *Untitled* features a geometric repetition of identical rectangular, translucent boxes made of green Plexiglas (sides and fronts) and stainless steel (tops and bottoms) arranged in a stack of ten with the space between each equaling six inches, the exact height of each box. Judd carefully orchestrated the voids as well as the solid boxes to create a rhythmic visual cadence. He used these intervals of negative space as volumetric material and to provide an objective theme of form rather than a metaphorical meaning. The fluorescent colors in this series are reminiscent of the light sculptures that Judd admired by his contemporary Dan Flavin (p. 72).

Judd wanted his materials to be viewed as significant elements in themselves—free from illusions, decoration, or virtuosity. Only by directly and matter-of-factly presenting the corporeality of the object could he address aesthetic experience in its most absolute state. Often, he employed the most basic of geometric forms, the cube, to further release his work from possible extraneous readings.

As with Ad Reinhardt (p. 64), Judd was more influenced by the painting of Kasimir Malevich (Russian, 1878–1935) and Piet Mondrian (Dutch, 1872–1944) than by the abstract expressionists. Upon Judd's death in 1994, fellow artist Richard Serra (p. 108) said, "By the time I arrived in New York in the late sixties, Judd's invention had already transformed the historical context. Judd's break had been so startling and abrupt that within three years abstract expressionism was out, minimalism was in."[1] Judd continuously investigated this repetitive, objective theme of form and space throughout his lifetime.

Later in his life Judd established his own art foundation—the Chinati Foundation—located in Marfa, a small Texan town near Mexico. In an attempt to revitalize the town, Judd purchased buildings that he planned to renovate and turn into venues for large-scale works of art, both his own and objects from his personal collection. Although Judd died before the major revitalization was realized, the foundation now exists as a major center for the display of works by Judd and other artists. LH

1 Richard Serra, "Donald Judd, 1928–1994," *Parkett*, no. 40/41 (June 1994), pp. 176–77.

Richard Artschwager

American, b. 1923

Since the early 1960s, Richard Artschwager has crossed the lines of contemporary art movements in his paintings and sculptures. His paintings, with their appropriated images, and his nonutilitarian, bluntly literal abstract furniture-sculptures have been associated with both pop art and minimalism. His pictures with painstakingly reproduced images from newspapers and magazines have been seen as examples of photorealism.

Yet Artschwager has never consistently fit into any one of these categories. Instead, using various means, he has steadily developed his central theme: how art imitates life and life imitates art. His chief concern has been how illusionistic devices are used in both art and non-art contexts. For example, he draws on the understanding that through the methods of perspective, three-dimensional objects can be represented as two-dimensional pictures and, conversely, through the application of two-dimensional patterns on three-dimensional objects, pictures are commonly literalized as the surfaces of objects.

Artschwager's operation of a furniture factory in New York from 1955 to 1965 was probably the chief catalyst in the development of the most distinctive aspects of his oeuvre: his penchant for reversing the functions of pictures and objects by making pictures that have the substance of objects and objects that have the surfaces of pictures, his use of furniture and building interiors and exteriors as his main motifs, and his

Polish Rider I
1970–71
Acrylic on Celotex
44 × 60³⁄₁₆ in. (111.8 × 152.9 cm)
Gift of Mrs. Robert B. Mayer
1984.2

126

frequent use of the industrial materials Formica and Celotex. An inexpensive building material used for walls and ceilings, Celotex has been Artschwager's preferred substitute for the painter's canvas since the early 1960s.

From 1970 to 1976, Artschwager created numerous paintings on Celotex featuring images of luxuriously furnished interiors copied from magazine illustrations. Among the best known are the four in the 1970–71 *Polish Rider* series, the first of which is in the MCA Collection. In this series all the paintings bear the same title, which refers to that of a painting by Rembrandt van Rijn (Dutch, 1606–1669) in the Frick Collection in New York. Though completely unlike Rembrandt's image, which depicts a horseman in a somber landscape, the MCA's

work appropriates its structure, by which spatial illusionism is achieved. While Rembrandt placed the figure of the horseman to block the vanishing point of his scene's perspectival lines, Artschwager left the perspectival lines of his American interior's floor, walls, and ceiling visible.

In this work, Artschwager made explicit the ongoing duality in art between the values of depth and surface that is only implicit in the arrested recession of space in Rembrandt's painting. Artschwager highlighted the illusory nature of the picture's "interior" by having it split apart over the bumpy surfaces of the Celotex, which, when viewed up close, causes the image to disintegrate

into an opaque "exterior," like the wall the Celotex is literally designed to be. Artschwager further externalized this interior image by framing it in aluminum, an industrial material.

Polish Rider I also conflates two otherwise distinct realms of social class and taste through its reference to materials. The interior depicted, with its Georgian dining room, appears upper-middle class, whereas the Celotex material on which it is depicted is commonly associated with lower-middle-class housing. By representing the upper-middle-class interior in lower-middle-class terms, Artschwager aimed to heighten our awareness of the class coding of interiors in general, both real and in the history of art, which communicate as maps of social standing. AP

Jackie Ferrara

American, b. 1929

Stacked Pyramid
1972
Cotton batting with glue on wood
24 × 52 × 13 in. (61 × 132.1 × 33 cm)
Gift of Lannan Foundation
1997.34

An artistic peer and friend of some of the minimalist artists who emerged in the 1960s, including Carl Andre (p. 110) and Sol LeWitt (p. 92), Jackie Ferrara was "discovered" when an art dealer saw her work at LeWitt's studio. Ferrara's sculptures, which she typically constructs with standard geometric units, employ many of the signal features of minimalism. Her "building block" approach to making sculptures reflects the minimalists' interest in breaking sculptural form into what they saw as its most basic elements. Throughout her career, Ferrara has maintained an interest in pattern, which she and other minimalists perceived as analogous to social systems.

Ferrara builds her sculptures by using an incrementally changing pattern of stacked or layered units. The increments impose rules on the work, and therefore maintain its relationship to systems. She emulates the processes of an architect, calculating the proportions of the sculpture on graph paper, plotting it from different perspectives, fashioning it in three dimensions, and employing architectural forms such as stairways, platforms, courtyards, pyramids, and niches. After 1980, she began creating large outdoor sculptures that increasingly approached the size of actual dwellings. In the 1980s and 1990s, Ferrara designed spaces for public use.

Her chief aim has been to create structures that encourage reflection and introspection. Many of her freestanding sculptures are larger than an architectural model but smaller than life-size, encouraging the projection of fantasy.

Her structures have often been compared to ancient places of worship — temples, ziggurats, mastabas — though Ferrara's stated intention is to create works with an ahistorical quality, simultaneously seeming ancient and futuristic.

Before 1972, Ferrara was making what she has called "funky" sculpture, using animal parts and ropes, among other things. A turning point came in 1971, when she bought a loft in New York that required her to do a great deal of carpentry. *Stacked Pyramid*, one of Ferrara's first signature stacked structures, is composed of units that are assembled in a pattern that decreases by increments of one. There are fourteen "bricks" on the lowest layer and fourteen layers, ending in one, the imaginary plateau point.

Stacked Pyramid, along with a series of four other stacked structures from 1973 that are also part of the MCA Collection, is one of the only works for which Ferrara used cotton batting. After 1973, she began using wood without cotton covering as her primary material, because wood is more durable and enables her to create more complex structures. The wood also has some of the absorbent surface quality of the cotton batting, which is soothing to the eye.

As she began creating elaborate wooden structures, Ferrara adopted new methods: instead of stacking loose units, she assembled wood works using glue, nails, and dowels. *Stacked Pyramid*, however, is stored in separate "bricks" and stacked for installation.

From her earliest structures to her most recent ones, Ferrara has maintained a duality between the systematic and the improvisational; although the increments determine the shape of her works, she chooses the increments intuitively. Unlike some minimalists, who emulated industrial production by contracting out the manufacture of editions of their works, Ferrara rarely deviates from making her works unique and with her own hands. A P

Ana Mendieta

American, b. Cuba 1948–1985

Untitled from the *Silueta* series
1973–1977/1991
Silver dye-bleach prints
Twelve parts; parts one, six, nine, ten:
16 × 20 in. (40.6 × 50.8 cm)
parts two, three, four, five, seven, eight, eleven,
twelve: 20 × 16 in. (50. 8 × 40.6 cm)
Ed: 7/20 aside from 4 artist's proofs
Partial and promised gift from The Howard and
Donna Stone Collection
2002.46.1–12

Ana Mendieta's *Silueta* series is a haunting synthesis of performance art with earth art, minimalism, body art, and feminism. In these works, created in Mexico, Mendieta traced her silhouette onto dirt, sand, and fields using stones, flowers, vegetation, fabric, and fireworks. While these works were performative, Mendieta enacted them without an audience. Her photographs and films remain as documents.

Although Mendieta began her artistic career as a painter, she was dissatisfied with the medium. She said, "my paintings were not real enough for what I wanted the images to convey, and by real I mean I wanted my images to have power, to be magic."[1] When Mendieta

began working outdoors with natural materials, a decisive shift occurred in her art. By using the earth, which she believed to be a living being, Mendieta sought a more direct involvement with its mysteries and powers. This notion of the living earth as a source of power is a tenet of Santería, the Afro-Cuban religion with roots both in Catholicism and the Yoruba religions native to Nigeria.

In 1973, while working in Mexico, Mendieta made her first earth body sculpture at the Mixtec ruins, a Zapotec burial site located at Yagul in the valley of Oaxaca. At this site, which is symbolic of an ancient culture's sacred passageway from one life to another, Mendieta

lay in a burial mound covered in flowers.[2] She intended the flowers to evoke rebirth and a rekindling of the site's origins as a shamans' school for initiation into the psychic realm. In another work she created a mold of her body by digging in the earth, as if reaching to ancestral spirits. About this time Mendieta wrote, "Plugging into Mexico was like going back to the source, being able to get some magic just by being there."[3]

This longing for a symbolic connection to her native land of Cuba was highly personal, yet had affinities with the emergence of Goddess consciousness, a feminist belief in the unification of the spiritual and material. For Mendieta, fusing her body with the earth was a spiritual act. She saw herself as the earth's conduit, representing and uncovering its power. Made with natural materials — sand, water, earth, flowers — subject to the elements, her works were ephemeral as nature itself. While this impermanence recalls *Spiral Jetty* by Robert Smithson (p. 90), Mendieta's physical relation with the land set her apart from male artists creating earthworks during the 1970s. Instead of creating large-scale earthworks to alter the viewer's relationship to the landscape, Mendieta created her art for herself: "My art is the way I reestablish the bonds that unite me to the universe."[4] TVE

1 Judith Wilson, "Ana Mendieta Plants," in Petra Barreras Del Rio, *Ana Mendieta, A Retrospective*, exh. cat. (New York: New Museum of Contemporary Art, 1987), p. 28.

2 Mary Jane Jacob, *Ana Mendieta: The "Silueta" Series, 1973 –1980*, exh. cat. (New York: Galerie Lelong, 1991, p. 13.

3 Judith Wilson, "Ana Mendieta Plants," in Petra Barreras Del Rio, *Ana Mendieta, A Retrospective*, exh. cat. (New York: New Museum of Contemporary Art, 1987), p. 31.

4 Ibid., p. 31.

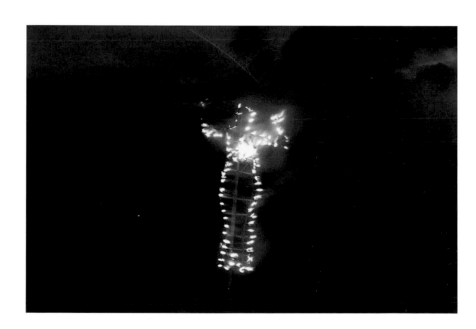

Christina Ramberg

American, 1946–1995

Throughout her twenty-five-year painting career, Christina Ramberg made artworks characterized by two main elements: highly finished surfaces and the use of visual metaphors for the psychic constraints on women. The majority of Ramberg's acrylic paintings on Masonite depict highly abstracted female bodies in various binding undergarments such as brassieres, bustiers, girdles, and dress shields that represent the restrictions placed on women. Using a controlled painting style to depict cylindrical bodies, with heads and feet cropped, Ramberg distances her subjects from the viewer, creating a sense of mystery and enigma. The abstracted figures — with their meticulously detailed areas of modeling, texture, and pattern — are composed of fragments of the female body: the back of a hairdo, for example, or the eyebrows, forehead, and hair, or the chest, torso, and arms. Partly in response to critics' assertions that Ramberg's work exploited women and

Sleeve Mountain #1 and #2
1973
Acrylic on fiberboard
Two panels, each: 25 1/16 × 10 3/4 in.
(63.6 × 27.3 cm)
Gift of Albert J. Bildner
1974.7.a – b

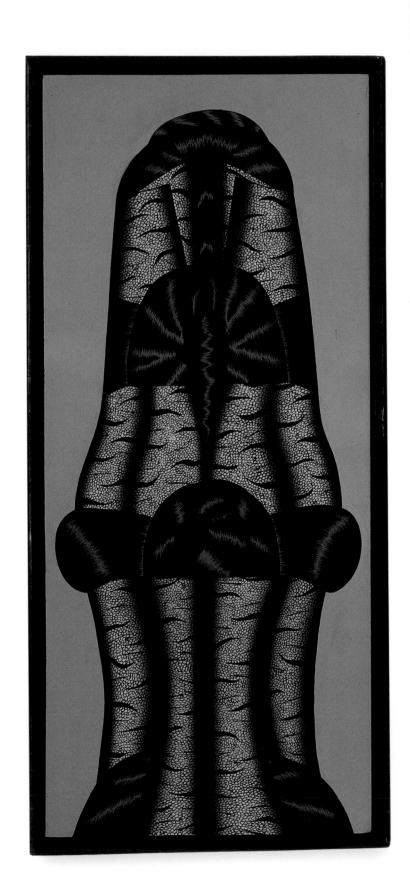

the body, the artist began to substitute the female form with objects such as chairs, lamps, and vases. This change opened her work to multiple associations and interpretations related to the notion of binding as frightening, erotic, and religious, which Ramberg welcomed.

Sleeve Mountain #1 and #2 form a diptych of abstract, slightly phallic shapes cropped at the bottom. Ramberg researched clothing design and fashion from a variety of historical periods and cultures. These two forms were inspired by designs for sleeves in Victorian fashion books. They incorporate the stylized representations of blue-black hair from previous paintings on an undulating green mesh body.

Ramberg examines the political and social dimensions of clothing and fashion through a lens of formal abstraction in order to suggest how the design of garments reflects broader social ideas and attitudes toward women. Her work is characterized by cartoonish imagery and an emphasis on the painting as an object; these features reflect the influence of Chicago imagist artists, such as Roger Brown (p. 134) and Philip Hanson (American, b. 1942). JRW

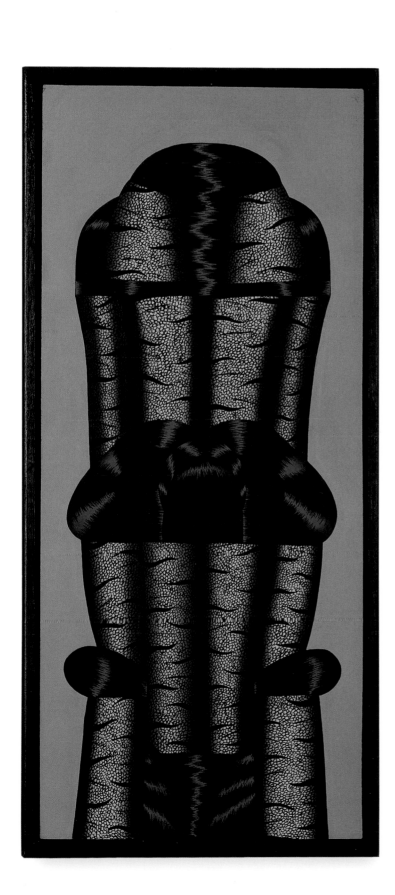

133

Roger Brown

American, 1941–1997

Whether depicting cityscapes, rural landscapes, topical and historical events and figures, or scenes of pure fantasy, the work of Roger Brown is always closely related to the theater. Brown extends theater's principles of exaggeration and artificiality to all manners of subjects, using hyperstylized imagery in his paintings, painted constructions, and found objects. Silhouetted figures with 1940s hairstyles, backlit in the rows of windows in high-rise buildings, are the voyeuristic hallmarks of Brown's paintings of urban scenes, while starkly contoured scallop-shaped hills resembling art deco design patterns are central features of his rural landscapes.

Brown's dramatic imagery, characterized by high contrast, repetition, and reduction of forms, identify him as a central figure in the Chicago tradition of imagism. His work developed along with others associated with this group, including Jim Nutt (p. 120), Ed Paschke (p. 118), and Christina Ramberg (p. 132). During the 1960s, Brown attended The School of The Art Institute of Chicago, the fertile ground of imagism, where he was influenced by "naive" sources of imagery such as the work of self-taught artists and the bold compositions and gripping use of caricature in the popular culture of comics and burlesque entertainment.

In 1973, Brown created paintings inspired by driving excursions he was taking at the time through the American South. One of these works, *Autobiography in the Shape of Alabama (Mammy's Door)*, is a tour-de-force combination of painting and object making, the major

Autobiography in the Shape of Alabama (Mammy's Door)
1974
Oil on canvas, mirror, wood, Plexiglas, photographs, postcards, and cloth shirt
89¾ × 48¾ × 18 in. (228 × 123.8 × 45.7 cm)
Gift of Maxine and Jerry Silberman
1976.41

134

modes in which Brown worked throughout his career. This three-sided work, made in the shape of Brown's native state of Alabama, is a rare example of autobiography in his work. It attaches to the wall by hinges as would a real door. On one side is a landscape painted with flat, patterned, cartoonish shapes of highly contrasting values, and vertically overlapping parts. Coordinate markings around the painting designate landmarks significant to Brown, including the house of his great grandmother Dizenia (Mammy) and his hometown of Opelika. In the lower right corner, the Gulf of Mexico is represented on a panel onto which a three-dimensional boat is mounted. The reverse side of the work is a fanciful reconstruction of a

door in Dizenia's house in Opelika. In Brown's version, the Z-shaped brace of the door serves as the Z in Dizenia's name, which is spelled out in wood. The six hooks on the door represent the six children of Dizenia's son, Brown's grandfather. On one of the hooks hangs a shirt that Mammy made for Brown when he was a boy. Inset wooden frames on the door showcase family photographs. A box in the upper center of the door labeled "PS Chicago" refers to Brown's place of residence at the time the work was made, and contains letters, photographs, small objects of sentimental value, and a key to symbols and records of family history. On the underside of the work is a painted and carved representation of one side of a guitar and an inscription addressed

to Mammy that reads "Thanks for Barbara Allen," the name of an Appalachian folk song Brown knew in his youth. The upper side of the guitar serves as the background of water on which the boat in the landscape sails.

Autobiography in the Shape of Alabama (Mammy's Door) is a synthesis of many modes of representation and perspectives. It joins the documentary and the expressive, the distant and the near, the verbal and the visual, object and image, the instant legibility of the style of Brown's work, and the protracted process of documenting his past. AP

Larry Clark

American, b. 1943

Tulsa
1961–1971/1980
Portfolio of gelatin silver prints
Fifty prints, each:
11 × 14 in. (27.9 × 35.6 cm) or
14 × 11 in. (35.6 × 27.9 cm)
Ed: 73/100
Gift of Lenore and Herbert Schorr
1983.110.2
2002.85.11
2002.85.20
2002.85.22

Larry Clark portrays drug and youth cultures in provocative photographs and films, as an insider and an observer. Early in his career, he was best known for his photographs published in two books, *Tulsa* (1971) and *Teenage Lust* (1983), and more recently for his controversial films depicting the less wholesome side of youth culture. Clark's subjects are considered out of the mainstream, engaging in dangerous or rebellious activities, mostly involving sex and drugs. Clark neither idealizes nor condemns his subjects; rather his eye is thoughtful, cinematic, and empathetic. Because Clark readily admits his desire to recapture his teenage years through his subjects, his photographs may be considered both documentary and autobiographical.

During his teen years in the 1960s, Clark's circle of friends in Tulsa, Oklahoma, was formed around drugs and prostitution. In 1963, 1968, and 1971, while studying professional photography in Milwaukee, Wisconsin,

Clark returned to Tulsa to take black-and-white pictures of his friends. Clark had hoped to make *Tulsa* a film, and in 1968 he used a 16mm camera to begin the project. He returned in 1971 after hearing of a renewed drug scene, and finished taking pictures for *Tulsa*, now widely regarded as his foremost work. Photographs from this book, arranged into three groupings by year, were subsequently printed in multiple-edition portfolios comprised of fifty images.

Tulsa begins with a short statement by Clark: "i was born in oklahoma in 1943. when i was sixteen i started shooting amphetamines. i shot with my friends everyday for three years and then left town but i've gone back through the years. once the needle goes in it never comes out [*sic*]." The group of photographs from 1963 includes images of Clark's male friends, looking out a window or in a mirror; groups of people

using drugs; and a couple injecting drugs into each other. The 1968 section includes stills from an unfinished movie he made about his friends. The section documenting the year 1971 marks a turn toward violence and death. Guns appear in many images: one friend lies on a bed after being accidentally shot in his leg, a woman has a black eye, a pregnant woman silhouetted against a window shoots up, a baby is buried. These photographs, even with dramatic lighting and composition that recall film noir and B movies, are not overtly sensational. Rather, Clark consistently asserts the humanity of his subjects in these intimate, psychologically complex portraits.

As he ages, Clark's insider/outsider status becomes increasingly ambiguous, yet his fascination with teenagers continues. *Teenage Lust* (1983), a compilation of photographs Clark took as he explored the United States, shows the sexual escapades of the younger siblings

of his *Tulsa* subjects and the Hispanic preadolescent pimps and pushers on Forty-second Street in New York. Unlike the *Tulsa* images, which Clark took while high, for *Teenage Lust,* Clark was strictly an observer of the sexually explicit situations he photographed. Initially, critics accused Clark of exploiting his subjects, as they would more than ten years later, after the release of his film *Kids* in 1995. Written by then nineteen-year-old Harmony Korine, *Kids* caused a moral uproar in its blatant and convincing portrayal of unsupervised urban thirteen and fourteen-year-olds having unprotected sex, drinking alcohol, and using drugs. Yet, Clark avoids a position of judgment, attempting an honest and objective portrayal of youth. He explored this approach in his quasi-collage work of the mid-1990s, which recalls pinup mosaics of teen idol and rock star posters. By juxtaposing newspaper text with headlines, popular icons, and found images of childhood, Clark explores

how media-derived conceptions of childhood differ vastly from reality. In 1993, Clark published the controversial series *The Perfect Childhood.*

For a career that has spanned more than forty years, Clark's relatively small body of work remains influential, and his print portfolios are often exhibited in museums. Clark's genre of personalized documentary photography can be seen as a precursor to the work of younger artists, such as Richard Billingham (British, b. 1970), Nobuyoshi Araki (Japanese, b. 1940), Nan Goldin (American, b. 1953), and Jack Pierson (p. 230) as a way to reveal private worlds in a public forum. JRW

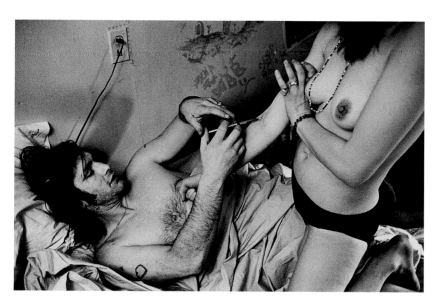

Cindy Sherman

American, b. 1954

Untitled, A

1975
Gelatin silver print
20 × 16 in. (50.8 × 40.6 cm)
Ed: 9/10
Gift of Lannan Foundation
1997.57

Untitled, B

1975
Gelatin silver print
20 × 16 in. (50.8 × 40.6 cm)
Ed: 9/10
Gift of Lannan Foundation
1997.58

Untitled, C

1975
Gelatin silver print
20 × 16 in. (50.8 × 40.6 cm)
Ed: 9/10
Gift of Lannan Foundation
1997.59

Untitled, D

1975
Gelatin silver print
20 × 16 in. (50.8 × 40.6 cm)
Ed: 9/10
Gift of Lannan Foundation
1997.60

Untitled, E

1975
Gelatin silver print
20 × 16 in. (50.8 × 40.6 cm)
Ed: 9/10
Gift of Lannan Foundation
1997.61

138

Since the mid-1970s, Cindy Sherman has consistently used specific artistic, cinematic, and popular media genres as frames of reference and recast them in insidious, transgressive ways, often with humorous, highly theatrical overtones. B movies, magazine centerfolds, fashion photography, fairy tales, old master painting, surrealist photography, and horror films have all served as fertile subject matter for her incisive investigations into the cultural assumptions and social mores of our time. Among Sherman's earliest works are a group of five untitled images of the artist herself performing the role of different characters through the use of simple props and a variety of exaggerated facial expressions. Made in 1975, these images are among the first examples of

Sherman's ongoing fascination with self-transformation as the basis for a body of work in which she has created a range of burlesque portrayals of various characters and types drawn from familiar popular cultural sources.

Sherman's *Untitled Film Stills,* made between 1977 and 1980, explore the range of female characters found in films, particularly B movies. The series numbers sixty-nine images total, five of which are in the MCA Collection. Described by Arthur Danto as "simultaneously and inseparably photographs and performances,"[1] they are related to work of the early and mid-1970s by such artists as Adrian Piper (p. 204) and Eleanor Antin (American, b. 1935) who photographically documented their engagement in performative situations and actions that involved self-transformation and role playing. Widely considered Sherman's most significant body of work, the *Untitled Film Stills* series perfectly mirrors the cultural assumptions of an era in which the power of the media in constructing identity, particularly that of women, formed the basis of

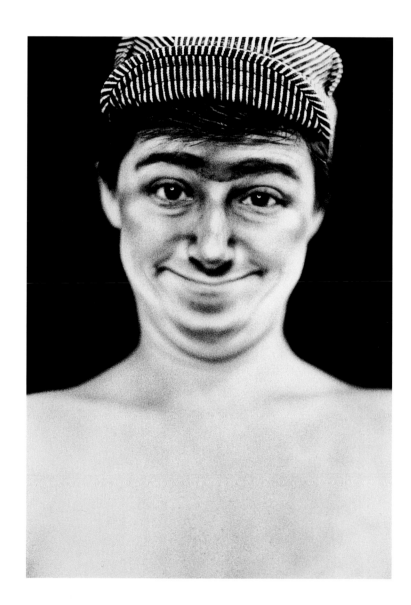

intensive critical analysis and theory. Sherman's *Untitled Film Stills* paralleled this critical trajectory and immeasurably influenced the development of postmodern theories about the fragmented, constructed nature of truth and identity.

In 1983–84, Sherman created a body of work inspired by fashion photography in which her penchant for the parodic dimensions of social satire and her enthusiasm for the grotesque come to the fore. *Untitled #137*, arguably the most powerful image of this series, completely undermines the viewer's expectation of the type of glamorous, polished female subject associated with high fashion photography. Clad in a chic ensemble, the woman portrayed in the image (again, the artist herself) appears dirty and deranged, with the vacant stare of a madwoman or a drug addict, against a suggestively "bloodied" backdrop. The artist clearly intended this and other images to be disjunctive and ridiculous, provoking reactions that range from horror to humor on the part of the viewer. With this series, Sherman demonstrated a more far-reaching range of fantasy and exaggeration as the basis of her imagery and began to reveal the

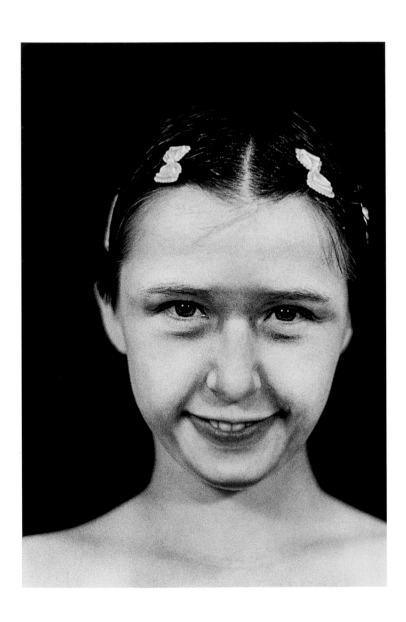

artificiality underlying her characterizations more overtly as the basis for her imagery.

The bizarre exaggeration and pointed use of fakery in the fashion series directly influenced Sherman's subsequent body of work inspired by fairy tales, several examples of which are represented in the MCA Collection. Images from this series, such as *Untitled #147, #153,* and *#188,* succeed most dramatically in being simultaneously horrific and comic in their morbid evocations of death and mayhem. Provocatively interweaving the real and the artificial both in her imagery and her choice of genres, Sherman parodies the conventions of these genres by exaggerating their modes of artifice and rendering them ambiguous — alternately seductive and repellent.

Stimulated by the shape-shifting conventions of fairy tales, these images offer a stunningly lurid portrayal of the artifacts of the monstrous.

During the first decade of Sherman's development, theorists and historians saw in her work the manifestation of a purely feminist critique of the media's construction of identity, though the subsequent evolution of her imagery

Untitled Film Still, #14
1978
Gelatin silver print
10 × 8 in. (25.4 × 20.3 cm)
Ed: 1/10
Gift of Lannan Foundation
1997.56

141

has profoundly complicated this reading. From the fairy tale series onward, her images have confounded the issue of sexual identity and the distinction between the body and its surrogate in works that are surreal, apocalyptic admixtures of rapture, nightmare, and vertigo. The dense emotive range of these images and Sherman's most recent series depicting a group of middle age female characters, which extend the ambiguously satiric tenor of some of her earliest photos, succeed in challenging the viewer's assumptions in complex and contradictory ways. With its combination of social critique, irreverent humor, and sense of perverse pleasure, Sherman's work can be understood in the tradition of artists ranging from Hieronymous Bosch (Dutch, 1450–1516) to Francisco Goya (Spanish, 1746–1828) to Hannah Höch (German, 1889–1978) in the way that it collapses our familiar references to the human body and destabilizes our understanding of its social and psychological identity. ES

1 Arthur Danto, *Cindy Sherman: Untitled Film Stills* (New York: Rizzoli, 1990), p. 11.

Untitled, #137
1984
Chromogenic development print
70½ × 47¾ in. (179.1 × 121.3 cm)
Ed: 2/5
Gerald S. Elliott Collection
1995.98

Untitled
1987
Chromogenic development print
40 × 30 in. (101.6 × 76.2 cm)
Ed: 1/35
Gift of the Men's Council
1987.3

Martin Puryear

American, b. 1941

Untitled
1975–1978
Osage orangewood, maple, and brass studs
86 × 49½ × 9 in. (218.4 × 125.7 × 22.9 cm)
Restricted gift of Collectors Group,
Men's Council, and Women's Board;
Vaklova Purchase Award and purchase grants
from the National Endowment for the Arts, and
the Illinois Arts Council Purchase Grant
1985.15

Martin Puryear's postminimal sculptures combine personal history and non-Western cultural traditions with wood crafting and aesthetic formalism. A culmination of many artistic and cultural influences, his artwork is both highly personal and abstract, reflecting Puryear's experiences as a Peace Corps volunteer in Sierra Leone and as a carpenter apprentice in Sweden. His handcrafted process and style link him to other sculptors such as H. C. Westermann (p. 54), Jackie Winsor (p. 156), Richard Hunt (p. 154), and Joel Shapiro (American, b. 1941), who have considered technique and skill to be of utmost importance. Although Puryear's sculptures have a sparse appearance, derived in part from the minimalist art of the 1960s, his interest in natural materials sets them apart from the industrially made, geometric work of artists such as Donald Judd (p. 124) and Carl Andre (p. 110). His refined sculptures display a tension between a raw, functional appearance and highly finished smooth surfaces as found in the work of early modern artists Hans Arp (German and French, 1887–1966), Isamu Noguchi (American, b. 1904), and Constantin Brancusi (Romanian, 1876–1957). Like Puryear, many of these artists looked to the art of non-Western cultures for inspiration.

In addition to wall sculptures such as *Untitled*, Puryear's freestanding sculptures and public projects, which are often quite large in scale, straddle a fine line between representation and abstraction by recalling various organic and anthropomorphic shapes. Some of these have suggestive titles that provide external references for the typically ambiguous works.

Puryear's primary medium is wood, although he has incorporated tar, wire, and animal hides in his sculptures, and more recently copper and bronze. He chooses various types of wood for their hue, density, and strength. *Untitled* is made of Osage orangewood, which is common in the rural area of Virginia where Puryear was raised. It is also the wood many Native Americans traditionally used for bows. For Puryear, the personal and historical significance of materials is as important as their physical and aesthetic attributes.

Using a slow, laborious process to create his sculptures, Puryear leaves the materials slightly rough to give a semblance of the natural material and handmade quality of the objects. Although Puryear's sculptures appear to be dense and solid, they are in fact quite fragile. His works suggest interior and exterior spaces with delicate curves and hollow vessels. In works such as *Untitled*, for example, linear contours cut through the negative space in and around the sculpture. Although it appears to be a bent piece of natural Osage orangewood, it is unclear at first whether the artist has manipulated the wood into this shape or if he found it that way. Upon closer inspection, it becomes apparent that the work is made of two different types of wood, joined together by brass studs and a wooden joint. The ends have clearly been carved into sharp points, to reveal the wood beneath the bark's surface. As such, it posits a larger question of how the distinctions of what is natural or artificial, real or virtual, manipulated or found become increasingly ambiguous in our technologically driven culture.
JRW

Brice Marden

American, b. 1938

Brice Marden uses abstraction and layers of pigment and wax in his paintings to evoke imagery and emotion for viewers, even as the works reflect his own experiences and inspirations. His many series of paintings are inspired by such diverse sources as nature — the moon, the seasons, the sea, the landscape — people, places, and the work of other artists, as well as by religious subjects such as the Annunciation of Mary. Hues of gray, green, and tan dominated his early paintings until the mid-1970s, when he began to use primary colors. The *Grove Group* paintings are considered pivotal in Marden's work as a turn away from murky tones toward colors inspired by the Mediterranean atmosphere.

In 1973, when he began spending summers in Hydra, Greece, Marden started a series of five paintings known as the *Grove Paintings*, part of a group of work that comprises drawings and collages. In his notebooks, Marden drew diagrams relating each band of color to the leaves, tree trunk, and earth of the surrounding olive groves. *Grove Group V* is made of three horizontal panels, the central one a grayish blue and the other two a grayish green. The complex colors exquisitely convey a mood or impression of the Greek landscape with a translucent depth, inviting viewers to meditate upon them.

Grove Group V
1976
Oil and wax on canvas
72 × 108 in. (182.9 × 274.3 cm)
Gerald S. Elliott Collection
1995.67.a – c

When Marden began making abstract paintings during the 1960s, minimalism was a predominant artistic vocabulary among his contemporaries. While his paintings have affinities with aspects of minimalism — they are created in series, and the nonrepresentational monochromatic panels endow the paintings with a sense of object-hood — the handcrafted properties of the oil paint and beeswax Marden uses distinguish his art as more closely related to the tradition of painting. His body of work recalls the evocative "zip" abstractions of Barnett Newman (American, 1905–1970) more than the industrially fabricated abstract steel sculptures of Donald Judd (p. 124), for instance. Marden also cites grid paintings by Jasper Johns (p.62) as highly influential in their limited formal structure, which he has imposed on his own work by using only rectangular canvases. Marden uses the "golden section" rectangle — in which the ratio of the whole to the larger part is equal to the ratio of the larger part to the smaller — to symbolize balance, stability, and universality.

Themes of nature and spirituality have continued to resonate within Marden's recent work. In the *Cold Mountain* series (1988–1992) he incorporated twisting gestural lines painted with tree branches or long-handled brushes. His use of color has also expanded to include more luminescent hues that absorb and reflect light. With his conceptual imagery, traditional references, and minimalist aesthetic, Marden's work continues to evoke poetic contemplation while pushing the limits of abstraction. JRW

John Cage

American, 1912–1992

A Dip in the Lake: Ten Quicksteps, Sixty-two Waltzes, and Fifty-six Marches for Chicago and Vicinity
1978
Felt-tip pen on map
53½ × 41½ in. (135.9 × 105.4 cm)
Restricted gift of Collectors Group, Men's Council, and Women's Board;
and National Endowment for the Arts Purchase Grant
1982.19

A Dip in the Lake is a musical score that John Cage created for the city of Chicago in 1978. The title suggests the spontaneity and playfulness of the quick steps, waltzes, and marches performed at dances, festivals, and parades. For this work, Cage linked points on a city map in an intricate grid of bright lines, using red, orange, yellow, green, blue, brown, and black felt-tipped pens. Cage then sent people to the points indicated by the intersection of lines, where they made audio recordings. A tape of sounds from each location was cut in varying lengths, determined by rolling dice. The tape was later spliced together to make a series of sound collages, which were played on loudspeakers at Chicago's 1982 New Music America Festival.

Chance is fundamental to Cage's work. His use of the I-Ching — a Chinese divination system that relies on chance — to make aesthetic decisions made possible an infinite range of options and departed from the more orderly approach of classic composition. Through chance, Cage explored the roles of intention, fate, and predetermination within a musical arrangement. The spirited, random quality he sought in his music began with a collection of ideas recorded through a series of influential essays and lectures he wrote in the 1950s.

The work of Cage and Marcel Duchamp (French, 1887–1968) formed the conceptual basis for the development of Fluxus during the 1960s and 1970s. Characterized by an experimental and nonrational approach to art making that existed outside the commercialized art system, Fluxus artists such as Dick Higgins (American, 1938–1998), Yoko Ono (American, b. Japan 1933), George Maciunas (American, b. Lithuania 1931–1978), Nam June Paik (American, b. Korea 1932), and George Brecht (American, b. 1925), among many others, sought to merge a spontaneous, performative, and humorous artistic practice with everyday life, working with film, theater, multiple objects, musical composition, photography, writing, and sound. In his essay "Back to the Future: Fluxus in Context" Andreas Huyssen wrote, "Cage demanded to free the pure materiality of sound and to emancipate noise from its oppressive exclusion from the realm of music. For sound to emerge, music had to be silent."[1]

Cage's early work had a profound effect on the work of Robert Rauschenberg (p. 70), Jasper Johns (p. 62), and choreographer Merce Cunningham; his embrace of ambient and environmental sound, as well as silence, has become a major impetus for younger artists and popular musicians working today such as Christian Marclay (Swiss, b. United States 1955) and Sonic Youth.
JS

1 Andreas Huyssen, "Back to the Future: Fluxus in Context," in *In the Spirit of Fluxus*, exh. cat. (Minneapolis: Walker Art Center, 1993), p. 148.

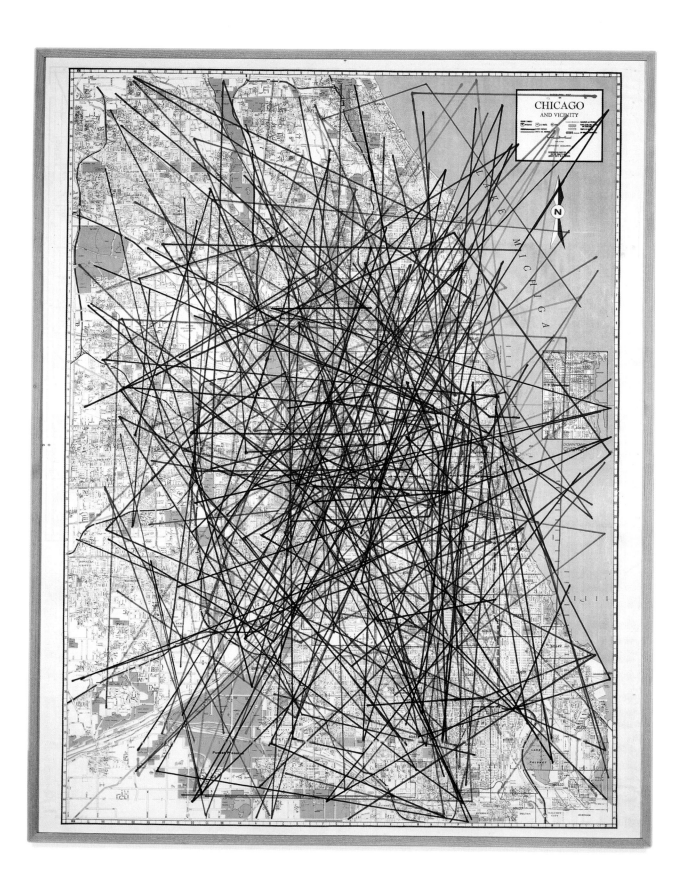

Gordon Matta-Clark

American, 1943–1978

Circus or The Caribbean Orange
1978
Silver dye-bleach prints
Two parts, installed: 42¼ × 64½ in. (107.3 × 163.8 cm)
Restricted gift of Mr. and Mrs. E. A. Bergman and Susan and Lewis Manilow
1978.1.a–b

The son of celebrated Chilean surrealist Roberto Matta (p. 42) and Anne Clark, Gordon Matta-Clark spent most of his youth in New York with his mother and his stepfather, the eminent writer Hollis Albert. Matta-Clark began his career in New York's then dilapidated SoHo district during the 1960s and 1970s when the rebellious fervor in liberal circles was at its height. He also worked with well-known earth and site artists such as Dennis Oppenheim (American, b. 1938), Robert Smithson (p. 90), and Christo (p. 76), as well as the performance artist Robert Wilson (American, b. 1941).

Entropy, abandonment, and the political and social implications of architecture as shelter profoundly interested Matta-Clark, who used the urban environment to comment on a "throwaway" culture and rigid modernist architecture. Using abandoned buildings as his raw material, he would make what he called "cuttings" — essentially drawing with saws and tools by carving into the structure of a standing building. Though many did not survive, some of his most legendary cuttings, such as *Pier In/Out* (New York, 1973) *Splitting: Four Corners* (New Jersey, 1974), *Bingo* (New York, 1974), and *Office Baroque* (Antwerp, 1977) are still intact.

In 1977, Matta-Clark was commissioned by the MCA to make a cutting from a recently acquired building (next to its former Ontario Street facility) that was to be renovated as an annex to the museum. In this cutting, titled *Circus* or *The Caribbean Orange*, Matta-Clark completed numerous incisions of various shapes through four floors. Three prominent circles (made with a chain saw) dissected the floors and defined a new space where visitors walked through for two weeks after the installation.

Matta-Clark documented all his cuttings, such as in this photographic diptych from *Circus* or *The Caribbean Orange,* for which he montaged photographs to create a complex view of the space. By manipulating the photographic image, Matta-Clark avoided presenting a single, conventional viewpoint, and instead created a multi-image work that embodied a sculptural vision. This photograph of *Circus* or *The Caribbean Orange* is composed of collaged photographs in two different-sized frames that are exhibited in a rectangular shape without an image in the lower left area. This empty space in the presentation of the photographs mimics the voids from the cuttings while the photographs both offer a disorienting view of the space and the illusion of the three-dimensionality of the original cutting. The photograph foregrounds its own medium by retaining the sprocket holes of the film roll and deep color from the printing edge; it also serves as evidence of the original cutting.

Matta-Clark derived the title *Circus* or *The Caribbean Orange* from two sources. "Circus" relates to the rings and circles used in a circus — a metaphoric reference to the relationship of the artist and viewer. According to Matta-Clark, the Caribbean technique of peeling oranges is to peel in a circular motion so that each slice is still connected to the prior, forming a spiral curl much like the concentric circles of the MCA cutting. *Circus* or *The Caribbean Orange* was the first and last museum commission that Matta-Clark completed. This cutting and the photographs that accompanied it were made just six months before he died, at age thirty-five. LH

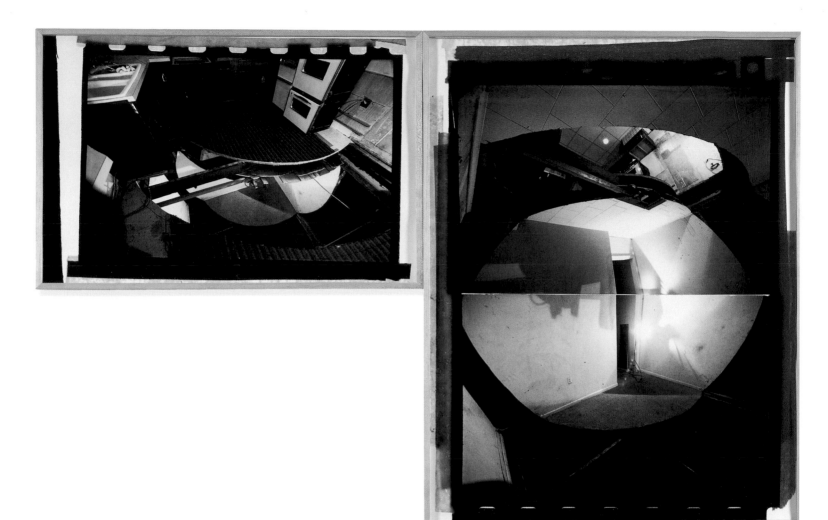

Raymond Pettibon

American, b. 1957

No Title (No Text: Black Electric Chair)
1978
Ink on paper
13⅞ × 10⅞ in. (35.2 × 27.6 cm)
Gift of Susan and Lewis Manilow
1999.46

No Title (To Dust Cover … Shut)
1984
Ink on paper
14 × 10⅛ in. (35.6 × 25.7 cm)
Gift of Susan and Lewis Manilow
1999.48

No Title (I don't know why)
1985
Ink on paper
10½ × 8⅜ in. (26.7 × 21.3 cm)
Gift of Susan and Lewis Manilow
1999.45

No Title (Begging to be Understood)
1991
Ink on paper
13⅞ × 11 in. (35.2 × 27.9 cm)
Gift of Susan and Lewis Manilow
1999.44

No Title (The Plague, There Throbbed)
1995
Ink on paper
15 × 11 1/16 in. (38.1 × 28.1 cm)
Gift of Susan and Lewis Manilow
1999.47

Raymond Pettibon is arguably the most prominent contemporary artist to specialize in drawings. Although he became recognized in the realm of fine art in the early 1980s, he was the unofficial artist of the punk music subculture of Los Angeles during the late 1970s and early 1980s, self-publishing photocopied booklets that he sold for less than two dollars. At the time, he also designed the promotional material for punk bands including Minutemen, Sonic Youth, and Black Flag, of which his brother, Gregory Ginn, was a member. He published approximately one hundred fanzines between 1978 and 1993, and to date has made more than 7,000 pen-and-ink drawings.

Pettibon's drawings from the late 1970s to the present retain some of the aesthetics of the punk subculture — the aggressive spontaneity, the anti-art refusal of polished appearances, and the macabre subjects and tone. Anarchic in spirit, Pettibon's interests are difficult to categorize. Nevertheless, a cynical attitude pervades his works that address delinquency, crime, killing, and the dark side of the 1960s and 1970s: the Vietnam War, figures such as Charles Manson and Patty Hearst, parodies of the summer of love, and a sense of youth counterculture gone awry. Pettibon depicts a world of alienation, dispossession, deviance, and disillu-

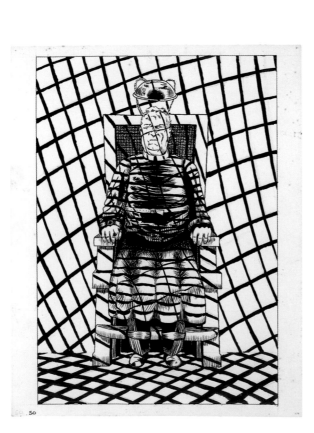

sionment with irreverent wit. His recurrent treatment of religious themes, featuring Jesus, the Bible, God, swords coming down from the sky, or even the image of praying money in *No Title (Begging to Be Understood)*, has a sardonic edge.

Pettibon's installation technique maintains the chaotic quality with which his drawings often depict the world. For exhibitions of his drawings in art galleries, he displays them in clusters that defy conventional ordering systems. Sometimes the drawings are clustered around a recurrent image. More often, they are grouped by the collection to which they belong, a practice that highlights the discontinuous character of his drawings but also acknowledges the creative role of the collector in making

intuitive, personal connections among the works. Pettibon's resistance to conventional ordering schemes extends to his unusual use of the cartoon format. The text and image relationships in Pettibon's drawings are rarely straightforward, clarifying, or even directly corresponding, forcing the viewer to make his or her own sense.

The group of drawings in the MCA Collection, ranging from 1978 to 1995, represents the major shifts in Pettibon's work since his beginning as a fanzine artist. Until about 1987, Pettibon used black ink almost exclusively and in many cases combined each drawing with a single phrase. By the 1990s, perhaps as a result of his increasing production for

art galleries or his evolution as a draftsman, his drawings showed a greater subtlety of line and complexity of imagery, and the introduction of color. He also began to experiment with different qualities, tones, and formats of paper, which enhance the effects of irregularity when the drawings are installed in clusters on the walls of galleries. The grouping in the MCA Collection indicates the difficulty of categorizing his subjects. Ultimately, that disjunction liberates the thoughts of artist and viewer alike, allowing new associations to emerge. AP

153

BEGGING TO BE UNDERSTOOD.

ALMOST MAKING OUT, WHILE I DO, THE JINGLE OF COIN.

(THE PLAGUE). THERE THROBBED NOT THERE A THOUGHT WHICH PIERCED THE PALL... THE PROCTOR TAKING OVER THE BELL-RINGING

HOT JURISDICTION. A CACOPHONY OF BELLS.

THE SOUNDS A MESS OF FRAZZLED NERVES.

Richard Hunt

American, b. 1935

Farmer's Dream
1980
Welded Corten steel
109 × 54 × 76½ in. (276.9 × 137.2 × 194.3 cm)
Gift of Mallinckrodt Group Inc.
in recognition of Richard A. Lenon
1994.1

In the 1930s Spanish sculptor Julio Gonzalez (1876–1942) wrote, "To project and draw in space with the help of new devices, to use this space and construct with it as if it were a newly acquired material — that is my endeavor."[1] While a student at The School of The Art Institute of Chicago (SAIC), Richard Hunt became interested in metal sculpture after a visit to an Art Institute exhibition of twentieth-century sculpture that included the work of Gonzalez, who assisted Pablo Picasso (Spanish, 1881–1973) with his early welded sculpture and also later influenced the open-form metal sculpture of David Smith (American, 1906–1965). Hunt uses particular materials — iron, steel, stainless steel, bronze, copper, and aluminum — in a way that echoes Gonzalez's conception of his work as drawing in space. Hunt's early work emphasized the presence of line in space, often recalling insect forms, while his later sculptures have a more substantial monumental presence. His work also encompasses a fully three-dimensional concept of sculpture that creates a unique perspective from each angle.

Hunt transforms metal scraps from junkyards into dynamic, surrealist forms that suggest plants, animals, machinery, and the human figure. Using a direct-metal welding technique, he combines both industrial and organic imagery. Hunt, who was born in Chicago, began making abstract sculptures out of various metals in the 1950s and has continued this practice, focusing on the importance of technique. Although his works display abstract formal qualities, most are inspired by mythological stories, African-American history, and the physical site of the sculpture. Many of the themes and forms of his early work, especially those evoking a sense of movement and flight, reappear in later works.

Hunt's large-scale commissions and public sculptures, including *Flight Forms* (2002) at Midway Airport, a sculpture for St. Procopius Abbey in Lisle, Illinois, and *Winged Forms* on the plaza of the Aon (formerly Amoco) building in Chicago's Loop, demand a different method of fabrication, and, unlike smaller works that he made in his studio, require collaboration. His public sculptures — including more than fifty in the Chicago area — respond to the location of their commission, reflecting the spirit and ideas of the space.

Farmer's Dream reflects elements of Hunt's experience growing up in the Midwest, as well as his family history. The idea for the work was initially inspired by Hunt's father, who was a sharecropper in rural Georgia before moving to Chicago during the Depression, and his mother, who was raised in Monmouth, Illinois. The arching plowlike form of the sculpture evokes an elegant version of farm machinery and movement. Although Hunt spent most of his childhood in the Englewood neighborhood on the South Side of Chicago, his interest in the intersection of natural and mechanical forms can easily be found in the context of farming, especially the numerous corn and soybean farms throughout the state. Hunt falls within a lineage of artists using mechanical and industrial materials to explore the idea of progress and technology from Gonzalez's "drawings in space" to Picasso's whimsical small sculptures made of bicycle seats and handlebars to the automobile assemblages of fellow SAIC alumnus John Chamberlain (American, b. 1927). J RW

1 *Picasso and the Age of Iron,* exh. cat. (New York: Solomon R. Guggenheim Museum, 1993), p. 284. First published in *Julio Gonzalez,* exh. cat. (Amsterdam: Stedelijk Museum, 1955).

Jackie Winsor

American, b. Canada 1941

Cheesecloth Piece
1981
Wood and cheesecloth
31½ x 31½ x 31½ in. (80 x 80 x 80 cm)
Gift of Lannan Foundation
1997.66

Jackie Winsor emerged in the early 1970s as part of the first wave of women to break into the male-dominated landscape of the art world. Along with artists such as Jackie Ferrara (p. 128), Eva Hesse (American, b. Germany 1936–1970), and Lynda Benglis (American, b. 1941), Winsor established herself as an important successor to early 1960s minimalism. She adopted certain aspects of minimalist object-making: simple, geometric forms, including cubes, spheres, cylinders, and pyramids, as well as the anti-illusionistic concept of the art object as a literal presence, analogous to another human body, that confronts the viewer and responds to its surroundings. Winsor has spoken of her sculptures as bodies. Yet she steers away from the variety of minimalism that emphasizes streamlined industrial finishes and out-sourced manufacturing. Concerned instead with calling attention to the process and duration of her objects' fabrication, Winsor makes each of her works by hand. Her labor-intensive, repetitive processes — such as wrapping, knotting, and repeatedly nailing her materials — result in works that evoke the passage of time. One of the first works for which Winsor became known, *Bound Grid* (1971–72) consists of a network of tree branches assembled into an irregular grid, with each joint of crossing branches heavily wrapped with twine into large balls.

Most of Winsor's sculptures take the form of large cubes built with wood, Sheetrock, or cement. She chose the cube because of what she considers to be its relative neutrality, which allows her to call attention to patterns and textures occurring within the form. Primarily concerned with the dynamism of forms, Winsor creates cubes that involve dramatic tensions between open and closed, opaque and porous, revealed and concealed membranes and chambers. With *Sheetrock Piece* (1976), Winsor began incorporating small square openings into the centers of all sides of her cubes, charging them with what she has spoken of as "concealed energy" and a sense of mystery.

Since 1985, Winsor has worked exclusively with concrete, but in the late 1970s and early 1980s she experimented with a wide variety of materials and treatments in her cubes. In *Painted Piece*, for instance, she applied fifty layers of paint to the interior and exterior of a plywood cube. She then attached the structure to the back of her car and dragged it around on all edges to reveal layers of different texture and color. In *Exploded Piece*, Winsor ignited explosives inside a concrete and plaster cube, then reassembled the blasted pieces in her characteristically painstaking way.

Cheesecloth Piece is a work from this experimental period. In it she explored the spatial and textural dynamics of a material not normally associated with art. Seamlessly wrapped around the wooden structure of Winsor's aperture-marked cube, the porous cheesecloth gives the structure a sense of lightness and, when viewed as a body, the feeling of skin. While the volume of the work is determined by the dimensions of the wooden cubic structure, the density is set by the diaphanous material. The openness of the material contrasts with the constriction of the small square openings, providing a dynamic tension between outside and inside. AP

Magdalena Abakanowicz

Polish, b. 1930

Cage
1981
Burlap, glue, and wood
66 × 46 × 61 in.
(167.6 × 116.8 × 154.9 cm)
Gift of Ralph I. and Helyn D. Goldenberg
1982.37.a–b

Magadalena Abakanowicz emerged as a unique presence in the arena of sculpture in the 1980s and has continued to create powerful bodies of work based on her experience of growing up and living in wartime, communist, and post-communist Poland. She began her career in the 1960s working with fiber in the rich tradition of Eastern European artisans who had honed their craft and experimented with a material often dismissed in contemporary art circles. Yet Abakanowicz, along with a few others such as Claire Zeisler (p. 106) and Ritzi (Romanian, b. 1941) and Peter Jacobi (Romanian, b. 1935), initiated a new approach to the medium. In her hands fiber transcends utilitarian application to exist as art, often expressing the brutal realities of her personal experience as well as demonstrating formal innovations never before realized. Huge forms woven out of sisal and other coarse fibers, called *Abakans*, marked her introduction to the international art world in the 1970s. Shown in groups, exhibitions of these works were an early, important form of installation art. Abakanowicz moved on to more representational forms in the 1980s, creating haunting tableaux of headless, often limbless figures. These truncated figures were both a personal statement — for she witnessed her mother's arm being blown off by gunfire during World War II — and a universal statement of people's many shortcomings, limitations, and failures to live up to their potential. Many of these works are molded burlap; this material forms the figural element in *Cage*.

The forms and processes of nature have always inspired Abakanowicz. Roughly hewn wood began appearing in her work in the early 1980s and has become in more recent years a primary medium. The wooden elements in *Cage* are objects salvaged from their intended purpose as they broke down and ceased to be useful. Portions of a pier, fence posts, and weathered planking make a cage in which the molded burlap figure sits, a resonant statement on man's existential crisis. The figure here, a mere shell trapped within the wooden structure, suggests how people box themselves into various cages, conceptual as well as physical. Yet Abakanowicz's background offers another reading. As a descendant from the great Tartar conqueror Houlagou-Kahn, and shaped by the horrors of World War II, when Jews from her village were summarily shot and her parents' estate was confiscated, Abakanowicz uses works like *Cage* to speak of man's dehumanizing and violent subjugation of others. The figure is too damaged to act. His arms and legs have been severed, preventing him from breaking out of his flimsy cage. The resigned slump of his back further underscores his bleak prospects. Among Abakanowicz's works, which are typically unsettling, *Cage* counts among her most searing statements about the human experience. LW

Julian Schnabel

American, b. 1951

By the time he created *Aorta*, Julian Schnabel had become a force on the American art scene. Eclectic in style and operatic in scale, Schnabel's artworks are titanic convergences of representation and abstraction, sculptural and painted elements, and text and image. His work, along with that of David Salle (p. 182) and Francesco Clemente (Italian, b. 1952), signaled a renewed interest in painting in the late 1970s. Incorporating unusual materials such as broken plates, deer antlers, or branches onto the surface of the wood, velvet, or as in *Aorta,* a sisal rug, Schnabel rejected painting's tradition of one-point perspective and natural representation, allowing him to develop enigmatic and emotionally charged imagery. Other artists who became more widely known during the 1980s, such as Sigmar Polke (p. 236) and Anselm Kiefer (p. 214), were similarly reevaluating the definition and history of painting by focusing on the use of everyday fabrics, materials, and objects in their work.

Throughout the 1980s, Schnabel cultivated a persona to match his imposing works, a braggadocio that led him to compare himself to old and modern masters, such as Giotto (Italian, 1266/67 or 1276–1337) and Vincent Van Gogh (Dutch, 1853–1890). The influence of Andy Warhol (p. 66) pervades Schnabel's entire oeuvre, though

Aorta
1981
Oil on sisal rug with wooden artist's frame
118 × 166 × 6¾ in. (299.7 × 421.6 × 17.1 cm)
Gerald S. Elliott Collection
1995.93

160

Schnabel cultivated a contrasting persona. Warhol fashioned a self-image that opposed the heroic model, appearing detached, evasive, and superficial, as opposed to brooding and intense — the conventional signs of the artist as visionary. The latter idea was reinforced by media representations of abstract expressionists of the 1940s and 1950s, such as Jackson Pollock (American, 1912–1956). Schnabel's persona, based on the heroic model, was exaggerated to become as parodic as Warhol's counterheroism.

With ironic and playful effects, he thwarts expectations of the relationship between form and content. Typically, Schnabel pairs formats or media that suggest either seriousness or baseness with subjects that have the opposite associations. The title *Aorta*, which refers to the main artery that carries blood from the heart to the rest of the body, identifies this as introspective, visceral art — in other words, as unmediated expressiveness following the model of abstract expressionism. This sense of seriousness pervades the large painting. The energetically applied paint, thickly congealed on the rough texture of the sisal rug, the heaviness of the rug surface itself, and the bloodred cross shape together imply Sturm und Drang; the presentation is positively baroque. Most of the shapes are indeterminate, composed of sloppy drips and slashes of color and vaguely totemic shapes reminiscent of works by Pollock.

The literal and figurative heaviness of the painting's forms, however, clashes with its subject. The only discernable forms in the painting are a man, a heart, and a tube attaching a valve of the heart to the man's genitals. With this bawdy humor in an otherwise lofty context, Schnabel creates a dissonance that tests the conventional expectations of representation in our culture. AP

161

Hollis Sigler

American, 1948–2001

Hollis Sigler's colorful drawings and paintings portray loosely autobiographical landscapes of dreams, emotions, and suffering. She consciously adopted a childlike, faux-naif style that contrasts markedly with the photo-realist style of her early paintings. She chose to work in this style to allow uninhibited access to feelings and ideas, while mitigating the emotional force within her work. Sigler, who noted that her work is about women from a female point of view, often depicted interiors and domestic trappings, which many feminist artists considered symbols of women's social space. However, certain works such as *She Wants to Belong To The Sky, Again*

present outdoor settings to evoke a sense of freedom and to reflect the changing demographic of women working outside of the home. The captions "she" or "her" in the paintings refer to the figure, which works as Sigler's alter ego as well as "everywoman."

She Wants to Belong To The Sky, Again is part of an earlier series from 1980 to 1981 entitled *Journey to Somewhere from Nowhere*, in which nine drawings tell the story of a frustrated suburban housewife futilely attempting to escape her surroundings. One of three oil paintings depicting scenes of fantasy, romance, and glamour, this work stands in stark

She Wants To Belong To The Sky, Again
1981
Oil on canvas with painted artist's frame
43⅛ × 61¼ in. (109.5 × 155.6 cm)
Illinois Arts Council Purchase Grant;
and Matching Funds
1982.25

162

contrast to Sigler's anguished drawings. In this fantastic image, a red dress, symbolizing the heroine of the narrative, floats upward into a rainbow sky, leaving behind a barren picnic scene. Sigler said that this series, which was inspired by childhood dreams of flight and the luminous color of paintings by Claude Monet (French, 1840–1926), also reflected her desire to abandon the symbols and formal conventions that she had developed in her work during the preceding years. A universal statement about the desire for escape, this ambiguous image allows for multiple interpretations concerning from what and where the woman is escaping. The text in Sigler's paintings, often the title of the work, conveys a direct narrative or description of what is taking place in the image.

The ambiguity of Sigler's earlier work was as deliberate as the overt personal messages of her work of the 1990s, including the *Breast Cancer Journal* (Sigler died of breast cancer) shown at the MCA and the *Palace of Passion* series. In these paintings, the struggles and complex emotions are focused on specific subjects. She depicted harsh emotional and psychological realities of women's domestic lives by using recognizable metaphoric and symbolic imagery. Sigler's continued use of an unsophisticated, expressive style, using oil pastels and colored pencils, as well as text and embellished frames, belies the serious and traumatic events portrayed in these paintings. Unlike that of the Chicago imagist artists, to whom she is often likened, Sigler's work recalls feminist art of the 1970s that employed traditionally female imagery to make political statements. Similarly, Sigler used domestic imagery to reflect an interior landscape of the female psyche, including her own, in the transitional early 1980s. JRW

John Ahearn

American, b. 1951

Clyde
1981
Acrylic on plaster and wood
26½ × 23 × 10 in. (67.3 × 58.4 × 25.4 cm)
Gift of Lannan Foundation
1997.17

164

John Ahearn's sculptures — plaster casts of people from his former South Bronx community — recall work by George Segal (p. 114). Unlike Segal, however, Ahearn maintains the identity of his sitters, reflecting his interest in representations of minorities during the early 1980s. Ahearn has worked with artists such as Jenny Holzer (p. 176) and Keith Haring (American, 1958–1990), whose art took the form of public interventions as means to circumvent galleries and museums and to reach a larger audience.

Since 1979, when he rented a storefront studio on Walton Street and 170th Street in the Bronx, Ahearn has undertaken a project of making bust and full-length casts that evolved into a public art collaboration, bringing art to people who are not usually exposed to the traditional art world as an attempt to counter the predominance of white men in the art world in the early 1980s. People passing by the storefront would watch and participate in Ahearn's work. Rigoberto Torres (b. 1960), a young Puerto Rican neighbor, has been Ahearn's collaborator for more than ten years. In 1993 their work was presented in the major exhibition *South Bronx Hall of Fame.* Like the early work of Chicago artist Iñigo Manglano-Ovalle (p. 256), Ahearn's art bridges racial, ethnic, and economic groups. As a white man, Ahearn has been criticized for representing "other" social groups of which he is not a part, and for promoting stereotypes. However, since the subjects choose to participate in the process, the sculptures incorporate their input, focusing on the unique qualities of individuals rather than on generalizations of an entire ethnic or economic group. He accomplishes this by casting each individual and capturing the details of their faces, necks, torsos, and arms. The process of casting each sitter takes about one hour. Ahearn applies gauze and a thick material called alginate directly to the body of the sitter. Then a plaster cast is made from the mold and painted.

The subject of *Clyde* is a welder who helped Ahearn in his studio at the Kelly Street Block Association Youth Center in the Bronx. Ahearn cast him in several poses — including holding a stick, as in this work, and with folded arms. The MCA's *Clyde* is one of a few pieces by Ahearn that address the theme of violence. It was inspired by a story Clyde told Ahearn of recent trouble he had in the neighborhood. Ahearn seeks to empower his subjects by allowing them to influence their own representations. The everyday, recognizable qualities of most of his subjects — who range from children to the elderly — reclaim negative images of Hispanics and African Americans that saturated the media and popular consciousness. Just as Ahearn crossed social boundaries by moving into the South Bronx, his work encourages conceptions of art, its role in society, and its audience to be redefined, exposing the diversity of his community's inhabitants to an insular art world. JRW

Richard Prince

American, b. Panama Canal Zone, 1949

Untitled (Sunset)
1981
Chromogenic development print
30 × 45 in. (76.2 × 114.3 cm)
Ed: 4/5
Gerald S. Elliott Collection
1995.79

Good News, Bad News
1989
Acrylic and screenprint on canvas
71 × 48 in. (180.3 × 121.9 cm)
Gerald S. Elliott Collection
1995.82

Richard Prince emerged around 1980 as part of a generation of appropriation artists, a group known for incorporating unaltered reproductions of fine art and mass media images into their works or evoking the styles of specific genres of media, such as advertisements and popular movies. Prince shared the "appropriation" label with such artists as Sherrie Levine (p. 186), Barbara Kruger (p. 178), Cindy Sherman (p. 138, and David Robbins (p. 190); like these artists, Prince aimed to expose and manipulate the conventions of fine art and mass media.

Prince first achieved notoriety with a group of works subtitled *Sunsets*, shown together at the Metro Pictures Gallery in New York in 1982. The MCA's *Untitled (Sunset)*, which employs images from travel-and-leisure magazine advertisements, belongs to this group. He first took black-and-white photographs of the advertisement illustration, then a commercial Photostat house enlarged and transferred them onto eleven-by-fourteen-inch acetate transparencies. He superimposed a screen of dots over the

enlarged image to give it a grainy, mechanical appearance. Prince then placed the transparency over a red-orange photograph of a second advertisement illustration. He achieved the out-of-focus effect in the red-orange photograph by taking close-up pictures of an ad and manipulating it under studio lighting.

Prince adopts commercial techniques and images not to imitate them but to make them seem unfamiliar and to undermine their original purpose. *Untitled (Sunset)* is disjunctive and surreal, the figures disengaged from the staged environment of the promotional image. By cropping the woman's head and, with it, her eyes, Prince disrupted the romantic connection between the man and the woman. The background, saturated with warm hues, suggests an explosion, which changes the scene from one of relaxation to one suggesting nuclear alarm. By altering key aspects of the original source, Prince reveals the conventionality of the advertisement's promise of paradise.

Good News, Bad News is an example of Prince's "joke" paintings, which he began in the late 1980s. This work is

divided into two main sections, which follow the conventions in cartoons for identifying caption and image. But they do not function in the usual way. Instead, the caption portion, the type under the line at the bottom of the painting, consists of the main text of a joke plus the beginning of its second iteration, with a slightly different opening line. The image portion consists of further disjointed images and text —

pictures of windows and beds appropriated from cartoons of the sort one might encounter in *Penthouse, Hustler,* or even *The New Yorker.* A handwritten joke, drafted successively in different versions with each one less effectively told, appears in the upper portion of *Good News, Bad News.* The last few versions are abruptly cropped, which exaggerates the bungled character of the subsequent versions. Both jokes represented in the painting are recognizable as part of a tradition of men's humor on the subject of adultery. But Prince's

strategy of repeating and varying the mechanisms of these jokes reveals the insecurity behind the macho laughter and critiques and undermines the source. Here, the joke is on the joke itself.

Whether in paintings or photographs, text or image, Prince's oeuvre, along with that of other appropriation artists, gives a nuanced and unprecedented analysis of consumer culture and the media. AP

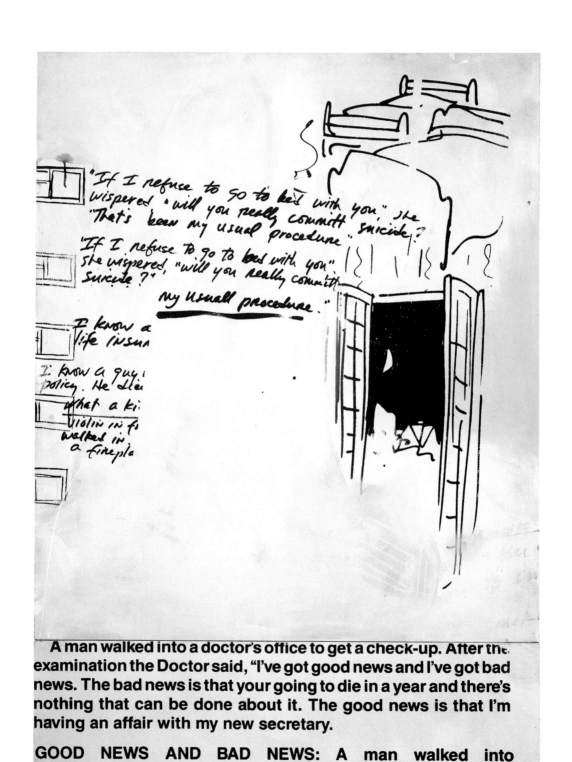

Jeff Koons

American, b. 1955

**New Hoover Deluxe Shampoo
Polishers, New Shelton Wet/Dry
10-Gallon Displaced Tripledecker**
1981/87
Polishers, vacuum cleaners, Plexiglas,
and fluorescent tubes
91 × 54 × 28 in. (231.1 × 137.2 × 71.1 cm)
Gerald S. Elliott Collection
1995.54

Lifeboat
1985
Bronze
Installed, approximately:
20½ × 87¼ × 62¾ in.
(52.1 × 221.6 × 159.4 cm)
Ed: 3/3
Gerald S. Elliott Collection
1995.56.a–c

Since his rise to prominence in the mid-1980s, Jeff Koons has been widely recognized for his investigation of how consumer products and their display communicate cultural values and arouse different states of mind. He has modeled his sculptures on consumer products and has manipulated store-bought items, exposing the subtleties of marketing, from the "body language" of store displays to the seductive properties of consumer goods themselves.

Koons's focus on consumer culture reflects the enduring legacy of 1960s pop artists such as Roy Lichtenstein (American, 1923–1997) and Andy Warhol (p. 66). Like works by Lichtenstein and Warhol, Koons's major series of works dramatize mass-cultural products, such as vacuum cleaners, sports equipment, mass-produced statuary and trinkets, pornographic imagery, and children's toys. Koons's agenda, unlike that of his 1960s predecessors, is to address people's psychological investment in particular consumable objects.

New Hoover Deluxe Shampoo Polishers, New Shelton Wet/Dry 10-Gallon Displaced Tripledecker belongs to the earliest body of work for which Koons became known. From approximately 1981 to 1987, he made a series of works entitled *The New*, featuring brand new vacuum cleaners in Plexiglas boxes, each lit underneath by rows of white fluorescent

tubes. The cleaners, in various arrangements and quantities, are isolated from their usual function. By displaying the pristine cleaners as purely visual objects, with dramatic fluorescent lighting and spotless Plexiglas encasing, Koons heightens the viewer's awareness of how such objects are designed to seduce consumers. The cleaners' anthropomorphic quality is emphasized by the way Koons stacks them in hierarchical relations and poses the machines' attachments in what seem to be communicative gestures. His indulgence in the allure of the surfaces of mass-cultural materials, which surpasses that of the pop artists, has influenced subsequent artists who address the phantasmagoric element of popular culture in their work, such as Mariko Mori (p. 264).

Koons's commentary on consumer culture extends to the consumption of fine art. In *New Hoover Deluxe Shampoo Polishers . . .* , he refers to major figures of 1960s minimalism. The Plexiglas cases are characteristic of the work of Donald Judd (p. 124) and the fluorescent tubes are signature features in Dan Flavin's art (p. 72). By using vacuum cleaners, Koons reveals the extent to which the minimalist aesthetic of clean, hard, geometric surfaces and industrial materials is an ideal vehicle for portraying the salesmanship associated with contemporary art. Koons suggests that simple, geometric structures seduce much like the display cases in stores that they resemble.

Lifeboat and *Rabbit* similarly demonstrate Koons's interest in reversing the function of appropriated objects. *Lifeboat*, a bronze cast of an inflated life raft, would no doubt drown its passengers. This work was first presented as a component of the exhibition *Equilibrium* (1985), which portrayed the sports industry as a site of existential floating and sinking, creating false hopes for achievement. That exhibition represented the second major series of works for which Koons achieved recognition: a variety of bronzed floatation equipment, specially constructed variations on fish tanks containing half-submerged basketballs (one is in the MCA Collection), and framed Nike posters.

Koons has often cast objects made from one material into another, exploring the emotional resonances and cultural connotations of materials. The transformation of plastic into bronze represents a translation from disposable and lightweight to precious and heavy (literally and figuratively). Moreover, casting *Lifeboat* in bronze increases the object's economic and cultural value as art, even as it destroys its original functional value.

For *Rabbit*, Koons had a plastic inflatable toy rabbit cast in stainless steel. The transformation from the plastic bunny with graphically animated features to a hard, uniform steel object in the shape of a bunny brings with it other changes that relate to psychological shifts in people's relationship to objects from childhood to adulthood: a change from the nonthreatening universe of cartoon fantasy to the robotic world of militarism and surveillance; a transition from the tactile experience of children's toys to the predominately visual one of art that one is not supposed to touch; a shift from unself-conscious absorption to self-consciousness in one's relationship to objects. A similar dynamic is in play in *Pink Panther,* a sculpture from Koons's *Banality* series, in which two pop culture figures are represented in ceramic, a traditional medium of decorative arts. The pink cartoon film character peers out innocently from the arms of a topless voluptuous blond — a hybrid Marilyn Monroe–Jane Mansfield playmate figure who exudes sexuality, and who, Koons has suggested, is about to gratify herself with the furry pink creature. Koons's perceptions about art in American culture continue to subvert expectations while probing significant issues about value in a consumerist society. AP

Rabbit
1986
Stainless steel
41 × 19 × 12 in. (104.1 × 48.3 × 30.5 cm)
Ed: 1/3 aside from 1 artist's proof
Partial gift of Stefan T. Edlis
and H. Gael Neeson
2000.21

Pink Panther
1988
Porcelain
41 × 20½ × 19 in.
(104.1 × 52.1 × 48.3 cm)
Ed: 1/3
Gerald S. Elliott Collection
1995.57

Tony Cragg

British, b. 1949

Red Bottle
1982
Plastic objects
108 × 33 × 3 in.
(274.3 × 83.8 × 7.6 cm)
Gerald S. Elliott Collection
1995.33

St. George and the Dragon
1985
Metal, plastic, and wood
72 × 102 × 40 in.
(182.9 × 259.1 × 101.6 cm)
Gerald S. Elliott Collection
1995.34

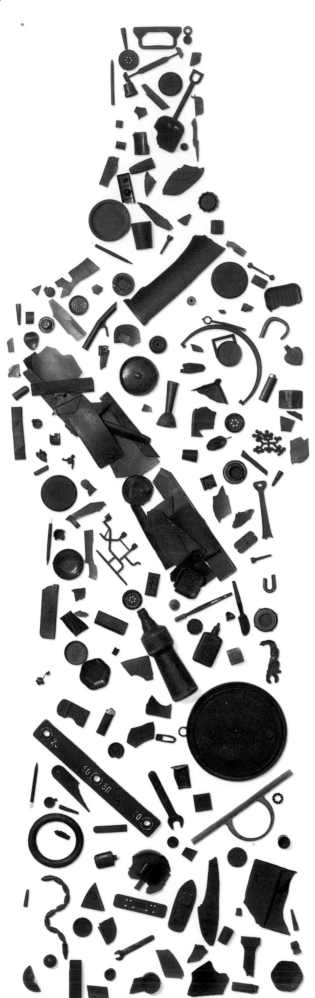

Throughout his career, Tony Cragg has attempted to fuse methods of art and science. Cragg, who began work as a biochemist, sees both disciplines as means of transcending a functional orientation to objects, and art as the sensual, tangible antidote to science's abstractions. Cragg has described his sculptures as "thinking models," revealing his approach to art as a series of propositions, or occasions for the viewer to ponder hypothetical variables and connections. Much of Cragg's sculpture studies the relationship of parts to the whole, stemming in part from his scientific understanding of matter as composed of particles and subparticles.

Cragg follows Richard Long (p. 194) and other British artists who struggled in the late 1960s with the legacy of the modernist sculptural tradition exemplified by Anthony Caro (b. 1924) and Henry Moore (1898–1986). Caro and Moore used welding and casting techniques to shape large masses of uniform materials. By contrast, Cragg's works, like Long's, forego the heroic stances of monumental abstractions for provisional, contingent arrangements of discrete objects. Cragg's floor and wall sculptures consist of found materials that are divided into parts and reunified based on one or more possibilities for connection — the physical congruence of neighboring parts, the uniformity of materials and of surfaces applied to otherwise disparate objects or materials, the repetition of a pattern of placement or type of object, and the resting or hanging of some parts on others.

In 1981 and 1982, Cragg created a number of works in various colors, each with different silhouettes recalling generic bottle shapes. In *Red Bottle*, a figural wall "drawing," Cragg used found objects sorted by color to create the bottle, whose shape he arrived at through an intuitive process in which he considered the possibilities of the materials' readymade shapes. Vessels and containers are significant in Cragg's work as symbols of unity and the joining of inside and outside, as ancient symbols of

mystery, and as metaphors for the body. *Red Bottle* also exemplifies the "thinking model" character of Cragg's works in its introduction of a philosophical problem regarding the identity of things. The bottle, made up of numerous non-bottle parts, is analogous to the relationship of all matter to its constituent particles: the particles are not thought of as identical to what they form together.

St. George and the Dragon is an example of the artist's large, freestanding sculptures, and in particular of his penchant for giving sculptural form to philosophical conundrums. The work is one of several from the mid-1980s with titles referring to legends and myths made with materials including PVC piping, trunks, jugs, tables, and chairs. According to the thirteenth-century legend, St. George slayed a dragon in order to rescue a king's daughter. St. George is traditionally depicted mounted on

a white horse, brandishing a sword that has been broken from his struggle with the winged and scaly dragon. In Cragg's version, what at first seem to be references to parts of the standard narrative and iconography — the PVC pipes perhaps standing in for a scaly-skinned dragon, the white jug for the horse — turn out to be red herrings. The viewer is left to attempt to identify objects in the work with either the saint or the dragon or the forces of good and evil they represent. The existence of three major items — a trunk, a vessel, and a ladder — entangled in the web of piping perpetually defers any pursuit of either/ or designations. A P

Bernd and Hilla Becher

Bernd, German, b. 1931
Hilla, German, b. 1934

Cooling Towers
1983
Gelatin silver prints
Twelve parts, each: 20 × 16 in.
(50.8 × 40.6 cm)
Gerald S. Elliott Collection
1995.31.a–l

Since the late 1950s, Bernd and Hilla Becher have photographed structures built during the Industrial Revolution in rural parts of Europe and the United States, such as water towers, grain elevators, silos, and water coolers. This husband-and-wife team has forged a genre of analytical and documentary photography in the lineage of Albert Renger Patzsch (German, 1897–1966) and August Sander (German, 1876–1964) by classifying its subjects into types, focusing on the formal similarities of seemingly disparate buildings. By using a typological model of categorization typically used in the disciplines of botany or ethnology, the Bechers aim to create groupings of images based on function, shape, material, and location.

The Bechers' photographs function as more than historical documents of these deteriorating structures. By choosing unused Industrial Revolution–era buildings, they remind viewers of the intellectual foundation for the current technological revolution. Furthermore, their seemingly banal subject matter suggested new possibilities for many later artists who have examined and categorized their environment through photographs. As proponents of objective or neutral photography, the Bechers want their subjects to be represented with as little intervention as possible. They take all of their black-and-white pictures, which have low horizons and

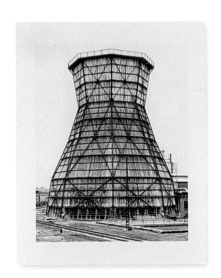

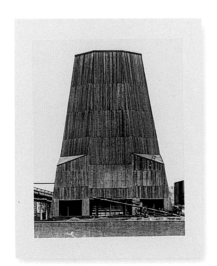

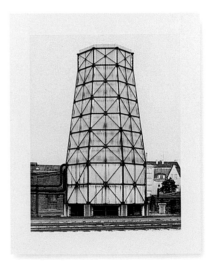

frontal views of buildings filling the image, on overcast days, when there are few shadows. They always make prints of the same size and usually exhibit them in groups of nine, in a three-by-three grid formation. The title of one of the Bechers' first books of photographs, *Anonymous Sculpture: A Typology of Technical Construction* (1970), reveals how they initially conceived of their project as an analysis of the aesthetic formal elements of the structures. It also points to the many anonymous architects, engineers, and carpenters who created these structures.

The Bechers have taken photographs of cooling towers since the 1950s and continue to do so. In some groupings of their works, they have incorporated prints made from negatives of early works along with photographs taken more recently. Unlike earlier versions, the 1983 work comprises twelve prints, exhibited in two rows of six. Cooling towers of this type, built for heavy industrial plants, are heat transfer systems. The heat from industrial machinery is transferred to water, which is piped into the cooling tower and cooled by forced air through the top. The cold water is then piped back into the plant. As photographs, these images compel the viewer to reconsider these structures as formal objects by comparing line, form, and shape. The Bechers captured a significant amount of detail on these hourglass structures, highlighting the intricate patterns of the crossbeams.

In the late 1960s, most critics placed the Bechers' photographs in the context of minimalism because they take on many of the conventions of conceptual and minimalist art, such as the use of a serial format and de-emphasizing the role of the artist. Pioneers of a significant conceptual model and language of photography, the Bechers have since become the leaders of German conceptual photography. As professors at the Kunstakademie Düsseldorf, their legacy can be seen in the work of their students Thomas Struth (p. 210), Thomas Ruff (p. 196), Candida Höfer (German, b. 1944), and Andreas Gursky (p. 290). JRW

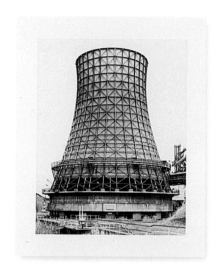  

 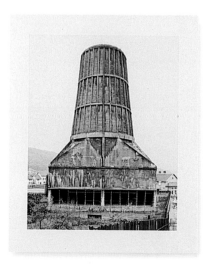 

Jenny Holzer
American, b. 1950

Truisms
1983
Electronic sign
6⁵/₁₆ × 60½ × 4¼ in. (16 × 153.7 × 10.8 cm)
Ed: 2/4
Partial gift of Dr. Paul and Dorie Sternberg
1986.66

Like her contemporary Barbara Kruger (p. 178), Jenny Holzer is concerned with the rhetoric of political propaganda and commercial advertising. Whereas Kruger juxtaposes pictures with words, Holzer focuses on the presentation of words, taking her cue from conceptual pioneers such as Bruce Nauman (p. 80) and Joseph Kosuth (p. 228). Holzer multiplies the expressive dimensions of words by using unexpected messages in a variety of signage formats, often placing them in ingenious public locations where a cross section of people will encounter them.

The *Truisms*, begun in 1978, are Holzer's first works in the style for which she became known. They began as single-sentence aphoristic statements of beliefs. Some sound like self-improvement rhetoric, as in "Fear is the greatest incapacitator" and "Go all out in Romance and let the chips fall wherever." Others espouse common beliefs, such as "You can't expect people to be something they're not" and "Humor is a release." Still others offer extremist and unpopular pronouncements, such as "Morals are for little people," "Old friends are better left in the past," and "Murder has its sexual side." Holzer uses the consistently deadpan tone of the platitude or well-worn cliché throughout the series. This tone as well as the alphabetical order of the *Truisms* counterbalances the statements' judgmental and contradictory nature. Holzer claims that the *Truisms* were initially inspired by the formidable reading list she was given upon her entry into the Whitney Museum of American Art's Independent Study Program in 1976–77. It included readings on art and literature, Marx, psychology, social and cultural theory, criticism, and feminism. The *Truisms*

started with the parodic process of oversimplifying complex ideas, and yet Holzer's attempt to condense intellectual history into pithy sayings belied her more serious quest at the time to develop a means of effective public address.

Although Holzer had composed all 193 *Truisms* by 1979, they have appeared in different formats and numbers since 1978. She picked between forty and fifty of them to use for posters she pasted first in 1978 on the facades of buildings in New York—at the entrance to banks, stores, or other spaces already saturated with signage. Holzer has also displayed them on T-shirts, caps, and books, and projected them onto the side of a house in Kassel, Germany, for the *Documenta* exhibition of 1982. In March of 1982, Holzer displayed a small selection of her *Truisms* on the 800-square-foot Specta-color Board above Times Square at

Broadway and Forty-second Street, a symbolic center of news and entertainment. This proved to be a breakthrough for Holzer, who for the first time used the medium that would become her signature format—the LED sign, composed of computer activated light-emitting diode lamps that display traveling texts and graphics in various colors and styles. The LED technology offers versatility in the presentation of words and graphics and offered significant storage of information. Holzer also liked the medium for its associations with authoritative rhetoric such as advertising and its flexibility in terms of placement. Holzer made an edition of eight (four with red letters and four in yellow-green) smaller LED signs for gallery display containing all 193 *Truisms*, one of which is featured here from the MCA Collection. One full loop of the *Truisms* takes twenty-six minutes and shows a variety of the LED sign's rhythmic variations in the presentation of the traveling text—beeping,

flashing, adjustments of speed, pausing, changes in font and width of characters, and different directional movements of letters and words— prompting the spectator to pause and reflect on his or her beliefs. A P

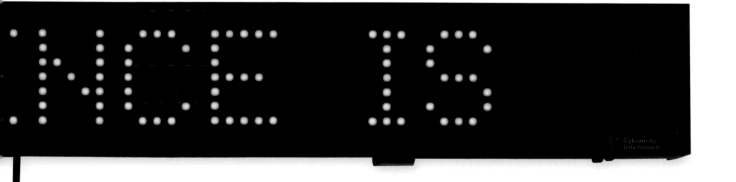

Barbara Kruger

American, b. 1945

Untitled (We construct the chorus of missing persons)
1983
Gelatin silver mural prints with painted artist's frame
121⅞ × 72⅞ × 2 in. (309.6 × 185.1 × 5.1 cm)
Restricted gift of Paul and Camille Oliver-Hoffmann
1984.22.a – c

This early work by Barbara Kruger is typical of the methods she has employed throughout her career: ambiguous but tangentially related combinations of image and text; imperatives or aggressive phrasing of the text, which implicate the viewer directly; and a use of pronouns that allows the subject and the object of a phrase to change according to a variable frame of reference.

The image of a woman's face with hair thinly veiling it provides a range of possibilities for meaning in relation to the text, which itself contains a dissonant combination of meanings. Although the word *missing* implies silencing, to "construct the chorus" of such "missing persons" suggests, on the contrary, that their absence gave them a voice. Perhaps Kruger is implying not only that "we" silence people, or women, but that by doing so "we" give voice to them. And if "we" speak *for* them, perhaps this is another form of silencing. Kruger raises myriad questions about political speech with just one carefully chosen juxtaposition of image and text. By establishing multiple meanings via the frames of reference and the subjects and objects of her texts and images, Kruger is able to challenge the authority of her commanding phrases and strong graphic compositions.

Kruger's layouts are informed by her years of work as a graphic designer beginning in the late 1960s, including her position as chief designer at *Condé Nast*. In her artwork, Kruger deliberately chooses attention-grabbing images, and then composes phrases that work with the images in a provocative and multifaceted way. Once she arrives at combinations, she makes photostats of the pictures, altering the size, cropping, and contrast to provide an image to be photographed again. She sends the final layouts to a photo studio, and has them enlarged to her specifications in black-and-white or color. Following the techniques of advertising and political propaganda, Kruger has used public space throughout her career, combining her characteristic pictures and words in the form of billboards that inspire a double take as one passes by on the street.

Her deliberate complication of verbal and visual representations has a long history in modern and contemporary art, extending from the surrealist experiments in word-and-image associations by René Magritte (p. 50) to the language games of Jasper Johns (p. 62), Joseph Kosuth (p. 228), and John Baldessari (p. 198). Kruger's work also extends a tradition of politically motivated art that attempts to challenge power structures. She and many like-minded artists of her generation — including Cindy Sherman (p. 138), Richard Prince (p. 166), and Jenny Holzer (p. 176) — saw art's political engagement as one that needed to come to terms with the power of the mass media in a more sophisticated way. Art could no longer oppose social institutions without recognizing the power of media to direct thought, and without learning to imitate its rhetoric. Kruger and other artists of her generation made a priority of seducing the viewer, as popular media does in advertising or propaganda, and then using art to raise provocative questions. AP

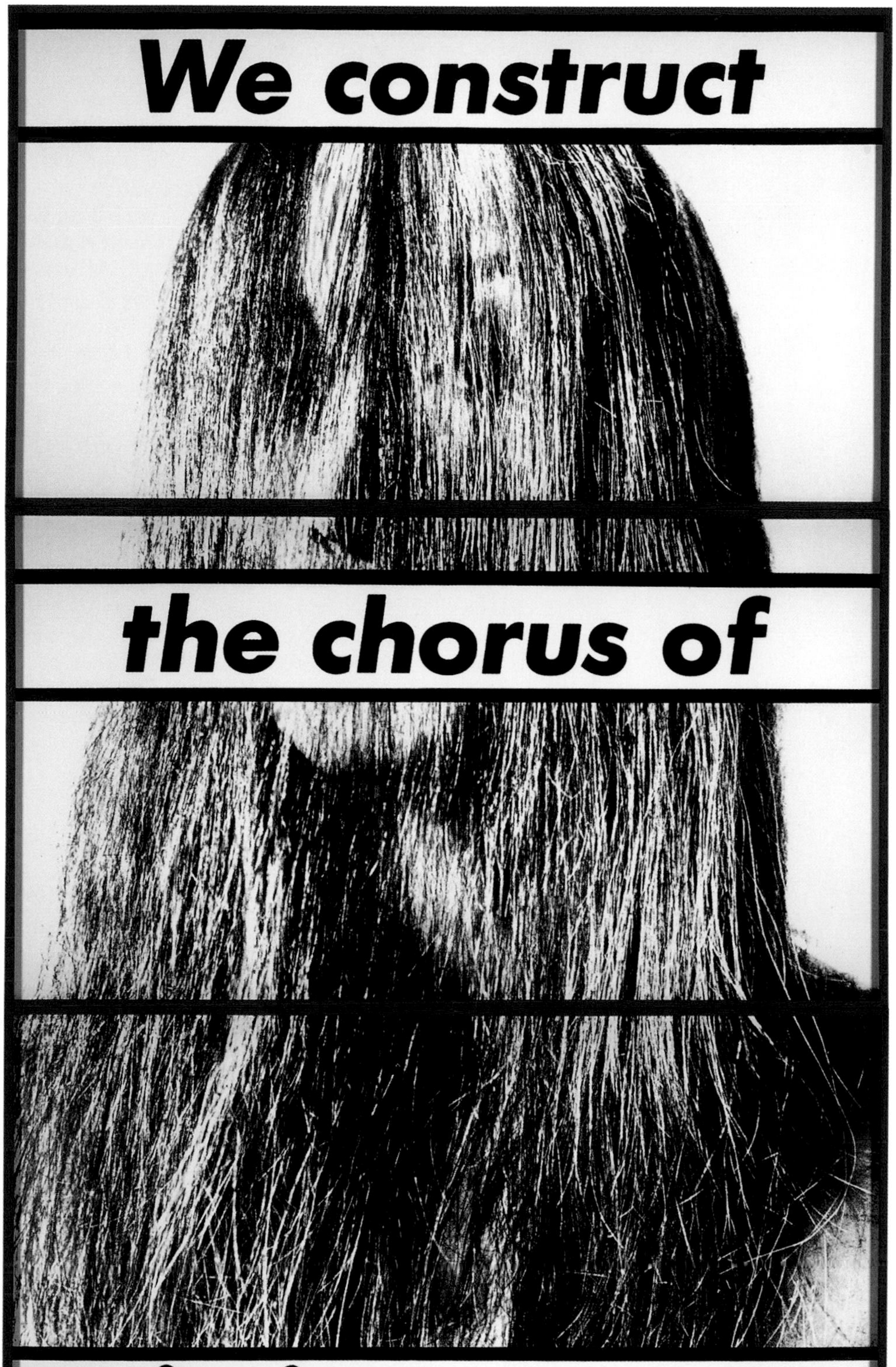
We construct
the chorus of
missing persons

Gilbert & George

Gilbert Proesch, British, b. Italy 1943
George Passmore, British, b. 1942

Winter Pissing
1983
Gelatin silver and chromogenic
development prints
95 × 79 in. (242 × 201 cm)
Gift of Anne and William J. Hokin
1991.10.a–p

The British duo Gilbert & George formed between 1967 and 1968 at St. Martin's School of Art in London, where the two young men met as students. Disillusioned by the aesthetic rigidity of Anthony Caro (British, b. 1924) and his "welding school" at St. Martin's, and eager to violate the boundaries of the dominant minimalist art-making practice there, they began making "living sculptures" with their own bodies. They felt that minimalism precluded human concerns. The best-known work from this period (1968–1972) is *The Singing Sculpture,* a performative work of varying duration in which the artists sing Flanagan and Allen's music hall song "Underneath the Arches" like music box figurines. Gilbert & George first developed their system of constructing composite works with their 1971 series of *Photo Pieces* — assemblages of framed photographs. Later, they hand-colored the individual photographic images and combined them in a grid, a style that has become their signature mode of production. While their work employs the formal language of photography, collage, and painting, Gilbert & George refer to their art as sculpture. Indeed, works such as *Winter Pissing,* with its individually framed parts, seem more like objects than conventional photographs or paintings.

Winter Pissing is from one of the most enigmatic groups of pictures Gilbert & George produced between 1981 and 1983. Unswerving in their adherence to their process, they produced the initial design with photographic images. Typically, Gilbert & George then cover the background surfaces of the work with bright, translucent color, allowing the underlying photo-based patterns to show through. In this group of pictures, however, the photographs are entirely or partly concealed by opaque color.

In this picture, Gilbert & George returned to enduring themes they developed early in their career: camaraderie, exultation in life's unappreciated moments, and the desire to demonstrate the fundamental nobility inherent in all people. The childhood game of "crossing swords," crisscrossing streams of urine, is a young boy's expression of close friendship, innocent transgression of parental codes of behavior, and creative collaboration. In winter climes, this game becomes a means of writing in the snow. A related work from the same year, *Friendship Pissing,* underscores the tender significance of these juvenile peccadilloes. *Winter Pissing* also evokes the sexual games of adults, particularly in gay culture, called water sports.

Since the beginning of their artistic and personal partnership, Gilbert & George have aspired to defy oppressive societal mores that condemn individuals who refuse conformity, particularly homosexuals. Challenging homophobic critics and their allies, Gilbert & George have made the intimate nature of their relationship implicit in work since *Queer* (1977). The good-natured naughtiness of the gesture in *Winter Pissing* is a manifesto of the inherent dignity in all people that Gilbert & George wish to reveal and explore. M R

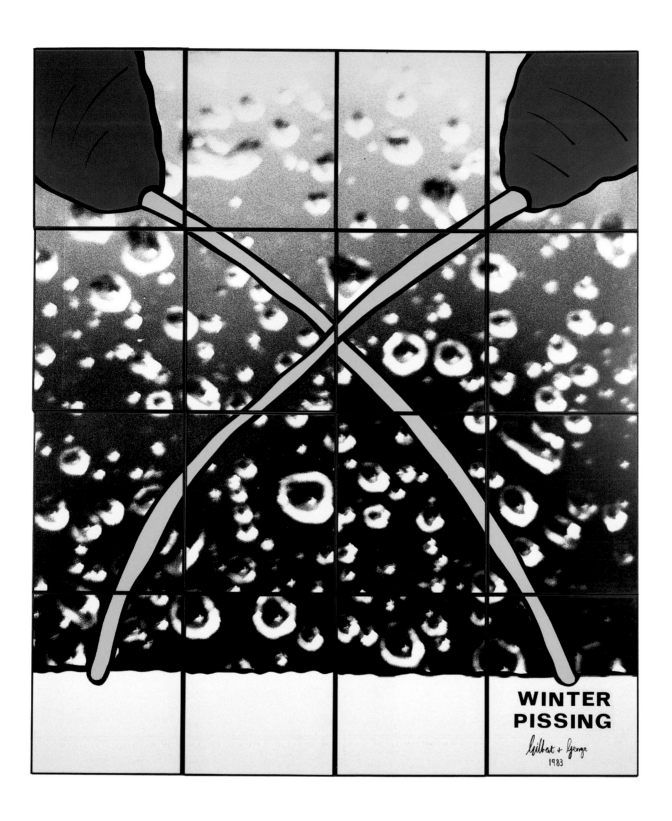

WINTER
PISSING

Gilbert + George
1983

David Salle

American, b. 1952

David Salle emerged at the beginning of the 1980s as a leading member of a group of artists examining the functions of various types of cultural representation, from the history of art to the mass media. Following the pluralism of the art world of the late 1970s, when no particular style or genre dominated, Salle and other artists of his generation investigated representation itself, rather than practicing one among many styles. Their tendency to appropriate pictures was inherited most directly from the previous generation of conceptual artists. A student of John Baldessari (p. 198) at the California Institute of the Arts, Salle assimilated Baldessari's conceptual practice of collecting imagery the way an anthropologist gathers and analyzes samples.

The relationship of images and objects in Salle's paintings is highly controlled, and the materials and images are typically constructed in layers. The first of three main layers Salle applied in *Din* consists of limblike cutouts of a predominantly green, patterned fabric embedded within areas of a green-tinted grisaille painting of a cluster of figures in loincloths. Salle often chooses imagery that conjures cultural stereotypes, such as the loincloths, to confront common assumptions about appearances and realities. In this first layer of *Din*, the figures' actions are obscured; the viewer sees only decorative patterns on the surface—the repetition of shapes between cloth and limbs, in the fabric itself, and among the bodies.

Din
1984
Oil and fabric on canvas with wood attachments
60⅛ × 84³⁄₁₆ × 20 in.
(152.7 × 213.8 × 50.8 cm)
Gift of Ralph I. and Helyn D. Goldenberg
1992.91

The second layer consists in part of broad, curved strokes of brown paint, which underscore patterns in the group of figures. Another component is a peach-colored outline of a reclining nude female wearing a bonnet, a type recognizable from an older tradition of European painting. The near nudity of the outlined figure corresponds to the near nudity of the grisaille figures. The outlined figure, however, is distinguished from the other figures by its peach color, which suggests white skin. The brown color of the other, less coherent strokes seems to indicate brown skin. The superimposition of the possibly European figure onto the brown other, is, perhaps, a metaphor for the act of representing others through the lens of European cultural ideas and standards. In 1984, the year Salle created *Din*, The Museum of Modern Art in New York mounted a highly controversial blockbuster exhibition, *Affinities of the Tribal and the Modern: Primitivism in Twentieth-Century Art*. Much critical response revolved around whether the exhibition perpetuated stereotypes of non-Western cultures. *Din* recalls "primitivist" works influenced by African art, which are distinguished by the representation of the other as irrational and unfathomable, yet full of aesthetically interesting "pattern."

The third layer of *Din*, which consists of a wooden hand and a table leg attached to the canvas, indicates Salle's skepticism toward representation. The leg suggests that the painting could be removed from the wall and used as a table. An attempt to position it in this way, however, would be absurd; the table would collapse. By evoking this scenario, Salle attempts to reveal the instability of representations. To do so, he obscured the imagery in the painting, presenting us with an insight into the nature of representation: like a din, a mixture of loud, discordant noises, representations have an inherently ironic function; by intensifying some aspects of reality they necessarily obscure others. A P

183

Christian Boltanski

French, b. 1944

Monument: Les enfants de Dijon is the first of several versions of a spiritually provocative installation of photographs, lights, and wires. In 1973, Christian Boltanski was invited by the Lentillères College of Secondary Education to create a work in a middle school in Dijon, France. Boltanski asked approximately 200 students for photographs of themselves, which he then rephotographed and installed in the school. Over a decade later, he reworked and reinstalled these photographs at Le Consortium, an exhibition site in Dijon.

This version of the work comprises sixty-eight magnified black-and-white photographs of Dijon schoolchildren installed in a darkened room. One hundred fifty-two tiny incandescent light-bulbs emit a somber glow, their spidery electrical wires falling indiscriminately in front of the images. The directness of the photographs in *Dijon* creates a frozen chorus of faces that ominously stare at the viewer while the accompanying lights suggest a variety of religious acts of remembrance. Boltanski used a border of photographed Christmas paper to frame the faces in colored, decorative shapes that are in stark contrast to the work's overarching sense of sadness and loss.

In *Monument: Les enfants de Dijon*, the sixty-eight images offer a documentation and inventory of the existence

**Monument: Les enfants de Dijon
(Monument: The Children of Dijon)**
1985
Gelatin silver and chromogenic development prints and light fixtures
Installed dimensions variable
Photographs: 11 × 9½ in. to 15¾ × 19¾ in.
(27.9 × 24.1 cm to 40 × 50.2 cm)
Gift of the William J. Hokin Family
2001.13

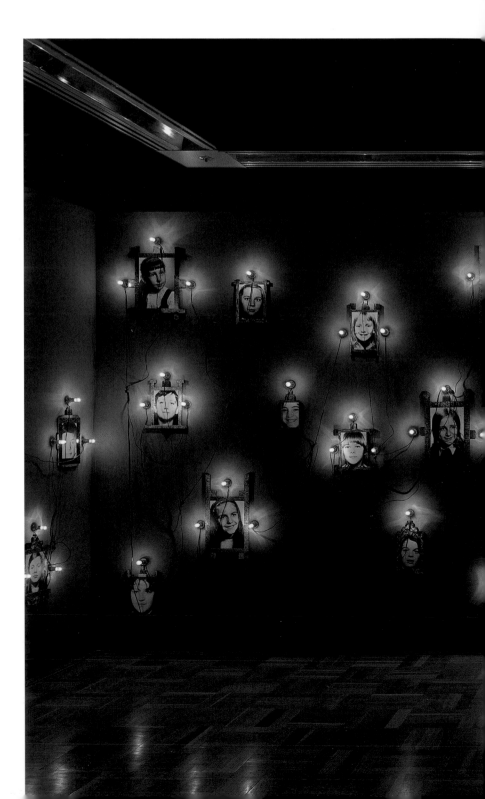

of each anonymous child. As in each of Boltanski's works, there are elements that suggest a human presence, such as second-hand clothes, letters, recycled materials, stacks of tin biscuit boxes (the early ones rusted by Boltanski's urine), and the faces of children. These remnants of lives lived or lost are an ever-present reminder of our own pasts and the blurred memories of childhood.

Boltanski's work has often been associated (whether intentionally or not) with memories of the Holocaust. In this installation, however, the photographs are of children from the 1970s who attended a newly constructed suburban school. *Monument: Les enfants de Dijon* was originally created to be exhibited at Le Consortium during a Catholic festival in France for All Saints Day, a holy day.

While Boltanski does not claim a religion, at various times in his career he has chosen to align himself with either Christianity or Judaism. (His mother was a Catholic writer and his father a Jewish doctor who, although he converted to Catholicism at an early age, feigned a divorce and hid in the family basement during the Occupation. He remained there until the liberation of France, weeks before Boltanski was born.) Though some of his early work leaned toward autobiography, the viewer can rarely be certain of the veracity of Boltanski's self-reflection. He often acknowledges that he has told so many lies about his childhood that he can no longer discern the truth.

Monument: Les enfants de Dijon is part of the larger series of individual works titled *Monuments*, in which Boltanski often used his characteristic rusted and flimsy metal frames to border the images. Constructed from inexpensive materials and originally secured to the wall with double-sided tape, they are not made of the traditional materials that one would associate with a monument. In spite of their ephemeral qualities, these works invoke a sense of sacredness and permanence. The spaces where Boltanski's *Monuments* are installed become holy sites, places of contemplation and memory. L H

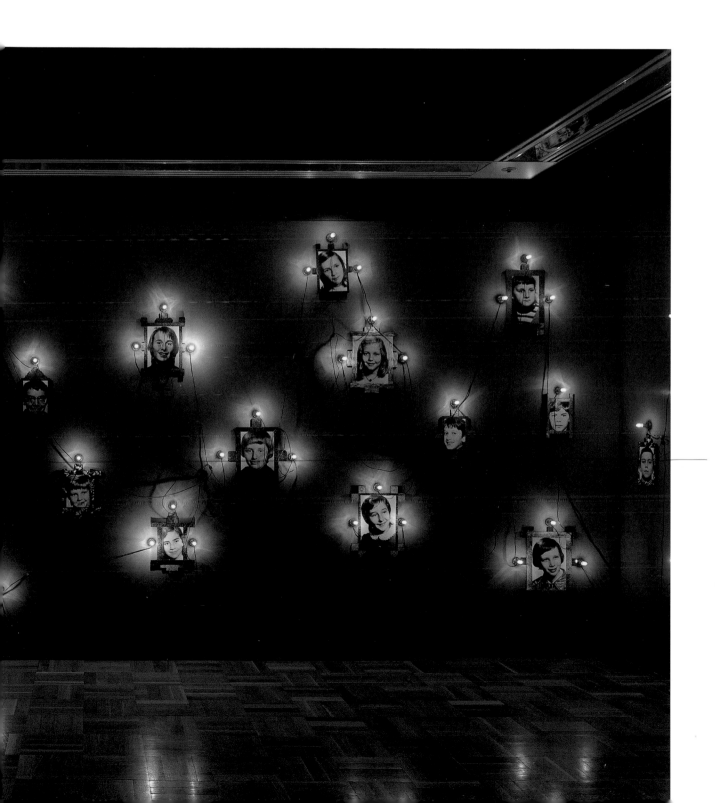

Sherrie Levine

American, b. 1947

Untitled (Gold Knots: 1)
1985
Acrylic on plywood with wooden
artist's frame
21⅛ × 17⅛ × 1¼ in. (53.6 × 43.5 × 3.2 cm)
Gift of Lannan Foundation
1997.43

Sherrie Levine explores the differences between original artwork and reproductions, compelling viewers to consider what people value in art. She has copied and made manipulated versions of works by modern masters and, by the early 1980s, had earned a reputation as one of the leading and most extreme of the appropriation artists. This group, known for manipulating found images to reveal conventions of representation, includes Richard Prince (p. 166), Barbara Kruger (p. 178), Louise Lawler (p. 208), David Salle (p. 182), and Cindy Sherman (p. 138), among others. Levine is best known for taking photographs of reproductions of works by famous modern photographers such as Edward Weston (American, 1886–1958) and Walker Evans (American, 1903–1975), thereby raising questions about issues of originality, authorship, and value.

The mid-1980s marks Levine's first move away from copying specific artworks. She next turned her attention to the conventions of abstract painting, reproducing what she saw as its "generic" characteristics. *Untitled (Gold Knots: 1)* is one of a group of similar works from that period in which Levine painted gold, leaflike shapes on the naturally occurring knots of plywood panels. The exposed plywood support refers to the renunciation of illusionism by some modernist artists and critic.

With a simple gesture, Levine challenged two contradictions of the modernist ideal of anti-illusionistic flatness. Her careful application of gold leaf, a material with historical and religious connotations of preciousness, questions the idea that stripping a surface bare is ever truly possible. Here, the gold adorns the surface in addition to concealing the support, which includes its natural markings. Not only does *Untitled (Gold Knots: 1)* conceal instead of reveal but it highlights the decorative appeal of abstract painting, despite the intellectual functions attributed to it by modernists. At the same time, Levine reminds us that revealing a "pure" surface may also be a fantasy; for surfaces like plywood are naturally irregular.

Levine's interest in how value in art is instantiated comes from a twentieth-century tradition of institutional critique initiated by Marcel Duchamp (French, 1887–1968) that extends to conceptualism. Levine has made this tradition a source of her reproductions. In 1991, she created multiple bronze versions of Duchamp's most notorious work, the porcelain urinal he presented in 1917 as his entry for the first major exhibition of art to be presented in the U.S. Whereas Duchamp's radical gesture tested the boundaries of acceptability and was rejected at the time, Levine reminds us of the extent to which this historical challenge to the institutions of art has since been enshrined within them. AP

Haim Steinbach

American, b. Israel 1944

Untitled (cabbage, pumpkin, pitchers) #1
1986
Plastic laminated wood shelf, ceramic pitchers
and tureen, and stuffed toy pumpkin
54³/₁₆ × 84 × 27½ in.
(137.6 × 213.4 × 69.8 cm)
Restricted gift of Anne and William J. Hokin and
Bernice and Kenneth Newberger Fund
1987.1 a – i

In the 1980s, Haim Steinbach focused on rituals of acquisition and display, exploring how meaning and value are assigned to objects and to people through their possessions. He shared these interests with a group of artists in the United States who also emerged in the 1980s, including Louise Lawler (p. 208) and Jeff Koons (p. 168). Like Koons, Steinbach makes sculptures and installations out of store-bought objects. However, while Koons often alters the materials of his borrowed objects, Steinbach's artistic intervention lies in his acts of selecting, positioning, and staging existing objects. This approach — an imitation of the rituals of the archaeologist, curator, or consumer — has many precedents in twentieth-century art, from the readymades of Marcel Duchamp (French, 1887–1968) to the work of younger artists such as Mark Dion (American, b. 1961) and Mike Kelley (p. 222).

Steinbach's view of his work as an "intervention" in the existing world of commodity circulation, and of himself as a user rather than maker of commodities, is reflected in the pricing structure of his work. Steinbach requires that collectors purchase the work as well as reimburse him separately for the exact cost of each of the objects used in it. This method makes it clear that his artistry is in his use of objects, not the objects themselves. As Steinbach began making more money as an artist, he included more expensive objects in his works. By 1987, he was buying collectible items, such as an eighteenth-century Dutch figurine, and expensive equipment, such as Universal weight-lifting machines.

Untitled (cabbage, pumpkin, pitchers) #1 is characteristic of Steinbach's works of the mid-1980s, which typically consist of store-bought items arranged on wedge-shaped shelves designed by the artist. In 1985, Steinbach began using a standardized but easily varied design for his shelves. They are always wedge-shaped and usually made of wood laminated in plastic. Their color, size, and number of units vary. The shelves simultaneously allude to commercial display shelving, modern-style domestic shelving, and minimalist sculpture in the manner of Donald Judd (p. 124) — references that allow Steinbach to conflate the rituals of advertising, domestic acquisition and display, and art. The store-bought nature of the objects on the shelves is another crucial aspect of Steinbach's shelf series. This choice both affirms and exposes the role of consumerism in how people define themselves. His process also draws a parallel between shopping and art making, both considered forms of self-expression.

In this work, Steinbach presents a ceramic "cabbage" soup tureen, stuffed toy pumpkin, and three ceramic black pitchers as though they are characters on a stage. Differences in shelf heights, sizes, and positions establish an order among inanimate objects that reflects human displays of social rank. An obnoxiously grinning stuffed-toy jack-o'-lantern dominates a row of identical black figures in profile and a solitary figure with a silver spoon in its surrogate mouth. Except for the pumpkin, all of these objects relate to food service. Instead of affirming the consumer's desire to use their possessions to aggrandize themselves, Steinbach uses such objects to address ideas about ostentation and concern with rank or social status. AP

David Robbins

American, b. 1957

Talent
1986
Gelatin silver prints
Eighteen parts, each: 10⅝ × 8⅝ in.
(27 × 21.9 cm)
and part f: 8⅝ × 10⅝ in. (21.9 × 27 cm)
Ed: 59/100
Gift of Hudson
1997.10.a – r

Following the model of conceptual artists who used their work to analyze social systems, artist and writer David Robbins creates artworks that examine prevalent values and behaviors in the art world, with special focus on how they overlap with or diverge from those in the entertainment industry and mass media. He has made films, assemblages, paintings, photographs, and video for television.

Robbins's penchant for dissecting the art world and the mass media was shared by many artists who rose to prominence and exhibited together during the 1980s, such as Richard Prince (p. 166), Barbara Kruger (p. 178), Jenny Holzer (p. 176), Jeff Koons (p. 168), Robert Longo (American, b. 1953), Allan McCollum (American, b. 1944), and Louise Lawler (p. 208).

Talent is an arrangement of head shots of eighteen contemporary artists. A standard of the entertainment industry, head shots conform to particular conventions, such as lighting, how the subject poses, and what facial expression he or she uses. By having artists photographed as if they were actors, Robbins questions the relationship between the art and entertainment worlds and examines the construction of public identity. According to Robbins,

> I hoped [*Talent*] would cause both avant-garde culture and entertainment culture to confront their habits of mind, framing the issue of criticality itself. It was my attempt to tip the critical and the noncritical into a perpetual motion of mutual critique, simultaneously indicting art's naive, excessive

190

Alan Belcher

Jenny Holzer

Michael Byron

Joel Otterson

Clegg and Guttmann

Steven Parrino

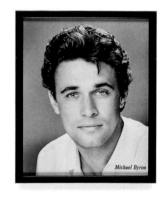
Robert Longo

Robin Weglinski

Ashley Bickerton

criticality and entertainment's smug, oafish complacency; art's chronic marginality and entertainment's brutish populism; art's fierce autonomy and entertainment's collaborative nature; art's addiction to disposable theory and entertainment's poverty of theory.[1]

Talent is successful in part because these artists "look the part" when posed, cropped, and lit as entertainers are. The illusion compels us to ask, "Is talent more a function of packaging than authentic characteristics?" Or, one may ask, "Have famous contemporary artists, so accustomed to media attention, already become akin to entertainers?" Robbins did a bit of "acting" himself, posing as an agent and hiring

a professional entertainment photographer to take head shots of the artists, who were instructed to pretend to be actors. He scheduled and paid for the photography, made sure the artists appeared, and told them to dress in black, gray, or white, and to take the event seriously.

The artists in *Talent* were photographed because they were Robbins's friends and artistic peers or those in the art world he admired and wanted to meet. However, as a portrait of the art world, the works is idiosyncratic, hardly representing in any systematic way artists of particular styles, attitudes, or even status. Since some were or are more famous than others, the subjective character of the expression "talent" becomes apparent. As the careers of the artists Robbins depicted continue to develop or recede over time, the meaning

of this work will continue to change. Yet it remains a portrait of a moment in which the idea of fame and media attention was inextricably related to that of art production.

In 1992, as a companion piece to *Talent*, Robbins made *Self Parody* (also in the MCA Collection). It consists of an array of black-and-white publicity shots, this time of comics (from Lucille Ball to Jerry Lewis) making funny or exaggerated facial expressions. Like *Talent, Self Parody* exemplifies Robbins's concept of "concrete comedy," in which the people or situations are real, not fictional. A P

1 David Rimanelli, "David Robbins: American Fine Arts Co.," *Artforum* 28, no. 4 (December 1989), p. 139.

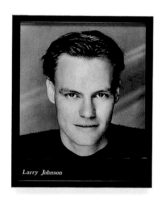

Larry Johnson

Cindy Sherman

Allan McCollum

Thomas Lawson

Jeff Koons

Gretchen Bender

Peter Nagy

Jennifer Bolande

David Robbins

Tony Tasset

American, b. 1960

Button Progression
1986
Leather cushions and wood
Installed, approximately: 22 × 196 × 19 in.
(55.9 × 497.8 × 48.3 cm)
Gift of Thea Westreich
1991.102.a – c

Along with other artists of this generation who came to maturity in Chicago such as Jeanne Dunning (p. 258) and Hirsch Perlman (b. 1960), Tony Tasset emerged in the mid-1980s. Critics, labeling these artists "neoconceptualists," noted that their work contrasted with the imagist idiom that had long been associated with artistic innovation in Chicago. Tasset and his peers instead extended aspects of 1960s and 1970s conceptual art — in Tasset's case, using art to analyze social systems. Tasset has employed a range of media, including sculpture, photography, and film, to comment on the processes that give value to art: conventions of production, consumption, installation, preservation, and publicity.

Button Progression is one of a group of works Tasset produced in the mid-1980s that explores the way art is put to unintended uses in the decorative schemes of collectors' homes and the institutional settings of galleries and museums. Among several works incorporating units of gray leather benches displayed either on the floor or mounted to the wall, *Button Progression* appears to be a hybrid of minimalist art and modernist furniture. The incremental increase in buttons, following a pattern of adding odd integers (three to the first and five to the next), recalls the rationalist strain within minimalism, in which a work's structure follows a serial formula,

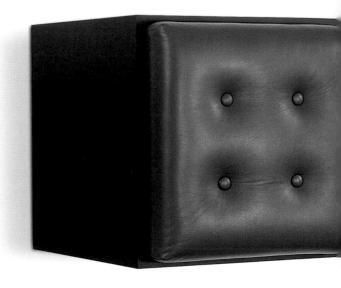

as in works by Sol LeWitt (p. 92). The wall-mounting of three-dimensional structures is characteristic of serial structures by Donald Judd (p. 124). Tasset deliberately appropriates impersonal and rationalist artistic styles to make works that resemble comfortable pieces of furniture. Ironically, by mounting benchlike structures on the wall, Tasset brings minimalism "down to earth." He exposes the underlying decorative aspects of minimalist structures — their affinity with modern design and the aesthetics of the modern homes and institutions into which they are assimilated. As the artist stated in 1986, "even a great work of art, once it has been placed in a home, will stylistically interact with the furniture."

Tasset's concern with the relationship of art to domestic and institutional interiors was inspired in large part by his experience as a gallery assistant at the Rhona Hoffman Gallery in Chicago in the early 1980s, where he installed the work of such artists as LeWitt, Judd, Richard Artschwager (p. 126), and Brice Marden (p. 146) in collectors' homes. In the process, he witnessed placement decisions involving all manners of aesthetic considerations, such as coordination with furniture and plants, which contradict the purist agenda of minimalism.

Tasset's art-handling experience must have also partially inspired *Abstraction with Wedges*, one of a number of works he exhibited in 1991 that address the precious treatment of art objects and the correlation of protection and permanence to value. In this work, Tasset designed and fabricated five wooden wedges of the sort used in the standard installation and movement of artworks, and used them to prop up a five-and-three-quarter-inch thick slab of transparent Plexiglas. This Plexiglas refers to minimalist artworks employing reductive geometry and industrial materials, as well as to materials used to protect works of art, as in the glazing of photographs and the construction of vitrines. AP

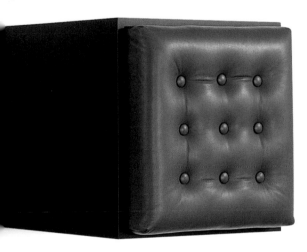

Abstraction with Wedges
1990
Plexiglas and poplar
5¾ × 44¼ × 43¼ in.
(14.6 × 112.4 × 109.9 cm)
Bernice and Kenneth Newberger Fund;
and Illinois Arts Council
Partners in Purchase Grant
1991.23.a – f

193

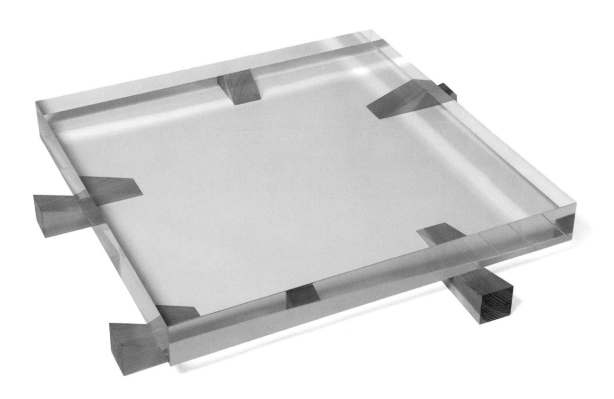

Richard Long
British, b. 1945

Fire Rock Circle
1987
Fire rock stones
Installed, approximately
16 × 110 in. diameter
(40.6 × 279.4 cm)
Gerald S. Elliott Collection
1995.64

Chicago Mud Circle
1996
Mud on wall
Approximately 24 ft. diameter (7.3 m)
Gift of David Meitus
1997.120

Richard Long has been recognized since the late 1960s for works that incorporate materials from the earth — such as wood, stones, mud, and water — into simple geometric forms, including lines, circles, crosses, and spirals. Long's works derive from his walks through a range of natural landscapes. At first, these walks were mainly in his native Bristol, England, but later came to include terrain in the United States, Africa, China, and South America. Throughout his career, Long has made works for display in both art galleries and in natural settings. He documents his outdoor works with photographs, which have become a sideline of his output, as have works on paper and artist's books.

Long is among the first generation of British sculptors to react against British modernist masters Anthony Caro (b. 1924) and Henry Moore (1898–1986), whose monumental, freestanding sculptures, made with uniform materials and joined by welding or casting, represent the idea of sculpture as the manipulation of appearances of gravity and light. Long contributed to the emergence of conceptual art as a time-based action as well as a product. In the early 1970s, Long's work seemed related to that of American contemporary artists who used the earth in their work, such as Robert Smithson (p. 90) and Michael Heizer (b. 1944). Yet Long has expressly distanced himself from those artists; he sees their insertion of machinery into the land as disruptive to nature. Rather, Long sees himself as a custodian of nature.

Fire Rock Circle and *Chicago Mud Circle* are representative of the range of Long's gallery works. *Fire Rock Circle* is one of numerous stone circles Long has produced, both in and outside of galleries. He provides instructions for the installation of such works, indicating the diameter, spacing, and patterning of irregularly shaped rocks in a variety of sizes and shapes into a perfectly circular form. For *Fire Rock Circle* and Long's other gallery works, the stones come from the unwanted remains of local quarries. Long never has stones especially cut for his works. The size and shape of his sculptures are determined to be proportionate to the spaces for which they are intended, allowing room for people to move freely around the works.

Chicago Mud Circle is one of numerous works Long has made since the early 1980s applying mud directly onto gallery walls. He made this work in one day, using his hands to "paint" with local mud. It debuted for the opening of the MCA's new building in the summer of 1996 and remains an irremovable part of the wall (when the work is not part of an exhibition, it is concealed by a temporary wall). Long's wall works function in the opposite way from those of Sol LeWitt (p. 92), whose wall drawings exist in the form of instructions that are infinitely reproducible. As with the *Fire Rock Circle*, *Chicago Mud Circle* is a balance of structure and spontaneity. A black, circular underpainting acts as a visual scaffolding for the exuberant gestures and splashes of the mud circle. AP

Thomas Ruff

German, b. 1958

Portrait (A. Wagner)
1985
Chromogenic development print
82½ × 65 in. (209.6 × 165.1 cm)
Ed: 2/4
Gift of Susan and Lewis Manilow
in honor of Gerald S. Elliott
1995.9

Portrait (Michael Van Ofen)
1987
Chromogenic development print
91¼ × 72¼ in. (231.8 × 183.5 cm)
Edition of 3
Gift of Susan and Lewis Manilow
in honor of Gerald S. Elliott
1995.10

Portrait (Carolin Kewer)
1988
Chromogenic development print
83 × 65 in. (210.8 × 165.1 cm)
Ed: 3/4
Gerald S. Elliott Collection
1995.90

Portrait (Heinz Haussman)
1988
Chromogenic development print
83 × 56 in. (210.8 × 165.1 cm)
Ed: 2/4
Gerald S. Elliott Collection
1995.91

Thomas Ruff studied at the Kunstakademie Düsseldorf, where influential photographers Bernd and Hilla Becher (p. 174) taught and where his fellow alumni include Thomas Struth (p. 210), Andreas Gursky (p. 290), and Candida Höfer (German, b. 1944). Although Ruff's work is characterized by a wide variety of subjects, he consistently examines perception and ways of looking. His *Nacht (Night)* series, begun in 1989, is taken from astrological negatives from a scientific observatory in Chile. Ruff carefully chose sections of the star clusters based on the composition of the negatives. He began making pictures in the early 1990s, influenced by the news media's portrayal of images taken with night vision equipment during the Gulf War. Later works borrow from propaganda posters and, unlike his earlier works, are decidedly more political than formal in content. A series of photographs from the late 1990s initiated a new subject of pornographic pictures taken from the Internet.

In an early series of portraits from the mid-1980s, Ruff photographed his subjects in three-quarter view or in profile, making portraits reminiscent of paintings. Out of this exercise he developed a formal series of large-scale images including *Portrait (A. Wagner)*, *Portrait (Heinz Hausmann)*, and *Portrait (Carolin Kewer)* that recall giant passport photos. Ruff systematically posed the sitters, often friends and acquaintances, with the same even lighting and frontal angle to evoke a sense of objectivity, as if the camera alone was capturing the image. He then enlarged the photographs to a monumental scale of five times life size. The untouched details of his subjects' faces are a visual map of various planes, textures, and surfaces. The frontal vantage point and framing of Ruff's portraits with their consistent cropping, lighting, and scale, echo the Bechers' typological approach to photography.

His portraits are often compared to a project by August Sander (German, 1876–1964), *Men of the Twentieth Century*, in which he took 540 portraits and photographically catalogued forty-five professional, social, and ethnic "types" in Germany. Unlike Sander's, Ruff's photographs are not typological studies of social groups. Rather than proposing a narrative reading of each portrait to associate with a larger social group, Ruff aimed to focus on the formal qualities that convey the physical individuality of each sitter. As he has said "let the machine do the work it would do anyway, why should I make things look different?" referring to the camera's ability to record visual details.

Ruff has embraced the creative possibilities of computer and digital manipulation of photographs in his recent series of photographs called *l.m.v.d.r*, based on the architecture of Ludwig Mies van der Rohe (German, 1886–1969). The series revisits a theme that

appeared in his work in the early 1980s and again in the early 1990s when he undertook a photographic series of European buildings that explored the hidden beauty of mundane architectural designs. Later, for the reopening of the Haus Lange and Haus Esters in Krefeld, Germany — Mies designs for private residences that are now contemporary art museums — Ruff was invited to photograph the buildings. Considering these long-standing modern icons with a renewed vigor, Ruff produced a series of images of the interiors and exteriors. Subsequently, The Museum of Modern Art, New York, asked Ruff to expand his series for inclusion in the 2001 exhibition *Mies in Berlin*. The subject of *d.p.b.02*, known as the Barcelona Pavilion, only existed for two years (1928–1930) until its reconstruction in 1986. Ruff examines the complexities of contemporary photographs by using all available technologies in this historically based project. Manipulating existing documentary black-and-white photographs, he employs techniques such as blurring and computer coloration to capture the speed and progress of what he calls "the locomotive of modern architecture."[1] JRW

1 "Mies Revisited." *Architecture* 90, no. 6 (June 2001) p. 103.

d.p.b.02
1999
Laserchrome and diasec
73⅝ × 111⅝ in. (187 × 283.5 cm)
Ed: 3/5
Partial gift of Pamela and Michael Alper
2001.14

197

John Baldessari

American, b. 1931

Fish and Ram
1988
Tempera on gelatin silver
and chromogenic development prints
Five parts, installed: 109¾ × 144¼ in.
(278.8 × 366.4 cm)
Restricted gift of Gerald S. Elliott;
Anne and William J. Hokin by exchange;
and National Endowment
for the Arts Purchase Grant
1989.2.a–e

Since the mid-1960s, John Baldessari has examined the nature of representation. His work offers solutions to such questions as: How does an image or text signify a message? How does the meaning of this message change when juxtaposed with other images and words? What happens when information in a representation is concealed or emphasized? Like other conceptual artists with whom he was associated in the late 1960s, including Lawrence Weiner (American, b. 1940), Joseph Kosuth (p. 228), Robert Heinecken (p. 100), Robert Barry (American b. 1936), and Douglas Huebler (American, b. 1924), Baldessari approached art as a kind of social science, akin to linguistics, anthropology, and sociology. Baldessari's participation in the genesis of conceptualism was recognized by his inclusion in *Information*, an exhibition of conceptual art at The Museum of Modern Art, New York, in 1970 that helped to codify the movement.

While many conceptual artists worked out of New York, Baldessari has lived in California throughout his career.

His influence on younger artists as a teacher at the California Institute of the Arts from 1970 to 1987 was profound. Among Baldessari's well-known students are David Salle (p. 182) and Eric Fischl (American, b. 1948).

Baldessari is best known for the photographic montages he began making in the 1980s. For *Fish and Ram*, he assembled six photographs drawn from B-movie and television stills that suggest the theme of subjugation. The fish, the woman wearing a fur shawl, and the ram represent hunting trophies. Images of a woman in fancy attire, a group of people moving in the same direction, a man beating another man, and soldiers in formation all represent social conformity and hierarchy. Each of the images in isolation would not necessarily carry the same thematic significance; yet the grouping reinforces parallels between the images.

Baldessari's constellation of pictures is complicated by his imposition of a variety of ordering schemes. The cluster of six photographs is divided into blocks of color and black-and-white images. The fish and ram are the only color images. The work thus divides into a comparison between the dominance of humans over animals and that of people or social systems over other people.

Baldessari modifies the images by cropping them and by using colored lines and colored and white circles to emphasize or conceal particular information and to direct associations made within the group of images. Most of the human faces in each image are cropped or concealed by circles. Baldessari has described his use of this device since the 1980s as a way of focusing attention on the typological quality of the people; de-emphasizing their faces also expands the viewer's consciousness of behavior, dress, and gesture. The colored lines emphasize and determine associations between specific parts of the images.

Meanwhile, the difference between the color of lines used in each image distinguishes the images from each other. Baldessari has explained his use of color-coded lines as an application of common cultural codes for color. For example, green signifies safety; red means danger. Through this device, Baldessari communicates the irony that seemingly benign images, like the woman in the evening dress, may actually represent something sinister. His work reveals not only an understanding of representation but also demonstrates how culturally loaded signs function in contemporary society. AP

199

Chuck Close

American, b. 1940

Cindy
1988
Oil on canvas
102 × 84 in. (259.1 × 213.4 cm)
Gift of Camille Oliver-Hoffmann
in memory of Paul W. Oliver-Hoffmann
1998.24

Since the late 1960s Chuck Close has painted, drawn, printed, and photographed portraits of himself, his family, and his fellow artists, focusing more on the way he creates the image than on the personalities of his sitters. For more than three decades he has devised systems of mark making to construct images based on deadpan "mug shot" photographs he takes himself. Using a grid, Close methodically transfers the information from the photographic sources, square by square, to a corresponding grid drawn onto a flat surface. The transposed photographic distortion, the often-visible underlying framework, and the enormity and intensity of the faces themselves heighten the artificiality of Close's portraits, emphasizing that the works are above all paint, evenly and laboriously distributed on a flat surface.

Though Close exhibited his early airbrushed portraits alongside the work of realist painters, his basic concerns were more aligned with those of the minimal and conceptual artists of the 1960s and 1970s. Countering the intuitive and highly personal aesthetics of abstract expressionism, artists such as Ad Reinhardt (p. 64), Sol LeWitt (p. 92), and Richard Serra (p. 108) set self-imposed guidelines reflecting their interest in control, repetition, and process in order to investigate form and material. Similarly, Close explores picture making through a predetermined system of rules that does not allow for much improvisation. It is the process of making, of both building up and deconstructing an image, that is the crux of his work.

After twenty years of painting monumental heads with airbrushed acrylic, colored pencil, watercolor, shards of paper pulp, and inked fingerprints, Close began using oil paint in 1986. Early in his career, he had consciously rejected this sensuous material as well as gestural brushwork in favor of something more mechanical and less personal. In his paintings of the mid- to late 1980s, Close's love of color and his suppressed painterly expressiveness were revealed and pushed further in his vibrant, loosely painted portraits of the 1990s. After a 1986 *Self-Portrait* and a series of dynamic portrayals of artist Lucas Samaras (American, b. Greece 1936), Close painted two quintessential 1980s artists: Francesco Clemente (Italian, b. 1952) and Cindy Sherman (p. 138), both of whom, like Close, use figurative imagery in their work. Close has continued to paint those he considers his family of artists, creating a virtual pantheon of New York artists at the end of the twentieth century.

Cindy is one of two large paintings of Sherman, who is best known for her photographs in which she herself depicts different female roles. She seems to have done just that for this sitting, donning big glasses, a ponytail, and casual dress. Both of Close's paintings of Sherman veer slightly from his typical, frontally posed compositions. Here, the pose is uncharacteristically asymmetrical — Sherman's head is tilted, and part of her hair and her right shoulder are cut out of the frame. Close also chose to use a grid that is oriented diagonally, emphasizing the slant of Sherman's head. Layers of orange, green, blue, and pink dabs of paint seem to vibrate within the tiny squares of Close's matrix, producing an overall warm flesh tone. Sherman's squinted eyes, penetrating gaze, and angled head challenge the viewer to determine whether this is the real Cindy or yet another character she is playing. SB

Ann Hamilton

American, b. 1956

Video group:
***(dissections . . . they said it was
an experiment • video)***
1988/1993
(the capacity of absorption • video)
1988/1993
(linings • video)
1990/1993
(aleph • video)
1992/1993
LCD monitor with color toned image,
30-minute video laser disc, and laser disc player
Four screens, each: 3½ × 4½ in.
(8.9 × 11.4 cm)
Ed: 6/9 aside from 2 artist's proofs
Bernice and Kenneth Newberger Fund;
restricted gift of Susan and Lewis Manilow and
Howard and Donna Stone
1995.12–15

In laboriously crafted installations, which often take the form of multiroom environments, Ann Hamilton investigates the systems and limits of language — both written and spoken — to convey physical experience. Often made with fragrant organic materials including algae, beeswax, and prairie grass, Hamilton's monumental dreamscapes of enigmatic textures and sounds appeal to all of the senses. From early photographs of "body objects" to recent videos and environments, her works often incorporate speech and text to address themes such as life and decay. Hamilton's study of fiber arts in the 1970s, as well as the emergence of performance and feminist art during that time, influenced her working methods indelibly.

Hamilton's work in the MCA Collection consists of four videos, displayed together on small monitors embedded in a wall, and named after the individual exhibitions in which they first appeared. *(dissections . . . they said it was an experiment • video)* debuted at the Santa Barbara Museum of Art in 1988. Hamilton positioned a man in a bathtub filled with paper ashes in the center of a long room. Rows of butterflies pinned as if in a scientific display covered one wall. A small shelf of fermentation bottles covered with red balloons was attached to the opposite wall. On the back wall hung a large transparency of a person struggling to hold a pot of "boiling" flowers. A table holding a glass of water was placed on the floor in front of it, and on the opposite wall a small monitor showed a person's neck deluged with water.

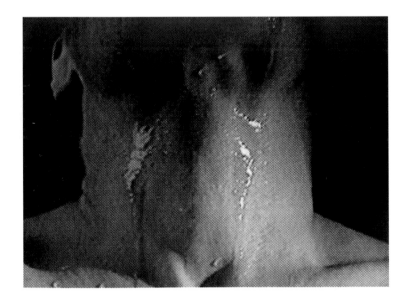 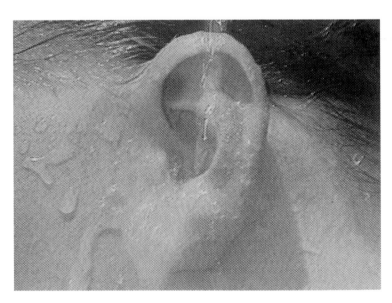

Hamilton created her next large-scale installation, *(the capacity of absorption • video),* for the Temporary Contemporary Exhibition space (now The Geffen Contemporary) at The Museum of Contemporary Art, Los Angeles, in 1988–89. Water, which Hamilton uses as a metaphor for spoken language, was the uniting element of this three-room installation, a work that sought to explore the reception of information by the ear. A large hoop, recalling the shape of a seventeenth-century speaking horn as well as that of a cochlea, displays a small video of water running into and over an ear. In another room, the brain is represented by a large buoy etched with a phrenology diagram. Hamilton describes the installation as "a metaphor for the way speech interrupts one's internal dialogue."[1] In it, she focuses on our ability to take in information through the ear, both consciously and unconsciously, as well as how disruptions of speech overpower the ability to experience through the other senses.

After receiving the Artist in Visual Arts Award Nine in 1990, Hamilton made *(linings • video)* (originally called *mufflings*). At one end of the room a video played a slow-motion image of water overflowing in a person's mouth, accompanied by an ambiguous sound of either human voices or windpipes. The walls were gridded with blue-green glass, and a carpet of prairie grass on the floor was covered with large sheets of glass. A large woven wire net filled with gray wool boots hung from the ceiling at the other end of the room. A humidifier filled the room with the odor of wet wool. This work explores the suffocation of speech or language as a parallel to the way culture suffocates nature.

Hamilton questioned the experience of one's body in relation to technological advances in *(aleph • video),* an installation for MIT's List Visual Arts Center in Cambridge, Massachusetts, in 1992. In a room with a floor of steel sheets, and walls covered with outdated scientific texts, an attendant sat at a table, slowly sanding the reflective material off mirrors. At the far end of the room, a small monitor embedded in the wall emitted the sound and image of stones rolling around the artist's mouth. Aleph, the first character of the Hebrew alphabet, refers to the initial formation of language and written words, but it also represents the shape of the larynx as the mouth moves in transition from silence to speech, an idea that repeatedly appears in Hamilton's work. JRW

1 Richard Smith, "Ann Hamilton," *New Art Examiner* 16, no. 8 (April 1989), p. 55.

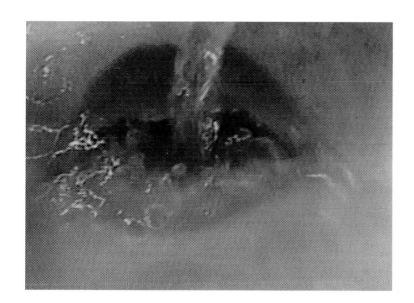

Adrian Piper

American, b. 1948

Cornered
1988
Video installation with birth certificates,
color video, monitor, table, and chairs
Dimensions variable
Bernice and Kenneth Newberger Fund
1990.4.a – p

Adrian Piper, who holds a PhD in philosophy and has taught and written widely, targets and confronts viewers by strategically asking them to question social, cultural, and racial stereotypes. In her pioneering 1960s performance pieces, she altered her appearance and engaged in deviant behavior in public places to spark reactions from passersby. Whether talking to herself repetitively or silencing herself by stuffing her mouth with a rag, Piper carefully noted the discomfort her abnormal activities incited in crowded buses, department stores, and other public places. Part conceptual art and part sociological experiment, Piper's performances lacked the characteristics that generally denote works as "art": they were not staged within museums or galleries and they lacked announced beginnings and endings. Rather, Piper's absurdist performances took place amidst the activities and settings of daily life, provoking subtle but telling effects. Unwitting observers of these actions summoned their defense mechanisms by looking the other way or ignoring the disturbance.

In Piper's major video installation *Cornered,* she strives to create a catalytic effect, addressing viewers frankly and directly, confronting their assumptions about race. Piper, an African American, directs her comments to white viewers who qualify her presence in their intellectual circles by construing her light complexion, composed demeanor, and conservative dress as attributes of their own racial group. Piper corners her audience with an aggressive confrontation of her experiential findings. "I'm black," she says, maintaining her guard as she "confesses" her racial identity. A table standing on end with legs exposed

backs the monitor into the corner wall; chairs arranged in a triangle face the monitor.

"I have no choice," she explains. "I'm cornered. If I tell you who I am, you become nervous and uncomfortable, or antagonized. But if I don't tell you who I am, I have to pass for white. And why should I have to do that?" The installation includes her father's two birth certificates, identifying him as black and white, respectively, hanging with the authority of legal documentation or the credentials of diplomas. Growing up in Harlem with two light-skinned black parents and attending on scholarship an elite private school where she was the only nonwhite student, Piper suffered what she termed the "gray experience." While traditional conventions classify those with a biracial lineage as black, for Piper, the criteria by which we determine race is not nearly as interesting as what we actually do about it. Piper calls on the viewer to acknowledge that he or she, too, may be merely passing for white.

Piper anticipates her audience's reactions to *Cornered* as they attempt to comprehend the implications of researching their black heritage. She calmly confronts these reactions, viewers' aversion to her aggressive approach, and their refusal to "get personal." "This is not an empty academic exercise," she reminds them, "This is real. And it has everything to do with you." The video concludes with the words, "Welcome to the Struggle," an invitation to and an implication of Piper's audience. H R

Jeff Wall

Canadian, b. 1946

Pleading
1988
Silver dye-bleach transparency and light box
54 × 73½ × 9¼ in. (137.2 × 186.7 × 23.5 cm)
Ed: 1/3 aside from 1 artist's proof
Gerald S. Elliott Collection
1995.106

Jeff Wall's large-scale photographs that represent scenes from everyday life were inspired by a range of sources from art history and literature. These include Old Master paintings by Titian (Italian, c. 1488 – 1576), paintings by Spanish masters Diego Velázquez (1599–1660) and Francisco de Goya (1746–1828), as well as Charles Baudelaire's essay "The Painter of Modern Life" (1863), which chronicles the artist Constantin Guys (French, 1802–1892) as he observes people in nineteenth-century Paris. Like Baudelaire's *flâneur*, who appreciated the ephemeral fashions of contemporary life, Wall looks to the world around him, often in his native Vancouver, for settings and locations that represent a larger scale of human experience. To prepare for many of his photographs of outdoor street scenes, Wall drives around watching people, then stages what he has observed.

Wall's narrative photographs depict modern-day moments of conflict and distress, focusing on women, minorities, immigrants, and children. Unlike works by other artists active during the conceptual era of the 1970s, Wall's pictorial photographs emerged from his love for dramatic history painting, which he studied as an art history doctoral student at London's Courtauld Institute. He experimented with filmmaking, and then returned to the studio, prompted by his "discovery" of a way to make dramatic photographs inspired by backlit bus stop advertisements. He had found an ideal medium that combined elements of cinema, painting, and photography, and was also ubiquitous in contemporary society.

Wall's first backlit photograph, *The Destroyed Room* (1978), signaled the beginning of his mature body of work. The color transparency placed in a light box has now become his signature style, and has been adopted by a number of younger artists for its reference to cinema and advertising and its saturated color. The large size of *The Destroyed Room* set a precedent for many later works, especially in its allusion to historical paintings, recalling *Death of Sardanapalus* (1827) by the French painter Eugène Delacroix (1798–1863). Nearly all of Wall's lightbox photographs, except *Pleading* and *In the Public Garden* (1993), are meticulously staged with actors, as if part of a film set. Unlike films, however, which usually attempt to simulate reality, Wall's pictures always contain elements that reveal the constructed nature of the photograph. His photographs from the early 1990s, such as *The Giant* (1992) and *The Vampire's Picnic* (1991), incorporate fantastic elements. Wall displays staged and nonstaged photographs together, diminishing the importance of the distinction in relation to the greater metaphorical interpretations of the scenarios.

Pleading was originally shot in London in 1986. It is an unstaged street photograph of a woman pleading with a man. The woman's all-black attire, and the presence of the woman to the left who is dressed identically, suggest that they are perhaps from a particular religious group. A group of similarly dressed people across the street erect a sign bearing two crosses, also indicating a religious affiliation. It is unclear what the woman is communicating to the man; however, the scene may be read as a struggle between individuals, or a struggle between cultures. Like many of Wall's photographs, this image depicts a precise moment in time while maintaining a level of ambiguity.

Wall merges fact and fiction in his photographs and at the same time, as an artist, art historian, and teacher, refers to art history and contemporary social issues. His generalized re-creations of events in a hyperrealist style act as snapshots of the distress of certain sectors of modern society, and, in the future, may serve as twentieth-century allegories in the tradition of history paintings. J RW

Louise Lawler

American, b. 1947

Since the early 1980s, Louise Lawler has posed questions about the social function of art in her photographs, installations, and provocative role-playing performances. For her 1982 exhibition at Metro Pictures Gallery in New York, Lawler presented an arrangement of works by the artists represented by the gallery at the time. This arrangement was to be sold for the price of the sum of all of the prices of the individual works plus a ten percent commission for Lawler, who played the role of dealer or auctioneer as well as curator and artist.

In 1984, Lawler began her best-known work, a series of photographs of arrangements of artworks in collectors' homes, corporate offices, museums, galleries, and auction houses. These photographs, as well as Lawler's installations of them, with texts and painted wall panels, focus on the relationship between art and the non-art elements that literally and figuratively frame them: a soup tureen under a painting by Jackson Pollock (American, 1912–1956) or the label next to a picture in an auction sales room listing the work's provenance. More recently, Lawler has exhibited crystal paperweights containing photographs of artworks arranged by curators, in which she examines the relationship of exhibitions to cultural tourism.

In the 1980s, many artists were interested in exposing and critiquing the conspicuous consumption of the period. Constant attention at the time

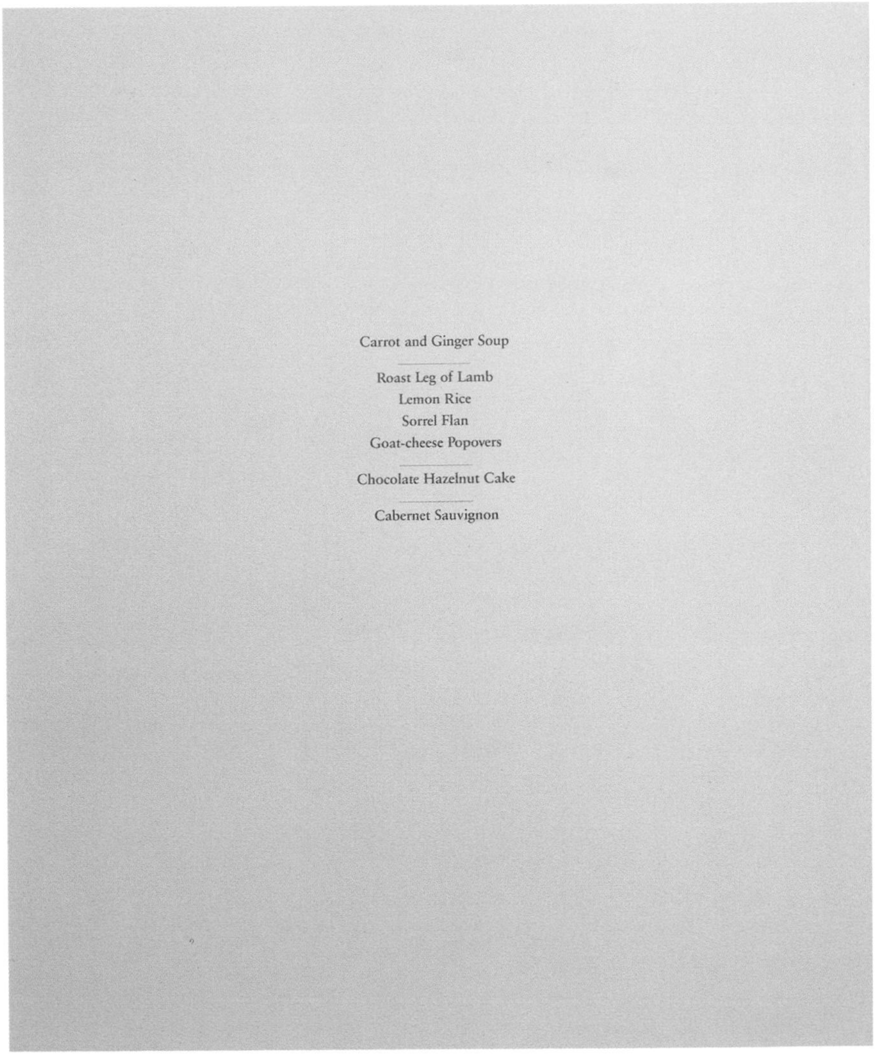

Between Reagan and Bush
1989
Silver dye-bleach print and transfer letters on painted wall
24 × 42 in. (61 × 106.7 cm)
Gerald S. Elliott Collection
1995.58.a–b

208

Carrot and Ginger Soup

Roast Leg of Lamb
Lemon Rice
Sorrel Flan
Goat-cheese Popovers

Chocolate Hazelnut Cake

Cabernet Sauvignon

in the popular media and art press dramatized the record-breaking prices of modern and contemporary works sold at auction. Lawler's quasi-sociological interest in art's status as commodity dovetailed with those of a wide range of her contemporaries. Some, like Sherrie Levine (p. 186), asked pointed questions about the relationship of art's value to the artist's signature, by rephotographing the works of famous photographers. Others, like Jeff Koons (p. 168) and Haim Steinbach (p. 188), examined the social psychology of consumer display techniques, creating works reminiscent of 1960s minimalist art.

Between Reagan and Bush consists of two juxtaposed parts. One is Lawler's framed photograph of works by Jeff Koons in storage before their installation for his much-hyped 1988 exhibition *Banality* at the Sonnabend Gallery in New York. The other is a painted wall panel of a menu taken from *The Silver Palate Cookbook*, a contemporary guide to entertaining geared toward elite consumers. The work in the MCA Collection is one of a series of six, each bearing the same title and framed photograph, but distinguished by the color of the wall panel and letters and by the particular menu chosen from the same cookbook. The title of this work identifies the policies of Presidents Ronald Reagan and George Bush as courses in a meal for upper-class consumption. Koons made the particular works in Lawler's photograph as a commentary on the relationship of taste to class, exaggerating the properties of kitsch objects for mass consumption in order to produce sculptures for elite consumption. Lawler's appropriation of the Koons sculptures, however, turns them back against themselves. With the giant pig sculpture in the foreground and the menu to the side of the photographs, Lawler uses Koons's work to represent what she sees as the gluttony of both elitist taste and politics, commenting on conspicuous consumption in the art market and culture at large. AP

209

Thomas Struth

German, b. 1954

Via Sanita, Naples
1989
Gelatin silver print
17⅛ × 23⅝ in. (43.5 × 60 cm)
Ed: 6/10
Gerald S. Elliott Collection
1995.105

Kunsthistorisches Museum I, Vienna
1989–1990
Chromogenic development print
mounted to Plexiglas
72 × 94 in. (182.9 × 238.7 cm)
Ed: 3/10
Gift of William J. Hokin,
the Dave Hokin Foundation
1993.24

Thomas Struth's photographs of visitors to cultural institutions and monuments, cityscapes, and family groupings probe the nuances of human relationships and social structures. Struth's work raises questions about cultural meaning, social significance, and authenticity of experience. His photographs examine the history of a specific location in relationship to the present, often symbolized by the presence of human figures whose activities in and relationship to these contexts are ambiguous.

Struth attended the Kunstakademie Düsseldorf, where his influential instructors included Bernd and Hilla Becher (p. 174) and Gerhard Richter (German, b. 1932). In his early documentary photographs of urban architecture, Struth adopted a boulevard perspective, with a symmetrical formal composition. This technique enhances the subtle and unique character of office and apartment buildings in such diverse settings as Düsseldorf, Chicago, New York, and Naples. Struth's black-and-white architectural photographs of the 1970s

and 1980s, such as *Via Sanita, Naples*, are void of figures; this absence compels the viewer to consider architecture and urban plans as social structures, manifestations of an implied but invisible human presence. Struth's later photographs of cities in Europe, the United States, and Asia document the bustling commercial life of urban centers at the end of the twentieth century. His family portraits, made from 1988 to 1990, function much like his other series in revealing social and psychological relationships. The subjects are all friends of Struth, and he allows them to choose the setting and arrange themselves. By adopting this formula, Struth reveals the subconscious relationships and organization among his subjects.

In 1989 Struth began a series of photographs taken in museum galleries of visitors looking at works of art, such as *One: Number 31* (1950) by Jackson Pollock (American, 1912–1956) at The Museum of Modern Art in New York and *La Grande Jatte* by Georges Seurat (French, 1859–1891) at The Art Institute of Chicago. Images such as these and

Kunsthistorisches Museum I, Vienna examine multiple, simultaneous levels of viewing, considering the museum as a cultural institution with well-established conventions and traditions. The act of looking is often private, yet in public institutions such as museums, the viewer's experience cannot be characterized as either purely private or public. Struth blurs the distinction further by taking photographs of people looking, who are in turn the object of the viewer's gaze.

In *Kunsthistorisches Museum I, Vienna*, Struth examines the interaction between monumental Renaissance paintings and disparate groups of visitors. A young, affluent couple in conversation on a bench in the middle of the gallery look tired and uninterested in the paintings. A large tour group in the corner takes notes as a docent speaks. A figure in a red jacket to the left looks across the room at the large painting on the far opposite wall. Opened in 1891 as a memorial to the patronage and collecting of the Hapsburg Dynasty, the Kunsthistorisches Museum in Vienna

is an institution deeply rooted in history and tradition. The architects designed the building in the Italian Renaissance style to link the artistic spirit of the Hapsburgs to that earlier artistically prosperous era.

Struth made two other photographs in this museum, *Kunsthistorisches Museum II* and *Kunsthistorisches Museum III* (both 1989), which depict a smaller group and an individual looking at the paintings. Struth is interested in who the museum visitors are and why they have come to the museums, posing

212

Todai-Ji Temple, Hall of the Great Buddha, Nara
1996
Chromogenic development print mounted to Plexiglas
69½ × 90½ in. (176.5 × 229.9 cm)
Ed: 6/10
Gift of LaSalle Bank
2000.15

questions about the relationship between today's viewers and historical buildings and artworks.

In *Milan Cathedral (Interior)*, Struth investigates the relationship, or the schism, between visitors — parishioners and tourists — to the historically rich, architecturally monumental location of the Milan Cathedral. Onlookers watch as a mass takes place and large paintings loom overhead, highlighted by natural and artificial lighting. In its multilayered study of observing, this photograph recalls Struth's series of museum photographs. Calling attention to the customarily fetishistic manner of

beholding art objects and creating an awareness of peoples' intervention in historical relationships through the act of looking, Struth's photographs pose important questions about the contemporary role of cultural and historical institutions.

Todai-ji Temple is from a series taken in Japan and China of views of significant religious buildings, as well as images of bustling urban centers of commerce. It portrays an impressive frontal view of the Great Buddha Hall of the Todai-ji Temple in Nara, Japan. Originally built in 752 A.D. as part of the

most ambitious religious complex and the center of imperially sponsored Buddhism, this wooden structure housed a fifty-three-foot-high Buddha. Unfortunately, as a result of various fires, the present building and Buddha were damaged and then reconstructed during the Edo period (1600–1868), with a few more recent structural enhancements. In this image, Struth used a wide boulevard perspective to invite the viewer into the temple's space, capturing passersby in the foreground. His insistently frontal view of this imposing structure is intended to underscore its historical resonance and ambiguous relationship to the present. JRW

213

Milan Cathedral (Interior), Milan
1998
Chromogenic development print
mounted to Plexiglas
74⅝ × 89 in. (189.5 × 226.1 cm)
Ed: 3/10
Restricted gift of LaSalle Bank, Antje
and John Jelinek, and Judith Neisser
2000.10

Anselm Kiefer

German, b. 1945

Banner
1990
Oil, lead, ash, rock, paper, and copper wire
on canvas
130 × 110¼ in. (330.2 × 280 cm)
Gift of Camille Oliver-Hoffmann
in memory of Paul W. Oliver-Hoffmann
1998.25

Anselm Kiefer, one of Germany's premier postwar artists, emerged in the early 1980s along with German and American peers such as Sigmar Polke (p. 236), Julian Schnabel (p. 160) and David Salle (p. 182). Kiefer employs heroic traditions and uses materials such as sand, straw, and lead as sculptural additions to his large, densely worked canvases. He has been both praised and condemned for his angst-ridden patriotism and his probing of Germany's collective conscience. His work attempts to reclaim a proud heritage while reconciling the horrors perpetrated by Nazis, as well as the suffering of the German people.

Banner is a typical example of Kiefer's large-scale and often ambiguous and multilayered paintings. Made as part of a series displayed as the *Lilit [Lilith]* paintings, *Banner* draws on Kiefer's interest in German mythology, history, and in particular the cabala, a system of Jewish mysticism. In cabalic texts, Lilith is the first wife of Adam, who refuses to take a subservient role. Historically, Lilith is often depicted with long, streaming hair and wings; in *Banner* Kiefer transmuted this traditional iconography into that of an airplane made of lead, trailing ribbands of lead and cloudy streams of white paint.

As is typical in Kiefer's works of this period, words play a preeminent role in *Banner*. The title links the work to historical paintings, such as *The Battle of Issus* (1529) by Albrecht Altdorfer (German, c. 1480–1538), in which a banner with text floats in the sky, as well as to the tradition of annunciation or visitation scenes in which angels or other divine messengers carry texts. The word *Atziluth* is inscribed in Kiefer's spindly handwriting across the rough, gray surface of *Banner*. In the cabala, Atziluth is the archetypal world — the divine world, the world of free will, or the world of emanations, with which Kiefer dealt extensively with in his seminal work from 1985 to 1988, *The Outpouring of the Sephiroth*. In *Banner*, the plane is flying toward the word *Atziluth* in the upper section of the painting, suggesting that Atziluth has not yet been achieved.

By conflating the idea of Lilith with that of an airplane and placing this iconography alongside the notion of Atziluth, Kiefer allows multiple readings. The cosmic struggle between forces of light and forces of dark in the cabala offer interpretations of the streamers and the streams of paint as literal emanations, symbolizing a basic tenet of the mystical writings. The streamers suggest that the plane is dive-bombing and letting out contrails, or has been hit and is streaming debris and smoke, calling to mind the bombing raids and air battles of World War II. Kiefer has frequently used the image of the airplane, and created a large-scale lead sculpture in the form of an airplane, *Melancholia*, also of 1990.

Other words, some partially obscured and numbered as if in a list, appear to the left of the airplane. The word *Azira* is scrawled on a scrap of cardboard attached to a lump of lead that dangles from the plane's longest lead streamers. The name *Berija* appears on the right wing of the airplane, and to the right and bottom of the airplane. Berija is the surname of the Russian secret police officer Lavrentija Berija, who ordered the deaths of more than 4,300 Polish officers in the forest of Katyn in 1940. The atrocity was long blamed on the Germans. In 1990, the Soviet Union admitted ordering and carrying out the killings, using German bullets to implicate the Nazis. This revelation was an important step in the reconciliation of Germany's responsibility for atrocities during World War II.

Born in Bavaria just two months before the final European battle of World War II, Kiefer studied informally in the early 1970s with Joseph Beuys (p. 122), who encouraged him to paint. Kiefer is also widely known for his large-scale woodblock prints, photography, and artist's books, usually taking the form of huge, sand-encrusted folios of distressed photographs. LW

Felix Gonzalez-Torres

American, b. Cuba 1957–1996

Untitled (The End)
1990
Offset prints on paper
22 × 28 × 22 in. (55.9 × 71.1 × 55.9 cm)
Restricted gift of Carlos and Rosa de la Cruz;
and Bernice and Kenneth Newberger Fund
1995.111

The universal sense of loss, love, and generosity evoked by the work of Felix Gonzalez-Torres is related to the artist's personal experiences, although his art is not strictly autobiographical. Issues related to AIDS, which took the life of his partner, Ross, and ultimately his own, inform much of his work, yet social and political references are secondary to the powerful ways in which his work suggests the transience of life.

Although his art, taking the form of stacks of paper, piles of candy, strings of lightbulbs, and billboards, shares formal similarities with earlier minimalist works, its conceptual framework relates more to postmodern ideologies of the 1980s and 1990s. Audiences were shocked and amused when the stack pieces, including *Untitled (The End)*, were first exhibited at the Andrea Rosen Gallery in New York in 1990. With these works, Gonzalez-Torres consciously overturned the traditions of art making to challenge the notion of art as a commodity and to subvert conventional rules and ideas about the precious nature of art objects. Viewers were encouraged to take a sheet from one of the many stacks such as *Untitled (Lover Boy)* and *Untitled (Blue Cross)*. The commercial paper and ink Gonzalez-Torres used were easily replenished, refuting the notion of a unique and handcrafted art object. In *Untitled (The End)*, a stack of white paper with a black border bleeding onto the edge, the framed blank white space suggests a place for the projection of ideas and memories. As the title intimates, the black edge may allude to mortality and the end of life.

Gonzalez-Torres's candy pieces, such as *Untitled (Portrait of Ross in LA)* (1991), which began concurrently with the stacks around 1989, are personal memorials to the suffering and death of the artist's partner. Each work is made of hundreds of pieces which, when separated from the group, become something new — a trace or memento of the larger work. The works represent a cycle of depletion and abundance, a metaphor for life and death, but they are also gifts or offerings to the public. Gonzalez-Torres considered these works complete when someone took a sheet of paper or piece of candy.

His other works, such as a large billboard of an image of an empty bed that was displayed around Manhattan and sculptures made of strings of lightbulbs, further exemplify themes of loss and remembrance. For his lightbulb pieces, Gonzalez-Torres specified the number of bulbs to be used, but left the arrangement or hanging unspecified. He did not make sketches or work in a studio; rather he would execute his ideas and display them for the first time in a gallery as an experiment. He also avoided forming a strong attachment to his works, imbuing them with an element of detachment. In a manner likened to Zen philosophy in its profound simplicity, Gonzalez-Torres's art reflects difficult lessons about detaching from the fear of losing what we value most. JRW

Cady Noland

American, b. 1956

Chainsaw Cut Cowboy Head
1990
Silk screen on aluminum with rope,
roll of tape, and cigarette box
60 × 60 × 19¼ in. (152.4 × 152.4 × 48.9 cm)
Gift of Susan and Lewis Manilow
1999.36.a – d

Cady Noland scrutinizes the exploitive side of the mass media. In installations and freestanding assemblages she has exhibited steadily since the mid-1980s, she exposes and reflects on how the media objectify, humiliate, and violate the privacy of people. Her installations, which often resemble mock public spaces and recall combinations of such disparate structures as children's jungle gyms and the gallows or fenced-off construction sites and crime scenes, allude to the combination of innocence and guilt that churns the mill of tabloid investigation and spectatorship. Her incorporation of found objects is similarly deliberate. Car tires, horse saddles, exit signs, chain-link fences, bungee cords, and scaffolding serve as metaphors for access and denial of access in her work; items such as beer cans, shopping carts, and silk-screened appropriations of newspaper and magazine images recall various kinds of consumption. Noland's titles — such as My Amusement, Sham Rage, Surrounded!!!, The Poster People, and Horror on the Hill — mimic sensational headlines.

Precursors for Noland's works are early 1960s images by Andy Warhol (p. 66), such as his Disaster series and views of Jackie Kennedy as a mourning widow. Noland's subjects are often the famous or infamous — movie stars, politicians and their spouses, "fallen" public figures, outlaws, celebrity criminals, terrorists, and victims — including Jackie Onassis, Lee Harvey Oswald, Betty Ford, and Patty Hearst — or stereotypical characters, such as cowboys, that appeal to voyeuristic impulses and a desire for limitless frontiers. The main component of Noland's assemblages is usually a silk-screened media image on an aluminum panel, leaning against the wall or propped up by a stand resembling a picture-frame backing. This form of flat sculpture counters the notion of sculpture as a voluminous object and conjures the false fronts of stage sets. The monochrome of the silk-screened images further adds to their sense of irreality.

Chainsaw Cut Cowboy Head is one of a number of freestanding works in which Noland has used cowboys and related references from Western films. It is also one of many such assemblages with holes or gashes in the aluminum panel, suggesting the violence of the story associated with the image and the violation of content occurring in the creation of stereotypes and media narratives. In this case, the holes in the figure's eye and ear humorously echo the figure's missing teeth, as well as the decapitation represented by the sculpture as just a "head." The Marlboro brand cigarettes recall the lone Marlboro Man used in the famous advertising campaign. Noland's big-sky country is the magazine layout, where the graphic designer's use of a role of masking tape may parallel the cowboy's lasso in its capture of imagery. A P

Ken Warneke

American, b. 1958

The Tyranny of Everyday Life
1990
Oil and acrylic on Masonite
41¾ × 35¾ in. (106 × 90.8 cm)
Gift of Mrs. M. A. Lipschultz,
Mr. and Mrs. E. A. Bergman, Nathan
Cummings, Grace and Edwin Hokin,
and Mrs. Richard L. Feigen by exchange
1991.24

The Tyranny of Everyday Life epitomizes the Kafkaesque quality of Ken Warneke's work. This allegory of compartmentalized, alienated, modern life is expressed in the form of a male figure whose body is gruesomely yet comically transformed into a murky, cloudlike formation of ambiguous substance — perhaps a heap of intestines or, as others have suggested, feces. A bureaucratic plumbing system, clogged with household objects that represent mundane, domestic activities, flows through the figure, whose expression is as blank as his features are precisely defined. Each vignette takes place in a psychologically and physically isolated white space, connected to other activities within the same tableau only mechanically, without any apparent larger purpose. The "wallpaper" background contrasts starkly with the simple, almost crude shapes and muted coloration of the superimposed pipe network, suggesting a disparity between this character's real life and his fantasy life, one that undoubtedly exacerbates the "tyranny of everyday life" for him.

This painting is one of a series Warneke initiated in 1988 in which purple figures metamorphose into insects with large, blankly staring human heads. The figures — including a locust-woman, spider-man, centipede-woman, termite-man, and cockroach-man — are portrayed against similar rococo-patterned, colored backgrounds. Each work in the series presents a different facet of the existential bankruptcy engendered by a technologically driven, utilitarian modern world, which Warneke depicts as a de-evolutionary force that turns people into insects. These darkly humorous portraits of the human condition recall the work of H. C. Westermann (p. 54) and Jim Nutt (p. 120), Warneke's predecessors in the Chicago art world.

Although many of Warneke's other painting series do not deal specifically with the theme of modernity, other aspects of this series represent ongoing concerns and methods in his oeuvre. His interest in portraying the absurdity of life lived robotically, for instance, comes across in another body of work he began in 1986, in which the figures of men and women are portrayed grabbing and flailing about each other's bodies in aimless, alienating sex acts that Warneke based on images from pornographic magazines. Warneke began painting figures in purple monochrome around 1986 as well, because of the color's contradictory associations with both the exalted side of life, as in the case of royalty, and the violated side of life, as in the color of bruised flesh.

Since his first recognized series of the mid-1980s, Warneke has thrived on the combination of opposites. A recurrent example is precisely rendered human facial features with indeterminate expressions. In a series begun in 1991, Warneke extended this aspect of his work by making paintings that are collages of facial features associated with certain ethnicities, races, and sexes. Painstakingly painted in numerous layers, these facial composites have an eerily dissonant quality. Warneke has employed such psychological disorientation in all of his work thus far — whether it involves a skewing of body parts or a slight mismatch in the relationship of figures to one another. In *The Tyranny of Everyday Life*, the dissonance is manifested both in the separation of figures and in the hybrid form of the central figure. AP

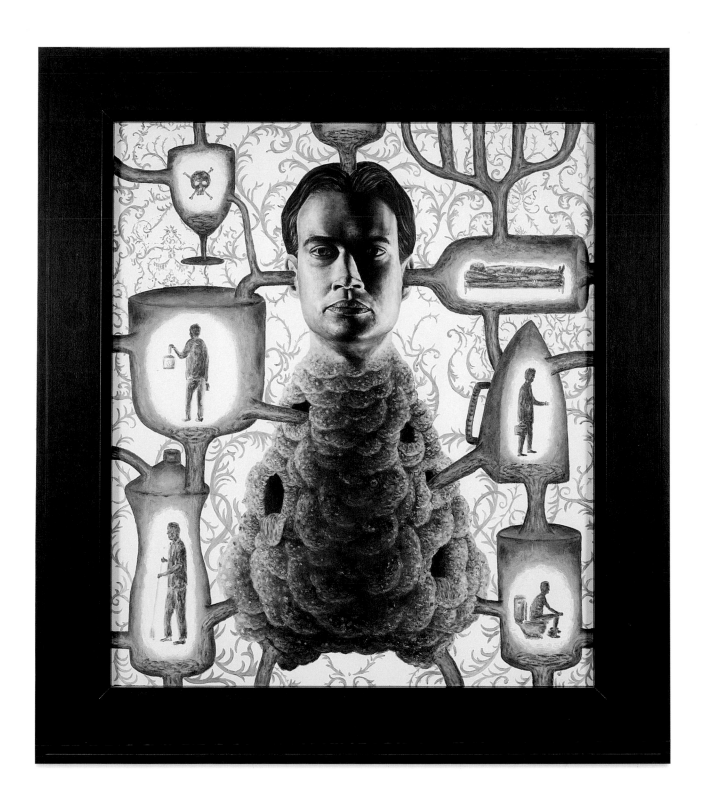

Mike Kelley

American, b. 1954

Mike Kelley explores how people assign value to objects by incorporating banal elements into his conceptual performances, paintings, sculptures, drawings, photographs, banners, and installations, often attempting to expose the dirty — and often, in Kelley's view, repressed — side of desire. Part of a generation of artists active in Los Angeles that included Chris Burden (p. 224), Paul McCarthy (b. 1947), and Charles Ray (b. 1953), Kelley focuses on the psychological power of art, presenting the converse side of America's clean and disposable consumer culture by incorporating pathetic and abject objects, such as discarded dolls. He infuses his work with an attitude reminiscent of adolescent rebellion that he says stems from his strict Catholic upbringing in a suburb of Detroit.

Throughout his career, Kelley has addressed various controversial subjects, including childhood sexuality, the relationship between creativity and criminality, and the hypocrisy of religion and politics, often using familiar forms,

including stuffed animals, cartoons, and brightly colored banners. Kelley first used old stuffed animals in *More Love Hours Than Can Ever be Repaid* (1987) and subsequently in installations such as the *Empathy Displacement* series, as well as an album cover for Sonic Youth's *Dirty* (1992).

Kelley uses handmade stuffed animals from secondhand stores to investigate the source of their value. Is it the materials and the time (or "love hours" as Kelley calls it) put into crafting the objects? Or are the objects valuable because of the human attributes and emotion projected onto them by the viewer? Kelley seeks to disrupt the commonly held associations of toys and stuffed animals with the purity of childhood in his provocative and often scatological installations. For Kelley, dolls symbolize adults' projection of idealized children and childhood, rather than nostalgic or romantic tokens of memory or the loss of innocence. Once used or dirty, such dolls are no longer useful and thus discarded, representing waste and death.

Craft Morphology Flow Chart
(details) 1991
Dolls and figures, gelatin silver prints, acrylic on paper, folding banquet tables, and folding card tables
Dimensions variable
Gift of Lannan Foundation
1997.41

Craft Morphology Flow Chart undermines the emotional effects of stuffed animals by pseudoscientifically categorizing 114 figures into formal typologies based on materials and construction techniques. The scientific model signals the idea of study and examination as Kelley suggests that we observe and study these objects to understand why they were thrown away. Each of the thirteen tables is devoted to a category of stuffed animal, such as sock monkeys, humanoids, aquatic figures, and crocheted dolls, and arranged by type, starting with humanoids and ending with the crocheted figures. Kelley measured sixty toys with a ruler and photographed them. The black-and-white images displayed on the wall document their comparative lengths. Additional figures that do not fall within one of the categories are placed on smaller tables, and a drawing by an archeological illustrator of the group of sock monkeys completes the installation. With the possibilities of emotional attachment thwarted, the objects are reduced to their negligible material value. By using such common materials, Kelley attempts to subvert the value systems of all commodities, from art to goods and services, and urges viewers to confront and challenge their psychological reactions to the abject. JRW

223

Chris Burden

American, b. 1946

The Other Vietnam Memorial

1991
Steel, aluminum, and etched
anodized copper plates
176 × 119 × 119 in.
(447 × 302.3 × 302.3 cm)
Gift of Lannan Foundation
1997.23

Chris Burden first gained notoriety in the 1970s through performance pieces in which he used his body as the subject for extreme, often violent actions with near-fatal components. In *Shoot* (1971), Burden had himself shot at close range, in the arm; he was crucified on top of a Volkswagen in *Transfixed* (1974); and he induced near-drowning for *Velvet Water* (1974). Burden often implicated his audiences, allowing either their distress or passivity to dictate the duration of his actions as in *Bodyworks* at the MCA in 1975.[1] Sculptural objects such as crucifixion nails, collectively titled *Relics*, almost always accompany footage of Burden's performances. These crucial fragments function as both evidence and souvenirs of the performance. Like Vito Acconci (p. 112), Burden is concerned with creating psychologically rich spaces that provoke and trouble the viewer. Burden has often incorporated architectural props such as raised platforms, ladders, and panels into his performances to suggest the uneasy, unequal relationship between performer and audience.

In *The Other Vietnam Memorial*, Burden addresses the emotionally charged genre of the public memorial, referring to Maya Lin's 1982 National Vietnam Veterans Memorial *The Wall* in Washington, D.C. Burden's memorial pays tribute to the three million Vietnamese killed during the war, mostly civilians, whose deaths have been largely overlooked by Americans. Standing more than thirteen feet high, *Memorial* is configured as a book with no ending, mirroring the continuance of grief caused by war and violence. The large, heavy copper pages, which the viewer may turn like the pages of a book, evoke the weight of the many victims of war. The imposing shiny metallic structure suggests sophisticated weaponry.

Formally, Burden's piece echoes aspects of Lin's memorial. The copper plates in *The Other Vietnam Memorial* are etched with millions of names, and as in the Vietnam Veterans Memorial, we are invited to touch and trace the letters in a gesture of grief and public guilt. But while Lin's monument identifies each victim by name, Burden offers an anonymous point of view. Because of the pervasive American media presence in Vietnam, the war was more often nameless than it was faceless. The vast number of Vietnamese casualties made it nearly impossible to compile an accurate list of names. Burden thus took 4,000 names from Vietnamese telephone books and altered them electronically to come up with a variety of combinations. According to James Tatum, Burden's work is "an imaginary monument to imagined victims, conceivable only because it is not designed for the public space that Vietnam Veterans Memorial occupies."[2] Burden's memorial uses the monument format with critical intent, illuminating the fatalities it is meant to ignore: nations hardly build war memorials to commemorate their enemy's dead. Like his earlier *Relics*, Burden's memorial attests to the reality of a past event, confirming the certainty of violence and staggering quantity of death while triggering America's collective memory and liability.
JS

1 For a discussion of this performance, see *Collective Vision* (MCA, 1996), p. 11.

2 James Tatum, "Memorials of the American War in Vietnam," in *Critical Inquiry* 22, no. 4 (summer 1996), pp. 639.

Alfredo Jaar

Chilean, b. 1956

Geography = War

1991
Duratrans, light boxes, 55-gallon metal barrels,
and water
Dimensions variable
Gift of Mr. and Mrs. M. A. Lipschulz, and
Maremount Corporation by exchange
1992.89.a–ddd

Alfredo Jaar has continually produced installations that incorporate light boxes, ubiquitous in advertising, to illuminate images of subjects that go unadvertised. In *Geography = War*, Jaar uses his characteristic light boxes and color transparencies, coupled with fifty-one fifty-five-gallon metal barrels, to dramatize the tragedy and horror of Western corporate exploitation abroad. Between August 1987 and May 1988, five Italian tankers carrying 35,000 tons of toxic waste arrived in Koko, Nigeria, where a farmer had agreed, for twenty-five cents a ton, or $100, to store the barrels on his land. Soon the drums began to deteriorate, leaking toxic waste into both the soil and water supply. The people of Koko, unwarned and ignorant of the effects of toxic waste, emptied some of the drums and used them to store food. Children played among them. Koko became a world of chemical burns, bleeding bodies, and contaminated food. The site has since become a research center for the study of toxic waste.

Jaar's installation consists of open barrels filled with water and lined with rust, suggesting danger and neglect. The viewer navigates the somber rows, peering over the barrels to catch the reflected photographic images from the light boxes suspended above the barrels. The faint outline of one's own reflection sometimes intrudes onto the picture plane, forcing the viewer to consider his or her role as both consumer and perhaps unwilling beneficiary in exploitative global economic practices.

226

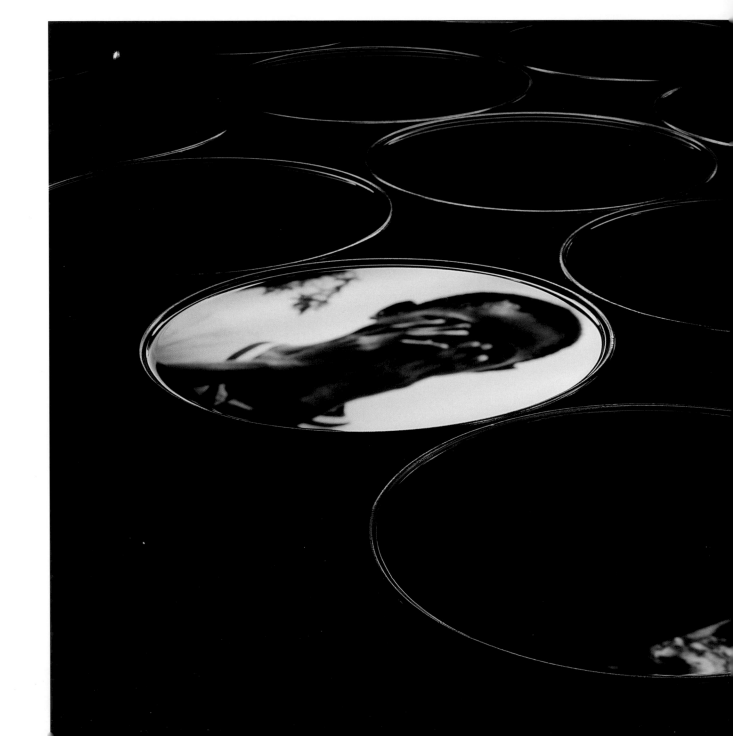

Jaar frustrates what Jacqueline Barnitz has called "the dramatic potential of the image"[1] through his unsentimental, almost banal rendering of Koko's citizens: a child covering his face with his hands, an elderly man standing, people digging through rubble.

Jaar's approach is in direct opposition to the often sensational and "compassionate" images found throughout the history of documentary photography. The Magnum Group, a prestigious Paris-based cooperative of photojournalists, embodied this latter approach. Founded in 1946 by Henri Cartier-Bresson and Robert Capa, among others, Magnum's heroic, exotic images appeared frequently in magazines such as *Life* and *Collier's*, revealing the exaggerated financial and cultural gap between America and the rest of the world.

Basing his work on firsthand research, Jaar often travels to the site in question. In August 1994, he traveled to Rwanda to work on The Rwanda Project, a four-year (1994–98) effort to question the lack of international intervention in the 1994 genocide that resulted in the mass murder of one million people. Jaar produced powerful public billboards showing the word *Rwanda* repeated many times, as well as a series of image-based installations.

Jaar's installation techniques are part of a larger phenomenon of artists working over the last twenty-five years who have often incorporated combinations of found objects, video, photographs, and text in complex multimedia works. Like that of Luis Camnitzer

(Uruguayan, b. Germany 1937) and Hans Haacke (German, b. 1936), Jaar's content sustains a commitment to global situations of urgency or neglect. Formally, his use of the photographic image in combination with found objects recalls the work of Felix Gonzalez-Torres (p. 216) and Ann Hamilton (p. 202). JS

1 Jacqueline Barnitz, "Conceptual Art and Latin America: A Natural Alliance," in *Encounters/ Displacements: Luis Camnitzer, Alfredo Jaar, Cildo Meireles*, exh. cat. (Austin: Archer M. Huntington Gallery, College of Fine Arts, University of Texas, 1992), p. 44.

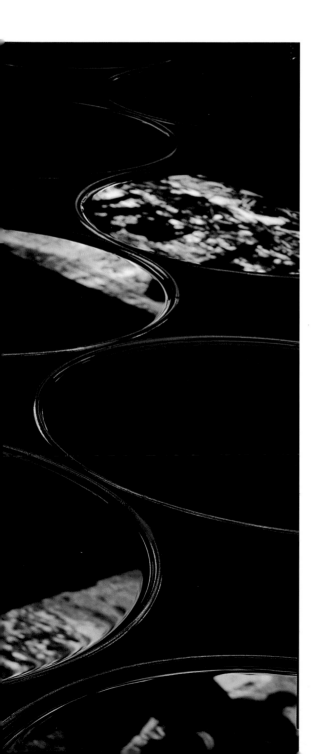

Joseph Kosuth

American b. 1945

No Number #6 represents Joseph Kosuth's fascination with language and the various rules associated with its use. One of the major figures in the development of conceptual art, Kosuth has been experimenting with text in neon since 1965, often exploring the disparity between what language claims to say and the meaning it evokes in different contexts. *No Number #6,* which reads "I am only *describing* language, not *explaining* anything," is part of a series of similar pieces. The red neon *No Number #5* states, "I can speak of experiencing a sentence," while *No Number #2* in blue neon reads, "The agreement of thought and reality consists in this, if I say falsely that something is *red*, then for all that, it isn't red." Kosuth does not presume to solve the contradictions of language with these pieces, but rather to draw attention to the limitations and possibilities of words. The influence of Viennese philosopher Ludwig Wittgenstein, particularly the exercises he designed to search for exact rules for language, is evident in Kosuth's work.

Kosuth has written several essays on the nature of artwork and what its performative function should be. He proposed the idea that art is wholly dependent on context and, by placing

No Number #6 (On Color, Blue)
1991
Neon tubing with argon gas and mercury
4 × 108 in. (10.2 × 274.3 cm)
Bernice and Kenneth Newberger Fund;
and National Endowment for the Arts Purchase
Grant
1991.5

something in a museum, it can be examined aesthetically, no matter how ordinary an object it may be. This idea explains his admiration for Marcel Duchamp (French, 1887–1968) and his experimentation with found objects. Kosuth disputes the formalist notion that people can have a natural and immediate experience of art, and that aesthetic judgments are involuntary and instinctive. He is concerned, rather, with the meaning infused by context and arrangement by the artist and by the viewer's awareness of how meaning is constructed.

Kosuth's intellectual interests affect his style far more than a particular artistic tradition or figure. Both Wittgenstein and Sigmund Freud influence his attention to language, and the way subjective experiences affect the significance of what is said. Kosuth takes deceptively simple statements or words and questions our assumptions and faith in the legitimacy of language to call attention to the signifying function of the artwork itself. He has demonstrated this interest in a variety of projects in which he juxtaposed artworks with written works, suggesting the notion that any text can and should be read for meaning, cultural or political significance, and individual sub-

jectivity. The artist has employed a variety of sources in his work — from literary figures like James Joyce to personalities in contemporary popular culture like Garry Trudeau and Lorena Bobbitt. Similarly, the written texts Kosuth examines span a broad range; he examines dictionaries, newspapers, and billboards for meaning, attempting to reveal how context can shift a neutral expression to something more sophisticated in structure. *No Number #6* embodies Kosuth's inquiry into the process of art and how we use language. MG

Jack Pierson
American, b. 1960

Scarface
1991
Metal and plastic sign lettering
Twenty-six parts, installed: 87 × 67 in.
(221 × 170.2 cm)
Gift of Zoe and Joel Dictrow
1997.76.a–z

Jack Pierson's work in various media captures a sense of loneliness, longing, and nostalgia in American culture. Drawing on a variety of myths, attitudes, symbols, and subtexts within popular culture, Pierson recovers discarded moments and objects and transforms them into meaningful experiences in impressionistic photographs, tableaux sculptures, ramshackle drawings, and sign-lettering assemblages. Pierson follows in the tradition of visual artists and writers of the past and present, such as Edward Hopper (American, 1882–1967), John Steinbeck, and Tennessee Williams, in portraying the wistful and crumbling grace of the urban and rural American landscape. In addition, his work incorporates frequent allusions to homoerotic desire with its romanticized images and coded references to gay culture.

Scarface is a unique variation on Pierson's signature sign-lettering works, most of which use a variety of found sign letters of differing shapes, sizes, and designs to create words and phrases or, recently, names of pop icons from years past. In these works, Pierson uses text as a sculptural element to evoke emotional states, suggesting a stylistic affinity with more radical forms of typography such as punk rock album designs or the darker connotation of anonymous ransom notes. *Scarface* departs from an immediately readable use of the letters by presenting a jumbled visual field of colors and shapes. The arrangement forms a word puzzle in which the viewer finds words — such as "sure" or "rest" — within the loosely structured square of letters. The work resembles a similar field of sign letters that Pierson created in 1991 titled *Deuce Lingo*, a field of red cinema letters and numbers that presents a more uniform yet no less arbitrary range of symbols.

Scarface, in its ordered yet somewhat chaotic array of shapes and forms, recalls *Broadway Boogie Woogie* paintings of the early 1940s by Dutch modernist Piet Mondrian (1872–1944) in its evocation of the hustle and bustle of the urban scene. One also feels a sense of the confusion and directionless activity of city life in the uneven and disorganized letters. The title — the nickname of the infamous gangster of the 1930s, Al Capone — alludes perhaps to the nostalgia that the sign-letters evoke. The brusque arrangement of the letters portrays a sense of aggression, as if a listing of the end of the alphabet had been forcibly rearranged and interrupted by other letters. *Scarface* provokes consideration of codes and their use in society — such as passwords for speakeasies in Capone's era of prohibition or the slang used in urban subcultures today — in the hidden messages and words contained within its mixture of letters. DM

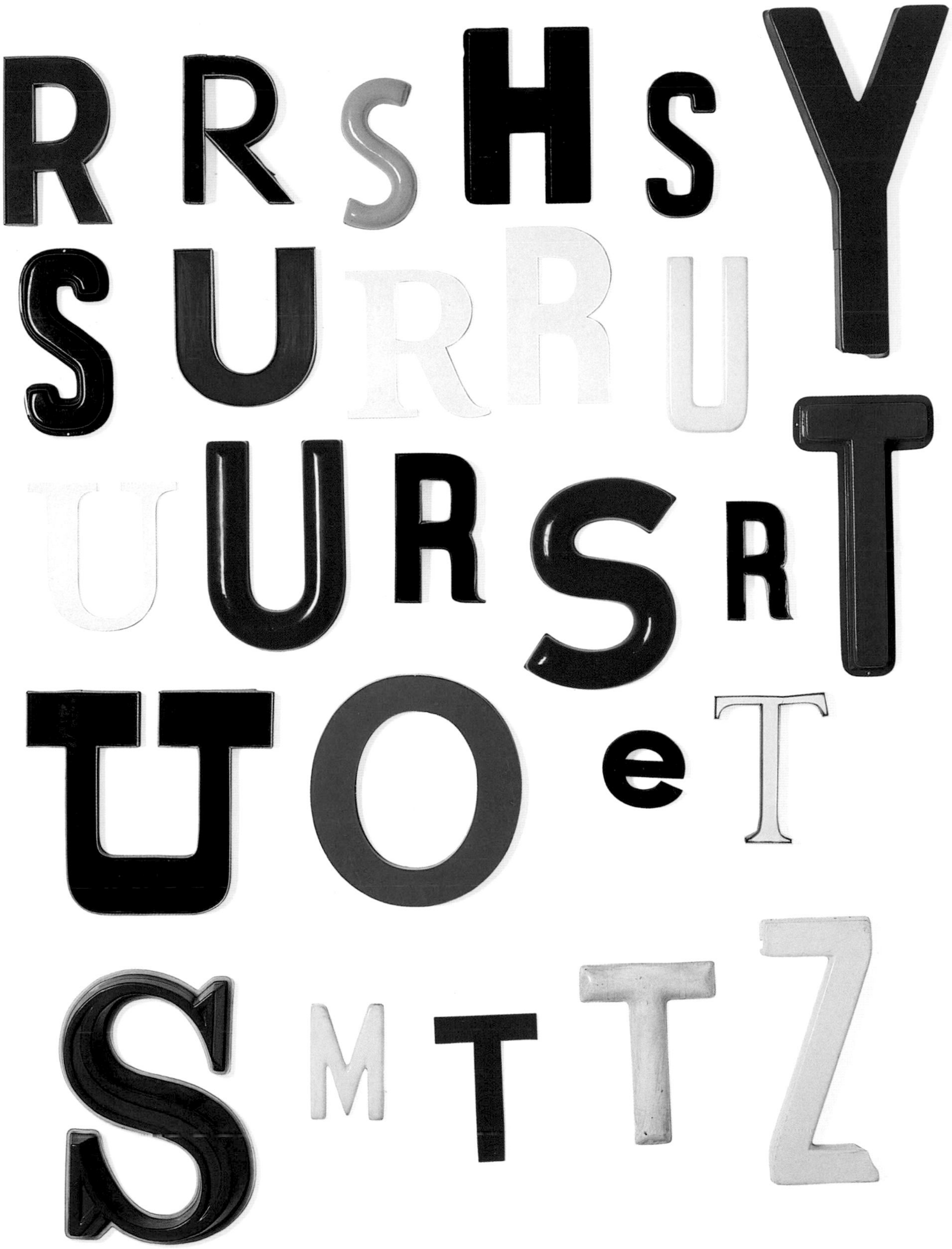
RRSHSY
SURRU
UURSRT
UOeT
SMTTZ

Gary Hume

British, b. 1962

Untitled
1991
Oil on panel
77 × 52 in. (195.6 × 132.1 cm)
Partial gift of Daryl Gerber Stokols
and Jeff Stokols
2002.78

Shortly after attending Goldsmith's College, London, in the late 1980s, Gary Hume took part in the seminal *Freeze* exhibition curated by artist Damien Hirst (British, b. 1965) in 1988. That exhibition launched the careers of so-called YBAs (Young British Artists), including Rachel Whiteread (b. 1963), Sarah Lucas (b. 1962), and Fiona Rae (b. 1963), who incorporated everyday and domestic materials into conceptually based art works. Gary Hume exhibited in *Freeze* his first series of paintings resembling doors — three large canvases coated in mint-green gloss paint — a subject he employed until 1992. Inspired by doors found in hospitals and other public buildings, Hume made a variety of monochrome and multicolored compositions with circles, squares, and rectangles, often evoking facial features. After 1988, Hume abandoned working with canvases and began painting on MDF board, Formica panels, and aluminum. The resulting works appeared more like sculptural objects than representations of doors. He expressed the metaphoric meaning of a door when he said "the door paintings are meant to evoke a sense of the future because a door is about moving in and out of the present into another place."[1]

Hume made the doors with a highly reflective household gloss paint that reflects the viewer's form onto the surface of the painting, while the paint also appears to change depending on the light. With variations of single and multipaneled doors and an idiosyncratic palette of saturated, acidic colors, including pink, tan, blue and brown, gray, and primary colors, as in *Untitled*, Hume began to explore the psychological and emotional effects of color. Recalling the first New York exhibition of Hume's doors at Matthew Marks Gallery, Brooks Adams described them as a "distinctive brand of hard edged, pop-inflected, quasi-absurdist, neo-Minimalism: slickly rendered, high-gloss painting of campy colours in 'mod' decors that at first glance appear to be geometric abstractions but turn out to be portraits of specific doors."[2]

Some works in the series have evocative titles such as *Incubus*, *Dream*, and *More Fucking Values* (all 1991). These works helped Hume establish his vocabulary as a painter and lay the groundwork for his ongoing innovations in form, abstraction, color, and subject matter. His later work employs a similar style of flattened forms and blocks of color but, unlike the doors, depict narrative, figurative, and decorative subjects including notorious radio disc jockey Tony Blackburn, actress Patsy Kensit, fashion models, and angels, as well as words, four-leaf clovers, and birds, among many other images. His everyday subjects become unfamiliar, with their flattened, abstracted forms and charged unnatural colors.

Hume's work recalls that of other British painters, such as Michael Craig-Martin (b. 1941), Patrick Caulfield (b. 1936), and Julien Opie (b. 1958) who work with stylized and simplified forms abstracted from reality and quoting directly from daily life and popular culture. J R W

1 Quoted in *Gary Hume Paintings*, exh. cat. (London: Institute of Contemporary Art; Bern, Switzerland: Kunsthalle Bern, 1995), p. 58.

2 Brooks Adams, "Thinking of You: An American's Growing, Imperfect Awareness," in *Sensation: Young British Artists from the Saatchi Collection*, exh. cat. (London: Royal Academy of Arts, 1997), p. 37.

Buzz Spector

American, b. 1948

Malevich: With Eight Red Rectangles

1991
Painted wood and books
96 × 80 in. (243.8 × 203.2 cm), variable depth
Ed: 1/3
Restricted gift of LaSalle Bank
1993.31.a – i

Buzz Spector is a poet who became a visual artist; his work is influenced by that of nineteenth-century French poet Stephane Mallarmé and Marcel Broodthaers (p. 116). Spector's use of text, literature, and books in his visual art and artist's books is in many ways an extension of his earlier writing. In 1978, he founded the Chicago-based journal *WhiteWalls*, which features poetry and artists' writings. His work has affinities to that of Ann Hamilton (p. 202), about whom he has written, in its physical manifestation of systems of knowledge and texts.

Like other conceptual artists who use unconventional and everyday materials to make statements about society, Spector has chosen books as his primary subject and object. His alterations of found books are metaphorical gestures that examine their relevance in contemporary culture. Spector addresses various issues related to books: specific texts, the role of the author, books as art, books as containers of knowledge, book collecting, and books as links between the present and past. His manipulations take on many forms, including tearing, carving, painting, embellishing, and stacking. Spector has also worked with photography, collage, postcards, and sculpture, in such works as the MCA's *Mallarmé* (1987/88) and *Malevich: With Eight Red Rectangles,* both of which focus on knowledge and the relationships among history, nostalgia, and contemporary life.

Malevich: With Eight Red Rectangles is based on the painting *Suprematism (with Eight Red Rectangles)* (1915) by Russian artist Kasimir Malevich (1878 – 1935). Malevich's avant-garde philosophy advocated a new state of consciousness, and even revolution, through the use of abstract forms reflecting pure feeling, devoid of external representation. Spector's work asserts the impossibility of replicating the impact of Malevich's original gesture by emphasizing the displacement of images, such as Malevich's pure abstractions. Similarly, the meaning discovered in books is remembered long after the books themselves are read. *Malevich: With Eight Red Rectangles* replicates the composition of the original painting with a large, freestanding white wall with recessed cutouts and eight corresponding red rectangles made with red books placed on the floor. The spine of each book contains information about the original painting usually found on a gallery label or checklist, such as the artist's name, title, date, medium, dimensions, and owner, with Buzz Spector's name and "1991" printed on the spine of one additional book. The pages of each book are blank, suggesting how in the context of Malevich's nonobjectivity, even emptiness is content. J RW

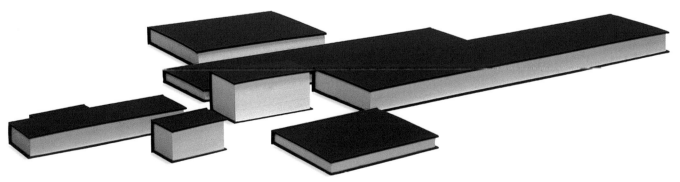

Sigmar Polke

German, b. 1941

Sigmar Polke's distrust of aesthetic and political dogmas pervades his work. Resisting the conformity of using one set of materials or a certain historical style, Polke creates his paintings using combinations of disparate techniques, such as drawing, collage, photography, silk screen, and installation elements, as well as a wide range of materials, including blankets, commercially printed fabrics, glass, scrim, resins, paint, unstable chemical compounds, minerals, and even meteorite dust. He appropriates imagery from such disparate sources as comics, advertisements, news photography, abstract expressionism, and eighteenth- and nineteenth-century prints. Evidence of Polke's distaste for purist aesthetics can be traced to his early work of the 1960s. In one well-known example, *Higher Beings Command:*

Paint the Upper Right Corner Black! (1969), Polke parodied the authoritarianism of then current trends in abstract painting and minimalism by painting a black triangle in the upper right corner of the canvas, which is blank except for the title stenciled at the bottom. In the context of Polke's education, even his choice to make paintings was contrarian. Joseph Beuys (p. 122), his instructor at the Kunstakademie Düsseldorf in the 1960s, habitually told his students that it was no longer acceptable to continue to paint in the post-Auschwitz period because painting was too withdrawn from engagement with life. Polke's art challenged this prescription by pushing the limits of what could define a painting further even than Robert Rauschenberg (p. 70), who greatly influenced Polke.

Ashes to Ashes

1992
Oil and ink on printed fabrics and velour
95½ × 157¾ in. (240 × 400.7 cm)
Gerald S. Elliott Collection
1995.78

236

Through the various stages of his work, Polke has consistently addressed the theme of conformity and its various manifestations — from the rationalism of capitalism, resulting in mass-production and mass-consumption, to the rationalism of post-Enlightenment political systems, which ironically brought about brutality on an unprecedented scale. Polke's interest in mass-production and consumption was sparked by his exposure to American pop art, especially that of Andy Warhol (p. 66) and Roy Lichtenstein (1923–1997). Polke's references to political systems became prominent mainly in the 1980s and 1990s, when his paintings also tended to reach a grand scale, like the one in the MCA Collection. Polke's work from this period includes references to Germany's Nazi past and the division between East and West Germany through imagery of watchtowers, prison bars, and concentration camps. In concert with these grim subjects, Polke often uses patterned fabrics. Though their combination is unexpected, both types of imagery convey social conformity and the inevitable link between the state and domestic existence, public and private spheres. Since the 1980s, Polke's work has counteracted various forms of aesthetic and political dogma through the cultivation of unpredictability and disjunction.

Ashes to Ashes exemplifies Polke's ongoing concern with the dualities of transformation versus rigidity, idiosyncrasy versus conformity. The title itself encapsulates these themes. The saying "ashes to ashes" refers to the cycle of life and death, in which the differences between things are obliterated in the beginning and the end of the life cycle. The imagery of the painting echoes the theme of sameness in life and death in its juxtaposition of rows of skulls with rows of polka dots. The artist frequently uses polka dots, which simultaneously represent sameness and, through a pun on Polke's last name, the individuality of the artist. The sameness exemplified by the rows of skulls and dots contrasts with the lavishly applied, irregularly shaped and spattered white paint, which the artist often employs as a way of literally and metaphorically breaking underlying patterns. A P

237

Hiroshi Sugimoto

Japanese, b. 1948

Hiroshi Sugimoto's interest in time has been the basis for his work for more than twenty years. His photographs examine the notion of metaphysical time in history, nature, and human constructions in an age in which time is one of the most valued commodities.

Photography depends on a certain relationship with time, namely the split-second condensation of a moment onto film. Sugimoto uses an eight-by-ten-inch camera to create black-and-white images of one of the four series of subjects he has worked on throughout his career — museum dioramas, empty movie theaters, a twelfth-century Buddhist temple in Kyoto, and seascapes — in addition to a series of architectural photographs begun in 1997.

Sugimoto took photographs of dioramas at the New York Museum of Natural History as an investigation into the frozen yet infinite sense of time presented by the taxidermic animals, artificial plants, and painted scenery. Similarly, he has photographed historical and popular effigies in wax museums. His movie theater series, in which he photographed the interiors of 1930s art-deco cinemas, as well as drive-in movie theaters, shows interiors with blank illuminated screens. Sugimoto's exposure time for each photograph was equal to the length of each film, effec-

Time Exposed
1991
Photolithographs and text on paper
and aluminum portfolio
Fifty-eight parts, each: 13⅞ × 18¼ in.
(35.2 × 46.4 cm)
Unnumbered first edition of 500
Gift of Maremont Corporation by exchange

South Pacific Ocean, Maraenui
1990
1993.25.19

Black Sea, Ozuluce
1991
1993.25.44

238

tively erasing the moving image and creating an eerie reversal of the light's source. His 1988 series *Hall of Thirty-Three Bays* depicts forty-eight nearly identical gilded sculptures of the Bodhisattva Kannon lined up in multiple rows in a Buddhist temple in Kyoto, presenting a spiritual notion of time. The repetition of the sculptures creates an infinite pattern of sameness. Only upon close inspection do reflections of light and shadows convey minute differences. His series of day and night seascapes also demands concentrated viewing to notice the intricacies and subtle differences between the photographs; from

afar they create a panorama of the horizon across time and continents.

The title of this series of seascapes, *Time Exposed*, refers to the representation of time in the images, as well as the effects of time on another edition of prints that Sugimoto has exhibited outdoors under the bleaching effects of the sun and natural effects of age. Sugimoto began the seascape series in 1980, when, as he has stated, he imagined an ancient man standing before the sea and naming it, thus using language to separate his inner and outer world. Traveling from places such as the Caribbean to the Black Sea to the Sea of Japan, Sugimoto consistently frames

equal parts of sky and sea with the horizon line at the center. The images are formal comparisons of the sky's gray tones, the hazy fog, and the water's wave pattern, reflecting the influence of minimalism. The horizon suggests looking ahead toward an unknown future.

The concept of this meditative work has been compared to the twenty-four-hour silent film, *Empire,* by Andy Warhol (p. 66) of the Empire State building. Unlike *Empire*, Sugimoto's timeless seascapes are devoid of any references to culture, industry, or technology, suggesting a meditation on the spiritual strength of nature and time. J RW

Sea of Japan, Hokkaido
1986
1993.25.6

Mediterranean Sea, Cassis
1989
1993.25.13

239

Lorna Simpson

American, b. 1960

Flipside
1991
Gelatin silver prints and Plexiglas plaque
Installed, approximately: 51¼ × 69¾ in.
(130.2 × 177.2 cm)
Ed: 3/3
Partial and promised gift from
The Howard and Donna Stone Collection
2002.62.a–c

Bio
1992
Internal dye diffusion transfer
process prints and engraved
Plexiglas plaques
Installed, approximately: 98 × 162 in.
(248.9 × 411.5 cm)
Gift of Maremont Corporation by exchange;
purchased through funds provided by
AT&T NEW ART/NEW VISIONS
1992.90 a–u

Lorna Simpson pairs visual signifiers such as hairstyles, black skin, and African masks with text to consider the symbolic construction of race and identity. She conveys racial classification with subtle language, using, in the words of Coco Fusco, "highly coded symbols of racial identity, or . . . of one's identification with blackness."[1] Simpson focuses on gender, making explicit the unspoken aspects of the African-American female experience. Like Jenny Holzer (p. 176), Barbara Kruger (p. 178), Adrian Piper (p. 204), and Carrie Mae Weems (American, b. 1953), Simpson is both informed by and examines social and cultural critique.

In 1991, Simpson began to examine how hair operates as a signifier of racial difference. In *Flipside* she juxtaposed a photograph of an African-American mask that recalls a 1960s American flip hairstyle with a photograph of the back of a woman's head and neck, whose hair is very short and curly. The text on the plaque reads "the neighbors were suspicious of her hairstyle," suggesting that the woman's refusal to assimilate into white cultural definitions of beauty by keeping her hair natural makes people question her role as a modern American woman. It is surprising to see the flipped hair on an African mask, since the origins of the style are assumed to be Caucasian. Simpson often photographs the back of her subjects to avoid the particulars of individuality and to focus on common issues that affect African Americans.

In *Bio*, stylized, repeated Polaroid photographs articulate a collective medical history. A figure stands with his or her back to the viewer, arms folded and

240

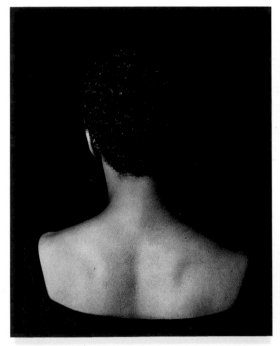 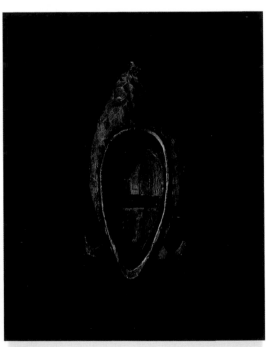

the neighbors were
suspicious of her hairstyle

hands in pockets, suggesting, perhaps, the impatience and restlessness of waiting in a hospital. Simpson locates her eighteen blood-red prints within one of three categories: "Biopsy," "Biography," and "Biology." Like John Baldessari (p. 198) and Bernd and Hilla Becher (p. 174), her arrangement of photographs depends on a vocabulary of comparative imagery. Spare and provocative, Simpson's work comes from a legacy of conceptual photography in which a series of images illustrates an idea.

A shrewd melancholy permeates *Bio*. Shoes represent the lower half of the body; one is missing above the Biopsy label, as though it were removed during surgery. Situated on plastic plaques, the wry observations "Choose general and you might lose a shelf of memory" and "Choose local and you'll remember too much," refer to anesthesia, but also function as veiled references to cultural amnesia regarding the deaths of black people in America over the last century. The black shoe boxes beneath the texts can be seen as figurative coffins, reinforcing the sense of loss.

Like Piper and Weems, Simpson initiates a complex discourse on race, siting the historic and contemporary institutional racism of American hospitals. "Bled to death outside of a hospital 60 years ago," refers to the period when, under Jim Crow laws, white hospitals would not treat black patients. In 1937, the jazz singer Bessie Smith bled to death outside a Memphis hospital after being refused treatment following a serious car accident. "Bled to death inside of a hospital last year" evokes vio-lence in black communities, while "tendency to keloid" refers to the raised scars more common in dark than light skin. The label "tendency to be prescribed antidepressants," under the "Biology" category, is characteristic of Simpson's way of revealing social constructs. Far from having the scientific authority of truth, this label comments less on the despair of black patients and more on the inclination of the medical establishment to make racist assumptions. JS/JRW

1 Coco Fusco, "Uncanny Dissonance: The Work of Lorna Simpson," in *English is Broken Here: Notes on the Cultural Fusion in the Americas* (New York: The New Press, 1991), p. 101.

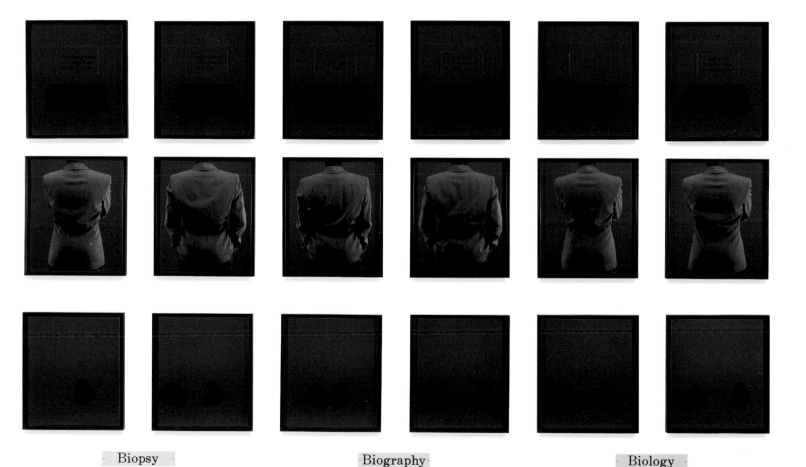

Biopsy   Biography   Biology

Glenn Ligon

American, b. 1960

Untitled

1992
Softground etchings, aquatint, spit bite, and
sugar lift on paper
Four parts, each: 25 × 17¼ in.
(63.5 × 43.8 cm)
Ed: 42/45
Gift of Sandra P. and Jack Guthman
2000.14.a – d

Since the 1980s, Glenn Ligon has explored the racial politics of language in a body of work that includes paintings, drawings, prints, installation works, and photographs. He examines the contemporary African-American experience, focusing especially in these five works on how racial identity has been represented in American historical documents and literature. His reinterpretations of these texts illustrate how authorship and literacy have shaped and reflected the course of race relations in the United States, giving primacy to the need for self-representation.

Ligon stencils short passages from significant African-American and European writers' texts in his paintings, lithographs, and etchings. He examines how the repetition of words conveys poignant ideas about black identity within a white dominated culture, often using first-person accounts that reflect broader experiences within the African-American community. In *Runaways* and *Narratives*, Ligon presents himself as the subject acting as a bridge between the past and present.

In *Untitled (Study #1 for Prisoner of Love)* the phrase "We are the ink that gives the white page a meaning" appears

repeatedly; at the bottom of the painting the black words against the white background become smudged. This text was taken from *Prisoner of Love* (1986) by Jean Genet. Similarly, in *Untitled: Four Etchings*, Ligon uses two succinct, charged sentences from Zora Neale Hurston's 1928 essay "How it Feels to be Colored Me": "I feel most colored when I am thrown against a sharp white background" and "I do not always feel colored." The other two etchings in the portfolio display the prologue of Ralph Ellison's first novel, *Invisible Man*

(1952),[1] in black text on a black background. As the words become illegible at the bottom of the prints, Ligon emphasizes the ideas in Ellison's text — namely that black people are treated as invisible in American society — rather than the words themselves.

In *White #11*, a canvas that from a distance looks completely black, Ligon confounds the viewer's expectation of text's legibility. He stenciled multiple phrases in black oil stick to cover a white background. The layers of words make the text, adopted from the book *White* written by British cultural historian Richard Dyer, nearly indecipherable,

undermining its purpose to communicate and creating an opposition between the way the painting looks and its title. Dyer's book addresses the representation of "whiteness" in popular films. The allover black canvas of *White #11* recalls monochromatic minimalist works by artists such as Agnes Martin (American, b. Canada 1912) and Ad Reinhardt (p. 64), yet in contrast to their strictly formal interests, Ligon directly addresses cultural histories and identity.

He uses historical images and texts to pose questions about the legacy of racism in America, recalling Kara

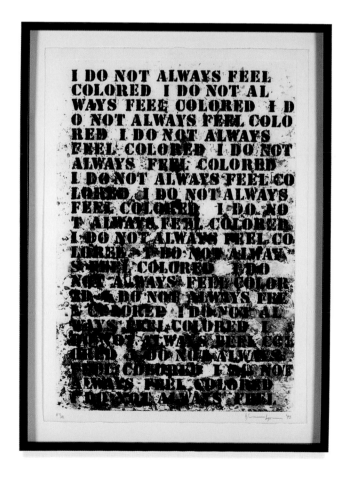

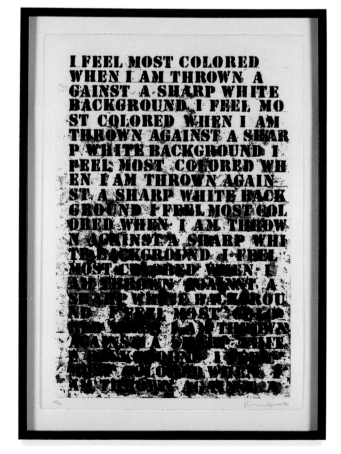

243

Walker's controversial silhouettes of pickaninny images (p. 272) and Lorna Simpson's combinations of photographs and searing texts (p. 240). The *Runaways* series refers to antebellum posters made by slave owners to announce the disappearance of slaves. These announcements described the slaves' physical attributes in the hope that they would be captured and returned. Ligon juxtaposed images, such as men with top hats with slaves in shackles, from slave narratives, newspaper ads, and antislavery pamphlets with texts written by friends who were asked to describe Ligon's appearance. In the late nineteenth century, during the post–Civil War era, former slaves wrote narratives to convey their personal experiences and to expose the reality of racism in the Northern "free" states. These narratives have increasingly been perceived not only as valuable historical documents, but as precursors to modern African-American literature. The prints in the *Narratives* series borrow the visual style of the title page of these documents through the use of font, design, and language, illuminating the racism inherent in the language. Multiple editions of narratives were sold in the tens of thousands at antislavery meetings. Often, a white man would write the title page, giving credibility to the black author, which Ligon mimics in the print "Black Like Me."

Ligon demonstrates the poignant effect of words to reflect individual stories as well as broader historical narratives, often providing the insight and emotion lacking from traditional versions of history. JRW

1 "I am an invisible man. No, I am not a spook like those who haunted Edgar Allan Poe; nor am I one of your Hollywood-movie ectoplasms. I am a man of substance, of flesh and bone, fiber and liquids — and I might even be said to possess a mind. I am invisible, understand, simply because people refuse to see me."

Untitled (Study #1 for Prisoner of Love)
1992
Oil on canvas
30½ × 20 in.
(77.5 × 50.8 cm)
Gift of Sandra P. and Jack Guthman
2000.11

Narratives
1993
Portfolio of etchings with chine collé
Nine parts, each:
28 × 21 in.
(71.1 × 53.3 cm)
Ed: 18/45 aside from 10 artist proofs
Gift of Sandra P. and Jack Guthman
2000.13.a–i

Runaways
1993
Portfolio of lithographs on paper
Ten parts, each:
19¾ × 23¾ in.
(50.2 × 60.3 cm)
Ed: 25/45 aside from 10 artist's proofs
Gift of Sandra P. and Jack Guthman
2000.12.a–j

White #11
1994
Oil paintstick on linen
84 × 60 in.
(213.4 × 152.4 cm)
Gift of Sandra P. and Jack Guthman
2000.9

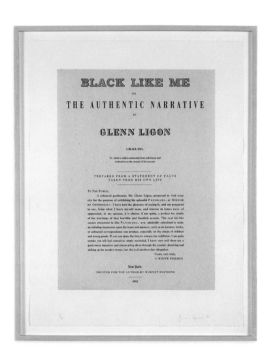

Andres Serrano

American, b. 1950

The Morgue (Knifed to Death I and II)
1992
Silver dye-bleach prints
Two parts, each: 49 × 59½ in.
(124.5 × 151.1 cm)
Ed: 2/3
Restricted gift of Carol and Douglas Cohen;
Lynn and Allen Turner; Ruth Horwich;
H. Gael Neeson and Stefan T. Edlis; and Gerald
S. Elliott by exchange
1996.4.a–b

Although the title of this pair of photographs alludes to a brutal murder, the images avoid prurient violence or idealizing sentimentality, conventional polarities for depicting death in popular fictional and journalistic media. Andres Serrano consistently chooses subjects and combinations of subjects toward which there is a deep-seated cultural ambivalence. His success in tapping into cultural taboos was demonstrated in 1989, when he became the target of controversy over National Endowment for the Arts funding as a result of his photograph *Piss Christ*, of a mass-produced crucifix immersed in urine.

In *The Morgue (Knifed to Death I and II)*, he features a subject's hands and wrists, where forensics experts have made incisions for an autopsy. The incisions are important because they have a purely pragmatic, clinical significance, while at the same time evoke a displaced form of stigmata. The dead body's denigration to the status of scientific specimen and its implied deification are represented simultaneously in these images. The arrangement of the photographs reveals another duality. With the hands appearing to reach toward each other, Serrano expressly intended this pair of photographs to resemble the barely touching, extended fingers of God and Adam in Michelangelo's *The Creation of Adam* on the Sistine Chapel ceiling.

This work is one of many within Serrano's 1992 series entitled *The Morgue (Cause of Death)*. For three months, Serrano photographed approximately ninety-five percent of the bodies that passed through a particular morgue.

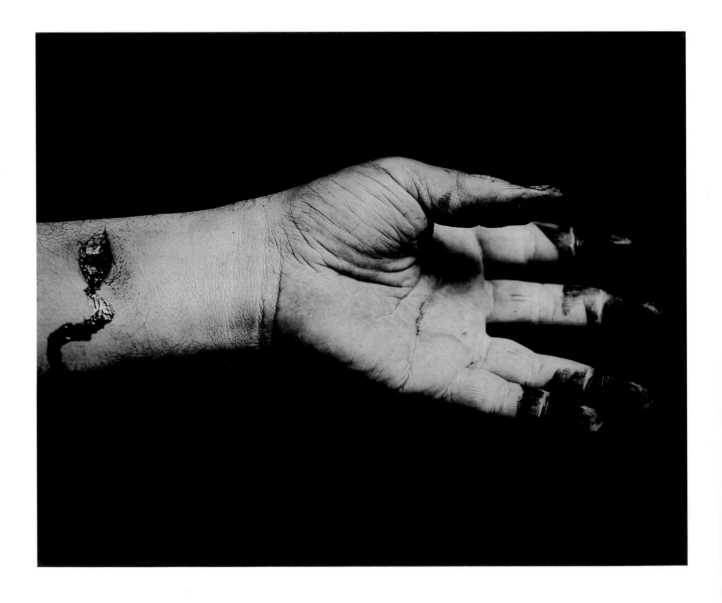

Some died violently — "stabbed to death," "hacked to death" — others accidentally or from disease — "drowned to death," "fatal meningitis." The morgue authorized Serrano's access on condition that neither the morgue nor the subjects be identifiable in his work. Serrano used this limitation to exploit the duality of impersonality versus intimacy toward his subjects. While he concealed the identifying features of the subjects, and cropped the images so that the body appears abstracted, Serrano, with his rich and sensual articulation of the subject's body, simultaneously reveals the subject's individual attributes.

Serrano began his first series, entitled *Bodily Fluids*, in 1985, delivering highly abstracted and theatrical depictions of such fluids as blood, milk, semen, and urine — all loaded with religious, scientific, and sociological significance. Serrano prefers subjects that invite mixed, and often conflicting, responses, attraction as well as repulsion. In the past, he has focused on religious statuary submerged in bodily fluids, formal portraits of homeless people, abstracted portraits of masked Ku Klux Klansmen, portraits of Catholic clergy in full regalia, and extreme close-ups of guns. Serrano strives to present his subjects in unexpected ways, so that we will see them anew and recognize our habits of stereotyping the subjects by good and evil, high and low. In part, his choice of religious subjects results from his conflicted view of his Catholic upbringing.

Since Serrano's aesthetic and symbolic models derive from painting traditions — he has expressed an ongoing fascination with Renaissance and Baroque painting — it is significant that he has chosen photography as his main medium. Photography allows him to conjure the modern aesthetics of scientific documentation as well as the theatricality of contemporary film, television, and print media — the primary distributors of cultural mythology in our time. Groundbreaking photographers of the early 1980s, such as Cindy Sherman (p. 138), Richard Prince (p. 166), and Barbara Kruger (p. 178) were influential for Serrano, in helping to secure photographers' equal stature to painters in the contemporary art world. AP

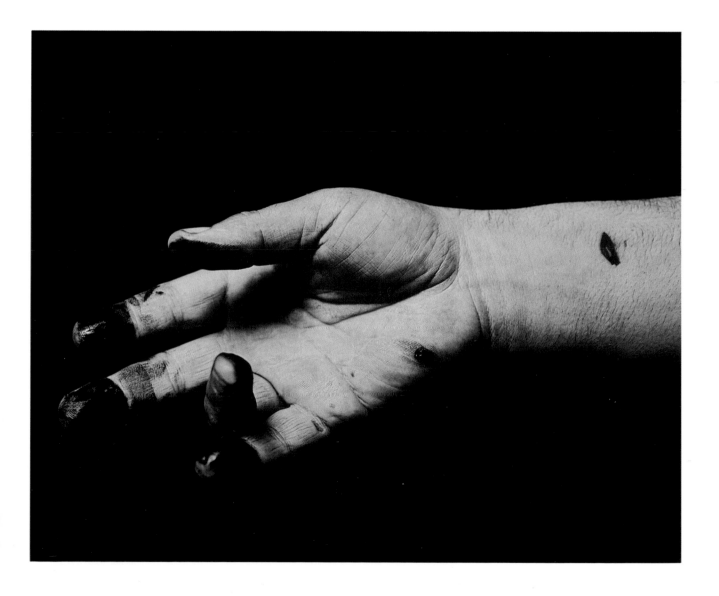

247

Tatsuo Miyajima

Japanese, b. 1957

Counter Circle No. 19
1993
LED, IC, wooden panel, and electrical wire
2¼ × 164 in. diameter (5.7 × 416.6 cm)
Bernice and Kenneth Newberger Fund, and restricted gift of Werner Kramarsky, Jackie Rabin, and Dedrea and Paul Gray
1997.74.a–d

For Tatsuo Miyajima, time is a metaphor for human behavior and beliefs. How people mark time — through science, technology, religion, and philosophy — reflects the way they define their place in society and the universe. Through particular measures of time, people organize their personal and collective lives and history. In his body of work, the artist incorporates references to Eastern and Western, ancient and modern concepts of time. Miyajima's works embody three principles he believes follow the nature of the universe itself: to keep changing, connect with everything, and continue forever.

The artist explicitly stated these principles in the program of a 1987 exhibition at the Gallery Lunami in Tokyo, in which he displayed three works representing each of the three concepts. By the end of 1987, Miyajima began using what would subsequently become his primary means of creating works that enact those core principles — the programmable LED digital counter. Since his international debut at the Venice Biennale in 1988, where he first exhibited works using this medium, Miyajima has become best known for his installations in darkened rooms of LED number counters in a variety of parts and spatial configurations, programmed to count at individual rates. They all embody his principles by offering a constantly changing display, having no terminal point, and, through the repetition of the same range of numbers in every part, represent the interconnectedness of things. His simpler installations involve singular shapes and fewer variables, such as displays of the counters in stationary circles or lines of counters on floors and walls. The more complicated works involve greater numbers of variables, including movement. In *U-Car* (1995), hundreds of digital counters counting one through nine at individual rates are

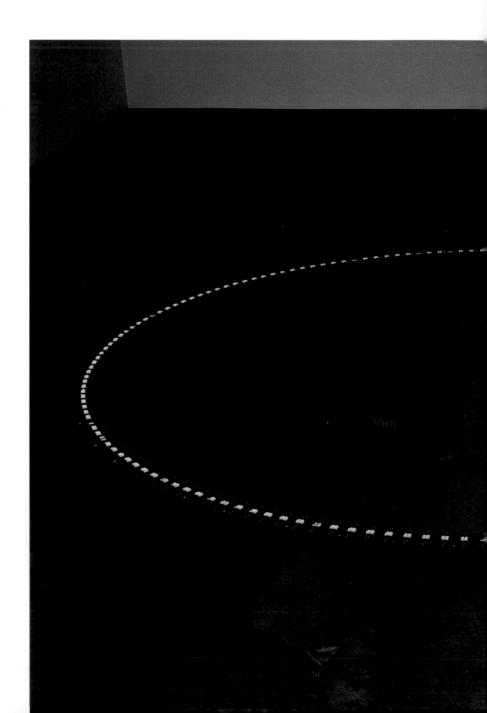

connected to battery-charged mechanisms programmed to change direction when they detect an obstacle. Whether his works have fewer or more variables, they combine elements of control and randomness, a translation of Miyajima's interest in chaos theory, which rejects determinism and attempts to explain irregularity and aperiodicity in nature.

Counter Circle No. 19 is one of a number of "counter circles" Miyajima has produced since 1988. In these works, Miyajima creates a circle — an ancient and universal symbol of eternal return — using modern LED technology. Miyajima's use of transcultural metaphors explains his refusal to use the figure zero in his counters. As the artist claims, zero has no counterpart in nature and is a specifically Western invention. When his counters reach nine, they darken momentarily before starting again at one. *Counter Circle No. 19*

consists of 184 green LED units arranged in a circle on the floor. Each unit counts one through nine, but the variable rates of the counters result in constantly changing and unique combinations of numbers. The different rates of the counters suggest a nonlinear notion of time. While all the counters count the same series of digits in the same order, many of them present different numbers at any given moment, a variation that the artist considers a metaphor for the uniqueness yet connectedness of the individual in society and the universe. As a societal model, this work also represents a utopian society, harmoniously ordered but without hierarchies. Defying the use of numbers to rank people and things, the circular structure of the work gives each number equal physical prominence in the installation. A P

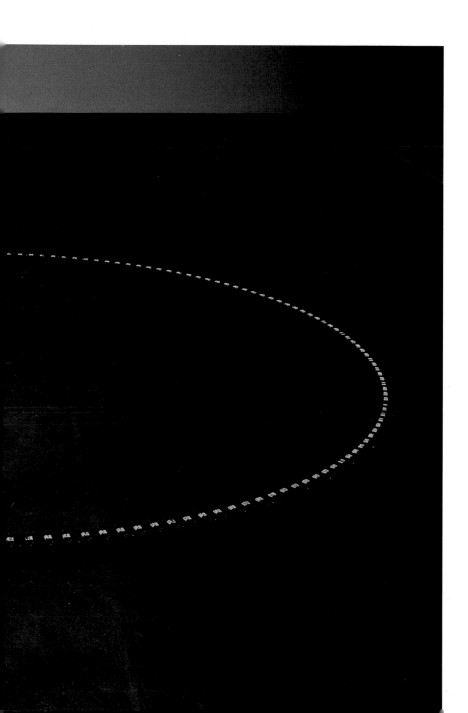

Stan Douglas

Canadian, b. 1960

Stan Douglas's video installations combine exhaustive research, evocative imagery, and rigorously conceptualized spatial arrangements to examine the psychological effects of media and popular culture on and in society. His works adopt the style and structure of a particular mass media form — such as a television advertisement or a Hollywood film — in order to dissect the way that form creates meaning and presents information to an audience. As such, his work offers a subtle political critique of how the mass media define and redefine history. Douglas uses space tactically in his installations, often incorporating multiple projections and complex sonic arrangements to emphasize the meaning of his work, creating an experience that affects the viewer on a physical as well as psychological and intellectual level.

Evening, which was commissioned by The Renaissance Society at The University of Chicago in 1994, addresses the shift in the late 1960s in the tone of television evening news reporting from an authoritative voice to what was described as "happy talk news": the delivery of even the most horrible and tragic events in an upbeat and comforting manner. (Importantly, other changes in news broadcasts, such as the transition from

Evening

1994
Color video installation
20 minutes
Dimensions variable
Ed: 2/2
Restricted gift of Frances and Thomas Dittmer and Bernice and Kenneth Newberger Fund
1996.40

250

a combination of black-and-white field footage with color studio footage to an all-color presentation, also occurred at this time.) The ABC network affiliate in Chicago, WLS, was the first to implement the "happy talk news" format in its broadcasts. This development occurred almost simultaneously with two of the most significant historical events in Chicago in the 1960s: the riot during the 1968 Democratic National Convention and the assassination of local Black Panther leaders Fred Hampton and Mark Clark in 1969.

Evening bridges an intuitive gap between these shocking local and national events from Chicago in the 1960s and the simultaneous development of a method of news broadcasting that served to anaesthetize television viewers to the grim realities presented to them. Douglas has fictionalized three television stations in the work, WBMB, WAMQ, and WCSL — sly allusions to the three real Chicago network stations WBBM (CBS), WMAQ (NBC), and WLS (ABC) — all of which are shown in different stages in the use of "happy talk news." The anchors, played by actors in the staged broadcasts, cover three different news stories: the murder of Hampton and Clark, the trial of the "Chicago Seven" (the political activists said to have incited the riot at the convention), and H. Ross Perot's failed mission to Hanoi to return American prisoners of war. A cacophonous soundtrack of the three anchors mediated by three "sound-domes" focuses the sound for the viewer. A troubling discrepancy develops between the increased "reality" of the visual news coverage (signified by the introduction of color broadcasting and the availability of live news footage) and the "mediated" presentation of the news being covered by the anchors. DM

William Kentridge

South African, b. 1955

Drawings for the film
History of the Main Complaint
1995–96

Charcoal and pastel on paper
27½ × 47¼ in. (69.8 × 120 cm)
Gift of Susan and Lewis Manilow
2001.25

Charcoal and pastel on paper
47¼ × 63 in. (120 × 160 cm)
Gift of Susan and Lewis Manilow
2001.26

William Kentridge's combinations of film, drawing, sculpture, prints, music, theater, and opera are distinguished by his intense reflections on the nature of public and private memory, individual and collective responsibility, the construction of history, and the shifting nature of identity. Though Kentridge has been working in Johannesburg since the mid-1970s as a graphic artist, filmmaker, theater director, actor, and set designer, he was largely unknown outside of South Africa until the dismantling of apartheid, and, with it the end of many countries' cultural boycott of South Africa in 1994. Though he is best known for his short animated films, Kentridge considers the activity of drawing at the basis of all of his work. He has stated, "I believe that in the indeterminacy of drawing, the contingent way that images arrive in the work, lies some kind of model of how we live our lives. The activity of drawing is a way of trying to understand who we are or how we operate in the world. It is in the strangeness of the activity itself that can be detected judgment, ethics, and morality."[1]

The centerpiece of Kentridge's extensive body of work is a series of eight narrative animated films that the artist has called *Drawings for Projection* (1989–1999). The films follow two characters — Soho Eckstein, the self-absorbed

wealthy mine owner and land developer who always wears a pin-striped suit, and Felix Teitlebaum, the romantic artist who is always shown nude and has an affair with Mrs. Eckstein — through their struggles in late apartheid and post-apartheid Johannesburg. Alter-egos of each other as well as of the artist, Soho and Felix reflect the disparity between individuals and the social and historical forces in their lives. Kentridge's films grow out of his successively reworked charcoal drawings, which he films and refilms through hundreds of alterations as he physically moves between paper and camera. The original images, buried beneath subsequent marks and erasures,

no longer exist except on film. The final image from each sequence, unless it is destroyed in the process, remains as an independent drawing. This laborious and deliberately rudimentary process, as well as the diaristic elements, evoke the artist's presence in these very personal, haunting narratives.

Felix in Exile, one of Kentridge's most memorable films and the fifth in the *Drawings for Projection* series, was made during the moments just preceding the first democratic elections in South Africa. It depicts the absorption of bodies into the bleak earth of Johannesburg's East Rand, underscoring the landscape's role as a reservoir of memory and history. Kentridge has said that

Felix in Exile questions "the way in which the people who had died on the journey to this new dispensation would be remembered — using the landscape as a metaphor for the process of remembering or forgetting."[2]

The fourteen drawings in the MCA Collection were used in the making of the film *History of the Main Complaint*, the sixth in the *Drawings for Projection* series. The work was commissioned for the exhibition *Faultlines: Inquiries into Truth and Reconciliation*, which was held in Cape Town in 1996. Like much of Kentridge's work, the film addresses the

issues of memory, truth, and reconciliation that gripped South Africa during the immediate postapartheid period, especially with the establishment of the Truth and Reconciliation Commission — public hearings held to recover lost histories, to make reparation to those who had suffered, and to provide amnesty. The film depicts Soho Eckstein in a coma lying in a hospital bed after an automobile accident and probes the interior landscape of the body and the streets of Johannesburg simultaneously. It tells a story about coming to terms with one's past actions and questions whether the

acceptance or acknowledgment of some type of responsibility will ultimately change one's behavior. *History of the Main Complaint* surveys Soho's guilt-ridden memory and his body, using powerful images of anatomy and medical equipment (specifically modern technologies that have the ability to look beneath the skin — MRIs, sonars, CT scans, and X rays). The film evolved from a sketch Kentridge was making for an opera project. Commissioned by the Kunsten-FESTIVALdesArts in Brussels to collaborate on a Monteverdi opera, he was experimenting to see whether there was a rapport between his

charcoal animation technique, Monteverdi's seventeenth-century music, and these twentieth-century medical systems.
SB

1 "Carolyn Christov-Bakargiev in conversation with William Kentridge," in Dan Cameron, Carolyn Christov-Bakargiev, and J. M. Coetzee, *William Kentridge* (London: Phaidon, 1999), p. 35.

2 Carolyn Christov-Bakargiev, *William Kentridge* (Brussels: Société des Expositions du Palais des Beaux-Arts de Bruxelles, 1998), p. 90.

Drawings for the film
History of the Main Complaint
1995–96

Charcoal and pastel on paper
22 × 30 in. (55.9 × 76.2 cm)
Gift of Susan and Lewis Manilow
2001.36

Charcoal and pastel on paper
31 ½ × 48 in. (80 × 121.9 cm)
Gift of Susan and Lewis Manilow
2001.29

Charcoal and pastel on paper
31 ½ × 47 ½ in. (80 × 120.6 cm)
Gift of Susan and Lewis Manilow
2001.35

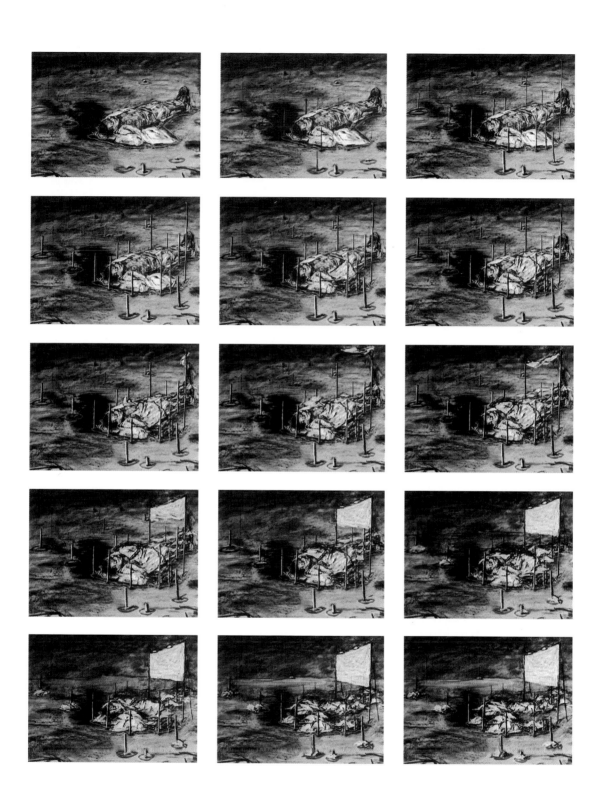

Sequence from the film *Felix in Exile*
1994
Color video projection
8 minutes, 43 seconds
Dimensions variable
Ed: 9/10
Gift of Susan and Lewis Manilow
2001.23

Iñigo Manglano-Ovalle

American, b. Spain 1961

Balsero
1994
Inflatable raft and inner tubes, marine vinyl, air-craft cable, and color video installation
Dimensions variable
Gift of Carlos and Rosa de la Cruz
1996.1

Le Baiser (The Kiss)
1999
Color video installation
Dimensions variable
Ed: 1/3 aside from 1 artist's proof
Restricted gift of the Sara Lee Corporation
1999.56

Iñigo Manglano-Ovalle employs aspects of minimalism and conceptual art in his video-based installations to examine how everyday objects and buildings reflect perceived social ideals. As an immigrant to the United States from Spain, some of his work emanates from personal experience around issues of identity. More recently he has undertaken a series of works in video and photography in which he considers the heroic aspirations of modern architecture.

Balsero is a multimedia installation that combines video and audio elements with an inflatable raft, clear vinyl, and steel cables. Its title refers to someone who travels by a *balsa*, a raft like those often used by illegal immigrants from Caribbean islands to the United States. A video monitor placed at the end of the raft shows a man from the back who alternately opens and clasps his hands behind his head. He appears to be floating in the raft, as he faces an endless view of the ocean and the sound of waves plays over speakers. Promise and possibility of a new life seem to await on the horizon. A close-up of human skin vibrates on a monitor that is connected to the raft by a suction cup and cable, a reminder of the many displaced people who undertake this journey. Steel cables suspend the raft and connect it to names of politically unstable cities (Hong Kong, Port-au-Prince, La Habana) as well as traditional U.S. immigrant ports of entry (New York, Los Angeles, Miami) stenciled on the walls. On a separate wall, the words Rio Bravo and Rio Grande—the Mexican and American names, respectively, for the river that borders Mexico and Texas—are connected by steel cables to two inner tubes partially hiding a second monitor face-up on the floor.

Balsero and other works by Manglano-Ovalle from the mid-1990s address various dichotomies surrounding the issue of immigration: legality and illegality, individual and state, upper and lower classes. Community-based projects such as *Tele-Vecindario: A Street Level Video Project* and the *Chicago City Life Low Rider Car Club* reflect these interests and often incorporate collaborative elements. *Tele-Vecindario*, for example, established a public video channel in the artist's neighborhood in Chicago, and has become a thriving project that has endured after his involvement ended. Manglano-Ovalle has since broadened the scope of his art beyond the Hispanic community, and taken on new formal and social issues including complex ethical questions in the fields of genetics, social engineering, and architecture.

Le Baiser (The Kiss) explores the relationship between the pervasive modern international style of Ludwig Mies van der Rohe's Farnsworth House (1945–1950) in Plano, Illinois, and domestic everyday living. The house, Mies's first private house in the United States, was designed for Dr. Edith Farnsworth as a weekend home outside Chicago, although its severe minimal design demanded too much maintenance for its owner. The elevated platform, white horizontal planes, and large glass windows create a structure that seems to float above the ground. In *Le Baiser*, Manglano-Ovalle created a suggestion of the house with a metal frame hanging from the ceiling that viewers can walk through. One of the windows is substituted with a video projection of the artist washing the windows in a caring gesture, like a kiss, in an attempt to humanize the "less is more" aesthetic of the home. Inside the house is a projection of a female DJ playing the song "Kiss," a remix of a guitar solo by the 1970s rock band Kiss, composed by sound artist Jeremy Boyle (American, b. 1975). The close physical proximity yet emotional distance between the DJ and the window washer reflects the strained relationship between Mies and Dr. Farnsworth due in part to the architect's unyielding vision that created a tension between theoretical and practical living spaces, while at the same time addressing issues of class in relationship to modernist residences. Manglano-Ovalle used the Farnsworth House as just one example of his examination and evaluation of twentieth-century social ideas in the twenty-first century. J R W

Jeanne Dunning

American, b. 1960

Study after "Untitled Landscape," 1987
1994–1995
Gelatin silver print with artist's frame
12 × 13 in. (30.5 × 33 cm)
Partial and promised gift from
The Howard and Donna Stone Collection
2002.26

The Extra Hair 2
1994
Silver dye-bleach print mounted to Plexiglas
with artist's frame
32½ × 16¾ in. (82.6 × 42.5 cm)
Ed: 3/3
Partial and promised gift from
The Howard and Donna Stone Collection
2002.28

The Pink
1996
Silver dye-bleach print mounted to Plexiglas
with artist's frame
74 × 52 in. (188 × 132.1 cm)
Ed: 2/3
Restricted gift of Collectors Forum
1996.8

Since her first solo gallery exhibition in 1987, Jeanne Dunning has been best known for her photographs and video installations that employ disconcerting imagery to expose people's feelings about their bodies. Often, she explores opposing notions such as attraction and repulsion, normalcy and deviance, and indulgence and denial to arouse contradictory feelings and reactions. In 1988, the artist exhibited enlarged passport-style photographs of women with just enough hair above their upper lip to confuse their otherwise feminine appearance. Other works present more extreme deviations from bodily norms and ideals, such as *The Extra Nipple* (1994), in which a woman presents a blemish on her outstretched tongue that resembles a nipple, and the *Extra Hair* series of photographs (1994), which show unusually long pubic hair dangling

from female torsos. In the video *On a Platter* (2000), a model stands steadfast while a substance leaks from her blouse onto a nearby table. The deadpan style of presentation accentuates the strangeness of the video.

Dunning's method of arousing the viewer's emotions through the suggestion of displaced or monstrous body parts recalls the practices of surrealists from the distorted photographs of female torsos by Man Ray (American, 1890–1976) to Hans Bellmer's drawings and sculptures of displaced and multiplied female body parts (p. 37) to the famous object of Freudian displacement by Meret Oppenheim (German, 1913–1985), her sexually suggestive fur-lined tea cup. In its use of surrealist methods to explore the body as a site of gender stereotyping, sexual repression, and the uncanny, Dunning's work can be compared to that of contemporaries such

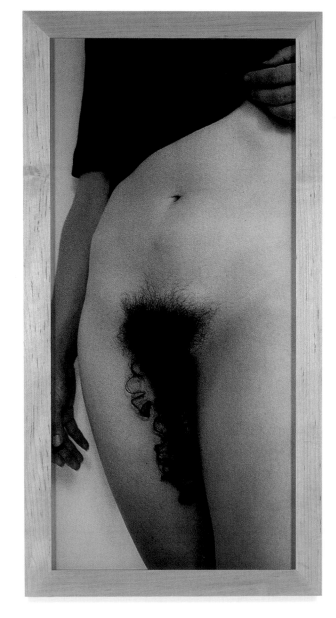

as Anne Wilson (American, b. 1949) and Ann Hamilton (p. 202) as well as Dunning's immediate precursor, Cindy Sherman (p. 138).

Dunning often composes extremely close-up photographs of body parts or fruits and vegetables that render them ambiguous but suggestive of intimate body parts. Her *Untitled Landscape* series (1987), for example, presents black-and-white images of mounds and strips of hair in varying shapes from indecipherable locations on the body so close up that they resemble examples of abstract landscape photography. *The Untitled Hole* series of the following year consists of enlarged close-ups of nostrils that vacillate between alluring abstract compositions and shockingly graphic representations of body parts.

The Pink is a prime example of Dunning's ability to make the familiar seem strange. The work was initially exhibited at Feigen Contemporary in Chicago in 1996 as part of an installation consisting of monochromatic six-by-four-foot photographs — *The Pink, The Yellow, The White, The Brown, The Red* — and a video monitor in the center of the room showing an infant repeatedly being fed and spitting food back out. The photographs show various vegetables and fruits, such as grapefruit, onions, and beets sitting in their juices. All of the photographs, which have since been dispersed as independent works, are extreme close-ups of their subjects that fill the entire composition, thus creating a shallow space reminiscent of the monochromatic abstract painting of the 1950s and 1960s. For Dunning's

generation, abstraction was associated with the advocacy of purity and reductionism in art. Her works violate the sanctity of art based on a reductionist rhetoric by evoking biological ooze and slime. In *The Pink,* the subject itself demonstrates the idea of breaking boundaries, with its bubbles and fluids flowing in and out of semi-porous membranes. The ambiguous imagery — is it luscious fruit or bacteria under a microscope? — is both seductive and repulsive. Dunning's desire to remind us of our bodies extends to the way she installs the work. The bottom of *The Pink* hangs one foot from the floor. This placement is a metaphor for her work's groundedness and contributes to the viewer's absorption in the image, which seems as though it is another body. A P

259

Jin Soo Kim

American, b. Korea 1950

Wall (from imprints)
1994–98
Steel and copper
78 × 78 × 12½ in. (198.1 × 198.1 × 31.8 cm)
Restricted gift of Robert and Sylvie Fitzpatrick, Roberta and Richard Lieberman, Sandra P. and Jack Guthman, Nancy A. Lauter and Alfred L. McDougal, Sukho and Yong Ja Kim, Antje and John Jelinek, Cleve E. Carney, Howard and Jacqueline Gilbert, and Susan and Robert Wislow
1998.54.a–f

Jin Soo Kim's *Wall (from imprints)* is a paradoxical structure, simultaneously dividing and uniting the surrounding spaces. While it forms a barrier, its transparency mediates between spaces. Each side is connected to the other through a delicate screen of hand-wrapped copper wires, calling to mind copper's function as a conduit of electricity. The warm glow of reflected light and tonal fluctuations in the copper soften the appearance of the rigid, cagelike metal grid. Kim gave the structure the semblance of animation, endowing it with human dimensions and a surrogate heart bundled inside its "breast."

Wall was first displayed in 1993 as part of a larger installation entitled *imprints*. Kim was invited to show her work in a 1994 exhibition at Atlanta's High Museum of Art titled *Equal Rights and Justice*, which commemorated the thirtieth anniversary of the death of Martin Luther King, Jr. For this exhibition, Kim chose to respond to the Los Angeles riots of 1992, during which racial antagonisms had manifested themselves in attacks on Korean-American shop owners and their property. For her installation, Kim collected interviews from African-American, Latino, and Korean-American residents of South Central Los Angeles and put paper fragments of the interviews, which she "wounded" with black graphite, onto steel panels that she wrapped with plaster "bandages." The works leaned against the walls like casualties, with rust from the steel bleeding through the bandages. The work in the MCA Collection derived from Kim's reworking of one of the structures she used for that exhibition.

Mending and healing have been themes in Kim's oeuvre since 1983, when she received her MFA from The School of The Art Institute in Chicago. Kim habitually uses discarded materials, including wire fencing, fabric scraps, broken pipes, rubber hoses, logs, sticks, and tires that she salvages from the street and abandoned buildings and yards. She ties, weaves, and wraps them in a repetitive process that she relates to rehabilitation (bandaging and swaddling) and preservation (burial and mummification). These processes are familiar to Kim, who worked as a hospital nurse until 1989. In the 1980s, she became known for works she called "environments" that engulfed entire rooms in dense, organic ganglia of found materials. Her works from the 1990s onward tend to be more geometric and systematically ordered, using grids and modular, architecturally legible structures as protective enclosures for found objects and scaffolds for wrapping and tying. Yet, throughout those years, Kim's works have retained an anthropomorphic quality. Her use of cloth against rusting metals recalls wounded bodies cared for and recuperated.

Kim's organic aesthetic and environmental approach dovetail with the traditions begun in the late 1960s of feminist art — in which the aesthetics of handcrafting and repetitive techniques associated with traditional women's work are exalted — and of process art. Kim's work is also grounded in her particular bicultural experience of industrialized societies. Raised in Korea in the 1950s and 1960s, Kim witnessed the introduction of an American machine culture of disposability to her home country, where it had been customary for people to reuse materials. When she moved to the United States in 1974, she experienced its industrial overproduction and waste firsthand. Kim's artistic process became a way to fuse the two cultures with which she continues to identify herself. AP

Judy Ledgerwood

American, b. 1959

Judy Ledgerwood's abstract paintings stem from color-field formalism and, like abstract expressionist works of the 1950s, examine notions of subjectivity and heroism. Her modernist inclinations are evident in the way she emphasizes the flat picture plane in order to investigate abstraction's roots and its relationship to beauty. The form of her paintings takes on an importance of its own, functioning independently of subject matter.

Driving Into Delirium is a large-scale painting representative of the kind of work Ledgerwood has been engaged in since the late 1970s. The viewer must stand back from the wide span of the work to view it in its entirety. The circular spots throughout appear to fall in slow motion, showcasing Ledgerwood's ability to use light, color, shape, and scale to suggest natural phenomena while remaining impenetrable and seductive. The pink, brown, and red shades evoke the body, suggesting skin, blood, excrement, and make-up. The painting is mostly a soft deep brown shade, marked all over with washed-out spots of a peach tone emanating through a thick chocolate-colored curtain. More dramatic are the circular spots of iridescent violet, bright siren red, and the daubs of lawn green, pink, and lavender paint that seem to be at once intentional and an afterthought.

Ledgerwood often seeks to explore the possibilities of aesthetic experience and the subjective response it can stimulate in a viewer. In her works, the eye must travel over a large canvas. The patience this process demands results in a kind of perceptual immediacy — the viewer feels as though he or she is being drawn in by the work. Like her predecessors in abstraction, Ledgerwood makes transcendent and personal inquiries in

Driving Into Delirium
1995
Oil and wax on canvas
72 × 144 in. (182.9 × 365.8 cm)
Gift of Donna and Howard Stone
2001.2

262

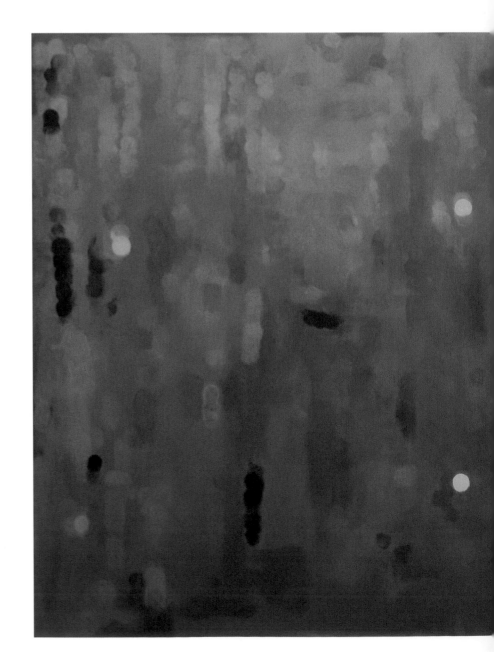

her art that are distinct from analytical reasoning. The resulting closeness between the artwork and the viewer is Ledgerwood's motive in inducing a sensual and aesthetic experience of the physical presence of the work.

Ledgerwood's painting has been compared to the work of such disparate painters as Barnett Newman (American, 1905–1970) and Brice Marden (p. 146) to landscape artists J. M. W. Turner (British, 1775–1851) and Caspar David Freidrich (German, 1774–1840). While her work is reminiscent of landscape paintings, Ledgerwood employs a more abstract and experiential mode aimed at the sublime. She has devised ways to subvert the typically masculine mark-making techniques of her predecessors, the abstract expressionists of the 1950s, who were concerned with the heroic and metaphysical possibilities latent in the artwork. To counteract what she calls "the male, exclamatory, ejaculatory mark,"[1] Ledgerwood uses a circular mark as a motif, allowing color and space to be less structured.

Art critic Michelle Grabner wrote about the uniqueness of Ledgerwood as an abstract painter in Chicago:

". . . there is still something more distinctive about Chicago abstraction, a nerve that separates it from activity on the coasts. . . Chicago's expansive geography, Bauhaus footing, and disposition for laboriously crafted surfaces combined with affection for the everyday, humanizes and makes colloquial a language Postmodernism made stale and cynical."[2]

Driving Into Delirium is an example of the kind of balance between surface beauty and emotional sensuality that characterizes Ledgerwood's particular brand of abstraction. M G

1 Judy Ledgerwood, "Speakeasy," *New Art Examiner* 23, no. 5 (January 1996), p. 14.

2 Michelle Grabner, "Lake Breeze: Referential Abstraction in Chicago," *New Art Examiner* 26, no. 1 (September 1998), p. 22.

Mariko Mori

Japanese, b. 1967

Birth of a Star

1995
3-D Duratrans, acrylic, light box, and audio CD
70³⁄₁₆ × 45¼ × 4¼ in.
(178.3 × 114.9 × 10.8 cm)
Ed: 1/2 aside from 1 artist's proof
Gift of The Peter Norton Family Foundation
1996.6.a–c

Sweeping advances in technology at the end of the twentieth century have inspired intriguing cultural transformations, from the ability to create highly realistic scenes with computer images to forms of music that make exclusive use of electronic devices. Artists in the 1990s have readily assimilated these new techniques to create works that frame the optimistic potential of advanced technology within the aesthetic traditions of the past. In her 1995 multimedia work *Birth of a Star*, Mariko Mori combines various elements of late twentieth-century culture, including computer-generated pop stars, fashion, and high-tech commercial presentation.

In this work, Mori transforms herself into a futuristic pop idol with plastic fashion accessories and a computer-generated makeover. It is accompanied by airy ambient music sung by the artist in Japanese. Mori's image reflects a range of art-historical and pop-cultural influences; it is simultaneously a cybernetic rendition of the famous painting by Sandro Botticelli (Italian, 1445–1510) and a monumentalized Japanese *anime* (animated film) or *manga* (comic book) character. (It eerily predates the creation of the computerized Japanese pop star Kyoko Date by one year.) The photograph's composition, which features a centrally placed figure who dominates the picture plane, is drawn from historical European modes of portraiture, while the method of presentation resembles the high-tech contemporary light-box format commonly seen in advertising.

Mori worked as a fashion model and studied fashion design prior to becoming an artist. The body of work immediately preceding *Birth of a Star* is largely comprised of photographs in which Mori posed on the streets of Tokyo costumed as a coquettish cyborg or a futuristic warrior from video games and comic books. Taking Cindy Sherman's *Untitled Film Stills* (p. 139) into the realm of sci-fi spectacle (and fulfilling the Warholian desire to become a machine) she presented a futuristic vision of femininity in this earlier body of work. *Birth of a Star* thus marks an important shift in Mori's career with its intense and exclusive use of computers to create otherworldly effects. This three-dimensional image anticipated Mori's ambitious and spectacular video installations such as *Nirvana* (1997) and *Dream Temple* (1999).

Mori's work combines elements from Eastern and Western cultures, often reflecting the artist's cross-cultural background as a Japanese-born woman who studied art in London and currently lives and works in New York and Tokyo. *Birth of a Star* was first shown in a 1995 solo exhibition of her work at Deitch Projects in New York, which was subtitled *Made in Japan*. This title cleverly alludes to Mori's ethnicity and to the popularity of Japanese products in the consumer culture of America in the 1980s. *Birth of a Star* celebrates this phenomenon while simultaneously calling attention to the synthetic shell of the celebrity's public persona: the "birth of the star" necessitates the development of a dazzling, elaborate masquerade to protect the vulnerable person within. DM

Tony Oursler

American, b. 1957

Tony Oursler portrays psychological disorders and distresses by animating inert objects with video projections of human faces along with uncanny recordings of human voices. Oursler's predecessors, Bill Viola (American, b. 1951) and Gary Hill (American, b. 1951), similarly explored the sculptural qualities of video, yet Oursler's influences are more related to his fellow Cal Arts alumnus and collaborator, Mike Kelley (p. 222). Oursler and Kelley, who formed the punk band The Poetics in the 1970s, use everyday found objects and materials in their work, a decidedly low-tech way to maintain a psychological attachment to the daily environment and popular culture. Kelley, for example, uses old rag dolls and folding card tables in works such as *Craft Morphology Flow Chart* (1991, pp. 222–23); Oursler uses floral-patterned fabric, dresses, and mattresses. The psychological tension in Oursler's work is heightened by the messages of despair and suspicion conveyed by the dolls and dummies that he uses as vehicles for exploring the way the mass media can distort our thinking.

In his work, Oursler seeks to illuminate the complex relationships among popular media and social realities such as crime, constructions of identity, and consumerism. He questions how simulacra such as television and movies influence our well-being and mental health by using video installations that aggressively engage viewers, often by subjecting them to shouted hostile phrases. In *Guilty,* a female figure is situated in a vulnerable position, trapped under a pink mattress. An empty pink dress serves as her body and her head is stuffed like a scarecrow's. A woman's face projected onto the compressed head yells accusatory remarks: "How could you want that? That's sick. That's

Guilty
1995
Color video installation, mattress,
dress, and pillow
Dimensions variable
Restricted gift of Dr. Paul and Dorie Sternberg
1996.2

sick. I know what you're thinking. I can feel it. I know what you want to do. It's written all over your face." The angry tone of the woman's voice makes the viewer feel as if he or she has actually done something wrong or is guilty of a perverse sexual advance.

Oursler's varied body of work, comprising videos, found and constructed sculptural objects, photos, drawings, and CD-ROMs, has been called a "techno-theater of cruelty" for its constant antagonistic taunting. Unlike earlier video artists, Oursler liberates video from the monitor. He began experimenting with dummies in 1989 as a way to investigate the cultural representations of the figure in and outside of the media. When the mini video projector arrived on the market, Oursler found the perfect medium for the faces of his subjects. He projects video recordings of actors (Tracy Leipold is a favorite) onto inanimate objects,

such as stuffed fabric in the shape of a head. His use of mimetic technology projected onto inanimate figures is a deliberate method of multilayered representation that devolves from real, to recorded, to projected, to simulated, and widens the space between the original and the copies, the real and the fictional. JRW

Pipilotti Rist

Swiss, b. 1962

Sip My Ocean
1996
Color video installation
9 minutes, 40 seconds
Dimensions variable
Ed: 2/3
Bernice and Kenneth Newberger Fund and restricted gift of Carol and Douglas Cohen
1996.39

Pipilotti Rist's *Sip My Ocean* is a humorously nostalgic wake-up call from a summer daydream. Two large video projections of sensually surreal and playful images converge in a corner while dreamy music surrounds the viewer. Much of the imagery shows various underwater scenes of the artist and her friends or of objects cascading to the ocean floor. These pleasant aquatic visions are complemented by Rist's acoustic rendition of Chris Isaak's moody and nostalgic song "Wicked Game." Fissures in the relaxed visual flow erupt in the occasional introduction of strikingly bizarre and incongruous scenes, such as solarized objects floating

through clouds and a human eye opening to reveal fiery explosions of volcanic lava. A similar phenomenon takes place when a muted voice (also Rist) suddenly enters the background of the song to scream the refrain, "I don't want to fall in love . . . with you."

In *Sip My Ocean*, Rist's use of a dual projection into a corner engulfs the viewer in images while the soundtrack fills the space with the wistful refrains of Isaak's song. This spatial use of video projection affects the viewer physically as well as visually, literally surrounding the viewer with oceanic visions and

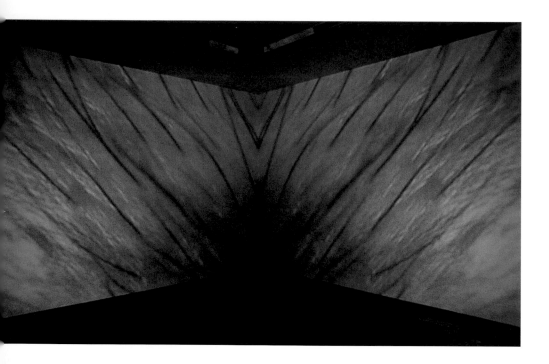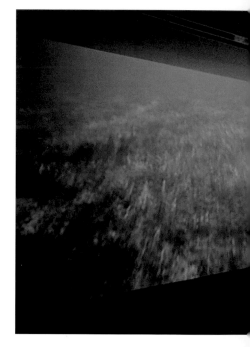

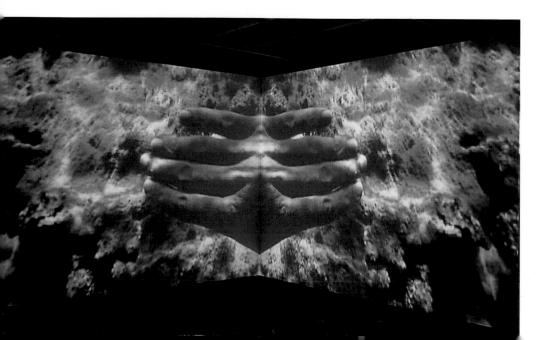

sounds of reverie. Rist's sonic interruption of screaming at the end of the song ushers in an unwelcome reminder of the real world and a rejection of the luxuriant feelings of romance evoked by the overall effect of her work. *Sip My Ocean* thus progresses from a lush reflection on bittersweet passion to a more disturbing and spiteful rejection of love. The anguished cry of "I don't want to fall in love . . . with you" is at once sour and slightly humorous in its delivery, sounding more like the echoes of a bratty child than the resistance of a lovelorn woman. The comical voice simultaneously complements the more pleasurable and lighthearted nature of the imagery while adding an undercurrent of malevolence and antagonism that affects the viewer on a more subconscious level.

Rist's video work has always combined humor and unexpected injections of unsettling elements into situations to provoke a psychological and often visceral response in the viewer. Her work reflects many of the changes that have occurred in the past decade of contemporary art, including the rapid ascension of video installation as an art medium, a more aggressive and sexually assertive sense of femininity, and an increasingly celebratory use of popular culture in art that has further blurred the lines between high and low culture. Rist's interests in music video and 1960s psychedelic culture and avant-garde movements such as Fluxus (especially the work of Nam June Paik [American, b. Korea 1932] and Yoko Ono [Japanese, b. 1933]) combine with a sweetly witty sensibility to produce videos and video installations that are entertaining and funny yet ultimately telling and affecting as well. DM

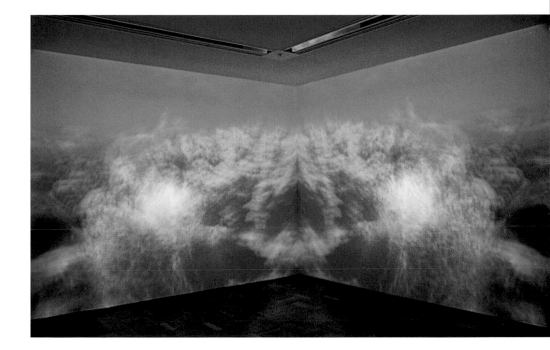

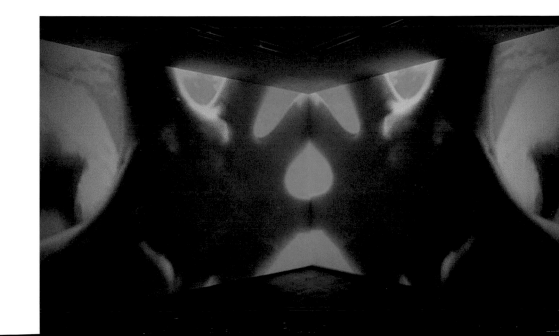

Kerry James Marshall

American, b. 1955

Kerry James Marshall's paintings reveal deeply embedded classical-art traditions yet are profoundly contemporary in their subject matter. Using a figurative style of imagery depicting African Americans in urban, suburban, and interior settings, Marshall makes large works that recall the grandeur and monumentality of traditional history painting. His commingling of references from art history and American history is evident in *Souvenir I*, one of a group of four paintings made in the late 1990s as a requiem to the decade of the 1960s and, in particular, the Civil Rights movement. Commemorating slain national and civil rights leaders Martin Luther King, Jr., John F. Kennedy, and Robert Kennedy, paintings for the *Souvenir* series depict these figures in a somber, reverent manner reminiscent of the souvenir commemorative objects popular in the black community. The *Souvenir* paintings also contain a multitude of symbols and allegorical references drawn from the iconographic traditions of art history. The most compelling of these is an angelic female figure, whose majestic form, adorned with glitter-encrusted golden wings, dominates the foreground of *Souvenir I*. Functioning as a solemn symbol of redemption, the angel is simultaneously an ordinary citizen, as was often the case in early Renaissance paintings, presented in the interior of her home in the seemingly mundane act of rearranging objects on a coffee table.

Souvenir I

1997
Acrylic, glitter, and paper on canvas
with grommets
108 × 157 in. (274.3 × 398.8 cm)
Bernice and Kenneth Newberger Fund
1997.73

In *Souvenir I*, Marshall reflects on the Civil Rights movement as a defining moment in recent American history, seen from the more equivocal vantage point of historical distance. The heroic scale of the painting allows Marshall to depict a scenario that seems larger than life. Each element in the tableau has extreme visual and symbolic importance. These range from the carefully rendered objects and furnishings in this clearly middle-class interior to the presence of a band of images of African-American cultural and political heroes deceased in the sixties — depicted as ghostly figures floating in the clouds along the top of the picture plane — to the application of glitter at junctures including the angel's wings, in the commemorative portraits, and as a decorative band along the bottom and sides of the canvas. Marshall characteristically fuses a range of painting techniques within each work, conjoining realism with abstraction and combining oil and acrylic with collage and other applied objects. Terrie Sultan has commented about his use of such techniques in the *Souvenir* series, "Here, the contradictory relationship between kitsch and commemoration is essential. The artist's glitter inventions — garlands, halos, fringe borders, clouds — emphatically state his understanding of history as a constant conflict between emotional immediacy and ironic distance."[1]

Marshall's rendition suggests an ambivalence about the legacy of the Civil Rights movement and its meaning from today's perspective. He points to the *Souvenir* series as an attempt to commemorate the pivotal events of the 1960s, mirroring the desires of the culture at large to lay the events and aspirations of the decade to rest. While the paintings from the *Souvenir* series embody the concept of history painting more fully than any of Marshall's previous projects, they do so in a way that is highly original. Departing from conventional narrative, they distill, encapsulate, and meditate in a rich and complex way on a period in our recent history, one with profound social and cultural implication for all Americans, from a distinctively African-American viewpoint. ES

1 Kerry James Marshall, Terrie Sultan, and Arthur Jafa, *Kerry James Marshall* (New York: Harry N. Abrams, 2000), p. 19.

Kara Walker

American, b. 1969

Presenting Negro Scenes Drawn Upon My Passage through the South and Reconfigured for the Benefit of Enlightened Audiences Wherever Such May Be Found, By Myself, Missus K. E. B. Walker, Colored
(details) 1997
Paper and watercolor on paper
Wall installation of sixty-five paper silhouettes, approximately: 13 × 150 ft. (4 × 45.7 m)
Gift of Susan and Lewis Manilow
1999.52

Truth and fiction collide in monumental proportion in Kara Walker's work. In her large-scale installations, Walker explicitly examines the psychological, historical, and social implications of slavery and the antebellum South. As such, racial stereotypes play a significant role in her work. Drawing on varied sources such as dime-store romance novels, contemporary literature, and narrative painting, Walker's images of mammies, pickaninnies, sambos, dandies, slave mistresses, pot-bellied plantation owners, and carpetbaggers crystallize in the form of the popular eighteenth- and nineteenth-century craft of cutting black paper into sharply defined portrait-silhouettes. Walker likens the silhouette to the racial stereotypes she explores:

> The silhouette says a lot with very little information, but that's also what the stereotype does. So I saw the silhouette and the stereotype as linked. Of course, while the stereotype, or the emblem, can communicate with a lot of people, and a lot of people can understand it, the other side of this is that it also reduces difference, reduces diversity to that stereotype."[1]

The title of this work, a play on historical slave narratives, refers to abolitionists' testimonials opposing slavery in the eighteenth and nineteenth centuries.

Presenting Negro Scenes . . . is a site-specific work that was originally made for an exhibition at The Renaissance Society at The University of Chicago in 1997. The paper cutout figures and landscape elements are adhered directly to the wall, immersing the viewer within the narrative. Standing alone against the white walls, the figures represent decidedly taboo subjects — sexual, scatological, or violent scenes that expose the desires, nightmares, and ghoulish thoughts that lurk within the American subconscious. Historical power relations are reversed, everyone is a victim and everyone is a perpetrator. The difference between pleasure and pain is difficult to discern. While these scenes present fictitious social and sexual interactions, each is loaded with tension that reveals itself the closer the imagery is examined. It is this tension, with its roots in the history of the American South and its indelible link to racism, that makes Walker's work relevant today. The installation brings cultural taboos out of hiding and confronts the racial tensions that have been both overt and sublimated in American society throughout the nation's history.

Walker's alluring yet highly disturbing imagery can be compared with works by contemporary artists such as Raymond Pettibon (p. 152) and Mike Kelley (p. 222). Like the large-scale paintings of Kerry James Marshall (p. 270), Walker's work employs African-American vernacular and alludes to heroically scaled history paintings of the past. The artist herself cites the politically charged, satirical works of German artists George Grosz (1893–1959) and Otto Dix (1891–1969) as important influences, as well as the biting racial parodies of painter Robert Colescott (American, b. 1925). sc

1 Quoted in Gary Garrels, *Kara Walker: Upon My Many Masters — An Outline*, exh. brochure (San Francisco: Museum of Modern Art, 1997), n.p.

David Hammons

American, b. 1943

In sculptures, installations, and performances, David Hammons elicits spiritual and cultural associations with his use of found objects. For him, spirituality is a broad notion that encompasses religious references as well as the idea of a life force or creative energy, personified in his musical heroes Sun Ra, Miles Davis, and Thelonius Monk. Early in his career, Hammons focused on references to African-American culture and spirituality, but more recently, inspired by travels in Europe and Asia during the 1990s, he has embraced a wider scope of influences. In an interview, Hammons stated, "There's so much talk about, to get people into cosmic consciousness, no one else is doing it. Artists are not supposed to be capitalists, we're supposed to be spiritualists, but everyone's capitalism is hard to reject. But we'll try to work on the spiritual and activate the third eye."[1]

The tension between artistic and commercial elements of art making has consistently been of interest to Hammons, who has aligned himself with self-taught "outsider artists." At the beginning of his career in the 1960s in Los Angeles, he made body prints with grease and margarine, work that reflected issues of racial and national identity at the fore during the Civil Rights era. The commercial success of these prints and other works on paper prompted the artist to change the direction of his work toward a junk aesthetic, using objects such as hair, rib bones, bottle caps, basketballs, cowrie shells, and shovels. Artist and writer Dawoud Bey (American, b. 1953) has likened Hammons's use of such objects to a West African tradition of *minkisi* in which fetish objects — endowed with spiritual properties — heal and protect a community from evil. Hammons's works directly address African-American and African culture and stereotypes, as

Praying to Safety
1997
Thai bronze statues, string, and safety pin
Installed: 36½ × 59¾ × 15 in.
(92.7 × 151.8 × 38.1 cm)
Restricted gift of Mr. and Mrs. J. Paul Beitler, Lindy Bergman, Carol and Douglas Cohen, Robert and Sylvie Fitzpatrick, Penny Pritzker and Bryan Traubert, Nancy A. Lauter and Alfred L. McDougal Charitable Fund, Ed and Jackie Rabin, Marjorie and Louis B. Susman, and Helyn D. Goldenberg
2000.5.a – d

274

a sardonic response to oppression and exploitation, while challenging the art establishment by using nontraditional art materials. The title of his first retrospective exhibition was *Rousing the Rubble*, an apt allegory for his spiritually charged "junk."

Hammons spent many years living and working in Harlem, then left the United States for Italy and other parts of Europe. These travels initiated his nomadic existence and introduced him to a wide range of cultural influences. In contrast to his earlier Afrocentric pieces, his current work draws from the specific histories and cultures of its location; Hammons has mined museums and cultural resources in Europe and Asia as he did his environment in Harlem.

Hammons often uses puns and humor to create multiple meanings in his works. *Higher Goals* (1986), a commission for the Public Art Fund in New York City in which he decorated

fifty-foot-high telephone poles with bottle caps and then topped them with basketball hoops, suggests that young African Americans seek something more than success as a famous athlete. For *Praying to Safety*, he placed two early nineteenth-century Thai Buddhist sculptures opposite each other with a safety pin precariously suspended on a string between them, calling to mind the daily struggle to find a balance between the material and spiritual worlds, the literal and the metaphorical. In many ways, Hammons's work centers around transcendence and the transformation of materials, language, history, traditions, and art institutions, so that new meanings can be assigned and new relationships formed. J R W

1 Deborah Menaker Rothschild, *Yardbird Suite, Hammons '93* (Williamstown, Mass.: Williamstown College Museum of Art, 1993).

275

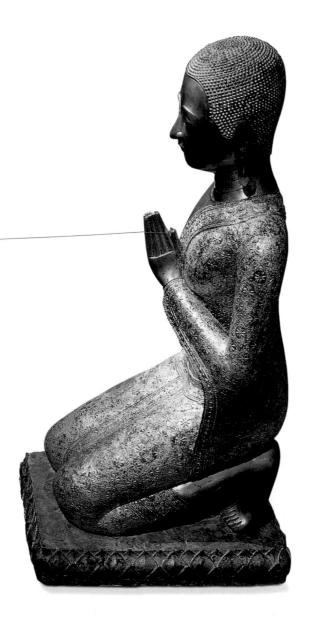

Jorge Pardo

American, b. Cuba 1963

Vince Robbins
1997
Plastic, steel, light bulbs, and electric wire
Dimensions variable
Restricted gift of Carlos and Rosa de la Cruz
1998.29

Jorge Pardo's work functions as both art and industrial design. Since the early 1990s, Pardo has designed chairs, tables, lamps, and other items. Although he is best known for designing furniture, Pardo has not limited himself to elements designed for interiors. In 1994 he began a four-year project to design a house for himself in the Mount Washington area of Los Angeles. Before moving in, Pardo opened the house as the extension of an exhibition of his work on view at The Museum of Contemporary Art, Los Angeles, in 1997. For that exhibition, Pardo focused on both interior design and the curatorial process, blurring the boundaries of both by arranging a selection of works he chose from MOCA's collection in the house. For the Chicago presentation of the exhibition, which was co-organized by the MCA and MOCA, Pardo exhibited a fully functional sailboat of his own design in the MCA's atrium.

Pardo extends conceptual artists' approach to art as defined by its institutional context. When Pardo's furniture is displayed in a gallery or museum, it is arranged in an unmovable and specific composition. Viewers relate to it as they would a sculpture or painting. When the work is part of a home, office, or restaurant, it functions more like furniture. Unlike many conceptual artists, who aimed to test the limits of what is considered art, Pardo wishes to maintain the multiple facets of his work.

Pardo's work also follows a significant twentieth-century lineage of attempts to integrate art and life through design, including the modernist movements of Russian constructivism, Dutch De Stijl, and the German Bauhaus. Yet Pardo departs from these earlier movements' pursuit of the new as well as their utopian goal to change social organization through design. While his spare, biomorphic forms recall the designs of early to mid-twentieth-century modernist designers such as Charles and Ray Eames and Alvar Aalto, Pardo selects and synthesizes elements from the recent past rather than continuing the utopian goals of the modernists who inspired him.

Pardo's work extends the minimal and postminimal artists' use of furniture, architectural constructions, and light to alter the exhibition site and the viewer's relationship to it. Other artists who have pioneered the use of furniture and architecture for this purpose include Robert Morris (p. 78) and Vito Acconci (p. 112). Dan Flavin (p. 72) and Robert Irwin (p. 86) have been innovators in the use of light to transform space.

Vince Robbins is simultaneously a lamp, an abstract art installation, and a portrait. It casts richly saturated, curved bands of orange-yellow light across everything in its radius, appearing to bend the surrounding walls as well as the room's emotional tone. Like all of Pardo's titles, *Vince Robbins* is deliberately cryptic. It matters less that the viewer recognize the specific name than know that it is, de facto, a reference to a person (a gallery assistant with whom Pardo worked). The "personality" of *Vince Robbins* will appear differently, depending on the circumstances of installation. This variability changes the face of the "portrait" but it also retains the work's identity as a functional lamp, which, in the context of a museum collection, is otherwise almost entirely subsumed by its identity as art. AP

276

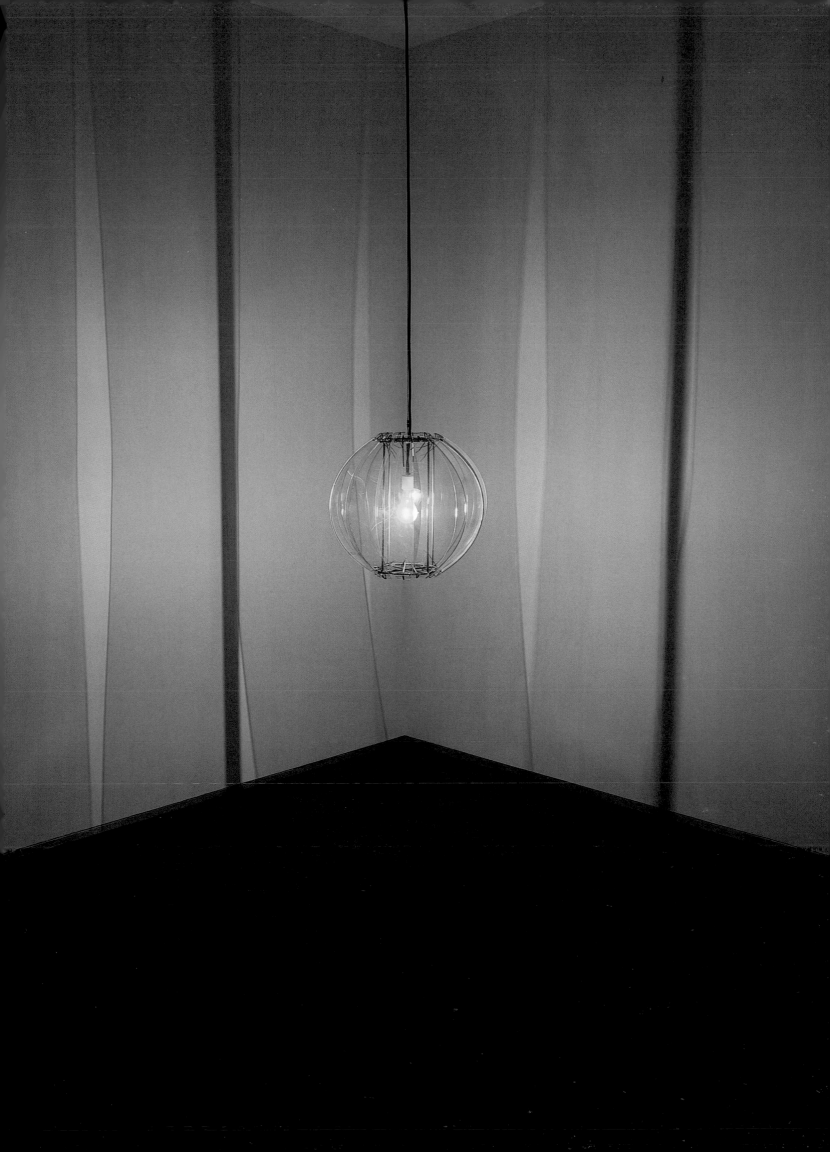

Jim Hodges

American, b. 1957

The end from where you are
1998
Silk, cotton, polyester, and thread
16 × 16 ft. (4.9 × 4.9 m)
Restricted gift in memory of John S. Baran with additional restricted support from the Meta S. and Ronald Berger Family Foundation
1999.4

Artists working at the end of the twentieth century have often returned to forms associated with notions of beauty. Flowers in particular have become a subject of interest, expressing a range of emotions and ideas about love, death, memory, mourning, and sexuality. These associations combine with aesthetic sensibilities culled from both late 1960s postminimalism and 1970s craft-oriented art in Jim Hodges's flower curtains, created between 1995 and 1998. Simultaneously strong and fragile, these works are visually and sculpturally charged from one angle, yet they dissolve into near-nothingness from another. *The end from where you are*, the coda in Hodges's series, is an elegantly somber arrangement of numerous black (and occasionally navy, maroon, and green) silk flowers that showers from the ceiling into a bundle on the floor.

In much of Hodges's work of the 1990s, everyday objects are used to represent a variety of emotions and memories for the artist and viewer alike. Large, beautiful works composed of a mosaic of mirror fragments split the viewer's reflected image in a poetic commentary on the figurative abstraction of our personality and our psyche. In this sense,

Hodges's work builds on the legacy of Felix Gonzalez-Torres (p. 216), who similarly combined subtle, evocative gestures of pristine beauty with powerfully personal and often political content. Much of Hodges's work also reveals an unexpected correlation between the natural world and human emotions or experiences. Works such as spider webs made from silver chains or shirts from various stages in Hodges's life combined to resemble the growth rings of a tree demonstrate his interest in finding connections between the world that surrounds us and the world of emotions inside us.

The simple and elegant presentation of a large field of silk flowers sewn together continues this pursuit of a poignantly human sensibility through the invocation of natural forms. While Hodges used a vibrant array of colors in previous flower curtain works, this work is composed almost entirely of black flowers. Artificial flowers, which have been used as a decorative element since ancient Egypt, lend the work a sense of household familiarity that balances its more transcendent connotations and appearance. According to Hodges, "the darkness in this work, like a darkening sky at the end of the day as the earth turns from the sun, brings the viewer to a place of quiet reflection." The immediate association of the flowers and the color black with death is overcome by the delicate juxtaposition of shapes within the work and the play of light through the translucent flowers and the spaces between them. *The end from where you are* thus encourages a sense of reverie in the careful appreciation of its complex and tenebrous beauty. DM

279

Shirin Neshat

Iranian, b. 1957

Turbulent
1998
Black-and-white video installation
Dimensions variable
Artist's proof aside from an edition of 3
Gift of Susan and Lewis Manilow
2000.22

Shirin Neshat, an Iranian artist who lives in New York, works within a system of binary oppositions; her personal and professional background, as well as her artwork, reflects both Eastern and Western influences. Born in Qazvin, a small religious city in northwestern Iran, Neshat came to California in 1974, and studied at the University of California at Berkeley. She was living in the United States when the Islamic Revolution overtook Iran in 1979 and the country was transformed into a rigid theocracy. After working in New York for several years, Neshat returned to Iran in 1990. The cultural and political changes she encountered there moved her to begin a new series of work that addressed the deep divisions between men and women, the religious and the secular, and pre- and postrevolutionary society in Iran. Although she had been a painter and involved in the visual arts since her days in California, Neshat's career began in earnest in 1993, when she embarked on film and photographic work related to Iran. The artist's status as both an Iranian and a woman heightened the controversy around her work and caused her to be exiled from her homeland; she still lives in New York and shoots her projects in countries neighboring Iran. In an interview with *Time* magazine, Neshat said, "Leaving [Iran] has offered me incredible personal development, a sense of independence that I don't think I would have had. But there's also a great sense of isolation. And I've permanently lost a complete sense of center. I can never call any place home. I will forever be in a state of in-between."[1]

Her attempt to negotiate these conflicting forces and images is central to her artwork. In *Turbulent*, she focuses on social segregation between men and

280

women. Iranian women are forbidden to sing or perform in front of a live audience, and this law provides a symbolic demarcation for the two parts of the film. Exhibited on two large screens opposite one another, *Turbulent* shows a man on one screen and a woman on the other, each on stage in identical auditoriums. In effect, they face one another while they perform, functioning as both subject and object, while engaging the viewer in a similar capacity. The male vocalist performs with his back to an audience of men, while the camera remains fixed on him. When he completes his song, a thirteenth-century poem by the mystic Rumi, he turns to the woman, who has been waiting and listening to his performance. She wears all black and sings to an empty auditorium while the camera whirls around her in an elliptical motion. Her voice has been altered by a computer and the sounds she makes are abstract. The emotional fervor

and chaotic tonal range of her performance are distinct from the harmonious vocals of her male counterpart.

In an interview with Lina Bertucci, Neshat stated, "Recently . . . I became very interested in how space and spatial boundaries are also politicized and are designed to lift personal and individual desire from the public domain and contain it within private spaces. Ultimately, men dominate public space and women exist for the most part in private space."[2] This sense of gender boundaries is addressed in *Turbulent,* and within the work's construct, Neshat plays with other dualities as well — black and white, presence and absence, alienation and transcendence, concrete and abstract sound, moving and fixed shooting, and rational and emotional power. The marginalized woman is afforded the power of inclusion through engagement

with the male performer as well as by those who view the work. Through exposing the limitations and imposed categories of this particular culture, Neshat transgresses them, using the transcendent power of music. MG

1 "Photo Essay — Shirin Neshat," from the *Time Europe* website: www.time.com/time/europe/photoessays/neshat (August 2000).

2 Lina Bertucci, "Shirin Neshat, Eastern Values," *Flash Art,* no. 197 (November/December 1997), p. 84.

281

Dan Peterman

American, b. 1960

Accessories to an Event (plaza)
(detail) 1998
Reprocessed plastic
Dimensions variable
Restricted gift of Sara Albrecht
and Bill Nygren
1998.28.a–j

Dan Peterman, one of the key members of the group of internationally recognized, Chicago-based conceptual artists who emerged in the late 1980s, works with ideas about recycling systems and recycled materials. Since the mid-1980s when he completed his MFA at The University of Chicago, he has kept a studio within The Resource Center, a recycling center on the border of Chicago's Hyde Park and Woodlawn, respectively the wealthiest and poorest of the city's South Side neighborhoods. Although Peterman is often described as an environmental artist, his intent expands upon any notion of this genre that implies merely honoring nature or condemning humanity's poor stewardship of the earth. Rather, he seeks to reveal processes by which people interact with both their natural and technological surroundings.

Often using modest objects or materials to examine interlocking social, political, and personal systems that make up life in the modern world, Peterman has made works from aluminum, plastics, and glass, or that feature recycling systems including composting, water purification, and the removal of toxic contaminants. Recycled plastics have provided a rich source of material for Peterman's works since the early 1990s, including *Accessories to an Event (plaza),* a commission by the MCA. *Accessories* is a variation of his public sculptures made from recycled plastic "timber" including such works as *Running Table* (1997), which took the form of a 100-foot-long picnic table placed in Chicago's Grant Park, a nod to *Running Fence* (1978), a work by Christo (p. 76).

Discrepancies among the complex systems of design, manufacturing, and distribution of consumer products, and the much less sophisticated efforts to deal with the waste associated with these products, are particularly fascinating to Peterman. He takes an essentially nonjudgmental approach to this situation; the human efforts to deal with

human problems represent a rich resource that allows Peterman to engage his viewers in "real world" conceptual art. In his case, the artwork is the thinking through of all the steps of the process that creates recycled plastic, including his or her own part in that system (which might include consuming milk or soda in plastic bottles).

The plastic planks that form *Accessories to an Event (plaza)* began their transformation into an artwork in the summer of 1998, when the bundled material was delivered to the MCA's large, open plaza facing Mies van der Rohe Way. Over the course of the summer, these planks were removed and redelivered, transformed into ten units — platforms, tables with attached benches, and planterlike structures — intended to be reconfigured, stacked, and displayed as the museum wishes, providing places where the public rests and eats lunch. *Accessories* is reminiscent of Vito Acconci's public sculptures of the 1980s and 1990s made from recycled materials and intended for actual use (including a work in the MCA Collection, *House of Used Parts* [1985, p. 113]). The MCA Collection features another work by Peterman, *Small Change* (1989), in which he fashioned crushed aluminum cans into three large "coins," the value of the aluminum equaling $100 at the time the piece was made. LW

Tony Fitzpatrick

American, b. 1958

Tony Fitzpatrick's fascination with the details of the images that surround him and the techniques of print media have fueled his development as one of the most significant contemporary printmakers. He expressed his deep engagement with American vernacular forms in *The Infinite Wager*, a suite of ten five-color etchings with aquatint focusing on notions of luck as represented in games of chance. Fitzpatrick, a product of Chicago's South Side — a group of neighborhoods legendary for street life, nightclubs, con games, and gambling of various sorts — has stayed close to his roots with *The Infinite Wager*. The son of a burial vault salesman who drove from funeral parlor to funeral parlor spinning Chicago stories to his often-errant progeny, Fitzpatrick was taken by his father's colorful cautionary tales. These prints grew out of his father's stories and were made as an homage to the elder Fitzpatrick shortly before his death in 1998. It is also the first of Fitzpatrick's suites of etchings to use primary colors, which he felt better illustrated the peculiar American vitality of gambling and jazz.

The Infinite Wager
1998
Portfolio of four and five-color etchings
on paper
Ten prints, each: 11⅜ × 10⅛ in.
(28.9 × 25.7 cm)
Ed: 8/45
Gift of Janice and Mickey Cartin
1998.44.1–10

284

Using various idioms and images associated with gaming and "good luck," some idiosyncratic, such as the "666," which refers to a jazz club formerly located at 666 South State Street in Chicago, and some universal, such as the hearts, diamonds, spades, and clubs of playing cards, a lucky horseshoe, and a wishbone, the artist creates active, multilayered compositions within the modest dimensions of each etching.

A poet and actor as well as a visual artist, Fitzpatrick is concerned not only with the imagery he depicts, but with the language he employs in each print's title, as well as in the narratives that can be constructed from the imagery. For example, in *Post Horse*, the racehorse is black, illustrating a superstition that it is unlucky to bet on an all-black horse, just as it is unlucky to have a black cat cross one's path. *Lucky Spider* refers to the betting on tarantula races, a Mexican peasant pastime that contrasts sharply with American horseracing, which requires a large investment and elaborate facilities. The *Jack Flower* serves as the "queen" of the suite, much like a queen in a deck of cards, and refers to the flowers gamblers would wear in their lapels. LW

285

Yinka Shonibare

British, b. 1962

Alien Obsessives, Mum, Dad and the Kids
1998
Wax printed cotton, plastic, and polyester
fiberfill on plastic and metal armatures
Installed: dimensions variable
Restricted gift of Donna and Howard Stone
1999.54.a–h

"I am beyond nationalism," Yinka Shonibare has said, "I cannot think in those terms because . . . I see them as artificial boundaries."[1] Born in London and raised in Nigeria, Shonibare works in a variety of media and genres, including sculptural installations, paintings, and photographs, focusing on such topics as national identity, race, class, and notions of authenticity. Often infusing his work with wit and parody, Shonibare appropriates quintessentially British imagery, both traditional and contemporary, such as a Victorian dandy or the English countryside, and combines it with elements from African history.

Standing approximately four feet high, the figures in *Alien Obsessives, Mum, Dad and the Kids* appear to have come from a 1950s science fiction film. Placed serendipitously within the gallery space, this "nuclear" family is enveloped in brightly colored African cloth. In this work, Shonibare exploits the ambiguous meanings attributed to the word *alien* to intriguing ends. Prior to the 1950s *Oxford English Dictionary* defined the word as something other or foreign. Today, the word also refers to an immigrant. Using the African cloth for the aliens' skin, Shonibare dovetails the popular understanding of the word *alien* with its longer standing definition. In so doing he shows that the concept of difference is profoundly mutable through time and

across cultures. The origins of the fabric reveal another complicated history. In the late nineteenth century this kind of fabric was designed in Indonesia and manufactured in Holland and Great Britain for exportation to West Africa and other parts of the world. The context and meaning of such material has changed over time: it is often worn today as a source of African national pride. Shonibare's use of this fabric in this and other sculptural works suggest the complexity of national identities, particularly in a postcolonial British context.

Shonibare has used African fabric in other works such as *Mr. And Mrs. Andrews without their Heads* (1998), a group of headless mannequins in tailored Victorian dresses in order to further address the complexity of postcolonial relations and to emphasize that European wealth has frequently been based on exploitation and plunder. In a series entitled *Diary of a Victorian Dandy* (1998), Shonibare photographed himself as a decadent nineteenth-century gentleman who enjoys a flamboyant lifestyle, offering a critique of the British class system that still prevails today. Like other artists in the MCA Collection such as Glenn Ligon (p. 242) and Lorna Simpson (p. 240), Shonibare puts forward a penetrating analysis of how definitions of identity are often influenced by race and ethnicity. sc

1 Fiona Lynch, *Birmingham Post*, March 1999, p. 53.

Sharon Lockhart

American, b. 1964

On Kawara: Whole and Parts, 1964—95,
Museum of Contemporary Art, Tokyo,
January 24 – April 5, 1998
1998
Chromogenic development prints
Four parts, installed: 64½ × 240 in.
(163.8 × 609.6 cm)
Ed: 2/6
Bernice and Kenneth Newberger Fund
2001.3.a – d

Enrique Nava Enedina: Oaxacan
Exhibition Hall, National Museum
of Anthropology, Mexico City
1999
Chromogenic development prints
Three parts, installed: 49 × 217½ in.
(124.5 × 552.5 cm)
Ed: 5/6
Partial gift of George and Lori Bucciero
1999.53.a – c

Since the mid-1990s, Sharon Lockhart has become recognized for her cinematically constructed photographs and photographically static films that investigate the relationship between the two media. She often uses serial imagery to create a narrative over successive images or to complicate the conceptual use of the photographic image as a factual document rather than as an expressive medium. Her work also focuses on everyday scenes and domestic situations that, despite their quotidian appearance and subject matter, often require elaborate staging and location research. Two of Lockhart's multiphotographic series, *On Kawara: Whole and Parts, 1964– 95, Museum of Contemporary Art, Tokyo, January 24–April 5, 1998* and *Enrique Nava Enedina: Oaxacan Exhibit Hall, National Museum of Anthropology,* depart from her use of staging, instead capturing moments that occurred in museums during visits to Japan and Mexico respectively. Both serve as important predecessors to the photographic and film projects she created in Brazil in 1999 as part of two anthropological kinship surveys she observed.

The museum's role as a site for the interpretation and representation of culture has become a powerful subject for artists in recent years, a tendency both works evoke. *On Kawara: Whole and Parts* comprises four photographs taken from the same angle that document the clockwork rotation of security guards at an exhibition of work by On Kawara (Japanese, b. 1933) at the Museum of Contemporary Art in Tokyo. Despite the seemingly identical nature of the images overall, barely noticeable differences in age, hairstyle, posture, and physiognomy begin to emerge upon closer inspection. Other details, such as the faint shifting of the sunlight through the entrance to the gallery, become apparent as well. Lockhart's photographic series operates in a similar fashion to the structuralist films of James Benning (American, b. 1942) and Michael Snow (Canadian, b. 1929) in their presentation of a series of seemingly similar images that change almost imperceptibly from one "frame" to the next. It also evokes the conceptual logic and spirit of the "date" paintings by On Kawara — uniformly colored serial works distinguished only by the date of their facture.

In *Enrique Nava Enedina*, a Mexican mason replacing tile in an anthropological museum is gradually enclosed by the glass structure that shields surrounding objects from dust. The three images present a portrait not only of Enrique himself, but of the two kinds of work — the physical replacement of the tile and the cultural "work" of anthropological interpretation — that occur within the institution. In addition to the overall social significance of the work, Lockhart has created a subtle visual play of reflective surfaces: the glass of the exhibition displays, the tinted glass of Enrique's walls, and the shiny marble surface of the floors. Her approach in this work was like an anthropologist categorizing other cultural practices through visual representation. The cultural "display" subtly critiques the reduction of Enrique's cultural identity to the sum of the historical artifacts surrounding him. In each image, Enrique maintains direct visual contact with the viewer while remaining shielded by the tinted glass structure. The viewer is engaged by his gaze yet kept at a distance by the tinted glass, which serves as both a physical shield and as a metaphoric allusion to the invisible cultural barrier between Enrique and the viewer. Lockhart directly addressed current debates regarding cross-cultural representation in *Enrique Nava Enedina*, demonstrating the necessity of gaining a more complete and complex understanding of other cultures through knowledge and appreciation of individuals. DM

Andreas Gursky

German, b. 1955

Prada III
1998
Chromogenic development print mounted on
Plexiglas with artist's frame
72 × 120 in. (182.9 × 304.8 cm)
Artist's proof aside from an edition of 6
Partial gift of Pamela and Michael Alper
2001.39

Avenue of the Americas
2001
Chromogenic development print mounted
on Plexiglas with artist's frame
81 × 140 3/8 in. (205.7 × 356.6 cm)
Ed: 2/6
Partial gift of Refco Group Ltd., LLC
2002.84

With brilliant color and precise clarity, Andreas Gursky creates striking, large-scale photographs. While many works present the grandeur of nature, increasingly Gursky's work captures the landscape of the contemporary world as transformed by twentieth-century global trade, travel, and finance. With keen attention to composition, color, balance and movement, Gursky presents dazzlingly compelling images of the contemporary world in its many manifestations.

During the 1980s Gursky studied at the Kunstakademie Düsseldorf, learning the rigorous methods of Bernd and Hilla Becher (p. 174), whose photographs take on elements of conceptual and minimal art. Initially adopting the Bechers' documentary approach and formal structure, he began to add color and digital revisions to his photographs.

Gursky uses a large-format camera, yielding photographs that offer a dual perspective: remarkable detail at close range and blurred abstraction at a distance. At first glance, the photographs look documentary. Gursky has modified many of them, however, cropping them, combining multiple viewpoints and time frames, and making other digital modifications. For *Chicago Board of Trade II*, an image of the derivatives (futures and options) exchange trading floor where traders meet to buy and sell agricultural and financial contracts, he shot a double exposure of the image to capture the swirling movements of the commodity traders in colorful trading jackets. With its compression of movement, people, and color, the image shows the Board of Trade in its surging, theatrical entirety.

Many elements of Gursky's work, especially his rigorous attention to pattern, line, and symmetry, resonate with abstract and minimalist art, as well as with aspects of contemporary culture. *Prada III* is part of a series of photographs of a single image of a pristine, shrinelike shelf with merchandise from the Italian fashion house Prada.

By reducing the central image to an unbroken parallel form, Gursky presents the shelf as a purely visual object. The image, which is reminiscent of Donald Judd's minimalist sculptures (p. 124), also resembles Dan Flavin's environments created using fluorescent light fixtures (p. 72).

Gursky's experiments with scale, perspective, and color coalesce in *Avenue of the Americas*, an image of the Hilton Hotel and Towers at Rockefeller Center on Sixth Avenue in New York. Shot at night, the photograph is dominated by monochromatic light emanating from the uniformly curtained rooms and the reflection of lights on the building's mirrored surface. By expanding the horizontality of the image, shrinking the depth of the picture plane, and minimizing the color, Gursky approaches formalist abstraction in this work. The horizontal planes of the windows are interrupted by the bisecting vertical banding of the building's glass panels, while the protruding diagonal panels further break up the grid of the image. The vertical buildings framing the edges of the photograph direct attention back to the central image. This inventive and painterly approach to the organization of perspective and space, combined with the enhancement of environments through digital manipulations and enormous scale, allows Gursky to create spectacular, idealized images of the contemporary world. TVE

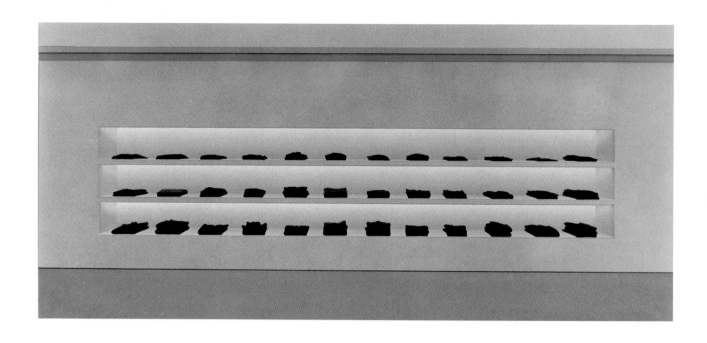

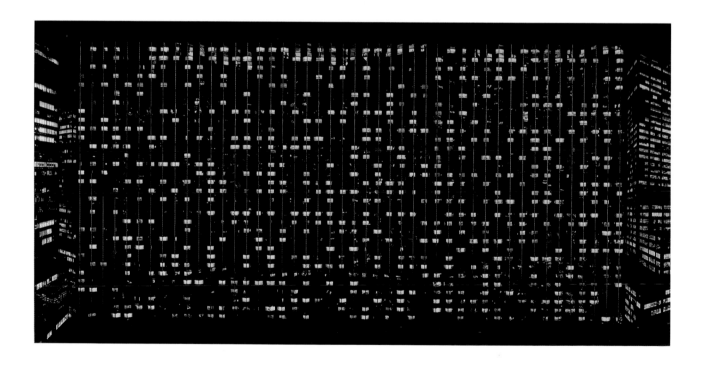

Chicago Board of Trade II
1999
Chromogenic development
print mounted on Plexiglas
with artist's frame
81½ × 132⅝ in.
(207 × 336.9 cm)
Ed: 3/6
Joseph and Jory Shapiro Fund
1999.59

Matthew Barney

American, b. 1967

The Cabinet of Frank Gilmore
1999
Vitrine with salt, epoxy resin,
nylon, polycarbonate honeycomb,
beeswax, and acrylic
46¾ × 47¹⁵⁄₁₆ × 37⅝ in.
(118.7 × 121.8 × 95.6 cm)
Restricted gift of the Sara Lee Corporation
1999.55

Cremaster 2: The Drone's Cell
1999
Chromogenic development print
with acrylic frame
43 × 54 in. (109.2 × 137.2 cm)
Ed: 2/6 aside from 2 artist's proofs
Partial and promised gift from The Howard and
Donna Stone Collection
2002.7

Crossing from film to video to sculpture, Matthew Barney is known for work that combines ritualized athletic endeavors with his personal mythology. In 1994 Barney began a five-part film series *Cremaster*, named after the muscle that controls the elevation of the testicles (in response to such stimuli as fear and cold); the cremaster also provides the first indication that a fetus is male. Each of the films was made out of sequence and with a specific geographic or architectural location as their focus: *Cremaster 4* (1994) was filmed on the Isle of Man in the Irish Sea; *Cremaster 1* (1995) at Bronco Stadium at Boise State University, Idaho; *Cremaster 5* (1997) in Budapest, Hungary; *Cremaster 2* (1999) on the Columbia Icefield, Alberta, Canada, and the Bonneville Salt Flats, Utah; and *Cremaster 3* (2002) in the Chrysler Tower and the Solomon R. Guggenheim Museum in New York. Barney's highly personal responses to each location make the landscape as important a character as those portrayed by the actors. In each film, Barney's central character accomplishes a quest that, as in classical mythology, forces him or her to overcome a series of escalating challenges before reaching a goal that reveals a physical or mental transformation.

In *Cremaster 2*, the plot is loosely based on the life of convicted killer Gary Gilmore (played by Barney), who was the subject of Norman Mailer's book *The Executioner's Song* (1979). Weaving in and out of the North American landscape, Barney's story revolves around Gilmore's demand to be executed according to the Mormon doctrine of

Blood Atonement after being convicted in Utah for the murders of two fellow Mormons. Gilmore's attempt to outsmart fate in his apparent use of religion for personal redemption, and his claim to be the illegitimate grandson of legendary magician Harry Houdini, are vital aspects of the film's plot. References ranging from the Mormon Church to country musician Johnny Cash to speed metal music abound in Barney's film of the ultimate anti-hero, who fought the American judicial system and ultimately could only win by losing his own life.

To accompany the film, Barney made sculptures, drawings, and photographs that are based on filmic elements. *The Cabinet of Frank Gilmore* and the photograph *Cremaster 2: The Drone's Cell*, refer to Gilmore's paternal grandfather and Gilmore himself, characters in *Cremaster 2*. The vitrine is made of nylon, beeswax, and plastic that form, in part, a chair (similar to one in the film) and a honeycomb structure that suggests features of the North American landscape. The photographic image portrays a film scene in which Gilmore is in the back seat of a 1966 Mustang (similar to a car he once owned) with a gun in his hand, moments before he kills a gas station attendant. The works meditate on fate and genealogy, incarceration and escape, metamorphosis and endurance — themes that typify the lives of both Gary Gilmore and Harry Houdini. SC

Paul Pfeiffer

American, b. 1966

*Fragment of a Crucifixion
(after Francis Bacon)*
1999
Color video installation
Image: 3 × 4 in. (7.6 × 10.2 cm)
Ed: 3/3 aside from 2 artist's proofs
Restricted gift of Kenneth C. Griffin
2000.8

Paul Pfeiffer's work introduced significant shifts in the production and presentation of video art at the end of the 1990s. Departing from the popular use of large-scale video projection — a format that brings the spectacle of the cinema into the gallery space — his small video monitor and projection works prompt an intimate relationship between the viewer and the moving image. Pfeiffer also incorporates state-of-the-art computer-imaging technology to seamlessly alter footage from films and sporting events and transforms them into strangely evocative examinations of human behavior. His fascination with the presence or absence of the body in architectural space, especially when the body is in extreme physical states of suffering, pleasure, or exertion, underpins much of his work to date. He often erases, manipulates, or replaces human figures with ghostly shadows, throwing the arena of events surrounding them into high relief.

Fragment of a Crucifixion presents footage of professional basketball player Larry Johnson celebrating a slam dunk with his signature performance of clenching his fists and shouting in wild-eyed abandon. The action is then placed on a loop, creating the illusion that the figure is perpetually locked in a back-and-forth motion of what appears to be either total ecstasy or dire anguish. Pfeiffer's removal of specific references (such as the name of the basketball team on Johnson's jersey) and mutation of the camera flashes into surreal bursts of light gives the scene a timeless and placeless quality. The diminutive size of the projection creates an unsettling sense of intimacy for viewing the strange mini-event of a man doomed to repeat his bizarre screaming fit of rapture or pain into eternity.

The subtitle of Pfeiffer's work refers to a painting by Francis Bacon (p. 44) of the same name in which a screaming, disembodied mouth hovers in the center of the composition in a manner similar to Johnson's frozen grimace. Bacon's best-known work, which depicts screaming male figures in indeterminate spaces, has often been viewed as reflecting the existential sense of hopelessness, grief, and angst in Britain and Europe after the cataclysmic years of World War II. Pfeiffer's *Fragment of a Crucifixion* points to the often ambiguous situation of the body in contemporary culture, for example, in the manipulation of the physical body through cosmetic surgery or dieting or the use of "morphing" in motion pictures or music videos. The exaggeration of the camera flashes also suggests the overwhelmingly spectacular nature of sporting events and other events in today's society and how their influence and impact has become all encompassing. In this work, Pfeiffer interrupts the flow of visual material from a sporting event by removing it from its original context and refashioning it to create an endless cycle of intense bodily movements and facial expressions. D M

Beat Streuli

Swiss, b. 1957

Chicago, July 99
(details)
1999
Silver dye-bleach transparencies on Plexiglas
Overall dimensions variable, each of
sixty-eight parts: 63 × 63 in. (160 × 160 cm)
Restricted gift of the Collectors Forum;
support for original commission from
Sara Albrecht and Bill Nygren
2000.17.1–17

Beat Streuli's *Chicago, July 99* is a series of seventeen dye-bleach transparencies on Plexiglas, designed to be mounted on the front windows of the MCA. The large images display pedestrians photographed in Chicago by Streuli in the summer, their faces reflecting the diversity of the city. Most of the photographs are bright close-ups of faces, capturing mainly individuals — a construction worker, business people, tourists, and young people — as well as some families. At night, back-lit by the museum's interior lights, the faces stand out, distinct and effulgent, as if on a movie screen at a drive-in. The sun's reflection on the windows obscures the images, which can be seen clearly only from the inside of the museum during the day. Because Streuli's photographs are specifically focused on the faces of people, the images lack explicit visual references to their setting. Within the museum, the Chicago skyline stands as a backdrop to the images in the window, behind the white of one subject's shirt or in the paleness of another's face. Streuli does not romanticize the urban landscape; just as the faces on the large transparencies speak for themselves, so does the city.

In past works, Streuli has also used city inhabitants as his subjects, magnifying them to the large scale of a billboard. The Chicago series is unique in its cheerful tone and focus on individuals. The Swiss artist, who has photographed in London, Tokyo, and New York, among other cities, thinks about his work as crossing disciplines. He explains, "It comes back to what I said about this old-fashioned idea of the crowd; it's a big Shakespearean drama when you look at it. After a while the pictures look like Hollywood stills too, they're about passion and suffering and joy."[1] In spite of this sense of glamour, Streuli's images are decidedly unaffected, capturing subjects in natural daylight as they are at any moment, thoughtful, engaged, laughing. There is a pleasant discrimination to Streuli's gaze that is familiar — his lens rests on people who seem suddenly attractive, the way we pause an extra second or

glance back at someone we pass because they have a striking look or energy.

Streuli entered into the contemporary art scene in the early 1990s and has been compared to Wolfgang Tillmans (German, b. 1968) and Nan Goldin (American, b. 1953). While these two artists also photograph apparently ordinary people for their work, their subjects are seldom as spontaneous or anonymous as Streuli's. His style has been associated with Jeff Wall (p. 206), who is similarly interested in the link between photography and film, and with the *flânerie* tradition, as in Charles Baudelaire's poetry and the work of the French surrealists. The figure of the flaneur is that of the individual traveling with confident curiosity among urban masses, wandering for no other reason than to look at the faces of a crowd and comprehend the city landscape. The practice involves a heightened mode of perception and poetic production aimed toward capturing a sense of immediacy. *Chicago, July 99* achieves this intimacy through the thoughtful attention of Streuli and looms from the windows of the museum, a tribute to the city. MG

1 David Brittain, interview of Beat Streuli in "The Crowd," *Creative Camera* (August/ September 1997), p. 36.

Tom Friedman

American, b. 1965

Untitled
1999
Cardboard and Styrofoam balls
100 × 30 × 17 in. (254 × 76.2 × 43.2 cm)
Restricted gift of the Nancy A. Lauter and Alfred
L. McDougal Charitable Fund, J. Ira and Nicki
Harris Foundation, Jacqueline S. Harris
Foundation, Orbit Fund, and Bernice and
Kenneth Newberger Fund
2000.20

Complicated visual and conceptual experiences embedded in a wide variety of materials characterize the work of the St. Louis–born, Massachusetts-based artist Tom Friedman. Friedman's work incorporates the lessons of late twentieth-century art even as it focuses on a highly personal point of view, capturing a childlike sense of wonder and discovery in the everyday as it explores the nature and meaning of art. Friedman's quest for deeper meaning leaves those who encounter his work more attuned to the strange nuances of the world and more sensitive to the grand pattern of our lives.

Working in a wide range of forms including sculpture, photography, and drawing, Friedman has amassed an impressive body of work during his relatively short career that defies easy characterization. He employs everyday materials, including Play Doh, sugar cubes, spaghetti, bubble gum, toothpicks, laundry detergent, and construction paper, using each material in a fairly traditional way, to construct a sculptural form or to explore the nature of the material itself. For example, in an untitled 1991 work, Friedman used laundry detergent as a substitute for snow to create a snow angel. In *Loop* (1993), he connected strands of cooked spaghetti end to end to create a continuous loop.

While Friedman's pieces initially engage the senses with their typically whimsical materials, the works themselves are hardly simplistic. The materials and his investigations of them serve as a point of departure from the known world in a journey to unfamiliar realms where the ordinary suddenly seems extraordinary. Often exploring the nature and limits of human perception, his works resonate with a multitude of associations. Scale shifts from the tiny to the huge are common in his work, adding to this sense of the extraordinary; one early work consists of a self-portrait carved into an aspirin, while the work in the MCA Collection is the legs and torso of a giant robot. Constructed from pieces of mat board and decorated with tiny balls of Styrofoam, *Untitled* seems like the impulsive work of a young boy, driven to build the robot of his imagination. Yet its gargantuan scale, especially considering the relatively flimsy materials from which it is constructed, surpasses any childhood imaginings. The robot becomes a modern colossus, risen up as if out of his packing crate, tiny bits of the protective Styrofoam still clinging to his body.

The human form, especially in full-body self-portraits, is a recurring motif in Friedman's work. He has created a three-quarters-scale standing self-portrait out of sugar cubes, and in one of his most disturbing works, a self-portrait meticulously crafted out of construction paper as if he had been ripped apart. In *Untitled*, the inhuman forms of the half-robot are poignant in their incompleteness. LW

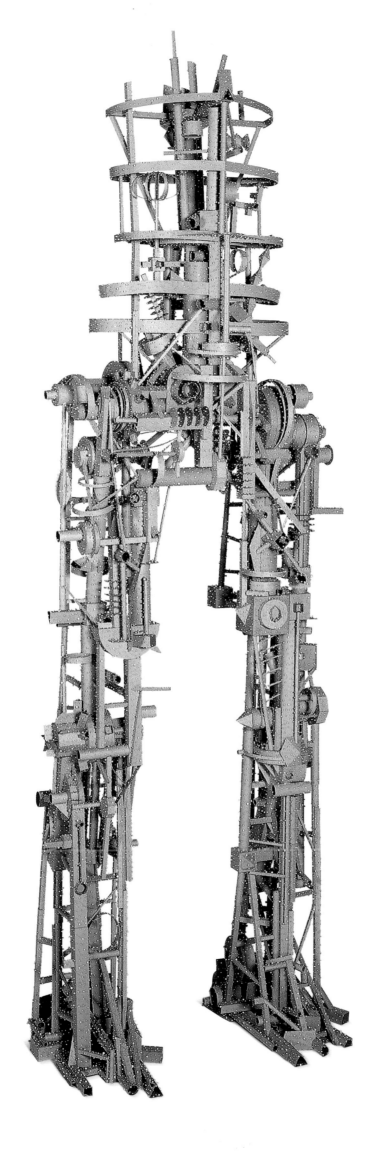

Arturo Herrera

Venezuelan, b. 1959

Behind the House III
1999
Wool felt
Four parts, installed: 102 × 296 in.
(259.1 × 751.8 cm)
Restricted gift of Nancy and Sandy Koltun
2000.16.a – d

In his collages, photographs, sculptures, wall paintings, and felt pieces Arturo Herrera explores the psychological associations of images abstracted from popular culture while leaving their meanings open-ended. The artist has said, "I am interested in the effect of nonlinear and associative readings on the viewer and the potential of painted space to be an intimate receptacle for the imagination and an aesthetic experience."

Herrera began making red, blue, black, and brown felt pieces in 1998. At first amorphous and ambiguous, these large works suggest ideas that may inspire images rather than representing them explicitly, often making oblique references to traditional landscape paintings as well as to his own collages and photographs. *Behind the House III* is a large piece comprising four red felt panels with driplike shapes cut out of the fabric, creating a vivid contrast of positive and negative forms. The work recalls Herrera's enigmatic black-and-white photographs of wooded landscapes, in which he used a mirror to create a reflective symmetry within the image, suggesting light seeping through trees as in mysterious fairy tale forest settings. The felt piece conveys a similar effect,

evoking the contours of light and dark shadows in a forest. The cutout technique stems from Herrera's collage works in which he carefully cut cartoons and Disney characters from coloring books and illustrated stories and recomposed them into ambiguous arrangements; a part of Bambi's leg, Snow White's skirt, and the seven dwarves' hats appear in flat compositions of paint and ink. He uses images from children's literature as a source to tap subconscious childhood memories, fragmenting the images to create a nonlinear narrative.

Herrera's use of felt as the primary material for his large-scale works has numerous associations with the avant-garde artists of the 1960s. Joseph Beuys (p. 122) used felt for its protective and natural symbolism, while Robert Morris (p. 78) used strips of heavy industrial felt in floor installations. The large size of Herrera's felt pieces recalls the monumental scale of abstract expressionist paintings, especially those of Jackson Pollock (American, 1912–1956).

Like many conceptual artists working today, Herrera is not limited by using only a few media to express his ideas. He works with the traditions

of painting, sculpture, relief, collage, and drawing in highly experimental and innovative ways to create hybrid forms. Some of his wall paintings are like drawings, the felt pieces have sculptural qualities, and his collages recall paintings, all while combining natural forms and popular culture in a collection of lyrical, evocative images. JRW

Giuseppe Gabellone

Italian, b. 1973

Giuseppe Gabellone laboriously constructs structures — some sleek and minimal, others biomorphic and earthy — frequently destroying them soon after he takes their photograph. The resulting images plumb our associations with documentary photography and with ideas of presence and absence. In the tradition of Italian artists working during the 1960s and 1970s such as Pino Pascali (1936 – 1968) and Mario and Marisa Merz (b. 1925 and 1931), Gabellone provokes questions about how materials convey meaning, reevaluating the properties of photography. By shifting the scale and exploiting the reproductive qualities of photographs, he creates enigmatic and evocative pictures.

Gabellone is first and foremost a sculptor. All of his works are part of his developing inquiry into the sculptural element of architecture. His photographs compel viewers to consider where their sculptural subjects have come from, what kind of nature generated them, whether they really existed somewhere before, or if, in our digital age, they are simply the result of some skillful manipulation. In fact everything in Gabellone's works existed in reality and was conceived and created by the artist. In the structure-sculpture he built exclusively for this untitled photograph, placed in a rough industrial space that contrasts with the smoothness of the sculpture and its fluid path, Gabellone created the basis for his own synthesis between the

Untitled
1999
Chromogenic development print
59$\frac{3}{8}$ × 96$\frac{1}{8}$ in. (150.8 × 244.2 cm)
Ed: 3/3
Restricted gift of Collectors Forum
2001.4

surreal, the contemporary, and the baroque. In this image, the structure (which Gabellone destroyed after taking the photograph) seems to have overgrown the space, suggesting continuous expansion.

In order to transform a photograph into an autonomous object, the artist believes that the subject-sculpture of the image needs to disappear from the world, so that what we see is the only reality we can absorb. All the labor invested into the making of the structure is the purpose of the final symbolic icon; the goal is, as in Taoist philosophy, the path. The effort is the content of the work, not the resulting object.

Gabellone creates a metaphysical experience in which viewers can only imagine the existence of the object. In extracting the sculpture from the space and re-creating it in the imagination of the viewer, he endows the object with a certain timelessness. Particularly in this work, the juxtaposition of the surreal structure with the banality of the space enhances the extraordinary and marvelous qualities in the final image.

The influence of modernist architecture and of the late nineteenth-century engineering feats such as the Eiffel Tower or New York's Coney Island roller coaster pervades this and other works by Gabellone. The spirit of his art can be characterized by constant challenges, not unlike the efforts of those pioneers of structural architecture, to generate new forms and visual innovation, at the same time paying tribute to the classical practice of sculpture. FB

305

Thomas Demand

German, b. 1964

Labor
2000
Chromogenic development print and Diasec
71 × 105½ in. (180.3 × 268 cm)
Ed: 1/6
Partial and promised gift from The Howard and
Donna Stone Collection
2002.18

Poll
2001
Chromogenic development print and Diasec
70 × 103 in. (177.8 × 261.6 cm)
Ed: 4/6
Restricted gift of Mr. and Mrs. Sanfred Koltun
2001.5

In his photographs of life-sized scenes constructed out of paper, Thomas Demand examines our expectations and assumptions about documentary photography. He fabricates settings that resemble actual places and events, approximating details and omitting human subjects entirely, photographs the scene, and then destroys his construction. In an age when an isolated image, rather than text, is often used to represent an entire story, Demand's reproductions raise doubts about the authenticity of images in the mass media and peoples' acceptance of such images as accurate and true.

Demand's enigmatically titled works are often based on photographs of historical situations. In *Badezimmer/ Bathroom* (1997), he re-created the photograph from German magazine *Der Spiegel* of the Beau Rivage Hotel bath-

room where German politician Uwe Barschel was found dead; the studio of Jackson Pollock (American, 1912–1956) appears in *Stall/Barn* (1997); *Raum/ Room* (1994) shows Hitler's headquarters after they were bombed in 1944; and *Studio* (1997) depicts the set of the German version of the 1950s game show *What's My Line?*

Poll was made during the highly contested manual recount of the ballots in the U.S. Presidential election of 2000. Demand found images of related events on the Internet, prompting his interest in the effect of digital images on our concept of reality and history. Although the volunteers and experts who examined faulty ballots during the recount are absent from the image, their tedious efforts are echoed in Demand's

306

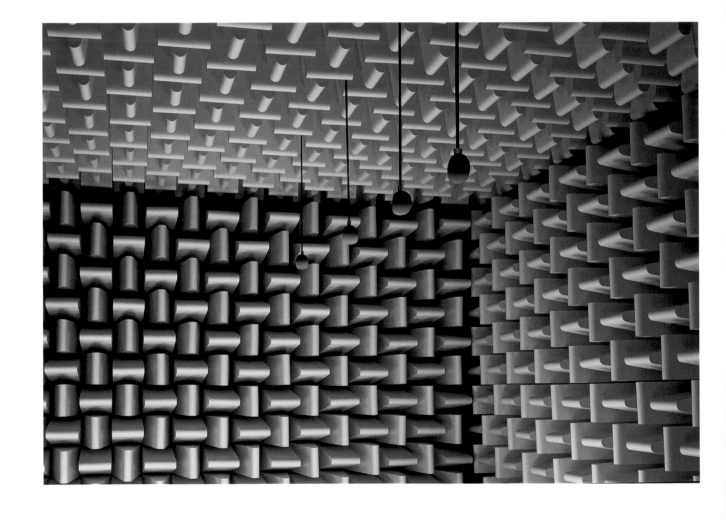

painstaking reconstruction of the event. The physical manifestation of the people's work, and more generally, the ideals of democracy, are represented in stacks of unmarked ballots. The photographs are approximately the same scale as Demand's construction, creating a fastidious representation of the actual event, however the scene appears abnormally perfect with no signs of human activity. Since the artist has not attempted to disguise the artificiality of the scenes, the paper construction is evident upon close inspection, drawing a comparison to the artificiality of images in the media.

As in *Poll*, Demand's exclusion of human subjects in *Labor* creates tension between the subject of the scene and his austere depiction of it, letting the viewers wonder what exactly they are looking at. The unfamiliar pattern of *Labor* is based on a specially engineered soundproof room with echo-absorbing beams in which BMW tests the noise levels of their cars as if they were speeding through the landscape. Three microphones hang from the ceiling to represent the simulated sound.

An understanding of Demand's pictures can be augmented by specific cultural knowledge — the images are instantly iconic and highly charged for those who recognize them, yet completely unfamiliar for others. However, recognition of the subjects is not always necessary, since the images in his works, from specific events to general images including escalators, airplane doors, and garages, evoke a broader narrative and provoke discussions about the ability of photography to represent the truth. J R W

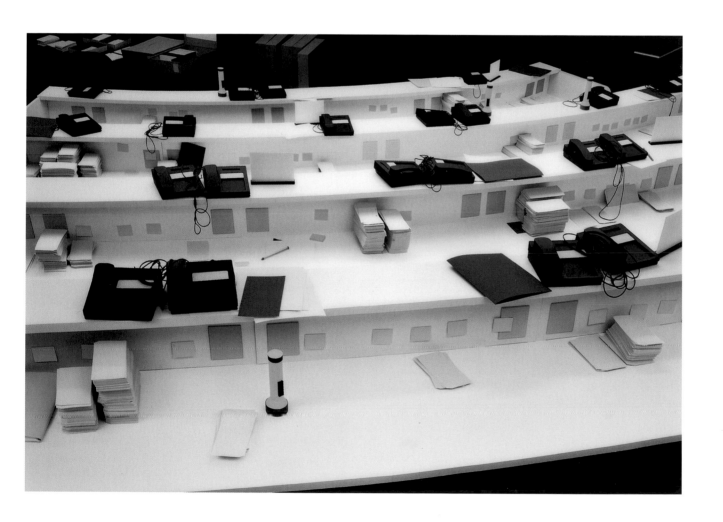

Jason Salavon

American, b. 1970

**The Top 25 Grossing Films
of All Time, 2 x 2**
2001
Color video installation
2 hours, 20 minutes
Dimensions variable
Ed: 1/5
Illinois Arts Council Purchase Grant and Bernice
and Kenneth Newberger Fund
2001.21

Jason Salavon is a conceptual artist who uses computer-manipulated data (he also designs his own software) and photographic as well as other media to create his artworks. Based in Chicago, he first established his reputation with a body of work that included computer-assisted composites of various similar images, such as *Every Playboy Centerfold, 1988–1997*, and a recent series featuring composites of numerous "typical" houses in New York, Chicago, and Los Angeles resulting in mysterious images that show the essential idea of home in each of these cities.

In 2000, Salavon began working with video projections, including *The Top 25 Grossing Films of All Time, 2 × 2*, which presents, as of the date of the work's making, a composite of the twenty-five top grossing movies. Through the process of color-averaging, in which the dominant color of a frame of a film is detected and enhanced, Salavon created a mesmerizing montage of luminous color that is projected onto a wall. Each of the twenty-five top grossing films is presented in a square divided into four rectangles occupying the position in the grid of color equivalent to its box-office position; thus *Titanic*, reduced to its essential colors, appears in the top right corner. Blues and whites, reflecting the color of sea, sky, and ice, dominate the *Titanic* square, in sharp contrast to the square immediately below it, which features the color-averaged frames of the animated film *The Lion King*—the highly saturated oranges of the African savanna and the lions themselves. No imagery appears, but the varying colors and rhythms that reflect how each film was edited are distinctive and ultimately recognizable. The longest film of the twenty-five, *Titanic*, dominates the work as the shorter films end and the squares they occupy fade away to black. In setting up a lyrical, constantly changing work of geometric abstraction, Salavon fuses the painterly with the dominant popular cultural form, film, creating an enjoyable and thought-provoking viewing experience. In reinterpreting the hours of imagery presented in these twenty-five movies as a moving "canvas" of light, Salavon demonstrates how people bring their unique perspectives to the common experiences that bind a culture.

In his reevaluation of how perception determines identity, Salavon has worked with both personal and cultural themes. He has explored his own body by photographing every square inch of it and creating, through a software program, a "flayed" image of himself arranged from darkest areas including hair and crevices to the lightest areas of his skin. He has examined films and the hold they have on the imagination through suites like *The Grand Unification Theory* (1997), which utilized and rearranged frames from four diverse films — *Star Wars*, *Snow White and the Seven Dwarfs*, *It's a Wonderful Life*, and *Deep Throat*. LW

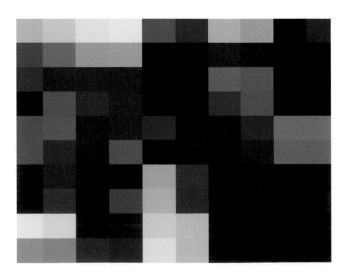

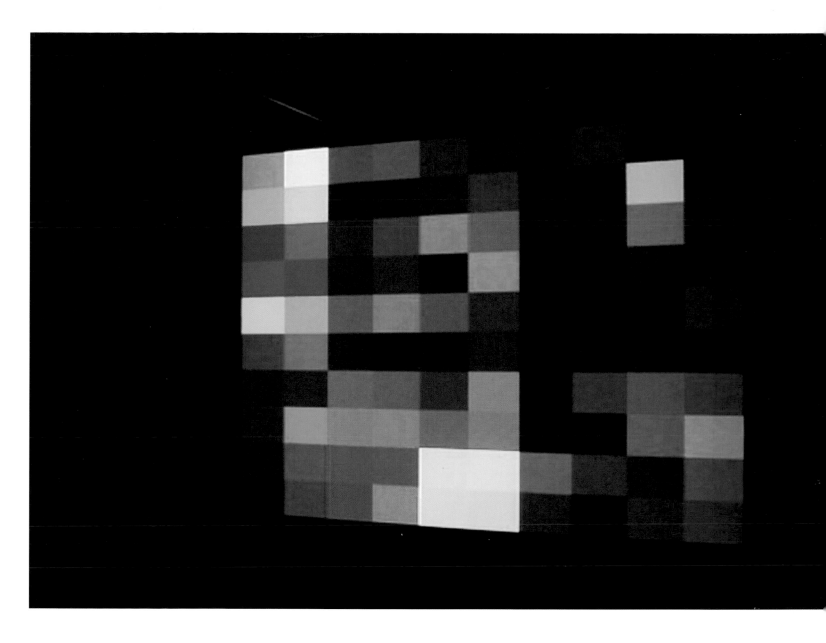
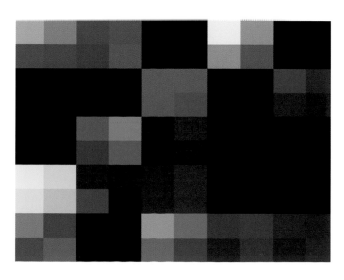

Maurizio Cattelan

Italian, b. 1960

Felix
2001
Oil on polyvinyl resin and fiberglass
26 × 6 × 20 ft. (7.9 × 1.8 × 6.1 m)
Ed: 1/2
The Edlis/Neeson Art Purchase Fund
2001.22

Maurizio Cattelan's giant cat, named *Felix* after the famous cartoon cat created in the early twentieth century by Otto Messmer, draws on popular culture and delves into our collective imagination and desire for spectacle. Cattelan has chosen a range of curious subjects for his works — the pope being struck down by a meteorite, a taxidermic horse hanging from the ceiling, a mannequin of himself in a Joseph Beuys felt suit (p. 123), this dinosaur-sized cat skeleton — all convincing representations of his version of reality, recalling fantastic surrealist imagery and always accompanied by a biting sense of humor. He often uses animals as stand-ins for the human figure, eliciting feelings of compassion and empathy with tragicomic overtones. He used real skeletons of a donkey, dog, cat, and rooster in his 1997 work *Love Lasts Forever*; a year later he made *Pluto*, a dog skeleton holding a newspaper in its mouth.

Cattelan's works take on eclectic forms in relationship to their installation sites, often revealing and undermining the conventions of art making and exhibitions in museums, galleries, and at international art fairs. In 2001, when visiting Chicago in preparation for a commission at the MCA, Cattelan was inspired by Sue — the most complete Tyrannosaurus rex ever discovered — at the Field Museum of Natural History. Measuring over forty-six feet in length with a tail that extends twenty-six feet in the air,

Felix is larger than his cross-town rival, who has become the Field Museum's signature attraction. Cattelan designed *Felix* for a particular space — the MCA atrium — but he also wanted his work to resonate with Sue, creating a conceptual dialogue across the city. At the Field, Cattelan learned that the skull displayed on Sue's skeleton was a cast, because the real one is too heavy to be displayed with the body. Considering what was most fascinating to the public about Sue — its scale, its historical and scientific significance, or its everyday name — Cattelan realized that fantasy is more important to viewers than reality or truth.

By treating art as a field study or a laboratory in which reality is reconstructed in all its complexity and contradiction, Cattelan plays with the power of the image, object, or scenario he creates to effectively communicate what text cannot. Because the cat skeleton is much larger than a human being, the usually benign animal seems intimidating, even frightening. As in his other works, with *Felix* Cattelan experiments with how viewers must suspend their disbelief in order to succumb to fantasy. He has said that when planning a work he first thinks of a very powerful image. The results, with their striking, often absurd and unreal subjects, linger in the memory. JRW

Donald Moffett

American, b. 1955

What Barbara Jordan Wore
2002
Installation of oil and enamel on linen with color video projection
Three parts, each: 45 × 60¼ in.
(114.3 × 153 cm)
Restricted gift of Nancy A. Lauter and Alfred L. McDougal, Judith Neisser, Thomas and Barbara Ruben, Faye and Victor Morgenstern Family Foundation, Ruth Horwich, and Funds from the 2001 Benefit Art Auction
2002.81.a–c

Donald Moffett, who was born in Texas and moved to New York in the late 1970s, was a founding member of the AIDS-activist collective Gran Fury, which flourished in the 1980s. When the group disbanded in the early 1990s, Moffett continued to make progressive art that challenged the status quo and sought out new aesthetic experimentation. More recently, he has worked in an increasingly abstract style, while anchoring his monochrome paintings with sociopolitical content. The work *What Barbara Jordan Wore* was featured in the MCA's *Donald Moffett: What Barbara Jordan Wore*, his first solo exhibition. The focus of this project was the ethical import of Barbara Jordan, one of the first African-American women to

be elected to the United States Congress. In these works, Moffett pushed the boundaries of monochromatic painting, experimenting with abstraction and representation, still and moving imagery, and audio and visual semiotics. Moffett has always infused his work with issues of social and political significance, affixing its aesthetic simplicity to real-world content.

The Watergate scandal and the Congressional hearings that followed are the focus of *What Barbara Jordan Wore*, especially the speech Jordan delivered to the House Judiciary Committee on July 25, 1974, in which she called upon the Committee to hold President Richard Nixon accountable

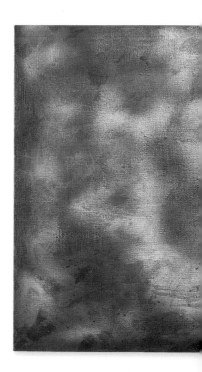

to the Constitution. The audio component of the work, Jordan's thirteen-minute speech played on a loop in the exhibition gallery, reinforces Moffett's interest in language as a tool to further the political dimensions of his work.

The three canvases that make up this work are painted dull gold with a video image projected on them. The uneven surface of oil paint functions unpredictably; the projected imagery changes as the viewer moves from one position to another. A close-up of Jordan as she reads her speech is projected on the first canvas. Her figure is enlarged and the focus of the work is not on her face, but the pink suit she wore, which Moffett tinted to an almost neon brightness. Another captures the citizens who witnessed the speech in Congress. Moffett blurred the faces in the crowd to an almost indistinct garden of colors — this canvas is the most impressionist of the three, absorbed most effectively from a distance where the subtle shifts of human movement and changing light can be grasped at once. On the third canvas, Moffett casts a short looped image of the Committee on the gold background in a seamless, nearly still way. Only occasional gestures evoke a haunting effect in the otherwise static piece.

While this work reflects Moffett's inclinations toward political and social discussion, it is unique both within his repertoire and in the field of abstraction. The imposition of video imagery on the monochromatic gold canvas creates a work that functions within the structure of painting but also has the kinetic power of film. With its rich use of color — gold and brown hues and the pink of Barbara Jordan's suit — along with the low and distinct sounds of Jordan's voice, this work is all-encompassing, capturing one's attention with both its visual complexity and innovation, as well as its ethical underpinnings and references to social content. MG

CATALOGUE OF SELECTED WO

Notes to the reader

This Catalogue includes information about the artists who are featured in the Selected Works section of this volume. Artists on the following pages are arranged in alphabetical order. Their names, nationalities, and birth-dates are followed by the page numbers on which they are featured in the Selected Works section. Throughout, Museum of Contemporary Art, Chicago, is abbreviated to MCA. This Catalogue does not list every work in the MCA Collection.

Captions

Dates
If a work was made over a period of more than one year, this is indicated with a dash: 1989–1990. If a work was conceived or made in one year and re-made in another, a slash separates the years: 1979/1989.

Materials
Materials are listed in order of their estimated proportionate use in the works. Found objects are identified by their former purposes or by their brand names when appropriate.

Dimensions
Measurements cited are the maximum dimensions of works in inches and centimeters. Height precedes width precedes depth. Most of the dimensions have been recorded to the nearest sixteenth of an inch and nearest millimeter. All other dimensions are taken from previously documented descriptions.

Credit lines
There are four classifications of gifts into the MCA Collection: full gifts; partial gifts, works with shared ownership; restricted gifts of moneys that are donated to purchase a work; and gifts by exchange, works purchased with funds from the sale of a deaccessioned work.

Provenance

Identities, locations, and dates of former ownership are given in chronological order up to the MCA's acquisition of the object. Original ownership is assumed to reside with the artist. Often a gallery is listed as the first owner. In most cases, unless noted, the work was consigned by a living artist to the gallery.

The date after each owner indicates when the work was acquired. If a direct transaction between one owner and another could not be found it is listed as unknown. Provenance is based on the following criteria: documents provided to the MCA at acquisition, correspondence to or from the artist or artist's estate or former owners, sales documents and other gallery records, and previously published histories of ownership. Agents of transfer, such as galleries, private dealers, and auction houses are included. For auctions, dates of sale and lot numbers are given.

Exhibition Histories

Exhibition histories are provided for each work that has been shown publicly, and arranged chronologically within each section. Exhibition information is documented based on one or more of the following sources, in order of precedence: museum or gallery records, exhibition catalogues, and exhibition reviews. The exhibition histories pertain only to the edition or object in the MCA Collection, except as noted. Dates indicate the full run of the exhibition. In some cases, objects may have been removed from one MCA exhibition before its end date to be included in another.

References

Bibliographic information is provided for each of the artists featured in this catalogue. Cited publications make reference to the objects catalogued here or provide general commentary on the selected artist.

Other works in the MCA Collection

Full captions are provided for all works in the MCA Collection by artists featured in this volume.

Magdalena Abakanowicz
Polish, b. 1930
p. 158

Cage
1981
Burlap, glue, and wood
66 × 46 × 61 in.
(167.6 × 116.8 × 154.9 cm)
Gift of Ralph I. and Helyn D. Goldenberg
1982.37.a–b

Provenance

Ralph I. and Helyn D. Goldenberg, Chicago, 1982.

MCA, 1982.

Exhibition History

Alterations, ARC/Musée d'Art Moderne de la Ville de Paris, Paris, January 13–February 21, 1981.

Magdalena Abakanowicz, MCA and the Chicago Public Library Cultural Center, November 6, 1982–January 2, 1983; Musée d'Art Contemporain, Montreal, February 10–March 27, 1983; Portland Art Museum and Portland Center for the Visual Arts, Oreg., February 28–April 22, 1984; Dallas Museum of Fine Arts, June 21–August 19, 1984; Frederick S. Wight Art Gallery of the University of California, Los Angeles, September 23–November 11, 1984.

Ten Years of Collecting, MCA, April 14–May 20, 1984.

Selections from the Permanent Collection, MCA, February 25–April 22, 1986.

Avant-Garde Art in the Eighties, Los Angeles County Museum of Art, April 21–July 12, 1987.

Images for Human Conduct: Selections from the Permanent Collection, MCA, July 31–September 1, 1987.

Magdalena Abakanowicz, Laumeier Sculpture Park, St. Louis, Mo., September 18–November 13, 1988.

Selections from the Permanent Collection Exhibition: Important Sculptural Works, MCA, April 25–July 8, 1989.

Modeling the Future: The New Museum and Key Works from the Permanent Collection, MCA, May 2–November 8, 1992.

Rings: Five Passions in World Art, High Museum of Art, Atlanta, July 4–September 29, 1996.

Envisioning the Contemporary: Selections from the Permanent Collection, MCA, June 21, 1997–April 5, 1998.

The Body Present: Effigies, Decoys, and Other Equivalents, MCA, January 19–May 12, 2002.

References

Jacob, Mary Jane. *Magdalena Abakanowicz*. Exh. cat. MCA; New York: Abbeville, 1982.

Jacob, Mary Jane et al. *Selections from the Permanent Collection, Vol. I*. MCA, 1984.

Rings: Five Passions in World Art. New York: Harry N. Abrams in association with the High Museum of Art, 1996. P. 122.

Sabbath, Lawrence. "The Weaving of Magic." *The Gazette* (Montreal), February 19, 1983, p. B8.

Other Works in the MCA Collection

Untitled, 1981
Charcoal on paper
39 3/8 × 29 5/8 in. (100 × 75.2 cm)
Gift of the artist
1982.36

Vito Acconci
American, b. 1940
p. 112

Stretch
1969
Gelatin silver prints, chalkboard spray paint,
chalk, and marker on foamcore
54 × 54 in. (137.2 × 137.2 cm)
Gerald S. Elliott Collection
1995.24

Provenance

Galerie Eric Franck, Geneva, mid-1980s.

Rhona Hoffman Gallery, Chicago, 1988.

Gerald S. Elliott, Chicago, 1988.

MCA, 1995.

Exhibition History

Vito Acconci, Stedelijk Museum, Amsterdam,
November 30, 1978 – January 14, 1979.

Vito Acconci: A Retrospective, 1969–1980, MCA,
March 21 – May 18, 1980.

*Vito Acconci Part 1: Early Works, Photographs
1969 – 1970*, Rhona Hoffman Gallery, Chicago,
January 8 – February 6, 1988.

*Affinities and Intuitions: The Gerald S. Elliott
Collection of Contemporary Art,* The Art Institute
of Chicago, May 12 – July 29, 1990.

*PC Focus: Conceptualism to Postconceptualism,
the 1960s to the 1990s*, MCA, August 22 –
November 8, 1992.

*Conceptual Photography from the Gerald S. Elliott
Collection*, MCA, February 6 – March 21, 1993.

*In the Shadow of Storms: Art of the Postwar Era
from the MCA Collection*, MCA, July 2, 1996 –
May 25, 1997.

Perspectives on Terrain, MCA, January 16 –
March 7, 1999.

House of Used Parts
1985
Aluminum ladders, doors, windows, wood,
canvas, and vinyl seat cushions
108 × 72 × 72 in. (274.3 × 182.9 × 182.9 cm)
Gerald S. Elliott Collection
1995.23

Provenance

Rhona Hoffman Gallery, Chicago, 1987.

Gerald S. Elliott, Chicago, 1987.

MCA, 1995.

Exhibition History

Making Shelter, Graduate School of Design,
Harvard University, Cambridge, Mass.,
April 1985.

Houses, Newhouse Gallery, Snug Harbor
Cultural Center, Staten Island, N.Y.,
December 1985 – January 5, 1986.

Vito Acconci: House of Used Parts, Mattress
Factory, Pittsburgh, Pa., 1986.

Vito Acconci: Domestic Trapping, Museum of
Contemporary Art, La Jolla, Calif., June 5 –
August 2, 1987; Neuberger Museum of Art,
State University of New York, Purchase, N.Y.,
September 17, 1987 – January 6, 1988; Aspen Art
Museum, Aspen, Colo., February 18 – April 17,
1988; Laumeier Sculpture Park, St. Louis, Mo.,
June 12 – September 4, 1988.

*Affinities and Intuitions: The Gerald S. Elliott
Collection of Contemporary Art,* The Art Institute
of Chicago, May 12 – July 29, 1990.

*Envisioning the Contemporary: Selections
from the Permanent Collection*, MCA,
June 21, 1997 – April 5, 1998 and
April 30, 1998 – February 7, 1999.

*Decades in Dialogue: Perspectives on the MCA
Collection*, MCA, February 27 – October 31, 1999.

References

Acconci, Vito. "Early Work: Moving My Body
into Place." *Avalanche* 6 (autumn 1972).

Acconci, Vito. "Projections of Hope."
Artforum 87, no. 3 (March 1988), p. 128.

Benezra, Neal, ed. *Affinities and Intuitions: The
Gerald S. Elliott Collection of Contemporary Art.*
Chicago: The Art Institute, 1990.

Jacob, Mary Jane et al. *Selections from the
Permanent Collection, Vol. I.* MCA, 1984.

Linker, Kate. *Vito Acconci.* New York:
Rizzoli, 1994.

Rickey, Carrie. "Vito Acconci: The Body
Impolitic." *Art in America* 68, no. 8
(October 1980), p. 118.

Schwartz, Ellen. "Vito Acconci: I Want to Put the
Viewer on Shaky Ground." *ARTnews* 80, no. 6
(June 1981), p. 93.

Vito Acconci: Photographic Works 1969 – 1970.
Exh. cat. Chicago: Rhona Hoffman Gallery,
1988.

Other Works in the MCA Collection

Claim Excerpts, 1971
Black-and-white video
62 minutes, 11 seconds
Unlimited edition
MCA purchase
1996.28

The Red Tapes (Parts I, II, and III), 1976
Black-and-white video
Part I: 43 minutes, 30 seconds;
Part II: 55 minutes; Part III: 55 minutes
Gift of the artist
1980.49.1–3

The Gangster Sister from Chicago, 1977
Walls, audiotape, and speakers
Installed: dimensions variable
Restricted gift of Young Hoffman Gallery and
Men's Council, and National Endowment for
the Arts Purchase Grant
1980.67

20 Foot Ladder for Any-Size Wall, 1979 – 1980
Etching on paper
Eight parts, each: 29 1/2 × 41 1/2 in.
(74.9 × 105.4 cm)
Ed: 3/15
Gift of L. A. Louver, Venice, Calif.
1991.64.a–h

Bridge Chairs for Sex and Gender, 1984
Enamel on aluminum ladder
110 × 127 9/16 × 17 11/16 in.
(279.4 × 324 × 44.9 cm)
Gift of Paul and Camille Oliver-Hoffmann
1984.55

John Ahearn
American, b. 1951
p. 164

Clyde
1981
Acrylic on plaster and wood
26 1/2 × 23 × 10 in. (67.3 × 58.4 × 25.4 cm)
Gift of Lannan Foundation
1997.17

Provenance

Brooke Alexander Inc., New York, 1981.

Lannan Foundation, Lake Worth, Fla., 1982.

MCA, 1997.

Exhibition History

Representation, Brooke Alexander, New York,
September – October 1981.

After Street Art, Boca Raton Museum of Art,
Boca Raton, Fla., April 28 – May 29, 1988.

*South Bronx Hall of Fame: Sculpture by John
Ahearn and Rigoberto Torres*, Contemporary Arts
Museum, Houston, September 13 – November,
1991; Witte de With, Rotterdam, Netherlands,
December 7, 1991 – January 26, 1992;
Contemporary Arts Center, Cincinatti, Ohio,
February 14 – April 18, 1992; The Contemporary
Museum, Honolulu, Hawaii, June 9 –
August 9, 1992.

*Images: Selections from the Lannan Foundation
Collection*, Lannan Foundation Gallery, Los
Angeles, December 3, 1992 – March 27, 1993.

John Ahearn: A Decade of Figurative Sculpture,
University Art Gallery, University of California,
San Diego, January 14 – February 26, 1995.

*Envisioning the Contemporary: Selections from the
Permanent Collection*, MCA, April 30, 1998 –
February 7, 1999.

The Possibilities of Citizenship, Lake Forest
College, Lake Forest, Ill., October 13 –
November 15, 2000.

*The Body Present: Effigies, Decoys, and Other
Equivalents*, MCA, January 19 – May 12, 2002.

References

Alexander, Brooke. "John Ahearn with Rigoberto
Torres." *Artforum* 25, no. 6 (February 1987),
pp. 115–16.

Cemablast, Robin. "Public Sculpture: Race, Sex,
and Politics." *ARTnews* 91, no. 3 (March 1992),
pp. 30–32.

317

Champions: John Ahearn. New York: Tony Shafrazi Gallery, 1983.

Cyphers, Peggy. "John Ahearn at Brooke Alexander." *Arts Magazine* 65, no. 10 (summer 1991), p. 96.

Figures: Forms and Expressions. Buffalo, N.Y.: Buffalo Fine Arts Academy, 1994.

Kramer, Jane. *Whose Art is it?* Durham, N.C.: Duke University Press, 1994.

Kuspit, Donald. "John Ahearn/Rigoberto Torres at the CAM." *Artforum* 30, no. 5 (January 1992), p. 110.

Pincus, Robert L. "From the Bronx, a Vision of Real People." *San Diego Tribune,* January 9, 1995, p. E6.

———. "Sculptures are Portraits of the Bronx." *San Diego Tribune,* February 5, 1995, p. D4.

"Public Art Yo-yo: What Goes Up, Comes Down." *Art in America* 80, no. 2 (February 1992), p. 29.

South Bronx Hall of Fame: Sculpture by John Ahearn and Rigoberto Torres. Exh. cat. Houston: Contemporary Arts Museum, 1991.

Taplin, Robert. "Dead or Alive: Molds, Modeling, and Mimesis in Representational Sculpture." *Sculpture* 13, no. 3 (May/June 1994), pp. 24–31.

Wainwright, Heather. "In the Neighborhood: A Critique of Social Activist Art." *Public Art Review* 9 (autumn/winter 1997), pp. 16–20.

Wylie, Charles. "John Ahearn: Clyde with Folded Arms, 1982–83." *Saint Louis Art Museum Bulletin* 21 (winter 1995), pp. 6–7.

Carl Andre

American, b. 1935
p. 110

Zinc-Lead Plain

1969
Zinc and lead
Thirty-six parts, installed: $3/8 \times 72 \times 72$ in. ($1 \times 182.9 \times 182.9$ cm)
Gerald S. Elliott Collection
1995.26.a–jj

Provenance

Paula Cooper Gallery, New York, 1985.

Gerald S. Elliott, Chicago, 1985.

MCA, 1995.

Exhibition History

Carl Andre: Sculpture 1958–1974, Kunsthalle Bern, Sperone, Switzerland, April 24–June 8, 1975.

Floor Show: Carl Andre, Richard Long, and Barry Le Va, Corcoran Gallery of Art, Washington, D.C., December 1976–January 1977.

Westkunst: Zeitgenössische Kunst seit 1939, Museen der Stadt Köln, Cologne, Germany, May 30–August 16, 1981. (Shown as part of *37 Pieces of Work,* 1969.)

Affinities and Intuitions: The Gerald S. Elliott Collection of Contemporary Art, The Art Institute of Chicago, May 12–July 29, 1990.

In the Shadow of Storms: Art of the Postwar Era from the MCA Collection, MCA, July 2, 1996–May 25, 1997.

Envisioning the Contemporary: Selections from the Permanent Collection, MCA, June 21, 1997–April 5, 1998 and April 30, 1998–February 7, 1999.

Selected Works from the Collection, MCA, October 14–November 26, 2000.

Original Language: Highlights from the MCA Collection, MCA, March 24–August 5, 2001.

Minimalismos, Museo Nacional Centro de Arte Reina Sofia, Madrid, July 10–October 8, 2001.

References

Bourdon, David. *Carl Andre: Sculpture 1959–1977.* Exh. cat. New York: Jaap Rietman, 1978.

———. "The Razed Sites of Carl Andre: A Sculptor Laid Low by the Brancusi Syndrome." *Artforum* 5, no. 2 (October 1966), pp. 15–17.

Serota, Nicholas. *Carl Andre: Sculpture 1959–1978.* Exh. cat. London: Whitechapel Art Gallery, 1978.

Siegel, Jeanne. "Carl Andre: Artworker." *Studio International* (November 1970), reprinted in Jeanne Siegel, ed. *Artworks: Discourse on the 60s and 70s.* New York: Da Capo, 1992. Pp. 129–39.

Tuchmann, Phyllis. "Background of a Minimalist: Carl Andre." *Artforum* 16, no. 7 (March 1978), pp. 29–33.

———. "An Interview With Carl Andre." *Artforum* 8, no. 10 (June 1970), pp. 55–61.

Waldman, Diane. *Carl Andre.* Exh. cat. New York: Solomon R. Guggenheim Museum, 1970.

Other Works in the MCA Collection

Untitled, 1963
Text on paper
$11 \times 8½$ in. (27.9×21.6 cm)
Gerald S. Elliott Collection
1995.25

Arcata Pollux, 1983
Western red cedar
$48 \times 36 \times 36$ in. ($121.9 \times 91.4 \times 91.4$ cm)
Gerald S. Elliott Collection
1995.27.a–g

Richard Artschwager

American, b. 1923
p. 126

Polish Rider I

1970–71
Acrylic on Celotex
$44 \times 60^3/_{16}$ in. (111.8×152.9 cm)
Gift of Mrs. Robert B. Mayer
1984.2

Provenance

Leo Castelli Gallery, New York, 1971.

Mr. and Mrs. Robert B. Mayer, Winnetka, Ill., 1971.

MCA, 1984.

Exhibition History

Radical Realism, MCA, May 22–July 4, 1971.

1978–1984 on long-term loan from the Robert B. Mayer Memorial Loan Collection to Miami University of Ohio Art Museum; exhibited when museum opened.

Ten Years of Collecting, MCA, April 14–May 20, 1984.

American Painting and Sculpture from 1968 to the Present: Selections from the Permanent Collection, MCA, December 12, 1984–January 22, 1985.

Permanent Collection Exhibition: Icon/Index, MCA, February 5–April 3, 1988.

Toward the Future: Contemporary Art in Context, MCA, May 5–July 1, 1990.

PUBLIC/public, Elvehjem Museum of Art, Madison, Wis., September 14–November 10, 1991.

PC Focus: Conceptualism to Postconceptualism, the 1960s to the 1990s, MCA, August 22–November 8, 1992.

Under Development: Dreaming the MCA's Collection, MCA, April 30–August 28, 1994.

In the Shadow of Storms: Art of the Postwar Era from the MCA Collection, MCA, July 2, 1996–May 25, 1997.

Envisioning the Contemporary: Selections from the Permanent Collection, MCA, June 21, 1997–April 5, 1998.

Transmute, MCA, August 21–November 7, 1999.

References

Baker, Elizabeth. "Artschwager's Mental Furniture." *ARTnews* 66, no. 9 (January 1968), pp. 48–49, 58–61.

Collective Vision. MCA, 1996.

Jacob, Mary Jane et al. *Selections from the Permanent Collection, Vol. I.* MCA, 1984.

Madoff, Steven Henry. "Richard Artschwager's Sleight of Mind." *ARTnews* 87, no. 1 (January 1988), pp. 114–21.

Richard Artschwager. Exh. cat. New York: Whitney Museum of American Art; London: W. W. Norton, 1988.

Richard Artschwager's Theme(s). Exh. cat. Buffalo, N.Y.: Albright-Knox Art Gallery, 1979.

van Bruggen, Coosje. "Richard Artschwager." *Artforum* 22, no. 1 (September 1983), pp. 44–51.

Other Works in the MCA Collection

Triptych, 1962
Formica on wood
37¾ × 54½ in. (95.9 × 138.4 cm)
Gift of Lannan Foundation
1997.19

Untitled, 1970
Spun fiber and wood
19¾ × 19 × 3¼ in. (50.2 × 48.3 × 8.3 cm)
Gift of Lannan Foundation
1997.20

Yes/No Ball, 1974
Bowling ball
10 in. diameter (25.4 cm)
Gift of the artist
1976.1

Fractal, 1987
Formica on wood
17 × 17 × 5½ in. (43.2 × 43.2 × 14 cm)
Ed: 5/25
Gift of the Ruttenberg Family in honor of the 90th birthday of David C. Ruttenberg
1999.27

Mirror, 1988
Formica on wood
35⁵⁄₁₆ × 24⁵⁄₁₆ in. (89.7 × 61.8 cm)
Ed: 8/25
Gift of the Ruttenberg Family in honor of the 90th birthday of David C. Ruttenberg
1999.28

Time Piece, 1989
Oil on wood, Formica, and aluminum
Two parts, installed: 25½ × 23½ × 5¼ in. (64.8 × 59.7 × 13.3 cm)
Ed: 5/30
Gift of the Ruttenberg Family in honor of the 90th birthday of David C. Ruttenberg
1999.29.a–b

Stretch, 1990
Acrylic on Celotex and wood
19½ × 20 in. (49.5 × 50.8 cm)
Gift of Judith Neisser
1995.17

Francis Bacon
British, b. Ireland 1909–1992
p. 44

Study for a Portrait

1949
Oil on canvas
58¹³⁄₁₆ × 51⁷⁄₁₆ in. (149.4 × 130.6 cm)
Gift of Joseph and Jory Shapiro
1976.44

Provenance

Hanover Gallery, London, 1949.

Gerald Corcoran, London.

Mrs. Helen Grigg, Uckfield, Sussex, England, before 1954.

Sotheby & Co., London, July 9, 1958, lot no. 188.

Richard L. Feigen & Co., Chicago, 1958.

Joseph and Jory Shapiro, Chicago, 1958.

MCA, 1976.

Exhibition History

Francis Bacon Paintings, Hanover Gallery, London, November 8–December 10, 1949.

XXVII Biennale di Venezia, British Pavilion, Venice, June 19–October 17, 1954.

Britisk Kunst 1900–1955, Kunstforeningen, Copenhagen, April 1956; Kunsternes Hus, Oslo, Norway, May–June 1956.

Francis Bacon: 12 Paintings 1947–1958, Richard Feigen Gallery, Chicago, July–August 1959.

New Images of Man, The Museum of Modern Art, New York, September 30, 1959–November 29, 1959; Baltimore Museum of Art, Md., January 10, 1960–February 7, 1960.

Surrealism, Rosenstone Art Gallery, Bernard Horwich Center, Chicago, May 11–21, 1966.

Selections from the Joseph Randall Shapiro Collection, MCA, December 20, 1969–February 2, 1970.

Artists View the Law in the Twentieth Century, The David and Alfred Smart Museum of Art, The University of Chicago, October 5–November 27, 1977.

Selections from the Permanent Collection and the Mayer Loan Collection, MCA, November 2, 1979–January 27, 1980.

Selections from the Permanent Collection, MCA, September 2–November 2, 1980.

Permanent Collection Exhibition, MCA, March 25–May 29, 1983.

Ten Years of Collecting, MCA, April 10–June 4 1984.

The Mr. and Mrs. Joseph Randall Shapiro Collection, The Art Institute of Chicago, February 23–April 14, 1985.

Francis Bacon, Tate Gallery, London, May 22–August 18, 1985; Stuttgart Staatsgalerie, Germany, October 6, 1985–January 5, 1986; Nationalgalerie, Berlin, February 6–March 31, 1986.

Images for Human Conduct: Selections from the Permanent Collection, MCA, July 31–September 1, 1987.

Selections from the Permanent Collection: Figurative Expressionism and Neo-Expressionism, MCA, April 25–July 8, 1989.

Francis Bacon, Hirshhorn Museum and Sculpture Garden, Smithsonian Institution, Washington, D.C., October 12, 1989–January 7, 1990; Los Angeles County Museum of Art, February 11–April 29, 1990; The Museum of Modern Art, New York, May 31–August 28, 1990.

Seventy-Fifth Anniversary Exhibition, The Arts Club, Chicago, May 11–June 26, 1992.

Venice Biennale (British Council), Museo Correr, Venice, June 13–October 10, 1993.

Negotiating Rapture: The Power of Art to Transform Lives, MCA, July 2–October 20, 1996.

Francis Bacon, Musée National d'Art Moderne, Centre Georges Pompidou, June 27–October 14, 1996; Haus der Kunst, Munich, November 4, 1996–January 31, 1997. (Included only in the Munich presentation).

Envisioning the Contemporary: Selections from the Permanent Collection, MCA, June 21, 1997–April 5, 1998.

Francis Bacon Exhibition 2000, Hugh Lane Municipal Gallery of Modern Art, North Dublin, June 1–August 31, 2000.

Original Language: Highlights from the MCA Collection, MCA, March 24–August 5, 2001.

People See Paintings: Photography and Painting from the MCA Collection, MCA, January 19–October 20, 2002.

References

Ades, Dawn and Andrew Forge. *Francis Bacon*. London: Tate Gallery and Thames and Hudson; New York: Harry N. Abrams, 1985.

Alley, Ronald. *Francis Bacon*. London and New York: Thames and Hudson, 1964.

Collective Vision. MCA, 1996.

Davies, Hugh and Sally Yard. *Francis Bacon*. New York: Abbeville, 1986.

Francis Bacon: Paintings. London: Marlborough Fine Art Ltd., 1985.

Francis Bacon. Paris: Musée National d'Art Moderne, Centre Georges Pompidou, 1996.

Francis Bacon: A Retrospective Exhibition. Exh. cat. New York: Harry N. Abrams, 1999. P. 60.

Gowing, Sir Lawrence. "Francis Bacon." In *Francis Bacon Paintings 1945–1982*. Tokyo: Tokyo Shimbun, 1983.

Jacob, Mary Jane et al. *Selections from the Permanent Collection, Vol. I*. MCA, 1984.

Sylvester, David. *Interviews with Francis Bacon 1962–1979*. London and New York: Thames and Hudson, 1980.

319

John Baldessari

American, b. 1931
p. 198

Fish and Ram

1988
Tempera on gelatin silver
and chromogenic development prints
Five parts, installed: 109¾ × 144¼ in.
(278.8 × 366.4 cm)
Restricted gift of Gerald S. Elliott;
Anne and William J. Hokin by exchange;
and National Endowment for the Arts
Purchase Grant
1989.2.a–e

Provenance

Margo Leavin Gallery, Los Angeles, 1988.

MCA, 1989.

Exhibition History

John Baldessari: Recent Work, Margo Leavin
Gallery, Los Angeles, April 9–May 14, 1988.

New Acquisitions: The MCA Collects, MCA,
November 23, 1991–January 26, 1992.

John Baldessari: A Retrospective, The Museum of
Contemporary Art, Los Angeles, March 25–
June 17, 1990; San Francisco Museum of
Modern Art, July 12–September 9, 1990;
Hirshhorn Museum and Sculpture Garden,
Smithsonian Institution, Washington, D.C.,
October 16, 1990–January 6, 1991; Walker Art
Center, Minneapolis, February 3–April 28, 1991;
Whitney Museum of American Art, New York,
July 10–October 13, 1991; Musée d'Art
Contemporain, Montreal, November 21, 1991–
February 13, 1992. (Included only in the Los
Angeles presentation.)

New Acquisitions: The Museum Collects, MCA,
November 23, 1991–January 26, 1992.

*PC Focus: Conceptualism to Postconceptualism,
the 1960s to the 1990s,* MCA, August 22–
November 8, 1992.

Transmute, MCA, August 21–
November 7, 1999.

References

Collective Vision. MCA, 1996.

Gardner, Colin. "A Systematic Bewildering."
Artforum 28, no. 4 (December 1989),
pp. 106–112.

Glueck, Grace. "From Nobody to Somebody:
John Baldessari, Artist of Ideas." *New York
Times,* April 4, 1990.

Goldstein, Ann. "John Baldessari." In
Reconsidering the Object of Art: 1965–1975. Exh.
cat. Los Angeles: The Museum of
Contemporary Art; Cambridge, Mass.: MIT
Press, 1995. Pp. 66–69.

Siegel, Jeanne. "John Baldessari: Recalling
Ideas." In Jeanne Siegel, ed. *Artwords 2:
Discourse on the Early 80s.* Ann Arbor, Mich.:
UMI Press, 1988. Pp. 37–50.

van Bruggen, Coosje. *John Baldessari.* Exh. cat.
Los Angeles: The Museum of Contemporary
Art; New York: Rizzoli, 1990.

Other Works in the MCA Collection

Three Eyes (with Gold Bug), 1987
Acrylic and photoemulsion on canvas
Four parts, installed: 91 × 111 in.
(231.1 × 281.9 cm)
Gift of anonymous donor
1993.28.a–d

Matthew Barney

American, b. 1967
p. 294

The Cabinet of Frank Gilmore

1999
Vitrine with salt, epoxy resin, nylon,
polycarbonate honeycomb, beeswax, and acrylic
46¾ × 47¹⁵/₁₆ × 37⅝ in.
(118.7 × 121.8 × 95.6 cm)
Restricted gift of the Sara Lee Corporation
1999.55

Provenance

Barbara Gladstone Gallery, New York, 1999.

MCA, 1999.

Exhibition History

*Age of Influence: Reflections in the Mirror of
American Culture,* MCA, March 14, 2000–
January 2, 2001.

*Original Language: Highlights from the MCA
Collection,* MCA, March 24–August 5, 2001.

Cremaster 2: The Drone's Cell

1999
Chromogenic development print
with acrylic frame
43 × 54 in. (109.2 × 137.2 cm)
Ed: 2/6 aside from 2 artist's proofs
Partial and promised gift from The Howard and
Donna Stone Collection
2002.7

Provenance

Barbara Gladstone Gallery, New York, 1999.

Howard and Donna Stone, Chicago, 2000.

MCA, 2002.

Exhibition History

*Age of Influence: Reflections in the Mirror of
American Culture,* MCA, March 14, 2000–
January 2, 2001.

*Original Language: Highlights from the MCA
Collection,* MCA, March 24–August 5, 2001.

References

Bryson, Norman. "Matthew Barney's
Gonadotrophic Cavalcade." *Parkett,* no. 45
(December 1995).

Flood, Richard. *Cremaster 2.* Minneapolis:
Walker Art Center, 1999.

Goodeye, Thyrza Nicols. "Matthew Barney 95
Suspension (Cremaster) Secretion (Pearl)
Secret (Biology)." *Parkett,* no. 45 (December
1995), pp. 67–73.

Onfray, Michel. "Mannerist Variations on
Matthew Barney." *Parkett,* no. 45 (December
1995), pp. 42–57.

Riley, Robert. *Matthew Barney: New Work.*
San Francisco: Museum of Modern Art, 1992.

Seward, Keith. "Matthew Barney and Beyond."
Parkett, no. 45 (December 1995), pp. 58–66.

Spector, Nancy. *The Cremaster Cycle.* Exh. cat.
New York: Solomon R. Guggenheim Museum,
2002.

Wakefield, Neville and Richard Flood. *Matthew
Barney: Pace Car for the Hubris Pill.* New York:
Distributed Art Publishers, 1996.

Wakefield, Neville, Thyrza Nicols Goodeye, and
Nancy Spector. *Matthew Barney.* New York:
Solomon R. Guggenheim Museum, 2002.

Other Works in the MCA Collection

Unit Bolus, 1988–1991
Cast petroleum jelly, stainless steel, and
electronic freezing device
28½ × 18 × 10 in. (72.4 × 45.7 × 25.4 cm)
Ed: 4/5
Gift of Cooperfund, Inc.
1993.14.a–e

RADIAL DRILL: OTTOgate, 1991
Gelatin silver print and prosthetic plastic
15³/₁₆ × 11⅜ × 1¾ in.
(38.6 × 28.9 × 4.4 cm)
Ed: 9/10
Gerald S. Elliott Collection
1995.28

Bernd and Hilla Becher

Bernd, German, b. 1931
Hilla, German, b. 1934
p. 174

Cooling Towers

1983
Gelatin silver prints
Twelve parts, each: 20 × 16 in.
(50.8 × 40.6 cm)
Gerald S. Elliott Collection
1995.31.a–l

Provenance

Sonnabend Gallery, New York, c. 1983–84.

Gerald S. Elliott, Chicago, 1989.

MCA, 1995.

Exhibition History

*Affinities and Intuitions: The Gerald S. Elliott
Collection of Contemporary Art,* The Art Institute
of Chicago, May 12–July 29, 1990.

*Conceptual Photography from the Gerald S. Elliott
Collection,* MCA, February 6–March 21, 1993.

Rephotographing the Subject, Museum of
Contemporary Photography, Chicago,
September 8–November 4, 1995.

*In the Shadow of Storms: Art of the Postwar Era
from the MCA Collection,* MCA, July 2, 1996–
May 25, 1997.

Adam Brooks: DeNaturalized, MCA,
February 14–July 5, 1998.

*Apposite Opposites: Photography from the MCA
Collection,* MCA, March 27–August 1, 1999.

*Original Language: Highlights from the MCA
Collection,* MCA, March 24–August 5, 2001.

References

Andre, Carl. "A Note on Bernd and Hilla Becher." *Artforum* 11, no. 4 (December 1972), pp. 59–61.

Becher, Bernd and Hilla. *Anonyme Skulpturen: Eine Typologie technischer Bauten.* Düsseldorf, Germany: Art Press, 1970.

Bernd and Hilla Becher. Eindhoven, Netherlands: Stedelijk van Abbemuseum, 1981.

Bernd and Hilla Becher: Tipologie, Typologien, Typologies. Venice: Forty-Fourth Biennale, 1990.

Collective Vision. MCA, 1996.

Freidus, Marc. *Typologies: Nine Contemporary Photographers.* Exh. cat. Newport Beach, Calif.: Newport Harbor Art Museum, 1991.

Garrels, Gary. *Photography in Contemporary German Art: 1960 to the Present.* Exh. cat. Minneapolis: Walker Art Center, 1992.

Grauerholz, A. and Anne Ramsden. "Photographing Industrial Architecture: An Interview with Hilla and Bernd Becher." *Parachute* 22, no. 1 (spring 1981), pp. 14–19.

Mascheck, Joseph. "Unconscious Formalism, A Response to Andre's Note on the Bechers." *Artforum* 11, no. 7 (March 1973), pp. 74–75.

Sante, Luc. "The Iron Age." *The New Republic* 213 (July 3, 1995), pp. 27–30.

Other Works in the MCA Collection

Cooling Tower (Kuehlturm), 1963–68
Gelatin silver print
24 × 19 in. (61 × 48.3 cm)
Partial and promised gift from The Howard and Donna Stone Collection
2002.10

Hans Bellmer
German, 1902–1975
p. 36

La toupie (The Top)
1938/1968
Oil on bronze
13¼ × 6¹³⁄₁₆ × 6 in. (33.7 × 17.3 × 15.2 cm)
Edition of 8 aside from 2 artist's proofs
Gift of Joseph and Jory Shapiro
1998.34

Provenance

André-Francois Petit, Paris, 1968.

Unknown.

Joseph and Jory Shapiro, Chicago, before 1975.

MCA, 1998.

Exhibition History

Hans Bellmer Drawing and Sculpture, MCA, May 3–June 22, 1975.

Staging Surrealism: A Succession of Collections 2, Wexner Center for the Arts, Columbus, Ohio, September 19, 1997–January 4, 1998.

Decades in Dialogue: Perspectives on the MCA Collection, MCA, February 27–October 31, 1999.

La Révolution Surréaliste, Musée National d'Art Moderne, Centre Georges Pompidou, Paris, February 27–June 24, 2002; Kunstsammlung Nordrhein-Westfalen, Düsseldorf, Germany, July 20–November 24, 2002.

References

Bellmer, Hans. *La Petite anatomie de l'image.* Paris: Eric Losfeld, 1957.

Krauss, Rosalind and Jane Livingston. *L'Amour Fou: Photography and Surrealism.* New York: Abbeville, 1985.

Licht, Ira. *Hans Bellmer: Drawings and Sculpture.* Exh. cat. MCA, 1975.

Webb, Peter. *Hans Bellmer.* London and New York: Quartet Books, 1985.

William and Norma Copley Foundation. *Bellmer.* London: P. Lund Humphries, 1961.

Joseph Beuys
German, 1921–1986
p. 122

Filzanzug (Felt Suit)
1970
Felt
67½ × 30¼ × 8½ in. (117.4 × 76.8 × 21.6 cm)
Ed: 87/100
Partial gift of Dr. Paul and Dorie Sternberg
1987.18.a–b

Provenance

Rene Bloch, Berlin, 1970.

Betty Gold, Los Angeles, 1970.

Herbert Palmer Gallery, Beverly Hills, Calif.

Dr. Paul and Dorie Sternberg, Glencoe, Ill., 1986.

MCA, 1987.

Exhibition History

Recent Acquisitions from the Permanent Collection, MCA, April 30–June 26, 1988.

Selections from the Permanent Collection, MCA, April 18–July 8, 1989.

Towards the Future: Contemporary Art in Context, MCA, May 5–July 1, 1990.

PC Focus: Conceptualism to Postconceptualism, the 1960s to the 1990s, MCA, August 22–November 8, 1992.

In the Shadow of Storms: Art of the Postwar Era from the MCA Collection, MCA, July 2, 1996–May 25, 1997.

Envisioning the Contemporary: Selections from the Permanent Collection, MCA, June 21, 1997–April 5, 1998 and April 30, 1998–February 7, 1999.

Adam Brooks: DeNaturalized, MCA, February 14–July 5, 1998.

Jana Sterbak, MCA, October 1, 1998–February 21, 1999.

Transmute, MCA, August 21–November 7, 1999.

The Body Present: Effigies, Decoys, and Other Equivalents, MCA, January 19–May 12, 2002.

Confronting Identities in German Art, 1800–2000, The David and Alfred Smart Museum of Art, The University of Chicago, October 3, 2002–January 2003.

References

Adriani, Gotz et al. *Joseph Beuys — Life and Works.* Woodbury, N.Y.: Barron's, 1979.

Borer, Alain. *The Essential Joseph Beuys.* Cambridge, Mass.: MIT Press, 1997.

Kuspit, Donald B. "Beuys: Fat, Felt, and Alchemy." *Art in America* 68, no. 5 (May 1980), pp. 79–88.

Schellmann, Jorg, ed. *Joseph Beuys: Multiples.* 6th ed. Munich and New York: Edition Schellmann, 1985.

Sharp, Willoughby. "An Interview with Joseph Beuys." *Artforum* 8, no. 4 (December 1969), pp. 40–47.

Tisdall, Caroline. *Joseph Beuys.* New York: Solomon R. Guggenheim Museum, 1979.

Christian Boltanski
French, b. 1944
p. 184

Monument: Les enfants de Dijon (Monument: The Children of Dijon)
1985
Gelatin silver and chromogenic development prints and light fixtures
Installed dimensions variable
Photographs: 11 × 9½ in. to 15¾ × 19¾ in. (27.9 × 24.1 cm to 40 × 50.2 cm)
Gift of the William J. Hokin Family
2001.13

Provenance

Galerie Ghislaine Hussenot, Paris, 1986.

William J. Hokin Family, Chicago, 1988.

MCA, 2001.

Exhibition History

Christian Boltanski Monuments, Le Consortium, Dijon, France, December 1985–1986.

The Art of Photography 1839–1989, Museum of Fine Arts, Houston, February 11–April 30, 1989.

New Art 3: Christian Boltanski, Cincinnati Art Museum, Ohio, October 22, 1994–January 16, 1995.

Crossings '97: France/Hawaii, The Contemporary Museum, Honolulu, October 7–November 11, 1997.

Christian Boltanski, MCA, January 19–March 24, 2002.

References

Gumpert, Lynn. *Christian Boltanski.* New York: Flammarion, 1994.

Gumpert, Lynn and Mary Jane Jacob. *Christian Boltanski: Lessons of Darkness.* Exh. cat. MCA; Los Angeles: The Museum of Contemporary Art; New York: New Museum of Contemporary Art, 1988.

321

Marsh, Georgia. "The White and the Black: An Interview with Christian Boltanski." *Parkett*, no. 22 (December 1989), pp. 36–40.

Moure, Gloria, Christian Boltanski, Jose Jimenez, and Jean Claire. *Christian Boltanski: Advent and Other Times.* New York: Rizzoli, 1997.

Semin, Didier, Christian Boltanski, Tamar Garb, Donald B. Kuspit, and Melvyn Bragg, ed. *Christian Boltanski.* London: Phaidon, 1997.

Reconstitution: Christian Boltanski. Exh. cat. London: Whitechapel Art Gallery, 1990.

Troisi, Sergio. *Christian Boltanski: Monte de Pieta.* Milan: Charta, 2002.

Other Works in the MCA Collection

Untitled from the *Monument* series, 1985
Gelatin silver and chromogenic development prints in tin frames and light fixtures
Installed: 81 × 44½ in. (205.7 × 113 cm)
Photographs: 8 × 6 in. (20.3 × 15.2 cm)
and 6 × 8 in. (15.2 × 20.3 cm)
Partial and promised gift from
The Howard and Donna Stone Collection
2002.12.a–ww

Tiroire (Drawer), 1988
Gelatin silver print, tin drawer, clothing, wire mesh, and electric lamp
Overall: dimensions variable
Drawer: 4¾ × 23⅝ × 15⅞ in.
(12 × 60 × 40.3 cm)
Photograph: 24 × 20⅛ in. (61 × 51.1 cm)
Partial and promised gift from The Howard and Donna Stone Collection
2002.11.a–c

Lee Bontecou
American, b. 1931
p. 88

Untitled
1966
Steel, wire, oil, and epoxy on fiberglass, canvas, leather, and light
78½ × 119 × 31 in. (199.4 × 302.3 × 78.7 cm)
Gift of Robert B. Mayer Family Collection
1991.85

Provenance

Leo Castelli Gallery, New York, 1966.

Robert B. Mayer Family Collection, Winnetka, Ill., 1966.

MCA, 1991.

Exhibition History

Lee Bontecou, MCA, March 25–May 7, 1972.

Part I: Thirtieth Anniversary, Leo Castelli Gallery, New York, January 31–February 27, 1987.

National Museum of Women in the Arts, Washington, D.C., March 11, 1987–November 8, 1990.

Long-term loan from the Robert B. Mayer Memorial Loan Collection to Miami University of Ohio Art Museum, Oxford, Ohio, December 31, 1991–March 22, 1995.

Monumental Statements, Miami University of Ohio Art Museum, Oxford, Ohio, November 6, 1992–May 16, 1993.

Envisioning the Contemporary: Selections from the Permanent Collection, MCA, June 21, 1997–April 5, 1998.

Age of Influence: Reflections in the Mirror of American Culture, MCA, March 14, 2000–January 2, 2001.

References

Americans 1963. Exh. cat. New York: The Museum of Modern Art, 1963.

Hadler, Mona. "Lee Bontecou: Heart of Conquering Darkness." *Source: Notes in the History of Art* 12 (autumn 1992), pp. 38–44.

———. "Lee Bontecou's 'Warnings.'" *Art Journal* 53, no. 4 (winter 1994), pp. 56–61.

Judd, Donald. "Lee Bontecou." *Arts Magazine* 39, no. 7 (April 1965), pp. 16–20.

Munro, Eleanor. *Originals: American Women Artists.* New York: Simon and Schuster, 1979.

Prokopoff, Stephen S. *Lee Bontecou.* Exh. cat. MCA, 1972.

Smith, Elizabeth A. T. "Abstract Sinister." *Art in America* 81, no. 9 (September 1993), pp. 82–87.

Victor Brauner
Romanian, 1903–1966
p. 38

L'objet qui rêve II (The Object that Dreams II)
1938
Oil on canvas
31¾ × 25⅝ in. (80.6 × 65.1 cm)
Gift of Joseph and Jory Shapiro
1992.53

Provenance

Richard L. Feigen & Co., Chicago, 1958.

Joseph and Jory Shapiro, Chicago, 1958.

MCA, 1992.

Exhibition History

Rosenstone Gallery, Bernard Horwich Center, Chicago, 1966.

Dada, Surrealism, and Their Heritage, The Museum of Modern Art, New York, March 27–June 9, 1968; Los Angeles County Museum of Art, July 16–September 8, 1968; The Art Institute of Chicago, October 19–December 8, 1968.

Selections from the Collection of Mr. and Mrs. Joseph Randall Shapiro, MCA, December 20, 1969–February 1, 1970.

The French Connection: Jewish Artists in the School of Paris 1900–1940, Works in Chicago Collections, Spertus Museum, Spertus Institute of Jewish Studies, Chicago, October 24–December 31, 1982.

Ten Years of Collecting, MCA, April 14–May 20, 1984.

Dada and Surrealism in Chicago Collections, MCA, December 1, 1984–January 27, 1985.

The Mr. and Mrs. Joseph Randall Shapiro Collection, The Art Institute of Chicago, February 23–April 14, 1985.

Permanent Collection: Promised Gifts Exhibition, MCA, October 3–November 28, 1989.

Staging Surrealism, Wexner Center for the Arts, Columbus, Ohio, September 19, 1997–January 4, 1998.

Victor Brauner: Surrealist Hieroglyphs, The Menil Collection, Houston, October 25, 2001–January 6, 2002.

Matta in America: Paintings and Drawings of the 1940s, The Museum of Contemporary Art, Los Angeles, September 30–January 6, 2002; Miami Art Museum, Fla., March 20–June 2, 2002; MCA, July 13–October 20, 2002. (Included only in the Chicago presentation.)

References

Feigen, Richard L. *Victor Brauner: Paintings from 1932–1958.* Exh. cat. Chicago: Richard L. Feigen & Co., 1959.

Jacob, Mary Jane et al. *Selections from the Permanent Collection, Vol. I.* MCA, 1984.

Lippard, Lucy, ed. "Victor Brauner." In *Surrealists on Art.* Englewood Cliffs, N.J.: Prentice Hall, 1970. Pp. 67–69.

Roditi, Edouard, ed. "Victor Brauner 1903–1966." In *Dialogues: Conversations with European Artists at Mid-Century.* San Francisco: Bedford Arts, 1990. Pp. 1–3.

Victor Brauner. Exh. cat. Paris: Réunion des Musées Nationaux in association with Musée National d'Art Moderne, Centre Georges Pompidou, 1972.

Victor Brauner: 1903–1966. Exh. cat. London: The Mayor Gallery, 1987.

Other Works in the MCA Collection

The Knight, 1949
Encaustic on board
33¼ × 25¼ in. (84.4 × 65.1 cm)
Gift of Joseph and Jory Shapiro
1998.35

Marcel Broodthaers

Belgian, 1924–1976
p. 116

1833......Le manuscrit
(1833......The Manuscript)

1969–1970
Vacuum-formed plastic
33⅝ × 47¼ in × ³⁄₁₆ in.
(85.4 × 120 × .8 cm)
Edition of 7
Restricted gift of Paul and Camille
Oliver-Hoffmann, Kunstadter Bequest Fund
in honor of Sigmund Kunstadter,
and anonymous donor
1983.68

1833......Le manuscrit
(1833......The Manuscript)

1969–1970
Vacuum-formed plastic
33⅝ × 47¼ × ³⁄₁₆ in.
(85.4 × 120 × .8 cm)
Edition of 7
Restricted gift of Paul and Camille
Oliver-Hoffmann, Kunstadter Bequest Fund
in honor of Sigmund Kunstadter,
and anonymous donor
1983.69

Provenance

Maria Gilissen Broodthaers, Brussels.

Marian Goodman Gallery, New York.

MCA, 1983.

Exhibition History

Selections from the Permanent Collection: American Painting and Sculpture from 1968 to the Present, MCA, December 12, 1983–January 22, 1984.

Ten Years of Collecting, MCA, April 14–May 20, 1984.

Word and Image, MCA, August 8–September 8, 1987 and October 3, 1987–January 10, 1988.

Permanent Collection Exhibition: Icon/Index, MCA, February 5–April 3, 1988.

Toward the Future: Contemporary Art in Context, MCA, May 5–July 1, 1990.

PC Focus: Conceptualism to Postconceptualism, the 1960s to the 1990s, MCA, August 22–November 8, 1992.

Under Development: Dreaming the MCA's Collection, MCA, April 30–August 28, 1994.

In the Shadow of Storms: Art of the Postwar Era from the MCA Collection, MCA, July 2, 1996–May 25, 1997.

Envisioning the Contemporary: Selections from the Permanent Collection, MCA, June 21, 1997–April 5, 1998 and April 30, 1998–February 7, 1999.

Decades in Dialogue: Perspectives on the MCA Collection, MCA, February 27–October 31, 1999.

References

Buchloch, Benjamin H. D., ed. *Broodthaers Writings, Interviews, Photographs*. Cambridge, Mass.: MIT Press, 1988.

Jacob, Mary Jane et al. *Selections from the Permanent Collection, Vol. I*. MCA, 1984.

Marcel Broodthaers. Exh. cat. Bern, Switzerland: Kunsthalle Bern, 1982.

Marcel Broodthaers. Exh. cat. London: Tate Gallery, 1980.

Marcel Broodthaers. Exh. cat. Minneapolis: Walker Art Center; New York: Rizzoli, 1989.

Ratcliff, Carter. "The Mold, the Mussel, and Marcel Broodthaers." *Art in America* 71, no. 3 (March 1983), pp. 134–37.

Other Works in the MCA Collection

La Soupe de Daguerre (Daguerre's Soup), 1975
Chromogenic development prints and paper label on board
21 × 20½ in. (53.3 × 52.1 cm)
Gerald S. Elliott Collection
1995.32

Roger Brown

American, 1941–1997
p. 134

Autobiography in the Shape of Alabama (Mammy's Door)

1974
Oil on canvas, mirror, wood, Plexiglas, photographs, postcards, and cloth shirt
89¾ × 48¾ × 18 in. (228 × 123.8 × 45.7 cm)
Gift of Maxine and Jerry Silberman
1976.41

Provenance

Phyllis Kind Gallery, Chicago, 1974.

Maxine and Jerry Silberman, Glencoe, Ill., 1974.

MCA, 1976.

Exhibition History

Seventy-First American Exhibition, The Art Institute of Chicago, June 15–August 11, 1974.

1967–1977: A View of a Decade, MCA, September 10–November 10, 1977.

Selected Sculpture from the Permanent Collection, MCA, March 24–July 1, 1979.

Selections from the Permanent Collection, MCA, May 3–August 31, 1980.

Roger Brown, Montgomery Museum of Fine Arts, Ala., October 5–November 23, 1980; Contemporary Arts Museum, Houston, December 12–January 19, 1981; MCA, February 13–April 12, 1981.

Permanent Collection, MCA, June–December 1981.

MCA Permanent Collection Exhibition, MCA, January 16–March 14, 1982.

Ten Years of Collecting, MCA, April 14–May 20, 1984.

Selections from the Permanent Collection: Portraits, MCA, December 12, 1984–April 13, 1985.

Toward the Future: Contemporary Art in Context, MCA, May 5–July 1, 1990.

Home Again, The Columbus Museum, Columbus, Ga., August 25–October 28, 1990.

Modeling the Future: The New Museum and Key Works from the Permanent Collection, MCA, May 2–November 8, 1992.

Chicago Imagism: A Twenty-Five Year Survey, Davenport Museum of Art, Iowa, December 3, 1994–February 12, 1995.

Art in Chicago: 1945–1995, MCA, November 16, 1996–March 23, 1997.

Roger Brown Memorial Exhibition, MCA, February 21–July 2, 1998.

References

Bowman, Russell. "An Interview with Roger Brown." *Art in America* 66, no. 1 (January–February 1978), pp. 106–11.

Gedo, John E. "Interviews with a Living Artist: The Art of Roger Brown." In *Perspectives on Creativity: The Biographical Method*. Norwood, N.J.: Ablex Publishing Co., 1992. Pp. 161–88.

Jacob, Mary Jane et al. *Selections from the Permanent Collection, Vol. I*. MCA, 1984.

Jannot, Mark. "Artist Provocateur." *Chicago* 43, no. 10 (October 1994), pp. 84–89, 118–21.

Lawrence, Sidney. *Roger Brown*. Exh. cat. Washington, D.C.: Hirshhorn Museum and Sculpture Garden, Smithsonian Institution; New York: George Braziller, 1987.

Roger Brown: Selected Paintings, 1973–1983. Exh. cat. Atlanta: Nexus Gallery, 1984.

Other Works in the MCA Collection

Ablaze and Ajar, 1972
Oil on canvas
70¼ × 47 in. (178.4 × 119.4 cm)
Bequest of Ruth S. Nath
1997.121

Criss Cross Country Groves and Show, 1973
Oil on canvas
40 × 70⅜ in. (101.6 × 178.8 cm)
Gift of Albert J. Bildner
1974.2

Mask for a Waitress, 1974
Oil on wood, metal, knives, spoons, forks, leather strap, mophead, and wheeled casters
51 × 9⅝ × 13 in. (129.5 × 24.4 × 33 cm)
Bequest of Ruth S. Nath
1997.123

Cosi Fan Tutte, 1979
Lithograph on paper
32½ × 24½ in. (82.6 × 62.2 cm)
Bequest of Ruth S. Nath
1997.122

Tornado Alley, 1986
Oil on canvas
24 × 72 in. (61 × 182.9 cm)
Gift of Ruth Horwich in honor of Lucinda Barnes
1998.1

Doctor's Building, c. 1988
Oil on canvas
18 × 12 in. (45.7 × 30.5 cm)
Gift of Dr. Melville D. Hartman
1998.4

323

Chris Burden

American, b. 1946
p. 224

The Other Vietnam Memorial

1991
Steel, aluminum, and etched
anodized copper plates
176 × 119 × 119 in.
(447 × 302.3 × 302.3 cm)
Gift of Lannan Foundation
1997.23

Provenance

Commissioned by Lannan Foundation, Los
Angeles, 1991.

MCA, 1997.

Exhibition History

Dislocations, The Museum of Modern Art,
New York, October 20, 1991–January 7,
1992.

*Lynn Davis: Egypt and Chris Burden: The
Other Vietnam Memorial and The Big Wheel*,
Lannan Foundation Gallery, Los Angeles,
June 27–October 31, 1992.

California Scheming, MCA, February 14–
May 31, 1998.

Adam Brooks: DeNaturalized, MCA,
February 14–July 5, 1998.

*Age of Influence: Reflections in the Mirror of
American Culture*, MCA, March 14, 2000–
January 2, 2001.

References

Chris Burden: Beyond the Limits. Exh. cat.
Vienna: MAK-Austrian Museum of Applied
Arts, 1996.

Chris Burden: 71–73. Los Angeles:
Burden, 1974.

Chris Burden: A Twenty-Year Survey. Exh. cat.
Newport Beach, Calif.: Newport Harbor Art
Museum, 1988.

Schimmel, Paul. "Leap into the Void:
Performance and the Object." In *Out of
Actions: Between Performance and the Object,
1949–1979*. Exh. cat. Los Angeles: The
Museum of Contemporary Art; London and
New York: Thames and Hudson, 1998.
Pp. 94–103.

Storr, Robert. "Chris Burden." *Dislocations*.
Exh. cat. New York: The Museum of Modern
Art, 1991. Pp. 26–28, 42, 43.

Tatum, James. "Memorials of the American War
in Vietnam." *Critical Inquiry* 22, no. 4 (summer
1996), pp. 634–50.

Other Works in the MCA Collection

16th Century Gunpowder, 1979
Mortar, pestle, charcoal, potassium nitrate,
sulfur, and printed text on paper in glass
and wood vitrine
12⅛ × 25 × 12 in. (30.8 × 63.5 × 30.5 cm)
Restricted gift of Angela and Rudolf Rossmann
1992.100.a–k

T.V.s and Hat, 1979
Televisions, hat, sign, and wood and
glass vitrine
16 × 21 × 16 in. (40.6 × 53.3 × 40.6 cm)
Gift of Lannan Foundation
1997.24.a–f

Pick, Bottle and Alcohol, 1979
Pick, glass bottle, sign, and wood and
glass vitrine
12 × 22 × 19 in. (30.5 × 55.9 × 48.3 cm)
Gift of Lannan Foundation
1997.25.a–e

Spy Kit, 1979
Radios, magnifying glass, lighter, tin box, cloth,
razor blade, and wood and glass vitrine
10¼ × 17 × 17 in. (26 × 43.2 × 43.2 cm)
Gift of Lannan Foundation
1997.26.a–k

Strangler Hunt Grows, 1979
Newspaper, postcard, gelatin silver print, mask,
and patch on paper
32¾ × 40¾ in. (83.2 × 103.5 cm)
Gift of Lannan Foundation
1997.27

Help Ma, 1979
Colored felt-tip pen, colored pencil, gelatin
silver prints, and cardboard mounted on paper
31⅞ × 40 in. (81 × 101.6 cm)
Gift of Lannan Foundation
1997.28

Spook Planes, 1979
Decals, postcard, and newspaper on paper
30 × 40 in. (76.2 × 101.6 cm)
Gift of Lannan Foundation
1997.29

John Cage

American, 1912–1992
p. 148

A Dip in the Lake: Ten Quicksteps, Sixty-two Waltzes, and Fifty-six Marches for Chicago and Vicinity

1978
Felt-tip pen on map
53½ × 41½ in. (135.9 × 105.4 cm)
Restricted gift of Collectors Group,
Men's Council, and Women's Board;
and National Endowment for the Arts
Purchase Grant
1982.19

Provenance

Margaret Roeder Fine Arts, New York, 1978.

MCA, 1982.

Exhibition History

John Cage: Scores and Prints, Whitney Museum
of American Art, New York, February 25–May 2,
1982; Albright-Knox Art Gallery, Buffalo, N.Y.,
May 18–June 27, 1982; Philadelphia Museum of
Art, September 11–October 3, 1982.

*Options 14: Selected Works by John Cage and
Other Composers,* MCA, July 6–August 29,
1982.

Permanent Collection Exhibition, MCA,
March 25–May 29, 1983.

Earth Art and Related Works from the Collection,
MCA, October 29, 1983–January 25, 1984.

Ten Years of Collecting, MCA, April 14–
May 20, 1984.

The Music of Art, Artrain, Detroit, Mich., 1985.

*John Cage: Partituren, Graphik, Zeichnungen,
Aquarelle,* Kunsthaus, Zurich, June 8–August
18, 1991; Stadtische Galerie Erlangen, Germany,
September 7–October 13, 1991.

*PC Focus: Conceptualism to Postconceptualism,
the 1960s to the 1990s,* MCA, August 22–
November 8, 1992.

Art on the Map, Chicago Cultural Center,
April 30–July 10, 1994.

*In the Shadow of Storms: Art of the Postwar Era
from the MCA Collection,* MCA, July 2, 1996–
May 25, 1997.

Perspectives on Terrain, MCA, January 16–
March 7, 1999.

References

Cage, John. *Silence: Lectures and Writings.*
Cambridge, Mass.: MIT Press, 1961.

Gena, Peter. *Options 14: Mayor Byrne's New
Music America '82.* MCA, 1982. P. 6.

Jacob, Mary Jane et al. *Selections from the
Permanent Collection, Vol. I.* MCA, 1984.

Wilding-White, Raymond. "John Cage Takes
Chances." *Chicago* 31, no. 7 (July 1982),
pp. 110–12.

Alexander Calder

American, 1898–1976
p. 48

Snow Flurry II

1951
Painted sheet metal and steel wire
96 × 96 in. diameter (243.8 × 243.8 cm)
Gift of Ruth and Leonard J. Horwich
1983.80

Provenance

Curt Valentin Gallery, New York.

James Goodman Gallery, New York.

Richard Gray Gallery, Chicago, 1966.

Ruth and Leonard J. Horwich, Chicago, 1966.

MCA, Chicago, 1983.

Exhibition History

Sixty-First American Exhibition of Paintings and Sculpture, The Art Institute of Chicago, October 21–December 5, 1954.

Twenty-Seventh Annual Exhibition by the Society of Contemporary American Art, The Art Institute of Chicago, April 11–May 21, 1967.

Alexander Calder: Mobiles and Stabiles, Grand Rapids Art Museum, Mich., May 18–August 24, 1969.

The Bergman Gallery, Cobb Hall, The University of Chicago, 1969.

Alexander Calder, a Retrospective Exhibition: Work from 1925 to 1974, MCA, October 26–December 8, 1974.

Ten Years of Collecting, MCA, April 13–June 10, 1984.

Toward the Future: Contemporary Art in Context, MCA, May 5–July 1, 1990.

Alexander Calder: From the Collection of the Ruth and Leonard J. Horwich Family, MCA, November 21, 1992–January 31, 1993.

Decades in Dialogue: Perspectives on the MCA Collection, MCA, February 27–October 31, 1999.

Matta in America: Paintings and Drawings of the 1940s, The Museum of Contemporary Art, Los Angeles, September 30–January 6, 2002; Miami Art Museum, Fla., March 20–June 2, 2002; MCA, July 13–October 20, 2002. (Included only in the Chicago presentation.)

Polychrome and Horizontal Bluebird

1954
Painted sheet metal and steel wire
39 × 63 in. diameter (99.1 × 160 cm)
Gift of Ruth Horwich
1991.92

Provenance

Perls Gallery, New York.

B.C. Holland Gallery, Chicago, 1965.

Ruth Horwich, Chicago.

MCA, 1991.

Exhibition History

Modeling the Future: The New Museum and Key Works from the Permanent Collection, MCA, May 2–November 8, 1992.

Alexander Calder: From the Collection of Ruth and Leonard J. Horwich Family, MCA, November 21, 1992–January 31, 1993.

The Nature of the Machine, Chicago Cultural Center, April 3–May 30, 1993.

In the Shadow of Storms: Art of the Postwar Era from the MCA Collection, MCA, July 2, 1996–May 25, 1997.

Decades in Dialogue: Perspectives on the MCA Collection, MCA, February 27–October 31, 1999.

Alexander Calder in Focus, MCA, December 23, 2000–August 19, 2001.

Alexander Calder in Focus: Works from the Leonard and Ruth Horwich Family Loan, MCA, July 20, 2002–April 2003.

References

Alexander Calder Foundation website (www.calder.org).

Collective Vision. MCA, 1996.

Grambye, Lars et al. *Alexander Calder: Retrospective.* Humlebaek, Denmark: Louisiana Museum of Modern Art, 1995.

Jacob, Mary Jane et al. *Selections from the Permanent Collection, Vol. I.* MCA, 1984.

Lipman, Jean. *Calder's Universe.* New York: Whitney Museum of American Art, 1968.

Warren, Lynne. *Alexander Calder from the Collection of the Ruth and Leonard J. Horwich Family.* MCA, 1992.

Other Works in the MCA Collection

Untitled, c. 1944
Steel and wire
47 × 46 in. diameter (119.4 × 116.8 cm)
Gift of Mary and Earle Ludgin Collection
1983.108

Brass in the Sky, 1947
Brass
48 × 120 in. diameter (121.9 × 304.8 cm)
Gift of Marshall Field's
1999.19

Cascading Snow, 1961
Painted sheet metal and steel wire
45 × 53 in. diameter (114.3 × 134.6 cm)
Gift of Ruth Horwich
1991.91

Cascade, 1963
Painted metal
17 1/8 × 12 1/2 in. diameter (43.5 × 31.8 cm)
Bequest of Ruth S. Nath
1998.7

Untitled, 1971
Gouache on paper
29 5/16 × 43 1/16 in. (74.4 × 109.4 cm)
Gift of Mr. and Mrs. Edward H. Weiss
1980.57

The River: Chicago, 1974
Gouache on paper
42 3/4 × 29 in. (108.6 × 73.7 cm)
Gift of Perls Gallery
1974.1

Flying Colors, 1976
Lithograph on paper
25 × 35 7/8 in. (63.5 × 91.1 cm)
Gift of Braniff International
1976.5

Maurizio Cattelan

Italian, b. 1960
p. 310

Felix

2001
Oil on polyvinyl resin and fiberglass
26 × 6 × 20 ft. (7.9 × 1.8 × 6.1 m)
Ed: 1/2
The Edlis/Neeson Art Purchase Fund
2001.22

Provenance

Marian Goodman Gallery, New York, 2001.

MCA, 2001.

Exhibition History

Felix, MCA, September 13, 2001–August 26, 2002.

References

Bonami, Francesco. "Every Artist Can Be a Man. The Silence of Beuys is Understandable." *Parkett,* no. 59 (September 2000), pp. 60–71.

Bonami, Francesco, Nancy Spector, and Barbara Vanderlinden. *Maurizio Cattelan.* London: Phaidon, 2000.

Bourriaud, Nicolas. "A Grammar of Visual Delinquency." *Parkett,* no. 59 (September 2000), pp. 34–49.

Cattelan, Maurizio. *Sixth Caribbean Biennial: A Project by Maurizio Cattelan.* Paris: Les Presses du Réel, 2001.

Gingeras, Alison M. "A Sociology Without Truth." *Parkett,* no. 59 (September 2000), pp. 50–59.

Maurizio Cattelan. Milan: Charta, 2000.

Rian, Jeff. "Maurizio Cattelan . . . Went Home." *Flash Art* 29, no. 190 (October 1996), p. 80.

325

Christo

Christo Javacheff
American, b. Bulgaria 1935
p. 76

Orange Store Front
1964–65
Painted wood, Masonite, Plexiglas, galvanized metal, pegboard, fabric, and electric lights
112½ × 101⅛ × 23⅞ in.
(285.8 × 256.8 × 60.6 cm)
Gift of Natalie and Irving Forman
1975.50

Provenance

Lo Guidice Gallery, Chicago, 1969.

Natalie and Irving Forman, Chicago, 1970.

MCA, 1975.

Exhibition History

Selected Sculpture from the Permanent Collection, MCA, March 23–July 1, 1979 and July 6–October 7, 1979.

Selections from the Permanent Collection, MCA, May 3–August 31, 1980 and September 2–November 2, 1980.

Permanent Collection Exhibition, MCA, March 25–May 29, 1983.

Selections from the Permanent Collection: American Painting and Sculpture from 1968 to the Present, MCA, December 12, 1984–January 22, 1985.

Nouveau Realism and Pop Art: Selections from the Permanent Collection, MCA, September 6–November 12, 1985.

Leo Castelli y Sus Artistas, Centro Cultural Arte Contemporaneo, Mexico City, June 25–October 18, 1987.

Toward the Future: Contemporary Art in Context, MCA, May 5–July 1, 1990.

PC Focus: Conceptualism to Postconceptualism, the 1960s to the 1990s, MCA, August 22–November 8, 1992.

In the Shadow of Storms: Art of the Postwar Era from the MCA Collection, MCA, July 2, 1996–May 25, 1997.

Decades in Dialogue: Perspectives on the MCA Collection, MCA, February 27–October 31, 1999.

Retrospective: Early Works, Martin-Gropius-Bau, Berlin, September 8–November 4, 2001.

Museum of Contemporary Art Packed (Chicago) — Project for January–March 1969
Collage, 1968
Graphite, fabric, oil, polyethylene, staples, and twine on mat board
21⅞ × 28 in. (55.6 × 71.1 cm)
Gift of William J. Hokin
1984.48

Provenance

Lo Guidice Gallery, Chicago, 1968.

William J. Hokin, Chicago, 1969.

MCA, 1984.

Exhibition History

The Permanent Collection, MCA, May 24–August 31, 1980.

Selections from the Permanent Collection, MCA, January 13–March 14, 1981.

American Painting and Sculpture: Selections from the Permanent Collection, MCA, June 28–August 19, 1985.

Site Cafe Installation, MCA, August 1985–January 1986.

Portraits: From the Permanent Collection of the MCA, College of DuPage Arts Center Gallery, Glen Ellyn, Ill., April 12–May 26, 1988.

Toward the Future: Contemporary Art in Context, MCA, May 5–July 1, 1990.

PC Focus: Private to Public, MCA, July 3–August 10, 1993.

Envisioning the Contemporary: Selections from the Permanent Collection, MCA, June 21, 1997–April 5, 1998.

References

Alloway, Lawrence. "Christo." *Studio International* 181, no. 931 (March 1971), pp. 97–99.

Bourdon, David. *Christo.* New York: Harry N. Abrams, 1970. P. 27.

———. "Christo's Storefronts." *Domus,* no. 435 (February 2, 1966), p. 49.

Fineberg, Jonathon. *Art since 1940: Strategies of Being.* New York: Harry N. Abrams, 1995.

Jacob, Mary Jane et al. *Selections from the Permanent Collection, Vol. I.* MCA, 1984.

Rosenberg, Karin, ed. *Christo: Wrap In, Wrap Out.* MCA, 1969.

Schellmann, Jorg, ed. *Christo Prints and Objects, 1963–1987.* Munich: Edition Schellmann; New York: Abbeville, 1988.

Other Works in the MCA Collection

Store Front I (Proposition pour salle 2 à la Galleria Nazionale d'Arte Moderna Roma), 1965–67
Collage with board, fabric, graphite, and paint on board
23¾ × 35½ in. (60.3 × 90.2 cm)
Gift of Century America Corporation, Chicago, Courtesy of William J. Hokin
1983.2

Museum of Contemporary Art (Packed-Project—About 20,000 Square Foot Surface), 1968
Canvas, twine, plastic, staples, graphite, colored pencil, and marker on paper
21⅞ × 27¾ in. (55.6 × 70.5 cm)
Gift of Mr. and Mrs. E. A. Bergman
1977.27

Project for the Museum of Contemporary Art-Chicago — 2,500 Square Foot, 1968
Gouache, fabric, graphite, marker, metal staples, and string on board
22 × 27¹⁵⁄₁₆ in. (55.9 × 71 cm)
Gift of MCA Permanent Collection Committee
1980.43

Museum of Contemporary Art-Chicago Project (Packed) 10,000 Sq. Feet of Tarpoline, 1968
Graphite, gelatin silver print, colored pencil, waxed string, fabric, marker, staples, plastic wrap, and transparent tape on bristol board
26⅝ × 20⅞ in. (67.6 × 53 cm)
Gift of Joseph and Jory Shapiro
1992.56

Wrapped Museum of Contemporary Art, Project for Chicago, 1969
Lithograph on paper
42⅛ × 32 in. (107 × 81.3 cm)
Artist's proof 1/10 aside from an edition of 60
Gift of William J. Hokin
1982.40

The Museum of Modern Art Wrapped (Project for the Museum of Modern Art-New York, June 1968), 1971
Lithograph on paper and gelatin silver print
27⅝ × 21⅝ in. (70.2 × 54.9 cm)
Ed: 29/100
Gift of Richard H. Templeton
1983.89

Chicago Magazines, Wrapped, 1980, 1980
Chicago magazines, polyethylene, and twine
12¼ × 9½ × 2 in. (31.1 × 24.1 × 5.1 cm)
Ed: 1/35 aside from 5 artist's proofs
Gift of the Men's Council
1980.52

Larry Clark

American, b. 1943
p. 136

Tulsa
1961–1971/1980
Portfolio of gelatin silver prints
Fifty prints, each:
11 × 14 in. (27.9 × 35.6 cm) or
14 × 11 in. (35.6 × 27.9 cm)
Ed: 73/100
Gift of Lenore and Herbert Schorr
1983.110.1–20
2002.85.1–30

Provenance

Robert Freidus Gallery, New York, 1980.

Lenore and Herbert Schorr, Los Angeles, c. 1980–81.

MCA, 1982.

Exhibition History

Images for Human Conduct: Selections from the Permanent Collection, MCA, July 31–September 1, 1987.

Adam Brooks: DeNaturalized, MCA, February 14–July 5, 1998.

Apposite Opposites: Photography from the MCA Collection, MCA, March 27–August 1, 1999.

Age of Influence: Reflections in the Mirror of American Culture, MCA, March 14, 2000–January 2, 2001.

References

Carson, L. M. Kit. "Review of *Tulsa*." *Rolling Stone* (March 16, 1972), p. 68.

Cheverton, Dick. "A Devastating Portrait of an American Tragedy." *Detroit Free Press*, November 7, 1971.

Crump, James. "Quasi-Documentary: Evolution of a Photographic Style." *New Art Examiner* 23, no. 7 (March 1996), pp. 22–28.

Esposito, Richard. "Ex-Addict Presents an Essay in Photos." *Daily News* (New York), September 30, 1979.

Freidus, Robert. "Larry Clark." *Arts Magazine* 54, no. 6 (February 1980), pp. 38–39.

Hughes, J. "Proof Sheet." *Popular Photography* 85, no. 6 (December 1979), p. 13.

Kelley, Mike. "In Youth is Pleasure." *Flash Art* 25, no. 164 (May/June 1992), pp. 82–86.

Lifson, Ben. "Ordinary People." *Village Voice*, October 22–28, 1980, p. 79.

Monk, Philip. "Larry Clark: Outlaw Artist." In *The American Trip*. Toronto: The Power Plant, 1996.

Thornton, Gene. "Practitioners with a Story to Tell." *New York Times*, September 30, 1979, sec. 2, p. 31.

Trebay, Guy. "Hot Flash? The Photographer from Tulsa Resurfaces." *Village Voice*, October 15–21, 1980, p. 1.

Yau, John. "Larry Clark at Robert Friedus." *Art in America* 67, no. 8 (December 1979), p. 116.

Zelevansky, Lynn. "Larry Clark." *Flash Art*, no. 101 (January/February 1981), p. 56.

Other Works in the MCA Collection

Untitled (KIDS), 1995
Portfolio of chromogenic development prints
Fifteen parts, each: 16 × 20 in.
(40.6 × 50.8 cm)
Ed: 10/25
Partial and promised gift from The Howard and Donna Stone Collection
2002.16.1–15

Chuck Close
American, b. 1940
p. 200

Cindy
1988
Oil on canvas
102 × 84 in. (259.1 × 213.4 cm)
Gift of Camille Oliver-Hoffmann
in memory of Paul W. Oliver-Hoffmann
1998.24

Provenance

The Pace Gallery, New York, 1988.

Camille and Paul W. Oliver-Hoffmann, Chicago, 1988.

MCA, 1998.

Exhibition History

Chuck Close: New Paintings, The Pace Gallery, New York, September 23–October 22, 1988.

Chuck Close, The Museum of Modern Art, New York, February 26–May 26, 1998; MCA, June 20–September 13, 1998; Hirshhorn Museum and Sculpture Garden, Smithsonian Institution, Washington, D.C., October 15, 1998–January 10, 1999; Seattle Art Museum, February 18–May 9, 1999; Hayward Gallery, London, July 22–September 19, 1999.

References

Greenberg, Jan and Sandra Jordan. *Chuck Close, Up Close.* London: DK Publishing, 1998.

Gregg, Gail. "The Making of a Retrospective." *ARTnews* 97, no. 4 (April 1998), pp. 142–47.

Hughes, Robert. "Close Encounters." *Time* 151, no. 14 (April 13, 1998).

Nemser, Cindy. "An Interview with Chuck Close." *Artforum* 8, no. 5 (January 1970), pp. 51–55.

Nochlin, Linda et al. "Four Close-Ups and One Nude." *Art in America* 87, no. 2 (February 1999), pp. 66–74, 172.

Peyton, Elizabeth and Chuck Close. "About Face — Chuck Close in Conversation with Elizabeth Peyton." *Parkett,* no. 60 (December 2000/January 2001), pp. 28–73.

Prose, Francine. "Distances and Faces of the Moon." *Parkett,* no. 60 (December 2000/January 2001), pp. 1–5.

Schjeldahl, Peter. *Chuck Close: Recent Paintings.* Exh. cat. New York: The Pace Gallery, 1991.

Soloman, Deborah. "The Persistence of the Portrait." *New York Times Magazine* (February 1, 1998).

Storr, Robert. *Chuck Close.* Exh. cat. New York: The Museum of Modern Art, 1998.

Storr, Robert. "Chuck Close." In *Realism and Its Doubles.* New York: Rizzoli, 1987. Pp. 9–23.

Other Works in the MCA Collection

Study for Frank, 1969
Crayon on gelatin silver print
14 × 11 in. (35.6 × 27.9 cm)
Gift of Bykert Gallery
1973.13

Susan, 1971
Color dye-transfer prints, plastic graph overlay, marker, and masking tape
Five parts, each: 24½ × 20½ in. (62.2 × 52.1)
Gift of Mrs. Robert B. Mayer
1987.17.a–e

Keith Four Times, 1975
Lithograph on paper
30 × 79 3/16 in. (76.2 × 201.1 cm)
Gift of Lynn and Allen Turner
1984.29

Tony Cragg
British, b. 1949
p. 172

Red Bottle
1982
Plastic objects
108 × 33 × 3 in. (274.3 × 83.8 × 7.6 cm)
Gerald S. Elliott Collection
1995.33

Provenance

Marian Goodman Gallery, New York.

Gerald S. Elliott, Chicago, before 1990.

MCA, 1995.

Exhibition History

Affinities and Intuitions: The Gerald S. Elliott Collection of Contemporary Art, The Art Institute of Chicago, May 12–July 29, 1990.

In the Shadow of Storms: Art of the Postwar Era from the MCA Collection, MCA, July 2, 1996–May 25, 1997.

Envisioning the Contemporary: Selections from the Permanent Collection, MCA, June 21, 1997–April 5, 1998 and April 30, 1998–February 7, 1999.

St. George and the Dragon
1985
Metal, plastic, and wood
72 × 102 × 40 in. (182.9 × 259.1 × 101.6 cm)
Gerald S. Elliott Collection
1995.34

Provenance

Donald Young Gallery, Chicago, 1985.

Gerald S. Elliott, Chicago, 1985.

MCA, 1995.

Exhibition History

Affinities and Intuitions: The Gerald S. Elliott Collection of Contemporary Art, The Art Institute of Chicago, May 12–July 29, 1990.

Envisioning the Contemporary: Selections from the Permanent Collection, MCA, April 30, 1998–August 1, 1999 and April 30, 1998–February 7, 1999.

References

Celant, Germano. *Tony Cragg.* London and New York: Thames and Hudson, 1996.

Collective Vision. MCA, 1996.

Serota, Nicholas. *Tony Cragg: The Turner Prize.* London: Tate Gallery and Patrons of New Art, 1988.

Tony Cragg. Exh. cat. Paris: Musée National d'Art Moderne, Centre Georges Pompidou, 1995.

Tony Cragg. London: The British Council, 1988.

Tony Cragg: Sculpture 1975–1990. London and New York: Thames and Hudson; Newport Beach: Newport Harbor Art Museum, 1991.

327

Other Works in the MCA Collection

Membrane, 1986
Wood, metal, and plaster
44½ × 46 × 32 in. (113 × 116.8 × 81.3 cm)
Gerald S. Elliott Collection
1995.35

Spill, 1987
Bronze
39 × 79 × 39 in. (99.1 × 200.7 × 99.1 cm)
Gerald S. Elliott Collection
1995.36

Loco, 1988
Wood
63 × 94½ × 86⅝ in. (160 × 240 × 220 cm)
Gerald S. Elliott Collection
1995.37

Thomas Demand

German, b. 1964
p. 306

Labor
2000
Chromogenic development print and Diasec
71 × 105½ in. (180.3 × 268 cm)
Ed: 1/6
Partial and promised gift from The Howard
and Donna Stone Collection
2002.18

Provenance

303 Gallery, New York, 2000.

Howard and Donna Stone, Chicago, 2000.

MCA, 2002.

Exhibition History

*Age of Influence: Reflections in the Mirror of
American Culture*, MCA, March 14, 2000 –
January 2, 2001.

Poll
2001
Chromogenic development print and Diasec
70 × 103 in. (177.8 × 261.6 cm)
Ed: 4/6
Restricted gift of Mr. and Mrs. Sanfred Koltun
2001.5

Provenance

303 Gallery, New York, 2001.

MCA, 2001.

Exhibition History

*People See Paintings: Photography and Painting
from the MCA Collection*, MCA, January 19 –
October 20, 2002.

References

Bonami, Francesco, Regis Durand, and Francois
Quintin. *Thomas Demand*. Paris: Fondation
Cartier pour l'Art Contemporain, 2000.

Demand, Thomas. "A Thousand Words:
Thomas Demand Talks about Poll."
Artforum 39, no. 9 (May 2001), pp. 144 – 45.

Durand, Regis. "Thomas Demand — Un Monde
de Papier." *Artpress*, no. 221 (February 1997),
pp. 40 – 45.

Princenthal, Nancy. "Thomas Demand."
Art/Text, no. 67 (November/December
1999/January 2000), pp. 64 – 69.

Spaid, Sue. "Thomas Demand." *Art/Text*,
no. 64 (February/March/April 1999), p. 84.

"Thomas Demand." *Parkett*, no. 62
(September 2001), pp. 104 – 143.

"Vik Muniz and Thomas Demand."
Blind Spot, no. 8 (1996), n.p.

Stan Douglas

Canadian, b. 1960
p. 250

Evening
1994
Color video installation
20 minutes
Dimensions variable
Ed: 2/2
Restricted gift of Frances and Thomas Dittmer
and Bernice and Kenneth Newberger Fund
1996.40

Provenance

David Zwirner Gallery, New York, 1994.

MCA, 1996.

Exhibition History (of both editions)

Stan Douglas, Institute of Contemporary Art,
London, September 2 – October 2, 1994.

Public Information: Desire, Disaster, Document,
Museum of Modern Art, San Francisco,
January 18 – April 30, 1995.

Stan Douglas, The Renaissance Society, The
University of Chicago, May 10 – June 10, 1995.

*A Notion of Conflict: A Selection of Contemporary
Canadian Art*, Stedelijk Museum, Amsterdam,
May 11 – June 11, 1995.

Video Spaces: Eight Installations, The Museum of
Modern Art, New York, June 22 – September 12,
1995.

*Everything That's Interesting is New: Dakis
Joannou Collection*, Athens School of Fine Art
"The Factory," Athens, Greece, January 20 –
April 20, 1996.

Stan Douglas, Musée d'Art Contemporain,
Montreal, February 2 – April 7, 1996.

*Envisioning the Contemporary: Selections from
the Permanent Collection*, MCA, June 21, 1997 –
April 5, 1998.

References

Augaitis, Daina et al. *Stan Douglas*. Exh. cat.
Vancouver: Vancouver Art Gallery, 1999.

Blase, Christoph. "Stan Douglas." In Burkhard
Rienschneider and Uta Grosenick, eds. *Art at
the Turn of the Millennium*. Cologne: Benedikt
Taschen, 1999. Pp. 130 – 33.

Cameron, Dan. "Stan Douglas." In *Cream:
Contemporary Art in Culture*. London: Phaidon,
1998. Pp. 100 – 103.

Watson, Scott et al, and Gilda Williams, ed.
Stan Douglas. London: Phaidon, 1998.

Jean Dubuffet

French, 1901 – 1985
p. 46

*La verrue sous le nez
(The Wart under the Nose)*
1951
Oil on board
28¾ × 23⅝ in. (73 × 60 cm)
Gift of Mr. and Mrs. E. A. Bergman
1978.43

Provenance

Unknown.

Galerie Lefebvre-Foinet, Paris.

Sidney Janis Gallery, New York, before 1964.

Mr. and Mrs. E. A. Bergman, Chicago, 1974.

MCA, 1978.

Exhibition History

Selected Works from the Permanent Collection,
MCA, July 6 – October 7, 1979.

Selections from the Permanent Collection, MCA,
May 3 – August 31, 1980.

MCA Permanent Collection Exhibition, MCA,
January 16 – March 14, 1982 and March 25 –
May 29, 1983.

Ten Years of Collecting, MCA, April 4 –
May 20, 1984.

Jean Dubuffet: Forty Years of His Art, The David
and Alfred Smart Museum of Art, The
University of Chicago, October 4 – December 2,
1984; Washington University Art Gallery, St.
Louis, Mo., January 19 – March 3, 1985.

*Selections from the Permanent Collection:
Figurative Expressionism and Neo-Expressionism*,
MCA, April 25 – July 8, 1989.

Toward the Future: Contemporary Art in Context,
MCA, May 5 – July 1, 1990.

*Realism, Figurative Painting, and the Chicago
Viewpoint*, MCA, July 20 – August 27, 1991.

*In the Shadow of Storms: Art of the Postwar Era
from the MCA Collection*, MCA, July 2, 1996 –
May 25, 1997.

*Envisioning the Contemporary: Selections from
the Permanent Collection*, MCA, June 21, 1997 –
April 5, 1998.

References

Danchin, Laurent. *Jean Dubuffet*. Paris:
Vilo International, 2001.

Jacob, Mary Jane et al. *Selections from the
Permanent Collection, Vol. I*. MCA, 1984.

*Jean Dubuffet 1943 – 1963: Paintings Sculptures
Assemblages*. Exh. cat. Washington, D.C.:
Smithsonian Institution, 1993.

MacGregory, John. "Plumbing the Depths."
Art & Antiques 8, no. 4 (April 1991), pp. 66 – 73.

Rowell, Margit. *Jean Dubuffet: A Retrospective*.
Exh. cat. New York: Solomon R. Guggenheim
Museum, 1973.

Selz, Peter. *The Work of Jean Dubuffet*. New York:
The Museum of Modern Art, 1962.

Machefer, 1954
Clinker and terra-cotta
15 × 6¼ × 4¼ in. (38.1 × 15.9 × 10.8 cm)
Gift of Joseph and Jory Shapiro
1998.37

The Happy Man, 1955
Watercolor and paper collage on paper
33⅛ × 17¾ in. (84.1 × 45.1 cm)
Gift of Lannan Foundation
1997.33

Jeanne Dunning
American, b. 1960
p. 258

Study after "Untitled Landscape," 1987
1994–1995
Gelatin silver print with artist's frame
12 × 13 in. (30.5 × 33 cm)
Partial and promised gift from
The Howard and Donna Stone Collection
2002.26

Provenance

Feigen, Inc., Chicago, 1995.

Howard and Donna Stone, Chicago, 1995.

MCA, 2002.

The Extra Hair 2
1994
Silver dye-bleach print mounted to Plexiglas
with artist's frame
32½ × 16¾ in. (82.6 × 42.5 cm)
Ed: 3/3
Partial and promised gift from
The Howard and Donna Stone Collection
2002.28

Provenance

Feigen, Inc., Chicago, 1994.

Howard and Donna Stone, Chicago, 1995.

MCA, 2002.

Exhibition History

Jeanne Dunning, MCA, November 12–
December 31, 1994.

The Pink
1996
Silver dye-bleach print mounted to Plexiglas
with artist's frame
74 × 52 in. (188 × 132.1 cm)
Ed: 2/3
Restricted gift of Collectors Forum
1996.8

Provenance

Feigen, Inc., Chicago, 1996.

MCA, 1996.

Exhibition History

Jeanne Dunning, Richard Feigen Inc., Chicago,
April 27–May 25, 1996.

No Harm in Looking, MCA, May 5–August 19,
2001.

References

Cruz, Amada. *Jeanne Dunning*. Exh. cat.
MCA, 1994.

Holliday, Taylor. "Nude Awakenings." *ARTnews*
98, no. 2 (February 1999), pp. 94–95.

Jeanne Dunning. Exh. cat. New York: Feigen
Contemporary; Tokyo: Tomio Koyama Gallery,
1997.

Jeanne Dunning. Exh. cat. Normal, Ill.: University
Galleries of Illinois State University Press, 1991.

Other Works in the MCA Collection

Study after "Untitled Landscape," 1987, 1987
Gelatin silver print with artist's frame
12¼ × 13⅛ in. (31.1 × 33.3 cm)
Gift of Hudson
1997.3

Head 3, 1989
Silver dye-bleach print mounted to Plexiglas
with artist's frame
25 × 17 in. (63.5 × 43.2 cm)
Artist's proof
Partial and promised gift from The Howard and
Donna Stone Collection
2002.23

Torso, 1990
Silver dye-bleach print mounted to Plexiglas
with cast rubber artist's frame
21½ × 17½ in. (54.6 × 44.4 cm)
Ed: 3/5
Gift of Steven P. Berkowitz
2001.15

Back, 1990
Silver dye-bleach print mounted to Plexiglas
with cast rubber artist's frame
21½ × 17½ in. (54.6 × 44.4 cm)
Ed: 1/5
Partial and promised gift from The Howard and
Donna Stone Collection
2002.21

Sample, 1990
Silver dye-bleach print mounted to Plexiglas
with artist's frame
23½ × 16¾ in. (59.7 × 42.5 cm)
Ed: 3/3
Partial and promised gift from The Howard and
Donna Stone Collection
2002.24

Sample 3, 1990
Silver dye-bleach print mounted to Plexiglas
with artist's frame
18 × 15 in. (45.7 × 38.1 cm)
Ed: 3/3
Partial and promised gift from The Howard and
Donna Stone Collection
2002.25

Sample 6, 1992
Silver dye-bleach print mounted to Plexiglas
with artist's frame
53¼ × 36⅞ in. (135.2 × 93.7 cm)
Ed: 1/3
Restricted gift of Raymond and Inez Saunders
1996.10

Untitled Hole, 1992
Silver dye-bleach print mounted to Plexiglas
with artist's frame
42¼ × 34¼ in. (107.3 × 87 cm)
Ed: 1/3
Partial and promised gift from The Howard and
Donna Stone Collection
2002.31

The Toe-Sucking Video, 1994
Color video
10 minutes
Ed: 4/10
Restricted gift of Collectors Forum
1996.9

The Third Breast, 1994
Silver dye-bleach print mounted to Plexiglas
with artist's frame
25½ × 39 in. (64.8 × 99.1 cm)
Ed: 2/3
Partial and promised gift from The Howard and
Donna Stone Collection
2002.30

Hand Hole, 1993/1996
Silver dye-bleach print mounted to Plexiglas
with artist's frame
26 × 25½ in. (66 × 64.8 cm)
Ed: 3/3
Partial and promised gift from The Howard and
Donna Stone Collection
2002.22

The Edge with Food, 1996
Silver dye-bleach print mounted to Plexiglas
with artist's frame
25⅛ × 21⅛ in. (63.8 × 53.6 cm)
Ed: 1/3
Partial and promised gift from The Howard and
Donna Stone Collection
2002.27

The Food, 1996
Silver dye-bleach print mounted to Plexiglas
with artist's frame
43¼ × 39½ in. (109.8 × 100.3 cm)
Ed: 3/3
Partial and promised gift from The Howard and
Donna Stone Collection
2002.29

Untitled with Food, 1996
Silver dye-bleach print mounted to Plexiglas
with artist's frame
42¼ × 28¼ in. (107.3 × 71.8 cm)
Ed: 3/3
Partial and promised gift from The Howard and
Donna Stone Collection
2002.32

329

Max Ernst
French, b. Germany, 1891–1976
p. 34

Loplop Introducing a Bird
1929/1957
Plaster, oil, and wood
40¼ × 48½ in. (102.2 × 123.2 cm)
Ed: 2/6
Gift of Joseph and Jory Shapiro
1991.25

Provenance

Alexander Iolas Gallery, New York, 1957.

Joseph and Jory Shapiro, Chicago, 1959.

MCA, 1991.

Exhibition History

Max Ernst, Alexander Iolas Gallery,
New York, 1957.

Surrealism Then and Now, The Arts Club,
Chicago, October 1–October 30, 1958.

*Selections from the Collection of Mr. and Mrs.
Joseph Randall Shapiro,* MCA, December 20,
1969–February 1, 1970.

Permanent Collection: Promised Gifts Exhibition,
MCA, October 10–November 28, 1981.

Ten Years of Collecting, MCA, April 4–
May 20, 1984.

Dada and Surrealism in Chicago Collections,
MCA, December 1, 1984–January 27, 1985.

*The Mr. and Mrs. Joseph Randall Shapiro
Collection,* The Art Institute of Chicago,
February 23–April 14, 1985.

New Acquisitions: The MCA Collects, MCA,
November 23, 1991–January 26, 1992.

PC Focus: Private to Public, MCA, July 3–
August 10, 1993.

*In the Shadow of Storms: Art of the Postwar Era
from the MCA Collection,* MCA, July 2, 1996–
May 25, 1997.

*Envisioning the Contemporary: Selections from
the Permanent Collection,* MCA, June 21, 1997–
April 5, 1998 and April 30, 1998–February 7, 1999.

*Matta in America: Paintings and Drawings of the
1940s,* The Museum of Contemporary Art, Los
Angeles, September 30–January 6, 2002; Miami
Art Museum, Fla., March 20–June 2, 2002;
MCA, July 13–October 20, 2002. (Included only
in the Chicago presentation.)

References

Jacob, Mary Jane et al. *Selections from the
Permanent Collection, Vol. I.* MCA, 1984.

Max Ernst: A Retrospective. Exh. cat. London:
Tate Gallery; Munich: Prestel, 1991.

Motherwell, Robert, ed. *The Dada Painters
and Poets.* 2d ed. New York: Wittenborn,
Schultz, 1951.

Nadeau, Maurice, and Richard Howard,
trans. *The History of Surrealism.* New York:
Macmillan, 1965.

Spies, Werner. *Max Ernst/Loplop: The Artist in
the Third Person.* New York: George Braziller,
1983.

Other Works in the MCA Collection

Bird Plaque, date unknown
Bronze
13¼ × 7⅛ × 6⅝ in. (33.6 × 18.1 × 16.8 cm)
Ed: 89/178
Gift of Joseph and Jory Shapiro
1998.39

Red Owl, 1952
Oil on canvas
41⅜ × 47⁷/₁₆ in. (105.1 × 120.5 cm)
Gift of Joseph and Jory Shapiro
1998.38

Jackie Ferrara
American, b. 1929
p. 128

Stacked Pyramid
1972
Cotton batting with glue on wood
24 × 52 × 13 in. (61 × 132.1 × 33 cm)
Gift of Lannan Foundation
1997.34

Provenance

Michael Klein, Inc., New York.

Lannan Foundation, Los Angeles, 1992.

MCA, 1997.

Exhibition History

Jackie Ferrara, A. M. Sachs Gallery, New York,
October 1973.

Jackie Ferrara Sculpture: A Retrospective, John
and Mable Ringling Museum of Art, Sarasota,
Fla., February 7–May 31, 1992; Indianapolis
Museum of Art, Ind., July 25–October 18, 1992;
Rose Art Museum, Brandeis University,
Waltham, Mass., November 19, 1992–
January 10, 1993.

*Floored: Sculpture from the Lannan Foundation
Collection,* Collection Foundation Gallery,
Los Angeles, April 8–August 13, 1995.

PC Focus: Jackie Ferrara, MCA, July 11–
September 27, 1998.

References

Bourdon, David, Nancy Princenthal, and Ileen
Sheppard-Gallagher. *Jackie Ferrara Sculpture: A
Retrospective.* Exh. cat. Sarasota, Fla.: John and
Mable Ringling Museum of Art, 1992.

Martin, Richard. "New York." *Art and Artists* 8,
no. 92 (November 1973), pp. 52–53.

Patton, Phil. "Sculpture the Mind Can Use."
ARTnews 81, no. 3 (March 1982), pp. 108–112.

Ratcliff, Carter. "Jackie Ferrara: An Architecture
of Intent." In *Jackie Ferrara.* Exh. cat. Coral
Gables, Fla.: Lowe Art Museum, 1982.

Yood, James. "Jackie Ferrara:
Indianapolis Museum of Art." *Artforum* 31,
no. 3 (November 1992), p. 112.

Other Works in the MCA Collection

Truncated Pyramid I, 1973
Cotton batting with glue on cardboard
72 × 24 × 24 in. (182.9 × 61 × 61 cm)
Gift of Lannan Foundation
1997.35

Truncated Pyramid II, 1973
Cotton batting with glue on cardboard
96 × 24 × 24 in. (243.8 × 61 × 61 cm)
Gift of Lannan Foundation
1997.36

Stainway, 1973
Cotton batting with glue on cardboard
32 × 37 × 70 in. (81.3 × 94 × 177.8 cm)
Gift of Lannan Foundation
1997.37

Tiered Circle, 1973
Cotton batting with glue on canvas
and plaster
10½ × 21½ in. diameter (26.7 × 54.6 cm)
Gift of Lannan Foundation
1997.38

Tony Fitzpatrick
American, b. 1958
p. 284

The Infinite Wager
1998
Portfolio of four and five-color etchings
on paper
Ten prints, each: 11⅜ × 10⅛ in.
(28.9 × 25.7 cm)
Ed: 8/45
Gift of Janice and Mickey Cartin
1998.44.1–10

Provenance

Janice and Mickey Cartin, Conn., 1998.

MCA, 1998.

References

Cartin, Mickey. *Bum Town.* Exh. cat. New York:
Bill Maynes Gallery, 1999.

Cartin, Mickey, Jonathan Demme, and Lynne
Warren. *Max and Gaby's Alphabet.* Exh. cat.
MCA, 2001.

Fitzpatrick, Tony. *The Infinite Wager.* Los
Angeles: Jonathan Novak Contemporary Art;
Chicago: Thomas McCormick Works of Art,
1999.

Kogan, Rick. "Bum Town: Artist Tony
Fitzpatrick's Ode to His Father and the City."
Chicago Tribune Magazine (July 30, 2000),
p. 16.

Zambreno, Kate. "Tony Fitzpatrick." *City Talk*
(Chicago), March 9, 2001, pp. 5–6.

Dan Flavin
American, 1933–1996
p. 72

*the alternative diagonals
of March 2, 1964 (to Donald Judd)*
1964
Fluorescent lights
145 × 12 × 4 in. (368.3 × 30.5 × 10.2 cm)
Ed: 1/3
Gerald S. Elliott Collection
1995.40

Provenance

Sperone Gallery, Turin, Italy, 1970.

Sperone Westwater, New York.

Young Hoffman Gallery, Chicago, late 1970s.

Gerald S. Elliott, Chicago, late 1970s.

MCA, 1995.

Exhibition History

Some Light, Kaymar Gallery, New York, 1964.

*Affinities and Intuitions: The Gerald S. Elliott
Collection of Contemporary Art,* The Art Institute
of Chicago, May 9–July 29, 1990.

*In the Shadow of Storms: Art of the Postwar Era
from the MCA Collection,* MCA, July 2, 1996–
May 25, 1997.

*Envisioning the Contemporary: Selections from
the Permanent Collection,* MCA, June 21, 1997–
April 5, 1998 and April 30, 1998–February 7, 1999.

Selected Works from the Collection, MCA,
October 14–November 26, 2000.

References

Burnham, Jack. "A Dan Flavin Retrospective in
Ottawa." *Artforum* 8, no. 4 (December 1969),
pp. 48–55.

Collective Vision. MCA, 1996.

*Dan Flavin, Fluorescent Lights, etc.: From Dan
Flavin.* Exh. cat. Ottawa: National Gallery of
Canada, 1969.

Flavin, Dan. " . . . in daylight or cool white."
Artforum 4, no. 4 (December 1965),
pp. 21–24.

———. "some other comments . . . more
pages from a spleenish journal." *Artforum* 6, no.
4 (December 1967), pp. 20–25.

———. "some remarks . . . excerpts
from a spleenish journal." *Artforum* 5, no. 4
(December 1966), pp. 27–29.

Judd, Donald. "In the Galleries."
Arts Magazine 38, no. 1 (April 1964), p. 31.

Kalina, Richard. "In Another Light." *Art in
America* 84, no. 6 (June 1996), pp. 68–73.

Tom Friedman
American, b. 1965
p. 300

Untitled
1999
Cardboard and Styrofoam balls
100 × 30 × 17 in. (254 × 76.2 × 43.2 cm)
Restricted gift of the Nancy A. Lauter and
Alfred L. McDougal Charitable Fund, J. Ira and
Nicki Harris Foundation, Jacqueline S. Harris
Foundation, Orbit Fund, and Bernice and
Kenneth Newberger Fund
2000.20

Provenance

Feature, New York, 1999.

MCA, 2000.

Exhibition History

Tom Friedman, MCA, July 8, 2000–October 1,
2000; Yerba Buena Center for the Arts, San
Francisco, November 4–January 28, 2001;
Aspen Art Museum, Aspen, Colo., February
16–April 15, 2001; Southeastern Center for
Contemporary Art, Winston-Salem, N.C.,
July 14–September 24, 2001; New Museum
of Contemporary Art, New York, October 11,
2001–January 17, 2002.

References

Cameron, Dan. "Same and Different." *Parkett,*
no. 64 (May 2002), pp. 52–63.

———. "Tom Friedman." In *Cream:
Contemporary Art in Culture.* London: Phaidon,
1998. Pp. 124–27.

Cooper, Dennis, Bruce Hainley, and Adrian
Searle. *Tom Friedman.* London: Phaidon, 2001

Frankel, David. "X-Acto Science: David Frankel
on Tom Friedman." *Artforum* 38, no. 10
(summer 2000), pp. 138–41.

Friedman, Tom. "Serious Playboys. Tom
Friedman in Conversation with John Waters."
Parkett, no. 64 (May 2002), pp. 78–91.

Johnson, Ken. "Friedman's Flea Circus."
Art in America 84, no. 5 (May 1996), pp. 78–81.

Matsui, Midori. "Mapping Your World. Tom
Friedman's Flexible Sculpture." *Parkett,* no. 64
(May 2002), pp. 64–77.

Platt, Ron. *Tom Friedman.* Exh. cat. Winston-
Salem, N.C.: Southeastern Center for
Contemporary Art, 2000.

Giuseppe Gabellone
Italian, b. 1973
p. 304

Untitled
1999
Chromogenic development print
59⅜ × 96⅛ in. (150.8 × 244.2 cm)
Ed: 3/3
Restricted gift of Collectors Forum
2001.4

Provenance

Studio Guenzani, Milan, 1999.

MCA, 2001.

Exhibition History

Giuseppe Gabellone, Fonds Régional d'Art
Contemporain du Limousin, Limoges, France,
December 10, 1999–February 26, 2000;
Fondazione Sandretto Re Rebaudengo per
L'Arte, Turin, Italy, September 30–November 19,
2000.

*Original Language: Highlights from the MCA
Collection,* MCA, March 24–August 5, 2001.

Giuseppe Gabellone, MCA, September 7,
2002–January 5, 2003.

References

Bonami, Francesco. *Giuseppe Gabellone.* Exh.
cat. MCA; Milan: Edizioni Charta, 2002.

———. "Giuseppe Gabellone." In *Cream:
Contemporary Art in Culture.* London: Phaidon,
1998.

Bonami, Francesco and Frederic Paul. *Giuseppe
Gabellone.* Limoges, France: Fonds Régional
d'Art Contemporain du Limousin; Turin, Italy:
Fondazione Sandretto Re Rebaudengo per
L'Arte, 1999.

Di Pietrantonio, Giacinto. "Conversation with
Giuseppe Gabellone." *Flash Art* 30, no. 195
(summer 1997), p. 127.

Gilbert & George
Gilbert Proesch, British, b. Italy 1943
George Passmore, British, b. 1942
p. 180

Winter Pissing
1983
Gelatin silver and chromogenic
development prints
95 × 79 in. (242 × 201 cm)
Gift of Anne and William J. Hokin
1991.10.a–p

Provenance

Crouel-Hussenot, Paris, 1983.

Anne and William J. Hokin, Chicago, 1987.

MCA, 1991.

Exhibition History

New Acquisitions: The MCA Collects, MCA, November 23, 1991 – January 26, 1992.

Transmute, MCA, August 21 – November 7, 1999.

References

Farson, Daniel. *Gilbert & George: A Portrait.* London: HarperCollins, 1999.

Gilbert and George. *The Words of Gilbert & George: With Portraits of the Artists from 1968 to 1997.* New York: Violette Editions, 1997.

Jahn, Wolf. *Gilbert & George.* Exh. cat. Milan: Museo d'Art Moderna, Città di Lugano, and Electra, 1994.

Ratcliff, Carter. *Gilbert & George: The Complete Pictures, 1971–1985.* New York: Rizzoli, 1986.

Richardson, Brenda. *Gilbert and George.* Baltimore, Md.: Baltimore Museum of Art, 1984.

Leon Golub

American, b. 1922
p. 58

Reclining Youth

1959
Lacquer on canvas
78¾ × 163½ in. (200 × 415.3 cm)
Gift of Susan and Lewis Manilow
1979.52

Provenance

Alan Frumkin Gallery, Chicago, 1959.

Susan and Lewis Manilow, Chicago, 1959.

MCA, 1979.

Exhibition History

New Images of Man, The Museum of Modern Art, New York, September 30 – November 29, 1959.

Leon Golub, A Retrospective Exhibition of Paintings from 1947 to 1973, MCA, September 7 – October 20, 1974.

Selections from the Permanent Collection, MCA, May 25 – 29, 1983.

Ten Years of Collecting, MCA, April 13 – June 10, 1984.

Leon Golub: Four Decades, New Museum of Contemporary Art, New York, September 21 – November 25, 1984; Museum of Contemporary Art, La Jolla, Calif., December 14, 1984 – January 25, 1985; MCA, February 8 – April 7, 1985; Montreal Museum of Fine Arts, April 18 – June 2, 1985; Corcoran Gallery of Art, Washington, D.C., July – September 8, 1985; Museum of Fine Arts, Boston, October 22, 1985 – February 2, 1986.

Selections from the Permanent Collection, MCA, August 19 – September 22, 1986.

Icon/Index, MCA, February 5 – April 3, 1988.

Art in Chicago 1945–1995, MCA, November 16, 1996 – March 23 1997.

Original Language: Highlights from the MCA Collection, MCA, March 24 – August 5, 2001.

Mercenaries I

1979
Acrylic on unstretched linen
120 × 166 in. (304.8 × 421.6 cm)
Gift of Lannan Foundation
1997.39

Provenance

Unknown.

Susan Caldwell, New York.

Private collector, 1985.

Sotheby's, N.Y., November 14, 1991, lot no. 243.

Lannan Foundation, Los Angeles, 1991.

MCA, 1997.

Exhibition History

Images: Selection from Lannan Foundation Collection, Lannan Foundation Gallery, Los Angeles, December 3, 1992 – March 27, 1993.

In the Shadow of Storms: Art of the Postwar Era from the MCA Collection, MCA, July 2, 1996 – May 25, 1997.

Envisioning the Contemporary: Selections from the Permanent Collection, MCA, June 21, 1997 – April 5, 1998 and April 30, 1998 – February 7, 1999.

Age of Influence: Reflections in the Mirror of American Culture, MCA, March 14, 2000 – January 2, 2001.

References

Collective Vision. MCA, 1996.

Golub. Exh. cat. New York: New Museum of Contemporary Art, 1984.

Jacob, Mary Jane et al. *Selections from the Permanent Collection, Vol. I.* MCA, 1984.

Leon Golub. Exh. cat. Malmö, Sweden: Malmö Konsthall, 1993.

Newman, Michael. "Interview with Leon Golub." In *Mercenaries and Interrogations.* Exh. cat. London: Institute of Contemporary Art, 1982. Pp. 4–11.

Olbricht, Hans-Ulrich, ed. *Leon Golub: Do Paintings Bite?: Selected Texts 1948–1996.* Ostfildern, Germany: Hatje Cantz, 1997. Pp. 197–202.

Siegel, Jeanne. "How Effective Is Social Protest Art?" (Vietnam, 1967). In *Artwords: Discourse on the 60s and 70s.* New York: De Capo, 1992. Pp. 101–119.

Other Works in the MCA Collection

Running Man, date unknown
Lithograph on paper
22¼ × 30 in. (56.5 × 76.2 cm)
Ed: 12/20
Gift of Samuel W. and Blanche M. Koffler
1984.46

Head XIII, 1958
Oil and lacquer on canvas
34⁵/₁₆ × 23¾ in. (87.2 × 60.3 cm)
Gift of Joseph and Jory Shapiro
1992.62

Head XXIII, 1958
Oil and lacquer on canvas
58½ × 44 in. (148.6 × 111.8 cm)
Gift of Walter and Dawn Clark Netsch
1994.17

Head II, 1959
Lacquer on canvas
44⅞ × 28⅞ in. (114 × 73.3 cm)
Gift of George Edson Danforth
1995.115

Two Battling Nude Men, c. 1965
Chalk on vellum
39 × 24 in. (99 × 61 cm)
Bequest of Ruth S. Nath
1998.11

South Africa, 1985
Lithograph on paper
22½ × 30½ in. (57.2 × 77.5 cm)
Ed: 55/90
Gift of the artist and Rhona Hoffman Gallery
1993.17

Felix Gonzalez-Torres

American, b. Cuba 1957–1996
p. 216

Untitled (The End)

1990
Offset prints on paper
22 × 28 × 22 in. (55.9 × 71.1 × 55.9 cm)
Restricted gift of Carlos and Rosa de la Cruz; and Bernice and Kenneth Newberger Fund
1995.111

Provenance

Andrea Rosen, New York/Cynthia Plehn, Santa Monica, Calif., 1990.

MCA, 1995.

Exhibition History

Felix Gonzalez-Torres, Andrea Rosen Gallery, New York, January 20 – February 24, 1990.

Felix Gonzalez-Torres, Solomon R. Guggenheim Museum, New York, March 3 – May 10, 1995; Centro Galego de Arte Contemporánea, Santiago de Compostela, December 12, 1995 – March 3, 1996; ARC-Musée d'Art Moderne de la Ville de Paris, April 18 – June 16, 1996; Kunstwerke Berlin, autumn 1996.

In the Shadow of Storms: Art of the Postwar Era from the MCA Collection, MCA, July 2, 1996 – May 25, 1997.

Envisioning the Contemporary: Selections from the Permanent Collection, MCA, June 21, 1997 – April 5, 1998 and April 30, 1998 – February 7, 1999.

Decades in Dialogue: Perspectives on the MCA Collection, MCA, February 27 – October 31, 1999.

Original Language: Highlights from the MCA Collection, MCA, March 24 – August 5, 2001.

References

Avgikos, Jan. "This Is My Body." *Artforum International* 29, no. 6 (February 1991), pp. 80–83.

Between Artists (Twelve Contemporary American Artists Interview Twelve Contemporary American Artists). Los Angeles: A.R.T. Press, 1996. Pp. 83–101.

Collective Vision. MCA, 1996.

Elger, Dietmar. *Felix Gonzalez-Torres*. Exh. cat. Ostfildern, Germany: Hatje Cantz, 1997.

Felix Gonzalez-Torres. Exh. cat. Hannover, Germany: Sprengel Museum, 1998.

Felix Gonzalez-Torres. Exh. cat. Los Angeles: The Museum of Contemporary Art, 1994.

Heartney, Eleanor. "Felix Gonzalez-Torres at Andrea Rosen." *Art in America* 78, no. 15 (May 1990), pp. 235–36.

McCoy, Pat. "Felix Gonzalez-Torres." *tema celeste* (April/May/June 1990), p. 54.

Spector, Nancy. *Felix Gonzalez-Torres*. New York: Solomon R. Guggenheim Museum, 1995.

Dan Graham
American, b. 1942
p. 96

Bedroom Dining Room Model House
1967
Chromogenic development prints
Two parts, each: 37¾ × 27⅝ in. (95.9 × 70.2 cm)
Gerald S. Elliott Collection
1995.42

Provenance

Marian Goodman Gallery, New York.

Gerald S. Elliott, Chicago, 1989.

MCA, 1995.

Exhibition History

Buildings and Signs, The Renaissance Society, The University of Chicago, September 3–October 1, 1978.

Affinities and Intuitions: The Gerald S. Elliott Collection of Contemporary Art, The Art Institute of Chicago, May 9–July 29, 1990.

PC Focus: Conceptualism to Postconceptualism, the 1960s to the 1990s, MCA, August 22–November 8, 1992.

Conceptual Photography from the Gerald S. Elliott Collection, MCA, February 6–March 21, 1993.

In the Shadow of Storms: Art of the Postwar Era from the MCA Collection, MCA, July 2, 1996–May 25, 1997.

References

Dan Graham: Public/Private. Exh. cat. Philadelphia: Levy Gallery for the Arts, Moore College of Art and Design, 1993.

A Dialogue about Recent American and European Photography. Exh. cat. Los Angeles: The Museum of Contemporary Art, 1991.

Graham, Dan. "Homes for America: Early Twentieth Century Possessable House to Quasi-Discrete Cell of '66." *Arts Magazine* 41, no. 3 (December 1966/January 1967), pp. 21–22.

———. *Rock My Religion Writings and Art Projects 1965–1990*. Cambridge, Mass.: MIT Press, 1993.

Huber, Hans Dieter, ed. *Dan Graham Interviews*. Ostfildern, Germany: Hatje Cantz, 1997.

Wall, Jeff. *Dan Graham's Kammerspiel*. Toronto: Art Metropole, 1996.

Andreas Gursky
German, b. 1955
p. 290

Prada III
1998
Chromogenic development print mounted on Plexiglas with artist's frame
72 × 120 in. (182.9 × 304.8 cm)
Artist's proof aside from an edition of 6
Partial gift of Pamela and Michael Alper
2001.39

Provenance

Matthew Marks Gallery, New York, 1998.

Pamela and Michael Alper, Chicago, 2001.

MCA, 2001.

Chicago Board of Trade II
1999
Chromogenic development print mounted on Plexiglas with artist's frame
81½ × 132⅝ in. (207 × 336.9 cm)
Ed: 3/6
Joseph and Jory Shapiro Fund
1999.59

Provenance

Matthew Marks Gallery, New York, 1999.

MCA, 2000.

Exhibition History

Andreas Gursky, Matthew Marks Gallery, New York, December 3, 1999–January 15, 2000.

Age of Influence: Reflections in the Mirror of American Culture, MCA, March 14, 2000–January 2, 2001.

Original Language: Highlights from the MCA Collection, MCA, March 24–August 5, 2001.

People See Paintings: Photography and Painting from the MCA Collection, MCA, January 19–October 20, 2002.

Avenue of the Americas
2001
Chromogenic development print mounted on Plexiglas with artist's frame
81 × 140⅜ in. (205.7 × 356.6 cm)
Ed: 2/6
Partial gift of Refco Group Ltd., LLC
2002.84

Provenance

Matthew Marks Gallery, New York, 2001.

Refco Group Ltd., LLC, Chicago, 2002.

MCA, 2002.

Exhibition History

Andreas Gursky, The Museum of Modern Art, New York, March 4–May 15, 2001; Museo Nacional Centro de Arte Reina Sofia, Madrid, July 12–September 23, 2001; Musée National d'Art Moderne, Centre Georges Pompidou, Paris, February 13–April 29, 2002; MCA, June 22–September 22, 2002 (not MCA edition).

References

Bradley, Fiona, Greg Hilty, and Lewis Briggs. *Andreas Gursky: Images*. Exh. cat. Liverpool: Tate Gallery, 1995.

Bryson, Norman. "The Family Firm—Andreas Gursky, German Photography." *Art/Text*, no. 67 (November 1999/January 2000), pp. 80–81.

Galassi, Peter. *Andreas Gursky*. Exh. cat. New York: The Museum of Modern Art, 2001.

Kimmelman, Michael. "Stun-Gun Reality, Magnificent in Its Artifice." *New York Times*, March 2, 2001, sec. B, pp. 31, 37.

Rugoff, Ralph. "World Perfect." *Frieze* 43 (November/December 1998), pp. 50–57.

Other Works in the MCA Collection

Bahnhof Porto, 1989
Chromogenic development print mounted on Plexiglas with artist's frame
58⅝ × 68 × 1¾ in. (148.9 × 172.7 × 4.5 cm)
Ed: 2/4
Gerald S. Elliott Collection
1995.43

333

Ann Hamilton
American, b. 1956
p. 202

Video group:
(the capacity of absorption • video)
1988/1993
(dissections . . . they said it was an experiment • video)
1988/1993
(linings • video)
1990/1993
(aleph • video)
1992/1993
LCD monitor with color toned image, 30-minute video laser disc, and laser disc player
Four screens, each: 3½ × 4½ in. (8.9 × 11.4 cm)
Ed: 6/9 aside from 2 artist's proofs
Bernice and Kenneth Newberger Fund; restricted gift of Susan and Lewis Manilow and Howard and Donna Stone
1995.12–15

Provenance

Sean Kelly Gallery, New York, 1993.

MCA, 1995.

Exhibition History

In the Shadow of Storms: Art of the Postwar Era from the MCA Collection, MCA, July 2, 1996 – May 25, 1997.

Envisioning the Contemporary: Selections from the Permanent Collection, MCA, June 21 – April 5, 1998 and April 30, 1998 – February 7, 1999.

Inside and Out: Contemporary Sculpture, Video, and Installations, Bass Museum of Art, Miami, Fla., May 16, 2001 – February 3, 2002.

References

Ann Hamilton: Present – Past, 1984 – 1997. Exh. cat. Lyon, France: Musée d'Art Contemporain de Lyon; Milan: Skira, 1998.

the body and the object: Ann Hamilton 1984 – 1996. Exh. cat. Columbus, Ohio: Wexner Center for the Arts, Ohio State University Press, 1996.

Collective Vision. MCA, 1996.

Outside the Frame: Performance and the Object. Exh. cat. Cleveland, Ohio: Cleveland Center for Contemporary Art, 1994.

Simon, Joan. *Ann Hamilton.* New York: Harry N. Abrams, 2002.

David Hammons

American, b. 1943
p. 274

Praying to Safety

1968
Thai bronze statues, string, and safety pin
Installed: 36½ × 59¾ × 15 in.
(92.7 × 151.8 × 38.1 cm)
Restricted gift of Mr. and Mrs. J. Paul Beitler, Lindy Bergman, Carol and Douglas Cohen, Robert and Sylvie Fitzpatrick, Penny Pritzker and Bryan Traubert, Nancy A. Lauter and Alfred L. McDougal Charitable Fund, Ed and Jackie Rabin, Marjorie and Louis B. Susman, and Helyn D. Goldenberg
2000.5.a – d

Provenance

Jeanne Greenberg, New York, 1997.

MCA, 2000.

Exhibition History

Age of Influence: Reflections in the Mirror of American Culture, MCA, March 14, 2000 – January 2, 2001.

Original Language: Highlights from the MCA Collection, MCA, March 24 – August 5, 2001.

References

Berger, Maurice. Interview of David Hammons in "Speaking Out: Some Distance to Go . . . ." *Art in America* 78, no. 9 (September 1990), pp. 78 – 85.

Bey, Dawoud. "In the Spirit of *Minkisi:* The Art of David Hammons." *Third Text,* no. 27 (summer 1994), pp. 45 – 54.

Cameron, Dan. "David Hammons: Coming in from the Cold." *Flash Art* 26, no. 168 (January/February 1993), pp. 68 – 71.

David Hammons: Rousing the Rubble. Exh. cat. New York: Institute for Contemporary Art; Cambridge, Mass.: MIT Press, 1991.

Diawara, Manthia. "Make it Funky." *Artforum* 36, no. 9 (May 1998), pp. 120 – 27.

19 Sixties: A Cultural Awakening Reevaluated. Exh. cat. Los Angeles: California Afro-American Museum Foundation, 1989.

Rothschild, Deborah Menaker. *Yardbird Suite, Hammons '93.* Exh. cat. Williamstown, Mass.: Williamstown College Museum of Art Press, 1993.

Robert Heinecken

American, b. 1931
p. 100

V.N. Pin Up (#1 of 2)

1968
Black-and-white film transparency on magazine page
12½ × 10 in. (31.8 × 25.4 cm)
Ed: 1/5
Gift of Daryl Gerber Stokols
1998.43

Provenance

Light Gallery, New York.

Private collection, U.S.

Karen Lennox Gallery, Chicago, 1997.

Daryl Gerber Stokols, Chicago, 1998.

MCA, 1998.

Exhibition History

Apposite Opposites: Photography from the MCA Collection, MCA, March 27 – August 1, 1999.

Robert Heinecken, Photographist: A Thirty-Five Year Retrospective, MCA, October 1 – November 28, 1999.

References

Coleman, A. D. "How, Heinecken Asks, Is Culture Affected by the Media?" *New York Observer,* August 3, 1989.

Enyeart, James, ed. *Heinecken.* Carmel, Calif. and New York: Friends of Photography/Light Gallery, 1980.

Hagen, Charles. "Robert Heinecken: An Interview." *Afterimage* 3, no. 10 (April 1976), pp. 18 – 12.

Johnston, Mark. "Contemporary American Photography: Part 1." In *Heinecken: Selected Works from 1966 – 1986.* Tokyo: Gallery MIN, 1986.

Parker, Fred R. Introduction to *Robert Heinecken: Photographic Work.* Pasadena, Calif.: Pasadena Art Museum, 1972.

Warren, Lynne, et al. *Robert Heinecken, Photographist: A Thirty-Five Year Retrospective.* Exh. cat. MCA, 1999.

Other Works in the MCA Collection

Are You Rea, 1964 – 68
Reproductions of photograms
Twenty-seven prints, each: 12¾ × 10 in.
(32.4 × 25.4 cm)
Ed: 327/500
Gift of Daryl Gerber Stokols
1998.42.1 – 27

Woman with Cats, 1998
Silver dye-bleach print mounted on foamcore
71½ × 29½ in. (181.6 × 74.9 cm)
Gift of Eileen Cowin and Jay Brecker
2000.26

Man Dealing the Four Elements, 1998
Silver dye-bleach print mounted on foamcore
71½ × 29½ in. (181.6 × 74.9 cm)
Gift of Joyce Neimanas
2000.27

Arturo Herrera

Venezuelan, b. 1959
p. 302

Behind the House III

1999
Wool felt
Four parts, installed: 102 × 296 in.
(259.1 × 751.8 cm)
Restricted gift of Nancy and Sandy Koltun
2000.16.a – d

Provenance

Brent Sikkema, New York, 1999.

MCA, 2000.

Exhibition History

Original Language: Highlights from the MCA Collection, MCA, March 24 – August 5, 2001.

References

Arturo Herrera. Chicago: The Renaissance Society, The University of Chicago Press, 1998.

Estep, Jan. "Arturo Herrera," *New Art Examiner* 25 (March 1998), pp. 50 – 51.

Grabner, Michelle. "Arturo Herrera, Renaissance Society & Wooster Gardens." *Art Press* (April 1998), pp. 80 – 81.

Helguera, Pablo. "Arturo Herrera: The Edges of the Invisible." *Art Nexus,* no. 33 (August/September/October 1999), pp. 48 – 52.

Hixson, Kathryn. "Arturo Herrera at Randolph Street Gallery." *Flash Art,* no. 184 (October 1995), p. 111.

Jim Hodges

American, b. 1957
p. 278

The end from where you are
1998
Silk, cotton, polyester, and thread
16 × 16 ft. (4.9 × 4.9 m)
Restricted gift in memory of John S. Baran with additional restricted support from the Meta S. and Ronald Berger Family Foundation
1999.4

Provenance

CRG Gallery, New York, 1998.

MCA, 1999.

Exhibition History

Jim Hodges: Every Way, MCA, January 16 – April 11, 1999; Institute of Contemporary Art, Boston, September 8 – October 23, 1999.

Age of Influence: Reflections in the Mirror of American Culture, MCA, March 14, 2000 – January 2, 2001.

References

Cruz, Amada. *Jim Hodges: Every Way.* Exh. cat. MCA, 1999.

Moreno, Gean. "Interview with Jim Hodges." *New Art Examiner* 27, no. 9 (June 2000), pp. 13–15.

Present Tense: Nine Artists in the Nineties. San Francisco: Museum of Modern Art, 1997.

Jenny Holzer

American, b. 1950
p. 176

Truisms
1983
Electronic sign
6⁵⁄₁₆ × 60½ × 4¼ in. (16 × 153.7 × 10.8 cm)
Ed: 2/4
Partial gift of Dr. Paul and Dorie Sternberg
1986.66

Provenance

Young Hoffman Gallery, Chicago, 1983.

Dr. Paul and Dorie Sternberg, Glencoe, Ill., 1983.

MCA, 1986.

Exhibition History

Museum of Contemporary Art on Michigan: Selections from the Permanent Collection, MCA, November 1, 1983 – January 1, 1984.

Ten Years of Collecting, MCA, April 13 – June 10, 1984.

Jenny Holzer, Dallas Museum of Art, October 28, 1984 – January 1, 1985.

American Painting and Sculpture: Selections from the Permanent Collection, MCA, June 28 – August 19, 1985.

Word and Image, MCA, October 3, 1987 – January 10, 1988.

New Acquisitions: The MCA Collects, MCA, November 23, 1991 – January 26, 1992.

PC Focus: Conceptualism to Postconceptualism, the 1960s to the 1990s, MCA, August 22 – November 8, 1992.

In the Shadow of Storms: Art of the Postwar Era from the MCA Collection, MCA, July 2, 1996 – May 25, 1997.

Decades in Dialogue: Perspectives on the MCA Collection, MCA, February 27 – October 31, 1999.

References

Foster, Hal. "Subversive Signs." *Art in America* 70, no. 10 (November 1982), pp. 88–92.

Jacob, Mary Jane et al. *Selections from the Permanent Collection, Vol. I.* MCA, 1984.

Jenny Holzer: Signs. Exh. cat. Des Moines, Iowa: Des Moines Art Center, 1986.

Siegel, Jeanne. "Jenny Holzer's Language Games." *Arts Magazine* 60, no. 4 (December 1985), pp. 64–68.

Waldman, Diane. *Jenny Holzer.* Exh. cat. New York: Solomon R. Guggenheim Museum and Harry N. Abrams, 1989.

Other Works in the MCA Collection

Living Series, 1980–82
Enamel on metal
Three parts, each: 21 × 23 in. (53.2 × 58.4 cm)
Ed: 1/5
Gift of Anne and William J. Hokin
1990.2.1–3

Selections from Under a Rock, 1986
Electronic sign
10 × 112½ × 4½ in. (25.4 × 285.8 × 11.4 cm)
Gerald S. Elliott Collection
1995.45

Gary Hume

British, b. 1962
p. 232

Untitled
1991
Oil on panel
77 × 52 in. (195.6 × 132.1 cm)
Partial gift of Daryl Gerber Stokols and Jeff Stokols
2002.78

Provenance

Daniel Weinberg Gallery, Los Angeles, 1991.

Daryl Gerber, Chicago, 1992.

MCA, 2002.

Exhibition History

Gary Hume Recent Paintings, Daniel Weinberg Gallery, Los Angeles, June 18 – July 18, 1991.

People See Paintings: Photography and Painting from the MCA Collection, MCA, January 19 – October 20, 2002.

References

Bovier, Lionel. "Definitely Something." *Parkett,* no. 48 (December 1996), pp. 19–21.

Dannatt, Adrian. "Gary Hume: The Luxury of Doing Nothing." *Flash Art* 28, no. 183 (summer 1995), pp. 97–99.

Gary Hume Paintings. Exh. cat. London: Institute of Contemporary Art; Bern, Switzerland: Kunsthalle Bern, 1995.

MacMillan, Ian. "Bold with Beauty." *Modern Painters* 9, no. 4 (winter 1996), pp. 36–39.

Robertson, Bryan. "The Real Thing." *Modern Painters* 12, no. 2 (summer 1999), pp. 25–28.

Sensation: Young British Artists from the Saatchi Collection. Exh. cat. London: Royal Academy of Arts, 1997.

Richard Hunt

American, b. 1935
p. 154

Farmer's Dream
1980
Welded Corten steel
109 × 54 × 76½ in. (276.9 × 137.2 × 194.3 cm)
Gift of Mallinckrodt Group Inc. in recognition of Richard A. Lenon
1994.1

Provenance

IMC Global, Inc., Lake Forest, Ill., 1980.

MCA, 1994.

Exhibition History

Statues into Sculpture: Twentieth-Century Selections from Midwest American Museums, White House (First Lady's Garden), Washington, D.C., October 11, 1994 – February 1995; Gibbes Museum of Art, Charleston, S.C., April 1 – June 30, 1995.

Chicago Park District, Seneca Park, Chicago, November 8, 1995 – April 3, 2002.

References

Castro, Jan Garden. "Richard Hunt: Freeing the Human Soul." *Sculpture* 17, no. 5 (May/June 1998), pp. 34–39.

Drell, Adrienne. "Sculptor Richard Hunt: Even His Trash is Art." *Chicago Sun-Times,* November 27, 1994, pp. 1, 16.

Kilian, Michael. "Contemporary Sculpture Finds Home in White House." *Chicago Tribune,* October 12, 1994.

Picasso and the Age of Iron. Exh. cat. New York: Solomon R. Guggenheim Museum, 1993. P. 284. First Published in *Julio González.* Exh. cat. Amsterdam: Stedelijk Museum, 1955.

Richard Hunt: Growing Forward. Exh. cat. Notre Dame, Ind: Snite Museum of Art, University of Notre Dame Press, 1996.

The Sculpture of Richard Hunt. Exh. cat. New York: The Museum of Modern Art, 1971.

Six Black Americans. Exh. cat. Trenton: New Jersey State Museum, 1980.

335

Untitled, c. 1963
Welded chromed steel
34 × 14 × 12 in. (86.4 × 35.6 × 30.5 cm)
Gift of Mark Maremont, Stephen Maremont,
and Kate Maremont Stone in memory
of Jill Fischer Maremont
1994.21

Small Hybrid, 1964
Steel
17½ × 9½ × 10 in. (44.4 × 24.1 × 25.4 cm)
Gift of Mr. and Mrs. Morton A. Sterling
1981.39

Kneehorn, 1965
Welded chromed steel
56¾ × 22 × 23½ in. (144.1 × 56.9 × 59.7 cm)
Bequest of Ruth S. Nath
1998.12

Robert Irwin

American, b. 1928
p. 86

Untitled

1965–67
Acrylic lacquer on shaped aluminum
60 in. diameter × 3½ in. (152.4 × 8.9 cm)
Gift of Lannan Foundation
1997.40

Provenance

The Pace Gallery, New York, 1993.

Lannan Foundation, Los Angeles, 1993.

MCA, 1997.

Exhibition History

Robert Irwin, The Museum of Contemporary Art,
Los Angeles, June 20–August 15, 1993;
Kolnischer Kunstverein, Cologne, Germany,
April 7–May 15, 1994; Musée d'Art Moderne de
la Ville de Paris, June 22–September 30, 1994;
Museo Nacional Centro de Arte Reina Sofia,
Madrid, January 31–April 17, 1995.

California Scheming, MCA, February 14–
May 31, 1998.

References

Allington, Edward. "Buddha Built My Hot Rod."
Frieze 38 (January/February 1998).

Butterfield, Jan. "The State of the Real and
Reshaping the Shape of Things" (1972).
In Sally Everett, ed. *Art Theory and Criticism:
An Anthology of Formalist, Avant-Garde,
Contextualist, and Postmodernist Thought.*
Jefferson, N.C. and London: McFarland and Co.,
1991.

Ferguson, Russell, ed. *Robert Irwin.* New York:
International Publications, 1993.

Licht, Ira. *Robert Irwin.* Exh. cat. MCA, 1975.

Sobchack, Vivian. Interview of Robert Irwin
in "From Space to Place: Vivian Sobchack
Talks to Robert Irwin." *Artforum* 32, no. 3
(November 1993).

Weschler, Lawrence, ed. *Being and Circumstance:
Notes Toward a Conditional Art.* Larkspur
Landing, Calif.: Lapis, 1985.

Weschler, Lawrence, ed. *Seeing Is Forgetting
the Name of the Thing One Sees: A Life of
Contemporary Artist Robert Irwin.* Berkeley:
University of California Press, 1982.

Alfredo Jaar

Chilean, b. 1956
p. 226

Geography = War

1991
Duratrans, light boxes, 55-gallon
metal barrels, and water
Dimensions variable
Gift of Mr. and Mrs. M. A. Lipschulz, and
Maremont Corporation by exchange
1992.89.a–ddd

Provenance

MCA, 1992.

Exhibition History

Alfredo Jaar: Geography=War, Virginia
Museum of Fine Arts, Richmond, Va.,
September 7–October 20, 1991;
MCA, April 30–August 2, 1992.

*In the Shadow of Storms: Art of the Postwar Era
from the MCA Collection,* MCA, July 2, 1996–
May 25, 1997.

*Envisioning the Contemporary: Selections from
the Permanent Collection,* MCA, June 21, 1997–
April 5, 1998 and April 30, 1998–February 7, 1999.

*Apposite Opposites: Photography from the MCA
Collection,* MCA, March 27–August 1, 1999.

References

Alfredo Jaar: Geography=War. Exh. cat.
Richmond, Va.: Anderson Gallery, Virginia
Commonwealth University Press and the
Virginia Museum of Fine Arts, 1991.

Barnitz, Jacqueline. "Conceptual Art and
Latin America: A Natural Alliance."
In *Encounters/Displacements: Luis Camnitzer,
Alfredo Jaar, Cildo Meireles.* Exh. cat. Austin:
Archer M. Huntington Gallery, College of
Fine Arts, University of Texas Press, 1992.

Collective Vision. MCA, 1996.

Encyclopedia of Photography. New York:
International Center of Photography, Pound
Press and Crown Publishers, 1984.

Grynsztejn, Madeleine. *Alfredo Jaar.* Exh. cat.
La Jolla, Calif.: Museum of Contemporary Art,
1990.

Jaar, Alfredo. *Let There Be Light: The Rwanda
Project 1994–1998.* Barcelona: ACTAR, 1998.

Ramírez, Mari Carmen. "Blueprint Circuits:
Conceptual Art and Politics in Latin America."
In *Latin American Artists of the Twentieth
Century.* Exh. cat. New York: The Museum of
Modern Art, 1993.

Guess Who Is Coming To Dinner, 1988
Duratrans and light box
20 × 20 × 5 in. (50.8 × 50.8 × 12.7 cm)
Ed: 5/5
Gerald S. Elliott Collection
1995.48

Cries and Whispers, 1988
Duratrans and light boxes
Two parts, each: 18 × 96 × 7 in.
(45.7 × 243.8 × 17.8 cm)
Gift of Howard and Donna Stone
1996.7.a–b

Geography=War (set of three artist proofs), 1989
Silver dye-bleach prints
Three parts, each: 10 × 8 in. (25.4 × 20.3 cm)
Artist's proof
Gift of the artist
1996.13.a–c

R, 1990
Silver dye-bleach transparency in
light box and mirrors
Installed, approximately: 132 × 40 × 24 in.
(335.3 × 101.6 × 61 cm)
Partial and promised gift from
The Howard and Donna Stone Collection
2002.35

Jasper Johns

American, b. 1930
p. 62

In Memory of My Feelings — Frank O'Hara

1961
Oil on canvas with objects
40¼ × 60 × 2⅞ in. (102.2 × 152.4 × 7.3 cm)
Partial gift of Apollo Plastics Corporation,
courtesy of Stefan T. Edlis and H. Gael Neeson
1995.114.a–d

Provenance

Leo Castelli Gallery, New York, 1961.

Mr. Ellin, 1962.

Dr. and Mrs. Eugene A. Eisner, Scarsdale,
New York, 1964.

Sotheby's, New York, May 20–21, 1983, lot. 437.

Apollo Plastics Corporation, Chicago, 1983.

MCA, 1995.

Exhibition History

Jasper Johns, Leo Castelli Gallery, New York,
January 12–February 7, 1963.

Drawing exhibition, Leo Castelli Gallery, New
York, May 1963.

Jasper Johns, The Jewish Museum, New York,
February 16–April 12, 1964.

*Jasper Johns: Paintings, Drawings, and Sculpture,
1954–1964,* Whitechapel Art Gallery, London,
December 2–31, 1964.

Jasper Johns, Pasadena Art Museum, Pasadena,
Calif., January 26–February 28, 1965.

Jasper Johns: A Retrospective Exhibition, Whitney Museum of American Art, New York, October 18, 1977–January 22, 1978; Museum Ludwig, Cologne, Germany, February 10–March 22, 1978; Musée National d'Art Moderne, Centre Georges Pompidou, Paris, April 18–June 4, 1978; Hayward Gallery, London, June 21–July 30, 1978; Seibu Museum of Art, Tokyo, August 19–September 26, 1978; Museum of Modern Art, San Francisco, October 20–December 10, 1978.

Pop Art 1955–1970, Art Gallery in New South Wales, Sydney, February 26–April 14, 1985; Queensland Art Gallery, Brisbane, Australia, May 1–June 6, 1985; National Gallery of Victoria, Melbourne, Australia, June 26–August 11, 1985.

Opening Installation, New Building, The Art Institute of Chicago, 1988–89.

Hand Painted Pop — American Art in Transition 1953–1962, The Museum of Contemporary Art, Los Angeles, December 6, 1992–March 7, 1993; MCA, April 3–June 20, 1993; Whitney Museum of American Art, New York, July 16–October 3, 1993.

Under Development, MCA, April 28–August 28, 1994.

In the Shadow of Storms: Art of the Postwar Era from the MCA Collection, MCA, July 2, 1996–May 25, 1997.

Jasper Johns: A Retrospective, The Museum of Modern Art, New York, October 16, 1996–January 14, 1997; Museum Ludwig, Cologne, Germany, March 7–June 1, 1997; Museum of Contemporary Art, Tokyo, June 28–August 17, 1997.

Jasper Johns: In Memory of My Feelings–Frank O'Hara, MCA, October 18, 1997–February 1, 1998.

In Memory of My Feelings: Frank O'Hara and American Art, The Museum of Contemporary Art, Los Angeles, July 11–November 14, 1999; Wexner Center, Columbus, Ohio, April 14–May 28, 2000; Parrish Art Museum, South Hampton, N.Y., June 11–July 23, 2000.

References

Bernstein, Roberta. *Jasper Johns's Paintings and Sculptures 1954–1974: The Changing Focus of the Eye*. Ann Arbor, Mich.: UMI Research Press, 1985. Pp. 78–89.

Collective Vision. MCA, 1996.

Ferguson, Russell. *In Memory of My Feelings: Frank O'Hara and American Art*. Los Angeles: The Museum of Contemporary Art, 1999. Pp. 127–36.

Francis, Richard. *Modern Masters: Jasper Johns*. New York: Abbeville, 1984.

Jasper Johns: Writings, Sketchbook Notes, Interviews. New York: The Museum of Modern Art, 1996.

Johnston, Jill. *Jasper Johns: Privileged Information*. London and New York: Thames and Hudson, 1996.

Orton, Fred. *Jasper Johns: The Sculptures*. Exh. cat. Leeds, England: Center for the Study of Sculpture, Henry Moore Institute, 1996. Pp. 44–55.

Varnedoe, Kirk. *Jasper Johns: A Retrospective*. Exh. cat. New York: The Museum of Modern Art, 1996.

Donald Judd
American, 1928–1994
p. 124

Untitled
1970
Stainless steel and Plexiglas
Ten parts, each: 6 × 27 × 24 in.
(15.2 × 68.6 × 61 cm)
Gerald S. Elliott Collection
1995.50.a–j

Provenance

Leo Castelli Gallery, New York, 1970.

L. M. Asher Family Collection, Los Angeles, 1970.

Unknown.

Gerald S. Elliott, Chicago, 1984.

MCA, 1995.

Exhibition History

Affinities and Intuitions: The Gerald S. Elliott Collection of Contemporary Art, The Art Institute of Chicago, May 12–July 29, 1990.

In the Shadow of Storms: Art of the Postwar Era from the MCA Collection, MCA, July 2, 1996–May 25, 1997.

Envisioning the Contemporary: Selections from the Permanent Collection, MCA, June 21, 1997–April 5, 1998 and April 30, 1998–February 7, 1999.

Decades in Dialogue: Perspectives on the MCA Collection, MCA, February 27–October 31, 1999.

Age of Influence: Reflections in the Mirror of American Culture, MCA, March 14, 2000–January 2, 2001.

Minimalismos, Museo Nacional de Arte Reina Sofia, Madrid, July 10–October 8, 2001.

References

Agee, William C. "Donald Judd in Retrospect: An Appreciation." In *Donald Judd*. Exh. cat. New York: The Pace Gallery, 1994. Pp. 5–17.

———. "Unit, Series, Site: A Judd Lexicon." *Art in America* 63, no. 3 (May/June 1975), pp. 40–49.

Benezra, Neal, ed. *Affinities and Intuitions: The Gerald S. Elliott Collection of Contemporary Art*. Exh. cat. Chicago: The Art Institute; London and New York: Thames and Hudson, 1990.

Carlson, Prudence. "Donald Judd's Equivocal Objects." *Art in America* 72, no. 1 (January 1984), pp. 114–18.

Collective Vision. MCA, 1996.

Haskell, Barbara. "Beyond Formalism." In *Donald Judd*. Exh. cat. New York: Whitney Museum of American Art and W. W. Norton, 1988.

Krauss, Rosalind. "Allusion and Illusion in Donald Judd." *Artforum* 4, no. 9 (May 1966), pp. 24–26.

Kuspit, Donald B. "Red Desert and Arctic Dreams." *Art in America* 77, no. 3 (March 1989), pp. 120–25.

Muller, Gregoire. "Donald Judd; Ten Years." *Arts Magazine* 47, no. 4 (February 1973), pp. 35–42.

Neisser, Judith. "A Magnificent Obsession." *Art & Auction* 10, no. 2 (December 1987), p. 109.

Poli, Francesco. "Big Boxes for Smaller Ones." *Contemporanea* 2, no. 2 (March/April 1989), pp. 61–62.

Serra, Richard. "Donald Judd, 1928–1994." *Parkett*, no. 40/41 (April 1994), pp. 176–77.

Smith, Brydon. *Donald Judd: Catalogue Raisonné of Paintings, Objects, and Wood-Blocks 1960–1974*. Ottawa: National Gallery of Canada, 1975.

Smith, Roberta. "Multiple Returns." *Art in America* 70, no. 3 (March 1982), pp. 112–14.

Tuchman, Phyllis. "Minimalism and Critical Response." *Artforum* 15, no. 9 (May 1977), pp. 26–31.

Yau, John. "Donald Judd." *Contemporanea* 2, no. 2 (March/April 1989), pp. 58–60.

Other Works in the MCA Collection

Untitled, 1965
Automobile lacquer on galvanized iron
6 × 27 × 24 in. (15.2 × 68.6 × 61 cm)
Gift of William J. Hokin
1978.52

Untitled, 1970
Anodized aluminum
6 × 110¾ × 6½ in. (15.2 × 281.3 × 16.5 cm)
Gerald S. Elliott Collection
1995.49

Untitled, 1978
Acrylic on plywood
19½ × 45 × 30½ in. (49.5 × 114.3 × 77.5 cm)
Gerald S. Elliott Collection
1995.51

Untitled, 1983
Plywood
39 × 216½ × 19⅝ in.
(99.1 × 549.9 × 49.9 cm)
Gerald S. Elliott Collection
1995.52.a–d

Untitled, 1984
Painted aluminum
11⅞ × 70⅞ × 11⅞ in.
(30.2 × 180.0 × 30.2 cm)
Gerald S. Elliott Collection
1995.53

337

Mike Kelley

American, b. 1954
p. 222

Craft Morphology Flow Chart

1991
Dolls and figures, gelatin silver prints,
acrylic on paper, folding banquet tables,
and folding card tables
Dimensions variable
Gift of Lannan Foundation
1997.41

Provenance

Rosamund Felsen Gallery, Los Angeles, 1991.

Lannan Foundation, Los Angeles, 1992.

MCA, 1997.

Exhibition History

Carnegie International, Carnegie Museum of Art,
Pittsburgh, Pa., October 19, 1991–February 16,
1992.

Mike Kelley, Kunsthalle Basel, Switzerland, April
5–May 24, 1992; Institute of Contemporary Art,
London, June 9–July 19, 1992.

Mike Kelley, Cape Musée d'Arte
Contemporain, Bourdeaux, France,
September 18–November 22, 1992.

*Radical Scavenger(s): The Conceptual Vernacular
in Recent American Art,* MCA, February 5–
April 17, 1994.

*Tables: Selections from the Lannan Foundation
Collection,* Lannan Foundation Gallery,
Los Angeles, October 9–January 9, 1994.

Paul McCarthy/Mike Kelley, Kunstverein,
Hamburg, Germany, March 23–May 15, 1995.

L'Informe: Mode d'Emploi, Musée National d'Art
Moderne, Centre Georges Pompidou, Paris,
May 22–August 26, 1996.

Mike Kelley: 1985–1996, Museu d'Art
Contemporani de Barcelona, Spain,
January 24–March 31, 1997; Rooseum Center
for Contemporary Art, Malmö, Sweden,
April 25–June 15, 1997; Stedelijk Van
Abbemuseum, Eindhoven, Netherlands,
July 5–August 31, 1997.

The Natural World, Vancouver Art Gallery,
Canada, October 10, 1997–January 24, 1998.

California Scheming, MCA, February 14–
May 31, 1998.

*Original Language: Highlights from the MCA
Collection,* MCA, March 24–August 5, 2001.

References

Carnegie International. Exh. cat. Pittsburgh, Pa.:
Carnegie Museum of Art, 1992.

Christie's New York Contemporary Art (Part II).
Auction cat. New York: Christie's, November 19,
1997. P. 156.

Duncan, Michael. "Kelley's Junk-Shop Pop." *Art
in America* 82, no. 6 (June 1994), pp. 84–98.

Kellein, Thomas. *Mike Kelley.* Basel: Edition
Cantz, 1992.

McKenna, Kristine. "The Taboo Artist."
Los Angeles Times (Calendar), Sunday, July 5, 1992,
pp. 4, 57, 66.

Mike Kelley: 1985–1996. Exh. cat. Barcelona:
Museu d'Art Contemporani de Barcelona, 1997.

Myers, Terry. "The Mike Kelley Problem."
New Art Examiner 21, no. 10 (summer 1994),
pp. 26–29.

Storr, Robert. "An Interview with Mike Kelley."
Art in America 82, no. 6 (June 1994),
pp. 90–93.

Other Works in the MCA Collection

Disembodied Militarism, 1988
Acrylic on paper
Six parts, each: 54 × 35¾ in. (137.2 × 90.8 cm)
Gift of Lannan Foundation
1997.42.a–f

Low Definition Presidency, 1993
Acrylic on paper
34½ × 22⁷⁄₁₆ in. (87.6 × 57 cm)
Gift of Howard and Donna Stone
1997.128

Mike Kelley and
Paul McCarthy (American, b. 1945)
Fresh Acconci, 1995
Color video
45 minutes
Unlimited edition
Bernice and Kenneth Newberger Fund
2002.77

William Kentridge

South African, b. 1955
p. 252

Felix in Exile

1994
Color video projection
8 minutes, 43 seconds
Dimensions variable
Ed: 9/10
Gift of Susan and Lewis Manilow
2001.23

Provenance

Stephen Friedman Gallery, London, 1996.

Susan and Lewis Manilow, Chicago, 1998.

MCA, 2001.

Exhibition History

William Kentridge, Hirshhorn Museum and
Sculpture Garden, Smithsonian Institution,
Washington, D.C., February 28–May 13, 2001;
New Museum of Contemporary Art, New York,
June 7–September 16, 2001; MCA, October 20,
2001–January 20, 2002; Contemporary Arts
Museum, Houston, March 1–June 2, 2002;
Los Angeles County Museum of Art, July 21–
October 6, 2002; South African National
Gallery, Cape Town, December 7, 2002–
March 23, 2003. (MCA edition was not included
in Cape Town presentation.)

History of the Main Complaint

1996
Color video projection
5 minutes, 50 seconds
Dimensions variable
Ed: 1/10
Gift of Susan and Lewis Manilow
2001.24

Exhibition History

William Kentridge, Hirshhorn Museum and
Sculpture Garden, Smithsonian Institution,
Washington, D.C., February 28–May 13, 2001;
New Museum of Contemporary Art, New York,
June 7–September 16, 2001; MCA, October 20,
2001–January 20, 2002; Contemporary Arts
Museum, Houston, March 1–June 2, 2002;
Los Angeles County Museum of Art, July 21–
October 6, 2002; South African National
Gallery, Cape Town, December 7, 2002–
March 23, 2003. (MCA edition was not included
in Cape Town presentation.)

Drawing for the film
History of the Main Complaint

1995–96
Charcoal and pastel on paper
27½ × 47¼ in. (69.8 × 120 cm)
Gift of Susan and Lewis Manilow
2001.25

Provenance

Stephen Freidman Gallery, London, 1996.

Susan and Lewis Manilow, Chicago, 1998.

MCA, 2001.

Exhibition History

William Kentridge, Hirshhorn Museum and
Sculpture Garden, Smithsonian Institution,
Washington, D.C., February 28–May 13, 2001;
New Museum of Contemporary Art, New York,
June 7–September 16, 2001; MCA, October 20,
2001–January 20, 2002; Contemporary Arts
Museum, Houston, March 1–June 2, 2002;
Los Angeles County Museum of Art, July 21–
October 6, 2002; South African National
Gallery, Cape Town, December 7, 2002–
March 23, 2003. (Not included in Cape Town
presentation).

Drawing for the film
History of the Main Complaint

1995–96
Charcoal and pastel on paper
47¼ × 63 in. (120 × 160 cm)
Gift of Susan and Lewis Manilow
2001.26

Provenance

Stephen Freidman Gallery, London, 1996.

Susan and Lewis Manilow, Chicago, 1998.

MCA, 2001.

Exhibition History

William Kentridge, Hirshhorn Museum and Sculpture Garden, Smithsonian Institution, Washington, D.C., February 28 – May 13, 2001; New Museum of Contemporary Art, New York, June 7 – September 16, 2001; MCA, October 20, 2001 – January 20, 2002; Contemporary Arts Museum, Houston, March 1 – June 2, 2002; Los Angeles County Museum of Art, July 21 – October 6, 2002; South African National Gallery, Cape Town, December 7, 2002 – March 23, 2003. (Not included in Cape Town presentation.)

Drawing for the film
History of the Main Complaint
1995 – 96
Charcoal and pastel on paper
31 ½ × 48 in. (80 × 121.9 cm)
Gift of Susan and Lewis Manilow
2001.29

Provenance

Stephen Freidman Gallery, London, 1996.

Susan and Lewis Manilow, Chicago, 1998.

MCA, 2001.

Exhibition History

William Kentridge, Hirshhorn Museum and Sculpture Garden, Smithsonian Institution, Washington, D.C., February 28 – May 13, 2001; New Museum of Contemporary Art, New York, June 7 – September 16, 2001; MCA, October 20, 2001 – January 20, 2002; Contemporary Arts Museum, Houston, March 1 – June 2, 2002; Los Angeles County Museum of Art, July 21 – October 6, 2002; South African National Gallery, Cape Town, December 7, 2002 – March 23, 2003. (Not included in Cape Town presentation.)

Drawing for the film
History of the Main Complaint
1995 – 96
Charcoal and pastel on paper
31 ½ × 47 ½ in. (80 × 120.7 cm)
Gift of Susan and Lewis Manilow
2001.35

Provenance

Stephen Freidman Gallery, London, 1996.

Susan and Lewis Manilow, Chicago, 1998.

MCA, 2001.

Drawing for the film
History of the Main Complaint
1995 – 96
Charcoal and pastel on paper
22 × 30 in. (55.9 × 76.2 cm)
Gift of Susan and Lewis Manilow
2001.36

Provenance

Stephen Freidman Gallery, London, 1996.

Susan and Lewis Manilow, Chicago, 1998.

MCA, 2001.

References

Benezra, Neal, Staci Boris, Dan Cameron, Lynne Cooke, and Ari Sitas. *William Kentridge.* Exh. cat. MCA; New York: New Museum of Contemporary Art and Harry N. Abrams, 2001.

Cameron, Dan, Carolyn Christov-Bakargiev, and J. M. Coetzee. *William Kentridge.* London: Phaidon, 1999.

Christov-Bakargiev, Carolyn. *William Kentridge.* Brussels: Société des Expositions du Palais des Beaux-Arts de Bruxelles, 1998.

Godby, Michael. "Memory and History in William Kentridge's *History of the Main Complaint.*" In Sarah Nuttall and Carli Coetzee, eds. *Negotiating the Past: The Making of Memory in South Africa.* Cape Town: Oxford University Press, 1998. Pp. 100 – 111.

Krauss, Rosalind. "'The Rock': William Kentridge's Drawings for Projection." *October,* no. 92 (spring 2000), pp. 3 – 35.

Other Works in the MCA Collection

Drawings for the film
History of the Main Complaint
1995 – 96

Charcoal and pastel on paper
47 ¼ × 63 in. (120 × 160 cm)
Gift of Susan and Lewis Manilow
2001.27

Charcoal and pastel on paper
31 ½ × 47 ½ in. (80 × 120.6 cm)
Gift of Susan and Lewis Manilow
2001.28

Charcoal on paper
27 × 40½ in. (68.6 × 102.9 cm)
Gift of Susan and Lewis Manilow
2001.30

Charcoal on paper
29½ × 41½ in. (74.9 × 105.4 cm)
Gift of Susan and Lewis Manilow
2001.31

Charcoal on paper
22 × 30 in. (55.9 × 76.2 cm)
Gift of Susan and Lewis Manilow
2001.32

Charcoal on paper
21¾ × 30 in. (55.9 × 76.2 cm)
Gift of Susan and Lewis Manilow
2001.33

Gouache and charcoal on paper
48 × 63 in. (121.9 × 160 cm)
Gift of Susan and Lewis Manilow
2001.34

Charcoal on paper
48 × 63 in. (121.9 × 160 cm)
Gift of Susan and Lewis Manilow
2001.37

Charcoal on paper
19¾ × 26 in. (50.2 × 66 cm)
Gift of Susan and Lewis Manilow
2001.38

Anselm Kiefer
German, b. 1945
p. 214

Banner
1990
Oil, lead, ash, rock, paper, and copper wire on canvas
130 × 110¼ in. (330.2 × 280 cm)
Gift of Camille Oliver-Hoffmann in memory of Paul W. Oliver-Hoffmann
1998.25

Provenance

Marian Goodman Gallery, New York, 1990.

Camille and Paul Oliver-Hoffmann, Chicago, 1990.

MCA, 1998.

Exhibition History

Anselm Kiefer, Marian Goodman Gallery, New York, May 5 – June 16, 1990.

Anselm Kiefer, Nationalgalerie Berlin, March 10 – May 20, 1991.

Decades in Dialogue: Perspectives on the MCA Collection, MCA, February 27 – October 31, 1999.

References

Arasse, Daniel. *Anselm Kiefer.* New York: Harry N. Abrams, 2001.

Francis, Richard and Sophia Shaw. "Anselm Kiefer." In *Negotiating Rapture: The Power of Art to Transform Lives.* Exh. cat. MCA, 1996.

Harten, Doreet LeVitte. *Anselm Kiefer: Lilith.* New York: Marian Goodman Gallery, 1991.

Huyssen, Andreas. "Kiefer in Berlin." *October,* no. 62 (autumn 1992), pp. 84 – 101.

Rosenthal, Mark. *Anselm Kiefer.* Exh. cat. Chicago: The Art Institute; Philadelphia: Philadelphia Museum of Art, 1987.

Schjeldahl, Peter. "The Art World: Anselm Kiefer at the Met." *The New Yorker* (January 18, 1999), p. 83.

Jin Soo Kim

American, b. Korea 1950
p. 260

Wall (from imprints)

1994–98
Steel and copper
78 × 78 × 12½ in. (198.1 × 198.1 × 31.8 cm)
Restricted gift of Robert and Sylvie Fitzpatrick,
Roberta and Richard Lieberman, Sandra P.
and Jack Guthman, Nancy A. Lauter and
Alfred L. McDougal, Sukho and Yong Ja Kim,
Antje and John Jelinek, Cleve E. Carney,
Howard and Jacqueline Gilbert, and
Susan and Robert Wislow
1998.54.a–f

Provenance

Zolla Lieberman Gallery, Chicago, 1998.

MCA, 1998.

Exhibition History

*Decades in Dialogue: Perspectives on the MCA
Collection,* MCA, February 27–October 31, 1999.

References

Jin Soo Kim: From Tacit Transit. Exh. cat.
Amherst: University of Massachusetts Press,
1993.

Tracks. Exh. cat. Hanover, N.H.: Jaffe-Friede and
Strauss Galleries, Hopkins Center, Dartmouth
College Press, 1999.

Warren, Lynne et al. *Art in Chicago, 1945–1995.*
Exh. cat. MCA, 1996. Pp. 262–63.

Wright, Beryl J. *Art at the Armory: Occupied
Territory.* Exh. cat. MCA, 1992. Pp. 97–99.

Other Works in the MCA Collection

Changmoon and Bal, 1990
Plaster and gauze on copper and steel
17 × 40 × 39 in. (43.2 × 101.6 × 99.1 cm)
Bernice and Kenneth Newberger Fund
1991.21

Franz Kline

American, 1910–1962
p. 52

Vawdavitch

1955
Oil on canvas
62¼ × 80¹¹⁄₁₆ (158.1 × 204.9 cm)
Gift of Claire B. Zeisler
1976.39

Provenance

Sidney Janis Gallery, New York, 1957.

Jane Wade Rosenberg, New York, 1958.

David Herbert Gallery, New York, 1958.

Fairweather-Hardin Gallery, Chicago, 1960.

Claire B. Zeisler, Chicago, 1961.

MCA, 1976.

Exhibition History

American Paintings: 1945–1957, Minneapolis
Institute of Arts, June 18–September 1, 1957.

Cross Currents, American Federation of the Arts,
New York; Winston-Salem Public Library, N.C.;
Vassar College, Poughkeepsie, N.Y.; University
Museum of Southern Illinois University,
Carbondale, Ill.; Art Alliance, Philadelphia;
Monticello Rotary Club, New York; Montclair Art
Association, N.J.; Cornell University, Ithaca,
N.Y.; Eastern Illinois University, Charleston, Ill.
1958–59.

*Exhibition of Contemporary Art from Chicago
Collectors,* The Bergman Gallery, Cobb Hall,
The University of Chicago, November 11–
December 9, 1968.

*Photography by Aaron Siskind in Homage to
Franz Kline,* The David and Alfred Smart
Museum of Art, The University of Chicago,
October 9–November 23, 1975.

MCA Permanent Collection Exhibition, MCA,
January 16–March 14, 1982.

Abstract Painting and Sculpture: 1950s–1980s,
MCA, October 22, 1985–April 13, 1986.

*Selections from the Permanent Collection:
Icon/Index,* MCA, February 5–April 3, 1988.

Toward the Future: Contemporary Art in Context,
MCA, May 5–July 1, 1990.

Romantic Modernism, Museum of Fine Arts,
Museum of New Mexico, Santa Fe, June 3–July
31, 1994.

Franz Kline: Black and White 1950–1961,
Menil Collection, Houston, September 8–
November 27, 1994; Whitney Museum of
American Art, New York, December 16, 1994–
March 5, 1995; MCA, March 25–June 4, 1995.
(Not included in the Houston presentation.)

*In the Shadow of Storms: Art of the Postwar Era
from the MCA Collection,* MCA, July 2, 1996–
May 25, 1997.

*Envisioning the Contemporary: Selections from
the Permanent Collection,* MCA, June 21, 1997–
April 5, 1998 and April 30, 1998–February 7, 1999.

*People See Paintings: Photography and Painting
from the MCA Collection,* MCA, January 19–
October 20, 2002.

References

Anfram, David. *Franz Kline: Black and White:
1950–1961.* Houston: The Menil Collection,
1994. Pp. 9–32.

Boyd, Williams. "Franz Kline and the Incredible
Lightness of Abstract Expressionism." *Modern
Painters* 7, no. 3 (autumn 1994), pp. 34–37.

Brach, Paul. "Urban Grit." *Art in America* 83,
no. 4 (April 1995), pp. 96–99.

Butler, Barbara. "Franz Kline—Retrospect." *Arts
Magazine* 37, no. 4 (January 1963), pp. 30–33.

Collective Vision. MCA, 1996.

De Kooning, Elaine. "Franz Kline: Painter of His
Own Life." *ARTnews* 61, no. 7 (November 1962),
pp. 28–31, 64–69. Reprinted from the Franz
Kline exhibition at the Washington Gallery of
Modern Art, Washington, D.C.

Jacob, Mary Jane et al. *Selections from the
Permanent Collection, Vol. I.* MCA, 1984.

Kline, Franz. *The Abstractions with Color.*
Washington, D.C.: Phillips Collection, 1979.
Pp. 9–23.

*Museum of Contemporary Art: Fifteen Years and
Beyond.* MCA, 1982.

Oeri, Georgine. "Notes on Franz Kline." In
Quadrum XII. Brussels, 1961.

Other Works in the MCA Collection

No. 3, 1948
Ink on paper
20⅛ × 29¾ in. (51.1 × 75.6 cm)
Gift of Susan and Lewis Manilow
1983.105

Jeff Koons

American, b. 1955
p. 168

New Hoover Deluxe Shampoo Polishers,
New Shelton Wet/Dry 10-Gallon
Displaced Tripledecker

1981/87
Polishers, vacuum cleaners, Plexiglas,
and fluorescent tubes
91 × 54 × 28 in. (231.1 × 137.2 × 71.1 cm)
Gerald S. Elliott Collection
1995.54

Provenance

Daniel Weinberg Gallery, Los Angeles, 1987.

Gerald S. Elliott, Chicago, 1988.

MCA, 1995.

Exhibition History

Encased Works, Daniel Weinberg Gallery, Los
Angeles, December 5, 1987–January 16, 1988.

Jeff Koons, MCA, July 1–August 28, 1988.

*Affinities and Intuitions: The Gerald S. Elliott
Collection of Contemporary Art,* The Art Institute
of Chicago, May 12–July 29, 1990.

*In the Shadow of Storms: Art of the Postwar Era
from the MCA Collection,* MCA, July 2, 1996–
May 25, 1997.

*Envisioning the Contemporary: Selections from
the Permanent Collection,* MCA, June 21, 1997–
April 5, 1998 and April 30, 1998–February 7, 1999.

*Decades in Dialogue: Perspectives on the MCA
Collection,* MCA, February 27–October 31, 1999.

Lifeboat

1985
Bronze
Installed, approximately: 20½ × 87¼ × 62¾ in.
(52.1 × 221.6 × 159.4 cm)
Ed: 3/3
Gerald S. Elliott Collection
1995.56.a–c

Provenance

Daniel Weinberg Gallery, Los Angeles, 1985.

Anthony Meier Fine Arts, New York, 1992.

Gerald S. Elliott, Chicago, 1992.

MCA, 1995.

Exhibition History

Jeff Koons, MCA, July 1–August 28, 1988.
(MCA edition was not included in this
exhibition.)

Jeff Koons, Museum of Modern Art,
San Francisco, December 10, 1992–
February 7, 1993.

*In the Shadow of Storms: Art of the Postwar Era
from the MCA Collection,* MCA, July 2, 1996–
May 25, 1997.

*Decades in Dialogue: Perspectives on the MCA
Collection,* MCA, February 27–October 31, 1999.

*Age of Influence: Reflections in the Mirror of
American Culture,* MCA, March 14, 2000–
January 2, 2001.

*Original Language: Highlights from the MCA
Collection,* MCA, March 24–August 5, 2001.

Rabbit
1986
Stainless steel
41 × 19 × 12 in. (104.1 × 48.3 × 30.5 cm)
Ed: 1/3 aside from 1 artist's proof
Partial gift of Stefan T. Edlis
and H. Gael Neeson
2000.21

Provenance

Sonnabend Gallery, New York, 1986.

Charles Saatchi, London, 1986.

Stefan T. Edlis and H. Gael Neeson,
Chicago, 1991.

MCA, 2000.

Exhibition History

Les Courtiers du Désir, Musée National d'Art
Moderne, Centre Georges Pompidou, Paris,
April 15–May 24, 1987.

Jeff Koons, MCA, July 1–August 28, 1988.
(MCA edition was not included in this
exhibition.)

D&S Ausstellung, Kunstverein Hamburg,
Germany, October 14–November 26, 1989.

Jeff Koons Retrospective, Stedelijk Museum,
Amsterdam, November 28, 1992–January 3,
1993.

Twenty Years, Twenty Artists, Aspen Art Museum,
Aspen, Colo., August 5–September 26, 1999.

*Original Language: Highlights from the MCA
Collection,* MCA, March 24–August 5, 2001.

*Trajected Traditions: Ceramics, Fibers, and
Metalsmiths,* Cranbrook Art Museum,
Bloomfield Hills, Mich., September 20,
2002–January 5, 2003.

Pink Panther
1988
Porcelain
41 × 20½ × 19 in.
(104.1 × 52.1 × 48.3 cm)
Ed: 1/3
Gerald S. Elliott Collection
1995.57

Provenance

Sonnabend Gallery, New York, 1988.

Gerald S. Elliott, Chicago, 1989.

MCA, 1995.

Exhibition History

*Affinities and Intuitions: The Gerald S. Elliott
Collection of Contemporary Art,* The Art Institute
of Chicago, May 12–July 29, 1990.

*Envisioning the Contemporary: Selections from
the Permanent Collection,* MCA, April 30, 1998–
January 1999.

*Original Language: Highlights from the MCA
Collection,* MCA, March 24–August 5, 2001.

References

Collective Vision. MCA, 1996.

Danoff, I. Michael. *Jeff Koons.* Exh. cat.
MCA, 1988.

Jeff Koons. Exh. cat. San Francisco: Museum of
Modern Art, 1992.

The Jeff Koons Handbook. London and New
York: Anthony d'Offay Gallery, Thames and
Hudson, 1992.

Muthesius, Angelika, ed. *Jeff Koons.* Cologne,
Germany: Benedikt Taschen GmbH, 1992.

Politi, Giancarlo. "Luxury and Desire: Interview
with Jeff Koons." *Flash Art,* no. 132
(February/March 1987), pp. 71–76.

Smith, Roberta. "Rituals of Consumption." *Art
in America* 76, no. 5 (May 1988), pp. 164–71.

Other Works in the MCA Collection

Three Ball Total Equilibrium Tank, 1985
Basketballs, sodium-chloride reagent in distilled
water, and glass vitrine with steel
support and air mounts
60½ × 48¾ × 13¼ in.
(153.7 × 123.8 × 33.7 cm)
Ed: 1/2
Gerald S. Elliott Collection
1995.55.a–k

Joseph Kosuth
American, b. 1945
p. 228

No Number #6 (On Color, Blue)
1991
Neon tubing with argon gas and mercury
4 × 108 in. (10.2 × 274.3 cm)
Bernice and Kenneth Newberger Fund;
and National Endowment for the Arts
Purchase Grant
1991.5

Provenance

Rhona Hoffman Gallery, Chicago, 1991.

MCA, 1991.

Exhibition History

New Acquisitions: The MCA Collects, MCA,
November 23, 1991–January 26, 1992.

*PC Focus: Conceptualism to Postconceptualism,
the 1960s to the 1990s,* MCA, August 22–
November 8, 1992.

*In the Shadow of Storms: Art of the Postwar Era
from the MCA Collection,* MCA, July 2, 1996–
May 25, 1997.

References

Battock, Gregory. *Idea Art.* New York:
E. P. Dutton & Co., 1973. Pp. 70–101.

Lippard, Lucy. *Six Years: The Dematerialization
of the Art Object from 1966–1972.* Berkeley:
University of California Press, 1972.
Pp. 146–49.

Timberman, Marcy. "Language, Thought, and
Reality, Joseph Kosuth at Margo Leavin Gallery."
Artweek 21, no. 3, September 27, 1990, p. 14.

Zevi, Adachiara. "Joseph Kosuth: The Context
Is the Stuff of Art." *L'Architettura* 45, no. 524
(June 1999), pp. 382–84.

Barbara Kruger
American, b. 1945
p. 178

**Untitled (We construct the chorus
of missing persons)**
1983
Gelatin silver mural prints with painted
artist's frame
121⅞ × 72⅞ × 2 in. (309.6 × 185.1 × 5.1 cm)
Restricted gift of Paul and Camille
Oliver-Hoffmann
1984.22.a–c

Provenance

Rhona Hoffman Gallery, Chicago, 1984.

MCA, 1984.

341

Exhibition History

New Works: Barbara Kruger, Rhona Hoffman Gallery, Chicago, March 13–April 3, 1984.

New American Photography: Barbara Kruger, Los Angeles County Museum of Art, January 17–March 17, 1985.

American Painting and Sculpture from 1968 to the Present: Selections from the Permanent Collection, MCA, June 28–August 19, 1985.

Slices of Life: The Work of Barbara Kruger, Krannert Art Museum, University of Illinois at Champaign-Urbana, October 4–November 9, 1986.

Images for Human Conduct: Selections from the Permanent Collection, MCA, July 31–September 1, 1987.

Word and Language, MCA, October 3, 1987–January 10, 1988.

Barbara Kruger Exhibition, National Gallery of Art, Private Bag, Wellington, New Zealand, March 4–May 1, 1988.

PC Focus: Conceptualism to Postconceptualism, the 1960s to the 1990s, MCA, August 22–November 8, 1992.

Transmute, MCA, August 21–November 7, 1999.

Barbara Kruger, The Museum of Contemporary Art, Los Angeles, October 17, 1999–February 13, 2000; Whitney Museum of American Art, New York, July 13, 2000–October 22, 2000.

References

Gambrell, Jamey. "What is Political Art Now?" *Village Voice*, October 15, 1985.

Goldstein, Ann. *Barbara Kruger*. Exh. cat. Los Angeles: The Museum of Contemporary Art, 1999.

Grunberg, Andy. "One Liner After Another." *New York Times*, March 31, 1984.

Lichtenstein, Therese. "Barbara Kruger." *Arts Magazine* 57, no. 9 (May 1983), p. 4.

Linker, Kate. *Love for Sale: The Words and Pictures of Barbara Kruger*. New York: Harry N. Abrams, 1990.

Squiers, Carol. "Diversionary (Syn)tactics: Barbara Kruger Has Her Way with Words." *ARTnews* 86, no. 2 (February 1987), pp. 76–85.

Other Works in the MCA Collection

Untitled (Who laughs last?), 1989
Photoengraving on magnesium
with artist's frame
25½ × 21½ × 3 in. (64.8 × 54.6 × 7.6 cm)
Gift of the artist and Mary Boone Gallery
1989.15

Wifredo Lam
Cuban, 1902–1982
p. 40

Anamu
1942
Oil on canvas
60 × 50 in. (152.4 × 127 cm)
Gift of Joseph and Jory Shapiro
1991.26

Provenance

Pierre Matisse Gallery, New York, 1944.

Francis J. Steegmuller, New York, 1946.

Joseph and Jory Shapiro, Chicago, before 1984.

MCA, 1991.

Exhibition History

Lam Paintings, Pierre Matisse Gallery, New York, June 6–24, 1944.

The United States Collects Pan-American Art, The Art Institute of Chicago, 1959.

Ten Years of Collecting, MCA, April 14–June 10, 1984.

In the Mind's Eye: Dada and Surrealism in Chicago Collections, MCA, December 1, 1984–January 27, 1985.

The Mr. and Mrs. Joseph Randall Shapiro Collection, The Art Institute of Chicago, February 23–April 15, 1985.

New Acquisitions: The MCA Collects, MCA, November 23, 1991–January 26, 1992.

Wifredo Lam and His Contemporaries 1938–1952, The Studio Museum in Harlem, New York, December 6, 1992–April 11, 1993.

In the Shadow of Storms: Art of the Postwar Era from the MCA Collection, MCA, July 2, 1996–May 25, 1997.

Envisioning the Contemporary: Selections from the Permanent Collection, MCA, June 21, 1997–April 5, 1998 and April 30, 1998–February 7, 1999.

Surrealism: A Cross-Cultural Perspective, Nassau County Museum of Art, Roslyn Harbor, N.Y., September 29, 2000–January 14, 2001.

Twentieth Century Exiles in America, Nassau County Museum of Art, New York, November 18, 2001–February 3, 2002.

Pierre Matisse and His Artists, The Pierpont Morgan Library, New York, February 14–May 19, 2002.

Matta in America: Paintings and Drawings of the 1940s, The Museum of Contemporary Art, Los Angeles, September 30, 2001–January 6, 2002; Miami Art Museum, Fla., March 20–June 2, 2002; MCA, July 13–October 20, 2002. (Included only in the Chicago presentation.)

References

Balderrama, Maria R., ed. *Wifredo Lam and His Contemporaries 1938–1952*. Exh. cat. New York: The Studio Museum in Harlem, New York, 1992.

Fletcher, Valerie, ed. *Crosscurrents of Modernism: Four Latin American Pioneers*. Exh. cat. Washington, D.C.: Hirshhorn Museum and Sculpture Garden, Smithsonian Institution, 1992. Pp. 167–227.

Fouchet, Max-Pol. *Wifredo Lam*. Balmes and Barcelona: Ediciones Polígrafa, S.A., 1976.

Griswold, William M. *Pierre Matisse and His Artists*. Exh. cat. New York: Pierpont Morgan Library, 2002.

Jacob, Mary Jane et al. *Selections from the Permanent Collection, Vol. I*. MCA, 1984.

Lam, Lou Laurin. *Wifredo Lam, Catalogue Raisonné of the Painted Work, Vol. I: 1923–1960*. Lausanne, Switzerland: Acatos, 1996.

Mosquera, Gerardo, ed. "Modernism from Afro-America: Wifredo Lam." In *Beyond the Fantastic: Contemporary Art Criticism from Latin America*. Cambridge, Mass.: MIT Press, 1996. Pp. 121–32.

Other Works in the MCA Collection

Annunciation, 1944
Oil on canvas
60¾ × 50¼ in. (154.3 × 127.6 cm)
Gift of Mr. and Mrs. E. A. Bergman
1977.28

Louise Lawler
American, b. 1947
p. 208

Between Reagan and Bush
1989
Silver dye-bleach print and transfer
letters on painted wall
24 × 42 in. (61 × 106.7 cm)
Gerald S. Elliott Collection
1995.58.a–b

Provenance

Metro Pictures Gallery, New York, 1989.

Gerald S. Elliott, Chicago, 1989.

MCA, 1995.

Exhibition History

Louise Lawler: How Many Pictures? Metro Pictures Gallery, New York, April 29–May 27, 1989.

Affinities and Intuitions: The Gerald S. Elliott Collection of Contemporary Art, The Art Institute of Chicago, May 12–July 29, 1990.

PC Focus: Conceptualism to Postconceptualism, the 1960s to the 1990s, MCA, August 22–November 8, 1992.

Conceptual Photography from the Gerald S. Elliott Collection, MCA, February 6–March 21, 1993.

In the Shadow of Storms: Art of the Postwar Era from the MCA Collection, MCA, July 2, 1996–May 25, 1997.

Adam Brooks: DeNaturalized, MCA, February 14–July 5, 1998.

Apposite Opposites: Photography from the MCA Collection, MCA, March 27–August 1, 1999.

References

Buskirk, Martha. "Interview of Louise Lawler." *October*, no. 70 (autumn 1994), pp. 104–8.

Decter, Joshua. "Louise Lawler: Minor Amusements of Art World Topicality." *Flash Art*, no. 148 (October 1989), pp. 127–28.

Elger, Dietmer and Thomas Weski. *Louise Lawler: For Sale*. Ostfildern, Germany: Hatje Cantz, 1994.

Fraser, Andrea. "In and Out of Place." *Art in America* 73, no. 6 (June 1985), pp. 122–29.

Goldberg, Vicki. "Ironic Icons." *American Photographer* 23 (September 1989), p. 70.

Johnson, Ken. "Louise Lawler at Metro Pictures." *Art in America* 77, no. 11 (November 1989), p. 191.

June Leaf
American, b. 1929
p. 104

Ascension of Pig Lady
1968
Acrylic on canvas with hand-sewn and stuffed figures, wood, and tin
123³⁄₈ × 174³⁄₄ × 8³⁄₁₆ in.
(313.4 × 443.9 × 20.8 cm)
Gift of Herbert and Virginia Lust
1983.12

Provenance

Allan Frumkin Gallery, New York, c. 1968–69.

Gallery Bernard, Chicago, 1969.

Herbert and Virginia Lust, Greenwich, Conn., 1969.

MCA, 1983.

Exhibition History

Street Dreams, Allan Frumkin Gallery, New York, December 7, 1968–January 4, 1969.

Thanks Sincerely June Leaf, Madison Art Center, Madison, Wis., December 21, 1973–February 17, 1974.

June Leaf: A Retrospective Exhibition, MCA, January 13–March 5, 1978.

New Acquisitions, MCA, March 25–May 29, 1983.

Museum of Contemporary Art on Michigan Avenue: Selections from the Permanent Collection, MCA, November 1, 1983–January 1, 1984.

Ten Years of Collecting, MCA, April 13–June 10, 1984.

American Painting and Sculpture from 1968 to the Present: Selections from the Permanent Collection, MCA, June 28–August 19, 1985.

June Leaf: A Survey of Painting, Sculpture, and Works on Paper, 1948–1991, Washington Project for the Arts Gallery, Washington, D.C., April 6–June 2, 1991; Addison Gallery of American Art, Phillips Academy, Andover, Mass., October–December 1991.

References

Adrian, Dennis. *June Leaf*. Exh. cat. Washington, D.C.: Washington Project for the Arts, 1991.

Art in Chicago 1945–1995. Exh. cat. MCA, 1996. P. 265.

Jacob, Mary Jane et al. *Selections from the Permanent Collection, Vol. I*. MCA, 1984.

June Leaf: A Retrospective Exhibition. Exh. cat. MCA, 1978.

Schulze, Franz. *Fantastic Images: Chicago Art since 1945*. Chicago: Follett, 1972. Pp. 14–17.

Thanks Sincerely June Leaf. Exh. cat. Madison, Wis.: Madison Art Center, 1973.

Yau, John. "Original Desire: June Leaf's Telling Art." *Arts Magazine* 66, no. 3 (November 1991), pp. 40–45.

Other Works in the MCA Collection

Red Painting, 1954
Oil on canvas
72 × 108 in. (182.9 × 274.3 cm)
Gift of Stuart Katz
1996.31

Arcade Women, 1956
Oil on canvas
69¹¹⁄₁₆ × 98⁵⁄₈ in. (177 × 250.5 cm)
Gift of Allan Frumkin
1978.42

Woman in Landscape, 1959
Charcoal on paper
Image: 46³⁄₁₆ × 29 in. (99.5 × 73.7 cm)
Gift of Susan and Lewis Manilow
1991.100

Dancer and Old Man, 1966
Oil on plaster and wood
14³⁄₄ × 11¼ × 7⁷⁄₈ in. (37.5 × 28.6 × 20 cm)
Gift of Susan and Lewis Manilow
1991.99

Woman at the Door, 1966
Oil on clay, wood, and glass
8¹⁄₈ × 5³⁄₈ × 7⁵⁄₈ in. (21 × 13.7 × 19.4 cm)
Gift of Susan and Lewis Manilow
1993.20

Character Yells at Storyteller, 1970
Watercolor on paper with collage
36¹⁄₈ × 23½ in. (91.8 × 59.7 cm)
Gift of Susan and Lewis Manilow
1991.98

There's More!, 1970
Lithograph on paper and ink and color wash on paper
15¼ × 11 in. (38.7 × 27.9 cm)
Gift of Peter Selz
1993.19.a–b

Characters Escaping, 1970
Gouache, ink, and collage on paper
11¹¹⁄₁₆ × 26 in. (29.7 × 66 cm)
Bequest of Ruth S. Nath
1998.13

Judy Ledgerwood
American, b. 1959
p. 262

Driving Into Delirium
1995
Oil and wax on canvas
72 × 144 in. (182.9 × 365.8 cm)
Gift of Donna and Howard Stone
2001.2

Provenance

Feigen, Inc., Chicago, 1995.

Donna and Howard Stone, Chicago, 1995.

MCA, 2001.

Exhibition History

Judy Ledgerwood, Feigen, Inc., Chicago, October 27–November 26, 1995.

People See Paintings: Photography and Painting from the MCA Collection, MCA, January 19–October 20, 2002.

References

Adcock, Craig. *Cold Days*. Exh. cat. Chicago: The Renaissance Society, The University of Chicago Press, 1999.

Grabner, Michelle. "Lake Breeze: Referential Abstraction in Chicago." *New Art Examiner* 26, no. 1 (September 1998), pp. 22–26.

Ledgerwood, Judy. "Speakeasy." *New Art Examiner* 23, no. 5 (January 1996), pp. 14–15.

Other works in the MCA Collection

Composition in Yellow and Grey, 1987
Oil and encaustic on canvas
90 × 120 in. (228.6 × 304.8 cm)
Gift of Wendy and John D. Cartland
1996.44

In Grey, 1989
Oil and encaustic on canvas
48¹⁄₈ × 96¹⁄₈ in. (122.2 × 244.2 cm)
Gift of Cooperfund, Inc.
1991.54

Study for Groovin' on Violet, 1996
Gouache on paper
Two panels, each: 40 × 60 in.
(101.6 × 152.4 cm)
Gift of the artist and Feigen Inc. Gallery
1996.15.1–2

Study for Groovin' on Lemon, 1996
Gouache on paper
Two panels, each: 40 × 60 in.
(101.6 × 152.4 cm)
Gift of the artist and Feigen Inc. Gallery
1996.16.1–2

343

Sherrie Levine

American, b. 1947
p. 186

Untitled (Gold Knots: 1)
1985
Acrylic on plywood with wooden
artist's frame
21⅛ × 17⅛ × 1¼ in. (53.6 × 43.5 × 3.2 cm)
Gift of Lannan Foundation
1997.43

Provenance

Baskerville+Watson, New York, 1985.

Bette and Herman Ziegler, New York, 1985.

Christie's, New York, February 24, 1993.

Lannan Foundation, Los Angeles, 1993.

MCA, 1997.

Exhibition History

Sherrie Levine, Baskerville+Watson, New York,
1985.

Tableaux Abstraits, Villa Arson, Nice, France,
July 11–September 28, 1986.

Directions: Sherrie Levine, Hirshhorn Museum
and Sculpture Garden, Smithsonian Institution,
Washington, D.C., March 9–May 30, 1988.

Art at the Edge: Sherrie Levine, High Museum
of Art, Atlanta, June 11–September 4, 1988.

*Envisioning the Contemporary: Selections from
the Permanent Collection,* MCA, June 21, 1997–
April 5, 1998 and April 30, 1998–February 7, 1999.

Examining Pictures: Exhibiting Paintings,
Whitechapel Art Gallery, London, May 7–
June 27, 1999; MCA, July 24–September 19, 1999;
Armand Hammer Museum, Los Angeles,
February 3–April 2, 2000.

References

Buskirk, Martha. "Interviews with Sherrie
Levine, Louise Lawler, and Fred Wilson."
October, no. 70 (autumn 1994), pp. 98–103.

Crimp, Douglas. "The Photographic Activity of
Postmodernism." *October,* no. 15 (winter 1980),
pp. 91–101.

———. *Pictures.* Exh. cat. New York: Artists
Space, 1977.

Foster, Hal. "Signs Taken For Wonders."
Art in America 74, no. 6 (June 1986), pp. 80–91.

Marincola, Paula, ed. *Image Scavengers:
Photography.* Exh. cat. Philadelphia: Institute
of Contemporary Art, 1982.

Marzoratti, Gerald. "Art in the (Re)Making."
ARTnews 85, no. 5 (May 1986), pp. 90–99.

Sherrie Levine: Fountain. Exh. cat. New York:
Mary Boone Gallery, 1991.

Sherrie Levine: Newborn. Exh. cat. Philadelphia:
Philadelphia Museum of Art; Frankfurt: Portikus
Frankfurt Am Main, 1993.

Taylor, Paul. "Sherrie Levine Plays with Paul
Taylor." *Flash Art,* no. 135 (summer 1987),
pp. 55–59.

Sol LeWitt

American b. 1928
p. 92

Serial Project, Set D
1966
Painted steel
15½ × 55½ × 55½ in. (39.4 × 141 × 141 cm)
Gerald S. Elliott Collection
1995.59

Provenance

Galerie Konrad Fischer, Düsseldorf, Germany,
c. 1967.

Hans Meyer, Düsseldorf, Germany.

Salvatore Ala, Milan.

Donald Young Gallery, Chicago, c. 1985.

Gerald S. Elliott, Chicago, 1985.

MCA, 1995.

Exhibition History

Sol LeWitt, Galerie Konrad Fischer, Düsseldorf,
Germany, January 6–February 3, 1968.

Sol LeWitt, Kunsthalle Bern, Switzerland,
October 7–November 19, 1972.

*Affinities and Intuitions: The Gerald S. Elliott
Collection of Contemporary Art,* The Art Institute
of Chicago, May 12–July 29, 1990.

*Decades in Dialogue: Perspectives on the MCA
Collection,* MCA, February 27–October 31, 1999.

**Wall Drawing No. 358: A 12" (30 cm)
Grid Covering the Wall. Within Each 12"
(30 cm) Square, One Arc from the Corner.
(The direction of the arcs and their
placement are determined by the
draftsman.)**
1981
Crayon and graphite grid on painted wall
Dimensions variable
Gerald S. Elliott Collection
1995.62

Provenance

John Weber Gallery, New York.

Gerald S. Elliott, Chicago.

MCA, 1995.

Exhibition History

Wallworks, John Weber Gallery, New York, 1986.

*Affinities and Intuitions: The Gerald S. Elliott
Collection of Contemporary Art,* The Art Institute
of Chicago, May 12–July 29, 1990.

*Fiftieth Anniversary of the Addison Gallery of
American Art,* Phillips Academy, Andover, Mass.,
May 9, 1991.

*In the Shadow of Storms: Art of the Postwar Era
from the MCA Collection,* MCA, July 2, 1996–
May 25, 1997.

*Envisioning the Contemporary: Selections from
the Permanent Collection,* MCA, June 21, 1997–
April 5, 1998 and April 30, 1998–February 7, 1999.

References

Collective Vision. MCA, 1996.

Garrels, Gary. *Sol LeWitt: A Retrospective.* Exh.
cat. San Francisco: Museum of Modern Art,
2000.

Legg, Alicia, ed. *Sol LeWitt.* Exh. cat. New York:
The Museum of Modern Art, 1978.

LeWitt, Sol. "Paragraphs on Conceptual Art."
Artforum 5, no. 10 (June 1967), p. 79.

Lippard, Lucy. "Sol LeWitt: Non-Visual
Structures." *Artforum* 5, no. 8 (April 1967),
pp. 42–46.

Sol LeWitt Structures 1962–1993. Exh. cat.
Oxford: Museum of Modern Art, 1993.

Stiles, Kristine and Peter Selz, eds. *Theories
and Documents of Conceptual Art: A Sourcebook
of Artists' Writings.* Berkeley: University
of California Press, 1996. Pp. 826–27.

Zevi, Adachiara, ed. *Sol LeWitt: Critical Texts.*
Rome: Graffiti, 1995.

Other Works in the MCA Collection

Drawing for Modular Cube/Base, 1967
Ink on paper
14½ × 17½ in. (36.8 × 44.4 cm)
Restricted gift of the Collectors Group, Men's
Council, Women's Board, Young Hoffman
Gallery, and National Endowment for the Arts
Purchase Grant
1978.60.1

Modular Cube/Base, 1967/1972
Painted wood
Cube: 15¼ × 15¼ × 15¼ in.
(38.7 × 38.7 × 38.7 cm)
Base: 2 × 45½ × 45½ in.
(5.1 × 114.9 × 114.9 cm)
Restricted gift of the Collectors Group, Men's
Council, Women's Board, Young Hoffman
Gallery, and National Endowment for the Arts
Purchase Grant
1978.60.a–b

Suite of 16 in Color, 1971
Lithographs on paper
Sixteen parts, each: 14 × 14 in.
(35.6 × 35.6 cm)
Ed: 34/50
Gift of Robert Cottle and Barbara Balkin Cottle
1983.42.1–16

Cube Structure Based on Five Modules # 75,
1971/77
Painted wood
24⅛ × 24⅛ × 24⅛ in.
(61.3 × 61.3 × 61.3 cm)
Gift of Roger and Neil Barrett
1994.22

Untitled, 1978
Etching on paper
20 × 20 in. (50.8 × 50.8 cm)
Gift of L. A. Louver, Venice, Calif.
1991.66

*Wall Drawing No. 311: Square, Circle, and Triangle
on Red, Yellow, and Blue,* 1978
Crayon and acrylic on wall
Dimensions variable
Gerald S. Elliott Collection
1995.60

Cube, 1979
Spray enamel on aluminum
11 × 11 × 11 in. (27.9 × 27.9 × 27.9 cm)
Ed: 1/5
Gift of the Men's Council
1980.45

1-2-3-4-5, 1980
Painted aluminum
25¼ × 99¼ × 32¾ in.
(64.1 × 252.1 × 83.2 cm)
Gerald S. Elliott Collection
1995.61.a–f

Untitled, 1986
Painted wood
78 × 27½ × 23 in.
(198.1 × 69.8 × 58.4 cm)
Gerald S. Elliott Collection
1995.63

One-, Two-, Three-, and Four-Part Combinations of Vertical, Horizontal, and Diagonal Left and Right Bands of Color, 1993–94
Gouache on paper
Sixty-four parts, each: 30 × 22 in.
(76.2 × 55.9 cm)
Restricted gift of Alsdorf Foundation, Lindy Bergman, Ann and Bruce Bachmann, Carol and Douglas Cohen, Frances and Thomas Dittmer, H. Gael Neeson and Stefan T. Edlis, Jack and Sandra P. Guthman, Anne and William J. Hokin, Judith Neisser, Susan and Lewis Manilow, Dr. Paul and Dorie Sternberg, Howard and Donna Stone, Lynn and Allen Turner, Martin E. Zimmerman, Mr. and Mrs. Burton W. Kanter, Ralph I. and Helyn D. Goldenberg, and Marcia and Irving Stenn
1994.13.a–lll

Bands of Color in Four Directions (Vertical), 1995
Woodcut on paper
33⅛ × 14¹⁄₁₆ in. (84.1 × 35.7 cm)
Ed: 20/45
Gift of the artist
1995.19

Glenn Ligon
American, b. 1960
p. 242

Untitled (Study #1 for Prisoner of Love)
1992
Oil on canvas
30½ × 20 in. (77.5 × 50.8 cm)
Gift of Sandra P. and Jack Guthman
2000.11

Provenance

Max Protetch Gallery, New York, 1992.

Sandra P. and Jack Guthman, Chicago, 1993.

MCA, 1996.

Untitled
1992
Softground etchings, aquatint, spit bite and sugar lift on paper
Four parts, each: 25 × 17¼ in.
(63.5 × 43.8 cm)
Ed: 42/45
Gift of Sandra P. and Jack Guthman
2000.14.a–d

Provenance

Max Protetch Gallery, New York, 1992.

Sandra P. and Jack Guthman, Chicago, 1993.

MCA, 2000.

Runaways
1993
Portfolio of lithographs on paper
Ten parts, each: 19¾ × 23¾ in.
(50.2 × 60.3 cm)
Ed: 25/45 aside from 10 artist's proofs
Gift of Sandra P. and Jack Guthman
2000.12.a–j

Provenance

Max Protetch Gallery, New York, 1993.

Sandra P. and Jack Guthman, Chicago, 1993.

MCA, 2000.

Exhibition History

Glenn Ligon: Runaways and Narratives, MCA, October 14–November 26, 2000.

Narratives
1993
Portfolio of etchings with chine collé
Nine parts, each: 28 × 21 in. (71.1 × 53.3 cm)
Ed: 18/45 aside from 10 artist proofs
Gift of Sandra P. and Jack Guthman
2000.13.a–i

Provenance

Max Protetch Gallery, New York, 1993.

Sandra P. and Jack Guthman, Chicago, 1993.

MCA, 2000.

Exhibition History

Glenn Ligon: Runaways and Narratives, MCA, October 14–November 26, 2000.

White #11
1994
Oil paintstick on linen
84 × 60 in. (213.4 × 152.4 cm)
Gift of Sandra P. and Jack Guthman
2000.9

Provenance

Max Protetch Gallery, New York, 1994.

Sandra P. and Jack Guthman, Chicago, 1994.

MCA, 2000.

Exhibition History

25 Americans: Painting in the 1990s, Milwaukee Art Museum, Milwaukee, Wis., September 8–November 5, 1995.

Un/Becoming, Institute of Contemporary Art, Philadelphia, January 17, 1998–March 8, 1998.

Age of Influence: Reflections in the Mirror of American Culture, MCA, March 14, 2000–January 2, 2001.

People See Paintings: Photography and Painting from the MCA Collection, MCA, January 19–October 20, 2002.

References

Glenn Ligon, New Work. Exh. cat. San Francisco: Museum of Modern Art, 1996.

Meyer, Richard. "Glenn Ligon: The Limits of Visibility." *Art/Text*, no. 58 (August/September/October 1997), pp. 32–35.

25 Americans: Painting in the 1990s. Exh. cat. Milwaukee, Wis.: Milwaukee Art Museum, 1995.

Un/Becoming. Exh. cat. Philadelphia: Institute of Contemporary Art, University of Pennsylvania Press, 1998.

Sharon Lockhart
American, b. 1964
p. 288

On Kawara: Whole and Parts, 1964–95, Museum of Contemporary Art, Tokyo, January 24–April 5, 1998
1998
Chromogenic development prints
Four parts, installed: 64½ × 240 in.
(163.8 × 609.6 cm)
Ed: 2/6
Bernice and Kenneth Newberger Fund
2001.3.a–d

Provenance

Blum & Poe, Santa Monica, Calif., 1998.

MCA, 2001.

Exhibition History

People See Paintings: Photography and Painting from the MCA Collection, MCA, January 19–October 20, 2002.

Enrique Nava Enedina: Oaxacan Exhibition Hall, National Museum of Anthropology, Mexico City
1999
Chromogenic development prints
Three parts, installed: 49 × 217½ in.
(124.5 × 552.5 cm)
Ed: 5/6
Partial gift of George and Lori Bucciero
1999.53.a–c

Provenance

Blum & Poe, Santa Monica, Calif., 1999.

George and Lori Bucciero, Chicago, 1999.

MCA, 1999.

Exhibition History

Age of Influence: Reflections in the Mirror of American Culture, MCA, March 14, 2000–January 2, 2001.

Sharon Lockhart, MCA, March 3–May 20, 2001; Museum of Contemporary Art, San Diego, Calif., June 9–September 3, 2001.

References

Anderson, Maxwell. *Whitney Biennial 2000 Exhibition*. Exh. cat. New York: Whitney Museum of American Art, 2000.

Burgi, Bernhard and Veit Görner. *Sharon Lockhart: Teatro Amazonas*. Exh. cat. Rotterdam, Netherlands: Nai, 1999.

Molon, Dominic and Norman Bryson. *Sharon Lockhart*. Exh. cat. MCA, 2001.

345

Other Works in the MCA Collection

Photo from the collection of João Damasceno/Interview Location/Survey of the Aripuanā River Region/Natal Community, Aripuanā River Interview Subject: João Damasceno/Interview Subjects: Alexandre de Oliveira Bento, José Luiz Cardoso, Maria de Jesus Araújo Ferreira/Anthropologist: Ligia Simonian/Photos from the collection of Alexandre de Oliveira Bento, 1999
Chromogenic development prints and gelatin silver prints
Six panels, one, six: 15⅞ × 12⅞ in.
(40.3 × 32.7 cm);
two, three: 26⅞ × 31¾ in. (68.3 × 80.6 cm);
four, five: 12⅞ × 15⅞ in. (32.7 × 40.3 cm)
Ed: 3/6
Partial and promised gift from The Howard and Donna Stone Collection
2002.40.a–f

Richard Long
British, b. 1945
p. 194

Fire Rock Circle
1987
Fire rock stones
Installed, approximately 16 × 110 in. diameter
(40.6 × 279.4 cm)
Gerald S. Elliott Collection
1995.64

Provenance

Donald Young Gallery, New York, 1987.

Gerald S. Elliott, Chicago, 1988.

MCA, 1995.

Exhibition History

Affinities and Intuitions: The Gerald S. Elliott Collection of Contemporary Art, The Art Institute of Chicago, May 12–July 29, 1990.

Painting: Singular Objects, National Museum of Modern Art, Tokyo, November 3–December 17, 1995; National Museum of Modern Art, Kyoto, Japan, January 5–February 18, 1996.

In the Shadow of Storms: Art of the Postwar Era from the MCA Collection, MCA, July 2, 1996–May 25, 1997.

Envisioning the Contemporary: Selections from the Permanent Collection, MCA, June 21, 1997–April 5, 1998 and April 30, 1998–February 7, 1999.

Age of Influence: Reflections in the Mirror of American Culture, MCA, March 14, 2000–January 2, 2001.

Chicago Mud Circle
1996
Mud on wall
Approximately 24 ft. diameter (7.3 m)
Gift of David Meitus
1997.120

Provenance

David Meitus, New York, 1996.

MCA, 1996.

Exhibition History

Envisioning the Contemporary: Selections from the Permanent Collection, MCA, June 21, 1997–April 5, 1998.

References

Appleton, Steven. "The Remote Artist." *Artweek* 20, no. 17, April 29, 1989, p. 6.

Benezra, Neal, ed., *Affinities and Intuitions: The Gerald S. Elliott Collection of Contemporary Art.* Exh. cat. Chicago: The Art Institute; London and New York: Thames and Hudson, 1990.

Christensen, Judith. "Re-creating Natural Harmony." *Artweek* 20, no. 30, September 23, 1989, p. 6.

Fuchs, R. H. *Richard Long: Circles, Cycles, Mud Stones.* Exh. cat. Houston: Contemporary Arts Museum, 1996.

Januszczak, Waldemar. "The Church of the New Art." *Flash Art,* no. 120 (January 1985), pp. 28–32.

Morgan, Robert C. "Richard Long's Poststructural Encounters." *Arts Magazine* 61, no. 6 (February 1987), pp. 76–77.

Jacob, Mary Jane and Graham Beal. *A Quiet Revolution: British Sculpture Since 1965.* Exh. cat. MCA; San Francisco: Museum of Modern Art in conjunction with Thames and Hudson, 1987.

Richard Long: Walking in Circles. Exh. cat. New York: George Braziller, 1991.

Taubeneck, Anne. "Art: Look, Yes, But Don't Touch." *Chicago Tribune,* April 13, 1997, sec. 7, p. 1.

Westfall, Stephen. "Earth Actions." *Art in America* 82, no. 10 (October 1994), pp. 114–15.

Other Works in the MCA Collection

Turf Circle, 1967/1989
Grass installation
Approximately: 1½ × 37 × 37 ft.
(.5 × 11.3 × 11.3 m)
Gift of Frances and Thomas Dittmer
1994.4

Watermarks, 1979
Gelatin silver prints and graphite on mat board
Two parts, each: 34⅞ × 48½ in.
(88.6 × 123.2 cm)
Gerald S. Elliott Collection
1995.65.a–b

Untitled, 1987
River Avon mud on rag board
60⅝ × 105 in. (154 × 266.7 cm)
Gift of Lannan Foundation
1997.44

René Magritte
Belgian, 1898–1967
p. 50

Les merveilles de la nature (The Wonders of Nature)
1953
Oil on canvas
30½ × 38⅝ in. (77.5 × 98.1 cm)
Gift of Joseph and Jory Shapiro
1982.48

Provenance

Alexander Iolas, New York, 1953.

Bodley Gallery, New York, 1955.

Joseph and Jory Shapiro, Chicago, c. 1955–56.

MCA, 1982.

Exhibition History

Exposition sur le thème La Sirène, La Sirène, Brussels, October 2, 1953–mid-October 1953.

Oeuvres récentes de René Magritte, La Sirène, Brussels, late October 1953.

Magritte, Iolas Gallery, New York, March 25–April 1957.

Magritte, The Renaissance Society, The University of Chicago, 1964.

Magritte, Arkansas Art Center, Little Rock, Ark., May 15–June 30, 1964.

Constant Companions, University of St. Thomas Art Department, Houston, October 28, 1964–February 7, 1965.

René Magritte, The Museum of Modern Art, New York, December 15, 1965–February 27, 1966; Rose Art Museum, Brandeis University, Waltham, Mass., April 3–May 1, 1966; The Art Institute of Chicago, May 27–July 4, 1966; Berkeley University Art Museum, Calif.; Pasadena Art Museum, Pasadena, Calif., August 2–September 4, 1966.

Selections from the Collection of Mr. and Mrs. Joseph Randall Shapiro, MCA, December 20, 1969–February 1, 1970.

MCA, May 1980.

Permanent Collection Exhibition, MCA, 1982.

Ten Years of Collecting, MCA, April 13–June 10, 1984.

Dada and Surrealism in Chicago Collections, MCA, December 1, 1984–January 27, 1985.

The Mr. and Mrs. Joseph Randall Shapiro Collection, The Art Institute of Chicago, February 23–April 14, 1985.

PC: Promised Gifts Exhibition, MCA, October 3–November 28, 1989.

Modeling the Future: The New Museum and Key Works from the Permanent Collection, MCA, May 2–November 8, 1992.

Surrealism: Revolution by Night, National Gallery of Australia, Canberra, March 13–May 2, 1993; Queensland Art Gallery, Brisbane, Australia, May 21–July 11, 1993; Art Gallery of New South Wales, Sydney, July 30–September 19, 1993.

In the Shadow of Storms: Art of the Postwar Era from the MCA Collection, MCA, July 2, 1996 – May 25, 1997.

Envisioning the Contemporary: Selections from the Permanent Collection, MCA, June 21, 1997 – April 5, 1998 and April 30, 1998 – February 7, 1999.

René Magritte Retrospective, Musées Royaux des Beaux-Arts de Belgique, Brussels, March 6 – June 28, 1998.

Transmute, MCA, August 21 – November 7, 1999.

René Magritte Retrospective, San Francisco Museum of Modern Art, May 5, 2000 – September 12, 2000.

People See Paintings: Photography and Painting from the MCA Collection, MCA, January 19 – October 20, 2002.

References

Ades, Dawn et al. *In the Mind's Eye: Dada and Surrealism*. MCA, 1984.

Breton, André. *Manifeste du surréalisme* (1924). In Maurice Nadeau, and Richard Howard, trans. *The History of Surrealism*. New York: Macmillan, 1965.

Collective Vision. MCA, 1996.

Ducasse, Isidore [Comte de Lautréamont, pseud.]. *Les chants de Maldoror, with Illustrations by René Magritte*. Brussels: La Boetie, 1948.

Jacob, Mary Jane et al. *Selections from the Permanent Collection, Vol. I*. MCA, 1984.

Soby, James Thrall. *René Magritte*. Exh. cat. New York: The Museum of Modern Art, 1965.

Sylvester, David. *Magritte*. New York: Harry N. Abrams, 1992.

Torczyner, Harry. *Magritte: Images and Ideas*. New York: Harry N. Abrams, 1979.

Waldberg, Patrick. *René Magritte*. Brussels: André de Rache, 1965.

Whitfield, Sarah and Michael Raeburn, and David Sylvester, ed., vols. II and III. *René Magritte Catalogue Raisonné*. Houston: Menil Foundation; Antwerp, Belgium: Fonds Mercator, 1997.

Other Works in the MCA Collection

Les rêveries du promeneur solitaire (Reveries of the Solitary Walker), 1926
Gouache, India ink, newspaper, music paper, and graphite on paper
23³⁄₈ × 17³⁄₄ in. (59.4 × 45.1 cm)
Gift of Joseph and Jory Shapiro
1992.64

Iñigo Manglano-Ovalle
American, b. Spain 1961
p. 256

Balsero
1994
Inflatable raft and inner tubes, marine vinyl, aircraft cable, and color video installation
Dimensions variable
Gift of Carlos and Rosa de la Cruz
1996.1

Provenance

Carlos and Rosa de la Cruz, Miami, Fla., 1994.

MCA, 1996.

Exhibition History

Balsero, Thomas Blackman Associates, Chicago, April 29 – June 3, 1994.

Correspondences/Korrespondenzen: 14 Artists from Berlin and Chicago, Berlinische Galerie fur Moderne Kunst, Berlin, November 18, 1994 – January 22, 1995; Chicago Cultural Center, April 22 – June 25, 1995. (Not included in the Chicago presentation.)

Xicano Progeny: Investigative Agents, Executive Council and Other Representatives from the Sovereign State of Azatlan, The Mexican Museum, San Francisco, April 1 – June 18, 1995.

Iñigo Manglano-Ovalle: Balsero, MCA, January 18 – April 6, 1997.

Transmute, MCA, August 21 – November 7, 1999.

Le Baiser (The Kiss)
1999
Color video installation
Dimensions variable
Ed: 1/3 aside from 1 artist's proof
Restricted gift of the Sara Lee Corporation
1999.56

Provenance

Max Protetch, New York, 1999.

MCA, 1999.

Exhibition History

Le Baiser, Institute of Visual Arts, Milwaukee, Wis., September 24 – November 28, 1999.

Age of Influence: Reflections in the Mirror of American Culture, MCA, March 14, 2000 – January 2, 2001.

Inigo Manglano-Ovalle, Cranbrook Art Museum, Bloomfield Hills, Mich., September 15 – November 24, 2001; Rose Art Museum, Brandeis University, Waltham, Mass., January 24 – April 7, 2002; Cleveland Center for Contemporary Art, Cleveland, Ohio, June 7 – August 11, 2002; Orange County Museum of Art, Newport Beach, Calif., January 18 – March 23, 2003; Palm Beach Institute of Contemporary Art, Lake Worth, Fla., April – May 2003.

References

Gamble, Allison. "Situated between Art and Social Service, 'The New Public Art' Struggles for Definition." *New Art Examiner* 21, no. 5 (January 1994), pp. 18 – 23.

Hofman, Irene and Anna Novakov. *Inigo Manglano-Ovalle*. Exh. cat. Bloomfield Hills, Mich.: Cranbrook Art Museum, 2001.

La Frontera/The Border Art about the Mexico/United States Border Experience. San Diego, Calif.: Centro Cultural de la Raza/Museum of Contemporary Art, 1993.

Moreno, Gean. "Iñigo Manglano-Ovalle and the Politics of Pleasure." *New Art Examiner* 28, no. 1 (September 2000), pp. 22 – 25, 46.

Palmer, Laurie. "Iñigo Manglano-Ovalle." *Frieze*, no. 27 (March/April 1996), p. 71.

Platt, Ron. *Iñigo Manglano-Ovalle: The Garden of Delights*. Winston-Salem, N.C.: Southeastern Center for Contemporary Art, 1998.

Rush, Michael. "Transparent Scenarios." *Art in America* 88, no. 10 (October 2000), pp. 134 – 37.

Snodgrass, Susan. "Iñigo Manglano-Ovalle at TBA Exhibition Space." *Art in America* 82, no. 9 (September 1994), p. 120.

Whitney Biennial 2000. New York: Whitney Museum of American Art, 2000.

Xicano Progeny: Investigative Agents, Executive Council and Other Representatives from the Sovereign State of Azatlan. Exh. cat. San Francisco: The Mexican Museum, 1995.

Other Works in the MCA Collection

Le Baiser/The Kiss I, 2000
Chromogenic development print mounted to Plexiglas
29 × 106 in. (73.7 × 269.2 cm)
Ed: 1/8
Partial and promised gift from The Howard and Donna Stone Collection
2002.41

Brice Marden
American, b. 1938
p. 146

Grove Group V
1976
Oil and wax on canvas
72 × 108 in. (182.9 × 274.3 cm)
Gerald S. Elliott Collection
1995.67.a – c

Provenance

Texas Gallery, Houston, 1976.

Mr. and Mrs. Edward R. Hudson, Jr., Fort Worth, Tex., 1976.

Gerald S. Elliott, Chicago, 1988.

MCA, 1995.

Exhibition History

A New Spirit in Painting, Royal Academy of Arts, London, winter 1981.

Affinities and Intuitions: The Gerald S. Elliott Collection of Contemporary Art, The Art Institute of Chicago, May 12–July 29, 1990.

Brice Marden: The Grove Group, Gagosian Gallery, New York, January 15–March 6, 1991.

In the Shadow of Storms: Art of the Postwar Era from the MCA Collection, MCA, July 2, 1996–May 25, 1997.

Envisioning the Contemporary: Selections from the Permanent Collection, MCA, June 21, 1997–April 5, 1998 and April 30, 1998–February 7, 1999.

References

Brice Marden: The Grove Group. Exh. cat. New York: Gagosian Gallery, 1991.

Brice Marden: Paintings, Drawings, and Prints 1975–1980. London: Whitechapel Art Gallery, 1981.

Collective Vision. MCA, 1996.

Poirier, Maurice. "Color-Coded Mysteries." *ARTnews* 84, no. 1 (January 1985), pp. 52–61.

Richardson, John. "Brice Marden's Abstract Heart." *Vanity Fair* (May 1999), pp. 168–77, 201–3.

Storr, Robert. "Brice Marden: Double Vision." *Art in America* 73, no. 3 (March 1985), pp. 118–25.

Westfall, Stephen. "Marden's Web." *Art in America* 80, no. 3 (March 1992), pp. 94–99.

Other Works in the MCA Collection

Tour IV, 1972
Oil and wax on canvas
96 3/8 × 47 1/2 in. (244.8 × 120.6 cm)
Gerald S. Elliott Collection
1995.66.a–b

8, 1987–88
Oil on linen
84 × 60 in. (213.4 × 152.4 cm)
Gerald S. Elliott Collection
1995.68

Marisol

Marisol Escobar
Venezuelan, b. France 1930
p. 68

Jazz Wall

c. 1962
Paper, paint, and found objects on wood
95 × 107 × 14 in. (241.3 × 271.8 × 35.6 cm)
Partial gift of Ruth Horwich
1998.48

Provenance

Ruth Horwich, Chicago, 1966.

MCA, 1998.

Exhibition History

Marisol, The Arts Club, Chicago, December 14, 1965–January 15, 1966.

Decades in Dialogue: Perspectives on the MCA Collection, MCA, February 27–October 31, 1999.

References

Berstein, Roberta. "Marisol's Self-Portraits: The Dream and the Dream." *Arts Magazine* 59, no. 7 (March 1985), pp. 86–89.

Gardner, Paul. "Who is Marisol?" *ARTnews* (May 1989), pp. 146–51.

Grove, Nancy. *Magical Mixtures: Marisol Portrait Sculpture.* Exh. cat. Washington, D.C.: The National Portrait Gallery, Smithsonian Institution, 1991.

Jacob, Mary Jane et al. *Selections from the Permanent Collection, Vol. I.* MCA, 1984.

Loring, John. *Marisol.* Exh. cat. New York: The New York Cultural Center, 1973. Pp. 5–7.

Marisol. Exh. cat. Chicago: The Arts Club, 1966.

Marisol. Exh. cat. New York: Marlborough Gallery, 1995.

Nemser, C. "Marisol." In *Art Talk: Conversations with Twelve Women Artists.* New York: Charles Scribner's Sons, 1975. Pp. 179–200.

Shulman, Leon. *Marisol.* Exh. cat. Worcester, Mass.: Davis Press, 1971.

Other Works in the MCA Collection

Printer's Box, 1956
Painted wood, plaster, and glass
16 1/2 × 21 3/4 × 2 in. (41.9 × 55.2 × 5.1 cm)
Gift of Joseph and Jory Shapiro
1992.65

Self-Portrait, 1961–62
Wood, plaster, marker, paint, graphite, human teeth, gold, and plastic
43 1/2 × 45 1/4 × 75 5/8 in.
(110.5 × 114.9 × 192.1 cm)
Gift of Joseph and Jory Shapiro
1992.66

Six Women, 1965–66
Wood, paint, mirrors, shoes, Formica, and plaster
69 × 105 × 52 in. (175.3 × 266.7 × 132.1 cm)
Gift of the artist
1968.1

Kerry James Marshall

American, b. 1955
p. 270

Souvenir I

1997
Acrylic, glitter, and paper on canvas with grommets
108 × 157 in. (274.3 × 398.8 cm)
Bernice and Kenneth Newberger Fund
1997.73

Provenance

Jack Shainman Gallery, New York, 1997.

MCA, 1997.

Exhibition History

Kerry James Marshall: Recent Paintings and Drawings, Addison Gallery of American Art at Phillips Academy, Andover, Mass., March 30–May 19, 1997.

Envisioning the Contemporary: Selections from the Permanent Collection, MCA, June 21, 1997–April 5, 1998.

Kerry James Marshall, The Renaissance Society, The University of Chicago, May 6–June 28, 1998; Brooklyn Museum of Art, New York, September 10–November 29, 1998; San Francisco Museum of Modern Art, January 22–May 2, 1999; Institute of Contemporary Art, Boston, June 6–August 22, 1999; Santa Monica Museum of Modern Art, Calif., December 17, 1999–February 28, 2000; Boise Art Museum, Idaho, May 20–July 30, 2000.

References

Camper, Fred. "Open Houses." *Chicago Reader,* May 8, 1998, sec. 1.

Kerry James Marshall: Mementos. Exh. cat. Chicago: The Renaissance Society, The University of Chicago Press, 1998.

Marshall, Kerry James, Terrie Sultan, and Arthur Jafa. *Kerry James Marshall.* New York: Harry N. Abrams, 2000.

Molesworth, Helen. "Project America: Kerry James Marshall." *Frieze,* no. 40 (May 1998), pp. 72–75.

Reid, Calvin. "Kerry James Marshall." *Bomb,* no. 62 (winter 1998), pp. 40–47.

Snodgrass, Susan. "Heroes and Martyrs." *Art in America* 86, no. 11 (November 1998), pp. 92–95.

Other Works in the MCA Collection

Study for Souvenir III, 1997
Charcoal on paper
30 1/2 × 42 in. (77.5 × 106.7 cm)
Gift of Susan and Lewis Manilow
1999.41

Study for Souvenir I, 1997
Charcoal on paper
30 1/2 × 42 in. (77.5 × 106.7 cm)
Gift of Susan and Lewis Manilow
1999.42

Matta

Roberto Matta
Chilean, b. 1911
p. 42

A Grave Situation

1946
Oil on canvas
55 × 77 1/8 in. (139.7 × 195.9 cm)
Gift of the Mary and Earle Ludgin Collection
1998.30

Provenance

Pierre Matisse Gallery, New York, 1946.

Mary and Earle Ludgin, Chicago, 1949.

MCA, 1998.

Exhibition History

Matta, Pierre Matisse Gallery, New York, April 11 – May 4, 1946.

Bloodflames, Hugo Gallery, New York, February 15 – 28, 1947.

Matta, The Museum of Modern Art, New York, September 10 – October 20, 1957. (Included only in the New York presentation.)

Matta: The First Decade, Rose Art Museum, Brandeis University, Waltham, Mass., May 8 – June 20, 1982.

The Mary and Earle Ludgin Collection, MCA, January 15 – March 13, 1983.

Primitivism in Twentieth-Century Art: Affinity of the Tribal and Modern, The Museum of Modern Art, New York, September 19, 1984 – January 15, 1985; Detroit Institute of Arts, Mich.; Dallas Museum of Art, June 23 – September 1, 1985.

Art of the Fantastic: Latin America, 1920 – 1987, Indianapolis Museum of Art, Ind., June 28 – September 13, 1987; The Queens Museum, Flushing, N.Y., October 10, 1987 – December 6, 1987; Center for the Fine Arts, Miami, Fla, January 15 – March 4, 1988; Centro Cultural / Arte Contemporaneo, Mexico City, March 25 – May 22, 1988.

La Femme Surréaliste, Musée Cantonal des Beaux-Arts de Lausanne, Switzerland, November 20, 1987 – February 28, 1988.

Permanent Collection: Promised Gifts Exhibition, MCA, October 3 – November 28, 1989.

Anxious Visions: Surrealist Art, University of California, Berkeley, October 3, 1990 – January 6, 1991.

Crosscurrents of Modernism: Four Latin American Pioneers, Hirshhorn Museum and Sculpture Garden, Smithsonian Institution, Washington, D.C., June 10 – September 7, 1992.

Decades in Dialogue: Perspectives on the MCA Collection, MCA, February 27 – October 31, 1999.

The Surrealists in Exile and the Beginning of the New York School, Museo Nacional Centro de Arte Reina Sofia, Madrid, December 14, 1999 – February 27, 2000.

Matta in America: Paintings and Drawings of the 1940s, The Museum of Contemporary Art, Los Angeles, September 30, 2001 – January 6, 2002; Miami Art Museum, Fla., March 20 – June 2, 2002; MCA, July 13 – October 20, 2002.

Let's Phosphoresce by Intellection #1
1950
Oil on canvas
58 × 69⅝ in. (147.3 × 176.8 cm)
Gift of Mr. and Mrs. E. A. Bergman
1976.45

Provenance

Sidney Janis, New York, 1951.

Muriel Kallis Newman Collection, Chicago, 1951.

Holland/Goldowsky Gallery, Chicago, c. 1956 – 58.

Mr. and Mrs. E. A. Bergman, Chicago, 1961.

MCA, 1976.

Exhibition History

Matta, Institute of Contemporary Art, London, January 16 – February 15, 1951; Sidney Janis Gallery, New York, April 16 – May 5, 1951.

Matta of Chile, Oils and Drawings, Pan-American Union, Washington, D.C., February 16 – March 15, 1955.

Matta, The Renaissance Society, The University of Chicago, March 30 – May 11, 1963.

Selected Works from the Permanent Collection, MCA, July 6 – October 7, 1979.

Selections from the Permanent Collection, MCA, May 3 – August 31, 1980.

Permanent Collection Exhibition, MCA, January 16 – March 14, 1982.

The Museum of Contemporary Art Selects: Paintings and Sculpture that Reflect Chicago's Best, MCA at Marshall Field's, State Street, Chicago, March 26 – April 5, 1984.

Dada and Surrealism in Chicago Collections, MCA, December 1, 1984 – January 27, 1985.

Toward the Future: Contemporary Art in Context, MCA, May 5 – July 1, 1990.

In the Shadow of Storms: Art of the Postwar Era from the MCA Collection, MCA, July 2, 1996 – May 25, 1997.

Envisioning the Contemporary: Selections from the Permanent Collection, MCA, June 21, 1997 – April 5, 1998 and April 30, 1998 – February 7, 1999.

The Surrealists in Exile and the Beginning of the New York School, Museo Nacional Centro de Arte Reina Sofia, Madrid, December 14, 1999 – February 27, 2000.

Matta in America: Paintings and Drawings of the 1940s, The Museum of Contemporary Art, Los Angeles, September 30, 2001 – January 6, 2002; Miami Art Museum, Fla., March 20 – June 2, 2002; MCA, July 13 – October 20, 2002. (Included only in the Chicago presentation.)

References

Collective Vision. MCA, 1996.

Dartnall, Colette, Elizabeth A. T. Smith, and William Rubin. *Matta in America: Paintings and Drawings of the 1940s.* Exh. cat. MCA; Los Angeles: The Museum of Contemporary Art, 2001.

Fletcher, Valerie. *Crosscurrents of Modernism: Four Latin American Pioneers.* Exh. cat. Washington, D.C.: Hirshhorn Museum and Sculpture Garden, Smithsonian Institution, 1992. P. 279.

Jacob, Mary Jane et al. *Selections from the Permanent Collection, Vol. I.* MCA, 1984.

Les Surréalistes en Exile et Les Débuts de l'école de New York. Exh. cat. Strasbourg: Musée d'Art Moderne et Contemporain, 2000.

Matta. Exh. cat. Paris: Musée National d'Art Moderne, Centre Georges Pompidou, 1985.

Matta: Surrealism and Beyond. Exh. cat. Milwaukee, Wis.: Haggery Museum of Art, Marquette University Press, 1997.

Onslow-Ford, Gordon. "Notes on Matta and Painting (1937 – 1941)." In Germana Ferrari. *Entretiens Morphologiques, Notebook No. 1, 1936 – 1944.* London: Sistan, 1987. Pp. 23 – 25.

Sawin, Martica. *Surrealism in Exile and the Beginning of the New York School.* Cambridge, Mass.: MIT Press, 1995.

Other Works in the MCA Collection

Untitled (Prime Ordeal), 1946
Oil on canvas
53½ × 75¼ in. (135.9 × 191.1 cm)
Gift of Joseph and Jory Shapiro
1974.25

Conference, 1957
Bronze
28¾ × 26⁷⁄₁₆ × 16¼ in. (73 × 67.2 × 41.3 cm)
Ed: 3/6
Gift of Joseph and Jory Shapiro
1992.68

Gordon Matta-Clark
American, 1943 – 1978
p. 150

Circus or The Caribbean Orange
1978
Silver dye-bleach prints
Two parts, installed: 42¼ × 64½ in. (107.3 × 163.8 cm)
Restricted gift of Mr. and Mrs. E. A. Bergman and Susan and Lewis Manilow
1978.1.a – b

Provenance

Young Hoffman Gallery, Chicago, 1978.

MCA, 1978.

Exhibition History

Gordon Matta-Clark, Visual Arts Gallery, University of Alabama, Birmingham, March 30 – April 18, 1980.

The Permanent Collection, MCA, May 24 – August 31, 1980.

Permanent Collection Exhibition, MCA, June 4 – August 1983.

Site Cafe Installation, MCA, August 1985 – January 1986.

Gordon Matta-Clark: A Retrospective, MCA, May 11 – August 18, 1985; University Art Museum, California State University, Long Beach, January 27 – March 2, 1986; Stedelijk Museum, Amsterdam, August 29 – October 12, 1986; Stadtisches Museum Abteiberg, Monchengladbach, Germany, November 9, 1986 – January 4, 1987; Kunsthalle Basel, Switzerland, January 24 – March 1, 1987; Le Nouveau Musée, Lyon/Villeurbanne, France, March 17 – May 10, 1987; Museum Van Hedendaagse Kunst Antwerpen, Belgium, June 17 – August 16, 1987; Porin Taideomuseu, Pori, Finland, September 7 – October 18, 1987; Carnegie Mellon University Art Gallery, Pittsburgh, Pa., February 13 – April 10, 1988; Brooklyn Museum, New York, May 13 – July 11, 1988; Mackenzie Art Gallery, Regina, Canada, August 7 – September 25, 1988; University Art Museum, University of California, Berkeley, October 12 – December 18, 1988; Musée d'Art Contemporain, Montreal, January 20 – April 9, 1989; Herbert F. Johnson Museum, Cornell University, Ithaca, N.Y., May 5 – July 2, 1989.

PC Focus: Conceptualism to Postconceptualism, the 1960s to the 1990s, MCA, August 22–November 11, 1992.

Gordon Matta-Clark, Instituto Valenciana de Arte Moderno, Centre Julio Gonzalez, Valencia, Spain, December 3, 1992–January 31, 1993; Musée Cantini, Marseilles, France, March 5–May 23, 1993; Serpentine Gallery, London, June 30–August 15, 1993.

In the Shadow of Storms: Art of the Postwar Era from the MCA Collection, MCA, July 2, 1996–May 25, 1997.

Apposite Opposites: Photography from the MCA Collection, MCA, March 27–August 1, 1999.

References

Adrian, Dennis. "A Cutout Sculptor Slices Up a Building." *Chicago Daily News*, February 4, 1978, p. 14.

Jacob, Mary Jane et al. *Selections from the Permanent Collection, Vol. I*. MCA, 1984.

Jacob, Mary Jane, Robert Pincus-Witten, and Joan Simon. *Gordon Matta-Clark: A Retrospective*. Exh. cat. MCA, 1985.

Kirshner, Judith Russi. *Circus — The Caribbean Orange*. MCA, 1978.

———. "Nonuments." In *Gordon Matta-Clark*. Exh. cat. Valencia, Spain: IVAM Centro Julio Gonzalez, 1993.

Lavin, Maud. "Gordon Matta-Clark and Individualism." *Arts Magazine* 58, no. 5 (January 1984), pp. 138–41.

Neff, John H. "Chicago's Special Art Museum." *The Art Gallery* 21, no. 6 (August/September 1978), pp. 42–46.

Simon, John. "Gordon Matta-Clark, 1943–1978." *Art in America* 66, no. 6 (November/December 1978), p. 13.

Other Works in the MCA Collection

Untitled, 1971–72
Marker and graphite on paper
30 × 22 in. (76.2 × 55.9 cm)
Gift of Anne Alpert and Jane Crawford
1985.31

Untitled, 1974
Cut paper
37¹⁵/₁₆ × 46¾ in. (96.4 × 118.7 cm)
Gift of Anne Alpert and Jane Crawford
1986.6

Circus or The Caribbean Orange, 1978
Silver dye-bleach print
39½ × 29½ in. (100.3 × 74.9 cm)
Restricted gift of Mr. and Mrs. E. A. Bergman and Susan and Lewis Manilow
1978.2

Untitled (Poster plan for 'Circus or The Caribbean Orange'), 1978
Gelatin silver prints, paper, ink, and masking tape on mat board
30 × 19⅞ in. (76.2 × 50.5 cm)
Gift of the artist
1980.38.1

Untitled (Elevation plan for 'Circus or The Caribbean Orange'), 1978
Ink, graphite, and transfer letters on paper on mat board
13½ × 20 in. (34.3 × 50.8 cm)
Gift of the artist
1980.38.2

Circus or The Caribbean Orange, 1978
Silver dye-bleach prints
24½ × 69 in. (62.2 × 175.3 cm)
Ed: 2/3
Partial and promised gift from The Howard and Donna Stone Collection
2002.45

Artist's paste-ups for MCA Exhibition catalogue, 'Circus,' 1979
Gelatin silver prints, masking tape, and graphite on mat board
Three parts, each: 20 × 30 in. (50.8 × 76.2 cm)
Gift of the artist
1980.39.1–3

Ana Mendieta
American, b. Cuba, 1948–1985
p. 130

Untitled from the *Silueta* series
1973–1977/1991
Silver dye-bleach prints
Twelve parts; parts one, six, nine, ten:
16 × 20 in. (40.6 × 50.8 cm)
parts two, three, four, five, seven, eight, eleven, twelve: 20 × 16 in. (50. 8 × 40.6 cm)
Ed: 7/20 aside from 4 artist's proofs
Partial and promised gift from The Howard and Donna Stone Collection
2002.46.1–12

Provenance

Galerie Lelong, New York, 1991.

Howard and Donna Stone, Chicago, 1994.

MCA, 2002.

References

Ana Mendieta, A Retrospective. Exh. cat. New York: New Museum of Contemporary Art, 1987.

Jacob, Mary Jane. *Ana Mendieta, The "Silueta" Series, 1973–1980*. Exh. cat. New York: Galerie Lelong, 1991.

Moure, Gloria. *Ana Mendieta*. Barcelona: Ediciones Polígraphia, S.A., 1996.

Other Works in the MCA Collection

Untitled, from the *Silueta* series, c. 1978
Gelatin silver print
16 × 20 in. (40.6 × 50.8 cm)
Bernice and Kenneth Newberger Fund
1995.112

Untitled (Leaf drawing), 1982
Drawing on dried ficus leaf
7 × 4⅜ in. (17.8 × 11.1 cm)
Bernice and Kenneth Newberger Fund
1995.113

Tatsuo Miyajima
Japanese, b. 1957
p. 248

Counter Circle No. 19
1993
LED, IC, wooden panel, and electrical wire
2¼ × 164 in. diameter (5.7 × 416.6 cm)
Bernice and Kenneth Newberger Fund; and restricted gift of Werner Kramarsky, Jackie Rabin, and Dedrea and Paul Gray
1997.74.a–d

Provenance

Richard Gray Gallery, Chicago, 1996.

MCA, 1997.

Exhibition History

Tatsuo Miyajima: Counter Groups, Richard Gray Gallery, Chicago, July 11–September 28, 1996.

Infinite Loop: Selected Light Works from the MCA Collection, MCA, December 9, 2000–January 15, 2001.

References

Artner, Alan. "Deceptively Cool, Tatsuo Miyajima Uses Digital Counters to Mark Mystic Moments." *Chicago Tribune*, July 19, 1996, sec. 7, p. 59.

Lingwood, James. "Keep Changing, Connect with Everything, Continue Forever." *Frieze*, no. 3 (March 1993), pp. 18–21.

Tatsuo Miyajima. Exh. cat. Hertogenbosch, Netherlands: Museum Het Kruithuis; Berlin: DAAD Galerie, 1991.

Tatsuo Miyajima: Big Time. Exh. cat. Fort Worth, Tex.: Modern Art Museum, 1996.

Tatsuo Miyajima — 133651. Exh. cat. Japan: Iwaki City Art Museum, 1992.

Wright, Beryl J. *Art at the Armory: Occupied Territory*. Exh. cat. MCA, 1992. Pp. 108–111.

Donald Moffett
American, b. 1955
p. 312

What Barbara Jordan Wore
2002
Installation of oil and enamel on linen with color video projection
Three parts, each: 45 × 60¼ in.
(114.3 × 153 cm)
Restricted gift of Nancy A. Lauter and Alfred L. McDougal, Judith Neisser, Thomas and Barbara Ruben, Faye and Victor Morgenstern Family Foundation, Ruth Horwich, and Funds from the 2001 Benefit Art Auction
2002.81.a–c

Provenance

Stephen Freidman Gallery, London and Marianne Boesky Gallery, New York, 2002.

MCA, 2002.

350

Exhibition History

What Barbara Jordan Wore, MCA, May 4–
September 8, 2002.

References

Lewis, Jim and Elizabeth A. T. Smith.
Donald Moffett: What Barbara Jordan Wore.
Exh. cat. MCA, 2002.

Myer, Richard. "This is to Enrage You: Gran Fury
and the Graphics of AIDS Activism." In Nina
Felshin, ed. *But is it Art? The Spirit of Art as
Activism.* Seattle: Bay Press, 1995.

Strange Ways: Here We Come. Exh. cat.
Vancouver: Fine Arts Gallery, The University of
British Columbia Press, 1990.

Torchia, Richard. *Blue [NY].* Exh. cat. Glenside,
Pa.: Beaver College Art Gallery Press, 1997.

Other Works in the MCA Collection

Untitled East (from "Blue NY"), 1997
Silver dye-bleach print with artist's frame
38¾ × 30¾ in. (98.4 × 78.1 cm)
Partial and Promised gift from The Howard
and Donna Stone Collection
2002.48

Mariko Mori

Japanese, b. 1967
p. 264

Birth of a Star

1995
3-D Duratrans, acrylic, light box, and audio CD
70³⁄₁₆ × 45¼ × 4¼ in.
(178.3 × 114.9 × 10.8 cm)
Ed: 1/2 aside from 1 artist's proof
Gift of The Peter Norton Family Foundation
1996.6.a–c

Provenance

Jeffrey Deitch Gallery, New York, 1995.

The Peter Norton Family Foundation,
Santa Monica, Calif., 1996.

MCA, 1996.

Exhibition History

*In the Shadow of Storms: Art of the Postwar Era
from the MCA Collection*, MCA, July 2, 1996–
May 25, 1997.

Mariko Mori, Andy Warhol Museum, Pittsburgh,
Pa., June 19–September 12, 1998.

Mariko Mori, MCA, October 10, 1998–
January 3, 1999.

Mariko Mori: Empty Dream, Brooklyn Museum
of Art, New York, April 8–August 1, 1999.

*People See Paintings: Photography
and Painting from the MCA Collection*, MCA,
January 19–October 20, 2002.

References

Corrin, Lisa, Carol S. Eliel, Margery King, and
Dominic Molon. *Mariko Mori.* Exh. cat. MCA;
London: Serpentine Gallery, 1998.

Kandel, Susan. "Mariko Mori."
In *Cream: Contemporary Art in Culture.*
London: Phaidon, 1998. Pp. 280–83.

Mariko Mori: Esoteric Cosmos. Exh. cat.
Kunstmuseum Wolfsburg, Wolfsburg,
Germany, 1999.

Robert Morris

American, b. 1931
p. 78

Portal

1965
Latex on aluminum
95¾ × 48¹⁄₁₆ × 12 in.
(243.2 × 122.1 × 30.5 cm)
Gift of Mrs. Robert B. Mayer
1984.3

Provenance

Green Gallery, New York, 1965.

Mr. and Mrs. Robert B. Mayer, Winnetka, Ill.,
1965.

MCA, 1984.

Exhibition History

*Selections from the Permanent Collection:
Important Sculptural Work*, MCA, April 25–
July 18, 1985.

Abstract Painting and Sculpture: 1950s to 1980s,
MCA, October 22, 1985–April 13, 1986.

*Pop Art, Minimalism, and Earth Art: The MCA's
Permanent Collection With Selected Loans*, MCA,
October 6–November 8, 1987.

Grounded: Sculpture on the Floor, University of
Michigan Museum of Art, Ann Arbor, Mich.,
April 7–June 3, 1990.

*In the Shadow of Storms: Art of the Postwar Era
from the MCA Collection*, MCA, July 2, 1996–
May 25, 1997.

References

Berger, Maurice. "Against Repression:
Minimalism and Anti-Form." In *Labyrinths:
Robert Morris, Minimalism, and the 1960s.* New
York: Harper & Row, 1989. Pp. 47–79.

Corcoran Gallery of Art. *Robert Morris.* Exh. cat.
Baltimore, Md.: Pridemark, 1969.

Judd, Donald. "Black, White, and Gray." *Arts
Magazine* 38, no. 6 (March 1964), pp. 36–38.

Robert Morris: The Mind/Body Problem. Exh. cat.
New York: Solomon R. Guggenheim Museum,
1994.

*Structures for Behavior: New Sculptures by Robert
Morris, David Rainovitch, Richard Serra, and
George Trakas.* Exh. cat. Ontario, Canada: Art
Gallery of Ontario, 1978.

Tucker, Marcia. *Robert Morris.* Exh. cat. New
York: Whitney Museum of American Art, 1970.

Other Works in the MCA Collection

Earth Projects, 1969
Portfolio of lithographs on paper
Ten parts, each: 22 × 30 in. (55.9 × 76.2 cm)
Ed: 4/125
Gift of Mrs. Robert B. Mayer
1978.3.1–12

Untitled, 1984
Acrylic on Hydrocal and oil on canvas
69½ × 86½ in. (176.5 × 219.7 cm)
Gerald S. Elliott Collection
1995.107

Bruce Nauman

American, b. 1941
p. 80

Untitled

1965
Fiberglass and polyester resin
Installed: 80 × 9 × 80 in.
(203.2 × 22.9 × 203.2 cm)
Gerald S. Elliott Collection
1995.69

Provenance

Nicholas Wilder Gallery, Los Angeles, 1966.

Leo Castelli Gallery, New York.

Mr. and Mrs. Eugene Schwartz, New York, 1968.

New Museum of Contemporary Art, New York.

Donald Young Gallery, Chicago, 1984.

Gerald S. Elliott, Chicago.

MCA, 1995.

Exhibition History

Bruce Nauman, Leo Castelli Gallery, New York,
January 27–February 17, 1968.

*Affinities and Intuitions: The Gerald S. Elliott
Collection*, The Art Institute of Chicago,
May 9–July 29, 1990.

*In the Shadow of Storms: Art of the Postwar Era
from the MCA Collection*, MCA, July 2, 1996–
March 26, 1997.

*Envisioning the Contemporary: Selections from
the Permanent Collection*, MCA, June 21, 1997–
April 5, 1998 and April 30, 1998–February 7, 1999.

Bound to Fail
from the portfolio *Eleven Color Photographs*

1966–67
Chromogenic development print
19⅞ × 23¾ in. (50.9 × 60.3 cm)
Ed: 8/8
Gerald S. Elliott Collection
1994.11.h

Self-Portrait as a Fountain
from the portfolio *Eleven Color Photographs*

1966–67
Chromogenic development print
19⅞ × 23¾ in. (50.9 × 60.3 cm)
Ed: 8/8
Gerald S. Elliott Collection
1994.11.k

351

Provenance

Leo Castelli Gallery, New York, 1970.

Nicholas Wilder Gallery, Los Angeles.

Leo Castelli Gallery, New York.

Gerald S. Elliott, Chicago, 1988.

MCA, 1994.

Exhibition History

Bruce Nauman, Museo Nacional Centro de Arte Reina Sofia, Madrid, November 30, 1993 – February 21, 1994; Walker Art Center, Minneapolis, April 10 – June 19, 1994; The Museum of Contemporary Art, Los Angeles, July 17 – September 25, 1994; Hirshhorn Museum and Sculpture Garden, Smithsonian Institution, Washington, D.C., November 3, 1994 – January 25, 1995; The Museum of Modern Art, New York, March 1 – May 23, 1995; Kunsthaus, Zurich, July 13 – October 8, 1995.

In the Shadow of Storms: Art of the Postwar Era from the MCA Collection, MCA, July 2, 1996 – May 25, 1997.

Wounds: Between Democracy and Redemption in Contemporary Art, Moderna Museet, Stockholm, Sweden, February 14 – April 19, 1998.

Le Temps, Vite, Musée National d'Art Moderne, Centre Georges Pompidou, Paris, January 1 – March 3, 2000.

Crossroads of American Sculpture, Indianapolis Museum of Art, Ind., October 14, 2000 – January 21, 2001; New Orleans Museum of Art, June 30 – September 2, 2001.

People See Paintings: Photography and Painting from the MCA Collection, MCA, January 19 – October 20, 2002.

Henry Moore Bound to Fail
1967/1970
Cast iron
25½ × 23 × 3½ in. (64.8 × 58.4 × 8.9 cm)
Unnumbered edition of 9, aside from 1 artist's proof
Gerald S. Elliott Collection
1995.71

Provenance

Blum/Helman Gallery, New York.

Joseph Helman Collection, New York.

Gerald S. Elliott, Chicago.

MCA, 1995.

Exhibition History

Affinities and Intuitions: The Gerald S. Elliott Collection, The Art Institute of Chicago, May 9 – July 29, 1990.

In the Shadow of Storms: Art of the Postwar Era from the MCA Collection, MCA, July 2, 1996 – May 25, 1997.

Envisioning the Contemporary: Selections from the Permanent Collection, MCA, June 21, 1997 – April 5, 1998 and April 30, 1998 – February 7, 1999.

Original Language: Highlights from the MCA Collection, MCA, March 24 – August 5, 2001

Three Dead-End Adjacent Tunnels, Not Connected
1979
Plaster and wood
21 × 115 × 104 in. (53.3 × 292.1 × 264.2 cm)
Gerald S. Elliott Collection
1995.73

Provenance

Leo Castelli Gallery, New York, 1980.

Donald Young Gallery, Chicago, 1983.

Galerie Daniel Templon, Paris, 1988.

Gerald S. Elliott, Chicago.

MCA, 1995.

Exhibition History

Bruce Nauman, Leo Castelli Gallery, New York, April 26 – May 17, 1980.

Bruce Nauman, Kunsthalle, Basel, Switzerland, July 13 – September 17, 1986; Musée d'Art Moderne de la ville de Paris, October 8 – December 7, 1986; Whitechapel Art Gallery, London, January 16 – February 22, 1987.

Andre, Flavin, LeWitt, Nauman, Serra, Galerie Daniel Templon, Paris, March 19 – April 25, 1987.

Affinities and Intuitions: The Gerald S. Elliott Collection, The Art Institute of Chicago, May 9 – July 29, 1990.

Recent Acquisitions, MCA, September 1 – November 1998.

Encounter: Nauman/Kcho, MCA, October 31 – November 28, 1999.

Original Language: Highlights from the MCA Collection, MCA, March 24 – August 5, 2001.

Life, Death, Love, Hate, Pleasure, Pain
1983
Neon
70⅞ in. diameter (180 cm)
Gerald S. Elliott Collection
1995.74

Provenance

Leo Castelli, New York, 1983.

Daniel Weinberg Gallery, Los Angeles, 1984.

Galerie Jean Bernier, Athens, 1984.

Barbara Gladstone Gallery, New York, 1986.

Gerald S. Elliott, Chicago, 1994.

MCA, 1995.

Exhibition History

Bruce Nauman: Recent Neons and Drawings, Daniel Weinberg Gallery, Los Angeles, February 8 – March 3, 1984.

Bruce Nauman, Galerie Jean Bernier, Athens, February 24 – March 22, 1986.

Encontros: Signs of Life, Fundação Calouste Gulbenkian, Modern Art Center, Lisbon, Portugal, May 30 – July 9, 1989.

Affinities and Intuitions: The Gerald S. Elliott Collection, The Art Institute of Chicago, May 9 – July 29, 1990.

In the Shadow of Storms: Art of the Postwar Era from the Museum of Contemporary Art, MCA, July 2, 1996 – March 26, 1997.

Envisioning the Contemporary: Selections from the Permanent Collection, MCA, June 21, 1997 – April 5, 1998 and April 30, 1998 – February 7, 1999.

Adam Brooks: DeNaturalized, MCA, February 14 – July 5, 1998.

Age of Influence: Reflections in the Mirror of American Culture, MCA, March 14, 2000 – January 2, 2001.

Chambres d'Amis (Krefeld Piece)
1985
Color video installation (*Good Boy Bad Boy*), audiotape (*One Hundred Live and Die*), and neon (*Hanged Man*)
Dimensions variable
Gerald S. Elliott Collection
1995.75.a–c

Provenance

Galerie Konrad Fischer, Düsseldorf, Germany, 1985.

Leo Castelli Gallery, New York.

Gerald S. Elliott, Chicago, 1988.

MCA, 1995.

Exhibition History

Dreissig Jahre durch die kunst, Museum Haus Lange and Museum Haus Esters, Krefeld, Germany, September 15 – December 1, 1985.

Bruce Nauman, Galerie Jean Bernier, Athens, February 24 – March 22, 1986.

Chambres d'Amis, Museum van Hedendaagse Kunst, Ghent, Belgium, June 20 – September 21, 1986.

Whitney Biennial 1987, Whitney Museum of American Art, New York, March 31 – July 5, 1987.

Affinities and Intuitions: The Gerald S. Elliott Collection, The Art Institute of Chicago, May 9 – July 29, 1990.

Bruce Nauman, Museo Nacional Centro de Arte Reina Sofia, Madrid, November 30, 1993 – February 21, 1994; Walker Art Center, Minneapolis, April 10 – June 19, 1994; The Museum of Contemporary Art, Los Angeles, July 17 – September 25, 1994; Hirshhorn Museum and Sculpture Garden, Smithsonian Institution, Washington, D.C., November 3, 1994 – January 29, 1995; The Museum of Modern Art, New York, March 1 – May 23, 1995; Kunsthaus, Zurich, July 13 – October 8, 1995.

Bruce Nauman Image/Text 1966 – 1996, Kunstmuseum Wolfsburg, Wolfsburg, Germany, May 24 – September 28, 1997; Musée National d'Art Moderne, Centre Georges Pompidou, Paris, December 16, 1997 – March 16, 1998; Hayward Gallery, London, July 16 – September 6, 1998; Museum of Contemporary Art, Helsinki, Finland, October 17, 1998 – January 6, 1999.

Hanging Carousel (George Skins a Fox)
1988
Color video installation with steel and polyurethane foam
204 in. diameter (518.2 cm) suspended 74½ in. (189.2 cm) above the floor
Gerald S. Elliott Collection
1995.76

Provenance

Sperone Westwater Gallery, New York, 1988.

Gerald S. Elliott, Chicago, 1991.

MCA, 1995.

Exhibition History

Bruce Nauman, Sperone Westwater Gallery, New York, September 10–October 15, 1988.

Bruce Nauman: Skulpturen und Installationen, 1985–1990, Museum fur Gegenwartskunst, Basel, Switzerland, September 23–December 10, 1990; Stadtische Galerie im Stadelschen Kunstintitut, Frankfurt, Germany, May 30–July 25, 1991.

Bruce Nauman, Museo Nacional Centro de Arte Reina Sofia, Madrid, November 30, 1993–February 21, 1994; Walker Art Center, Minneapolis, April 10–June 19, 1994; The Museum of Contemporary Art, Los Angeles, July 17–September 25, 1994; Hirshhorn Museum and Sculpture Garden, Smithsonian Institution, Washington, D.C., November 3, 1994–January 25, 1995; The Museum of Modern Art, New York, March 1–May 23, 1995; Kunsthaus, Zurich, July 13–October 8, 1995.

Transmute, MCA, August 21–November 7, 1999.

"... the nearest faraway place ..." Dia Center for the Arts, New York, May 10–June 17, 2001.

Rats and Bats
(Learned Helplessness in Rats II)
1988
Color video installation with Plexiglas
Dimensions variable
Gerald S. Elliott Collection
1995.77

Provenance

Leo Castelli Gallery, New York, 1988.

Sperone Westwater Gallery, New York, 1989.

Gerald S. Elliott, Chicago, 1989.

MCA, 1995.

Exhibition History

Group show, Leo Castelli Gallery, New York, 1988.

Affinities and Intuitions. The Gerald S. Elliott Collection, The Art Institute of Chicago, May 9–July 29, 1990.

Bruce Nauman: Skulpturen und Installationen, 1985–1990, Museum fur Gegenwartskunst, Basel, Switzerland, September 23–December 10, 1990; Stadtische Galerie im Stadelschen Kunstintitut, Frankfurt, Germany, May 30–July 25, 1991.

Metropolis: International Art Exhibition Berlin 1991, Martin-Gropius-Bau, Berlin, April 20–July 21, 1991.

Lyon Biennial of Contemporary Art, Lyon Museum of Contemporary Art, France, December 19, 1995–March 18, 1996.

Encounter: Nauman/Kcho, MCA, October 31–November 28, 1999.

Original Language: Highlights from the MCA Collection, MCA, March 24–August 5, 2001.

References

Benezra, Neal. "Empowering Space: Notes on the Sculpture of Bruce Nauman." In *Affinities and Intuitions: The Gerald S. Elliott Collection of Contemporary Art.* Chicago: The Art Institute, 1990. Pp. 58–69.

Bruce Nauman. Exh. cat. London: Whitechapel Art Gallery; Basel, Switzerland: Kunsthalle Basel, 1986. Pp. 15–16, 28–29.

Bruce Nauman: 25 Years with Leo Castelli. New York: Rizzoli, 1994.

Collective Vision. MCA, 1996.

Livingston, Jane and Marcia Tucker. *Bruce Nauman: Work from 1965 to 1972.* Exh. cat. Los Angeles: Los Angeles County Museum of Art; New York: Praeger, 1973.

Morgan, Robert C. "Eccentric Abstraction and Postminimalism." *Flash Art,* no. 144 (January/February 1989), pp. 73–81.

Richardson, Brenda. *Bruce Nauman: Neons.* Exh. cat. Baltimore, Md.: Baltimore Museum of Art, 1982. Pp. 13–36.

Saltz, Jerry. "Assault and Battery, Surveillance and Captivity." *Arts Magazine* 63, no. 8 (April 1989), pp. 13–14.

Sharp, Willoughby. "Nauman Interview." *Arts Magazine* 44, no. 5 (March 1970), pp. 22–27.

Simon, Joan. "Breaking the Silence: An Interview with Bruce Nauman." *Art in America* 76, no. 9 (September 1988), pp. 141–49, 203.

Simon, Joan, Kathy Halbreich, and Neal Benezra. *Exhibition Catalogue and Catalogue Raisonné, Bruce Nauman.* Minneapolis: Walker Art Center, 1994.

Storr, Robert. "Bruce Nauman: Doing What Comes Unnaturally." *Parachute* 73 (January/February/March 1994), pp. 12–16.

Tucker, Marcia. "PheNAUMANology." *Artforum* 9, no. 4 (December 1970), pp. 38–43.

Van Bruggen, Coosje. *Bruce Nauman.* New York: Rizzoli, 1988.

———. "Entrance Entrapment Exit." *Artforum* 24, no. 10 (summer 1986), pp. 88–96.

Other Works in the MCA Collection

Mold for a Modernized Slant Step, 1966
Plaster
Installed: 18¼ × 14½ × 13⅜ in. (46.4 × 36.8 × 34 cm)
Gerald S. Elliott Collection
1995.70.a–b

Waxing Hot from the portfolio *Eleven Color Photographs,* 1966–67
Chromogenic development print
19¹⁵⁄₁₆ × 19¹⁵⁄₁₆ in. (50.6 × 50.6 cm)
Ed: 8/8
Gerald S. Elliott Collection
1994.11.a

Finger Touch Number 1 from the portfolio *Eleven Color Photographs,* 1966–67
Chromogenic development print
19¾ × 23⅝ in. (50.2 × 60 cm)
Ed: 8/8
Gerald S. Elliott Collection
1994.11.b

Feet of Clay from the portfolio *Eleven Color Photographs,* 1966–67
Chromogenic development print
22½ × 23½ in. (55.2 × 59.7 cm)
Ed: 8/8
Gerald S. Elliott Collection
1994.11.c

Finger Touch With Mirrors from the portfolio *Eleven Color Photographs,* 1966–67
Chromogenic development print
19⅞ × 23⅝ in. (50.5 × 60 cm)
Ed: 8/8
Gerald S. Elliott Collection
1994.11.d

Untitled from the portfolio *Eleven Color Photographs,* 1966–67
Chromogenic development print
19¹⁵⁄₁₆ × 23¹¹⁄₁₆ in. (50.6 × 60.2 cm)
Ed: 8/8
Gerald S. Elliott Collection
1994.11.e

Coffee Spilled Because the Cup Was Too Hot from the portfolio *Eleven Color Photographs,* 1966–67
Chromogenic development print
19⁷⁄₁₆ × 23⅛ in. (49.4 × 58.7 cm)
Ed: 8/8
Gerald S. Elliott Collection
1994.11.f

Coffee Thrown Away Because it was Too Cold from the portfolio *Eleven Color Photographs,* 1966–67
Chromogenic development print
19¹⁵⁄₁₆ × 23¾ in. (50.6 × 60.3 cm)
Ed: 8/8
Gerald S. Elliott Collection
1994.11.g

Bound to Fail from the portfolio *Eleven Color Photographs,* 1966–67
Chromogenic development print
19⅞ × 23⅝ in. (50.5 × 60 cm)
Ed: 8/8
Gerald S. Elliott Collection
1994.11.h

Drill Team from the portfolio *Eleven Color Photographs,* 1966–67
Chromogenic development print
20 × 23⁷⁄₁₆ in. (50.8 × 59.5 cm)
Ed: 8/8
Gerald S. Elliott Collection
1994.11.i

Eating my Words from the portfolio *Eleven Color Photographs,* 1966–67
Chromogenic development print
19⅜ × 23³⁄₁₆ in. (49.2 × 60.5 cm)
Ed: 8/8
Gerald S. Elliott Collection
1994.11.j

Run from Fear, Fun from Rear, 1972
Neon
Two parts,
Part a: 8 × 46 × 2¼ in. (20.3 × 116.8 × 5.7 cm)
Part b: 7¼ × 44½ × 2¼ in. (18.4 × 113 × 5.7 cm)
Ed: 4/6
Gerald S. Elliott Collection
1995.72.a–b

353

Shit and Die, 1985
Drypoint on paper
15¾ × 22½ in. (40 × 57.2 cm)
Ed: 31/38
Gift of the Ruttenberg Family in honor of the
90th birthday of David C. Ruttenberg
1999.33

Live or Die (State I), 1985
Lithograph on paper
16 × 12 in. (40.6 × 30.5 cm)
Ed: 7/25
Gift of the Ruttenberg Family in honor of the
90th birthday of David C. Ruttenberg
1999.34

Live or Die (State II), 1985
Lithograph on paper
16 × 12 in. (40.6 × 30.5 cm)
Ed: 11/25
Gift of the Ruttenberg Family in honor of the
90th birthday of David C. Ruttenberg
1999.35

Elliott's Stones, 1989
Granite
Six stones, each approximately:
3¾ × 39⅞ × 25⅝ in. (9.5 × 101.3 × 65.1 cm)
Gerald S. Elliott Collection
1995.2.a–f

Above Yourself (Study for 'Elliott's Stones'), 1989
Graphite on paper
26 × 39¼ in. (66 × 99.7 cm)
Gerald S. Elliott Collection
1995.3

After Yourself (Study for 'Elliott's Stones'), 1989
Graphite on paper
26 × 39¼ in. (66 × 99.7 cm)
Gerald S. Elliott Collection
1995.4

Before Yourself (Study for 'Elliott's Stones'), 1989
Graphite on paper
26 × 39¼ in. (66 × 99.7 cm)
Gerald S. Elliott Collection
1995.5

Behind Yourself (Study for 'Elliott's Stones'), 1989
Graphite on paper
26 × 39¼ in. (66 × 99.7 cm)
Gerald S. Elliott Collection
1995.6

Beneath Yourself (Study for 'Elliott's Stones'),
1989
Graphite on paper
26 × 39¼ in. (66 × 99.7 cm)
Gerald S. Elliott Collection
1995.7

Beside Yourself (Study for 'Elliott's Stones'), 1989
Graphite on paper
26 × 39¼ in. (66 × 99.7 cm)
Gerald S. Elliott Collection
1995.8

354

Shirin Neshat
Iranian, b. 1957
p. 280

Turbulent
1998
Black-and-white video installation
Dimensions variable
Artist's proof aside from an edition of 3
Gift of Susan and Lewis Manilow
2000.22

Provenance

Patrick Painter, Inc., Santa Monica, Calif., 1998.

Susan and Lewis Manilow, Chicago, 1998.

MCA, 2000.

Exhibition History

Unfinished History, Walker Art Center,
Minneapolis, October 18, 1998–January 10,
1999; MCA, January 30–April 4, 1999
(not MCA edition).

*Original Language: Highlights from the MCA
Collection*, MCA, March 24–August 5, 2001.

References

Ali, Salwat. "Lifting the Veil." *Art Review*
(November 2, 2001).

Bertucci, Lina. "Shirin Neshat, Eastern Values."
Flash Art 30, no. 197 (November / December
1997), pp. 84–87.

Miller, Paul. "Shirin Neshat's Turbulent."
Parkett, no. 54 (December 1998 / January 1999),
pp. 157–64.

"Photo Essay — Shirin Neshat." *Time Europe*
(August 2000), website: www.time.com/time/
europe/photoessays/neshat.

Other Works in the MCA Collection

On Guard, 1997
Ink on gelatin silver print
40 × 60 in. (101.6 × 152.4 cm)
Artist's proof aside from an edition of 3
Partial and promised gift from
The Howard and Donna Stone Collection
2002.49

Cady Noland
American, b. 1956
p. 218

Chainsaw Cut Cowboy Head
1990
Silk screen on aluminum with rope,
roll of tape, and cigarette box
60 × 60 × 19¼ in. (152.4 × 152.4 × 48.9 cm)
Gift of Susan and Lewis Manilow
1999.36.a–d

Provenance

American Fine Arts Co., New York, 1990.

Susan and Lewis Manilow, Chicago, 1991.

MCA, 1999.

Exhibition History

*Original Language: Highlights from the MCA
Collection*, MCA, March 24–August 5, 2001.

References

Bonami, Francesco. "Cady Noland:
Claustrophobic Lawn." *Flash Art* 31, no. 201
(summer 1998), pp. 122–25.

Nichols Goodeve, Thyrza. "Art as Encyclopedia,
History as Vaudeville." *Parkett*, no. 46 (May
1996), pp. 92–95.

Relyea, Lane. "Hi-Yo Silver: Cady Noland's
America." *Artforum* 31, no. 5 (January 1993),
pp. 50–55.

———. "Holy Crusade." *Parkett*, no. 46 (May
1996), pp. 72–75.

Jim Nutt
American, b. 1938
p. 120

Summer Salt
1970
Vinyl paint over plastic and enamel
on wood and Masonite
61¼ × 36 × 3½ in. (155.6 × 91.4 × 8.9 cm)
Gift of Dennis Adrian
in honor of Claire B. Zeisler
1980.30.1

Provenance

Phyllis Kind Gallery, Chicago, 1970.

Dennis Adrian, Chicago, 1971.

MCA, 1980.

Exhibition History

Phyllis Kind Gallery, Chicago, c. 1970–71.

Selections from the Permanent Collection, MCA,
May 3–August 31, 1980.

*Selections from the Permanent Collection and the
Robert B. Mayer Memorial Loan*, MCA,
January 13–February 8, 1981.

Permanent Collection Exhibition, MCA, June–
December, 1981.

Selections from the Dennis Adrian Collection,
MCA, January 30–March 14, 1982.

Ten Years of Collecting, MCA, April 14–June 10,
1984.

*The Figure in Chicago Art: Selections from the
Permanent Collection*, MCA, February 19–
March 31, 1985.

*The Museum of Contemporary Art at
333 W. Wacker: Chicago Artists from the Permanent
Collection*, MCA, July 10–August 21, 1987.

*Portraits: From the Permanent Collection of the
MCA*, College of DuPage Arts Center Gallery,
Glen Ellyn, Ill., April 12–May 26, 1988.

Toward the Future: Contemporary Art in Context,
MCA, May 5–July 1, 1990.

Jim Nutt Retrospective, Milwaukee Art Museum, Wis., June 17–August 28, 1994; Henry Art Gallery, University of Washington, Seattle, September 14–November 20, 1994; National Museum of American Art, Smithsonian Institution, Washington, D.C., February 10–May 21, 1995; Contemporary Arts Center, Cincinnati, Ohio, July 8–September 6, 1995.

Art in Chicago, 1945–1995, MCA, November 16–March 23, 1997.

References

Alloway, Lawrence. "Art." *Nation* (October 5, 1974), pp. 317–18.

Bonesteel, Michael. "Hairy, Scary, Odd, and Daring." *Chicago Reader*, February 12, 1982, p. 34.

Bowman, Russell. "Words and Images: A Persistent Paradox." *Art Journal* 45, no. 4 (winter 1985), pp. 335–43.

Cameron, Dan. "Nutt's Progress." *Arts Magazine* 58, no. 8 (April 1984), pp. 66–69.

Gedo, Mary Mathews. "Dennis Adrian Collection." *Arts Magazine* 56, no. 8 (April 1982), p. 9.

Halstead, Whitney. "Jim Nutt." *Arts Magazine* 49, no. 2 (October 1974), pp. 46–47.

Jacob, Mary Jane et al. *Selections from the Permanent Collection, Vol. I.* MCA, 1984.

Jim Nutt Retrospective. Exh. cat. Milwaukee, Wis.: Milwaukee Art Museum, 1994.

Schulze, Franz. *Fantastic Images: Chicago Art since 1945.* Chicago: Follett, 1972. P. 169.

Selections from the Dennis Adrian Collection. Exh. cat. MCA, 1982.

Vine, Richard. "Where the Wild Things Were." *Art in America* 85, no. 5 (May 1997), pp. 98–111.

Other Works in the MCA Collection

Quaffed, 1969–1970
Graphite, colored pencil, and crayon on paper
25½ × 40 in. (64.8 × 101.6 cm)
Gift of Dennis Adrian in honor of
Mr. and Mrs. Morton G. Neumann
1980.30.2

Armed, c. 1970s
Colored pencil on paper
24 × 36 in. (61 × 91.4 cm)
Gift of Susan and Lewis Manilow
1999.43

a sweet note of regret . . ., 1970
Etching on paper
Plate: 2⅝ × 4⁵⁄₁₆ in. (6.7 × 11 cm)
Edition of 15
Gift of Howard and Donna Stone
1993.21

Where Did He Come From?
Why Doesn't He Leave?, 1971
Acrylic on paper and metal
9¼ × 8¼ × 5¼ in. (23.5 × 21 × 13.3 cm)
Gift of Muriel and Albert Newman
in honor of John Neff
1982.16

She Seams Up Set, 1971
Acrylic on paper
7¾ × 7 in. (19.7 × 17.8 cm)
Gift of Gerald S. Elliott
1989.1

He's Not Allowed to Look, However, 1973
Colored pencil on paper and acrylic on mat board
34½ × 27 in. (87.6 × 68.6 cm)
Gift of Joseph and Jory Shapiro
1976.8

Don't, 1975
Graphite on paper with artist's frame
14⅜ × 13⅜ in. (36.5 × 34 cm)
Bequest of Ruth S. Nath
1998.15

M.C.A.'s first BIG 10 yrs., 1977
Acrylic on portfolio
23⅛ × 31½ in. (58.7 × 80 cm)
Gift of Carol and Douglas Cohen
1991.67.1

I'm not stopping from the portfolio
M.C.A.'s first BIG 10 yrs., 1977
Etching on paper
Plate: 3¹⁵⁄₁₆ × 6⅞ in. (10 × 17.5 cm)
Artist's proof 4/5 aside from an edition of 50
Gift of Carol and Douglas Cohen
1991.67.2

you hoo-little boy from the portfolio
M.C.A.'s first BIG 10 yrs., 1977
Etching on paper
Plate: 3¹⁵⁄₁₆ × 4⁵⁄₁₆ in. (10 × 11 cm)
Artist's proof 4/5 aside from an edition of 50
Gift of Carol and Douglas Cohen
1991.67.3

oh! My goodness (NO NO) from the
portfolio *M.C.A.'s first BIG 10 yrs.*, 1977
Etching on paper
Plate: 9⅞ × 11⅞ in. (25.1 × 30.2 cm)
Artist's proof 4/5 aside from an edition of 50
Gift of Carol and Douglas Cohen
1991.67.4

your so coarse (tish tish) from the
portfolio *M.C.A.'s first BIG 10 yrs.*, 1977
Etching on paper
Plate: 8¹⁵⁄₁₆ × 7¹⁵⁄₁₆ in. (22.7 × 20.2 cm)
Artist's proof 4/5 aside from an edition of 50
Gift of Carol and Douglas Cohen
1991.67.5

your so coarse (tish tish), 1977
Etching on paper
Plate: 8¹⁵⁄₁₆ × 7¹⁵⁄₁₆ in. (22.7 × 20.2 cm)
Ed: 11/50 aside from 4 artist's proofs
Gift of Holleb & Coff, Attorneys
1998.45

swell!!, 1981
Colored pencil on craft paper
12 × 14⅛ in. (30.5 × 35.9 cm)
Bequest of Sandra Jorgensen
1999.24

Claes Oldenburg
American, b. Sweden 1929
p. 74

Green Beans
1964
Vinyl, and acrylic on plaster
Eighteen parts, each: 2 × 11¾ × 5 in.
(5.1 × 29.8 × 12.7 cm)
Gift of Anne and William J. Hokin
1996.5.a–r

Provenance

Sidney Janis Gallery, New York, 1964.

Richard Bellamy Gallery, New York, 1964.

Leon Kraushar, Long Island, New York.

Karl Ströher, Darmstadt, Germany, 1968.

Sotheby's, New York, May 2, 1989, lot. 15.

Anne and William J. Hokin, Chicago, 1989.

MCA, 1996.

Exhibition History

Exhibition of Recent Work by Claes Oldenburg, Sidney Janis Gallery, New York, April 7–May 2, 1964.

Six From the East, San Francisco Art Institute, April 15–May 22, 1966.

Sammlung 1968 Karl Stroher, Neue Pinakothek, Haus der Kunst, Munich, June 14–August 9, 1968; Ausstellung der Deutschen Gesellschaft für Bildende Kunst e.V. (Kunstverein Berlin) und der Nationalgalerie der Staatlichen Museen Preussischer Kulturbesitz in der Neuen Nationalgalerie Berlin, March 1–April 14, 1969; Städtische Kunsthalle, Düsseldorf, Germany, April 25–June 17, 1969; Kunsthalle Bern, Switzerland, July 12–August 17 and August 23–September 28, 1969.

In the Shadow of Storms: Art of the Postwar Era from the MCA Collection, MCA, July 2, 1996–May 25, 1997.

L'Informe: le modernisme à rebours, Musée National d'Art Moderne, Centre Georges Pompidou, Paris, May 21–August 26, 1996.

Envisioning the Contemporary: Selections from the Permanent Collection, MCA, June 21, 1997–April 5, 1998 and April 30, 1998–February 7, 1999.

Age of Influence: Reflections in the Mirror of American Culture, MCA, March 14, 2000–January 2, 2001.

Sculpture in the Form of a Fried Egg
1966/1971
Canvas, dyed cotton, and expanded polystyrene
122 in. diameter (309.9 cm)
Gift of Anne and William J. Hokin
1986.65

Provenance

Margo Leavin Gallery, Los Angeles, 1981.

Anne and William J. Hokin, Chicago, 1981.

MCA, 1986.

Exhibition History

Claes Oldenburg: Objects into Monuments, Pasadena Art Museum, Pasadena, Calif., December 7, 1971 – February 6, 1972; Berkeley Art Museum, Berkeley, Calif., February 28 – April 9, 1972; William Rockhill Nelson Art Gallery, Kansas City, Mo., May 11 – June 18, 1972; Fort Worth Art Museum, Tex., July 10 – August 20, 1972; Des Moines Art Center, Iowa, September 18 – October 29, 1972; The Art Institute of Chicago, January 20 – February 25, 1973.

Pop, Minimalism, and Earth Art: Selections from the Permanent Collection, MCA, May 6 – July 2, 1987.

L'Informe: le modernisme à rebours, Musée National d'Art Moderne, Centre Georges Pompidou, Paris, May 21 – August 26, 1996.

In the Shadow of Storms: Art of the Postwar Era from the MCA Collection, MCA, July 2, 1996 – May 25, 1997.

Envisioning the Contemporary: Selections from the Permanent Collection, MCA, June 21, 1997 – April 5, 1998 and April 30, 1998 – February 7, 1999.

Transmute, MCA, August 21 – November 7, 1999.

References

Claes Oldenburg: An Anthology. New York: Solomon R. Guggenheim Museum and Harry N. Abrams, 1995.

Claes Oldenburg Raw Notes. Halifax, Nova Scotia, Canada: Nova Scotia College of Art and Design Press, 1973.

Collective Vision. MCA, 1996.

Glueck, Grace. "Soft Sculptures or Hard — They're Oldenburgers." *New York Times Magazine* (September 21, 1969).

Jacob, Mary Jane et al. *Selections from the Permanent Collection, Vol. I.* MCA, 1984.

Judd, Donald. "In the Galleries: Claes Oldenburg." *Arts Magazine* 38, no. 10 (September 1964), p. 63.

Rose, Barbara. "Claes Oldenburg's Soft Machines." *Artforum* 5, no. 10 (June 1967), pp. 30 – 35.

Schmidt, K. K. *Karl Stroher: Sammler und Sammlung.* Stuttgart, Germany: Dr. Cantz-sche Druckerei, 1982. P. 311.

Soloman, Alan and U. Mulas. *New York: The New Art Scene.* New York: Holt, Rinehart, and Winston, 1967. P. 209.

Visual Forms of Expressionism 1960 – 70: Sammlung Karl Stroher. Darmstadt, Germany: Hessisches Landesmuseum, 1970.

Other Works in the MCA Collection

Flying Pizza from the portfolio *New York Ten 1966,* 1964
Lithograph on paper
16⅞ × 22⅛ in. (42.9 × 56.2 cm)
Ed: 128/200
Gift of Edward Weiss
1981.51.9

Feasible Monument for a Chicago Site: Giant Cuff Link Using Picasso Head (Picasso's Cuff Link), 1969
Spray enamel, half-tone print mounted on foil, graphite, felt-tip pen, crayon, cardboard, wood, nails, and Plexiglas
28 × 24 × 19 in. (71.1 × 61 × 48.3 cm)
Gift of Anne and William J. Hokin
1986.56

Raw Notes, 1974
Artist's book
Closed: 10¹⁵⁄₁₆ × 7½ × 1⅛ in.
(27.8 × 19 × 2.8 cm)
Gift of Mr. and Mrs. Robert Vogele
1986.2.1

The Office. A Typewriter Print, 1974
Lithograph on paper
Open: 32¹⁵⁄₁₆ × 22⁷⁄₁₆ in. (83.7 × 57 cm)
Ed: 6/50 aside from 12 artist's proofs
Gift of Mr. and Mrs. Robert Vogele
1986.2.2

Raw Notes, 1974
Portfolio
Closed: 11¹¹⁄₁₆ × 8⅜ × 1¹⁵⁄₁₆ in.
(29.7 × 21.3 × 4.9 cm)
Gift of Mr. and Mrs. Robert Vogele
1986.2.3

Bat Spinning at the Speed of Light, 1975
Lithograph on paper
37⅛ × 25 in. (94.3 × 63.5 cm)
Ed: 18/60
Gift of the Men's Council
1980.50

Emerald Pill, 1977
Enamel on cast aluminum, and stainless steel
6 × 2⅜ in. diameter (15.2 × 6 cm)
Ed: 1/35
Gift of the Men's Council
1978.4

Model of Proposed Facade for the MCA, In the Shape of a Geometric Mouse, 1977
(based on a 1967 drawing)
Watercolor, graphite, and ink on mat board, cardboard, and foamcore
18 × 23½ × 23¼ in. (45.7 × 59.7 × 59.1 cm)
Gift of the artist
1978.37

Soft Alphabet, 1978
Screenprint on wood, muslin, sand, and talc
Box: 2⅞ × 29³⁄₁₆ × 22⅛ in.
(7.3 × 74.1 × 56.2 cm)
Ed: 14/16
Gift of Anne and William J. Hokin
1987.8

Soft Saxophone (Black, Yellow, Red), 1992
Lithograph on paper
35 × 43¾ in. (88.9 × 111.1 cm)
Ed: 22/30
Gift of the artist and Brooke Alexander Editions
1993.22

Tony Oursler
American, b. 1957
p. 266

Guilty
1995
Color video installation, mattress, dress, and pillow
Dimensions variable
Restricted gift of Dr. Paul and Dorie Sternberg
1996.2

Provenance

Metro Pictures Gallery, New York, 1995.

MCA, 1996.

Exhibition History

Zeichen & Wunder. Niko Pirosmani (1862 – 1918) und die Kunst der Gegenwart. (Signs & Wonders. Niko Pirosmani (1862 – 1918) and Recent Art), Kunsthaus, Zurich, March 31 – June 18, 1995; Centro Galego de Arte Contemporanea, Santiago de Compostela, Spain, July 20 – October 20, 1995.

1995 Carnegie International, Carnegie Museum of Art, Pittsburgh, Pa., November 4, 1995 – February 18, 1996.

In the Shadow of Storms: Art of the Postwar Era from the MCA Collection, MCA, July 2, 1996 – May 25, 1997.

Tony Oursler: Guilty, MCA, August 31 – November 10, 1996.

Transmute, MCA, August 21 – November 7, 1999.

No Harm in Looking, MCA, May 5 – August 19, 2001.

References

Introjection: Tony Oursler, Mid-Career Survey, 1976 – 1999. Exh. cat. Williamstown, Mass.: Williams College Museum of Art, 1999.

Matthew Barney, Tony Oursler, Jeff Wall. Munich: Sammlung Goetz, 1996.

Tony Oursler: Videotapes, Dummies, Drawings, Photographs, Viruses, Light, Heads, Eyes, and CD-ROM. Exh. cat. Hannover, Germany: Kunstverein Hannover, 1998.

Jorge Pardo
American, b. Cuba 1963
p. 276

Vince Robbins
1997
Plastic, steel, light bulbs, and electric wire
Dimensions variable
Restricted gift of Carlos and Rosa de la Cruz
1998.29

Provenance

Friedrich Petzel Gallery, New York, 1997.

MCA, 1998.

Exhibition History

Rooms with a View: Environments for Video, Solomon R. Guggenheim Museum, New York, April 14–June 15, 1997.

Transmute, MCA, August 21–November 7, 1999.

References

Bush, Kate. "Design For Life." *Frieze,* no. 36 (September/October 1997), pp. 52–57.

Cruz, Amada. *Jorge Pardo.* Exh. cat. Los Angeles: The Museum of Contemporary Art; MCA, 1997.

Drohojowska-Philp, Hunter. "Welcome to the House that Jorge Built." *Los Angeles Times,* October 11, 1998, pp. 62, 82.

Grabner, Michelle. "Jorge Pardo: Living Without Boundaries." *Sculpture* 16, no. 10 (December 1997), pp. 38–41.

Ed Paschke

American, b. 1939
p. 118

Japanese Cowboy

1969
Oil on canvas
14 × 10 in. (35.6 × 25.4 cm)
Gift of Susan and Lewis Manilow
1993.8

Provenance

Marianne Deson Gallery, Chicago, 1976.

Susan and Lewis Manilow, Chicago, 1976.

MCA, 1993.

Exhibition History

Ed Paschke, Marianne Deson Gallery, Chicago, 1976.

In the Shadow of Storms: Art of the Postwar Era from the MCA Collection, MCA, July 2, 1996–May 25, 1997.

Envisioning the Contemporary: Selections from the Permanent Collection, MCA, June 21, 1997–April 5, 1998.

Adria

1976
Oil on canvas
96⅛ × 74 in. (244.2 × 188 cm)
Gift of Susan and Lewis Manilow
in honor of Dennis Adrian
1988.6

Provenance

Galerie Darthea Speyer, Paris, 1976.

Susan and Lewis Manilow, Chicago, 1977.

MCA, 1988.

Exhibition History

Ed Paschke, Galerie Darthea Speyer, Paris, November 1976.

Museum of Contemporary Art Permanent Collection Exhibition, MCA, January 16–March 14, 1982.

Museum of Contemporary Art on Michigan: Selections from the Permanent Collection, MCA, November 1, 1983–January 1, 1984.

Ten Years of Collecting, MCA, April 14–June 10, 1984.

Selections from the Permanent Collection: Portraits, MCA, December 12, 1984–April 13, 1985.

Ed Paschke, Lowe Art Museum, University of Miami, Coral Gables, Fla., December 15, 1988–January 29, 1989.

Toward the Future: Contemporary Art in Context, MCA, May 5–July 1, 1990.

Modeling the Future: The New Museum and Key Works from the Permanent Collection, MCA, May 2–November 8, 1992.

Chicago Imagism: A Twenty-Five Year Survey, Davenport Museum of Art, Iowa. December 3, 1994–February 12, 1995.

In the Shadow of Storms: Art of the Postwar Era from the MCA Collection, MCA, July 2, 1996–March 26, 1997.

Art in Chicago, 1945–1995, MCA, November 16–March 23, 1997.

References

Adams, Brooks. "The Progress of Ed Paschke." *Art in America* 70, no. 9 (October 1982), pp. 114–22.

Benezra, Neal. *Ed Paschke.* New York: Hudson Hills; Chicago: The Art Institute, 1990. Pp. 34–35, 152.

Collective Vision. MCA, 1996.

Ed Paschke: Selected Works 1967–1981. Exh. cat. Chicago: The Renaissance Society, The University of Chicago Press, 1982.

"Ed Paschke's *Adria.*" *Chicago Daily News,* November 20, 1976.

Elliott, David. "Collector Adrian: A Gambler Who Loves Wild Cards." *Chicago Sun-Times,* February 14, 1982, pp. 7, 21.

Gedo, Mary Matthews. "Dennis Adrian Collection." *Arts Magazine* 56, no. 8 (April 1982), p. 9.

Holg, Garrett. "MCA Uses Strength as Building Block 'Toward Future.'" *Chicago Sun-Times,* June 17, 1990, pp. 11, 13.

Jacob, Mary Jane et al. *Selections from the Permanent Collection, Vol. I.* MCA, 1984.

Lyon, Christopher. "Surrealism Sets Tone of MCA Retrospective." *Chicago Sun-Times,* May 13, 1984, p. 22.

Museum of Contemporary Art: Fifteen Years and Beyond. MCA, 1982. P. 24.

Rice, Barry. "Five Uneasy Pieces." *Chicago Magazine* (July 1996), pp. 22–24.

Vishny, Michelle. "An Interview with Ed Paschke." *Arts Magazine* 55, no. 4 (December 1980), pp. 146–49.

Williams, Kevin M. "10 Most-Vaunted." *Chicago Sun-Times,* July 2, 1996.

Other Works in the MCA Collection

Memorial, 1968
Oil on canvas
32 × 24 in. (81.3 × 61 cm)
Gift of Susan and Lewis Manilow
1993.7

Sunburn, 1970
Oil on canvas
27⅞ × 37¹⁵⁄₁₆ in. (70.8 × 96.4 cm)
Gift of Muriel and Albert Newman
in honor of Dennis Adrian
1982.17

Heavy Shoes, 1970
Oil on canvas
44¼ × 38 in. (112.4 × 96.5 cm)
Gift of Joseph and Jory Shapiro
1992.70

Hair Bag, 1971
Oil on canvas
34 × 20 in. (87.4 × 50.8 cm)
Bequest of Ruth S. Nath
1998.17

Drawing for "Turds in Hell," 1972
Oil, ink, and graphite on paper
19 × 24¾ in. (48.3 × 62.9 cm)
Gift of Gerald S. Elliott
1981.17

Elcina, 1973
Oil on canvas
60 × 38 in. (152.4 × 96.5 cm)
Gift of Albert J. Bildner
1974.5

Lucy, 1973
Oil on canvas
59⅞ × 38 in. (152.1 × 96.5 cm)
Gift of Albert J. Bildner
1974.6

Casey, 1975
Oil on canvas
48 × 20 in. (121.9 × 50.8 cm)
Bequest of Ruth S. Nath
1998.16

Metal de Bleu (Blue Metal), 1977
Oil on canvas
32 × 22 in. (81.3 × 55.9 cm)
Bequest of Ruth S. Nath
1998.18

Nervosa, 1980
Oil on canvas
46 × 42 in. (116.8 × 106.7 cm)
Gift of Judith Neisser
1994.6

Bistro, 1981
Lithograph on paper
32¼ × 41¼ in. (81.9 × 104.8 cm)
Ed. 7/35 aside from 10 artist's proofs
Gift of Jeanne Marienthal-Weislow
1986.53

Execo, 1983
Color lithograph on paper
34¼ × 24 in. (87 × 61 cm)
Ed: 3/40 aside from 10 artist's proofs
Gift of the Business Committee for the Arts, Inc., commissioned for its Seventeenth Annual Business in the Arts Award Program
1983.40

Kontata, 1984
Lithograph on paper
34¼ × 24 in. (87 × 61 cm)
Subscriber's Proofs: VII/X aside from
an edition of 45 and 10 artist's proofs
Gift of Jeanne Marienthal-Weislow
1986.46

Ed Paschke,
Stephan Meyers (American, b. 1968);
Ellen Sandor (American, b. 1942); and
Janine Fron (American, b. 1969)
No Fumare por Favore (No Smoking Please),
1997
Rotated computer interleaved Lightjet
Duratrans and Kodalith films on Plexiglas
with light box
30 × 40 in. (76.2 × 101.6 cm)
Ed: 3/6
Gift of Ellen Sandor and Ed Paschke
1998.51

Dan Peterman

American, b. 1960
p. 282

Accessories to an Event (plaza)

1998
Reprocessed plastic
Dimensions variable
Restricted gift of Sara Albrecht
and Bill Nygren
1998.28.a–j

Provenance

MCA commission, 1998.

Exhibition History

Dan Peterman: Accessories to an Event (plaza),
MCA, July 15, 1998 – November 26, 2001.

Semi-permanent. Parts of this work are on
display every year.

References

Hixson, Kathryn. "Dan Peterman: Recycle."
New Art Examiner 28, no. 2 (October 2000),
pp. 26 – 29.

Kirshner, Judith Russi. "Dan Peterman."
Artforum 33, no. 7 (March 1995), pp. 94 – 95.

Peterman, Dan. *Thank You for Your Patronage:
Chairs from Street Carts: A Project by Daniel
Peterman*. Chicago: The Resource Center and
the Men's Council of the MCA, 1989.

Peterman, Dan and Lynne Warren. *Dan
Peterman: Options 48: Sulfur Cycle*. MCA, 1994.

Vendrame, Simona. "Sublime Garbage." *tema
celeste* (January/February 2001), pp. 56 – 61.

Williams, Kevin M. "Waste's No Picnic:
Artist's Plastic Table Makes Big Statement."
Chicago Sun-Times, April 22, 1997, p. 4.

Other Works in the MCA Collection

Small Change, 1989
Densified, recycled aluminum cans
Three parts, each: 8 × 40 in. diameter
(20.3 × 101.6 cm)
Gift of Maremont Corporation by exchange
1993.13.1 – 3

Raymond Pettibon

American, b. 1957
p. 152

No Title (No Text: Black Electric Chair)

1978
Ink on paper
13⅞ × 10⅞ in. (35.2 × 27.6 cm)
Gift of Susan and Lewis Manilow
1999.46

No Title (To Dust Cover...Shut)

1984
Ink on paper
14 × 10⅛ in. (35.6 × 25.7 cm)
Gift of Susan and Lewis Manilow
1999.48

No Title (I don't know why)

1985
Ink on paper
10½ × 8⅜ in. (26.7 × 21.3 cm)
Gift of Susan and Lewis Manilow
1999.45

No Title (Begging to be Understood)

1991
Ink on paper
13⅞ × 11 in. (35.2 × 27.9 cm)
Gift of Susan and Lewis Manilow
1999.44

No Title (The Plague, There Throbbed)

1995
Ink on paper
15 × 11 1/16 in. (38.1 × 28.1 cm)
Gift of Susan and Lewis Manilow
1999.47

Provenance

Regen Projects, Los Angeles.

Susan and Lewis Manilow, Chicago,
c. 1994–97.

MCA, 1999.

Exhibition History

Raymond Pettibon, The Renaissance Society,
The University of Chicago, September 13 –
November 14, 1998; The Drawing Center,
New York, February 21 – April 11, 1999;
Philadelphia Museum of Art, May 2 –
June 27, 1999.

*Drawing on the Figure: Works on Paper of the
1990s from the Manilow Collection*, MCA,
March 18 – June 25, 2000.

The Possibilities of Citizenship, Lake Forest
College, Lake Forest, Ill., October 13 –
November 15, 2000.

References

Buchloh, Benjamin H. D. "Raymond Pettibon:
Return to Disorder and Disfiguration." *October*,
no. 92 (2000), pp. 37 – 51.

Duncan, Michael. "Pettibon's Talking
Pictures." *Art in America* 87, no. 3 (March 1999),
pp. 106 – 9, 129.

James, Elizabeth. "Raymond Pettibon:
Kunsthalle." *Artforum* 33, no. 10 (summer 1995),
p. 116.

Loock, Ulrich, ed. *Raymond Pettibon*. Exh. cat.
Bern, Switzerland: Kunsthalle Bern, 1995.
Pp. 7 – 12, 28.

Temkin, Ann and Hamza Walker, eds. *Raymond
Pettibon: A Reader*. Philadelphia: Philadelphia
Museum of Art, 1998.

Other Works in the MCA Collection

No Title (Without Much Reading), 1989
Ink on paper
30¼ x 22½ in. (76.8 x 57.2 cm)
Gift of Hudson
1997.8

Paul Pfeiffer

American, b. 1966
p. 296

*Fragment of a Crucifixion
(after Francis Bacon)*

1999
Color video installation
Image: 3 × 4 in. (7.6 × 10.2 cm)
Ed: 3/3 aside from 2 artist's proofs
Restricted gift of Kenneth C. Griffin
2000.8

Provenance

The Project, New York, 1999.

MCA, 2000.

Exhibition History

Paul Pfeiffer, The Project, New York,
November 19, 2000 – January 7, 2001.

*Original Language: Highlights from the MCA
Collection*, MCA, March 24 – August 5, 2001.

*People See Paintings: Photography and Painting
from the MCA Collection*, MCA, January 19 –
October 20, 2002.

References

Anderson, Maxwell. *Whitney Biennial: 2000
Exhibition*. Exh. cat. New York: The Whitney
Museum of American Art, 2000.

Hunt, David. "Man Trap." *Frieze*, no. 53
(summer 2000), pp. 98 – 99.

Siegel, Katy. "Paul Pfeiffer." *Artforum* 38,
no. 10 (summer 2000), pp. 174 – 75.

Jack Pierson

American, b. 1960
p. 230

Scarface

1991
Metal and plastic sign lettering
Twenty-six parts, installed: 87 × 67 in.
(221 × 170.2 cm)
Gift of Zoe and Joel Dictrow
1997.76.a – z

Provenance

Tom Cugliani Gallery, New York, 1991.

Zoe and Joel Dictrow, New York, 1991.

MCA, 1997.

Exhibition History

Envisioning the Contemporary, MCA,
June 21, 1997 – April 5, 1998.

Decades in Dialogue: Perspectives on the MCA Collection, MCA, February 27 – October 31, 1999.

Original Language: Highlights from the MCA Collection, MCA, March 24 – August 5, 2001.

Jack Pierson, Regrets, Museum of Contemporary Art, North Miami, Fla., May 16 – August 25, 2002.

References

Boston School. Exh. cat. Boston: Institute of Contemporary Art; Allston, Mass.: Primal Media, 1995.

Goodrow, Gérard A. and Peter Weiermair, ed. *Jack Pierson: The Lonely Life.* Zurich: Edition Stemmle, 1997.

Grosenick, Uta and Burkhard Reimschneider, eds. *Art at the Turn of the Millennium.* Cologne, Germany: Taschen, 1999.

Jack Pierson: Traveling Show. Exh. cat. MCA, 1995.

Pierson, Jack. *All of a Sudden.* New York: Power House Cultural Entertainment, 1999.

Other Works in the MCA Collection

Angel Youth, 1984 – 1995
Chromogenic development prints
Thirteen parts, six at: 20 × 30 in.
(50.1 × 76.2 cm)
and seven at: 30 × 20 in. (76.2 × 50.1 cm)
Ed: 2/25
Restricted gift of The Dave Hokin Foundation
1995.119.1 – 13

Adrian Piper

American, b. 1948
p. 204

Cornered

1988
Video installation with birth certificates,
color video, monitor, table, and chairs
Dimensions variable
Bernice and Kenneth Newberger Fund
1990.4.a – p

Provenance

John Weber Gallery, New York, 1990.

Feigen, Inc., Chicago, 1990.

MCA, 1990.

Exhibition History

Adrian Piper: Reflections 1967–1987, Alternative Museum, New York, April 18 – May 30, 1989; Nexus Contemporary Art Center, Atlanta, November – December 1987; Goldie Paley Gallery, Philadelphia, February – March 1989; University of Colorado Art Gallery, Boulder, March 1990; Power Plant Gallery, Toronto, Canada, May – June 1990; Wooster Art Museum, Wooster, Ohio, August 29 – October 4, 1990; Lowe Art Museum, University of Miami, Coral Gables, Fla., December 24, 1990 – January 27, 1991; Santa Monica Museum of Art, Santa Monica, Calif., February – March 18, 1991; Washington Project for the Arts, Washington, D.C., June 18 – August 30, 1991.

Adrian Piper: Close to Home, University of Iowa, Iowa City, February 2 – March 2, 1991.

Adrian Piper, Ikon Gallery, Birmingham, England, September 21 – November 2, 1991; Cornerhouse, Manchester, England, January 18 – February 23, 1992; Cartwright Hall, Bradford, England, March 21 – May 10, 1992; Kettle's Yard, Cambridge, England, July 23 – September 6, 1992; Kunstverein, Munich, October 6 – November 22, 1992.

New Acquisitions: The MCA Collects, MCA, November 23, 1991 – January 26, 1992.

Dislocations, The Museum of Modern Art, New York, October 16, 1991 – January 7, 1992.

Mistaken Identities, University Art Museum, University of California at Santa Barbara, November 11 – December 20, 1992; Museum Folkwang, Essen, Germany, February 11 – March 31, 1993; Forum Stadtpark, Graz, Austria, April 29 – May 30, 1993; Neues Museum Weserburg/Forum Langenstraße, Bremen, Germany, June 6 – August 15, 1993; Louisiana Museum of Modern Art, Copenhagen, September 17 – November 14, 1993; Western Gallery, Western Washington University, Bellingham, Wash., January 5 – February 13, 1994.

Civil Rights Now, Montgomery Museum of Fine Arts, Montgomery, Ala., January 19 – March 13, 1994.

Outside the Frame: Performance and the Object, Cleveland Center for Contemporary Art, Ohio, February 11 – May 1, 1994; Blaffer Gallery, Houston, June 10 – July 31, 1994; Snug Harbor Cultural Center, Staten Island, N.Y., October 23 – January 8, 1995.

Adrian Piper, Jacob Lawrence Gallery, University of Washington, Seattle, April 12 – April 25, 1994.

I + the Other, Dignity for All: Reflections on Humanity, Stichting Artimo (under auspices of Red Cross Amsterdam), June 13 – August 21, 1994.

Cornered, 1988, by Adrian Piper, Rice University Art Gallery, Houston, January 19 – March 2, 1995.

Mistaken Identities, Africas 95, Biennial of Johannesburg, Art Gallery of New South Wales, Sydney, Australia, February 28 – April 30, 1995.

Decide Who You Are, University Gallery at State University of New York, Purchase, N.Y., March 4 – April 25, 1995.

Cornered, Paula Cooper Gallery, Inc., Chicago, June 9 – July 28, 1995

In the Shadow of Storms: Art of the Postwar Era from the MCA Collection, MCA, July 2 – March 25, 1997.

Envisioning the Contemporary: Selections from the Permanent Collection, MCA, June 21, 1997 – April 5, 1998 and April 30, 1998 – February 7, 1999.

Who Are You? Selected Works by Adrian Piper, Davis Museum and Cultural Center, Wellesley, Mass., March 11 – August 16, 1998.

MEDI(T)Ations: Adrian Piper's Videos, Installations, Performances, and Soundworks, 1968 – 1992, MCA, March 27 – July 11, 1999; The Museum of Contemporary Art, Los Angeles, August 6 – November 5, 2000; New Museum, New York, October 26, 2000 – January 21, 2001; The Andy Warhol Museum, Pittsburgh, Pa., March 3 – May 13, 2001; The Center for Contemporary Art, Cincinnati, Ohio, June 23 – August 19, 2001.

Adrian Piper: A Retrospective, 1965 – 2000, Mt. St. Vincent University, Halifax, Nova Scotia, July 8 – August 30, 2000; New Museum of Contemporary Art, New York, October 26, 2000 – January 21, 2001; The Andy Warhol Museum, Pittsburgh, Pa., March 4 – May 13, 2001; Cleveland Center for Contemporary Art, Ohio, June 23 – August 19, 2001; Weatherspoon Art Gallery, N.C., September 23 – December 16, 2001; Generali Foundation, Vienna, May 16 – August 25, 2002; Institute d'Art Contemporain, Lyon/Villeurbanne, France, January 15 – April 15, 2003; Museu d'Art Contemporani de Barcelona, June – September 2003.

Issues of Identity in Recent American Art, Gibson Gallery at State University of New York, Potsdam, March 12 – April 24, 2001; University Galleries, Illinois State University, Normal, Ill., June 12 – September 9, 2001; The Ewing Gallery of Art and Architecture, University of Tennessee, October 11 – November 8, 2001; Ben Shahn Galleries, William Patterson University, Wayne, N.J., January 31 – March 8, 2002; Samek Art Gallery, Bucknell University, Lewisburg, Pa., March 18 – April 14, 2002.

Double Life, Generali Foundation, Vienna, May 10 – August 12, 2001.

References

Berger, Maurice and Adrian Piper. *Adrian Piper: A Retrospective, 1965–2000.* Baltimore, Md.: Baltimore County Fine Arts Gallery, University of Maryland Press, 2000.

Collective Vision. MCA, 1996.

Johnson, Ken. "Being & Politics." *Art in America* 78, no. 9 (September 1990), pp. 154 – 60.

Masterson, Piers. "Adrian Piper and Brenda Croft." *Art Monthly*, no. 178 (July/August 1994), pp. 32 – 33.

Piper, Adrian. *Out of Order, Out of Sight, Vols. I and II.* Cambridge, Mass.: MIT Press, 1999.

Wilson, Judith. "In Memory of the News and of Our Selves: The Art of Adrian Piper." *Third Text* 16/17 (autumn/winter 1991), pp. 39 – 64.

Witzling, Mara R., ed. *Voicing Today's Visions: Writings by Contemporary Female Artists.* New York: Universe, 1994.

Sigmar Polke

German, b. 1941
p. 236

Ashes to Ashes

1992
Oil and ink on printed fabrics and velour
95½ × 157¾ in. (240 × 400.7 cm)
Gerald S. Elliott Collection
1995.78

Provenance

Gerald S. Elliott, Chicago, 1993.

MCA, 1995.

Exhibition History

In the Shadow of Storms: Art of the Postwar Era from the MCA Collection, MCA, July 2, 1996–May 25, 1997.

Sigmar Polke: A Retrospective Exhibition, Kunst-und Ausstellungshalle der Bundesrepublik Deutschland, Bonn, Germany, June 7–October 12, 1997; Nationalgalerie im Hamburger Bahnhof-Museum fur Gegenwart, Berlin, October 30, 1997–Feburary 15, 1998.

Decades in Dialogue: Perspectives on the MCA Collection, MCA, February 27–October 31, 1999.

Transmute, MCA, August 21–November 7, 1999.

People See Paintings: Photography and Painting from the MCA Collection, MCA, January 19–October 20, 2002.

References

Hentschel, Martin and Kevin Power. "Sigmar Polke: An Irreducible and Multiform Reality." *Flash Art* 29, no. 190 (October 1996), pp. 86–93.

Liebman, Lisa. "Sigmar Polke." *Artforum* 36, no. 5 (January 1998), pp. 89–90.

Moos, David. "Clairvoyant Memories: The Time of Sigmar Polke." *Art/Text*, no. 62 (August/September/October 1998), pp. 58–65.

Sigmar Polke: Illumination. Exh. cat. Minneapolis: Walker Art Center, 1995.

"Sigmar Polke's Art." *Warhol Beuys Polke.* Exh. cat. Milwaukee, Wis.: Milwaukee Art Museum, 1987. Pp. 97–101.

"Special Issue on Sigmar Polke." *Parkett*, no. 30 (December 1991).

Richard Prince

American, b. Panama Canal Zone, 1949
p. 166

Untitled (Sunset)

1981
Chromogenic development print
30 × 45 in. (76.2 × 114.3 cm)
Ed: 4/5
Gerald S. Elliott Collection
1995.79

Provenance

Barbara Gladstone Gallery, New York, 1981.

Gerald S. Elliott, Chicago, 1989.

MCA, 1995.

Exhibition History

Image Scavengers: Photography, Institute of Contemporary Art, Philadelphia, December 8, 1982–January 30, 1983.

Richard Prince, Centre National d'Art Contemporain de Grenoble, France, 1988.

Affinities and Intuitions: The Gerald S. Elliott Collection, The Art Institute of Chicago, May 9–July 29, 1990.

Conceptual Photography from the Gerald S. Elliott Collection, MCA, February 6–March 21, 1993.

Transmute, MCA, August 21–November 7, 1999.

People See Paintings: Photography and Painting from the MCA Collection, MCA, January 19–October 20, 2002.

Good News, Bad News

1989
Acrylic and screenprint on canvas
71 × 48 in. (180.3 × 121.9 cm)
Gerald S. Elliott Collection
1995.82

Provenance

Barbara Gladstone Gallery, New York, c. 1989–1990.

Gerald S. Elliott, Chicago, 1990.

MCA, 1995.

Exhibition History

PC Focus: Conceptualism to Postconceptualism, the 1960s to the 1990s, MCA, August 22–November 8, 1992.

Conceptual Photography from the Gerald S. Elliott Collection, MCA, February 6–March 21, 1993.

Transmute, MCA, August 21–November 7, 1999.

References

Deitcher, David. "Review of Richard Prince at Metro Pictures." *Art in America* 70, no. 6 (summer 1982), p. 144.

Image Scavengers: Photography. Exh. cat. Philadelphia: Institute of Contemporary Art, 1982.

Linker, Kate. "On Richard Prince's Photographs." *Arts Magazine* 57, no. 103 (November 1982), pp. 120–22.

Robbins, David. "Interview with Richard Prince." *Aperture*, no. 100 (autumn 1985), pp. 6–13.

Salvioni, Daniela. "On Richard Prince: Anthropological Findings of What Makes the American Libido Tick." *Flash Art*, no. 142 (October 1988), pp. 88–89.

Squiers, Carol. "Is Richard Prince a Feminist?" *Art in America* 81, no. 11 (November 1993), pp. 114–19.

Taylor, Paul. "Richard Prince Interview." *Flash Art*, no. 142 (October 1988), pp. 90–91, 121, 123.

Other Works in the MCA Collection

Untitled (three women's hands with gloves), 1980
Chromogenic development prints
Three parts, each: 27 × 40 in. (68.6 × 101.6 cm)
Gerald S. Elliott Collection
1995.81.a–c

Untitled (Four Perfume Containers), 1980
Chromogenic development prints
Four parts, each: 20 × 24 in. (50.8 × 61 cm)
Gift of Barbara Gladstone
2000.33.a–d

Two or Three Worlds, 1986
Chromogenic development print
86 × 48 in. (218.4 × 121.9 cm)
Ed: 1/2
Gift of Anne and William J. Hokin
1987.7

Super Heavy Santa, 1986
Chromogenic development print
86 × 48 in. (218.4 × 121.9 cm)
Artist's proof aside from an edition of 2
Gerald S. Elliott Collection
1995.80

Martin Puryear

American, b. 1941
p. 144

Untitled

1975–1978
Osage orangewood, maple, and brass studs
86 × 49½ × 9 in. (218.4 × 125.7 × 22.9 cm)
Restricted gift of Collectors Group, Men's Council, and Women's Board; Vaklova Purchase Award and purchase grants from the National Endowment for the Arts, and the Illinois Arts Council Purchase Grant
1985.15

Provenance

James Brookens, Washington, D.C., 1978.

Donald Young Gallery, Chicago, 1984.

MCA, 1985.

Exhibition History

Martin Puryear, Protetch-McIntosh Gallery, Washington, D.C., May 9–June 3, 1978.

Young Hoffman Gallery, Chicago, 1980.

Young Hoffman Gallery, Chicago, 1982.

American Painting and Sculpture from 1968 to the Present: Selections from the Permanent Collection, MCA, June 28–August 19, 1985.

Selected Recent Acquisitions from the Permanent Collection, MCA, February 8 – April 22, 1986.

Chicago Artists from the Permanent Collection, MCA, July 13 – August 21, 1987.

Selections from the Permanent Collection: Important Sculptural Works, MCA, April 25 – July 8, 1989.

Toward the Future: Contemporary Art in Context, MCA, May 5 – July 1, 1990.

In the Shadow of Storms: Art of the Postwar Era from the MCA Collection, MCA, July 2, 1996 – May 25, 1997.

Envisioning the Contemporary: Selections from the Permanent Collection, MCA, June 21, 1997 – April 5, 1998.

References

Benezra, Neal and Robert Storr. *Martin Puryear.* Chicago: The Art Institute; London and New York: Thames and Hudson, 1991.

Davies, Hugh Marlais and Helaine Posner. *Martin Puryear.* Exh. cat. Amherst, Mass.: University Gallery, University of Massachussetts at Amherst Press, 1984.

Forgey, Benjamin. "Draftmanship and Woodsmanship." *ARTnews* 77, no. 1 (January 1978), p. 121.

Martin Puryear: Public and Personal. Exh. cat. Chicago: Chicago Office of Fine Arts, 1987.

Christina Ramberg

American, 1946 – 1995
p. 132

Sleeve Mountain #1 and #2

1973
Acrylic on fiberboard
Two panels, each: 25 1/16 × 10 3/4 in.
(63.6 × 27.3 cm)
Gift of Albert J. Bildner
1974.7.a – b

Provenance

Albert J. Bildner, São Paulo, Brazil, c. 1973 – 74.

MCA, 1974.

Exhibition History

The School of The Art Institute Fellowship Exhibition, The Art Institute of Chicago, May 19 – June 24, 1973.

Made in Chicago, XII Bienal de São Paulo, Brazil, October – November 1973; National Collection of the Arts, Smithsonian Institution, Washington, D.C., October 31 – December 29, 1974; MCA, January 11 – March 2, 1975.

Chicago 77, Ohio State University, Columbus, November 1 – December 7, 1977.

Eleven Chicago Painters, Florida State University Gallery, Tallahassee, February 12 – March 3, 1978.

Contemporary Chicago Painters, University of Northern Iowa Gallery of Art, Cedar Falls, April 2 – April 30, 1978.

Selections from the Permanent Collection — A Major Show, MCA, May 3 – August 31, 1980.

Permanent Collection Exhibition, MCA, January 16 – March 14, 1982.

Chicago Imagists, Kansas City Art Institute, Kansas City, Mo., September 17 – October 10, 1982.

Joseph Yoakum: His Influence on Contemporary Art and Artists, Carl Hammer Gallery, Chicago, January 13 – February 17, 1984.

Ten Years of Collecting, MCA, April 13 – June 10, 1984.

Alternative Spaces: A History in Chicago, MCA, June 23 – August 19, 1984.

The Figure in Chicago: Selections from the Permanent Collection, MCA, February 19 – March 31, 1985.

Chicago Artists from the Permanent Collection, MCA, July 10 – August 21, 1987.

Portraits from the Permanent Collection of the MCA, College of DuPage Arts Center Gallery, Glen Ellyn, Ill., April 12 – May 26, 1988.

References

Christina Ramberg Drawings. Chicago: Gallery 400, College of Architecture and the Arts, University of Illinois at Chicago Press, 2000.

Christina Ramberg: A Retrospective 1968 – 1988. Exh. cat. Chicago: The Renaissance Society, The University of Chicago, 1988.

Contemporary Chicago Painters. Cedar Falls: University of Northern Iowa Gallery of Art Press, 1978.

Made in Chicago. Exh. cat. Washington, D.C.: National Collection of Fine Arts, Smithsonian Institution, 1974.

Spector, Buzz. "Christina Ramberg." *Artforum* 27, no. 2 (October 1988), pp. 153 – 54.

Taylor, Sue. "Christina Ramberg at The Renaissance Society." *Art in America* 76, no. 6 (June 1988), p. 166.

Who Chicago? An Exhibition of Contemporary Imagists. Exh. cat. Sunderland, Tyne, and Wear, England: Ceolfrith Gallery, Sunderland Arts Center, 1980.

Other Works in the MCA Collection

Muscular Alternative, 1979
Acrylic on Masonite
47 1/4 × 35 1/4 in. (120 × 89.5 cm)
Bequest of Sandra Jorgensen
1999.25

Robert Rauschenberg

American, b. 1925
p. 70

Retroactive II

1963
Oil, silk screen, and ink on canvas
80 × 60 in. (203.2 × 152.4 cm)
Partial gift of Stefan T. Edlis
and H. Gael Neeson
1998.49

Provenance

Galerie Ileana Sonnabend, Paris, 1964.

Leo Castelli Gallery, New York, 1966.

Mary Harari, Johannesburg, 1966.

Sotheby Parke-Bernet, New York, October 23, 1975, lot no. 428.

Galerie Beyeler, Basel, Switzerland, 1975.

James Goodman Gallery, New York.

Greenberg Van Doren Gallery, St. Louis, 1979.

James Corcoran Gallery, Los Angeles, 1979.

Private collection, New York, c. 1979.

Richard L. Feigen & Co., New York, 1982.

Stefan T. Edlis, Chicago, 1982.

MCA, 1998.

Exhibition History

Salon de Mai, Galerie Ileana Sonnabend, Paris, May 1964.

Robert Rauschenberg, Museum Haus Lange and Museum Haus Esters, Krefeld, Germany, September 12 – October 18, 1964.

Robert Rauschenberg Bilder Zeichnungen Lithos, Amerika Haus, West Berlin, January 8 – February 4, 1965.

Prospect/Retrospect: Europa 1946 – 1976, Stadtische Kunsthalle, Düsseldorf, Germany, October 20 – 31, 1976.

Arte USA, Fundacion Juan March, Madrid, February 9 – March 31, 1977; Fundacion Joan Miró, Barcelona, April 15 – June 12, 1977.

Two Hundred Years of American Paintings from Private Chicago Collections, Terra Museum of American Art, Evanston, Ill., June 25 – September 2, 1983.

Pop Art, Montreal Museum of Fine Arts, October 23, 1992 – January 24, 1993.

Under Development: Dreaming the MCA's Collection, MCA, April 30 – August 28, 1994.

Decades in Dialogue: Perspectives on the MCA Collection, MCA, February 27 – October 31, 1999.

The American Century: Art and Culture 1900 – 2000, Whitney Museum of American Art, New York, September 23, 1999 – February 27, 2000.

Age of Influence: Reflections in the Mirror of American Culture, MCA, March 14, 2000 – January 2, 2001.

Les Années Pop, Musée National d'Art Moderne, Centre Georges Pompidou, Paris, March 7 – June 18, 2001.

361

References

Arnason, H. H. *History of Modern Art: Painting, Sculpture, Architecture.* Englewood Cliffs, N.J.: Prentice Hall; New York: Harry N. Abrams, 1968. P. 580.

Ashberry, John. "U.S. Takeover Paris." *New York Herald Tribune,* May 24, 1964, p. 5.

Barotte, René. "Pour ses vingt ans le Salon de Mai consacre le 'Pop Art.'" *Elle,* no. 961 (May 1964).

Feinstein, Roni. *Robert Rauschenberg: The Silk-screen Paintings 1962–64.* New York: The Whitney Museum of American Art, 1990. P. 155.

Guttenberg, Lauren M. "The Image of Venus in the Work of Robert Rauschenberg." Master's thesis, The School of The Art Institute of Chicago, 1995.

Hopps, Walter. *Robert Rauschenberg: The Early 1950s.* Houston: Menil Collection, Houston Fine Art Press, 1991.

Kotz, Mary Lynn. *Rauschenberg, Art and Life.* New York: Harry N. Abrams, 1990.

Lucie-Smith, Edward. *Lives of the Great Twentieth-Century Artists.* London: Weidenfeld and Nicholson, 1986. P. 320.

Olson, Roberta M. "Rauschenberg, the Extraordinary Ragpicker." *Soho Weekly News,* March 31, 1977, p. 19.

Ragon, Michel. "L'Art de homo ludens." *Jardin des Arts,* no. 157 (December 1967), p. 43.

———. "Rauschenberg: la vendette de l'ecole de New York." *Beaux-Arts* (June 23–July 6, 1965), p. 4.

Rauschenberg Overseas Culture Exchange. Washington, D.C.: National Gallery of Art, 1991.

Robert Rauschenberg. Washington, D.C.: National Collection of Fine Arts, Smithsonian Institution, 1976–77.

Robert Rauschenberg Drawings 1958–1968. New York: Acquavella Contemporary Art., 1986.

Robert Rauschenberg: A Retrospective. New York: Solomon R. Guggenheim Museum, 1998.

Rose, Barbara. Interview of Robert Rauschenberg in *Rauschenberg.* New York: Vintage Books, 1987.

Other Works in the MCA Collection

Dante's Inferno, 1964
Portfolio with offset facsimiles on paper, lithograph on paper, and book
Portfolio: 2½ × 18¾ × 18½ in.
(6.4 × 47.6 × 47 cm)
Thirty-four facsimiles, each: 14½ × 11½ in.
(36.8 × 29.2 cm)
Lithograph: 15⅝ × 16⅛ in. (39.7 × 41 cm)
Book: 16⅞ × 17¼ × 1 in.
(42.8 × 43.8 × 2.5 cm)
Ed: 88/300
Gift of Mrs. Robert B. Mayer
1991.60.1–37

Cardbird IV, 1971
Collage of corrugated cardboard with photo offset and screen printing
38½ × 39¼ in. (97.8 × 99.7 cm)
Ed: 22/75
Gift of Century America Corporation, Chicago, courtesy of William J. Hokin
1983.6

Cardbird VII, 1971
Collage of corrugated cardboard with photo offset and screen printing
33 × 33¼ in. (83.8 × 84.5 cm)
Ed: 22/75
Gift of Century America Corporation, Chicago, courtesy of William J. Hokin
1983.7

Untitled, 1972
Watercolor, photo-transfer, newspaper rubbings, masking tape, colored pencil, graphite, and paper collage on paper
30⅝ × 22½ in. (77.8 × 57.2 cm)
Gift of Joseph and Jory Shapiro
1976.13

Ad Reinhardt
American, 1913–1967
p. 64

Abstract Painting
1962
Oil on canvas
60 × 60 in. (152.4 × 152.4 cm)
Gift of William J. Hokin
1981.44

Provenance

Noah Goldowsky, New York, 1962.

William J. Hokin, Chicago, 1966.

MCA, 1981.

Exhibition History

Den Inre och den Yttre Rymden (The Inner and the Outer Space); An Exhibition Devoted to Universal Art, Moderna Museet, Stockholm, Sweden, December 26, 1965–February 20, 1966.

Ad Reinhardt: Paintings, The Jewish Museum, New York, November 23, 1966–January 15, 1967.

Permanent Collection Exhibition, MCA, January 16–March 14, 1982.

Permanent Collection Exhibition, MCA, March 25–May 29, 1983.

Ten Years of Collecting, MCA, April 14–June 10, 1984.

Selections from the William J. Hokin Collection, MCA, April 20–June 16, 1985.

Toward the Future: Contemporary Art in Context, MCA, May 5–July 1, 1990.

In the Shadow of Storms: Art of the Postwar Era from the MCA Collection, MCA, July 2, 1996–May 25, 1997.

Envisioning the Contemporary: Selections from the Permanent Collection, MCA, June 21, 1997–April 5, 1998 and April 30, 1998–February 7, 1999.

Age of Influence: Reflections in the Mirror of American Culture, MCA, March 14, 2000–January 2, 2001.

People See Paintings: Photography and Painting from the MCA Collection, MCA, January 19–October 20, 2002.

References

Ad Reinhardt: Black Paintings 1951–1967. Exh. cat. New York: Marlborough Gallery, Inc., 1970.

"Ad Reinhardt: Three Statements." *Artforum* 4, no. 7 (March 1966), pp. 34–35.

Collective Vision. MCA, 1996.

Hulten, K. G., ed. *Den Inre och den Yttre Rymden (The Inner and the Outer Space); An Exhibition Devoted to Universal Art.* Exh. cat. Stockholm: Moderna Museet, 1965.

Jacob, Mary Jane et al. *Selections from the Permanent Collection, Vol. I.* MCA, 1984.

Lippard, Lucy. *Ad Reinhardt.* New York: Harry N. Abrams, 1981.

———. *Ad Reinhardt: Paintings.* Exh. cat. New York: The Jewish Museum, 1966.

Masheck, Joseph, ed. "Five Unpublished Letters from Ad Reinhardt to Thomas Merton and Two in Return." *Artforum* 17, no. 4 (December 1978), pp. 23–27.

Rose, Barbara. *Art-as-Art: The Selected Writings of Ad Reinhardt.* New York: Viking Press, 1975.

Smith, Walter. "Ad Reinhardt's Oriental Aesthetic." *Smithsonian Studies in American Art* 4, no. 3/4 (summer/autumn 1990), pp. 23–45.

Other Works in the MCA Collection

Untitled from the Wadsworth Athenaeum portfolio *Ten Works by Ten Painters,* 1964
Screenprint on paper, and folder
24 × 20 in. (61 × 50.8 cm)
Ed: 280/500
Gift of Mrs. Robert B. Mayer
1991.61.10.a–b

Untitled from the portfolio *New York International 1965,* c. 1965
Screenprint on Plexiglas
11¹⁵⁄₁₆ × 11¹⁵⁄₁₆ in. (30.3 × 30.3 cm)
Ed: 75/225
Gift of Edward Weiss
1981.52.6

Pipilotti Rist
Swiss, b. 1962
p. 268

Sip My Ocean
1996
Color video installation
9 minutes, 40 seconds
Dimensions variable
Ed: 2/3
Bernice and Kenneth Newberger Fund and restricted gift of Carol and Douglas Cohen
1996.39

362

Provenance

Gilli Stampa, Stampa Gallery, Basel, Switzerland, 1996.

MCA, 1996.

Exhibition History

Pipilotti Rist: Sip My Ocean, MCA, July 2 – August 25, 1996.

Pippilotti Rist: Sip My Ocean, MCA, May 23 – August 2, 1998.

Pipilotti Rist, Pitti Discovery, Florence, May 20 – June 5, 1999.

Cinematic Expression: Contemporary Video and Film, Jack S. Blanton Museum of Art, University of Texas, Austin, June 18 – August 8, 1999.

Pipilotti Rist, Fabric Workshop and Museum, Philadelphia, October 26, 1999 – February 19, 2000.

Pipilotti Rist, Art Gallery at the College of New Jersey, Ewing, October 11 – November 8, 2000.

Original Language: Highlights from the MCA Collection, MCA, March 24 – August 5, 2001.

Outer and Inner Space: A Video Exhibition in Three Parts, Virginia Museum of Fine Arts, Richmond, January 10 – March 17, 2002.

Sip My Ocean, Arizona State University Art Museum, Tempe, August 31, 2002 – January 5, 2003.

References

Molon, Dominic. *Pipilotti Rist: Sip My Ocean.* MCA, 1996.

Myers, Terry. "Grist for the Mill." *Art/Text,* no. 61 (May / June / July 1998), pp. 32 – 35.

Spector, Nancy. "The Mechanics of Fluids." *Parkett,* no. 48 (December 1996), pp. 83 – 85.

David Robbins

American, b. 1957
p. 190

Talent

1986
Gelatin silver prints
Eighteen parts, each: 10⅝ × 8⅝ in. (27 × 21.9 cm)
and part f: 8⅝ × 10⅝ in. (21.9 × 27 cm)
Ed: 59/100
Gift of Hudson
1997.10.a – r

Provenance

Hudson, New York, 1987.

MCA, 1997.

Exhibition History

Metro Pictures Gallery, New York, March 28 – April 25, 1987.

Fake Ecstasy With Me, MCA, July 12 – October 12, 1997.

Apposite Opposites: Photography from the MCA Collection, MCA, March 27 – August 1, 1999.

David Robbins, Institute of Visual Arts, Milwaukee, Wis., September 22 – November 22, 2000.

References

Decter, Joshua. "New York in Review." *Arts Magazine* 64, no. 7 (February 1990), p. 94.

Estep, Jan. "Do You Consider This a Career?" *New Art Examiner* 26, no. 2 (October 1998), pp. 26 – 31.

Morgan, Susan. "Write When You Get Work." *Artscribe International,* no. 65 (September / October 1987), pp. 52 – 54.

Olander, William. "Fake: A Meditation on Authenticity." In *Fake.* Exh. cat. New York: New Museum of Contemporary Art, 1987.

Rimanelli, David. "David Robbins, American Fine Arts Co." *Artforum* 28, no. 4 (December 1989), p. 139.

Other Works in the MCA Collection

Self-Parody, 1993
Gelatin silver prints
Eighteen parts:
seventeen parts: 10 × 8 in. (25.4 × 20.3 cm);
one part: 8 × 10 in. (20.3 × 25.4 cm)
Gift of James Mark Pedersen
1999.20.a – r

Dieter Roth

German, 1930 – 1998
p. 102

Stemplekasten (Rubber Stamp Box)

1968
Rubber stamps, inkpads, and instruction sheet in box
Box closed: 2½ × 11⅛ × 11⅛ in. (6.4 × 28.2 × 28.2 cm)
Gift of the artist
1984.24

Provenance

MCA, 1984.

Exhibition History

Options 19: Dieter Roth, MCA, February 18 – April 1, 1984.

Multiformity, MCA, July 6 – July 28, 2002.

References

Conzen, Ina. *Dieter Roth: Die Haut der Welt.* Exh. cat. Stuttgart, Germany: Staatsgalerie, 2000. P. 114.

Philpot, Clive. "Contemporary Artists and Their Books." In *Artists' Books.* Stuttgart, Germany: Institute for Foreign Cultural Relations and Authors, 1995. P. 102.

Roth, Dieter. *Gesammelte Werke, Band 36, 96 Piccadillies: Postkarten von Werken 1968 – 1977.* Stuttgart, Germany: Edition Hansjörg Mayer, 1977.

Other Works in the MCA Collection

96 Piccadillies, 1977
Artist's book
9½ × 7⅛ in. (24.1 × 18.1 cm)
Gift of Peter Giblin
1979.34.1

Self-Portrait as Piccadilly-Eros (Speedy Drawing), 1977
Graphite on paper
9 1/16 × 13 in. (23 × 33 cm)
Gift of Peter Giblin
1979.34.2

96 Piccadillies, 1977
Artist's book
9½ × 7⅛ in. (24.1 × 18.1 cm)
Gift of Martha D. Klein
1979.51.1

Self-Portrait as Piccadilly-Eros (Speedy Drawing), 1977
Graphite on paper
9 1/16 × 13 in. (23 × 33 cm)
Gift of Martha D. Klein
1979.51.2

2 times 5 BATS, 1978
Portfolio of offset prints and graphite on paper
Eleven prints and title page, each: 19⅞ × 13¾ in. (50.5 × 34.9 cm)
Drawing: 19 × 25 in. (48.3 × 63.5 cm)
Ed: 46/100
Gift of Steven Sohacki
1979.24.1–12

2 times 5 TROPHIES, 1978
Portfolio of offset prints and graphite on paper
Nine prints and title page, each: 19 ⅝ × 13⅞ in. (49.8 × 35.2 cm)
Drawing: 19 × 25 in. (48.3 × 63.5 cm)
Ed: 98/100
Gift of Robert S. Wax
1979.25.1–10

2 times 5 DOGS, 1979
Portfolio of lithographs on paper and graphite on paper
Eleven prints and title page, each: 19⅝ × 13⅞ in. (50.5 × 34.9 cm)
One print: 17 ¾ × 12 11/16 in. (45 × 32.2 cm)
Drawing: 19 × 25¼ in. (48.3 × 64.1 cm)
Ed: 22/100
Gift of Robert Layton
1979.21.1–14

Thomas Ruff

German, b. 1958
p. 196

Portrait (A. Wagner)

1985
Chromogenic development print
82½ × 65 in. (209.6 × 165.1 cm)
Ed: 2/4
Gift of Susan and Lewis Manilow in honor of Gerald S. Elliott
1995.9

Provenance

Fred Hoffman Gallery, Santa Monica, Calif., 1988.

Susan and Lewis Manilow, Chicago, 1989.

MCA, 1995.

Exhibition History

New Acquisitions: Works on Paper, MCA, July 24–September 21, 1997.

Apposite Opposites: Photography from the MCA Collection, MCA, March 27–August 1, 1999.

Age of Influence: Reflections in the Mirror of American Culture, MCA, March 14, 2000–January 2, 2001.

Portrait (Michael Van Ofen)
1987
Chromogenic development print
91¼ × 72¼ in. (231.8 × 183.5 cm)
Edition of 3
Gift of Susan and Lewis Manilow in honor of Gerald S. Elliott
1995.10

Provenance

Robin Lockett Gallery, Chicago.

Susan and Lewis Manilow, Chicago, 1989.

MCA, 1995.

Exhibition History

New Acquisitions: Works on Paper, MCA, July 24–September 21, 1997.

Apposite Opposites: Photography from the MCA Collection, MCA, March 27–August 1, 1999.

Age of Influence: Reflections in the Mirror of American Culture, MCA, March 14, 2000–January 2, 2001.

Portrait (Carolin Kewer)
1988
Chromogenic development print
83 × 65 in. (210.8 × 165.1 cm)
Ed: 3/4
Gerald S. Elliott Collection
1995.90

Provenance

303 Gallery, New York, 1988.

Gerald S. Elliott, Chicago, 1989.

MCA, 1995.

Exhibition History

Thomas Ruff, 303 Gallery, New York, April 25–May 6, 1989.

Affinities and Intuitions: The Gerald S. Elliott Collection of Contemporary Art, The Art Institute of Chicago, May 12–July 29, 1990.

PC Focus: Conceptualism to Postconceptualism: The 1960s to the 1990s, MCA, August 22–November 8, 1992.

People See Paintings: Photography and Painting from the MCA Collection, MCA, January 19–September 1, 2002.

Portrait (Heinz Haussman)
1988
Chromogenic development print
83 × 56 in. (210.8 × 165.1 cm)
Ed: 2/4
Gerald S. Elliott Collection
1995.91

Provenance

303 Gallery, New York, 1988.

Gerald S. Elliott, Chicago, 1989.

MCA, 1995.

Exhibition History

Thomas Ruff, 303 Gallery, New York, April 25–May 6, 1989.

Affinities and Intuitions: The Gerald S. Elliott Collection, The Art Institute of Chicago, May 9–July 29, 1990.

PC Focus: Conceptualism to Postconceptualism, the 1960s to the 1990s, MCA, August 22–November 8, 1992.

Conceptual Photography from the Gerald S. Elliott Collection, MCA, February 6–March 21, 1993.

Apposite Opposites: Photography from the MCA Collection, MCA, March 27–August 1, 1999.

Age of Influence: Reflections in the Mirror of American Culture, MCA, March 14, 2000–January 2, 2001.

People See Paintings: Photography and Painting from the MCA Collection, MCA, January 19–October 20, 2002.

d.p.b.02
1999
Laserchrome and diasec
73⅝ × 111⅝ in. (187 × 283.5 cm)
Ed: 3/5
Partial gift of Pamela and Michael Alper
2001.14

Provenance

Galerie Philip Nelson, Paris.

Pamela and Michael Alper, Chicago, 2001.

MCA, 2001.

Exhibition History

People See Paintings: Photography and Painting from the MCA Collection, MCA, January 19–October 20, 2002.

References

Birnbaum, Daniel. "Thomas Ruff." *Artforum* 35, no. 3 (November 1996), pp. 93, 127.

Garrels, Gary. *Photography in Contemporary German Art: 1960 to the Present.* Exh. cat. Minneapolis: Walker Art Center, 1992.

Myers, Terry. "Thomas Ruff: 303 Gallery." *Art/Text,* no. 62 (August/September/October 1998), pp. 82–83.

Pocock, Philip. "Thomas Ruff." *Journal of Contemporary Art* 6, no. 1 (summer 1993), pp. 78–86.

Rubinstein, Meyer Raphael. "Apollo in Düsseldorf." *Arts Magazine* 64, no. 2 (October 1988), pp. 41–43.

Ruff, Thomas. *Thomas Ruff: Andere Portraits + 3D.* Ostfildern, Germany: Hatje Cantz, 1995.

Wulffen, Thomas. "Thomas Ruff." *Flash Art* 26, no. 168 (January 1993), pp. 64–67.

Ed Ruscha
American, b. 1937
p. 94

Every Building on The Sunset Strip
1966
Artist's book
First edition
MCA Purchase
AB1981.584

Provenance

Printed Matter, Inc., New York, 1966.

MCA, 1981.

Exhibition History

Artists' Books and Recordings: Selections from the Permanent Collection, MCA, September 14–December 1, 1985.

Vast, N.A.M.E. Gallery, Chicago, November 17, 1995–January 13, 1996.

Artists' Books from the Permanent Collection, MCA, 1997.

Ed Ruscha Resource Gallery, MCA, November 4, 2000–February 2, 2001.

Whiskey A-Go-Go from The Sunset Strip series
1966/1995
Gelatin silver print
20 × 29 9/16 in. (50.8 × 75.1 cm)
Ed: 16/25 aside from 8 artist's proofs
Bernice and Kenneth Newberger Fund
1996.41.1

Gazzarri's Supper Club from The Sunset Strip series
1966/1995
Gelatin silver print
19¾ × 29 5/16 in. (50.2 × 74.4 cm)
Ed: 16/25 aside from 8 artist's proofs
Bernice and Kenneth Newberger Fund
1996.41.2

Schwab's Pharmacy from The Sunset Strip series
1976/1995
Gelatin silver prints
20⅛ × 29 9/16 in. (51.1 × 75.1 cm)
Ed: 16/25 aside from 8 artist's proofs
Bernice and Kenneth Newberger Fund
1996.41.3

**Greenblatt's Deli from
The Sunset Strip series**
1976/1995
Gelatin silver print
20 3/16 × 29 7/8 in. (51.3 × 75.9 cm)
Ed: 16/25 aside from 8 artist's proofs
Bernice and Kenneth Newberger Fund
1996.41.4

**Filthy McNasty's from
The Sunset Strip series**
1976/1995
Gelatin silver print
20 1/8 × 29 7/8 in. (51.1 × 75.9 cm)
Ed: 16/25 aside from 8 artist's proofs
Bernice and Kenneth Newberger Fund
1996.41.5

**Liquor Locker from
The Sunset Strip series**
1976/1995
Gelatin silver print
20 1/8 × 29 7/8 in. (51.1 × 75.9 cm)
Ed: 16/25 aside from 8 artist's proofs
Bernice and Kenneth Newberger Fund
1996.41.6

Provenance

Patrick Painter, Santa Monica, Calif, 1995.

MCA, 1996.

Exhibition History

New Acquisitions: Works on Paper, MCA,
July 24 – September 21, 1997.

*Apposite Opposites: Photography from the MCA
Collection,* MCA, March 2 – August 1, 1999.

Ed Ruscha Resource Gallery, MCA, November 4,
2000 – February 2, 2001.

References

Castleman, Riva. *A Century of Artists' Books.*
New York: The Museum of Modern Art, 1994.

Drucker, Johanna. *The Century of Artists' Books.*
New York: Granary Books, 1995.

Edward Ruscha Editions 1959 – 1999. Exh. cat.
Minneapolis: Walker Art Center, 1999.

Guest, Tim, ed. *Books by Artists.* Toronto:
Art Metropole, 1981.

Livet, Anne. *The Works of Edward Ruscha.* Exh.
cat. San Francisco: Museum of Modern Art;
New York: Hudson Hills, 1982.

Lyons, Joan, ed. *Artists' Books: A Critical
Anthology and Sourcebook.* Rochester, N.Y.:
Visual Studies Workshop, 1985.

Rosenzweig, Phyllis. "Sixteen (and Counting):
Ed Ruscha's Books." In *Ed Ruscha.* Washington,
D.C.: Hirshhorn Museum and Sculpture
Garden, Smithsonian Institution; Oxford:
Museum of Modern Art, 2000.

Schaffner, Ingrid. *Deep Storage.* Munich: Prestel,
1998. Pp. 240 – 42.

Sunshine and Noir: Art in L.A. 1960 – 97. Exh. cat.
Humlebaek, Denmark: Louisiana Museum of
Modern Art, 1997.

Other Works in the MCA Collection

News, Mews, Pews, Brews, Stews & Dues, 1970
Portfolio of organic screenprints on paper
Six prints, each: 23 × 31 1/4 in.
(58.4 × 80.6 cm)
Edition of 125
Gift of Nicolo Pignatelli
1979.29.1 – 9

Soil, 1971
Gunpowder and powdered pigment on paper
11 1/2 × 29 1/4 in. (29.2 × 74.3 cm)
Gift of Gerald S. Elliott
1978.48

People Yawning, 1982
Lithograph on paper
47 3/8 × 25 in. (120.3 × 63.5 cm)
Ed: 21/40
Gift of Robert Cottle and Barbara Balkin Cottle
1983.43

Words Without Thoughts, 1986
Acrylic on canvas
54 × 60 in. (137.2 × 152.4 cm)
Gift of Lannan Foundation
1997.49

Robert Ryman
American, b. 1930
p. 60

Untitled No. 25
1960
Oil on canvas
52 3/4 × 52 3/4 in. (133.9 × 133.9 cm)
Gerald S. Elliott Collection
1995.92

Provenance

Saatchi Collection, London, 1984.

Vivian Horan Fine Art, New York, c. 1990.

Larry Gagosian Gallery, New York.

Marc Blondeau S. A., Paris.

Stephen Mazoh, Inc., New York, 1993.

Gerald S. Elliott, Chicago, 1993.

MCA, 1995.

Exhibition History

*Bilderstreit. Widerspruch, Einheit und Fragment in
der Kunst seit 1960,* Museum Ludwig, Cologne,
Germany, April 8 – June 28, 1989.

*In the Shadow of Storms: Art of the Postwar Era
from the MCA Collection,* MCA, July 2, 1996 –
May 25, 1997.

*Envisioning the Contemporary: Selections from
the Permanent Collection,* MCA, June 21, 1997 –
April 5, 1998 and April 30, 1998 – February 7, 1999.

Adam Brooks: DeNaturalized, MCA, February
14 – July 5, 1998.

Examining Pictures: Exhibiting Paintings,
Whitechapel Art Gallery, London, May 7 –
June 27, 1999; MCA, July 24 – September 19,
1999; Armand Hammer Museum, Los Angeles,
February 3 – April 2, 2000.

*People See Paintings: Photography and Painting
from the MCA Collection,* MCA, January 19 –
October 20, 2002.

References

McEvilley, Thomas. "Absence Made Visible."
Artforum 30, no. 10 (summer 1992), pp. 92 – 96.

Sauer, Christel and Peter Pasquill, trans.
"Robert Ryman — An Introduction." In *Robert
Ryman.* Exh. cat. Zurich: Kunsthalle für
Internationale Neue Kunst, 1980. N.p.

Storr, Robert. "Simple Gifts." In *Robert Ryman.*
Exh. cat. London: Tate Gallery, 1993. Pp. 9 – 45.

Wood, Christopher S. "Ryman's Poetics." *Art in
America* 82, no. 1 (January 1994),
pp. 62 – 71.

Jason Salavon
American, b. 1970
p. 308

**The Top 25 Grossing Films
of All Time, 2 x 2**
2001
Color video installation
2 hours, 20 minutes
Dimensions variable
Ed: 1/5
Illinois Arts Council Purchase Grant and Bernice
and Kenneth Newberger Fund
2001.21

Provenance

Peter Miller Gallery, Chicago, 2001.

MCA, 2001.

References

BitStreams: Art in the Digital Age. Exh. brochure.
New York: Whitney Museum of American Art,
2001.

Camper, Fred. "Jason Salavon at Peter Miller."
Chicago Reader, April 20, 2001, sec. 2, p. 30.

Grabner, Michelle. *Jason Salavon.* Exh. brochure.
Glen Ellyn, Ill.: Gahlberg Gallery, College of
DuPage, 1999.

Hawkins, Margaret. "Finding Meaning in the
Mundane." *Chicago Sun-Times,* April 13, 2001,
p. 24.

Stein, Lisa. "Bits and Bytes Yield Brilliant Works
of Art." *CityTalk* (Chicago), April 13, 2001, p. 21.

David Salle
American, b. 1952
p. 182

Din
1984
Oil and fabric on canvas with wood
attachments
60 1/8 × 84 3/16 × 20 in.
(152.7 × 213.8 × 50.8 cm)
Gift of Ralph I. and Helyn D. Goldenberg
1992.91

365

Provenance

Mary Boone Gallery, New York, 1984.

Ralph I. and Helyn D. Goldenberg, Chicago, 1985.

MCA, 1992.

Exhibition History

School of Visual Arts, New York, October 1–20, 1984.

Mary Boone Gallery, New York, May 1985.

Selected Recent Acquisitions from the Permanent Collection, MCA, February 8–April 22, 1986.

David Salle, Institute of Contemporary Art, Philadelphia, October 9–November 30, 1986; Whitney Museum of American Art, New York, January 14–March 29, 1987; The Museum of Contemporary Art, Los Angeles, April 20–June 14, 1987; Art Gallery of Ontario, Toronto, July 17–September 17, 1987; MCA, November 21, 1987–January 10, 1988.

Permanent Collection: Promised Gifts Exhibition, MCA, October 3–November 28, 1989.

Toward the Future: Contemporary Art in Context, MCA, May 5–July 1, 1990.

New Acquisitions from the Permanent Collection, MCA, February 6–March 21, 1993.

In the Shadow of Storms: Art of the Postwar Era from the MCA Collection, MCA, July 2, 1996–May 25, 1997.

Decades in Dialogue: Perspectives on the MCA Collection, MCA, February 27–October 31, 1999.

References

Foster, Hal. "The 'Primitive' Unconscious of Modern Art, or White Skin Black Masks." In Hal Foster, ed. *Recodings: Art, Spectacle, Cultural Politics.* Seattle: Bay Press, 1985. Pp. 181–210.

Kardon, Janet and Lisa Phillips. *David Salle.* Exh. cat. Philadelphia: Institute of Contemporary Art, University of Pennsylvania Press, 1986.

Pincus-Witten, Robert. "An Interview with David Salle." *Flash Art*, no. 123 (summer 1985), pp. 35–36.

Schjeldahl, Peter. *Salle.* New York: Vintage Books, 1987.

Taylor, Paul. "How David Salle Mixes High Art and Trash." *New York Times*, January 11, 1987, sec. 6, pp. 28, 39–40.

Tuten, Frederick. "David Salle: At the Edges." *Art in America* 85, no. 9 (September 1997), pp. 78–83.

Whitney, David, ed. *David Salle.* New York: Rizzoli, 1994.

Julian Schnabel
American, b. 1951
p. 160

Aorta
1981
Oil on sisal rug with wooden artist's frame
118 × 166 × 6¾ in. (299.7 × 421.6 × 17.1 cm)
Gerald S. Elliott Collection
1995.93

Provenance

Mary Boone Gallery, New York, 1981.

Saatchi Collection, London, 1982.

Larry Gagosian Gallery, New York, 1989.

Gerald S. Elliott, Chicago, 1989.

MCA, 1995.

Exhibition History

Julian Schnabel, Tate Gallery, London, June 30–September 5, 1982.

Julian Schnabel, Leo Castelli Gallery, New York, April 30–June 4, 1983.

Julian Schnabel and Georg Baselitz, Akron Art Museum, Akron, Ohio, June 18–August 28, 1983.

Zeitgeist, Martin-Gropius-Bau, Berlin, 1983.

Affinities and Intuitions: The Gerald S. Elliott Collection of Contemporary Art, The Art Institute of Chicago, May 12–July 29, 1990.

Decades in Dialogue: Perspectives on the MCA Collection, MCA, February 27–October 31, 1999.

References

Julian Schnabel. Exh. cat. Amsterdam: Stedelijk Museum, 1982.

Julian Schnabel Paintings 1975–1986. Exh. cat. London: Whitechapel Art Gallery, 1986.

Kuspit, Donald. "Julian Schnabel." In Jeanne Siegel, ed. *Art Talk: The Early 80s.* New York: De Capo, 1988.

McGuigan, Cathleen. "Julian Schnabel: 'I Always Knew It Would Be Like This.'" *ARTnews* 81, no. 6 (summer 1982), pp. 88–94.

Ratcliff, Carter. "Art to Art: Julian Schnabel." *Interview* (October 1980).

Schnabel, Julian. *CVJ: Nicknames of Maitre D's & Other Excerpts from Life.* New York: Random House, 1987.

————. "The Patients and the Doctors." *Artforum* 22, no. 6 (February 1984), pp. 54–59.

Warrick Reed, Dupuy. "Julian Schnabel: The Truth of the Moment." *Arts Magazine* 54, no. 3 (November 1979), pp. 86–91.

Other Works in the MCA Collection

Painting for Allan Moss, 1981
Oil on jute
108 × 120 in. (274.3 × 304.8 cm)
Gift of Cooperfund, Inc.
1992.6

Untitled, 1988
Oil on tarpaulin
126 × 96½ in. (320 × 245.1 cm)
Gerald S. Elliott Collection
1995.94

George Segal
American, 1924–2000
p. 114

Man in Bar
1969
Plaster, tempera on metal, wood, and cloth
60½ × 24½ × 12⅜ in.
(153.7 × 62.2 × 31.4 cm)
Gift of Mr. and Mrs. E. A. Bergman
1974.12

Provenance

Sidney Janis Gallery, New York, 1970.

Mr. and Mrs. E. A. Bergman, Chicago, 1970.

MCA, 1974.

Exhibition History

Jewish Artists of the Twentieth Century, Maurice Spertus Museum of Judaica, Chicago, October 5–January 30, 1975.

George Segal: Sculptures, Walker Art Center, Minneapolis, October 29, 1978–January 7, 1979; San Francisco Museum of Modern Art, February 18–April 1, 1979; Whitney Museum of American Art, New York, May 16, 1979–July 8, 1979.

Selections from the Permanent Collection and the Robert B. Mayer Memorial Loan, MCA, January 13, 1980–February 8, 1981.

The Window in Twentieth-Century Art, Neuberger Museum at State University of New York, Purchase, N.Y., September 20, 1986–January 18, 1987; Contemporary Arts Museum, Houston, April 18–June 29, 1987.

George Segal: Works of 1959–1989, Sofia Imber Contemporary Art Museum of Caracas, Venezuela, 1989.

Modeling the Future: The New Museum and Key Works from the Permanent Collection, MCA, May 2–November 8, 1992.

Under Development: Dreaming the MCA's Collection, MCA, April 30–August 28, 1994.

The Body Present: Effigies, Decoys, and Other Equivalents, MCA, January 19–May 12, 2002.

References

Friedman, Martin and Graham W. J. Beal. *George Segal: Sculptures.* Exh. cat. Minneapolis: Walker Art Center, 1978.

George Segal: Environments. Philadelphia: Institute of Contemporary Art, University of Pennsylvania Press, 1976.

George Segal, A Retrospective: Sculptures, Paintings, and Drawings. Exh. cat. Montreal: Montreal Museum of Fine Arts, 1997.

George Segal: Sculpture. Miami, Fla.: Lowe Art Museum, University of Miami Press, 1983.

George Segal: Works of 1959 to 1989. Caracas, Venezuela: Sofia Imber Contemporary Art Museum of Caracas, 1991.

Hawthorne, Don and Sam Hunter. *George Segal.* New York: Rizzoli, 1989.

Kramer, Hilton. "George Segal, a Retrospective: Sculptures, Paintings, and Drawings." *The New Criterion* 17, no. 1 (September 1998), pp. 46–47.

Livingstone, Marco. *George Segal Retrospective.* Montreal: Montreal Museum of Fine Arts, 1998. Pp. 92–96.

Richard Serra
American, b. 1939
p. 108

Prop
1968
Lead antimony
86¼ × 60 × 57 in. (219.1 × 152.4 × 148.8 cm)
Gift of Mrs. Robert B. Mayer
1978.44 a–b

Provenance

Leo Castelli Gallery, New York, 1968.

Mr. and Mrs. Robert B. Mayer, Winnetka, Ill., 1969.

MCA, 1978.

Exhibition History

Contemporary Art from the Robert B. Mayer Collection, The David and Alfred Smart Museum of Art, The University of Chicago, January 21– March 15, 1976.

Richard Serra, Stedelijk Museum, Amsterdam, November 18, 1977–January 2, 1978.

Selected Sculpture from the Permanent Collection, MCA, March 23–July 1, 1979.

MCA Permanent Collection Exhibition, MCA, January 16–March 14, 1982.

Permanent Collection: Earth Art, MCA, October 29, 1982–January 25, 1983.

Permanent Collection Exhibition, MCA, June 4– August 1983.

American Painting and Sculpture from 1968 to the Present: Selections from the Permanent Collection, MCA, June 28–August 19, 1985.

Pop Art, Minimalism, and Earth Art, MCA, May 6–July 2, 1987 (at 333 W. Wacker); October 6–November 8, 1987 (at MCA).

Selections from the Permanent Collection: Sculptural Work, MCA, April 25– July 8, 1989.

Toward the Future: Contemporary Art in Context, MCA, May 5–July 1, 1990.

Power: Its Myths and Mores in American Art, 1961–1991, Indianapolis Museum of Art, Ind., September 5–November 3, 1991; Akron Art Museum, Akron, Ohio, January 18–March 21, 1992; Virginia Museum of Fine Arts, Richmond, Va., May 11–July 12, 1992.

In the Shadow of Storms: Art of the Postwar Era from the MCA Collection, MCA, July 2, 1996– May 25, 1997.

Envisioning the Contemporary: Selections from the Permanent Collection, MCA, June 21, 1997– April 5, 1998 and April 30, 1998–February 7, 1999.

Age of Influence: Reflections in the Mirror of American Culture, MCA, March 14, 2000– January 2, 2001.

References

Bois, Yve-Alain. "Richard Serra." *Artforum* 36, no. 5 (May 1998), p. 96.

Collective Vision. MCA, 1996.

Crimp, Douglas. "Serra's Public Sculpture: Redefining Site Specificity." In Laura Rosenstock, ed. *Richard Serra Sculpture*. New York: The Museum of Modern Art, 1986. Pp. 41–55.

Jacob, Mary Jane et al. *Selections from the Permanent Collection, Vol. I*. MCA, 1984.

Krauss, Rosalind E. "Richard Serra Sculpture." In Laura Rosenstock, ed. *Richard Serra Sculpture*. New York: The Museum of Modern Art, 1986. P. 20.

Stuckey, Charles F. "Minimalism: The Early Years." In Neal Benezra, ed. *Affinities and Intuitions, The Gerald S. Elliott Collection of Contemporary Art*. Exh. cat. Chicago: The Art Institute, 1990. Pp. 17–28.

Other Works in the MCA Collection

Another Look at a Corner, 1985
Hot-rolled Corten steel plates
Two parts, each: 54 × 54 × 1½ in.
(137.2 × 137.2 × 3.8 cm)
Gerald S. Elliott Collection
1995.95.a–b

Five Plate Pentagon, 1988
Hot-rolled Corten steel plates
Five parts, each: 66 × 61 × 2 in.
(154.9 × 154.9 × 5.1 cm)
Gerald S. Elliott Collection
1995.96.a–e

Andres Serrano
American, b. 1950
p. 246

The Morgue (Knifed to Death I and II)
1992
Silver dye-bleach prints
Two parts, each: 49 × 59½ in.
(124.5 × 151.1 cm)
Ed: 2/3
Restricted gift of Carol and Douglas Cohen, Lynn and Allen Turner, Ruth Horwich, H. Gael Neeson and Stefan T. Edlis; and Gerald S. Elliott by exchange
1996.4.a–b

Provenance

Paula Cooper Gallery, New York, 1992.

MCA, 1996.

Exhibition History

Aperto 1993, La Biennale di Venezia, Venice, June 13–October 10, 1993 (ed: 2/3).

Andres Serrano: The Morgue (Cause of Death), Paula Cooper Gallery, New York, January 23– February 20, 1993.

Andres Serrano, Center for Contemporary Art, Ujazdowski Castle, Warsaw, Poland, January 17–February 23, 1994; Moderna Galerija Ljubliana, Slovenia, March 1–April 3, 1994; Magazin4 Vorarlberger Kunstverein, Bregenz, Austria, May–June 1994.

Reflex, Vienna Secession, Vienna, April 12–24, 1994.

Andres Serrano: Works 1983–1993, Institute of Contemporary Art, University of Pennsylvania, Philadelphia, November 12, 1994–January 15, 1995; New Museum of Contemporary Art, New York, January 27–April 9, 1995; Center for Fine Arts, Miami, Fla., May 6–June 30, 1995; Contemporary Arts Museum, Houston, September 30–November 26, 1995; MCA, December 9, 1995–February 4, 1996; Malmö Konsthall, Malmö, Sweden, March 30–May 19, 1996. (Included only in the Malmö presentation).

Absolute Landscape: Between Illusion and Reality, Yokohama Museum of Art, Japan, February 1– March 30, 1997.

Apposite Opposites: Photography from the MCA Collection, MCA, March 27–August 1, 1999.

Transmute, MCA, August 21–November 7, 1999.

People See Paintings: Photography and Painting from the MCA Collection, MCA, January 19– October 20, 2002.

References

Andres Serrano: Works 1983–1993. Exh. cat. Philadelphia: Institute of Contemporary Art, University of Pennsylvania Press, 1994.

Bonami, Francesco. "Andres Serrano at Paula Cooper and Vik Muniz at Stux." *Flash Art* 26, no. 170 (May/June 1993), p. 83.

Budney, Jen, Emanuela de Cecco, Helena Kontova, and Giancarlo Politi. "Andres Serrano: Between Benetton and Caravaggio." *Flash Art* 28, no. 184 (October 1995), pp. 68–72.

Chimpen, Augusto. "Andres Serrano." *Art Nexus*, no. 15 (January/February/March 1995), pp. 108–9.

Harold, Jim. "Andres Serrano, The Sea of Possibility." *Art and Design* 12, no. 9/10 (September/October 1997), pp. 8–9.

Harold, Jim and Mark Durden. "The Morgue." *Creative Camera*, no. 326 (February/March 1994), pp. 10–15.

Lifson, Ben. "Andres Serrano at Paula Cooper." *Artforum* 31, no. 8 (April 1993), p. 94.

Saltz, Jerry. "Andres Serrano at Paula Cooper." *Art in America* 81, no. 5 (May 1993), p. 124.

Taylor, Victor Zamudio. "Andres Serrano, the Soul Needs to Know How to Walk." *Art Nexus*, no. 18 (October/November/December 1995), pp. 72–77.

Other Works in the MCA Collection

Nomads (Payne), 1990
Silver dye bleach print
40 × 32½ in. (101.6 × 82.6 cm)
Ed: 2/10
Partial and promised gift from
The Howard and Donna Stone Collection
2002.60

367

Cindy Sherman

American, b. 1954
p. 138

Untitled, A

1975
Gelatin silver print
20 × 16 in. (50.8 × 40.6 cm)
Ed: 9/10
Gift of Lannan Foundation
1997.57

Untitled, B

1975
Gelatin silver print
20 × 16 in. (50.8 × 40.6 cm)
Ed: 9/10
Gift of Lannan Foundation
1997.58

Untitled, C

1975
Gelatin silver print
20 × 16 in. (50.8 × 40.6 cm)
Ed: 9/10
Gift of Lannan Foundation
1997.59

Untitled, D

1975
Gelatin silver print
20 × 16 in. (50.8 × 40.6 cm)
Ed: 9/10
Gift of Lannan Foundation
1997.60

Untitled, E

1975
Gelatin silver print
20 × 16 in. (50.8 × 40.6 cm)
Ed: 9/10
Gift of Lannan Foundation
1997.61

Provenance

Metro Pictures Gallery, New York, 1993.

Linda Cathcart Gallery, Santa Monica, Calif., 1993.

Lannan Foundation, Los Angeles, 1993.

MCA, 1997.

Exhibition History

Facts and Figures: Selections from the Lannan Foundation Collection, Lannan Foundation Gallery, Los Angeles, October 22, 1994 – February 26, 1995.

Cindy Sherman Retrospective, The Museum of Contemporary Art, Los Angeles, November 2, 1997 – February 1, 1998; MCA, February 28 – May 31, 1998; Galerie Rudolfinum, Prague, June 25 – August 23, 1998; Musée d'Art Contemporain de Bordeaux, France, February 6 – April 25, 1999; Museum of Contemporary Art, Sydney, June 4 – August 29, 1999; Art Gallery of Ontario, Toronto, October 1, 1999 – January 2, 2000.

Instrumentalized Vision: From the World in a Box to Images on a Screen, The Getty Research Institute, Los Angeles, November 13, 2001 – February 3, 2002.

Untitled Film Still, #14

1978
Gelatin silver print
10 × 8 in. (25.4 × 20.3 cm)
Ed: 1/10
Gift of Lannan Foundation
1997.56

Provenance

Rhona Hoffman Gallery, Chicago, 1981.

Russell Bowman, Milwaukee, Wis., 1987.

Sotheby's, New York Contemporary Art, Part II, November 11, 1993, sale 6495 lot 215.

Lannan Foundation, Los Angeles, 1993

MCA, 1997.

Exhibition History

New Acquisitions: Works on Paper, MCA, July 24 – September 21, 1997.

Adam Brooks: DeNaturalized, MCA, February 14 – July 5, 1998.

Lovesexy: Identity and Desire in the MCA Collection, MCA, January 19 – April 21, 2002.

Untitled, #137

1984
Chromogenic development print
70½ × 47¾ in. (179.1 × 121.3 cm)
Ed: 2/5
Gerald S. Elliott Collection
1995.98

Provenance

Metro Pictures Gallery, New York, 1984.

Gerald S. Elliott, Chicago, 1984.

MCA, 1995.

Exhibition History

Cindy Sherman, National Art Gallery, Wellington, New Zealand, June 17 – August 13, 1989; Waikato Museum of Art and History, Hamilton, New Zealand, August 30 – October 8, 1989.

Affinities and Intuitions: The Gerald S. Elliott Collection of Contemporary Art, The Art Institute of Chicago, May 12 – July 29, 1990.

Conceptual Photography from the Gerald S. Elliott Collection, MCA, February 6 – March 21, 1993.

In the Shadow of Storms: Art of the Postwar Era from the MCA Collection, MCA, July 2, 1996 – May 25, 1997.

Decades in Dialogue: Perspectives on the MCA Collection, MCA, February 27 – October 31, 1999.

Age of Influence: Reflections in the Mirror of American Culture, MCA, March 14, 2000 – January 2, 2001.

Untitled

1987
Chromogenic development print
40 × 30 in. (101.6 × 76.2 cm)
Ed: 1/35
Gift of the Men's Council
1987.3

Provenance

MCA Men's Council commission.

Exhibition History

Portraits: From the Permanent Collection of the MCA, Arts Center Gallery, College of DuPage, Glen Ellyn, Ill., April 12 – May 26, 1988.

The Insistent Subject: Photographing Time and Again, MCA, September 8 – November 4, 1995.

References

Collective Vision. MCA, 1996.

Cruz, Amada, Elizabeth A. T. Smith, and Amelia Jones. *Cindy Sherman Retrospective.* Exh. cat. MCA; Los Angeles: The Museum of Contemporary Art, 1997.

Danto, Arthur. *Cindy Sherman: Untitled Film Stills.* New York: Rizzoli, 1990.

Other Works in the MCA Collection

Untitled Film Still, #8, 1978
Gelatin silver print
8 × 10 in. (20.3 × 25.4 cm)
Ed: 1/10
Gift of Lannan Foundation
1997.52

Untitled Film Still, #9, 1978
Gelatin silver print
8 × 10 in. (20.3 × 25.4 cm)
Ed: 1/10
Gift of Lannan Foundation
1997.55

Untitled Film Still, #29, 1979
Gelatin silver print
8 × 10 in. (20.3 × 25.4 cm)
Ed: 1/10
Gift of Lannan Foundation
1997.53

Untitled Film Still, #49, 1979
Gelatin silver print
8 × 10 in. (20.3 × 25.4 cm)
Ed: 1/10
Gift of Lannan Foundation
1997.54

Untitled, #153, 1985
Chromogenic development print
65½ × 47½ in. (166.4 × 120.6 cm)
Ed: 4/6
Gift of Gerald S. Elliott by exchange
1985.41

Untitled, #147, 1985
Chromogenic development print
49½ × 72¾ in. (125.7 × 184.8 cm)
Ed: 1/6
Gerald S. Elliott Collection
1995.99

Untitled, #152, 1985
Chromogenic development print
71 1/4 × 48 1/2 in. (181 × 123.2 cm)
Ed: 5/6
Gerald S. Elliott Collection
1995.100

Untitled, #166, 1986
Chromogenic development print
55 1/2 × 32 3/4 in. (141 × 83.2 cm)
Ed: 1/6
Gift of Lannan Foundation
1997.62

Untitled, #167, 1987
Chromogenic development print
60 1/4 × 90 1/4 in. (153 × 229.2 cm)
Ed: 4/6
Gift of Susan and Lewis Manilow in honor of
Gerald S. Elliott
1993.10

Untitled, #172, 1987
Chromogenic development print
72 1/2 × 48 1/2 in. (184.2 × 123.2 cm)
Ed: 1/6
Gift of Susan and Lewis Manilow
in honor of Gerald S. Elliott
1993.11

Untitled, #188, 1989
Chromogenic development print
45 1/4 × 67 in. (114.9 × 170.2 cm)
Ed: 3/6
Gerald S. Elliott Collection
1995.101

Yinka Shonibare
British, b. 1962
p. 286

Alien Obsessives, Mum, Dad and the Kids
1998
Wax printed cotton, plastic, and polyester
fiberfill on plastic and metal armatures
Installed: dimensions variable
Restricted gift of Donna and Howard Stone
1999.54.a – h

Provenance

Stephen Friedman Gallery, London, 1998.

MCA, 1999.

Exhibition History

Tablet, the Tabernacle, London, 1998.

Yinka Shonibare Alien Obsessives, Norwich
Gallery, Norwich School of Art and Design, Vt.,
November 26 – December 18, 1998.

Dressing Down, Ikon Gallery, Birmingham,
England, February 10 – April 4, 1999.

Heaven, Kunsthalle, Düsseldorf, Germany,
July 30 – October 17, 1999; Tate Liverpool,
England, December 9, 1999 – February 27, 2000.

*Age of Influence: Reflections in the Mirror of
American Culture,* MCA, March 14, 2000 –
January 2, 2001.

Vision Boo1, Malmö, Sweden, May 17 –
September 16, 2001.

*Double Dress: Yinka Shonibare, A Nigerian/British
Artist,* The Israel Museum, Jerusalem, May 30 –
October 29, 2002.

References

Cameron, Dan. *Nka: Journal of Contemporary
African Art,* no. 11/12, 2000.

Enwezor, Okwui. "Yinka Shonibare: The Joke Is
on You." *Flash Art* 30, no. 197 (November/
December 1997), pp. 96 – 97.

Guha, Tania. "Yinka Shonibare." *Third Text,*
no. 37 (summer 1994), pp. 87 – 90.

Lynch, Fiona. *Birmingham Post,* March 1999,
p. 53.

Ratnam, Niru. *Art Monthly,* no. 225 (April 1999),
pp. 40 – 41.

Waxman, Lori. "Yinka Shonibare: Camden Arts
Centre, London." *New Art Examiner* 28, no. 3
(November 2000), pp. 36 – 37.

Hollis Sigler
American, 1948 – 2001
p. 162

She Wants To Belong To The Sky, Again
1981
Oil on canvas with painted artist's frame
43 1/8 × 61 1/4 in. (109.5 × 155.6 cm)
Illinois Arts Council Purchase Grant;
and Matching Funds
1982.25

Provenance

Barbara Gladstone Gallery, New York, 1981.

MCA, 1982.

Exhibition History

A Journey to Somewhere from Nowhere,
University of South Florida Art Galleries,
Tampa, February 19 – March 12, 1982.

Eight Artists: The Anxious Edge, Walker Art
Center, Minneapolis, April 25 – June 13, 1982.

Recent Acquisitions to the Permanent Collection,
MCA, September – October 1982.

Selections from the Permanent Collection, MCA,
March 25 – May 29, 1983.

Ten Years of Collecting, MCA, April 14 – May 20,
1984.

*The Figure in Chicago Art: Selections from the
Permanent Collection,* MCA, February 19 –
March 31, 1985.

Selections from the Permanent Collection, MCA,
August 19 – September 28, 1986.

*Hollis Sigler: Paintings, Drawings, and Prints
1976 – 1986,* Akron Art Center, Akron, Ohio,
November 14, 1986 – January 18, 1987; Gallery of
the Chicago Public Library Cultural Center,
Chicago, January 24 – March 21, 1987.

Chicago Artists from the Permanent Collection,
MCA, July 10 – August 21, 1987.

Word and Image, MCA, August 1 –
September 8, 1987.

Partners in Purchase: Selected Works 1976 – 1989,
Illinois Arts Council, State of Illinois Art Gallery,
Chicago, September 18 – November 9, 1989.

*Realism, Figurative Painting, and the Chicago
Viewpoint,* MCA, July 20 – August 27, 1991.

Small Details, Lakeview Museum of Art and
Science, Peoria, Ill., 1994.

*In the Shadow of Storms: Art of the Postwar Era
from the MCA Collection,* MCA, July 2, 1996 –
November, 1996.

Art in Chicago, 1945 – 1995, MCA, November 16 –
March 23, 1997.

*Envisioning the Contemporary: Selections from
the Permanent Collection,* MCA, June 21, 1997 –
April 5, 1998.

References

Boris, Staci. *Hollis Sigler: Breast Cancer Journal.*
Exh. cat. MCA, 1994.

Eight Artists: The Anxious Edge. Exh. cat.
Minneapolis: Walker Art Center, 1982.

Horsfield, Kate and Lyn Blumenthal. "Interview
with Hollis Sigler." *Profile* 3, no. 2 (March 1983).

Love, Susan and James Yood. *Hollis Sigler's
Breast Cancer Journal.* New York: Hudson Hills,
1999.

Schwartzman, Allan. *A Journey to Somewhere
from Nowhere.* Tampa: University of South
Florida Art Galleries Press, 1982.

Storr, Robert. "Hollis Sigler at Barbara
Gladstone." *Art in America* 70, no. 4 (April
1982), p. 142.

Taylor, Sue. "Hollis Sigler and Dan Ramirez."
New Art Examiner 1, no. 6 (March 1983),
pp. 9, 29.

Westfall, Stephen. "Hollis Sigler." *Arts Magazine*
56, no. 9 (May 1982), pp. 32 – 33.

Other Works in the MCA Collection

Discover Hidden Talents, Develop Special Abilities,
1981
Oil on canvas with painted artist's frame
47 1/16 × 65 in. (119.5 × 165.1 cm)
Gift of The Robert A. Lewis Fund in honor of
William and Polly Levey
1982.8

He Could Never Declare His Love to Her, 1981
Oil pastel on paper
28 × 34 in. (71.1 × 86.4 cm)
Gift of Hollis Sigler
1999.7

Inside She Was Bleeding, 1981
Oil pastel on paper
28 × 34 in. (71.1 × 86.4 cm)
Gift of Hollis Sigler
1999.8

He Passed Her His Poisoned Heart, 1981/1999
Oil pastel on paper
28 × 34 in. (71.1 × 86.4 cm)
Gift of Hollis Sigler
1999.9

369

She Wanted More, 1981/1999
Oil pastel on paper
28 × 34 in. (71.1 × 86.4 cm)
Gift of Hollis Sigler
1999.10

He Was Heartless, She Was Poison, 1981/1999
Oil pastel on paper with painted artist's frame
28 × 34 in. (71.1 × 86.4 cm)
Gift of Hollis Sigler
1999.11

Everything Money Can Buy, 1981/1999
Oil pastel on paper with painted artist's frame
28 × 34 in. (71.1 × 86.4 cm)
Gift of Hollis Sigler
1999.12

He Was Always Hungry for Power, 1981/1999
Oil pastel on paper with painted artist's frame
28 × 34 in. (71.1 × 86.4 cm)
Gift of Hollis Sigler
1999.13

There Is A Doubt, She Could Be Right, 1982
Lithograph on paper
27 × 31 in. (68.6 × 78.7 cm)
Ed: 29/35
Gift of Hollis Sigler
1999.15

They Were Right, They Are Perfect, 1982
Lithograph on paper
27 × 31 in. (68.6 × 78.7 cm)
Ed: 27/35
Gift of Hollis Sigler
1999.16

She Always Thought She Was Wrong, 1982
Lithograph on paper
27 × 31 in. (68.6 × 78.7 cm)
Ed: 26/35
Gift of Hollis Sigler
1999.17

She Was Tired of Filling Her Heart With Hopeless Dreams, 1983
Lithograph on paper
27 × 31 in. (68.6 × 78.7 cm)
Ed: 33/35
Gift of Hollis Sigler
1999.18

When You Least Expect It, 1986
Hand-colored lithograph in Plexiglas box
13 × 16 3/8 × 8 3/8 in. (33 × 41.6 × 21.3 cm)
Ed: 1/35
Gift of the Men's Council
1986.33

Some Kind of Love, 1992
Oil on canvas with painted artist's frame
49 1/2 × 61 1/2 in. (125.7 × 156.2 cm)
Gift of Hollis Sigler
1999.6

From Me All Things Proceed and to Me They Must Return, 1992
Oil pastel on paper
36 × 75 in. (91.4 × 190.5 cm)
Ed: 29/35
Gift of Hollis Sigler
1999.14

Lorna Simpson
American, b. 1960
p. 240

Flipside
1991
Gelatin silver prints and Plexiglas plaque
Installed, approximately: 51 1/4 × 69 3/4 in.
(130.2 × 177.2 cm)
Ed: 3/3
Partial and promised gift from
The Howard and Donna Stone Collection
2002.62.a–c

Provenance

Josh Baer Gallery, New York, 1991

Howard and Donna Stone, Chicago, 1991.

MCA, 2002.

Exhibition History

Lorna Simpson: For the Sake of the Viewer, MCA, November 21, 1992–March 14, 1993; The Contemporary Museum, Honolulu, Hawaii, June 8–August 1, 1993; Contemporary Arts Center, Cincinnati, Ohio, September 5–November 7, 1993; Henry Art Gallery, University of Washington, Seattle, November 24, 1993–February 6, 1994; The Studio Museum in Harlem, New York, February 25–April 30, 1994; Tel Aviv Museum of Art, Israel, August 30–October 27, 1994.

Rhapsody: Selections from Valley Collections, Arizona State University Art Museum, Tempe, February 10–May 13, 2001.

Bio
1992
Internal dye diffusion transfer process prints and engraved Plexiglas plaques
Installed, approximately: 98 × 162 in.
(248.9 × 411.5 cm)
Gift of Maremont Corporation by exchange; purchased through funds provided by AT&T NEW ART/NEW VISIONS
1992.90 a–u

Provenance

Josh Baer Gallery, New York, 1992.

Rhona Hoffman Gallery, Chicago, 1992.

MCA, 1992.

Exhibition History

Lorna Simpson, Rhona Hoffman Gallery, Chicago, March 6–April 4, 1992.

Lorna Simpson, Josh Baer Gallery, New York, May 16–June 20, 1992.

Lorna Simpson: For the Sake of the Viewer, MCA, November 21, 1992–March 14, 1993; The Contemporary Museum, Honolulu, Hawaii, June 8–August 1, 1993; Contemporary Arts Center; Cincinnati, Ohio, September 5–November 7, 1993; Henry Art Gallery, University of Washington, Seattle, November 24, 1993–February 6, 1994; The Studio Museum in Harlem, New York, February 25–April 30, 1994; Tel Aviv Museum of Art, Israel, August 30–October 27, 1994.

In the Shadow of Storms: Art of the Postwar Era from the MCA Collection, MCA, July 2, 1996–May 25, 1997.

Apposite Opposites: Photography from the MCA Collection, MCA, March 27–August 1, 1999.

References

Albee, Edward. *The Death of Bessie Smith.* New York: Signet, 1959. Pp. 24–25.

Collective Vision. MCA, 1996.

Fusco, Coco. "Uncanny Dissonance: The Work of Lorna Simpson." In *English Is Broken Here: Notes on Cultural Fusion in the Americas.* New York: The New Press, 1995. Pp. 97–102. Originally published in *Lorna Simpson.* Exh. cat. Hamilton, N.Y.: Colgate University Press, 1991.

hooks, bell. "Yearning: An Aesthetic of Blackness." In *Race, Gender, and Cultural Politics.* Boston: South End Press, 1990. Pp. 103–113.

Mercer, Kobena. "Black Hair/Style Politics." In *Welcome to the Jungle: New Positions in Black Cultural Studies.* New York: Routledge, 1994. Pp. 97–128.

Simpson, Lorna and Sarah J. Rodgers. *Lorna Simpson: Interior/Exterior, Full/Empty.* Exh. cat. Columbus, Ohio: Wexner Center for the Arts, Ohio State University Press, 1997.

Willis, Deborah. "Eyes in the Back of Your Head: The Work of Lorna Simpson." In *Lorna Simpson (Untitled 54).* Exh cat. San Franscisco: The Friends of Photography, 1992.

Wright, Beryl J. and Saidya V. Hartman. *Lorna Simpson: For the Sake of the Viewer.* Exh. cat. MCA, 1992.

Other Works in the MCA Collection

Tricks Are For, 1987
Gelatin silver prints and engraved Plexiglas plaques
Panel one: 51 × 33 1/4 in. (129.5 × 84.4 cm)
Panel two: 41 × 35 1/4 in. (104.1 × 89.5 cm)
Panel three: 41 × 50 3/4 in. (104.1 × 128.9 cm)
Panel four: 37 × 38 3/4 in. (94 × 98.4 cm)
Partial and promised gift from The Howard and Donna Stone Collection
2002.64.a–g

Necklines, 1989
Gelatin silver prints and engraved Plexiglas plaques
Installed, approximately: 68 1/2 × 70 in.
(174 × 177.8 cm)
Ed: 1/2
Partial and promised gift from The Howard and Donna Stone Collection
2002.63.a–e

Two Sisters and Two Tongues, 1991
Color Polaroids
Installed, approximately: 32 1/2 × 83 1/4 in.
(81.8 × 211.5 cm)
Ed: 1/2
Gift of Susan and Lewis Manilow in honor of Gerald S. Elliott
1993.32.a–f

She, 1992
Color Polaroids and engraved Plexiglas plaques
Installed, approximately: 29 × 85 1/4 × 2 in.
(73.7 × 216.5 × 5.1 cm)
Ed: 3/4
Gift of Judith Neisser
1996.3.a–e

Wigs (Portfolio), 1994
Waterless lithograph on felt
Installed, approximately: 72 × 162½ in.
(182.9 × 412.8 cm)
Ed: 4/15
Gift of Rhona Hoffman Gallery and the artist
1996.19.a–ll

The Clock Tower, 1995
Serigraph on felt panels
Twelve parts, each: 33½ × 22½ in.
(85.1 × 57.2 cm)
Ed: 2/3
Bernice and Kenneth Newberger Fund
1996.42.a–l

Robert Smithson
American, 1938–1973
p. 90

A Nonsite (Franklin, New Jersey)
1968
Painted wooden bins, limestone,
gelatin silver prints and typescript
on paper with graphite and transfer
letters, mounted on mat board
Bins installed: 16½ × 82¼ × 103 in.
(41.9 × 208.9 × 261.6 cm);
Board: 40¹/₁₆ × 30¹/₁₆ in. (101.8 × 76.4 cm)
Gift of Susan and Lewis Manilow
1979.2.a–g

Provenance

Dwan Gallery, New York, 1968.

Susan and Lewis Manilow, Chicago, 1979.

MCA, 1979.

Exhibition History

Earthworks, Dwan Gallery, New York,
October 5–30, 1968.

Probing the Earth: Contemporary Land Projects,
Hirshhorn Museum and Sculpture Garden,
Smithsonian Institution, Washington, D.C.,
October 27, 1977–January 2, 1978; Museum of
Contemporary Art, La Jolla, Calif., January 27–
February 26, 1978; Seattle Art Museum,
March 23–May 21, 1978.

Selected Sculpture from the Permanent Collection,
MCA, March 23–July 1, 1979 and July 6–
October 7, 1979.

The Permanent Collection, MCA, May 24–
August 31, 1980.

Robert Smithson: Sculpture, Herbert F. Johnson
Museum, Cornell University, Ithaca, N.Y.,
November 14–December 21, 1980; Walker Art
Center, Minneapolis, February 8–March 22,
1981, MCA, April 10–June 14, 1981; Museum of
Contemporary Art, La Jolla, Calif., August 14–
September 25, 1981; Laguna Gloria Art
Museum, Austin, Tex., November 13, 1981–
January 10, 1982; Whitney Museum of American
Art, New York, February 16–April 18, 1982.

Robert Smithson: Retrospective, Paris
ARC/Musée d'Art Moderne de la Ville de Paris,
November 30, 1982–January 16, 1983.

*Earth Art and Related Works from the Permanent
Collection,* MCA, October 29, 1983–January 25,
1984.

Ten Years of Collecting, MCA, April 13–June 10,
1984.

*Transformations in Sculpture: Four Decades of
American and European Art,* Solomon R.
Guggenheim Museum, New York, 1985.

*American Painting and Sculpture from 1968 to
the Present: Selections from the Permanent
Collection,* MCA, June 28–August 19, 1985.

Pop, Minimalism, and Earth Art, MCA,
October 6–November 8, 1987.

*The New Sculpture 1965–1975: Between
Geometry and Gesture,* Whitney Museum of
American Art, New York, February 20–June 3,
1990; The Museum of Contemporary Art, Los
Angeles, February 17–July 7, 1991.

Toward the Future: Contemporary Art in Context,
MCA, May 5–July 1, 1990.

*PC Focus: Conceptualism to Postconceptualism,
the 1960s to the 1990s,* MCA, August 22–
November 8, 1992.

*Robert Smithson: Une Retrospective, Le Paysage
Entropique 1960–1973,* IVAM, Centre Julio
Gonzalez, Valencia, Spain, April 22–June 13,
1993 (as *Robert Smithson: El Paisage Entropico
Una retrospectiva 1960–1973*); Musée d'art
Contemporain, Galeries Contemporaines des
Musées de Marseilles, France, September 23–
December 11, 1994; Palais des Beaux-Arts,
Brussels, Belgium, June 16–August 28, 1994.

Robert Smithson/Tony Tasset: Site/Nonsite, MCA,
October 7–December 3, 1995.

*In the Shadow of Storms: Art of the Postwar Era
from the MCA Collection,* MCA, July 2, 1996–
May 25, 1997.

Robert Smithson, Museet for Samtidskunst,
Oslo, Norway, February 27, 1999–May 5, 1999;
Moderna Museet, Stockholm, Sweden, June 16,
1999–September 1, 1999; Arken Museum of
Modern Art, Copenhagen, Denmark, October 2,
1999–January 16, 2000.

eccovention, The Contemporary Arts Center,
Cincinnati, Ohio, June 21–August 25, 2002.

Mirror Stratum
1966
Mirrors
10⅛ × 35 × 35 in. (25.7 × 88.9 × 88.9 cm)
Gift of Ralph I. and Helyn D. Goldenberg
1982.26

Provenance

John Weber Gallery, New York.

Ralph I. and Helyn D. Goldenberg.

MCA, 1982.

Exhibition History

*Earthart and Related Works from the Permanent
Collection,* MCA, October 19, 1983–January 25,
1984.

Ten Years of Collecting, MCA, April 13–June 10,
1984.

*Abstract Painting and Sculpture: 1950s–1980s—
Selections from the Permanent Collection,* MCA,
October 22, 1985–April 13, 1986.

*Modeling the Future: The New Museum and Key
Works from the Permanent Collection,* MCA,
May 2–November 8, 1992.

Robert Smithson Retrospective, IVAM, Valencia,
Spain, April 22–June 20, 1993; Musée de
Marseilles, France, September 24–December 17,
1994; Palais des Beaux Arts, Brussels, June 16–
August 28, 1994; Art Gallery of Ontario,
Toronto, May 1–July 30, 1995.

References

Capasso, Nicholas. "Environmental Art:
Strategies for Reorientation in Nature." *Arts
Magazine* 59, no. 5 (January 1985), pp. 73–77.

Collective Vision. MCA, 1996.

Glueck, Grace. "Moving Mother Earth."
New York Times, October 6, 1968, p. D38.

Holt, Nancy, ed. "Smithson's Non-Site Sights,
an Interview with Anthony Robbin."
In *The Writing of Robert Smithson: Essays with
Illustrations.* New York: New York University
Press, 1979. P. 157.

Jacob, Mary Jane et al. *Selections from the
Permanent Collection, Vol. I.* MCA, 1984.

Kurtz, Bruce. "Review: Robert Smithson at the
Whitney." *Art in America* 70, no. 4 (April 1982),
pp. 135–36.

Lippard, Lucy. *Six Years: The Dematerialization of
the Art Object from 1966 to 1972.* New York:
Praeger, 1973.

Robbin, Anthony. "Smithson's Non-Site Sights."
ARTnews 29, no. 2 (February 1969), pp. 50–53.

Ruwedel, Mark. "The Land as Historical
Archive." *American Art* 10, no. 1 (spring 1996),
pp. 36–41.

Other Works in the MCA Collection

Blueprint for Glass Stratum, 1967
Photocopy on paper
13½ × 22⅛ in. (33.5 × 56.2 cm)
Gift from the Estate of the artist
1982.29.a–b

The Spiral Jetty, 1970
16mm color film
35 minutes
Gift of Muriel K. Newman
1978.40

Movie Script for Broken Circle, Holland, c. 1970
Graphite on paper
12⅝ × 11¹/₁₆ in. (32.1 × 28.1 cm)
Gift of Ruth and Robert Vogele
1986.1

Buzz Spector
American, b. 1948
p. 234

Malevich: With Eight Red Rectangles
1991
Painted wood and books
96 × 80 in. (243.8 × 203.2 cm), variable depth
Ed: 1/3
Restricted gift of LaSalle Bank
1993.31.a–i

Provenance

Roy Boyd Gallery, Chicago, 1991.

MCA, 1993.

Exhibition History

Knowledge: Aspects of Contemporary Art, University Art Museum, Santa Barbara, Calif., January 8–February 23, 1992; Santa Monica Museum of Art, Calif., April 2–June 14, 1992; North Carolina Museum of Art, Raleigh, August 8–October 25, 1992.

Buzz Spector: Cards and Letters, Roy Boyd Gallery, Santa Monica, Calif., February 29–March 28, 1992.

Buzz Spector: Further Re:Collections, Roy Boyd Gallery, Chicago, June 4–July 6, 1993.

References

McCracken, David. "Buzz Spector Comments on Art and Artists." *Chicago Tribune,* June 25, 1993, sec. 7, p. 56.

Pagel, David. "Buzz Spector Reconfigures Malevich Masterpiece." *Los Angeles Times,* March 12, 1992, p. F14.

Relyea, Lane. "Buzz Spector at Roy Boyd Gallery." *Artforum* 30, no. 9 (May 1992), p. 124.

Other Works in the MCA Collection

Stone Book (Astounding Revelations), 1983
Altered book with stones
9¼ × 12¼ in. (23.5 × 31.1 cm)
Gift of Roy Boyd Gallery, Chicago
1984.9

Stone Book, 1983
Altered book with stones and shells
8 × 11¾ in. (20.3 × 29.8 cm)
Restricted gift of Ira G. Wool and Illinois Arts Council Purchase Grant
1984.10

Library, 1984
Altered book pages, rocks, and wood
11 × 61¾ × 12¾ in. (27.9 × 156.8 × 32.4 cm)
Gift of Howard and Donna Stone
1995.122.a–w

Mallarmé, 1987–88
Wooden curio cabinet, gold leaf on glass, book, and shell
56 × 26 × 14½ in.
(142.2 × 66 × 36.8 cm)
Restricted gift of LaSalle Bank
1997.72.a–c

Strata, 1989
Silk screen on paper, bookcase, and books
Installed, approximately: 96 × 63 × 12 in.
(243.8 × 160 × 30.5 cm)
Gift of Tom and Linda Heagy
2000.23.a–aaa

Decorum, 1989
Graphite, ink, gesso, wax, and postcards on paper
78 × 78 in. (198.1 × 198.1 cm)
Gift of Tom and Linda Heagy
2000.24

Waterfalls, 1991
Postcards, paper, and aluminum
71 × 10½ × 8¼ in. (180.3 × 26.7 × 21 cm)
Bernice and Kenneth Newberger Fund
1991.22.a–b

Malevich, 1992
Screenprint with embossing on paper
22⅝ × 19⅛ in. (57.5 × 48.6 cm)
Artist's proof aside from an edition of 20
Gift of the artist
1994.8

MCA Piece, 1998
Altered book
Closed: 8⅝ × 5¾ × 1⅛ in.
(21.9 × 14.6 × 2.8 cm)
Gift of the artist
1998.52

Haim Steinbach

American, b. Israel 1944
p. 188

Untitled (cabbage, pumpkin, pitchers) #1

1986
Plastic laminated wood shelf, ceramic pitchers and tureen, and stuffed toy pumpkin
54³⁄₁₆ × 84 × 27½ in.
(137.6 × 213.4 × 69.8 cm)
Restricted gift of Anne and William J. Hokin and Bernice and Kenneth Newberger Fund
1987.1 a–i

Provenance

Rhona Hoffman Gallery, Chicago, 1986.

MCA, 1987.

Exhibition History

Recent Acquisitions: The Permanent Collection, MCA, August 1–November 3, 1987.

Selections from the Permanent Collection: Important Sculptural Works, MCA, April 25–July 8, 1989.

Toward the Future: Contemporary Art in Context, MCA, May 5–July 1, 1990.

PC Focus: Conceptualism to Postconceptualism, the 1960s to the 1990s, MCA, August 22–November 8, 1992.

Envisioning the Contemporary: Selections from the Permanent Collection, MCA, April 30, 1998–February 7, 1999.

Decades in Dialogue: Perspectives on the MCA Collection, MCA, February 27–October 31, 1999.

References

Budney, Jed. "Haim Steinbach." *Flash Art* 29, no. 191 (November/December 1996), pp. 88–92.

Cotter, Holland. "Haim Steinbach: Shelf Life." *Art in America* 76, no. 5 (May 1988), pp. 156–63, 202.

Damaged Goods: Desire and the Economy of the Object. Exh. cat. New York: New Museum of Contemporary Art, 1986. Pp. 13–34.

Objectives: The New Sculpture. Exh. cat. Newport Beach, Calif.: Newport Harbor Art Museum, 1990. Pp. 154–62.

Beat Streuli

Swiss, b. 1957
p. 298

Chicago, July 99

(detail)
1999
Silver dye-bleach transparencies on Plexiglas
Overall: dimensions variable, each of sixty-eight parts: 63 × 63 in. (160 × 160 cm)
Restricted gift of the Collectors Forum; support for original commission from Sara Albrecht and Bill Nygren
2000.17.1–17

Provenance

MCA, 2000.

Exhibition History

Beat Streuli, MCA, October 14, 1999–June 5, 2000.

Semi-permanent. Parts of this work are on display every year.

References

Beat Streuli, City. Exh. cat. Düsseldorf, Germany: Kunsthalle Düsseldorf; Zurich: Kunsthalle Zurich; Ostfildern-Ruit, Germany: Hatje Cantz, 1999.

Brittain, David. Interview of Beat Streuli in "The Crowd." *Creative Camera* (August/September 1997), pp. 35–38.

Danto, Arthur. "Beat Streuli's Gesamtkunstwerk." *Parkett,* no. 54 (December 1998/January 1999).

Heartney, Eleanor. "Beat Streuli and Adrian Schiess at the New York Kunsthalle." *Art in America* 85, no. 6 (June 1997), p. 112.

Verzotti, Giorgio. "A Flash." *Artforum* 34, no. 1 (September 1995), pp. 68–71.

Zdanovics, Olga. "Beat Streuli." *Art Papers* 24, no. 3 (May/June 2000), p. 48.

Thomas Struth

German, b. 1954
p. 210

Via Sanita, Naples

1989
Gelatin silver print
17⅛ × 23⅝ in. (43.5 × 60 cm)
Ed: 6/10
Gerald S. Elliott Collection
1995.105

Provenance

Luhring Augustine Gallery, New York, 1989.

Gerald S. Elliott, Chicago, 1989.

MCA, 1995.

Exhibition History

John Kessler, Stephen Prina, Thomas Struth, Luhring Augustine Gallery, New York, March 16– April 15, 1989.

Affinities and Intuitions: The Gerald S. Elliott Collection of Contemporary Art, The Art Institue of Chicago, May 12–July 29, 1990.

Kunsthistorisches Museum I, Vienna
1989–1990
Chromogenic development print
mounted to Plexiglas
72 × 94 in. (182.9 × 238.7 cm)
Ed: 3/10
Gift of William J. Hokin,
The Dave Hokin Foundation
1993.24

Provenance

Marian Goodman Gallery, New York, 1990.

MCA, Eleventh Benefit Art Auction, October 16, 1993, lot. 45.

William J. Hokin, The Dave Hokin Foundation, Chicago, 1993.

MCA, 1993.

Exhibition History

Thomas Struth, Marian Goodman Gallery, New York, September 11–October 13, 1990.

Thomas Struth, Museum Photographs, Hirshhorn Museum and Sculpture Garden, Smithsonian Institution, Washington, D.C., May 21–August 16, 1992; Kunsthalle, Hamburg, Germany, November 11, 1993– January 16, 1994.

In the Shadow of Storms: Art of the Postwar Era from the MCA Collection, MCA, July 2, 1996– May 25, 1997.

Adam Brooks: DeNaturalized, MCA, February 14–July 5, 1998.

Apposite Opposites: Photography from the MCA Collection, MCA, March 27–August 1, 1999.

People See Paintings: Photography and Painting from the MCA Collection, MCA, January 19– October 20, 2002.

Todai-Ji Temple, Hall of the Great Buddha, Nara
1996
Chromogenic development print
mounted to Plexiglas
69½ × 90½ in. (176.5 × 229.9 cm)
Ed: 6/10
Gift of LaSalle Bank
2000.15

Provenance

Marian Goodman Gallery, New York, 1996.

LaSalle Bank, Chicago, 1997.

MCA, 2000.

Exhibition History

Original Language: Highlights from the MCA Collection, MCA, March 24–August 5, 2001.

Milan Cathedral (Interior), Milan
1998
Chromogenic development print
mounted to Plexiglas
74⅝ × 89 in. (189.5 × 226.1 cm)
Ed: 3/10
Restricted gift of LaSalle Bank, Antje and John Jelinek, and Judith Neisser
2000.10

Provenance

Marian Goodman Gallery, New York, 1999.

MCA, 2000.

Exhibition History

Age of Influence: Reflections in the Mirror of American Culture, MCA, March 14, 2000– January 2, 2001.

Original Language: Highlights from the MCA Collection, MCA, March 24–August 5, 2001.

People See Paintings: Photography and Painting from the MCA Collection, MCA, January 19– October 20, 2002.

References

Belting, Hans. *Thomas Struth Museum Photographs.* Munich: Schirmer/Mosel, 1998.

Collective Vision. MCA, 1996.

Hapgood, Susan. "Thomas Struth at Marian Goodman Gallery." *Art in America* 79, no. 1 (January 1991), pp. 125–26.

Kuspit, Donald. "Thomas Struth — Marian Goodman." *Artforum* 29, no. 4 (December 1990), pp. 132–33.

Loock, Ulrich. "Thomas Struth." *Creative Camera* 5 (May 1988), pp. 14–19.

Saltz, Jerry. "What Is the Reason for Your Visit to This Museum?" *Arts Magazine* 65, no. 5 (January 1991), pp. 13–14.

Schwabsky, Barry. "Thomas Struth." *Arts Magazine* 65, no. 4 (December 1990), p. 83.

Thomas Struth. Exh. cat. Dallas: Dallas Museum of Art, 2002.

Thomas Struth — Photographs. Exh. cat. Chicago: The Renaissance Society, The University of Chicago Press, 1990.

Thomas Struth, Strangers, and Friends. Exh. cat. Boston: Institute of Contemporary Art; Cambridge, Mass.: MIT Press, 1994.

Other Works in the MCA Collection

Via Giovanni a Mare, Naples, 1988
Gelatin silver print
17 × 23½ in. (43.2 × 59.7 cm)
Unnumbered edition of 10
Gerald S. Elliott Collection
1995.103

Via Medina, Naples, 1988
Gelatin silver print
17 × 23½ in. (43.2 × 59.7 cm)
Unnumbered edition of 10
Gerald S. Elliott Collection
1995.104

The Shimada Family, Yamaguchi, 1986, 1989
Chromogenic development print
17 × 23½ in. (43.2 × 59.7 cm)
Ed: 4/10
Gerald S. Elliott Collection
1995.102

Hiroshi Sugimoto
Japanese, b. 1948
p. 238

Time Exposed
1991
Photolithographs and text on paper
and aluminum portfolio
Fifty-eight parts, each: 13⅞ × 18¼ in.
(35.2 × 46.4 cm)
Unnumbered first edition of 500
Gift of Maremont Corporation by exchange
1993.25.1–58

Provenance

Fraenkel Gallery, San Francisco, 1991.

MCA, 1993.

Exhibition History

Envisioning the Contemporary: Selections from the Permanent Collection, MCA, June 21, 1997– April 5, 1998.

References

Brougher, Kerry. *Hiroshi Sugimoto.* Exh. cat. Los Angeles: The Museum of Contemporary Art, 1993.

Bryson, Norman. "Hiroshi Sugimoto's Metabolic Photography." *Parkett,* no. 46 (1996), pp. 120–23.

Camhi, Leslie. "Time Traveler." *ARTnews* 98, no. 2 (February 1999), pp. 92–93.

Cooke, Lynne and Mark Francis, eds. "Hiroshi Sugimoto." In *Carnegie International 1991.* Vol. 2. Pittsburgh: The Carnegie Museum of Art, 1991. P. 128.

Denson, G. Roger. "Satori Among the Stills." *Parkett,* no. 46 (1996), pp. 143–51.

Feldman, Melissa E. "Hiroshi Sugimoto." *Art Monthly,* no. 208 (July/August 1997), pp. 29–30.

Kellein, Thomas. *Time Exposed.* Exh. cat. Basel, Switzerland: Kunsthalle Basel; New York and London: Thames and Hudson, 1995.

Koplos, Janet. "Through a Japanese Viewfinder." *Art in America* 85, no. 3 (March 1997), pp. 84–85.

Other Works in the MCA Collection

Sanju San-gen-do, The Hall of Thirty-three Bays, 1995
Gelatin silver print
18¾ × 23¾ in. (47.6 × 60.3 cm)
Restricted gift of Paul and Dedrea Gray in memory of Joseph Randall Shapiro
1996.21

Tony Tasset

American, b. 1960

p. 192

Button Progression

1986
Leather cushions and wood
Installed, approximately: 22 × 196 × 19 in.
(55.9 × 497.8 × 48.3 cm)
Gift of Thea Westreich
1991.102.a–c

Provenance

Feature, Chicago, 1986.

Thea Westreich, New York, 1986.

MCA, 1991.

Exhibition History

*PC Focus: Conceptualism to Postconceptualism,
the 1960s to the 1990s*, MCA, August 22–
November 8, 1992.

*Decades in Dialogue: Perspectives on the MCA
Collection*, MCA, February 27–October 31, 1999.

Abstraction with Wedges

1990
Plexiglas and poplar
5¾ × 44¼ × 43¼ in.
(14.6 × 112.4 × 109.9 cm)
Bernice and Kenneth Newberger Fund; and
Illinois Arts Council Partners in Purchase Grant
1991.23.a–f

Provenance

Rhona Hoffman Gallery, Chicago, 1991.

MCA, 1991.

Exhibition History

Tony Tasset, Rhona Hoffman Gallery, Chicago,
January 4–26, 1991.

New Acquisitions: The MCA Collects, MCA,
November 23, 1991–January 26, 1992.

Art in Chicago, 1945–1995, MCA, November 16,
1996–March 23, 1997.

Selections from MCA Collection, MCA,
October 14–November 26, 2000.

References

Anxious Objects. Exh. cat. Normal, Ill.: University
Galleries, Illinois State University Press, 1987.

Henry, Gerrit. "Tony Tasset at Christine Burgin."
Art in America 75, no. 6 (June 1987), pp. 157–58.

Hixson, Kathryn. "Transcendence to
Transformation: The Art of Tony Tasset." *New
Art Examiner* 27, no. 8 (May 2000), pp. 34–37.

Kirshner, Judith Russi. "The Benefit of Doubt
or Loving Modernism to Death." *Artforum* 27,
no. 3 (November 1998), pp. 106–111.

Tony Tasset: Recent Works. Exh. cat. London:
Karsten Schubert Ltd. in association with
Christine Burgin, New York, 1987.

Other Works in the MCA Collection

Museum Abstraction, 1986
Painted wood and Naugahyde cushions
Wall component: 35⅞ × 83⅝ × 4 in.
(91.1 × 212.4 × 10.2 cm)
Bench: 17 × 81 × 25½ in.
(43.2 × 205.7 × 64.8 cm)
Gift of Susan and Lewis Manilow
1991.101.a–b

Wedge Bench, 1986
Painted Medite and leather
32 × 60 × 19 in. (81.3 × 152.4 × 48.3 cm)
Gift of Susan and Lewis Manilow
1993.33

Cloth Drop, 1990
Cloth, gelatin silver print, and wood frame
Cloth: 143 × 117 in. (363.2 × 297.2 cm)
Framed photograph: 14½ × 16½ in.
(36.8 × 41.9 cm)
Gift of the artist
1995.120.a–c

Untitled, 1993
Enamel on Medite
18 × 36 × 18 in. (45.7 × 91.4 × 45.7 cm)
Gift of Hudson
1997.13

Robert Smithson (Las Vegas), 1995
Silver dye-bleach print
83 × 49 × 3 in. (210.8 × 124.5 × 7.6 cm)
Ed: 1/3
Gift of the artist and Rhona Hoffman Gallery;
restricted gift of Jack and Sandra P. Guthman
1995.123

Richard Tuttle

American, b. 1941

p. 98

Purple Octagon

1967
Dyed canvas
54¹³⁄₁₆ × 55½ in. (139.2 × 141 cm)
Gift of William J. Hokin
1982.69

Provenance

Betty Parsons Gallery/Noah Goldowsky, New
York, 1967.

William J. Hokin, Chicago, 1969.

MCA, 1982.

Exhibition History

Betty Parsons Gallery, New York, 1967.

*Thirty-First Biennial Exhibition of Contemporary
American Painting*, Corcoran Gallery of Art,
Washington, D.C., February 1–March 16, 1969.

Permanent Collection Exhibition, MCA,
March 25–May 29, 1983.

Toward the Future: Contemporary Art in Context,
MCA, May 5–July 1, 1990.

*Jorge Pardo with rotating works from the
Permanent Collection*, MCA, January 25–
February 2, 1997.

*Envisioning the Contemporary: Selections from
the Permanent Collection*, MCA, June 21, 1997–
April 5, 1998 and April 30, 1998–February 7, 1999.

*People See Paintings: Photography and Painting
from the MCA Collection*, MCA, January 19–
October 20, 2002.

References

Pincus-Witten, Robert. "The Art of Richard
Tuttle." *Artforum* (February 1970), pp. 62–67.

———. *Postminimalism*. London: Out of
London Press, 1997.

Tuttle, Richard, Herausgegeben Von Jochen
Poetter, ed. *Richard Tuttle Chaos, Die the Form*.
New York: Distributed Art Publishers, 1994.

Tuttle, Richard, Jennifer Gross, and Matthias
Haldemann, ed. *Richard Tuttle: Replace the
Abstract Picture Plane*. Ostfildern, Germany:
Hatje Cantz, 2001.

Von Erich, Franz and Richard Tuttle. *Richard
Tuttle: Perceived Obstacles*. Cologne, Germany:
Buchhandlung Walther Konig, 2001.

Whitney, Kathleen. "Richard Tuttle:
No Way You Can Frame It." *Sculpture Magazine*
(March 1998), pp. 33–37.

Kara Walker

American, b. 1969

p. 272

Presenting Negro Scenes Drawn Upon My Passage through the South and Reconfigured for the Benefit of Enlightened Audiences Wherever Such May Be Found, By Myself, Missus K. E. B. Walker, Colored

1997
Paper and watercolor on paper
Wall installation of sixty-five paper silhouettes,
approximately: 13 × 150 ft. (4 × 45.7 m)
Gift of Susan and Lewis Manilow
1999.52

Provenance

Wooster Gardens, New York, 1997.

Susan and Lewis Manilow, Chicago, 1997.

MCA, 1999.

Exhibition History

Kara Walker, The Renaissance Society, The
University of Chicago, January 22–February 23,
1997.

*Age of Influence: Reflections in the Mirror of
American Culture*, MCA, March 14, 2000–
January 2, 2001.

References

Armstrong, Elizabeth et al. *No Place
(Like Home)*. Exh. cat. Minneapolis: Walker
Art Center, 1997.

Garrels, Gary. *Kara Walker: Upon My Many
Masters — An Outline*. Exh. brochure. San
Francisco: Museum of Modern Art, 1997.

Janus, Elizabeth, "As American as Apple Pie."
Parkett, no. 59 (September 2000), pp. 130–41.

Salz, Jerry. "Ill-Will and Desire." *Flash Art* 29,
no. 191 (November/December 1996), pp. 82–86.

Shaw, Gwendolyn Dubois. "Final Cut." *Parkett*,
no. 59 (September 2000), pp. 129–33.

Sheets, Hilarie M. "Cut It Out." *ARTnews* 101,
no. 4 (April 2002), pp. 126–29.

Subotnick, Ali. "Kara Walker." *Make* 92 (2002), pp. 25–27.

Walker, Hamza. "Nigger Lover or Will There Be Any Black People in Utopia?" *Parkett*, no. 59 (September 2000), pp. 152–58.

Jeff Wall
Canadian, b. 1946
p. 206

Pleading
1988
Silver dye-bleach transparency and light box
54 × 73½ × 9¼ in. (137.2 × 186.7 × 23.5 cm)
Ed: 1/3 aside from 1 artist's proof
Gerald S. Elliott Collection
1995.106

Provenance

Marian Goodman Gallery, New York, c. 1988–89.

Gerald S. Elliott, Chicago, 1989.

MCA, 1995.

Exhibition History

Affinities and Intuitions: The Gerald S. Elliott Collection of Contemporary Art, The Art Institute of Chicago, May 12–July 29, 1990.

Conceptual Photography from the Gerald S. Elliott Collection, MCA, February 6–March 21, 1993.

In the Shadow of Storms: Art of the Postwar Era from the MCA Collection, MCA, July 2, 1996– May 25, 1997.

Envisioning the Contemporary: Selections from the Permanent Collection, MCA, June 21, 1997– April 5, 1998 and April 30, 1998–February 7, 1999.

Original Language: Highlights from the MCA Collection, MCA, March 24–August 5, 2001.

People See Paintings: Photography and Painting from the MCA Collection, MCA, January 19– October 20, 2002.

References

Barents, Els. "Typology, Luminescence, Freedom." In *Jeff Wall Transparencies.* New York: Rizzoli, 1987.

Brougher, Kerry. *Jeff Wall.* Exh. cat. Los Angeles: The Museum of Contemporary Art, 1997.

Crow, Thomas. "Profane Illuminations: The Social History of Jeff Wall." In *Modern Art in the Common Culture.* New Haven, Conn.: Yale University Press, 1996.

Dufour, Gary. "Against the Reality/Fiction of History." In *Jeff Wall 1990.* Exh. cat. Vancouver: Vancouver Art Gallery, 1990.

Jeff Wall. MCA; Paris: Galerie National Jeu de Paume; London: Whitechapel Art Gallery, 1995.

Jones, Bill. "False Documents." *Arts Magazine* 64, no. 9 (May 1990), pp. 51–55.

Jones, Bill. "The Truth is Out There." *On Paper* 1, no. 6 (July/August 1997), pp. 20–23.

Reid, Calvin. "Jeff Wall." *Arts Magazine* 64, no. 4 (December 1989), p. 79.

Vine, Richard. "Wall's Wager." *Art in America* 84, no. 4 (April 1996), pp. 86–93.

Other Works in the MCA Collection

Diagonal Composition, 1995
Silver dye-bleach transparency and light box
19½ × 22½ × 5 in. (49.5 × 57.2 × 12.7 cm)
Ed: 4/10
Partial and promised gift from
The Howard and Donna Stone Collection
2002.66

Andy Warhol
American, 1928–1987
p. 66

Troy Diptych
1962
Silk-screen ink on synthetic polymer paint on canvas
81 × 110¾ in. (205.7 × 281.3 cm)
Gift of Mrs. Robert B. Mayer
1984.1.a–b

Provenance

Stable Gallery, New York, c. 1962–63.

Mr. and Mrs. Robert B. Mayer, Winnetka, Ill., 1963.

MCA, 1984.

Exhibition History

Contemporary Art from the Robert B. Mayer Collection, The David and Alfred Smart Museum of Art, The University of Chicago, January 21– March 26, 1976.

Museum of Contemporary Art on Michigan: Selections from the Permanent Collection, MCA, November 1, 1983–January 1, 1984.

Ten Years of Collecting, MCA, April 13– June 10, 1984.

Nouveau Realism and Pop Art: Selections from the Permanent Collection, MCA, September 6– November 12, 1985.

Selections from the Permanent Collection, MCA, February 25–April 22, 1986.

Pop, Minimalism, and Earth Art, MCA, October 6–November 8, 1987.

Andy Warhol: A Retrospective, The Museum of Modern Art, New York, February 1–May 2, 1989; The Art Institute of Chicago, May 31– August 13, 1989; Hayward Gallery, London, September 7–November 5, 1989; Museum Ludwig, Cologne, Germany, November 20, 1989–February 11, 1990; Palazzo Grassi, Venice, February 24–May 27, 1990; Musée National d'Art Moderne, Centres Georges Pompidou, Paris, June 19–September 10, 1990.

Toward the Future: Contemporary Art in Context, MCA, May 5–July 1, 1990.

Modeling the Future: The New Museum and Key Works from the Permanent Collection, MCA, May 2–November 11, 1992.

In the Shadow of Storms: Art of the Postwar Era from the MCA Collection, MCA, July 2, 1996– May 25, 1997.

Envisioning the Contemporary: Selections from the Permanent Collection, MCA, June 21, 1997– April 5, 1998 and April 30, 1998–February 7, 1999.

Hall of Mirrors: Art and Film since 1945, The Museum of Contemporary Art, Los Angeles, March 17–July 28, 1996; The Wexner Center for the Arts, Columbus, Ohio, September 21, 1996–January 5, 1997; Palazzo delle Esposizioni, Rome, June–September 1997; MCA, October 11, 1997–January 25, 1998.

Decades in Dialogue: Perspectives on the MCA Collection, MCA, February 27–October 31, 1999.

References

Bourdon, David. *Warhol.* New York: Harry N. Abrams, 1989.

Collective Vision. MCA, 1996.

"Collectors: A Life of Involvement." *Time* 91, no. 13 (March 29, 1968), pp. 68–75.

Crone, Rainer, and John W. Gabriel, trans. *Andy Warhol.* New York: Praeger, 1970. Pp. 69, 110–11.

Fineberg, Jonathan. *Art since 1940: Strategies of Being.* New York: Harry N. Abrams, 1995. Pp. 250–59.

Garrels, Gary, ed. *The Works of Andy Warhol.* Seattle: Bay Press, 1989.

Jacob, Mary Jane et al. *Selections from the Permanent Collection, Vol. I.* MCA, 1984.

Judd, Donald. "Andy Warhol." *Arts Magazine* 37, no. 4 (January 1963), p. 49.

McShine, Kynaston, ed. *Andy Warhol: A Retrospective.* New York: The Museum of Modern Art, 1989.

Schirmer's Visual Dictionary. Munich: Schirmer/Mosel, 1990.

Superstar. Produced and directed by Chuck Workman. 87 min. Marlin Lewis Entertainment Ltd, 2000, 1990. DVD.

Other Works in the MCA Collection

Jacqueline Kennedy I from the portfolio *Volume I — Eleven Pop Artists 1965,* c. 1965
Screenprint on paper
23¹⁵/₁₆ × 20 in. (60.8 × 50.8 cm)
Ed: 27/200
Gift of Edward Weiss
1981.49.1

Jacqueline Kennedy II from the portfolio *Volume II — Eleven Pop Artists 1965,* 1965
Screenprint on paper
23¾ × 20¾ in. (60.3 × 52.7 cm)
Edition of 200
Gift of Edward Weiss
1981.50.5

Untitled from the portfolio *Ten Works by Ten Painters,* 1965
Screenprint on paper, and folder
20 × 24 in. (50.8 × 61 cm)
Ed: 280/500
Gift of Mrs. Robert B. Mayer
1991.61.3.a–b

Campbell's Soup Cans II, 1969
Screenprints on paper
Ten prints, each: 35 × 23 in. (88.9 × 58.4 cm)
Ed: 17/250
Gift of Beatrice Cummings Mayer
1991.89.1–10

Vote McGovern (The McGovern Poster), 1972
Screenprint on paper
42 × 42 in. (106.7 × 106.7 cm)
Gift of Beatrice Cummings Mayer
1991.90

Sigmund Freud from the portfolio *Ten Jews of the Twentieth Century*, 1980
Screenprint on paper
40 × 32 in. (101.6 × 81.3 cm)
Gift of Jeanne Marienthal-Weislow
1981.46

Gertrude Stein from the portfolio *Ten Jews of the Twentieth Century*, 1980
Screenprint on paper
40 × 32 in. (101.6 × 81.3 cm)
Gift of Jeanne Marienthal-Weislow
1981.47

Ken Warneke
American, b. 1958
p. 220

The Tyranny of Everyday Life
1990
Oil and acrylic on Masonite
41¾ × 35¾ in. (106 × 90.8 cm)
Gift of Mrs. M. A. Lipschultz,
Mr. and Mrs. E. A. Bergman, Nathan
Cummings, Grace and Edwin Hokin,
and Mrs. Richard L. Feigen by exchange
1991.24

Provenance

Dart Gallery, Chicago, c. 1990–91.

MCA, 1991.

Exhibition History

Human, Suburban Fine Arts Center, Highland Park, Ill., September 6–October 2, 1991.

New Acquisitions: The MCA Collects, MCA, November 23, 1991–January 26, 1992.

Haunting Images: Paintings of Reference and Metaphor, Foster Art Gallery, University of Wisconsin, Eau Claire, March 4–24, 1992.

Decades in Dialogue: Perspectives on the MCA *Collection*, MCA, February 27–October 31, 1999.

References

Carroll, Patty. *Spirited Visions: Portraits of Chicago Artists*. Champaign-Urbana, Ill.: University of Illinois Press, 1991.

Recent Art in Chicago. Exh. brochure. New York: Artist's Space, 1986.

Warren, Lynne et al. *Art in Chicago, 1945–1995*. Exh. cat. MCA, 1996. Pp. 226, 289.

Yood, James. "Purplexity and Ambiguity in Warneke." *Artforum* 29, no. 9 (May 1991), pp. 124–27.

H. C. Westermann
American, 1922–1981
p. 54

Memorial to the Idea of Man If He Was an Idea
1958
Pine, bottle caps, cast-tin toys, glass, metal, brass, ebony, and enamel
56½ × 38 × 14¼ in. (143.5 × 96.5 × 36.2 cm)
Gift of Susan and Lewis Manilow
1993.34

Provenance

Alan Frumkin Gallery, Chicago, 1958.

Lori and Lewis Manilow, Chicago, 1958.

MCA, 1993.

Exhibition History

H. C. Westermann: Recent Work, Allan Frumkin Gallery, Chicago, 1958.

New Images of Man, The Museum of Modern Art, New York, September 30–November 29, 1959; Baltimore Museum of Art, Md., January 9–February 7, 1960.

The New American Realism, Worcestor Art Museum, Mass., February 18–April 4, 1965.

Seven Decades: 1895–1965, Crosscurrents in Modern Art, Public Education Association of the City of New York, April 26–May 21, 1966.

Sculpture since 1945: A Generation of Innovation, The Art Institute of Chicago, June 23–August 27, 1967.

H. C. Westermann, Los Angeles County Museum of Art, November 26, 1968–January 12, 1969; MCA, January 29–March 2, 1969.

H. C. Westermann, Whitney Museum of American Art, New York, May 17–July 16, 1978; New Orleans Museum of Art, La., August 25–October 15, 1978; Des Moines Art Center, Iowa, November 13–December 25, 1978; Seattle Art Museum, January 17–February 25, 1979; San Francisco Museum of Modern Art, March 30–May 20, 1979.

Permanent Collection Exhibition on Michigan Avenue, MCA, November 1, 1983–January 1, 1984.

Permanent Collection: Promised Gifts Exhibition, MCA, October 3–November 28, 1989.

Toward the Future: Contemporary Art in Context, MCA, May 5–July 1, 1990.

Under Development: Dreaming the MCA's Collection, MCA, April 30–August 28, 1994.

Art in Chicago, 1945–1995, MCA, November 16, 1996–March 23, 1997.

Envisioning the Contemporary: Selections from the Permanent Collection, MCA, June 21, 1997–April 5, 1998 and April 30, 1998–February 7, 1999.

H. C. Westermann, MCA, June 30–September 23, 2001; Hirshhorn Museum and Sculpture Garden, Smithsonian Institution, Washington, D.C., February 14–May 12, 2002; The Museum of Contemporary Art, Los Angeles, June 9–September 8, 2002; Menil Collection, Houston, October 4, 2002–January 5, 2003.

W.W.I General, W.W.II General, W.W.III General
1962
Pine, plywood, and fluorescent alkyd enamel
19¾ × 34½ × 13 in. (50.2 × 87.6 × 33 cm)
Gift of Mrs. Robert B. Mayer
1984.4

Provenance

Allan Frumkin Gallery, Chicago, 1962.

Mr. and Mrs. Robert B. Mayer, Winnetka, Ill., 1964.

MCA, 1984.

Exhibition History

Recent Sculpture by H. C. Westermann, Allan Frumkin Gallery, New York, October 8–26, 1963.

Permanent Collection Exhibition, MCA, March 25–May 29, 1983.

Ten Years of Collecting, MCA, April 14–June 10, 1984.

Toward the Future: Contemporary Art in Context, MCA, May 5–July 1, 1990.

Under Development: Dreaming the MCA's Collection, MCA, April 30–August 28, 1994.

In the Shadow of Storms: Art of the Postwar Era from the MCA Collection, MCA, July 2, 1996–May 25, 1997.

Rosebud
1963
Douglas fir, plate-glass mirror, brass, ink, and rubber bumpers
24¼ × 19¾ × 9¼ in. (61.6 × 50.2 × 23.5 cm)
Partial gift of Ruth Horwich
2001.6

Provenance

Alan Frumkin Gallery, Chicago, 1963.

Leonard J. and Ruth Horwich, Chicago, mid-1960s.

MCA, 2001.

Exhibition History

H. C. Westermann, Los Angeles County Museum of Art, November 26, 1968–January 12, 1969; MCA, January 29–March 2, 1969.

H. C. Westermann, Whitney Museum of American Art, New York, May 17–July 16, 1978; New Orleans Museum of Art, La., August 25–October 14, 1978; Des Moines Art Center, Iowa, November 13–December 25, 1978; Seattle Art Museum, January 17–February 25, 1979; San Francisco Museum of Modern Art, March 30–May 20, 1979.

Recent Glass Sculpture: A Union of Ideas, Milwaukee Art Museum, Milwaukee, Wis., September 5–November 2, 1997.

H. C. Westermann, MCA, June 30–September 23, 2001; Hirshhorn Museum and Sculpture Garden, Smithsonian Institution, Washington, D.C., February 14–May 12, 2002; The Museum of Contemporary Art, Los Angeles, June 9–September 8, 2002; Menil Collection, Houston, October 4, 2002–January 5, 2003.

Billy Penn
1976
Galvanized sheet metal, steel, pine, bronze, and aluminum alkyd paint
79¼ × 42½ × 29⅝ in.
(201.3 × 108 × 75.2 cm)
Gift of Alan and Dorothy Press
1979.1

Provenance

Xavier Fourcade, New York, 1976.

Alan and Dorothy Press, Chicago, 1979.

MCA, 1979.

Exhibition History

Selected Sculpture from the Permanent Collection, MCA, March 23–July 1, 1979.

Groups III, Waddington Galleries, London, February 5–March 1, 1980.

H. C. Westermann at the Serpentine, Serpentine Gallery, London, December 5, 1980–February 8, 1981.

The Image in American Painting and Sculpture, 1950–1980, Akron Art Museum, Akron, Ohio, September 12–November 8, 1981.

MCA Permanent Collection Exhibition, MCA, January 16–March 14, 1982.

Ten Years of Collecting, MCA, April 14–June 10, 1984.

American Painting and Sculpture from 1968 to the Present: Selections from the Permanent Collection, MCA, June 28–August 19, 1985.

Toward the Future: Contemporary Art in Context, MCA, May 5–July 1, 1990.

Modeling the Future: The New Museum and Key Works from the Permanent Collection, MCA, May 2–November 8, 1992.

Under Development: Dreaming the MCA's Collection, MCA, April 30–August 28, 1994.

Envisioning the Contemporary: Selections from the Permanent Collection, MCA, April 30, 1998–February 7, 1999.

H. C. Westermann, MCA, June 30–September 23, 2001; Hirshhorn Museum and Sculpture Garden, Smithsonian Institution, Washington, D.C., February 14–May 12, 2002; The Museum of Contemporary Art, Los Angeles, June 9–September 8, 2002; Menil Collection, Houston, October 4, 2002–January 5, 2003.

References

Adrian, Dennis. "Some Notes on H. C. Westermann." *Art International* 7, no. 2 (February 1963), pp. 52–55.

Anonymous. "Fishhooks in the Memory." *Time* (December 20, 1968), pp. 66–69.

"The Art of H. C. Westermann." *Artforum* 6, no. 1 (September 1967), pp. 16–22.

Barrette, Bill, ed. *Letters from H. C. Westermann*. New York: Timken, 1988.

Collective Vision. MCA, 1996.

Jacob, Mary Jane et al. *Selections from the Permanent Collection, Vol. I*. MCA, 1984.

Lucie-Smith, Edward. "London Letter: Chicago Artists." *Art International* 24, no. 7/8 (March/April 1981), pp. 128–31.

McCarthy, David. "H. C. Westermann's Brinkmanship." *American Art* (autumn 1996), pp. 50–69.

Rooks, Michael and Lynne Warren. *H. C. Westermann: Exhibition Catalogue and Catalogue Raisonné of Objects*. MCA; New York: Harry N. Abrams, 2001.

See America First: The Prints of H. C. Westermann. Chicago: The David and Alfred Smart Museum of Art, The University of Chicago Press, 2001.

Other Works in the MCA Collection

Emaculate Conception, c. 1940s
Oil and gold leaf on canvas
32 × 19¹⁵⁄₁₆ in. (81.3 × 50.6 cm)
Gift of Mrs. E. A. Bergman
1991.78

Untitled, c. 1954–55
Watercolor on paper with painted artist's frame
22⅞ × 10¼ in. (58.1 × 26 cm)
Gift of Mrs. E. A. Bergman
1991.77

Untitled, 1954
Acrylic on canvas
39½ × 29½ in. (100.3 × 74.9 cm)
Gift of Herbert K. Reis in memory of his sister, Jory Graham
1983.77

City, 1954
Wood, concrete, paint, glass, lead, stained glass, wire, and sandpaper
74¼ × 11 × 10¾ in. (188.6 × 27.9 × 27.3 cm)
Gift of Stefan T. Edlis
1986.59

Untitled, c. 1954–55
Oil on canvas
40 × 30 in. (101.6 × 76.2 cm)
Gift of Mrs. E. A. Bergman
1991.76

The Old Eccentric's House, 1956–57
Birch-veneer plywood, spruce lath, and mirror
18¾ × 18¾ × 33¼ in.
(47.6 × 47.6 × 84.4 cm)
Gift of anonymous donor
1980.32

Two Acrobats and A Fleeing Man, 1957
Fir, pine, and lead
12 × 20¼ × 1½ in. (30.5 × 51.4 × 3.8 cm)
Gift of Susan and Lewis Manilow
1984.6

He Whore, 1957
Plywood, vermilion, oak, maple, walnut, fir, birch, mirror, paint, chromium-plated brass, cork, rope, and U.S. dimes
23½ × 11½ × 20 in. (59.7 × 29.2 × 50.8 cm)
Gift of Susan and Lewis Manilow
1993.35

Death Ship of No Port, 1957
Pine, canvas, bronze, wire, and paint
24¼ × 30½ × 3⅝ in. (61.6 × 77.5 × 9.2 cm)
Gift of John F. Miller
1995.121

Mad House, 1958
Pine, plywood, glass, brass, galvanized sheet metal, enamel, cast-tin toy, lead soldier, paper découpage, mirror, and U.S. penny
38⅛ × 17½ × 21 in. (96.8 × 44.4 × 53.3 cm)
Gift of Joseph and Jory Shapiro
1978.5

The Rascette, 1961
Painted wood
24 × 14 × 10 in. (61 × 35.6 × 25.4 cm)
Gift of anonymous donor
1982.50

Untitled (for Gregory N. Westermann), 1979
Vermilion, bird's-eye maple, and brass
Closed: 7⅜ × 9⅞ × 6⅞ in.
(18.7 × 25.1 × 17.5 cm)
Gift of Gregory N. Westermann in memory of H. C. Westermann
2000.18

Jackie Winsor
American, b. Canada 1941
p. 156

Cheesecloth Piece
1981
Wood and cheesecloth
31½ × 31½ × 31½ in. (80 × 80 × 80 cm)
Gift of Lannan Foundation
1997.66

Provenance

Paula Cooper Gallery, New York, c. 1981–82.

Margo Leavin Gallery, Los Angeles, 1984.

William J. Hokin, Chicago, 1984.

Christie's, New York, May 2, 1991, lot. 225.

Lannan Foundation, Los Angeles, 1991

MCA, 1997.

Exhibition History

Jackie Winsor: New Work, Paula Cooper Gallery, New York, February–March 1982.

Jackie Winsor/Barry Ledoux Sculpture, Hayden Gallery, MIT, Cambridge, Mass., December 1983–January 1984.

American Woman Artists Part II: The Recent Generation, Sidney Janis Gallery, New York, February 1984.

American Sculpture, Margo Leavin Gallery, Los Angeles, July 17–September 15, 1984.

Selections from the William J. Hokin Collection, MCA, April 20–June 16, 1985.

Abstraction: Selections from the Lannan Foundation Collection, Lannan Foundation Gallery, Los Angeles, October 12, 1991–February 8, 1992.

Percept/Image/Object: Selections from the Lannan Foundation Collection, Lannan Foundation Gallery, Los Angeles, February 26–May 15, 1994.

Envisioning the Contemporary: Selections from the Permanent Collection, MCA, June 21, 1997–April 5, 1998 and April 30, 1998–February 7, 1999.

References

Jackie Winsor/Barry Ledoux. Exh. cat. Cambridge, Mass.: Hayden Gallery, MIT Press, 1983.

Jackie Winsor. Exh. cat. New York: The Museum of Modern Art, 1979.

Mifflin, Margot. "Jackie Winsor: Pieces of Life." *ARTnews* 91, no. 6 (summer 1992), pp. 100–105.

Sobel, Dean. *Jackie Winsor.* Exh. cat. Milwaukee, Wis.: Milwaukee Art Museum, 1991.

Claire Zeisler

American, 1903–1991
p. 106

Rosemary

1968
Jute and wool on steel armature
60 × 48 in. diameter (152.4 × 121.9 cm)
Gift of Mrs. Robert B. Mayer
1983.35

Provenance

Richard L. Feigen & Co., Chicago, 1968.

Mr. and Mrs. Robert B. Mayer, Winnetka, Ill., 1968.

MCA, 1983.

Exhibition History

Robert B. Memorial Loan to Asheville Art Museum, N.C., 1976–1983.

AIC Retrospective, The Art Institute of Chicago, February 10–May 20, 1979.

Claire Zeisler, Whitney Museum of American Art, New York, December 14, 1984–March 10, 1985.

American Painting and Sculpture from 1968 to the Present: Selections from the Permanent Collection, MCA, June 28–August 19, 1985.

Chicago Artists from the Permanent Collection, MCA, July 10–August 21, 1987.

Selections from the Permanent Collection: Important Sculptural Works, MCA, April 25–July 8, 1989.

Envisioning the Contemporary: Selections from the Permanent Collection, MCA, April 30, 1998–February 7, 1999.

References

Claire Zeisler: A Retrospective. Exh. cat. Chicago: The Art Institute, 1979.

Jacob, Mary Jane et al. *Selections from the Permanent Collection, Vol. I.* MCA, 1984.

Lyon, Christopher. "A Woman of Fiber." *Chicago Magazine* (November 1985), pp. 159–63.

Warren, Lynne et al. *Art in Chicago, 1945–1995.* Exh. cat. MCA, 1996. P. 293.

Other Works in the MCA Collection

Fragments and Dashes, 1978–1980
Beads, chamois, cotton, feather, raw wool, shells, stones, and wood in Plexiglas case
4½ × 44½ × 15½ in. (11.4 × 113 × 39.4 cm)
Restricted gift in honor of the artist's birthday
1983.36

Reproduction Credits

The photographs in this book were taken by James Isberner, staff photographer, or Joe Ziolkowski, former staff photographer, with the exception of the following:

84 (top) Courtesy Donald Young Gallery, Chicago

84 (bottom) Courtesy Konrad Fischer Galerie

87 Courtesy Pace Wildenstein, New York

235 Courtesy of the artist. Photo by Jody Zellen

240 Courtesy Sean Kelly Gallery, New York

250–51 Courtesy David Zwirner Gallery, New York

268–69 (bottom left, bottom center) Courtesy The Fabric Workshop and Museum

291 (top) Courtesy Matthew Marks Gallery, New York

295 Courtesy Barbara Gladstone Gallery, New York. Photo by Michael James O'Brien

306 Courtesy 303 Gallery, New York

308–9 Courtesy of the artist and Peter Miller Gallery, Chicago

Individual works of art appearing in this catalogue may be protected by copyright in the United States of America or elsewhere, and may not be reproduced in any form without the permission of the copyright owners.

The following credits appear at the request of the artist or the artist's representatives:

12, 48–49 © 2002 Estate of Alexander Calder / Artists Rights Society (ARS), New York

17, 73 © 2002 Estate of Dan Flavin / Artists Rights Society (ARS), New York

20, 151 © 2002 Estate of Gordon Matta-Clark / Artists Rights Society (ARS), New York

35 © 2002 Artists Rights Society (ARS), New York / ADAGP, Paris

37 © 2002 Artists Rights Society (ARS), New York / ADAGP, Paris

39 © 2002 Artists Rights Society (ARS), New York / ADAGP, Paris

41 © 2002 Artists Rights Society (ARS), New York / ADAGP, Paris

42–43 © 2002 Artists Rights Society (ARS), New York / ADAGP, Paris

45 © 2002 Artists Rights Society (ARS), New York / DACS, London

47 © 2002 Artists Rights Society (ARS), New York / ADAGP, Paris

51 © 2002 C. Herscovici, Brussels / Artists Rights Society (ARS), New York

52–53 © 2002 The Franz Kline Estate/ Artists Rights Society (ARS), New York

58–59 © 1959 and © 1979 Leon Golub

62–63 © Jasper Johns/Licensed by VAGA, New York

65 © 2002 Estate of Ad Reinhardt / Artists Rights Society (ARS), New York

66–67 © 2002 Andy Warhol Foundation for the Visual Arts / ARS, New York

69 Art © Marisol/Licensed by VAGA, New York

71 © Robert Rauschenberg/Licensed by VAGA, New York

74–75 © 1964 and © 1966 Claes Oldenburg

76–77 © 1965 and © 1968 Christo

79 © 2002 Robert Morris / Artists Rights Society (ARS), New York

80–85 © 2002 Bruce Nauman / Artists Rights Society (ARS), New York

87 © 2002 Robert Irwin / Artists Rights Society (ARS), New York

90–91 Art © Estate of Robert Smithson / Licensed by VAGA, New York

92–93 © 1966 and ©1981 Sol LeWitt

106–7 © 1968 Claire Zeisler

109 © 2002 Richard Serra / Artists Rights Society (ARS), New York

110–11 Courtesy of the artist and Paula Cooper Gallery, New York

112–13 © 1969 and © 1985 Vito Acconci

115 Art © The George and Helen Segal Foundation / Licensed by VAGA, New York

116–17 © 2002 Artists Rights Society (ARS), New York / SABAM, Brussels

123 © 2002 Artists Rights Society (ARS), New York / VG Bild-Kunst, Bonn

125 Art © Donald Judd Foundation / Licensed by VAGA, New York

126–27 © 1971 Richard Artschwager

128–29 © 1972 Jackie Ferrara

134–35 Courtesy The School of the Art Institute of Chicago and the Brown Family

146–47 Courtesy Matthew Marks Gallery, New York

149 © 1993 John Cage Trust

159 © 1981 Magdalena Abakanowicz

174–75 © 1983 Bernd and Hilla Becher

176–77 © 2002 Jenny Holzer / Artists Rights Society (ARS), New York

181 © 1983 Gilbert & George

182–83 © David Salle/Licensed by VAGA, New York

187 Courtesy of the artist and Paula Cooper Gallery, New York

201 © 1988 Chuck Close

202–3 © 1993 Ann Hamilton and Sean Kelly Gallery, New York

205 © 1988 Adrian Piper

208–9 © 1989 Louise Lawler

221 © 1990 Ken Warneke

231 © 1991 Jack Pierson

233 Courtesy of Matthew Marks Gallery, New York

246–47 Courtesy of the artist and Paula Cooper Gallery, New York

252–55 © 1994 and © 1996 William Kentridge

257 © 1994 and © 1999 Iñigo Manglano-Ovalle

261 © 1994 Jin Soo Kim

265 © 1995 Mariko Mori

268–69 (bottom row, left and center) Courtesy The Fabric Workshop and Museum

280–81 © 1998 Shirin Neshat. Courtesy Barbara Gladstone Gallery, New York

291–93 Courtesy Matthew Marks Gallery, New York

294–95 © 1999 Matthew Barney. Courtesy Barbara Gladstone Gallery, New York

306–7 Courtesy 303 Gallery, New York

308–9 © 2001 Jason Salavon

311 © 2001 Maurizio Cattelan

Museum of Contemporary Art, Chicago

Authors' Acknowledgments

Preparing this catalogue — the first publication of substantial size and scope documenting the MCA Collection in the museum's thirty-five-year history — has been a pleasure and a privilege. We have been grateful for the opportunity over the last five years to research these remarkable works of art: to reflect on their significance, to find connections among them, and to tell the story of their existence through provenance and exhibition histories. We hope this book will serve as an important contribution to contemporary art scholarship.

This volume functions not as an exhaustive catalogue of works in the MCA Collection, but as a selection of the museum's most important and influential works. We based our final selection on the following criteria: works reflecting the periods, styles, and artists whose works we hold in depth; the most significant works by the most influential artists of our time; and a balance of local, national, and international artists from different cultural backgrounds, reflecting the MCA's ongoing commitment to building a diverse collection.

With Pritzker Director Robert Fitzpatrick and Associate Director Greg Cameron at the helm, we have benefited from the sustained support and encouragement necessary to complete such a massive and long-range undertaking. James W. Alsdorf Chief Curator Elizabeth Smith's thoughtful guidance at every stage of this project has provided an outstanding model, and her belief in the book's importance has made preparing it an even more rewarding process. The initial organizers of the Collection catalogue project, former Director Kevin E. Consey and former Curator of Collections Lucinda Barnes, also deserve recognition for the timely initiation of this important undertaking.

Many writers contributed to this catalogue. Elizabeth Smith's compelling essay introduces the MCA Collection with a particular focus on the museum's art historical strengths, providing a fresh view of the works illustrated in this book. In addition, we are grateful to the following MCA staff for contributing entries to the catalogue: Manilow Senior Curator Francesco Bonami, Director of Collections and Exhibitions Lela Hersh, Curator Lynne Warren, Associate Curator Staci Boris, Associate Curator Dominic Molon, Assistant Curator Michael Rooks, Curatorial Assistant Sylvia Chivaratanond, and Curatorial Coordinator Tricia Van Eck. We also extend our gratitude to former MCA interns Jenni Sorkin and Heather Ring and to former Susman Curatorial Fellow Monika Gehlawat for contributing entries. In addition, we thank the MCA Curatorial staff for advising on which artists and works to feature.

Numerous interns over the duration of the project made important contributions: Weena Perry, Alison Gass, Jenni Sorkin, Heather Ring, Lan Nguyen, Anna Taylor, Amy Rogaliner, Ingrid Messer, Lauren Douville, Lara Taylor, Marisa Sanchez, Tania Zubkus, Megan Green, Kate Ross, Kathleen Fitzgerald, and Taro Nettleton deserve high praise. Jennifer Zukerman, former Susman Curatorial Fellow, skillfully assisted with research for this catalogue.

We gratefully acknowledge our editorial staff, led by Associate Director of Publications Kari Dahlgren, who ably edited the manuscript for this book and oversaw its production. We have appreciated her insight and dedication throughout. Former Associate Director of Publications Michael Sittenfeld contributed in many significant ways to the early stages of this catalogue, while Editorial Assistant Trisha Beck provided invaluable assistance with all aspects of the text. Former Editor Tony Neuhoff, Catherine A. Steinmann, and editorial interns Apsara di Quinzio, Juliet Do, and Conner Perkins also contributed. We are enormously proud of the catalogue's thoughtful design by Hal Kugeler, Director of Design and Publications, whose expertise enhanced this volume in countless ways.

For checking the accuracy of the object information about the works of art featured in this catalogue, we thank Registrar Jennifer Draffen and Assistant Registrar Jude Palmese. As Director of Collections and Exhibitions, Lela Hersh's oversight of the museum's registrarial function made archival research in her department progress smoothly and effortlessly.

Unless otherwise credited, the photographs in the catalogue were taken by Jamie Isberner. For securing the rights of reproduction and coordinating the photography for every object in the catalogue, we thank Coordinator of Rights and Reproductions Zoe Donnell. Former Coordinator of Rights and Reproductions Stacey Gengo also contributed in the book's earlier stages. Much of our research was ably facilitated by former librarians Janice Dillard and Dennis McGuire.

The Development Department worked tirelessly to raise funds for this catalogue, and we appreciate the priority they gave to this project. MCA Associate Director Greg Cameron has supported the book since its inception, as did former Director of Development Chris Jabin. Current Director of Development Patrick McCusker has continued this enthusiasm and support. We also recognize former Manager of Foundation and Government Relations Janine Perron, current Foundation and Government Relations Manager, Julie Havel, and Sarah Kirby, Manager of Individual Giving, for their efforts. We would also like to thank Benjamin Kim, former Coordinator of Foundation and Government Relations.

Myriad aspects of this catalogue were enabled by the visionary philanthropy of the Elizabeth F. Cheney Foundation, which was able to see the value of our project in 1997 in its very early stages. The Foundation made a substantial commitment that funded the book's research, writing, and editing. We are likewise indebted to the Lannan Foundation for their generous contribution to this project, and to the Furthermore Foundation for underwriting the book's complex production. We are especially grateful to Donna and Howard Stone and Ruth Horwich for their help in making possible every aspect of this catalogue and exhibition.

We would also like to thank the innumerable artists, galleries, archives, libraries, museums, auction houses, and collectors who so readily and kindly searched through their records to provide details about artworks, exhibition dates, and provenance.

Julie Rodrigues Widholm
Curatorial Assistant, Museum of Contemporary Art, Chicago

Alison Pearlman
Former Assistant Curator, Museum of Contemporary Art, Chicago

Selected Works from the Museum of Contemporary Art, Chicago, Collection

Index of Artists

Life, Death, Love, Hate, Pleasure, Pain

383

Museum Staff

Janet Alberti

Matti Allison

Duncan Anderson

Kimberly Aubuchon

Phillip Bahar

Francesco Bonami

Staci Boris

Elysia Borowy

Michelle Brandt

Kennon Brown

Nicole Bryant

Greg Cameron

Sylvia Chivaratanond

Sherrie Corbin

Amy Corle

Tony Cornelious

Gina Crowley

Andrew Cuison

Lauren Cumbia

Yolanda Cesta Cursach

Kari Dahlgren

Lynn Davis

Warren Davis

Tim Davison

Zoe Donnell

Jennifer Draffen

Helen Dunbeck

Diana Fabian

Robert Fitzpatrick

Anthony Fobbs

Brian Francisco

Nikki Frisinger

Judy Gooden

Meredith Gray

John Gustafson

Hillary Hanas

Matthew Hanner

Jennifer Harris

Julie Havel

Sharon Hawkins

Mary Heathcott

Lela Hersh

Steve Hokanson

Carol Nasaw Hurvitz

Jamie Isberner

Natalie Jacobson

Sue Jaquith

Renee Jessup

Lisa Johnson

Kythzia Jurado

Connor Kalista

Natasha Karpasov

Susan Kieffer

Sarah Kirby

Hal Kugeler

Suzanne Lampert

Carmen Larios

Julie Marie Lemon

Joel Liveris

Karla Loring

Lea Lovelace

Brad Martin

Patrick McCusker

Larry McElroy

Don Meckley

Dominic Molon

Derek Moore

Stephanie Morgan

Richard Norwood

Dennis O'Shea

Gretchen Orendorf

Jude Palmese

Phongtorn Phongluantum

Robin Parker

Laurie Poindexter

Tomasz Poplawski

June Puntahachart

Yasmil Raymond

Willie Reives

Mary Richardson

Michael Riley

Michael Rooks

Mykl Ruffino

Eddie Sallie

Jared Sheldon

Cary Shoda

Scott Short

Elizabeth Smith

Earnest Sterling

Rebecca Swayze

Peter Taub

Jennifer Thielen

Joni Todd

Tricia Van Eck

Erika Varricchio

Igor Vygovsky

Karin Warch

Lynne Warren

Julie Weinstein

Kristi Widgery

Julie Rodrigues Widholm

Robert Wisniewski

Janet Wolski

Wendy Woon

Full time, August 2002